Peabody Picture Vocabulary Test–III (PPVT-III)

Scales of Independent Behavior–Revised (SIB-R)

Standardized Test for the Assessment of Reading (S.T.A.R.)

*Stanford Achievement Test Series, Tenth Edition (SESAT, SAT, TASK)

Stanford Diagnostic Mathematics Test 4 (SDMT4)

*Stanford-Binet Intelligence Scale, Fifth Edition (SB5)

STAR Early Literacy Computer-Adaptive Diagnostic Assessment

STAR Math

*Teacher's Report Form for Ages 6 to 18 (TRF)

*Temperament and Atypical Behavior Scale (TABS)

Terra Nova, Second Edition

Test for Auditory Comprehension of Language, Third Edition (TACL-3)

*Test of Early Mathematics Ability, Third Edition (TEMA-3)

*Test of Early Reading Ability, Third Edition (TERA-3)

Test of Language Development, Primary: Third Edition (TOLD-P:3)

Test of Language Development–Intermediate: 3 (TOLD-I:3)

Test of Nonverbal Intelligence–3 (TONI-3)

*Test of Phonological Awareness, Second Edition: Plus (TOPA 2+)

Test of Reading Comprehension–3 (TORC-3)

*Test of Silent Word Reading Fluency (TOSWRF)

Test of Visual-Motor Integration (TVMI)

Test of Written Language–3 (TOWL-3)

Test of Written Spelling–4 (TWS-4)

Tests of Achievement and Proficiency (TAP)

*Vineland Adaptive Behavior Scales, Second Edition (VABS II)

Wechsler Individual Achievement Test, Second Edition (WIAT-2)

*Wechsler Intelligence Scale for Children–IV (WISC-IV)

*Wechsler Preschool and Primary Scale of Intelligence–III (WPPSI-III)

Wide Range Achievement Test 3 (WRAT3)

Woodcock Diagnostic Reading Battery (WDRB)

Woodcock-Johnson Psychoeducational Battery–III (WJ-III)

Young Children's Achievement Test (YCAT)

*Youth Self-Report (YSR)

Assessment

In Special and Inclusive Education
Tenth Edition

John Salvia
The Pennsylvania State University

James E. Ysseldyke
University of Minnesota

with

Sara Bolt
Michigan State University

HOUGHTON MIFFLIN COMPANY

Boston • New York

Publisher: *Pat Coryell*
Senior Sponsoring Editor: *Sue Pulvermacher-Alt*
Development Editor: *Julia Giannotti*
Editorial Assistant: *Dayna Pell*
Senior Project Editor: *Bob Greiner*
Editorial Assistant: *Katherine Leahey*
Senior Art and Design Coordinator: *Jill Haber Atkins*
Composition Buyer: *Chuck Dutton*
Manufacturing Coordinator: *Brian Pierogostini*
Marketing Manager: *Laura McGinn*

Cover Image: *"Natural Forces #4" © 1997 by Ann Schroeder. Photo by David Caras.*

Printed in the U.S.A.

Library of Congress Catalog Number: 2005932943

Instructor's exam copy:
ISBN-10: 0-618-73233-0
ISBN-13: 978-0-618-73233-3

For orders, use student text ISBNs:
ISBN-10: 0-618-69269-X
ISBN-13: 978-0-618-69269-9

1 2 3 4 5 6 7 8 9-DOC-10 09 08 07 06

CONTENTS

PREFACE

As indicated by the title of the tenth edition, *Assessment: In Special and Inclusive Education*, we continue to be concerned about assessing the performance and progress of students with disabilities regardless of whether their education occurs in general or special education settings. Many of the same issues that have plagued educational assessment and decision making remain today. New issues have also come to the fore as a result of the 2004 Reauthorization of the Individuals with Disabilities Improvement Act (IDEA); this legislation has drawn attention to a new way to assess students with learning disabilities. In addition, philosophical differences continue to result in considerable dispute over the value of standardized and unstandardized test administration, objective and subjective scoring, generalizable and ungeneralizable measurement, interpersonal and intrapersonal comparisons, and so forth. After carefully considering the various approaches to assessment, we remain committed to approaches that facilitate data-based decision making. Thus we believe students and society are best served by the objective, reliable, and valid assessment of student abilities and meaningful educational results.

Our position is based on several conclusions. First, the IDEA requires objective assessment, largely because it usually leads to better decision making. Second, we are encouraged by the substantial improvement in assessment devices and practices over the past twenty plus years. Third, although some alternatives are merely unproven, other innovative approaches to assessment—especially those that celebrate subjectivity—have severe shortcomings that have been understood since the early 1900s. Fortunately, much of the initial enthusiasm for those approaches is already beginning to wane. Fourth, we believe it is unwise to abandon effective procedures without substantial evidence that the proposed alternatives are really better. Too often, we learned that an educational innovation was ineffective at high human cost. Finally, objective assessment is mandated in federal legislation.

However, our commitment is not the same as unqualified acceptance. From the first edition of *Assessment* we have criticized poor assessment procedures and practices that fall short of accepted standards. Although we recognize that objective assessment has improved, there is still much room for improvement. Some tests are still published with poor technical characteristics. Many achievement tests need to become even more authentic, more contextualized, and less disconnected with learning and instruction. Some paradigms for data-based decision making with demonstrated efficacy in some situations need additional validation before extending their use. We welcome the renewed interest in assessment. We hope that better theory and practice will emerge from the heated debates. These are indeed exciting times.

Audience for This Book

Assessment: In Special and Inclusive Education, Tenth Edition, is intended for a first course in assessment taken by those whose careers require understanding and informed use of assessment data. The primary audience is made up of those who are or will be teachers in special education at the elementary or secondary level. The secondary audience is the large support system for special educators: school psychologists, child development specialists, counselors, educational administrators, nurses, preschool educators, reading specialists, social workers, speech and language specialists, and specialists in therapeutic recreation. Additionally, in today's reform climate, many classroom teachers enroll in the assessment course as part of their own professional development. In writing for those who are taking their first course in assessment, we have assumed no prior knowledge of measurement and statistical concepts.

Purpose

Students have the right to an appropriate education in the least restrictive educational environment. Decisions regarding the most appropriate environment and the most appropriate program for an individual should be data-based. Assessment is one part of the process of collecting the data necessary for educational decision making, and the administration of tests is one part of assessment. Unfortunately, tests have sometimes been used to restrict educational opportunities; many assessment practices have not been in the best interests of students. Those who assess have a tremendous responsibility; assessment results are used to make decisions that directly and significantly affect students' lives. Those who assess are responsible for knowing the devices and procedures they use and for understanding the limitations of those devices and procedures.

Teachers are confronted with the results of tests, checklists, scales, and batteries almost daily. This information is intended to be useful to them in understanding and making educational plans for their students. But the intended use and actual use of assessment information have often differed. However good the intentions of test designers, misuse and misunderstanding of tests may well occur unless teachers are informed consumers and users of tests. To be an informed consumer and user of tests, a teacher must bring to the task certain domains of knowledge, including knowledge of the basic uses of tests, the important attributes of good tests, and the kinds of behaviors sampled by particular tests. This text aims at helping education professionals acquire that knowledge.

The New Edition

Coverage The tenth edition retains the style and content of the first nine editions. It continues to offer evenhanded, documented evaluations of standardized tests in each domain; straightforward and clear coverage of basic assessment concepts; and illustrations of applications to the decision-making process. Most chapters have been updated, and several have been revised substantially. The organization of the tenth edition is changed. We have added a fifth part, "Decision Making," that contains three substantially revised chapters ("Teacher Decision Making," "Making Entitlement Decisions," and "Making Accountability Decisions"). In addition, we have added a new chapter to this part, Chapter 30, "Assessing Response to Instruction," as described below.

In addition, the IDEA has been revised. While many provisions of the law remain unchanged in the new IDEA, there is one notable change for members of the assessment community. Schools are now allowed to use response to intervention to identify students with learning disabilities.

New and Revised Tests

One of the most notable changes is a reduction in the number of tests reviewed in Part 4. We have opted to place tests that are less frequently used on our website. Access the Online Study Center/Online Teaching Center for this text by visiting http://college.hmco.com/pic/salvia10e.

There are several new and revised tests, including the Asperger Syndrome Diagnostic Scale (ASDS), Developmental Test of Visual-Motor Integration (VMI), Behavioral and Emotional Rating Scale, Second Edition (BERS-2), Bender Visual Motor Gestalt Test, Second Edition (BVMGT-2), Dynamic Indicators of Basic Early Literacy Skills, Sixth Edition (DIBELS), Gilliam Asperger's Disorder Scale (GADS), Vineland Adaptive Behavior Scales, Second Edition (VABS II), Stanford-Binet Intelligence Scale, Fifth Edition (SB5), Temperament and Atypical Behavior Scale (TABS), Comprehensive Mathematical Abilities Test (CMAT), Group Mathematics Assessment and Diagnostic Evaluation (G·MADE), The Test of Phonological Awareness, Second Edition: Plus (TOPA 2+), Test of Silent Word Reading Fluency (TOSWRF), Wechsler Intelligence Scale for Children–Fourth Edition (WISC-IV), Stanford Achievement Test Series (SESAT, SAT, TASK), Test of Early Reading Ability, Third Edition (TERA-3), and Test of Early Mathematics Ability, Third Edition (TEMA-3). These new tests are indicated by an asterisk in the list of all tests reviewed in this edition, which appears on the inside front cover and first page of this book.

New Chapters

The following are brand-new chapters to this edition:

- Chapter 15, "How to Evaluate a Test," takes the reader through four steps: picking a test; understanding a test's purposes, content, procedures, and scores; evaluating a test's norms, reliability, and validity; and reaching a summary evaluation of a test.

- Chapter 30, "Assessing Response to Instruction" (RTI), discusses the fundamental assumptions in assessing RTI; definitions of RTI; measurement concepts in RTI models; dimensions of assessment of RTI; purposes of assessing RTI; examples of RTI assessment models; and issues and considerations.

New and Revised Chapter Content

The following chapters are substantially revised.

- Chapter 9, "Adapting Tests to Accommodate Students with Disabilities"

- Chapter 16, "Assessment of Intelligence: An Overview"
- Chapter 21, "Assessment of Academic Achievement with Multiple-Skill Devices"
- Chapter 23, "Assessment of Mathematics"
- Chapter 26, "Assessment of Social and Emotional Behavior"
- Chapter 28, "Teacher Decision Making" (Chapter 15 in 9th ed.)
- Chapter 29, "Making Entitlement Decisions" (Chapter 16 in 9th ed.)
- Chapter 31, "Making Accountability Decisions" (Chapter 29 in 9th ed.)

Organization   Part 1, "Assessment: An Overview," places testing in the broader context of assessment: Assessment is described as a multifaceted process, the kinds of decisions made using assessment data are delineated, and basic terminology and concepts are introduced. In Chapter 3, "Legal and Ethical Considerations in Assessment," we describe the ways assessment practices are regulated and mandated by legislation and litigation. In Part 2, "Basic Concepts of Measurement," we give readers an understanding of the measurement principles needed to comprehend and apply the content in Parts 3, 4, and 5.

In Parts 3 and 4, we review the most commonly used assessment instruments and approaches. In Part 3, "Assessment in Classrooms," we address the kinds of assessments that typically take place in classroom settings. The focus of these chapters is on observations, teacher-made tests, and non-test-based approaches that are designed specifically to provide information on effective instruction. In Part 4, "Assessment Using Formal Measures," we review formal (usually standardized) testing that occurs for the most part outside of classrooms. Test evaluations follow a similar format. Initially we describe the kinds of behaviors sampled by tests in the domain; then we describe specific tests. For each test, we examine the kinds of behaviors it samples, the adequacy of its norms, the kinds of scores provided, and evidence for technical adequacy (reliability and validity). Consistent with our earlier editions, we evaluate the technical adequacy of tests in light of the standards set by three professional associations (the American Psychological Association, the American Educational Research Association, and the National Council on Measurement in Education) in their document entitled *Standards for Educational and Psychological Testing* (1999). Test evaluations are virtually a handbook for assessment practitioners.

In Part 5, "Decision Making," we discuss the numerous decisions made in special and inclusive educational settings. Chapter 28 discusses the instructional decisions that precede and follow eligibility decisions. Chapter 29 discusses how entitlement decisions are made. Chapter 30, a new chapter, discusses how response to intervention can and is used to make instructional and entitlement decisions. Chapter 31 discusses the use of large-scale assessments to evaluate educational outcomes and make decisions about accountability. Part 5 concludes with a discussion of the future of assessment.

All chapters end with a summary of chapter content and various activities to facilitate student understanding of the chapter's major concepts. Many have additional readings, several sites on the Internet, and questions for review and thought. Two appendixes at the end of the text contain areas of the normal curve and the equations used in the text. Complete references for in-text citations follow the appendixes.

End-of-chapter Print Resources and Technology Resources have been substantially updated. New websites have been added for students to visit in order to find additional information related to each chapter. We selected websites that we believed were relevant to the materials presented in the chapter and that were likely to endure—that is, sites maintained by publishers, professional or scientific organizations, or university research centers with a record of longevity. The websites were active at the time we prepared the text, but we are, of course, not responsible for their continued presence. In addition, new readings have been added to most chapters.

Assessment is a controversial topic; we have attempted to be objective and evenhanded in our review and portrayal of current assessment practices.

Online Teaching Center and Online Student Center

These websites extend the textbook content and provide resources for further exploration into assessment practices. They offer links to relevant websites, test reviews from prior editions, appendixes from the text, and additional resources helpful for students and instructors.

The marginal website icon will direct you to additional tests on the website (http://college.hmco.com/pic/salvia10e). Test development is an ongoing process. It is our intent to review new tests as they become available and to place the reviews on the Houghton Mifflin website.

Online Study Center
General Resources

New to the text's website are Houghton Mifflin's Video Cases. Available online and organized by topic, each "case" is a 4- to 6-minute module consisting of video files presenting actual classroom scenarios that depict the complex problems and opportunities teachers face every day. The video clips are accompanied by "artifacts" to provide background information and allow preservice teachers to experience true classroom dilemmas in their multiple dimensions.

Acknowledgments

Over the years, many people have assisted in our efforts. In the preparation of this edition, we express our sincere appreciation to Tom Frank for his continuing contributions to the section on hearing assessment. We also appreciate the assistance of Ruth Nelson for her work on the Instructor's Resource Manual with Test Items, which accompanies this text. We also thank Julia Giannotti for her assistance throughout the development of this edition. We remain indebted to Lisa Mafrici, Senior Developmental Editor, and Sue Pulvermacher-Alt, Sponsoring Editor, for their ongoing support for *Assessment: In Special and Inclusive Education*. Finally, a special thank you to Loretta Wolozin, who sponsored eight of the previous editions.

John Salvia
Jim Ysseldyke
Sara Bolt

Assessment

PART 1

Assessment: An Overview

School personnel regularly use assessment information to make important decisions about students. Part 1 of this text looks at basic considerations in psychological and educational assessment of students, as well as introducing concepts and principles that constitute a foundation for informed and critical use of terms and the information they provide.

Chapter 1 describes assessment and includes a delineation of the types of decisions that are made using assessment that can support the three areas, or domains, that are assessed and societal concerns about assessment. Chapter 2 covers steps in the assessment process, and broader concerns about assessment. Chapter 3 takes up fundamental legal and ethical issues in assessment.

Assessment of Students

ASSESSMENT TOUCHES EVERYONE'S LIFE. IT ESPECIALLY AFFECTS THE LIVES OF PEOPLE who work with children and who work in schools. As you begin this course on assessment of students, consider the following:

- You apply for a part-time job to work your way through school. You learn that, as part of the application process, you must take a test of word-processing speed and a personality test.

- Mr. and Mrs. Johnson receive a call from their child's third-grade teacher, who says he is concerned about Morgan's performance on a reading test. He would like to refer Morgan for further testing to see whether Morgan has a learning disability.

- Mr. and Mrs. Esquirol tell you that their son is not eligible for special education services because he scored "too high" on an intelligence test.

- In response to publication of test results showing that U.S. students rank low in comparison to students in other industrialized nations, the U.S. Secretary of Education issues a call for higher educational standards for all students.

- The superintendent of schools in a large urban district learns that only 40 percent of the students in her school district who took the state graduation test passed it.

- Your local school district asks for volunteers to serve on a task force to design a measure of technological literacy to use as a test with students.

Assessment is a process of collecting data for the purpose of making decisions about individuals and groups, and this decision-making role is the reason that assessment touches so many people's lives. A quick perusal of newspaper headlines shows that assessment is one of the most hotly debated issues among not only educators but also the general public. People react strongly when test scores are used to make interpersonal comparisons in which they or those they love look inferior. Entire communities are keenly interested when test scores from their schools are reported and compared with scores from schools in other communities. We expect that you would have strong positive or negative reactions to the use of test scores to make decisions about whether you or your child could enter college, be promoted to the next grade, receive special education, be put in a program for gifted and talented students, or graduate. You would probably question the kinds of tests used, the skills or behaviors they measured, and their technical adequacy. Probably no other activity that takes place in education brings with it so many challenges. In this text, you will learn about assessment practices, the kinds of decisions made, the types of tests used, and the technical adequacy of these tests.

Assessment takes place on a large stage, and there are many players. School personnel have always used test information to make decisions about what students have learned, as well as what and where they should be taught. Throughout their professional careers, teachers, guidance counselors, school social workers, school psychologists, and school administrators are required to give, score, and interpret a wide variety of tests. Because professional school personnel routinely receive test information from their colleagues within the schools and from community agencies outside the schools, they need a working knowledge of important aspects of testing.

School districts are increasingly being held accountable for the performance of their pupils. Parents, the general public, legislators, and bureaucrats want to know the extent to which students are profiting from their schooling experiences. Educators estimate that students attending U.S. public schools take more than 300 million standardized tests each year. School district personnel use these tests to document the achievement of a population of students that gets more diverse every year. Some states have put plans into place to make the size of teachers' pay increases and the resources individual schools receive dependent on (among very few other things) the magnitude of student gains on achievement tests. New kinds of assessments, such as performance assessments and portfolio assessments, are being used and refined. (Educators refer to these new forms of assessment as "alternative assessments" and sometimes as "authentic assessments.") Federal education policy contains specific expectations for states to develop high educational standards and to use tests to measure the extent to which students meet the standards. The Elementary and Secondary Education Act signed into law in 2002 calls for schools to assess and report on the progress of all students annually. The Individuals with Disabilities Education Act (IDEA) requires that schools and states report on the performance and progress of all students with disabilities. Clearly, assessment is in the forefront of activities in education.

In this text, we address primarily the use of tests to make educational decisions about individuals and groups. We also describe the use of tests in making accountability decisions for schools and school systems. We examine norm-referenced or standardized tests, reporting on each measure's suitability for particular types of decisions. We include chapters on performance assessment and the use of portfolios, teacher-made tests, assessment of instructional environments, and outcomes-based accountability, recognizing shifts and tension points in assessment practices today. Our coverage of assessments is broad, including both formal and informal assessments, multiple methods for collecting information, and the many purposes for which the collected information is used.

Testing Is One Part of Assessment

Testing consists of administering a particular set of questions to an individual or group of individuals to obtain a score. That score is the end product of testing. Testing may be part of the larger process known as assessment; however, testing and assessment are not synonymous. Assessment in educational settings is a multifaceted process that involves far more than just administering a test. When we assess students, we consider the way they perform a variety of tasks in a variety of settings or contexts, the meaning of their performance in terms of the total functioning of each individual, and the likely explanations for those performances. High-quality assessment procedures take into consideration the fact that anyone's performance on any task is influenced by (1) the demands of the task itself, (2) the history and characteristics the individual brings to the task, and (3) the factors inherent in the context in which the assessment is carried out.

We have defined assessment as the process of collecting data for the purpose of making decisions about students. When we assess students, we measure their competence. Specifically, we measure their progress toward attaining those competencies their schools or parents want them to master. In schools, we are concerned about competence in three domains in which teachers provide interventions: academic, behavioral (including social), and physical.

Historically in special and remedial education, and now increasingly in general education settings, the focus of assessment has been on measuring student progress toward instructional goals or outcomes and on diagnosing the need for special programs and related services. For example, we may want to know whether Antoine needs special services to assist him in developing reading skills (need for service in an academic domain) or the extent to which Ellen is developing physically at a normal rate (progress decision in the physical domain). Figure 1.1 shows the 13 kinds of decisions that use assessment information and the three domains in which these decisions are made. Throughout this book we always try to be very specific in our discussions of assessment activities, and to differentiate assessment practices on the basis of the domain and the kind of decisions being made. We try never to talk about assessment by itself, but instead about assessment for a specific purpose. Note that we have organized the 13 kinds of decisions into four major types: (1) prereferral classroom decisions, (2) entitlement decisions, (3) postentitlement classroom decisions, and (4) accountability/outcomes decisions.

FIGURE 1.1
The Assessment
Decision–Problem
Area Matrix

	Academic	Behavioral	Physical
Problem Area			

Prereferral Classroom Decisions

Provision of Special Help or Enrichment

Referral to an Intervention Assistance Team

Provision of Intervention Assistance

Entitlement Decisions

Screening

Referral

Exceptionality

Documentation of Special Learning Needs

Eligibility

Postentitlement Classroom Decisions

Instructional Planning

Setting

Progress Evaluation

Accountability/Outcome Decisions

Program Evaluation

Accountability

Types of Decisions

The decisions that use assessment information are varied and complex, and they occur in and out of classrooms. Some are decisions about who is eligible for the benefits of special education services, some are about planning instructional interventions for students, and others are about the extent to which students are benefiting from services they receive. In Table 1.1, we list and briefly define the 13 kinds of decisions. The table and the following discussion are organized around the four types just identified.

Prereferral Classroom Decisions
When students show academic, behavioral, or physical difficulties, their classroom teacher typically tries out a number of teaching alternatives. Most states now require that teachers implement and document the effectiveness of several alternative instructional approaches before they are allowed to refer students for formal assessment. These prereferral classroom decisions center on whether to

TABLE 1.1   Decisions Made Using Assessment Information

	Decision Area	Question to Be Answered
Prereferral Classroom Decisions	Provision of special help or enrichment	Should the student be provided with remediation, compensation, or enrichment so that difficulty in learning can be overcome?
	Referral to an intervention assistance team	Should the teacher seek the assistance of an intervention assistance team (composed of other teachers) in planning instructional interventions for an individual student?
	Provision of intervention assistance	Should the intervention assistance team provide the student with intensified remediation, compensation, or enrichment?
Entitlement Decisions	Screening	Is more intensive assessment necessary?
	Referral to a child study team	Should the student be referred for formal psychoeducational evaluation, to be conducted by members of a child study team?
	Exceptionality	Does the child meet state criteria for assigning a disability label or a label of gifted and talented?
	Special or unique learning needs	Does the student have special learning needs that require special education assistance so that the outcomes of schooling can be achieved?
	Eligibility	Is the student eligible for special education services?
Postentitlement Classroom Decisions	Instructional planning	What should a teacher teach, and how should he or she teach?
	Setting	Where should students be taught?
	Progress evaluation	To what extent are students making progress toward specific instructional goals?
Accountability/ Outcomes Decisions	Program evaluation	Are specific instructional programs working as school personnel want them to work?
	Accountability	To what extent is education working for students? (Accountability decisions usually are made at the national, state, or school district level.)

provide special help or enrichment, refer the student to an intervention assistance team, or provide intervention assistance.

Provision of Special Help or Enrichment

Teachers use classroom tests, daily observations, and interviews to decide whether a student is in need of special assistance. Generally, when a student's rate of progress is 20 to 50 percent of that of other students, the teacher has reason to provide special help. When a student's progress is significantly better than that of other students, there is reason to provide enrichment. The process of collecting and using data to decide to provide special help or enrichment is an assessment process. The assessment decision is a judgment by the teacher that the student is not as competent as other students (or is working above the level of other students) and needs special assistance (or enrichment). Special assistance does not mean special education services. Rather, the help may be in the form of tutoring, Title I assistance, assignment of a study buddy, or adaptation of classroom materials and instruction. Special assistance may be designed to remediate a deficiency, compensate for a disability, or provide enrichment. The assistance may also be provided at home. Parents may assist the student with homework or hire a tutor.

Referral to an Intervention Assistance Team

The teacher uses both assessment information obtained as a part of continuous monitoring of student progress and information derived from monitoring the success of efforts to provide special help. The teacher uses assessment information to make judgments or observations that the student is having difficulty acquiring or retaining behavioral or academic skills. Skill acquisition may require simultaneous elimination of undesirable skills or behaviors.

When the student does not make satisfactory progress even with special help, the teacher may seek assistance from an *intervention assistance team (IAT)*, usually composed of general education teachers whose role is to help one another come up with ways to teach difficult-to-teach students. The IAT (sometimes called a prereferral team, teacher assistance team [TAT], mainstream assistance team [MAT], or schoolwide assistance team [SWAT]) works as a problem-solving team. Sometimes the members of the IAT gather data through observation, interview, or testing. When they do so, they are engaging in assessment. The interventions that are developed and put in place by IATs often are called "prereferral interventions" because they occur prior to formal referral for child study.

Which students do teachers refer to IATs? Although that question can be answered simply—they refer students who bother them—it is not easy to predict whether a student will be referred. Different teachers are bothered by different behaviors, although some behaviors and characteristics will probably bother most, if not all, teachers. Effective teachers use data to support their belief that students need further assistance.

Provision of Intervention Assistance

In 1980 very few states required prereferral interventions. Currently, about three fourths of the states do. The prereferral intervention (or intervention assistance) process has been put in place in states and local school districts in an effort to reduce referral for testing and overidentification of students as needing special education services. The process is based on the notion that many of the difficulties for which students are formally referred can be alleviated by adjusting classroom interventions. The purpose of prereferral intervention in fact is twofold: (1) to try to alleviate difficulties and (2) to document the kinds of techniques that do and do not improve student outcomes.

One of the best examples of prereferral intervention is found in Iowa, where a mandatory problem-solving process is used to systematically examine the nature and severity of an education-related problem. The focus is on developing effective educational interventions. Steps in the Iowa problem-solving process are shown in Table 1.2.

Each local education agency, in conjunction with a regional area education agency, attempts to resolve problems or behaviors of concern directly in the general education environment, prior to conducting a full and individual evaluation. General education interventions include teacher consultation with special educators and collaboration among general educators in attempts to improve student performance. Activities are documented and include (1) measurable and goal-directed attempts to resolve problems and behaviors of concern, (2) communication with parents, (3) collection of related data, (4) intervention design and implementation, and (5) systematic monitoring of student progress and of the effects of the intervention. If these general education interventions do not alleviate the academic or behavior problem, a full and individual intervention is conducted.

Entitlement Decisions

Screening

Screening is the process of collecting data to decide whether more intensive assessment is necessary. Implicit in screening is the notion that students' difficulties may go unnoticed if teachers do not test for them. It is assumed, for example, that a student might have a hearing difficulty or cognitive deficit that would go unrecognized without screening. Because there is some variability in teachers' tolerances for and awareness of various problems, there may be students in classrooms who are exceptional but are not having their needs met. School districts want to find these students and provide special services to them, so screening programs are started.

Screening decisions are essentially administrative in nature. All students in particular schools or school districts are given preliminary tests to identify those who differ significantly from their classmates (in either a positive or a negative sense) and therefore may be eligible for special education services. Just as vision and hearing tests are routinely given to identify pupils with vision or hearing problems, intelligence tests may be administered to identify students who need special attention, either because of limited intellectual capacity or because of

----

TABLE 1.2	Steps in the Iowa Problem-Solving Process

Description of the problem. The problem or behavior of concern is described in objective, measurable terms that focus on alterable characteristics of the individual and the environment, and describe the degree of discrepancy between the demands of the educational setting and the individual's performance.

Data collection and problem analysis. A systematic data-based process for examining all that is known about the problem is used to identify interventions that have a high likelihood of success. Relevant data are collected in multiple settings using multiple sources and methods. The data collection procedures are individually tailored, valid, and reliable, and allow for frequent and repeated measurement of the effectiveness of proposed interventions.

Intervention design and implementation. Interventions are chosen and designed based on the preceding analysis, the defined problem, parent input, and professional judgments about their potential effectiveness. They are described in an intervention plan that includes goals and strategies, a progress monitoring plan, a decision-making plan for summarizing student progress and analyzing the extent to which it is appropriate, and the names of the responsible parties. Interventions are implemented as developed and can be modified on the basis of objective data and with the agreement of the responsible parties.

Progress monitoring. Systematic monitoring of student progress includes regular and frequent data collection, and analysis of individual performance across time. Interventions are modified as frequently as necessary based on this monitoring.

Evaluation of intervention effects. The effectiveness of interventions is evaluated through a systematic procedure in which patterns of individual performance are analyzed, summarized, and compared to initial levels of performance.

SOURCE: Adapted from Special Education Rules, Iowa Department of Education, 1998; Reschly & Ysseldyke, 2002; Tilly, 2002.

highly superior intellectual ability. Achievement tests, measures of what has been taught to and learned by students, are routinely given to identify students who are experiencing academic difficulty and for whom further assessment may be appropriate.

Screening is an initial stage during which students who may evidence a particular problem, disorder, disability, or disease are sorted out from the general population. Screening has its origins in medicine and uses terminology from medical screening practices. We speak of individuals who perform poorly on screening measures as being "at risk"; we describe individuals as "false positives" when they perform poorly on screening measures but do well on later follow-up assessments, which show that they do not have the condition for which they were screened. Sometimes students show no problems at the time of screening and are considered "normal," but later they evidence the very problems for which screening was conducted. These students are said to be "false negatives."

TABLE 1.3   Hits and Misses in Making Screening Decisions

	Reality	
Result of Screening	*Student Has a Certain Characteristic*	*Student Doesn't Have the Characteristic*
Student has a certain characteristic	Hit	False positive
Student doesn't have the characteristic	False negative	Normal

Finally, when we talk about the accuracy of screening decisions, we often speak of the "hit rate" (proportion of accurate positive decisions) for screening. Table 1.3 shows the relationship between screening decisions and accurately diagnosed conditions.

Screening takes place at all levels of education. Children are screened before they enter kindergarten or first grade to determine their academic readiness in terms of language, cognitive, and motor development, and social and emotional functioning. We want to know the competencies they do and do not have. They may also be given vision and hearing screening tests. After they are tested, their performance is compared with standards established by those who make the screening tests. For example, if two thirds of the children who took the test when it was being developed scored 300 points or better, children who score below 300 could be considered at risk. Test developers usually provide cutoff scores to help educators make decisions. Sometimes students are denied school entrance if they score low on a screening test (parents are asked to delay school entry until the child is deemed ready to enter school), and sometimes low performance results in the child's being marked for observation and monitoring. School administrators vary greatly in their views on which skills, abilities, and behaviors students need in order to enter school. Many view all children as ready for school and focus their efforts on getting the schools ready for students.

Screening also is used throughout the school years to identify students who need extra attention because their performance is markedly different from normal or average performance. When this screening is done, student performance is judged *relative to that of others*. Cutoff scores are based on the average performance of students at various ages or grade levels. The scores of this norm group are used in deciding whether more testing is necessary. Decisions about performance usually are based on single snapshots of student performance or behavior. Decisions about progress usually are made by looking at student performance over time, often using the same test. Judgments about student competence or progress over time may also be made *relative to an absolute standard*. Absolute standards typically are statements about the competencies schools want students to have at specific points in time (such as graduation or completion of grade 9).

At some point, educators may come to believe that a student's academic or behavioral needs are so different that they cannot be met using the current approaches and that the child needs special education to achieve desired outcomes. When students' scores indicate a special need, they may be referred for psychoeducational assessment and given individually administered psychological and educational tests. These tests help to determine the specific reasons for a student's performance on a screening measure.

Referral

When a student fails to make satisfactory progress, even with the help of an IAT, the student may be referred for formal psychoeducational evaluation. *Referral* usually is a formal process involving the completion of a referral form and a request for a team of professionals to decide whether a student's academic, behavioral, or physical development warrants the provision of special education services. The team of professionals is usually called a "child study team," although in some states and districts within states these teams go by other names: In Colorado and Massachusetts, they are called "individualized education plan (IEP) teams"; in Texas, "admission, review, and dismissal (ARD) teams." Child study teams make two kinds of decisions: decisions about exceptionality (whether the child is disabled or gifted) and decisions about special learning needs. These teams are composed of general education teachers, special education teachers, one or more administrators, the student's parents, and related services personnel, such as the school psychologist, nurse, social worker, and counselor, depending on the nature of the case. Recent surveys show that each year, 3 to 5 percent of the students in public schools are referred for psychological and educational assessment. About 92 percent of those students who are referred are tested, and about 73 percent of those who are tested are declared eligible for special education services (Algozzine, Christenson, & Ysseldyke, 1982; Ysseldyke, Vanderwood, & Shriner, 1997).

Exceptionality

In making exceptionality decisions, the child study team decides whether a student meets the eligibility criteria for special education as specified by the state in which the student lives. If, for example, the student must be shown to have both an IQ below 70 and deficits in adaptive behavior in order to be categorized as a student with mental retardation, one or more team members will administer tests to see whether the child scores below the required levels. The team does the official assigning of an exceptionality category, and the criteria used to make the decision are state-established criteria. For example, teams identify, according to state criteria, categorical conditions such as blind, deaf, mentally retarded, emotionally disturbed, and learning disabled. They also decide whether youngsters are gifted or talented. Given that some students have multiple disabilities, teams must identify the category under which services will be provided. Teams are required to gather assessment information, and it is illegal to base exceptionality decisions on a single test.

Documentation of Special or Unique Learning Needs

Child study teams also make decisions about whether students have special learning needs that require provision of special education services. For example, they may document that a student who is blind or visually impaired experiences academic difficulties without instruction in Braille or the use of large-print books. They make a formal statement that the student has special learning needs that require special education assistance, and they link these learning needs to statements about the kinds of assistance required. Increasingly, child study teams rely on the data they receive from those who have conducted prereferral interventions with individual children.

Eligibility

Before the Education for All Handicapped Children Act was passed in 1975, eligibility, labeling, and placement decisions typically were made by administrators or school psychologists. Members of the U.S. Congress, acting on the belief that individual decision making was capricious and too often wrong, decided that these decisions should be made by teams using multiple sources of information.

Before a student may be declared eligible for special education services, he or she must be shown to have an exceptionality (a disability or a gift or talent) *and* to have special learning needs. It is not enough to be disabled or to have special learning needs. Students can be disabled and not require special education. Students can have special learning needs but not meet the state criteria for being declared disabled. Students who receive special education (1) have diagnosed disabilities (or special gifts or talents), (2) have special learning needs, and (3) need special education services to achieve educational outcomes.

In addition to the classification system employed by the federal government, every state has an education code that specifies the kinds of students considered to be disabled. States have different names for the same disability. For example, in California, some students are called "deaf" or "hard of hearing"; in other states, such as Colorado, the same kinds of students are called "hearing impaired." Different states have different standards for classification of the same disability. In Pennsylvania, the maximum IQ for individuals with mental retardation is 80; in Minnesota, the maximum IQ is 70; in California, an African American student cannot be classified as having mental retardation on the basis of an individual intelligence test. Some states consider gifted students to be exceptional and entitled to special education services; other states do not.

In late 2004 Congress reauthorized the IDEA. It provided new alternative ways to declare students eligible for special education services. Specifically, it removed the requirement that students have a severe discrepancy between ability and achievement in order to be considered learning disabled. As of the writing of this edition, the U.S. Department of Education had not yet specified regulations and guidelines defining the new alternatives. These regulations and guidelines may affect eligibility. For more information, visit the website for this text and click on your textbook. New IDEA provisions are posted.

Online Study Center
General Resources

Postentitlement Classroom Decisions

Instructional Planning

Inclusive education teachers are able to take a standard curriculum and plan instruction around it. Although curricula vary from district to district—largely as a function of the values of community and school—they are appropriate for most students at a given age or grade level. However, what should teachers do for those students who differ significantly from their peers or from district standards in their academic and behavioral competencies? These students need special help to benefit from classroom curriculum and instruction, and school personnel must gather data to plan special programs for these students.

Three kinds of decisions are made in instructional planning: (1) what to teach, (2) how to teach it, and (3) what expectations are realistic. Deciding what to teach is a content decision, usually made on the basis of a systematic analysis of the skills that students do and do not have. Scores on tests and other information help teachers decide whether students have specific competencies. Test information may be used to determine placement in reading groups or assignment to specific compensatory or remedial programs. Teachers also use information gathered from observations and interviews to decide what to teach. They obtain information about how to teach by trying different methods of teaching and monitoring students' progress toward instructional goals. Finally, decisions about realistic expectations are always inferences, based largely on observations of performance in school settings and performance on tests.

With the increased attention given to learning disabilities and with federal and state requirements for individualized education programs for exceptional students, we have seen an expansion in the use of curriculum-based assessment procedures in planning instructional efforts. The merits and limitations of tests in planning specific education programs are discussed in several chapters in Parts 3 and 4 of this text. Instructional planning for students with disabilities involves development of an individualized educational plan. The IEP and the components required to be included in it are described in the chapter "Assessment of Intelligence: Individual Tests."

Setting

Setting decisions are often called "placement decisions." Educators determine where to put students so that they may receive the most appropriate services. Students with disabilities are educated in different kinds of settings, and the settings vary in their location, the kinds of other students enrolled, and the kind of curriculum taught. Federal law and regulations allow for a "continuum of alternative placements," and educators must decide which setting is least restrictive to the student. The law says that each public agency must ensure

1. that to the maximum extent appropriate, children with disabilities, including children in public or private institutions or other care facilities, are educated with children who are nondisabled; and

2. that special classes, separate schooling, or other removal of children with disabilities from the regular educational environment occurs only if the

nature or severity or the disability is such that education in regular classes with the use of supplementary aids and services cannot be achieved satisfactorily (§300.550).

The continuum of alternative placements must include these placements: instruction in regular classes, special classes, special schools, home instruction, and instruction in hospitals and institutions. In addition, provision must be made for supplementary services (such as resource rooms or itinerant instruction) to be provided in conjunction with regular class placement.

Setting decisions must be made by an IEP team that includes the parents and other persons knowledgeable about the student. Student placements must be determined at least annually, based on the child's IEP, and must be as close as possible to the child's home. Unless their IEPs indicate otherwise, children are to be educated in the school they would attend if they were nondisabled. Federal law also requires that, in selecting educational placements, school personnel give consideration to any potential harmful effect on the child or on the quality of services that he or she needs. Students with disabilities are not to be removed from general education classrooms solely because of needed modifications in the general curriculum (§300.552). It is incumbent on school personnel to demonstrate that students are educated in the least restrictive setting that is appropriate, not simply a setting in which they can physically be put.

Progress Evaluation

Parents, teachers, and students have a right and a need to know how students are progressing in school. How do we know whether students are learning and developing competence? One way to know, of course, is to rely on our observations of a student's behavior and our own feelings about and impressions of the student's work. Just as a parent evaluates a child's development on the basis of general impressions or observations, so teachers evaluate students' progress on the basis of subjective general impressions.

Teachers also collect assessment information to decide whether their students are making progress. They may give unit tests, or they may evaluate portfolios of the students' work (sometimes called "portfolio assessment"). The data that are collected as part of the process of evaluating pupil progress are used to fine-tune education programs or to make changes in teaching strategies. Some of the data collected in progress evaluations tell teachers and parents whether specific instructional objectives have been achieved.

When tests are used to make progress evaluation decisions, it is critical that there be good correspondence between the test and the curriculum. When discussing tests, we must distinguish between attainment and achievement. *Attainment* is what an individual has learned, regardless of where it has been learned. *Achievement* is what has been learned as a result of instruction in the schools. Any test of factual information measures attainment; however, a test of factual information is an achievement test only if it measures what has been directly taught. Only achievement tests can be used to monitor pupil progress. It would be pointless to use a test that did not assess what a teacher had taught.

The best way to collect data for the purpose of evaluating individual students' progress is to sample the skills that are being taught. This method allows teachers to measure the extent to which students have mastered content and to chart their progress toward meeting instructional objectives.

Accountability/
Outcome Decisions   Assessment information is used to make decisions about the extent to which educational programs in school systems are working. It is also used to make decisions about the extent to which education is working for all students, including students with disabilities.

Program Evaluation

Assessment data are collected to evaluate specific programs. Here the emphasis is on gauging the effectiveness of the curriculum in meeting the goals and objectives of the school. School personnel typically use this information for school-wide curriculum planning. For example, schools can compare two approaches to teaching in a content area by (1) giving tests at the beginning of the year, (2) teaching two comparable groups two different ways, and (3) giving tests at the end of the year. By comparing students' performances before and after, the schools are able to evaluate the effectiveness of the two competing approaches.

The process of assessing educational programs can be complex if numerous students are involved and if the criteria for making decisions are written in statistical terms. For example, an evaluation of two instructional programs might involve gathering data from hundreds of students and comparing their performances using many statistical tests. Program costs, teacher and student opinions, and the nature of each program's goals and objectives might be compared to determine which program is more effective. This kind of large-scale evaluation probably would be undertaken by a group of administrators working for a school district.

Of course, program evaluations can be much less formal. For example, Martha is a third-grade teacher. When Martha wants to know the effectiveness of an instructional method she is using, she does her own evaluation. Recently, she wanted to know whether having students complete activities in their basal readers was as effective as having them use language experience activities. She compared students' written products using both methods and concluded that the use of language experience activities was a better way to help them achieve competence.

Accountability

Public schools in the United States have come under increasing criticism over the past two decades. In 1983 a special study panel commissioned by the U.S. Department of Education issued a report entitled *A Nation at Risk*, which raised concerns about education in the United States and about the accomplishments of U.S. students. Increasingly, parents want reports on how students are doing in their schools, legislators want to know how the schools are doing, and policy makers want data on the educational performance of the nation's youth. School personnel regularly administer tests to students, engage in portfolio assessment or performance assessment, and issue reports on the achievement of the students in their schools. Such practices are sometimes called "outcomes-based accountability practices."

Making Assessment Decisions

We have described assessment as the process of collecting data for the purpose of making decisions about students. However, assessment and decision making are seldom straightforward. Students are not uniformly referred, tested, declared eligible, placed in special education, and then taught. Rather, the assessment process proceeds differently in different places for different students. Decisions made about students are neither sequential nor mutually exclusive. For example, a teacher may be providing Dominic with special assistance in reading, during which time the speech-language pathologist may administer a language screening test to him.

Sometimes it takes a long while to go through the sequence of decisions; at other times, the interval from screening or referral to provision of services is very short. Some students perform poorly on a screening measure and are referred immediately to an IAT or child study team. Other students come to the attention of the IAT only after the teacher has provided considerable assistance and the student has not profited to the extent desired. Referral may result from a teacher's observations, a parent's request, or the student's own request. IATs may try a number of interventions, and then students who fail to perform as expected will be referred to the child study team. Assessment is dynamic and ongoing. After the declaration of eligibility for services and specification of learning needs for a student, teachers continue to observe how the student performs under differing circumstances and to modify instruction accordingly (Algozzine, Ysseldyke, & Elliott, 1997).

Context can affect assessment practices. Some students are not referred to an intervention assistance team because their general education class teacher has special expertise in dealing with their disability. Other students with particular disabilities are more likely to receive assistance in one district or state than in another.

When is assessment started? Timing is largely a function of the severity of a disability. The assessment and decision-making process may be shortened in some instances, such as when a parent of a child with severe disabilities initiates a referral. Parents know very early in a child's life that severe disabilities are present. They may contact their family physician, who may need very little time to decide that a child has a disability—it may be readily apparent. But sometimes it is necessary for assessment personnel to engage in extensive assessment to ascertain whether a child has a developmental disorder. In general, it takes longer to decide to declare students with mild disabilities eligible for special education services than it does to make the same decision for students with severe disabilities. Some disabilities do not show up until students are in school and experience difficulty with schoolwork.

Assessment Domains

Assessment relies on the specification and verification of problems for the purpose of making different kinds of decisions. We just described the kinds of decisions that are made in educational settings. We now describe three kinds of problems with which assessment is usually concerned: academic problems, behavior problems, and physical problems.

Academic Problems

The most common reason students are referred for psychological or educational assessment is that a teacher or parent believes that they are not performing as well academically as could be expected. Teachers usually make that decision on the basis of their observations of pupil performance in core content areas: reading, mathematics, and written language and communication. When referring students to IATs or child study teams for assessment, teachers must specify their concerns. Teachers who refer students for assessment because of vague "reading problems" provide diagnostic personnel with limited information. To the extent that teachers describe and specify the nature of a student's problems (for example, "Rachel is the poorest reader in the class and consistently has difficulty associating letters with sounds"), they help diagnostic personnel. Some very effective teachers regularly gather information about pupil progress in academic content areas and use those data to make decisions about special assistance or to refer students.

Academic competence is nearly always assessed in making exceptionality and eligibility decisions. For example, a student referred for reading problems might be given a reading test to provide a comparison of his or her reading skills with those of other students in the school or even the nation. The results of the test would be used to verify or disconfirm the existence of a problem. Academic performance is also usually assessed in making instructional planning decisions. In deciding what to teach a student, the teacher or team must specify which academic competencies the student already has.

Behavior Problems

Students are often referred for psychological or educational assessment because they demonstrate behavior problems. Students for whom severe behavior problems can be specified and verified are often declared eligible for special education services. Behavior problems include failure to get along with peers, delinquent activities, and excessive withdrawal, as well as disruptive and noncompliant behavior. For example, Ms. Swanson might be troubled because Larry is so quiet and withdrawn. She might begin to verify that this is actually the problem by counting the frequency of Larry's interactions with his peers. A low count would not, by itself, indicate a problem. Therefore, Ms. Swanson might select another boy whose behavior she judged to be appropriate and count the frequency of his interactions with his peers. She could then verify that Larry interacted much less frequently than a boy who had no problem interacting. Ms. Swanson might plan a social skills training program for Larry to increase the number of positive interactions that he has with his classmates. She could systematically collect data on the effectiveness of this new program and reach some decisions about Larry's progress.

Physical Problems   Physical problems include sensory disabilities (such as in vision or hearing), problems of physical structure (for example, spina bifida or cerebral palsy), and chronic health problems (such as diabetes or asthma). Severe physical problems are often brought to the attention of parents by physicians before a child enters school. When a child with a severe physical problem enters school, the parents may supply the school with specific information from physicians, confirming and specifying the physical nature of the child's problem.

Milder, but nonetheless important, problems that have not been noticed by the parents are often discovered during routine screening. For example, suppose White Haven Area School District requires that the school nurse, Mr. Slique, regularly conduct hearing tests (such as a pure-tone audiometric test for hearing within the specific range). When he screens the first-grade students, Mr. Slique notes that Jane has a 65-decibel loss in her more sensitive ear. A hearing loss of such magnitude, if confirmed, would have serious educational implications and would necessitate substantial educational modifications so that Jane could profit from her education. However, the screening assessment was conducted in the nurse's room, which was not soundproofed, and with equipment that had not been checked recently for accuracy. Therefore, Mr. Slique decides that it would be best to have an audiologist see Jane and diagnose her hearing problem. He works with the child study team to refer Jane to the audiologist for more extensive testing of her hearing.

Assessment and Society

The students we teach in assessment classes often come with questions about the role that testing plays in social decision making. They ask such questions as "Is it fair to place students in special education on the basis of their performance on a test?" "What do tests say about a person?" and "Should an employer decide whether to hire a person on the basis of how that person does on a test?" Our students also question the use of tests in making decisions about college entrance or admission to graduate school. Throughout this text, when appropriate, we address these and other issues surrounding the use of tests in schools. Testing does play a critical role in schools and in society. Many times, tests are used to make high-stakes decisions that may have a direct and significant effect on individuals' life opportunities or on the continued funding of schools and school systems. The joint committee of three professional associations that developed a set of standards for test construction and use has addressed the kinds of issues our students often raise:

> Educational and psychological testing are among the most important contributions of behavioral science to our society, providing fundamental and significant improvements over previous practices. Although not all tests are well developed nor are all testing practices wise and beneficial, there is extensive evidence documenting the effectiveness of well-constructed tests for uses supported by validity evidence. The proper use of tests can result in wiser decisions about individuals and programs than would be the case without their use and also can provide a

route to broader and more equitable access to education and employment. The improper use of tests, however, can cause considerable harm to test-takers and other parties affected by test-based decisions (American Educational Research Association, American Psychological Association, & National Council on Measurement in Education, 1999).

SUMMARY

Testing is part of a larger concept: assessment. Assessment data are used to document the competencies that students do or do not have and to clarify and verify the existence of educational problems in the areas of academic functioning, behavioral and social adaptation, and physical development. Assessment provides data to facilitate decision making. Thirteen kinds of decisions are made using assessment information: decisions about provision of special help or enrichment, referral to an intervention assistance team, provision of intervention assistance, screening, referral to a child study team, exceptionality, documentation of a special or unique learning need, eligibility, instructional planning, setting, progress evaluation, program evaluation, and accountability. Many complex social, political, and ethical issues arise when tests are used to make important decisions about individuals. Assessment is an important activity, and it is critical that it be done right.

QUESTIONS FOR CHAPTER REVIEW

1. What is the difference between testing and assessment?
2. Attack or defend this generalization: Different kinds of data are needed for the purpose of making different kinds of educational decisions.
3. What five kinds of decisions are made in determining whether students are entitled to special education services?
4. Imagine that, as a member of a debate team, you are required to take the position that educational

and psychological tests are either detrimental or beneficial to society. Select the position that you wish to take, and provide an argument for your position.

PROJECT

Three types of problems—academic, behavioral, and physical—which could be highly related, are specified and verified through assessment procedures. Create a case in which these three problems are interrelated, and identify the implications that this complexity has for assessment procedures after the student has been referred for behavior problems.

RESOURCES FOR FURTHER INVESTIGATION

Print Resources

Algozzine, B. A., Ysseldyke, J. E., & Elliott, J. (1997). *Strategies and tactics for effective instruction* (2nd ed.). Longmont, CO: Sopris West.

Ysseldyke, J. E., Vanderwood, M., & Shriner, J. (1997). Changes over the past decade in special education referral to placement probability: An incredibly reliable practice. *Diagnostique, 23*(1), 193–201.

Technology Resources

AMERICAN EDUCATIONAL RESEARCH ASSOCIATION
www.aera.net
This website provides information to professionals interested in educational research and its practical application. The organization is divided into 12 divisions,

and information on assessment is located in the following areas: Teaching and Teacher Education, School Evaluation and Program Development, and Measurement and Research Methodology.

American Psychological Association (APA)
www.apa.org
This connects to the APA website, where it is possible to search for information about psychology, education, and employment opportunities. There is also information on APA membership and publications.

National Education Association
www.nea.org
This is the home page for this national organization of teachers and educators. There is an information center about public education and a resource room containing tips for teachers to help students learn.

U.S. Department of Education
www.ed.gov/index.html
This page provides news and information about the government's educational initiatives. There is a listing of programs, services, publications, and products.

Council for Exceptional Children (CEC)
www.cec.sped.org
The CEC home page disseminates information on special education issues and legislation, scholarships and awards for students with special needs, and CEC services. It often contains information on assessment.

Practical Assessment, Research, & Evaluation
http://pareonline.net
This website is an online journal that provides research articles about assessment.

Regional Resource and Federal Center (RRFC) Network
www.dssc.org/frc/rrfc.htm
This is a network of seven technical assistance agencies (six Regional Resource Centers [RRCs] and one Federal Resource Center) funded by the U.S. Department of Education, Office of Special Education Programs. The RRFC Network delivers technical assistance to state education agencies, helping them improve special education policies, programs, and practices. The RRCs regularly track assessment legislation.

Council of Chief State School Officers (CCSSO)
www.ccsso.org
CCSSO is a nationwide nonprofit organization composed of public officials who lead the departments responsible for elementary and secondary education in the 50 states, the U.S. extrastate jurisdictions, the District of Columbia, and the Department of Defense Education Activity.

Education Week
www.edweek.org/ew/index.html
This is the website of the weekly publication of current local, state, national, and international education news.

CHAPTER 2

Assessment Processes and Concerns

IN THE CONTEXT OF EDUCATION, ASSESSMENT IS PERFORMED TO GAIN AN UNDER-standing of an individual learner's strengths and weaknesses in order to make appropriate educational decisions. Any textbook description of this interactive, individualized, and complex process is necessarily general and linear; thus, to some extent, descriptions of data collection and decision making can distort and oversimplify these processes. This chapter begins with a description of the process of collecting data to gain an understanding of a student's strengths and weaknesses. It ends with a description of frequently voiced concerns about assessment and subsequent decision making.

Underlying this chapter is the belief that the best educational decisions are based on information; usually, better decisions are based on more information. Although good decisions can be based on a flash of insight, more often they are the result of generating hypotheses, carefully amassing information, carefully analyzing that information for consistencies and inconsistencies, and then deciding whether there is sufficient evidence to support or reject the hypotheses.

The Process of Assessment

When a student is experiencing difficulty in school, two related and complementary types of assessment should be performed. First, the instruction a student has received is assessed to ascertain whether the student's difficulties stem from inappropriate curriculum or inadequate teaching. When instruction is found to be inadequate, the student should be given appropriate instruction to see whether it alleviates the difficulty. When appropriate instruction fails to remediate the difficulty, further assessment of the student is carried out. Each approach is described in this section.

Assessing Instruction

Until the early 1980s most assessment activities in school settings consisted of efforts to assess the learner. Yet school personnel often have difficulty developing instructional recommendations solely on the basis of information about the characteristics of students. Englemann, Granzin, and Severson (1979) recommended that assessment begin with instructional diagnosis "to determine aspects of instruction that are inadequate, to find out precisely how they are inadequate, and to imply what must be done to correct their inadequacy" (p. 361). In this approach, assessment consists of systematic analysis of instruction in terms of its appropriateness for the learner. Two dimensions are usually considered when instruction is assessed: instructional challenge and instructional environment.

Instructional Challenge

For instruction to be effective, it must be possible for the learner, with a reasonable effort, to master the information (the facts, skills, behaviors, or processes) being taught. If the degree to which information challenges a learner is thought of as a continuum, we can think of material as ranging from too easy (unchallenging), through about right in degree of difficulty (appropriately challenging), to too difficult (overly challenging).

Unchallenging Content

Instruction that is too easy for a student teaches information that requires no additional practice for acquisition or retention; the student understands the information and can use it. Usually, unchallenging instruction occurs for two reasons. First, a teacher may hold previously mastered goals as the current goals of instruction. Thus the teacher teaches what the student already knows. Obviously, if a student already has met the goal, additional instruction or practice wastes time and bores the student. Second, the pace of challenge may be too slow. In this case, a teacher initially provides instruction on new information but fails to recognize when the student has mastered it. Here, too, time is wasted, and the student is bored. Needed levels of mastery vary with the capabilities of individual students and the design of the curriculum. However, as a rule of thumb, educators frequently use a criterion of a 95 percent correct response rate as the point beyond which students no longer need even independent practice.

Appropriately Challenging Content

Instruction that is appropriately challenging is, of course, neither too easy nor too difficult. Moreover, such instruction is usually motivating because students can see that, with some effort, they will succeed. Depending on the student and the task, challenging material usually produces rates of correct student response of between 85 and 95 percent.

Overly Challenging Content

Instruction that is too difficult for a student attempts to teach information for which the student lacks significant prerequisites. This problem occurs for two related reasons. First, instruction can be too challenging if a student lacks facts, concepts, behaviors, or strategies on which the new instruction is based. Two examples illustrate: (1) If students do not understand addition, they will probably be unsuccessful in learning multiplication beyond some rote memorization; (2) if students do not understand that deciduous trees go dormant in the winter, they may not grasp the difference between dead trees and healthy but dormant ones.

Second, instruction can be too difficult when its pace is too fast. In this case, the student has been exposed to prerequisite information but has not yet mastered it. For example, a youngster may still be learning to control writing movement when the teacher moves on to printing letters. As a result, the student may still be concentrating on pencil grip instead of learning how specific letters are formed.

Like information that is too easy, what is too difficult for a student varies with the capabilities of the student and the design of the curriculum. However, educators generally believe that, when average students cannot respond with about 85 percent accuracy, the material is too difficult; for students with severe cognitive handicaps, rates of correct response of less than 90 percent may indicate that the material is too challenging for guided practice. When instruction is too challenging, students do not learn efficiently and often experience frustration; such students are occasionally called "curriculum casualties."

Instructional Environment

Instruction involves more than appropriate curriculum. It is a complex activity, the outcomes of which depend on the interaction of many factors. Recognition of this fact has led to efforts to assess the qualitative nature of students' instructional environments (Ysseldyke & Christenson, 2002).

Assessment of the instructional environment consists of systematically analyzing the extent to which those factors that are known to make a difference in pupils' learning are present in the instruction that students receive. Since the early 1970s psychologists and educators have learned much about the attributes of instruction that result in efficient and motivated learning. Yet, in many classrooms, instruction is not particularly effective. Too often, teachers use a strategy of "cover and pray": They talk about the content and pray that the students learn it. In these classrooms, students are exposed to information, not taught; teachers hope that students somehow learn the information, but they do not assess to make sure that their students have learned it. In these classrooms, some students master the curriculum because they are sufficiently capable of learning from exposure or are taught by their parents. Others do not master the curriculum and become teaching disabled. Through no fault of their own, their learning is not commensurate with their abilities. Thus, when students experience difficulty learning, a necessary component of assessment is evaluating the quality of the instruction that students have received. Although the chapter "Portfolio Assessment" deals in greater detail with the ecology of instruction, two dimensions of instruction (classroom management and learning management) are worth describing here.

Classroom Management

Classroom management refers to a collection of organizational goals centered on using time wisely in order to maximize learning and on maintaining a safe classroom environment that is conducive to student learning. In classrooms that are poorly organized, students lose learning opportunities because of disruptions by other students, ineffective grouping, poor transitions between activities, and so forth. In contrast, well-organized classrooms have clearly stated and well-understood procedures, consistent consequences for student behavior, and student freedom within a structured environment.

Learning Management

The organization and management of the classroom to ensure learning require careful attention to detail. Essentially, teachers must oversee the learning situation. Effective teachers do the following:

- Demonstrate what is to be learned and then provide adequate opportunities for meaningful rehearsal and guided and independent practice with appropriate materials until skills become automatic
- Give students immediate, specific, and corrective feedback about their performances and provide opportunities to correct mistakes
- Reinforce desired outcomes
- Stress understanding, application, and transfer of information

Assessing Learners

When students have received appropriate instruction but are still experiencing academic or behavioral problems, school personnel usually begin to assemble existing information to document the nature of the problem (that is, to identify specific learning strengths and weaknesses) and to generate hypotheses about the problem's likely cause.

Kinds of Information   A test is only one of several assessment techniques or procedures available for gathering information. During the process of assessment, data from observations, recollections, tests, and professional judgments all come into play.

Observations

Observations can provide highly accurate, detailed, verifiable information, not only about the person being assessed, but also about the surrounding contexts. Observations can be categorized as either nonsystematic or systematic.

Nonsystematic Observation   In *nonsystematic,* or informal, *observation,* the observer simply watches an individual in his or her environment and notes the behaviors, characteristics, and personal interactions that seem significant. Nonsystematic observation tends to be anecdotal and can be subjective and unreplicable. However, nonsystematic observations can provide the basis for determining what to observe systematically.

Systematic Observation   In *systematic observation,* the observer sets out to observe one or more precisely defined behaviors. The observer specifies observable events that define the behavior and then counts the frequency or measures the frequency, duration, amplitude, or latency of the behaviors. The observer must be careful to observe the important behaviors and characteristics—not just those that are convenient to measure.

Disadvantages of Observations   There are three potential disadvantages in using observations to collect information: imperfect observation, time demands, and distortion of the context of observation.

A substantial body of research indicates that humans often imperfectly observe, interpret observations, and reach decisions based on their observations. Two types of imperfect observation are particularly noteworthy: the halo effect and expectancy.

The *halo effect* is the tendency to make subjective judgments on the basis of general attributes. Thus one characteristic of a subject, such as race, may alter the way in which the subject's peer interactions are seen. Salvia and Meisel (1980) have documented the impact on observation of several student characteristics: social class, given names, surnames, race, facial attractiveness, and labels of exceptionality. The halo effect is most likely to influence observations when the behavior or attributes under consideration are not easily observed, are not clearly defined, involve reactions of other people, or are of high moral importance. Conversely, providing observers with systematic training in observation, specific observation procedures, and highly objective situations can substantially reduce or eliminate biased observations (Salvia & Meisel, 1980).

Expectancy is the tendency to see behaviors that are consistent with one's beliefs about what should happen; the observers never would have seen these behaviors with their own eyes unless they already believed in them. For example, teachers are more likely to observe improved behavior on the part of their classes when they believe that their interventions are effective. Expectancy is most likely to influence observations when teachers have beliefs about instructional and behavior interventions, and when the behavior is difficult to observe or not clearly defined. The most effective way to prevent expectancies from influencing observations is to keep observers blind—that is, uninformed about who is receiving intervention or about the nature of the intervention. However, this technique is very difficult to implement in schools.

The second disadvantage of observation is that it can be very time consuming. The more precisely and carefully observations are made, the more time consuming they become. Thus an assessor pays for accurate information by not being able to collect other information.

The third disadvantage is that the very presence of an observer may distort or otherwise alter the situation to such a degree that the behavior of the individual being observed also is altered. For example, students may be hesitant to misbehave when an outsider is observing in the classroom.

Recollections

Recalled observations and interpretations of behavior and events are frequently used as an additional source of information. People who are familiar with the student can be very useful in providing information through interviews and rating scales.

Interviews   Interviews can range in structure from casual conversations to highly structured processes in which the interviewer has a predetermined set of questions that are asked in a specified sequence. Generally, the more structured the interview is, the more accurate are the comparisons of the results of several different interviews.

Rating Scales   *Rating scales* can be considered the most formal type of interview. Rating scales allow questions to be asked in a standardized way and to be accompanied by the same stimulus materials, and they provide a standardized and limited set of response options. The two most commonly used types of response options are Likert-like scaling and frequency estimates. With *Likert scales,* a person is usually required to agree or disagree with a statement by indicating whether he or she strongly agrees, agrees, disagrees, or strongly disagrees. Occasionally, this type of scale has a neutral midpoint (neither agree nor disagree). With *frequency estimates,* a person responds by indicating how often a behavior or situation occurs. The estimate may be verbal (always, frequently, seldom, or never) or numerical (more than 95 percent of the time, between 50 percent and 95 percent of the time, and so on).

Disadvantages of Recollections   In addition to having some of the same disadvantages associated with direct observation, recollections suffer from two other disadvantages. First, the longer the time is between observation and recollection, the greater is the chance that some memory distortion will occur. For example, important details may be forgotten, and some things that are generally consistent with the remembrance may be invented. Second, individuals may not be truthful. People may be unwilling to divulge painful or embarrassing details. They may alter what they tell an interviewer according to what they believe the interviewer hopes to hear. They may provide information selectively or over- or understate problems to further their own agendas. For example, parents who do not want their child placed in special education may assert that a child's school avoidance is infrequent, even though it is a daily problem.

Tests

A *test* is a predetermined set of questions or tasks for which predetermined types of behavioral responses are sought. Tests are particularly useful because they permit tasks and questions to be presented in exactly the same way to each person tested. Because a tester elicits and scores behavior in a predetermined and consistent manner, the performances of several different test takers can be compared, no matter who does the testing. Hence, tests tend to make many contextual factors in assessment consistent for all those tested. The price of this consistency is that the predetermined questions, tasks, and responses may not be equally relevant to all students.

Basically, two types of information—quantitative and qualitative—result from the administration of a test. *Quantitative data* are the actual scores achieved on the test. An example of quantitative data is Lee's score of 80 on her math test. *Qualitative data* consist of other observations made while a student is tested; they tell us how Lee achieved her score. For example, in earning a score of 80 on her math test, Lee may have solved all of the addition and subtraction problems, with the exception of those that required regrouping. On a language test, Henry may have performed best on measures of his ability to define words, while demonstrating a weakness in comprehending verbal statements. When tests are used in assessment, it is not enough simply to know the scores a student earned on a given test; it is important to know how the student earned those scores.

Interpreting Quantitative Test Performance   Once gathered, quantitative data must be interpreted: What do the numbers mean? Interpretation occurs along two dimensions: performance standards and informational context. First, the meaning of a student's performance on a test depends on the standard against which the performance is compared. For example, if Juan got 75 percent correct on his weekly spelling test, his teacher might want to know how other students did on that test (that is, a comparative standard), or the teacher might evaluate Juan's performance on an absolute basis (for example, he did not get 90 percent correct, but he improved his score over that on his previous test). Second, the meaning of a specific performance depends on the other information that has been amassed; in other words, the performance must be contextualized to show how it relates to the other information that has been collected. These two dimensions are often related. Depending on the purpose of assessment and the context, assessors may select test procedures that will provide a particular kind of interpretive information.

All tests should be objective in the sense that there are predetermined answers or standards for scoring a response. Legally, assessments must be objective in the sense that the attitudes, opinions, and idiosyncrasies of the examiner do not affect scoring; any two examiners should score a response in the same way. Objective scoring, per se, does not imply fair scoring; it implies only predetermined criteria and standardized scoring procedures. A subjective test, by contrast, lacks a predetermined correct answer. Therefore, the examiner's subjective judgments, attitudes, and opinions can affect the scoring. Many people erroneously define an essay test as a subjective test. Such a test can be objective if there are predetermined, explicit criteria for correct responses, so that the same response would be assigned the same score by two or more examiners.

Normative Standards   Most assessments that occur outside of the classroom are norm-referenced—that is, an individual's performance is compared with the performance of many peers. In norm-referenced assessment, although the learning of particular content or skills is important, the resulting score is used primarily to ascertain the extent of differential learning, which allows the tester to rank individuals from those who have learned many skills to those who have learned few.

Commercially prepared *norm-referenced devices* typically are designed primarily to do one thing: yield a distribution of scores that distinguish the performances of individuals. They allow the tester to discriminate among the performances of a number of individuals and to interpret how one person's performance compares with those of other individuals with similar characteristics. Thus a person's performance on a test is measured in reference to the performances of others who are presumably like that person in other respects.

Commercially prepared norm-referenced tests are standardized on groups of individuals representative of all children, and typical performances for students of certain ages or in certain grades are obtained. The raw score that an individual student earns on a test, which is the number of questions answered correctly, is compared with the raw scores earned by other students. A *transformed score,* such as a percentile rank, is used to express the given student's standing in the group of all children of that age or grade.

Classroom teachers, counselors, psychologists, speech and language therapists, and others may create their own assessment devices for their own purposes. The primary differences between commercially prepared and custom-made tests are the representatives of the comparison group (see the chapter "Norms") and the specificity of the content (see the discussion of content validity in the chapter "Validity"). Teacher-made tests are illustrative of the class of custom-made tests. Teachers usually limit the group with whom an individual's performance is compared. Thus, as one example, a teacher may compare Juan's performance only with that of his classmates—not with that of all students in the same grade. Moreover, what Juan is asked to do (the content of the test) usually reflects the classroom curriculum directly. Thus Juan's teacher learns how Juan compares with other students in the classroom who have received the same instruction on the same content. As a second example, Jim's special education teacher might want to know whether Jim can be integrated into a regular fourth-grade class for reading instruction. This teacher could ask the general education class teacher to nominate two or three other students who are reading at an acceptable level. The special education teacher could assess Jim's reading and the reading of these nominated students to ascertain whether Jim is reading as well as his peers. If he is, his reading skills are sufficient for integration.

Absolute Standards   In contrast to norm-referenced tests, *criterion-referenced tests* do not indicate a person's relative standing in skill development; they measure a person's mastery of particular information and skills in terms of absolute standards. Thus criterion-referenced tests provide answers to specific questions, such as "Does Maureen spell the word *dog* correctly?" "Does Geraldo read beginning fourth-grade material with 90 percent accuracy?" "Has Jennifer passed 75 percent of the questions on the driver's test?" In criterion-referenced assessment, the emphasis is on passing one or a series of questions. The test giver is interested in what the particular individual can and cannot do, rather than in how that individual's performance compares with those of other people.

When teachers use criterion-referenced tests, the items are often linked directly to specific instructional objectives and therefore facilitate the writing of such objectives. Test items frequently sample sequential skills, enabling a teacher not only to know the specific point at which to begin instruction, but also to plan those instructional aspects that follow directly in the curricular sequence.

School personnel use different terms to refer to assessment activities that are parts or derivatives of criterion-referenced assessment, including, for example, curriculum-based assessment, objective-referenced assessment, performance or direct assessment, and formative evaluation of student progress. *Curriculum-based assessment* is defined as "a procedure for determining the instructional needs of a student based on the student's ongoing performance with existing course content" (Tucker, 1985, p. 200). In *objective-referenced assessment,* tests are referenced to specific instructional objectives rather than to the performance of a peer group or norm group. Pupil performance is evaluated by measuring whether the student has met specific objectives. In performance assessment, a student is required to perform specific skills; the teacher does not make inferences about the student's ability to perform the skill. For example, rather than inferring writing skill from tests of writing mechanics and spelling, a teacher would ask a student to write a story. Finally, *formative evaluation* refers to the assessment of progress toward a long-term or major objective (see Bloom, Hastings, & Madaus, 1971).

The Individuals with Disabilities Education Act (IDEA) includes a requirement that states specify standards (results) that will be met by all students, including students with disabilities and with limited English proficiency. The law also specifies that school districts will report annually to their state and that the state will report annually to the U.S. Department of Education the extent to which all students are making progress toward or meeting the state standards. Standards differ in the different states. The practice of measuring and reporting progress toward meeting these absolute standards is often referred to as standards-referenced assessment.

Comparing Normative and Absolute Standards   Interpretation of a student's performance in both normative and absolute terms is useful in special education. No single form of interpretive information is preferred in all situations.

Obviously, when normative comparisons are required, norm-referenced assessments should be made. Norm-referenced interpretations are usually required in screening decisions. For example, if Suang has 20/100 vision, she sees things at 20 feet that normal individuals see at 100 feet. Suang's poor vision, as compared with others', warrants further assessment and treatment. Norm-referenced interpretations are usually required for decisions about exceptionality when a cognitive handicap is suspected; tests of intelligence are always norm referenced.

When tests are administered to help the classroom teacher plan and evaluate instructional programs for children, criterion-referenced interpretations are recommended. For example, when planning a program for an individual student, a teacher obviously should be more concerned with identifying the specific skills that the student does or does not have than with knowing how the student compares with others.

School districts and states typically use both normative and absolute standards in making accountability decisions. They typically use the results of norm-referenced tests to report on the performance of students in their district or state in comparison with those in a test's norm group. They also use standards-referenced tests to assess performance relative to state standards and report on the relative (comparative) progress of students in their various schools or districts.

Professional Judgments

Assessment requires judgment, and the judgments and assessments made by others can play an important role in assessment. When a diagnostician (the person responsible for performing an assessment) lacks competence to render a judgment, the judgments of those who possess the necessary competence are essential. Diagnosticians seek out other professionals to complement their own skills and background. Thus referring a student to various specialists (hearing specialists, vision specialists, reading teachers, and so on) is a common and desirable practice in assessment. Judgments by teachers, counselors, psychologists, and practically any other professional school employee may be useful in particular circumstances.

Expertise in making judgments is often a function of familiarity with the student being assessed. Teachers regularly express professional judgments; for example, report card grades represent the teacher's judgment of a student's academic progress during the marking period; referrals for psychological evaluation represent a different type of judgment, based on experience with many students and observations of the particular student. Judgments represent both the best and the worst of assessment data. Judgments made by conscientious, capable, and objective individuals can be invaluable aids in the assessment process. Inaccurate, biased, and subjective judgments can be misleading at best and harmful at worst.

The Gathering of Information

Information can be categorized as describing either how a person is functioning now or how a person has functioned in the past. Obviously, the distinction between current and historical information blurs, and the point at which current information becomes historical information depends in part on the particular fact or bit of information. For example, if Johnny had his appendix removed three years ago, we know he currently has no appendix. However, if Johnny was a poor reader two years ago while in the first grade, he may or may not be a poor reader today.

Using Extant Information

There are three general sources of information available to school personnel: cumulative records, student products, and anecdotal records.

Cumulative Records State law requires schools to maintain files on each student. Thus schools maintain extensive records about students and sometimes about their families. Although there is some variability from state to state and district to district, these files are likely to contain basic identifying information (such as name, address, and birth date), current educational status (such as grade and school), and basic educational history. This history may contain previous report cards, results of standardized tests, and attendance records. The cumulative records of exceptional students will also probably contain the results of individually administered tests, reports from other professionals (such as language or occupational therapists), multidisciplinary team evaluations, individualized education plans, assorted state-required paperwork, and perhaps medical information. Thus a student's cumulative record contains a potential wealth of information about that student's development. This information may be useful in deciding whether a problem is chronic or recent, what has been tried with the student, who the important persons in the student's educational life are, and so forth.

Although these records are not public in the sense that anyone can read them, access to them can be gained legally in two ways. First, anyone in the school with a legitimate need for the information can obtain access. Thus, for example, a school psychologist, teacher, or counselor may inspect the permanent files of students with whom he or she is working. Second, parents may authorize professionals working with their children to exchange information with professionals outside the schools. Thus, for example, parents can authorize their family physician to provide information to a school psychologist about their child's medications or health; parents can authorize teachers or school psychologists to provide information to the family physician about the effect of medication on the student's activity level and attention.

Student Products Students generate volumes of permanent products: essays, drawings, completed worksheets and tests, and so forth. Although some of these products invariably find their way home, a number of products may remain in the teacher's possession. Some teachers assemble portfolios of student work, keep their own files of student work, and display student work in the classroom. Teachers also maintain summaries of student work. These summaries can take the form of charts of student progress or evaluations recorded in a grade book. Permanent products and grades are useful sources of information about a student's current level of performance and accomplishment. A student's work can be compared with the permanent products created by other students of similar age and expected outcomes.

Anecdotal Records Some teachers keep personal notes about unusual occurrences during the school year. These notes may be prepared for several reasons, two of which are especially noteworthy. First, anecdotal records may be useful in documenting the characteristics of problem behaviors and the conditions under which they occur. For example, a teacher might note the antecedents and consequences of a problem behavior in order to form hypotheses about effective interventions. Second, anecdotal records may be useful in providing a fuller record to justify or document a teacher's actions. For example, a teacher might document a parent's concerns mentioned during a telephone conversation in order to establish a record of parent contacts.

Limitations of Extant Information   Extant information has three limitations of which diagnosticians must be aware. First, someone must cull currently important information from other recorded information. Second, a diagnostician cannot control what information was collected in the past; crucial bits of information may never have been collected. Third, the conditions under which the information was collected are unknown or often difficult to evaluate.

Gathering New Data

There are three advantages to having and using current information. The first is the most obvious: Current information describes a person's current behavior and characteristics. Information about current status is required for most educational decisions. Second, the diagnostician can select the specific information needed to make the desired decisions. This advantage is particularly relevant because assessment is dynamic. Frequently, information leads to further questions that require additional information to answer. Third, current information can be verified.

Putting It Together

As shown in Table 2.1, there are eight general classes of diagnostic information sources (four historical types and four current ones). The classification depends on the source of information, the currency of the information (current or historical), and the kinds of information collected (tests, observations, and so forth).

No single diagnostician has the time, competence, or opportunity to collect all possible types of information. In cases in which specialized information is needed, diagnosticians must rely on the observations, tests, and judgments of others. If a behavior occurs infrequently or is demonstrated only outside of school, the diagnostician may have to rely on the observations and judgments of others who have more opportunity to collect the information—parents or perhaps ward attendants in institutional settings. For example, throwing a tantrum at bedtime obviously does not occur at school; however, without specific reasons to distrust parental reports, most diagnosticians would accept these reports of such behavior as accurate. Moreover, if the problem was intermittent, a diagnostician would have to spend several evenings at the child's home to get a firsthand estimate of the frequency and severity of the tantrums.

Finally, it is usually the responsibility of a team to integrate the information and make decisions. Teams and the types of decisions they make are discussed in the chapters "Making Entitlement Decisions" and "Assessment of Intelligence: An Overview."

Educational Prognosis

Assessment and educational decision making involve explicit or implicit predictions. A prognosis may be offered for students in their current environment and life circumstances or in some therapeutic or remedial environment. For ex-

TABLE 2.1	Examples of Different Types of Historical and Current Diagnostic Information

| Type of Information | Time at Which Information Is Gathered | |
	Historical	*Current*
Observations	Previous individualized education plans prepared by teachers or psychologists	Anecdotal records placed in personal files by teacher
	Disciplinary notes in permanent file	Momentary time sampling of on-task behavior
Recollections	Student's developmental history previously given by parent	Interviews with former teachers of target student
	Rating scale completed the previous year by parent or teacher	Rating scale completed this year by parent or teacher
Tests	Scores from first-grade screening test	Scores on an individual intelligence test
	Scores from third-grade group achievement tests	Results of criterion-referenced tests given by teacher
Judgments	Physician's diagnosis of attention deficit disorder	Teacher's decision to refer student for evaluation
	Grades from previous teachers	Multidisciplinary team's classification of student having a learning disability

ample, knowing that Harry has mental retardation and has not profited from instruction leads to the predictions that (1) he probably will not profit from the same types of instruction in the future; (2) he may fall farther behind the other children and perhaps even develop problem behaviors; and (3) if he is placed in an environment where he can receive more individual attention and specially designed instruction, he should make more progress academically and socially.

In education, as in most other human service ventures, predictions are often not sufficiently sophisticated to allow mathematical specification. Rather, diagnosticians rely on developmental theory and intervention research to make hypotheses about the variables that should influence outcomes or that should intensify or attenuate a given variable's impact. In reaching decisions and making predictions, they then weigh a child's current life circumstances and developmental history in light of various contextual factors.

Current Life Circumstances

Any interpretation of an individual's performance and predictions about future success must include an understanding of that individual's current circumstances. Current life circumstances include the student's family, community and friends, and physical abilities and health.

Family A student's family life contributes enormously to that student's ability to profit educationally. Yet, too frequently, there are significant challenges at home: families headed by a single parent, families in which both parents work or neither parent works, and families that are homeless. Some families are simply dysfunctional. Because of either increasing awareness and reporting of problems or increasing family stress, educators seem to be seeing more students from families with histories of physical, sexual, psychological, or substance abuse. For students who experience difficulties in both school and home, the prognosis frequently is not good. No matter how well intentioned they are, school personnel seldom can assume the family's nurturing role to overcome the effects of a dysfunctional milieu that affects a student's life for 18 or more hours each day.

A student's acculturation is also of great importance. Attitudes and values, especially in the early years, are shaped by the family. These attitudes and values have an important relationship to success in school and later life. Beliefs about the worth of schooling, the relationship between effort and outcome, and the ability to overcome adversity are all important to school success. Culturally determined attitudes about gender roles can have negative effects, for example, when they limit a girl's or a young woman's educational options. Willingness to take risks, to trust and cooperate with a relatively unfamiliar adult, and to give substantial effort to tasks similarly influences school performance. Finally, a student's working knowledge of the public culture (that is, societal mores and values, standard American English, and the fund of general and specific cultural information) influences performance on school-related tasks.

Community and Friends As a child grows older, community and friends play increasingly important roles. To the extent that they are dysfunctional, the student is at risk of failing in school and in life. Two concerns are especially noteworthy. The first is the safety of the community. For some students, the trip to school is literally a matter of life and death; murder is the leading cause of death in some age groups of children, and the risks are especially great for children of color. Some students must daily pass by crack houses or roving gangs ready to steal clothing or lunch money, and there are metal detectors at the school entrance. The second concern relates to the values instilled by community and friends. When a student's community and friends value education, the student has an enhanced prognosis for success in school and in the rest of life.

Physical Abilities and Health Sensory and physical limitations have serious implications for assessment and schooling. Vision, hearing, and physical handicaps have long-term implications for instruction and assessment; different instructional and assessment procedures may be used with such students. Acute health conditions can produce short-term sensory or physical limitations; for example, otitis media may result in temporary hearing loss.

A student's health and nutritional status can play an important role in the student's performances on a wide variety of tasks and on academic development in general. Sick or malnourished children are apt to be lethargic, inattentive, and perhaps irritable. A temporary illness, such as the flu, can result in lost or reduced opportunities for learning. Moreover, children from economically impoverished backgrounds tend to be at greater risk of physical or health limitations for two reasons: (1) Their physical environments may be more hazardous, and (2) their parents may lack the funds to secure medical treatment.

Developmental History

A person's current life circumstances are shaped by the events that make up his or her history of development. Deleterious events may have profound effects on physical and psychological development. Physical and sensory limitations may restrict a student's opportunity to acquire various skills and abilities. A history of poor health or poor nutrition may result in missed opportunities to acquire various skills and abilities. An individual's history of reward and punishment can shape what that person will achieve and how that person will react to others. In short, it is not enough to assess a student's current level of performance; those who assess must also understand what has shaped that current performance.

Contextual Factors

In addition to the skills, characteristics, and abilities a pupil brings to any task, other factors affect the assessment process. How another person interprets or re-acts to various behaviors or characteristics can determine whether an individual will even be assessed. For example, some teachers do not understand that a certain amount of physical aggression is typical of young children or that verbal aggression is typical of older students. Such teachers may refer normally aggressive children for assessment because they have interpreted aggression as a symptom of some underlying problem.

The theoretical orientation of the diagnostician also plays an important part in the assessment process. Diagnosticians' backgrounds and training may predispose them to look for certain types of pathologies. Just as Freudians may look for unresolved conflicts and behaviorists may look for antecedents and consequences of particular behaviors, diagnosticians may let their own theoretical orientation color their interpretation of particular information.

Finally, the conditions under which a student is observed or the conditions under which particular behaviors are elicited can influence that student's performance. For example, the level of language used in a question or the presence of competing stimuli in the immediate environment can affect a pupil's responses.

Decision Making

Diagnosticians reach an understanding of a student by integrating information about current performance with information about current life circumstances and developmental history. They try to make sure that their understanding is not tainted by subjectivity or by personal values and beliefs. Combined with their knowledge of appropriate practices and legal requirements, their understanding guides decision making and predictions about future performance. For example, a decision to classify a student as exceptional is reached when the assessor makes a judgment that, when all things are considered, the student fits a particular diagnostic category. Obviously, such a decision requires thorough knowledge of the criteria that define a category, in addition to detailed knowledge of the student and his or her current life circumstances.

Assessment Concerns

Decisions in school frequently have important, and occasionally lifelong, consequences. The procedures for gathering data and conducting assessments are matters that are rightfully of great concern to the general public—both individuals who are directly affected by the assessments (such as parents, students, and classroom teachers) and individuals who are indirectly affected (for example, taxpayers and elected officials). These matters are also of great concern to individuals and agencies that license or certify assessors to work in the schools. Finally, these matters are of great concern to the assessment community. For convenience, the concerns of these groups are discussed separately; however, the reader should recognize that many of the concerns overlap and are not the exclusive domain of one group or another. Thus the final portion of this section discusses the social validity of an assessment in relationship to various groups.

Concerns of the General Public

The individuals who are affected by educational decisions are rightly concerned about assessment procedures. They want, and deserve, good decisions. However, any decision can have undesired consequences. Decision making creates "haves" and "have nots." Most people who take a test for a driver's license pass the test; some people fail the test and are denied driving privileges. College entrance tests determine admission for some students and exclusion for others. In the same way, decisions about special and remedial education have consequences. Some consequences are desired, such as extra services for students who are entitled to special education. Other consequences are unwanted, such as denial of special education services or diminished self-esteem resulting from a disability label.

Moreover, the desirability of some decisions varies, depending on the student. For example, a decision that a child with mental retardation is eligible for special education may be greeted enthusiastically by some parents but rejected by other parents. Concerns of laypeople generally surface when the educational decisions have undesired consequences and are viewed as undemocratic, elitist, or just unfair.

Fairness

Fairness is an imprecise concept both psychometrically and legally. It is probably best viewed as a marker for a class of conditions and situations in which the outcomes are thought to be disadvantageous, inaccurate, or wrong. Thus issues of fairness usually imply dissatisfaction with an outcome. Allegations of unfair procedures might focus on any of the following complaints.

Lack of Opportunity   Equal opportunity to learn is a complex and often highly charged issue. The issue is not whether a student lacks a particular skill or whether an assessment fairly ascertains what skills a student does and does not possess. The issue is the meaning of absent skills and information. When a student lacks information and skill because of restricted or different opportunities to learn, inferences about what that lack of information or skill means must be made with the greatest of care. For example, tests of intelligence assume that test takers have had comparable opportunity to acquire the information and concepts elicited. When a student has not had that opportunity, inferences about intelligence are dubious. Lack of opportunity probably has as many causes as any social malady. The following list is intended to be illustrative, not exhaustive.

- *Inadequate district resources.* In most states, the costs of education are borne largely by local school districts, which rely on property taxes. Because the assessed value of property located within district boundaries varies from district to district, some districts have a larger tax base than others. Thus the same rate of taxation produces less revenue in poorer districts than in richer districts. Moreover, poorer districts usually tax at much higher rates while generating less revenue than wealthier districts. Limited district resources translate directly into lost opportunities for students: teachers with emergency certificates, rather than complete qualifications; curriculum narrowing, resulting in a lack of enrichment or advanced courses; old materials; lack of equipment such as computers, laboratory equipment, or equipment for vocational shop classes; and so forth.

- *Inadequate instruction.* A teacher or a district's curriculum may not cover essential content, leading students to be tested on material and concepts that were never taught or were inadequately taught.

- *Student deficiencies.* Through no fault of their own, students may be unable to take advantage of adequate resources. For example, acute or chronic illness may restrict a student's opportunity to learn material.

- *Inadequate home supervision.* Parents may not (1) ensure that children get enough sleep, (2) limit television viewing time, (3) encourage completion of homework, or (4) stress the value of education.

Ethnic and Gender Bias   Related to questions of opportunity are issues of ethnic, racial, and gender bias. Although we struggle to achieve a society in which the accomplishments of all individuals are valued, not all groups are treated equally. The issue of ensuring unbiased assessment for an individual from a minority group has a long history in the law, philosophy, and education. Three aspects of the issue are particularly relevant to this section of this book.

1. *Representation of individuals from diverse backgrounds in assessment materials.* Test materials should present people of color and women in both nonstereotypic and traditional roles and situations. It is widely believed that failure to do this has a chilling effect on students of color and young women and girls.

2. *Experiential opportunities of individuals from diverse backgrounds.* To the extent that students of color, girls, and young women undergo different

acculturation, test materials should account for differences in experiential background for acquiring the tested skills, information, and values. For example, tests should have an equal number of questions that are more advantageous for males and questions that are more advantageous for females. (This is usually determined empirically by identifying items on which either boys or girls score higher.) Alternatively, test makers could delete questions that elicit pronounced differences in results between males and females or among members of culturally diverse groups.

3. *Language and concepts.* The language and concepts describing students of color and women and girls should not be racist or sexist.

Subjective Scoring   It is frequently thought to be inappropriate to assess student performance when the criteria for scoring student responses are subjective. Although students who receive the benefit of subjective scoring may not complain, assessors should be prepared to defend an indefensible position when questioned by students who are penalized by subjective scoring procedures. Most people would have trouble accepting scoring criteria that cannot be explicated; for example, a teacher might say to a student that this is a "B" paper without being able to explain how the paper differed from an "A" paper. A subjective criterion of "I know one when I see one" is seldom acceptable to people who have not produced "one."

Similarly, when instructors with the same background and qualifications as the assessor reach different judgments about a student's work, that judgment is seldom satisfactory to students who receive lower grades. For example, almost all the professors in the education department use one definition of a behavioral objective, but Professor Smith uses a different definition. When students are accustomed to producing objectives that meet the wider definition of all previous instructors, they may argue with Professor Smith's judgment in considering their objectives to be wrong.

Finally, if criteria for scoring are not explicit and objective, marking student answers wrong can lead to accusations of gender, racial, or ethnic discrimination.

Unequal Treatment   Students and parents expect marking standards to be applied consistently. Perhaps no situation is more troubling than when two students receive different scores for essentially the same product. When no cheating is suspected, one would expect student work to be marked uniformly.

Unfair Comparisons   People are frequently sensitive about the people with whom they (or their children) are compared. Thus comparison groups should be appropriate. It would be inappropriate to compare an 8-year-old's elapsed time in a 100-meter dash with that of a 16-year-old. Moreover, comparative evaluations should make logical sense. For example, high school and college students frequently complain when examinations are graded on a curve because this practice requires that some students get lower grades. In the worst case, even students who knew the material well could receive a poor grade.

Finally, comparisons should take into account issues of diversity. Years ago, test publishers frequently excluded people of color from comparison groups used to establish norms; European American people were apparently thought to be the only people of interest. Such comparisons failed to take into account the potential impact of cultural differences associated with ethnic or racial differences. Today, most test authors and publishers have moved beyond such simplistic conceptualizations of comparison groups and have included individuals from all of the larger minority groups in the United States. Nonetheless, even these more broadly representative norms may be unsuitable for use with students who are members of smaller minority groups (those that make up 1 percent of the population or less). When testing students from numerically small minorities that differ substantially in acculturation, there is no simple answer to the question of whether to make normative comparisons. In some cases, where no inferences are made about underlying ability (for example, oral reading), normative comparisons might be legitimate. In other cases (for example, in the assessment of intelligence or adaptive behavior), such comparisons are probably unwise.

Face Validity

An evaluation procedure should bear a logical relationship to the decision that is to be made. Although there is much more to valid assessment than the mere appearance of the test (see the chapter "Validity"), what is being asked should make intuitive sense to the test taker or to his or her parents. For example, an employment test should obviously have something to do with work to be done by the prospective employee. In the same way, school tests should be authentic in that they should measure outcomes sought by the school.

Concerns of Certification Boards

Certification and licensure boards establish standards to ensure that assessors are appropriately qualified to conduct assessments, and these boards also sanction professionals for practicing beyond their competence. Test administration, scoring, and interpretation require different degrees of training and expertise, depending on the kind of test being administered and the degree of interpretation required to obtain meaning from the test taker's performance. Although most teachers can readily administer or learn to administer group intelligence and achievement tests, as well as classroom assessments of achievement, a person must have considerable training to score and interpret most individual intelligence and personality tests. Therefore, all states certify teachers and psychologists who work in the schools on the basis of formal training and, sometimes, on the demonstration of competence.

When pupils are tested, we should be able to assume that the person doing the testing has adequate training to administer the test correctly. We also should be able to assume that the tester can establish rapport with pupils, because students generally perform best in an atmosphere of trust and security. We further assume that the tester knows how to administer the test correctly. Testing consists of standardized presentation of stimuli. To the extent that the person giving the test does not correctly present the questions or materials, the obtained scores lose interpretability. We also assume that the person who administers a test knows how to score the test. Correct scoring is a prerequisite to attaining a meaningful picture of a student. Finally, we assume that accurate interpretations can and will be made.

Obviously, professionals should administer only those tests that they are qualified to administer. Too often, unfortunately, we hear of people with no training in individual intelligence testing who nonetheless administer individual intelligence tests, or we see people with no formal training in personality assessment administering or interpreting personality tests. Such tests may look easy enough to give; however, the correct administration, scoring, and interpretation are complex. Because tests are so often used to make decisions that will affect a child's future, having a skilled observer or tester is especially important.

Concerns of Assessors

Although those responsible for making educational decisions are also concerned with fair and valid testing, their concerns are generally more precise and detailed. There are four generally held areas of concern: accuracy, generalizability, meaning, and utility.

Accuracy

Accuracy is rightly considered a property of the diagnostician. Observations should not distort or incorrectly represent reality—diagnosticians must see what is there. No matter what form assessment takes, the diagnostician must always categorize a student's behavior or products. For example, in classifying behavior, an observer might ask the question, "Did Bob hit Harry?" In this case, the diagnostician uses explicit or implicit criteria to make a judgment about Bob's behavior; that is, the diagnostician has a definition of "hit" and decides whether Bob's behavior matches that definition. Similarly, when a diagnostician tests Bob, Bob's responses are classified as correct, partially correct, or incorrect; that is, the diagnostician has a definition of "correct" and decides whether Bob's response matches that definition.

Inaccuracies occur in assessment because a diagnostician has applied criteria incorrectly or inconsistently and therefore has made decisions that are in error. Errors occur when a diagnostician either allows a definition to drift or change over time, or loses focus or objectivity. The situation in which observations are made has a substantial impact on the accuracy of the observations. For example, accuracy can be jeopardized when the behavior is difficult to observe, when there are too many behaviors to observe, when the decision rules are too complex, or when the definition of behavior is unclear or insufficiently detailed. As the chapter "Reliability" shows, it is possible to estimate the accuracy of observations.

Generalizability

Seldom are educators and psychologists interested in a single behavior or response at one specific time in one context. Usually, diagnosticians want to generalize a student's performance along three dimensions: domain, times, and settings.

Generalization to a Larger Domain   Usually, diagnosticians want to generalize from a student's performance on a few questions to that student's performance on all other similar items. For example, when a student is given a math quiz containing 10 multiplication facts, the teacher would like to infer that student's knowledge of all 100 multiplication facts. To allow generalization to other related performances, the sample of behavior must be sufficiently large. Moreover, the behavior sample must be representative of the domain. Thus a teacher might be willing to generalize answering 10 multiplication facts to general knowledge of multiplication facts but should be unwilling to infer skill in all facets of multiplication (such as solving problems with two multiplicands) because the sample is not representative of the entire domain.

Generalization to Other Times   In most cases, a diagnostician would like to assume that behavior observed on one occasion will be observed on similar future occasions. For example, if Kim knows 10 multiplication facts today, we would like to assume that she will know those same facts tomorrow and next week. In this sense, every observation is a prediction.

Although assessments are usually stable, they are not invariably stable. Luck is not stable; a student who makes a lot of lucky guesses today may not be so lucky tomorrow. Behaviors and skills that are emerging are unlikely to be stable. For example, a student who is learning consonant sounds will not consistently give the correct sound for a consonant until the information is mastered.

Unusual conditions in the student being examined often produce unstable results. If Abdul has a cold or otitis media, he may not do what he is otherwise capable of doing on a test. Similarly, unusual conditions in the assessment setting may produce unstable results. For example, if Abdul is distracted during a test, his performance may not indicate what he usually can do.

Generalization to Other Settings   Just as assessors are concerned with generalization to larger domains and other times, they are also concerned with generalization to other settings. For example, if Jill reads accurately in school, we would like to assume that she can read materials of similar difficulty at home. When behavior and skills fail to generalize to other settings, teachers and psychologists frequently look for differences across the settings in an attempt to ascertain what conditions or stimuli functionally control the behavior.

Meaning

Implicit in the preceding discussion is the idea that accurately observed and generalizable behavior may have meaning beyond what is directly observed. For example, a child's completion of a human-figure drawing may represent artistic ability, intellectual ability, various personality traits, or perceptual-motor skill. None of these constructs is observable; they are inferred from behavior and products that are observable, and the inferences to be made vary, depending on the student's opportunity to learn.

Students all come to school with unique background experiences in educational, social, and cultural environments—background experiences that are inextricably intertwined with their school experiences. Diagnosticians often must try to unravel these relationships. One of the most common examples is when psychologists assess a student's intellectual ability. To some extent, all tests of intelligence measure cultural learning in some form (for example, language, general information, and social values). Moreover, the inference drawn from the results of intellectual testing is that students who have learned more than other students from comparable backgrounds have more ability to learn.

However, when cultural backgrounds vary, differences in what has been learned cannot be attributed to the ability to learn. A simple example illustrates the problem. A child may be asked to name the four seasons of the year, and the correct (keyed) answer is "summer, fall, winter, and spring." However, in some parts of the country, many boys and girls associate seasons with hunting; thus, they might respond, "buck, doe, rabbit, and turkey." Their response, although not the keyed response, is not wrong; it represents different *acculturation,* different background experiences and opportunities to learn in both formal and informal settings.

A similar problem occurs when commercially prepared achievement tests are used. When a student's curriculum does not address tested information (or does not address it comprehensively), the student has not had comparable opportunity to learn that information. Inferences about the student's ability to profit from instruction are, at best, tenuous.

Finally, acculturation is a matter of experiential background rather than of gender, skin color, race, or ethnic background (although one's acculturation may be associated with any of these). When we say that a child's acculturation differs from that of the majority, we are saying that the child's experiential background differs. It is that different experience, not the child's ethnic origin, for example, that leads the child to respond differently from the children on whom the test was standardized.

Another way in which opportunity affects the meaning of a student's performance is the presence of a disability. Not only do students with disabilities frequently undergo different acculturation, but their sensory and physical limitations can have a significant impact on tested performance. A test or an individual test item invariably measures an individual's ability to receive a stimulus and then express a response. Skill in the content area measured by a test cannot be measured accurately if meeting the stimulus and response demands of a question is beyond the capabilities of the student.

Common sense tells us that, if a student cannot read directions or write responses, a test requiring these abilities is inappropriate. In such cases, the test measures inability in reading directions or writing answers, rather than skill or ability in the content being assessed. A student with a severe visual disability may know the content of a written test but earn a low score because of visual impairment. A student with a severe physical disability may know the content of the test but not answer any questions correctly because of an inability to write. Similarly, students with communication disorders may know the answers to the questions a tester asks but be unable (or unwilling) to respond to even the most sensitively administered individual test that requires oral answers. Children with physical or sensory handicaps may also perform more slowly than nonhandicapped children; a test that awards points for the speed, as well as the accuracy, of response would not be a valid test of such a child's mastery of content.

A major clue to the meaningfulness of a test is the presence of individuals of different backgrounds and abilities in the standardization sample. When students from diverse backgrounds and with diverse physical abilities are included, test authors have the possibility of discovering whether their test materials are meaningful (as well as unbiased) for children from a variety of backgrounds. When students from diverse backgrounds and with diverse physical abilities are included in the norms in the same proportions in which they are found in the general population, the derived scores are potentially meaningful.

Utility

Finally, diagnosticians are concerned about the usefulness of their assessment procedures. Several topics could be considered in a discussion of utility, but two—efficiency and sensitivity—are particularly relevant for our purposes.

Efficiency *Efficiency* refers to the speed and economy of data collection. Diagnosticians try to gather a wide variety of general information, sacrificing some accuracy to delineate the problem, and then focus their efforts with more accurate and sensitive, but time-consuming, assessments. Usually, highly accurate and specific information takes longer to accumulate than less accurate and less specific information.

For example, group-administered tests are far more efficient than individually administered tests. However, a group test often provides substantially less information than an individual test does. Most group tests survey content rather than provide detailed information about a student's abilities and weaknesses. In addition, valuable qualitative information cannot be collected because of the format of group tests. The examiner may provide oral directions for younger children, but for children beyond the fourth grade, the directions usually are written. The examiner typically cannot rephrase, probe, clarify, or prompt to elicit a student's best performance or control the tempo and pace of the testing or interrupt or terminate the test when a student becomes fatigued.

The scoring of group-administered tests is also more efficient because students usually write or mark answers rather than make extended responses that take more time to score; indeed, because most group tests are machine scored, examiners seldom see a student's responses to individual questions. Similarly, teacher judgments or ratings of behavior are more efficient to collect than systematic behavioral observations; however, behavioral observations tend to be more accurate and are usually less subject to various biases.

Sensitivity *Sensitivity* refers to the ability of an assessment procedure to detect small differences across groups of students and within individual students. Sensitivity is especially important when assessments are made to ascertain whether students have made relatively small changes as a result of instruction or when di-agnosticians want to make fine discriminations among test takers. For instruction to be both sensitive and efficient, the narrow range of development in which the student is functioning is assessed with sufficient items to discriminate. Thus the teacher or psychologist must have an accurate idea of where a student currently functions.

Social Validity of Assessment

Social validity refers to consumers' access to and satisfaction with the assessment procedures. Three classes of consumers are relevant in this discussion: (1) parents and students, (2) diagnosticians, and (3) school administrators.

Parents and Students

For parents and students, social validity generally translates into issues of access and disposition. *Access* refers to the availability of the assessment. For example, can parents and students get to the physical location where the assessment will be conducted? Is the assessment scheduled at a convenient time? Because of the large number of families with a single parent or with two parents who work, finding a convenient time and location often means that teachers and psychologists must work outside of normal school hours. Disposition refers to the willingness of students or parents to complete the assessment. For students, this means giving their best efforts during assessment; for parents, this means cooperating during interviews, completing questionnaires, and participating in decision making.

Diagnosticians

For diagnosticians, social validity translates into issues of ease of administration and utility. If diagnosticians find a particular test or approach undesirable, it is less likely that they will use that approach. Many relatively worthwhile tests stay on the shelf because they are very difficult to administer or score. Others are not used because school personnel do not like the test items, format, or some other aspect of the test. Still others are not used because school personnel believe the measures provide meaningless or useless information.

School Administrators

For administrators, the acceptability of an assessment procedure often becomes an issue of money and risk management. A key responsibility of administrators is to manage money. Thus, when two assessment procedures produce comparable information, the less expensive one (in terms of both personnel time and direct cost) is preferred. Thus procedures that result in fewer completed assessments or assessments that require overtime pay for diagnosticians are typically not used if there are comparable procedures that do not make such demands on resources. Similarly, if an assessment procedure increases the risk of litigation or due-process proceedings, it is less likely to be used than procedures with minimal risk.

SUMMARY

When a student is experiencing difficulty in school, the instruction the student has received is assessed to ascertain the probable cause of that student's difficulties. A curriculum is inappropriate when it is too easy or too hard; instruction can be ineffective because of poor classroom management (lack of organization, disruptive behavior, poor transitions, and so forth) or poor learning management (lack of opportunity for student practice, lack of feedback, poor match of level of instruction to student skill level, failure to teach for higher-level thinking skills, and so forth). Students who experience difficulties and have had inadequate instruction should be given appropriate instruction before it is assumed that the students themselves are the root of the problem.

When instruction is deemed appropriate, the learners are assessed. A variety of information from multiple sources is usually collected or pulled together from existing data. This information may take the form of nonsystematic or systematic observations, interviews, rating scales, tests, and judgments of other professionals. Student performances may be evaluated by comparing them with the performances of other students or with an absolute standard (such as a criterion of 90 percent correct). This information is used to make predictions about students, either in their current situation or in some alternative (such as therapeutic) situation. A variety of factors are considered in reaching a prognosis: the student's family situation, community ties and friendships, physical abilities and health, and developmental history.

Because the process of assessment is quite complex and educational decisions frequently have lifelong consequences, people are rightfully concerned about the entire process. Parents and the general public are frequently concerned about fairness, equal opportunity, ethnic and gender bias, and the appearance of proper assessment procedures. Individuals charged with overseeing the qualifications of persons conducting assessments are rightfully concerned about diagnostician qualifications and training. Also, diagnosticians themselves are concerned about the accuracy, generalizability, meaning, and

utility of the information they collect to facilitate decision making.

QUESTIONS FOR CHAPTER REVIEW

1. Identify three different ways to begin an assessment. Describe an optimal sequence of activities for assessing a student.
2. What are two factors that may have a significant effect on a student's performance during assessment?
3. When and why might you want to administer a group test individually?
4. What is the difference between a norm-referenced and a criterion-referenced test? Cite an advantage of each.
5. How might you evaluate the extent to which students you assess are acculturated in a manner that is comparable to those in a test's norm group?
6. Lupe's parents have just moved into the area. Lupe was enrolled in second grade a few weeks before the annual standardized achievement tests are administered. The decision is made to let her take the tests in Mr. Peño's room, although he is not her teacher, because he speaks Spanish (the language that Lupe speaks at home). Is this sufficient to ensure test validity for Lupe? Why or why not?
7. In this text we identified several concerns about the fairness of assessments. Create a scenario for at least two of the concerns, showing specifically the ways in which each is important to testing students with disabilities.

PROJECT

Interview a school principal or a person who tests students about the standardized achievement tests administered in a local school or school district. Specifically ask about how children with disabilities are involved in the standardized assessments. How do the policies and practices compare with those recommended in this textbook?

RESOURCES FOR FURTHER INVESTIGATION

Print Resources

Boehm, A. E., & Weinberg, R. A. (1997). *The classroom observer: A guide for developing observation skills* (3rd ed.). New York: Teachers College Press.

Christenson, S. L., & Ysseldyke, J. E. (1989). Assessing student performance: An important change is needed. *Journal of School Psychology, 27,* 409–426.

Deno, S. L. (1985). Curriculum-based assessment: The emerging alternative. *Exceptional Children, 52,* 219–232.

Deno, S. L. (1986). Formative evaluation of individual school programs: A new role for school psychologists. *School Psychology Review, 15,* 358–374.

Fuchs, L. S., & Fuchs, D. (Eds.). (1986). Linking assessment to instructional intervention: An overview. *School Psychology Review, 15*(3).

Howell, K. W. (1986). Direct assessment of academic performance. *School Psychology Review, 15,* 324–335.

Lentz, F. E., & Shapiro, E. S. (1986). Functional assessment of the academic environment. *School Psychology Review, 15,* 346–357.

Shapiro, E. S. (1996). *Academic skills problems: Direct assessment and intervention* (2nd ed.). New York: Guilford Press.

Shapiro, E. S., & Kratochwill, T. R. (Eds.) (2000). *Behavioral assessment in schools: Theory, research, and clinical foundations* (2nd ed.). New York: Guilford Press.

Ysseldyke, J. E., & Christenson, S. L. (1987a). Evaluating students' instructional environments. *Remedial and Special Education, 8,* 17–24.

Ysseldyke, J. E., & Christenson, S. L. (2002). *Functional assessment of academic behavior: Creating effective learning environments.* Longmont, CO: Sopris West.

Technology Resources

PATHWAYS TO SCHOOL IMPROVEMENT
www.ncrel.org/sdrs
Click on the Assessment topic button to find information about critical issues in assessment and links to other assessment pages. Also, click on the search button to do a keyword search for articles about critical issues in assessment.

CRESST HOME PAGE
www.cse.ucla.edu/index6.htm
The National Center for Research on Evaluation, Standards, and Student Testing home page provides access to a large amount of assessment information, including newsletters, technical reports, videos, CD-ROMs, papers, and resources.

NATIONAL INSTITUTE ON STUDENT ACHIEVEMENT, CURRICULUM, AND ASSESSMENT
www.ed.gov/offices/OERI/SAI/index.html
The National Institute on Student Achievement, Curriculum, and Assessment home page has links to several sites that describe projects that are ongoing in areas such as assessment, content standards, and other research projects designed to improve student achievement.

INSTITUTE OF EDUCATION SCIENCES
www.ed.gov/about/offices/list/ies/index.html
This site provides information on the condition of education, practices that improve academic achievement, and the effectiveness of federal and other education programs.

CHAPTER 3

Legal and Ethical Considerations in Assessment

MUCH OF THE PRACTICE OF ASSESSING STUDENTS IS THE DIRECT RESULT OF LEGISLA-tion, guidelines, and court cases. If you were to interview directors of special education in your area and ask them why students are assessed, they might initially tell you that students are assessed in order to provide information about how best to teach them. Pressed harder, these directors would probably tell you that students are assessed because assessment is required by law. They might also tell you that specific kinds of students (for example, some minority students) are not assessed because in some instances such assessments have been forbidden by the court. Federal laws mandate that students be assessed before they are entitled to special education services. Such laws also mandate that there be an individualized education program for every student with a disability and that instructional objectives for each of these students be derived from a comprehensive individualized assessment.

In this chapter, we first examine legislation that has affected assessment. We then talk about some of the ethical standards for assessment that have been developed by professional associations. We close the chapter by reviewing guidelines for the collection, maintenance, and dissemination of pupil records.

Laws

Eight laws (some are revisions of earlier laws by the same name) have had important effects on assessment practices: Section 504 of the Rehabilitation Act of 1973 (Public Law 93-112); the Education for All Handicapped Children Act of 1975 (Public Law 94-142); the 1986 Amendments to the Education for All Handicapped Children Act (Public Law 99-457); the Individuals with Disabilities Education Act of 1990 (IDEA; Public Law 101-476); the Americans with Disabilities Act of 1992 (ADA; Public Law 101-336); the 1997 Amendments to the Individuals with Disabilities Education Act (Public Law 105-17); the 2001 Elementary and Secondary Education Act (No Child Left Behind Act; Public

Law 107-110); and the 2004 reauthorization of the IDEA. Table 3.1 lists the major provisions of these eight laws.

Section 504 of the Rehabilitation Act of 1973

Section 504 of the Rehabilitation Act of 1973 (Public Law 93-112) prohibits discrimination against persons with disabilities. The act states:

> No otherwise qualified handicapped individual shall, solely by reason of his handicap, be excluded from the participation in, be denied the benefits of, or be subjected to discrimination in any program or activity receiving federal financial assistance.

TABLE 3.1	Major Federal Laws and Their Key Provisions
Act	**Provisions**
Section 504 of the Rehabilitation Act of 1973 (Public Law 93-112)	It is illegal to deny participation in activities or benefits of programs, or to in any way discriminate against a person with a disability solely because of the disability. Individuals with disabilities must have equal access to programs and services. Auxiliary aids must be provided to individuals with impaired speaking, manual, or sensory skills.
Education for All Handicapped Children Act of 1975 (Public Law 94-142)	Students with disabilities have the right to a free, appropriate public education. Schools must have on file an individualized education program for each student determined to be eligible for services under the act. Parents have the right to inspect school records on their children. When changes are made in a student's educational placement or program, parents must be informed. Parents have the right to challenge what is in records or to challenge changes in placement. Students with disabilities have the right to be educated in the least restrictive educational environment. Students with disabilities must be assessed in ways that are considered fair and nondiscriminatory. They have specific protections.
1986 Amendments to the Education for All Handicapped Children Act (Public Law 99-457)	All rights of the Education for All Handicapped Children Act are extended to preschoolers with disabilities. Each school district must conduct a multidisciplinary assessment and develop an individualized family service plan for each preschool child with a disability.
Individuals with Disabilities Education Act of 1990 (IDEA; Public Law 101-476)	This act reauthorizes the Education for All Handicapped Children Act. Two new disability categories (traumatic brain injury and autism) are added to the definition of students with disabilities. A comprehensive definition of transition services is added.
Americans with Disabilities Act of 1992 (ADA; Public Law 101-336)	Discrimination on the basis of disability is prohibited in employment, services rendered by state and local governments, places of public accommodation, transportation, and telecommunication services.
1997 Amendments to the Individuals with Disabilities Education Act (Public Law 105-17)	These amendments add a number of significant provisions to IDEA and restructure the law. A number of changes in the IEP and participation of students with disabilities in state- and districtwide assessments are mandated. Significant provisions on mediation of disputes and discipline of students with disabilities are added. Funding of special education is restructured.

TABLE 3.1	Major Federal Laws and Their Key Provisions (*cont.*)
2001 Elementary and Secondary Education Act (No Child Left Behind Act; Public Law 107-110)	Targeted resources are provided to help ensure that disadvantaged students have access to a quality public education (funds Title 1).
	The act aims to maximize student learning, provide for teacher development, and enhance school system capacity.
	The act requires states and districts to report on Annual Yearly Progress for all students, including students with disabilities.
	The act provides increased flexibility to districts in exchange for increased accountability.
	The act gives parents whose children attend schools on state "failing schools list" an option to move their students to another school.
	Students in "failing schools" are eligible for supplemental education services.
2004 Reauthorization of IDEA	Students with disabilities are to be taught by a highly qualified teacher. Teachers must possess full state special education certification or pass a state special education licensing exam and hold another teaching certificate.
	New approaches are introduced to determine overidentification.
	The state must have measurable annual objectives for students with disabilities.
	Districts are not required to use severe discrepancy between ability and achievement in identifying LD students.
	A new Center for Special Education Research is established.

If the Office of Civil Rights (OCR) of the U.S. Department of Education finds that a state education agency (SEA) or local education agency (LEA) is not in compliance with Section 504 and that district chooses not to act to correct the noncompliance, OCR may withhold federal funds from that SEA or LEA.

Most of the provisions of Section 504 were incorporated into and expanded in the Education for All Handicapped Children Act of 1975 (Public Law 94-142) and the Americans with Disabilities Act of 1992 (Public Law 101-336). Section 504 and the Americans with Disabilities Act are broader than the Education for All Handicapped Children Act because their provisions are not restricted to a specific age group or to education. Section 504 is the law most often cited in court cases involving either employment of people with disabilities or appropriate education in colleges and universities for students with disabilities. Section 504 has been used to secure services for students with conditions not formally listed in the disabilities education legislation. For example, since the 1980s, Section 504 has been used to get services for students who have attention deficit disorders, which are not classified as disabilities within the Individuals with Disabilities Education Act.

The Education for All Handicapped Children Act of 1975

Education is a responsibility of the state rather than the federal government. No provision of the U.S. Constitution mandates education. Yet every state has compulsory education laws which require students to attend school. In 1975 the U.S. Congress passed a compulsory special education law, the Education for All Handicapped Children Act (often known by its congressional number, Public Law 94-142). That law was designed to serve four major purposes:

1. To guarantee that special education services are available to children who need them

2. To ensure that decisions about providing services to students with disabilities are made in fair and appropriate ways

3. To set clear management and auditing requirements and procedures for special education at all levels of government

4. To provide federal funds to help states educate students with disabilities

Much of what happens in assessment is directly mandated by one of the four provisions of Public Law 94-142. These provisions are described in the section on the 1997 Amendments to IDEA.

The 1986 Amendments to the Education for All Handicapped Children Act

In 1986 Congress passed a major set of amendments to the Education for All Handicapped Children Act, extending all rights and protections of the law to preschoolers with disabilities. The provisions of this set of amendments, Public Law 99-457, requires states to provide a free, appropriate public education to children ages 3 through 5 years with disabilities by school year 1990–1991. In addition, these amendments provide grants to states so they can offer interdisciplinary educational services both to infants and toddlers with disabilities and to their families. Thus states now have a significant incentive to serve children with disabilities from birth through age 2 years. This bill also expands Public Law 94-142 by requiring that noneducational federal, state, and local resources and services be made available to all children with disabilities. Federal or state-funded agencies other than schools can no longer argue that they cannot provide services to children if the services can be provided by schools.

Public Law 99-457 specifies that each school district use a multidisciplinary assessment to develop an individualized family service plan (IFSP) for each child. The IFSP must include the following:

▓ A statement of the child's present level of cognitive, social, speech and language, and self-help development

▓ A statement of the family's strengths and needs related to enhancing the child's development

▓ A statement of the major outcomes expected for the child and family

▓ Criteria, procedures, and timelines for measuring progress

▓ A statement of the specific early intervention services necessary to meet the unique needs of the child and family, including methods, frequency, and intensity of service

▓ Projected dates for initiation and expected duration of services

▓ The name of the person who will manage the case

▓ Procedures for transition from early intervention into a preschool program

The Individuals with Disabilities Education Act

The Individuals with Disabilities Education Act of 1990 (Public Law 101-476) is a reauthorization of Public Law 94-142. Congress renamed the Education for All Handicapped Children Act and reaffirmed a national intention to support alternative education for students with special learning needs. To reflect contemporary practices, Congress replaced references to "handicapped children" with "children with disabilities." Two new disability categories (autism and traumatic brain injury) were added, and a comprehensive definition of transition services (services to ensure smooth movement from school to postschool activities) was added. The law also specifies that schools must develop individualized transition plans for students who are 16 years of age or older.

The Americans with Disabilities Act

The purpose of the Americans with Disabilities Act of 1992 (Public Law 101-336) is to extend to people with disabilities civil rights equal to those guaranteed without regard to race, color, national origin, gender, and religion through the Civil Rights Act of 1964. ADA prohibits discrimination on the basis of disability in employment, in the provision of services by state and local governments, in places of public accommodation, in the provision of transportation, and in the provision of telecommunication services, such as telephones. It states that employers cannot discriminate against individuals with disabilities. Employers must use employment application procedures (including assessments) that enable individuals with disabilities to apply for jobs. In making decisions about whom to hire, promote, or discharge, employers are not allowed to take into account a person's disability. Individuals with disabilities should not be paid differently than others, they have the same rights to job training, and they are to have the same privileges of employment as others.

The 1997 Amendments to the Individuals with Disabilities Education Act

The IDEA amendments of 1997 (Public Law 105-17) clarify and add to the 1990 IDEA. In the following sections we describe those parts of the law that are directly applicable to assessment of students with disabilities.

The Individualized Education Program (IEP) Provisions

Public Law 94-142 specifies that all students with disabilities have the right to a free, appropriate public education and that schools must have an *individualized education plan (IEP)* for each student with a disability. In the IEP, school personnel must specify the long-term and short-term goals of the instructional program. IEPs must be based on a comprehensive assessment by a multidisciplinary team. We stress that assessment data are collected for the purpose of helping team members specify the components of the IEP. The team must specify not only goals and objectives, but also plans for implementing the instructional program. They must specify how and when progress toward accomplishment of objectives will be evaluated. Figure 3.1 illustrates an IEP for a student in a Minnesota school district. Note that specific assessment activities that form the basis for the program are listed, as are specific instructional goals or objectives. IEPs are to be formulated by a multidisciplinary child study team that meets

FIGURE 3.1
An Individualized
Education Program

INDIVIDUALIZED EDUCATION PROGRAM

11/11/02
Date

Thompson   J.
STUDENT: Last Name   First   Middle
                                                      5.3   *8/4/92*

School of Attendance   Home School   Grade Level   Birthdate/Age

School Address   School Telephone Number

Child Study Team Members

LD Teacher
Case Manager

Homeroom teacher
Name   Title

Parents
Name   Title

Facilitator (school psychologist)
Name   Title

Speech pathologist
Name   Title

Name   Title   Name   Title

Summary of Assessment Results

IDENTIFIED STUDENT NEEDS: ___ *Reading from last half of*
DISTAR II – present performance level _____

_____

_____

LONG-TERM GOALS: ___ *To improve reading achievement level by at*
least one year's gain. To improve math achievement to grade level.
To improve language skills by one year's gain. _____

_____

SHORT-TERM GOALS: ___ *Master Level 4 vocabulary and reading*
skills. Master math skills in basic curriculum. Master
spelling words from Level 3 list. Complete units 1-9 from
Level 3 curriculum. _____

_____

MAINSTREAM MODIFICATIONS: _____

_____

_____

(continued)

Description of Services to Be Provided

Type of service	Teacher	Starting date	Amt. of time per day	OBJECTIVES AND CRITERIA FOR ATTAINMENT
SLD Level III	*LD Teacher*	*11/11/02*	*2½ hrs*	*Reading: Will know all vocabulary through the "Honeycomb" level. Will master skills as presented through DISTAR II. Will know 123 sound-symbols presented in "Sound Way to Reading."* *Math: Will pass all tests at basic 4 level.* *Spelling: 5 words each week from Level 3 list.* *Language: Will complete units 1-9 of the grade 4 language program. Will also complete supplemental units from "Language Step by Step."*

General education classes	Teacher	Amt. of time per day	OBJECTIVES AND CRITERIA FOR ATTAINMENT
		3½ hrs	*Out-of-seat behavior: Sit attentively and listen during general education class discussions. A simple management plan will be implemented if he does not meet this expectation. General education modifications of social studies: Will keep a folder in which he expresses through drawing the topics his class will cover. Modified district social studies curriculum. No formal testing will be done. An oral reader will read text to him, and oral questions will be asked.*

The following equipment, and other changes in personnel, transportation, curriculum, methods, and educational services will be made:

DISTAR II reading program spelling Level 3; "Sound Way to Reading" program; vocabulary tapes

Substantiation of least restrictive alternatives: *The planning team has determined the student's academic needs are best met with direct SLD support in reading, math, language, and spelling.*

Anticipated Length of Plan: __*1 yr*__   The next periodic review will be held: __*May 2003*__

☐ I do approve this program placement and the above IEP

☐ I do not approve this placement and/or the IEP

☐ I request a conciliation conference

———————————————————
PARENT/GUARDIAN

———————————————————
PRINCIPAL or Designee

with the parents. Parents have the right to agree or disagree with the contents of the program.

In 1997 amendments, Congress mandated a number of changes to the IEP. The core IEP team was expanded to include both a special education teacher and a general education teacher. The new law also specifies that students with disabilities are to be included in state- and districtwide assessments, and that states must report on the performance and progress of all students, including students with disabilities. The IEP team must decide whether the student will take the test with or without accommodations, or take an alternative assessment.

Protection in Evaluation Procedures Provisions

Congress included a number of specific requirements in Public Law 94-42. These requirements were designed to protect students and help ensure that assessment procedures and activities would be fair, equitable, and nondiscriminatory. Specifically, Congress mandated eight provisions:

1. Tests are to be selected and administered so as to be racially and culturally nondiscriminatory.
2. To the extent feasible, students are to be assessed in their native language or primary mode of communication (such as American Sign Language or communication board).
3. Tests must have been validated for the specific purpose for which they are used.
4. Tests must be administered by trained personnel in conformance with the instructions provided by the test producer.
5. Tests used with students must include those designed to provide information about specific educational needs, not just a general intelligence quotient.
6. Decisions about students are to be based on more than their performance on a single test.
7. Evaluations are to be made by a multidisciplinary team that includes at least one teacher or other specialist with knowledge in the area of suspected disability.
8. Children must be assessed in all areas related to a specific disability, including—where appropriate—health, vision, hearing, social and emotional status, general intelligence, academic performance, communicative skills, and motor skills.

Least Restrictive Environment (LRE) Provisions

In writing the Education for All Handicapped Children Act, Congress wanted to ensure that, to the greatest extent appropriate, students with disabilities would be placed in settings that would maximize their opportunities to interact with students without disabilities. Section 612(S)(B) states:

To the maximum extent appropriate, handicapped children ... are educated with children who are not handicapped, and that special classes, separate schooling, or other removal of handicapped children from the regular educational environment occurs only when the nature or the severity of the handicap is such that education in regular classes with the use of supplementary aids and services cannot be achieved satisfactorily.

The LRE provisions arose out of court cases in which state and federal courts had ruled that, when two equally appropriate placements were available for a student with a disability, the most normal (that is, least restrictive) placement was preferred.

Due-Process Provisions

In Section 615 of Public Law 94-142, Congress specified the procedures that schools and school personnel would have to follow to ensure due process in decision making. Specifically, when a decision affecting identification, evaluation, or placement of a student with disabilities is to be made, the student's parents or guardians must be given both the opportunity to be heard and the right to have an impartial due-process hearing to resolve conflicting opinions.

Schools must provide opportunities for parents to inspect the records that are kept on their children and to challenge material that they believe should not be included in those records. Parents have the right to have their child evaluated by an independent party and to have the results of that evaluation considered when psychoeducational decisions are made. In addition, parents must receive written notification before any education agency can begin an evaluation that might result in changes in the placement of a student.

In the 1997 amendments to IDEA, Congress specified that states must offer mediation as a voluntary option to parents and educators as an initial part of dispute resolution. If mediation is not successful, either party may request a due-process hearing.

The No Child Left Behind Act of 2001

The No Child Left Behind Act of 2001 (Public Law 107-110) is the reform of the federal Elementary and Secondary Education Act. Signed into law on January 8, 2002, the act has several major provisions that affect assessment and instruction of students with disabilities and disadvantaged students. The law requires stronger accountability for results by specifying that states must have challenging state educational standards, test children in grades 3–8 every year, and specify statewide progress objectives that ensure proficiency of every child by grade 12. The law also provides increased flexibility and local control, specifying that states can decide their standards and procedures, but at the same time must be held accountable for results. Parents are given expanded educational options under this law, and students who are attending schools judged to be "failing schools" have the right to enroll in other public schools, including public charter schools. A major provision of this law is called "putting reading first," a set of provisions ensuring an all-out effort to have every child reading by the end of third grade. These provisions will provide funding to schools for intensive reading interventions for children in grades K–3. Finally, the law specifies that all students have the right to be taught using "evidence-based instructional methods"; that is, teaching methods proven to work. The provisions of this law require that states include all students, among them students with disabilities and English-language learners, in their statewide accountability systems.

2004 Reauthorization of IDEA

The Individuals with Disabilities Education Act was reauthorized in 2004. Several of the new requirements of the law have special implications for assessment of students with disabilities. After much debate, Congress removed the requirement that students must have a severe discrepancy between ability and achievement in order to be considered learning disabled. It replaced this provision with a grant of permission to states and districts to use data on student responsiveness to intervention in the making of eligibility decisions. We now provide in this textbook a full chapter on "Assessing Response to Instruction." Congress also specified that states must have measurable goals, standards or objectives for all students with disabilities.

Ethical Considerations

Professionals who assess students have the responsibility to engage in ethical behavior. Many professional associations have put together sets of ethical standards to guide the practice of their members; many of these standards relate directly to assessment practices. Here we cite a number of important ethical considerations, borrowing heavily from the American Psychological Association's (1992) *Ethical Principles of Psychologists and Code of Conduct* and the National Association of School Psychologists' (2002) *Principles for Professional Ethics*. We have not cited the standards explicitly, but we have distilled from them a number of specific ethical considerations.

Responsibility for the Consequences of Professional Work

The assessment of students is a social act that has specific social and educational consequences. Those who assess students use assessment data to make decisions about the students, and these decisions can significantly affect an individual's life opportunities. Those who assess students must accept responsibility for the consequences of their work, and they must make every effort to be certain that their services are used appropriately. In short, they are committed to the application of professional expertise to promote improvement in the quality of life available to the student, family, school, and community. For the individual who assesses students, this ethical standard may mean refusing to engage in assessment activities that are desired by a school system but that are clearly inappropriate.

Recognition of the Boundaries of Professional Competence

Those who are entrusted with the responsibility of assessing and making decisions about students have differing degrees of competence. Not only must professionals regularly engage in self-assessment to be aware of their own limitations, but they should also recognize the limitations of the techniques they use. For individuals, this sometimes means refusing to engage in activities in areas in which they lack competence. It also means using techniques that meet recognized standards and engaging in the continuing education necessary to maintain high standards of competence.

As schools become increasingly diverse, professionals must demonstrate sensitivity in working with people from different cultural and linguistic backgrounds, and with children who have different types of disabling conditions. Assessors should have experience working with students of diverse backgrounds and should demonstrate competence in doing so, or they should refrain from assessing and making decisions about such students.

Confidentiality of Information

Those who assess students regularly obtain a considerable amount of very personal information about those students. Such information must be held in strict confidence. A general ethical principle held by most professional organizations is that confidentiality may be broken only when there is clear and imminent danger to an individual or to society. Results of pupil performance on tests must not be discussed informally with school staff members. Formal reports of pupil performance on tests must be released only with the permission of the persons tested or their parents or guardians.

Those who assess students are to make provisions for maintaining confidentiality in the storage and disposal of records. When working with minors or other persons who are unable to give voluntary informed consent, assessors are to take special care to protect these persons' best interests.

Adherence to Professional Standards on Assessment

A joint committee of the American Educational Research Association, the American Psychological Association, and the National Council on Measurement in Education (1999) publishes a document entitled *Standards for Educational and Psychological Testing*. These standards specify a set of requirements for test development and use. It is imperative that those who develop tests behave in accordance with the standards and that those who assess students use instruments and techniques that meet the standards.

In Parts 3 and 4 of this text, we review commonly used tests and talk about the extent to which those tests meet the standards. We provide information to help test users make informed judgments about the technical adequacy of specific tests. There is no federal or state agency that acts to limit the publication or use of technically inadequate tests. Only by refusing to use technically inadequate tests will users force developers to improve them. After all, if you were a test developer, would you continue to publish a test that few people purchased and used? Would you invest your company's resources to make changes in a technically inadequate test that yielded a large annual profit to your firm if people continued to buy and use it the way it was?

Test Security

Those who assess students are expected to maintain test security. It is expected that assessors will not reveal to others the content of specific tests or test items. At the same time, assessors must be willing and able to back up with test data decisions that may adversely affect individuals.

Pupil Records: Collection, Maintenance, and Dissemination

Policies and standards for the collection, maintenance, and dissemination of information about children must balance two sometimes conflicting needs. Parents and children have a basic right to privacy; schools need to collect and use information about children (and sometimes parents) in order to plan appropriate educational programs. Schools and parents have a common goal: to promote the welfare of children. In theory, schools and parents should agree on what constitutes and promotes a child's welfare, and in practice, schools and parents generally do work cooperatively.

Yet there have been situations in which there has been no cooperation or in which schools have operated against the best interests and basic rights of children and parents. School personnel have often flagrantly disregarded the rights to privacy of parents and children. Educationally irrelevant information about the personal lives of parents, as well as subjective, impressionistic, unverified information about parents and children, has been amassed by some schools. Parents and children have been denied access to pupil records, and therefore they have effectively been denied the opportunity to challenge, correct, or supplement those records. Conversely, schools have on occasion irresponsibly released pupil information to public and private agencies that had no legitimate need for or right to the information. Worse yet, parents and children were often not even informed that the information had been accumulated or released.

Abuses in the collection, maintenance, and dissemination of pupil information were of sufficient magnitude that the Russell Sage Foundation convened a conference in 1969 to deal with the problem. The voluntary guidelines developed at that conference (Goslin, 1969) have been widely accepted, implemented, and incorporated into federal laws.

In 1974 many of these recommended guidelines became federal law when the Family Educational Rights and Privacy Act (Public Law 93-380, commonly called the Buckley amendment) was enacted. The basic provisions of the act are quite simple. All educational agencies that accept federal money (preschools, elementary and secondary schools, community colleges, and colleges and universities) must grant parents the opportunity to inspect and challenge student records; if records are found to be inaccurate, parents have the right to correct them. The only records to which parental access may be denied are the personal notes of teachers, supervisors, administrators, and other educational personnel that are kept in the sole possession of the maker of the records. (Students age 18 years or older are given the same rights as parents in regard to their own records.) Also, educational agencies must not release identifiable data without the parents' written consent. Violators of the provisions of the Family Educational Rights and Privacy Act are subject to sanctions; federal funds may be withheld from agencies found to be in violation of the law.

The remainder of this chapter deals with specific issues and principles in the collection, maintenance, and dissemination of pupil information.

Collection of Pupil Information

Schools collect massive amounts of information about individual pupils and their parents. As we said in the chapter "Assessment of Students," information can be used for a number of legitimate educational decisions: special assistance, referral, screening, exceptionality, eligibility, instructional planning, pupil evaluation, setting, and program evaluation decisions. Considerable data must be collected if a school system is to function effectively, both in delivering educational services to children and in reporting the results of its educational programs to the various community, state, and federal agencies to which it may be responsible.

Consent

In its section on procedural safeguards, the Individuals with Disabilities Education Act mandates that prior written notice be given to the parents or guardians of a child whenever an educational agency proposes to initiate or change (or refuses to initiate or change) either the identification, evaluation, or educational placement of the child, or the provision of a free and appropriate education to the child. It further requires that the notice fully inform the parent, in the parent's native language, regarding all appeal procedures available. Thus schools must inform parents of their right to present any and all complaints regarding the identification, evaluation, or placement of their child; their right to an impartial due-process hearing; and their right to appeal decisions reached at a due-process hearing—if necessary, by bringing civil action against a school district.

The collection of research data requires the individual informed consent of parents. Various professional groups, such as the American Psychological Association and the National Association of School Psychologists, consider the collection of data without informed consent to be unethical; according to the Buckley amendment, it is illegal to experiment with children without prior informed consent. Typically, informed consent for research-related data collection requires that the pupil or parents understand (1) the purpose of and procedures involved in the investigations, (2) any risks inherent in participation in the research, (3) the fact that all participants will remain anonymous, and (4) the participants' option to withdraw from the research at any time.

Verification

Verifying information means ascertaining or confirming the information's truth, accuracy, or correctness. Depending on the type of information, verification may take several forms. For observations or ratings, verification means confirmation by another individual. For standardized test data, verification means conducting a reliable and valid assessment. (The concepts of reliability and validity are defined and discussed in detail in the chapters "Reliability" and "Validity.")

Unverified information can be collected, but every attempt should be made to verify such information before it is retained in a student's records. For example, serious misconduct or extremely withdrawn behavior is of direct concern to the schools. Initial reports of such behavior by a teacher or counselor are typically based on unverified observations. The unverified information provides hints, hypotheses, and starting points for diagnosis. However, if the data are not confirmable, they should not be collected and must not be retained. Similarly, data from unreliable tests should, we believe, be considered unverified information unless other data are presented to confirm the results.

Maintenance of Pupil Information

The decision to keep test results and other information should be governed by three principles: (1) retention of pupil information for limited periods of time, (2) parental rights of inspection and amendment, and (3) assurance of protection against inappropriate snooping. First, the information should be retained only as long as there is a continuing need for it. Only verified data of clear educational value should be retained. A pupil's school records should be periodically examined, and information that is no longer educationally relevant or no longer accurate should be removed. Natural transition points (for example, promotion from elementary school to junior high) should always be used to remove material from students' files.

The second major principle in the maintenance of pupil information is that parents have the right to inspect, challenge, and supplement student records. Parents of children with disabilities or with special gifts and talents have had the right to inspect, challenge, and supplement their children's school records for some time. Parents or guardians must be given the opportunity to examine all relevant records with respect to the identification, evaluation, and educational placement of the child; the free and appropriate public education of the child; and the opportunity to obtain an independent evaluation of the child. Again, if parents have complaints, they may request an impartial due-process hearing to challenge either the records or the school's decision regarding their child. The 1997 reauthorization of IDEA specifies further that parents have the right to (1) be accompanied and advised by counsel and by individuals with special knowledge or training with respect to the problems of children with disabilities; (2) present evidence and confront, cross-examine, and compel the attendance of witnesses; (3) have a written or electronic verbatim record of such a hearing; and (4) have written findings of facts and decisions.

The third major principle in the maintenance of pupil records is that the records should be protected from snoopers, both inside and outside the school system. In the past, secretaries, custodians, and even other students have had access, at least potentially, to pupil records. Curious teachers and administrators who had no legitimate educational interest had access. Individuals outside the schools, such as credit bureaus, have often found it easy to obtain information about former or current students. To make sure that only individuals with a legitimate need have access to the information contained in a pupil's records, it is recommended that pupil records be kept under lock and key. Adequate security mechanisms are necessary to ensure that the information in a pupil's records is not available to unauthorized personnel.

Dissemination of Pupil Information

Educators need to consider both access to information by officials and dissemination of information to individuals and agencies outside the school. In both cases, the guiding principles are (1) the protection of pupils' and parents' rights to privacy and (2) the legitimate need to know particular information, as demonstrated by the person or agency to which the information is disseminated.

Access Within the Schools

Those desiring access to pupil records should sign a form stating why they need to inspect the records; a list of people who have had access to their child's files and the reasons that access was sought should be available to parents. The provisions of the Buckley amendment state that

> all persons, agencies, or organizations desiring access to the records of a student shall be required to sign a written form which shall be kept permanently with the file of the student, but only for inspection by the parents or student, indicating specifically the legitimate educational or other interest that each person, agency, or organization has in seeking this information (§438, 4A).

When a pupil transfers from one school district to another, that pupil's records are also transferred. The Buckley amendment is very specific as to the conditions of transfer. When a pupil's file is transferred to another school or school system in which the pupil plans to enroll, the school must (1) notify the pupil's parents that the records have been transferred, (2) send the parents a copy of the transferred records if the parents so desire, and (3) provide the parents with an opportunity to challenge the content of the transferred data.

Access for Individuals and Agencies Outside the Schools

School personnel collect information about pupils enrolled in the school system for educationally relevant purposes. There is an implicit agreement between the schools and the parents that the only justification for collecting and keeping any pupil data is educational relevance. However, because the schools have so much information about pupils, they are often asked for pupil data by potential employers, credit agencies, insurance companies, police, the armed services, the courts, and various social agencies. To divulge information to any of these sources is a violation of this implicit trust unless the pupil (if over age 18) or the parents request that the information be released. Note that the courts and various administrative agencies have the power to subpoena pupil records from schools. In such cases, the Buckley amendment requires that the parents be notified that the records will be turned over in compliance with the subpoena.

Except in the case of the subpoena of records or the transfer of records to another school district, no school personnel should release any pupil information without the written consent of the parents. The Buckley amendment states that no educational agency may release pupil information unless "there is written consent from the student's parents specifying records to be released, the reasons for such release, and to whom, and with a copy of the records to be released to the student's parents and the student if desired by the parents" (§438, b2A).

Communicating in Language the General Public Can Understand

Those who assess students have a responsibility to make certain that the information they disseminate is put in the hands of authorized persons and is used to help the individual assessed. Assessment findings are to be communicated in language readily understood by the school staff members. In communicating written information, those who assess students must be certain that their interpretations of test results are clear and in language that is easily understood, so that the information may be used for the betterment of the student assessed.

SUMMARY

The practice of assessing students takes place in a social, political, and legal context. Much assessment takes place because it is mandated by law. School personnel are required to assess students before declaring them eligible for special education services. The major piece of legislation that currently serves as a guide for assessment activities is the 1997 Amendments to the Individuals with Disabilities Education Act (Public Law 105-17). The law reauthorizes the Individuals with Disabilities Education Act of 1990 (Public Law 101-476), which included provisions specifying that (1) schools must have individualized education programs for students, (2) students must be educated in least restrictive environments, and (3) students who are assessed have due-process rights. The law also specifies a number of ways in which students who are evaluated are to be protected.

Public Law 99-457, a set of amendments to the Education for All Handicapped Children Act, was enacted in 1986 (1) to extend the right to an education to include preschoolers with disabilities and (2) to extend the right to noneducational federal, state, and local resources and services to all children with disabilities.

The 2001 Elementary and Secondary Education Act (also called the No Child Left Behind Act) mandates that educational standards are for all students and that state education agencies must test and report on the performance and progress of all students in grades 3–8 every year. This law governs states' large-scale assessment efforts.

Those who assess students have certain ethical responsibilities. They are responsible for the consequences of their actions and for recognizing the limits of their competence. There are specific requirements for confidentiality of information obtained in assessment and for keeping the content of tests secure. Those who assess students should adhere to the professional standards outlined in *Standards for Educational and Psychological Testing.*

Schools are entrusted with the lives of children. Each day, decisions are made that are intended to be in the children's best interests. These decisions are based on both objective information and professional interpretation of that information. The schools must exercise their power over the lives of children very carefully. When school personnel collect data, they must make sure that the data are educationally relevant; their authority does not include the power to snoop and pry needlessly. The schools need latitude in deciding what information is educationally relevant, but the parents must have the right to check and halt the school's attempts to collect some types of information. Parents' informed consent to the collection of information about their children is basic to the family's right to privacy.

The schools should periodically examine all pupil records and destroy all information that is not of immediate or long-term utility, or that has not been verified. The information that is retained must be guarded. Parents and students over age 18 years must be given the opportunity to examine records, to correct or delete information, and to supplement the data contained in files. Sometimes the release of information that has been gathered could be damaging or embarrassing to children and their families. Schools must not release data to outside agencies except under subpoena or with the written consent of parents or a pupil who is over age 18. As in all areas of testing and data maintenance, common sense and common decency are required.

QUESTIONS FOR CHAPTER REVIEW

1. What were the major purposes of Public Law 94-142, the Education for All Handicapped Children Act of 1975? How did the 1997 Amendments to the Individuals with Disabilities Education Act update Public Law 94-142? What new provisions were added?

2. What four things must be specified in an individualized education plan?

3. Identify and explain the importance of three ethical considerations that are relevant to assessment practices.

4. Assume that you are a researcher who is about to conduct a study on reading comprehension in the schools. Write a letter to the parent of a potential subject that would meet the requirements of the law regarding informed consent about research participation. Make up information about the study if you need to do so, but be as brief as you can, remembering that parents will differ in research sophistication and reading ability.

PROJECT

Visit various special education settings (general education classrooms, resource rooms, self-contained classrooms, special schools). Write or discuss how each can be described as a least restrictive appropriate environment for an individual student.

RESOURCES FOR FURTHER INVESTIGATION

Print Resources

American Educational Research Association, American Psychological Association, & National Council on Measurement in Education. (1999). *Standards for educational and psychological testing.* Washington, DC: American Educational Research Association.

Sage, D. D., & Burrello, L. C. (1988). *Public policy and management in special education.* Englewood Cliffs, NJ: Prentice-Hall.

Yell, M. (1998). *The law and special education.* Upper Saddle River, NJ: Prentice-Hall.

Ysseldyke, J. E., Algozzine, B., & Thurlow, M. L. (1999). Legal issues in special education. In *Critical issues in special education* (3rd ed.; ch. 8). Boston: Houghton Mifflin.

Zerkel, P., & Richardson, S. N. (1988). *A digest of Supreme Court decisions affecting education* (2nd ed.). Bloomington, IN: Phi Delta Kappa Educational Foundation.

Technology Resources

EDLAW, Inc.
www.edlaw.net
EDLAW, Inc., provides access to legal documents associated with the Individuals with Disabilities Education Act, selected IDEA regulations, Section 504 of the Rehabilitation Act, and related education resources. There is also a link to a home page of legal briefs concerning education.

IDEA Law and Resources
www.cec.sped.org/law_res/doc/
This page provides links to the Council for Exceptional Children's analysis and comments as well as official government publications dealing with Public Law 108-466.

U.S. Department of Education
www.ed.gov
This website includes major press releases from the U.S. Department of Education, as well as summaries of laws and policies on the assessment of students with disabilities.

PART 2

Basic Concepts of Measurement

Part 2 deals with basic statistical and measurement concepts. Chapter 4 is intended for the person with little or no background in descriptive statistics; it contains a discussion of the major concepts necessary for understanding most of the remaining chapters in this part and later parts of the book. Chapter 5 discusses the scores typically used in norm-referenced and criterion-referenced assessment. The most frequently used scores in norm-referenced assessment compare a student with other students who make up the test norms. Criterion-referenced scores are most often used in classrooms. The two most useful types of criterion-referenced scores are percentage correct (accuracy) and rate of correct responses (fluency). Chapter 6 discusses how normative samples are usually obtained and the important characteristics of individuals in these samples. Chapter 7 provides an introduction to reliability and is often the most difficult chapter for students. This chapter deals with (1) the important concept that scores are fallible and (2) the amount of error associated with scores. Chapter 8, the last chapter in this part of the text, introduces the concept of test validity. *Validity,* the extent to which a test or other procedure leads to valid inferences about tested performance, is *the* most important and inclusive aspect of a test's technical adequacy. Chapters 9 and 10 deal with two fundamental areas of concern in assessment. Chapter 9 discusses how some students require adaptations and modifications to testing procedures in order to participate in large-scale assessments or to be individually assessed. Chapter 10 discusses issues involved in testing students with limited English proficiency.

Chapters 4 through 8 provide the basic statistics and psychometric theory that are the foundations of test development and use. We realize that numbers and formulas often scare both beginning students and seasoned veterans. Yet they sit at the heart of testing. Chapters 9 and 10 deal with special issues of validity that are so important and ubiquitous that they require their own chapters. Everyone who uses tests and test results must understand both in order to evaluate students fairly and intelligently.

The reader should bear in mind that many nuances and subtleties of basic statistics and measurement are not discussed, and no derivations or proofs are presented. We explain psychometric theory from a classical perspective and provide equations and computational examples to show how particular numbers are obtained, as well as to provide material for a logical understanding of critical measurement concepts. However, some widely used tests are constructed using item-response (or latent trait) theory. (For an overview of this orientation and associated procedures, visit the website for this text.) Finally, we alert the reader that this text has many audiences, some of whom may have advanced understanding of other theories and statistical procedures which are clearly beyond the scope of this book. For these readers, we identify advanced multivariate statistical procedures used to validate specific hypotheses, but we provide no explanations of the procedures. Thus Part 2 and the remaining sections of this book emphasize the basic technical information that a consumer needs to understand in order to interpret most tests.

CHAPTER 4

Descriptive Statistics

WE USE *DESCRIPTIVE STATISTICS* TO DESCRIBE OR SUMMARIZE DATA. IN TESTING, THE data are scores: several scores on one individual, one score on several individuals, or several scores on several individuals. Descriptive statistics are calculated using the basic mathematical operations of addition, subtraction, multiplication, and division, as well as simple exponential operations (squares and square roots); advanced knowledge of mathematics is not required. Although many calculations are repetitive and tedious, calculators and computers facilitate these calculations, and for many applications, test authors provide tables of all the pertinent descriptive statistics. This chapter deals with the basic concepts needed for an understanding of descriptive statistics: scales of measurement, distributions, measures of central tendency, measures of dispersion, and measures of relationship (correlation).

Scales of Measurement

The ways in which data can be summarized depend on some characteristics of the scores that are to be described. With some types of scores, we can use all the basic mathematical operations; with other types of scores, none of the basic mathematical operations can be used. The scale on which performances are measured determines how we can describe those performances. There are four types of measurement scales: nominal, ordinal, ratio, and equal interval (Stevens, 1951).

Ordinal and equal-interval scales are the most frequently used scales in norm-referenced measurement. Nominal and ratio scales are seldom used. The four scales are distinguished on the basis of the relationship between adjacent, or consecutive, values on the measurement continuum. An adjacent value in this case means a potential or possible value, rather than an obtained or measured value. In Figure 4.1, which depicts a portion of a yardstick, the possible values are any points between 2 inches and 6 inches, measured in intervals of eighths of an inch. Any two consecutive points (for instance, 3⅛ inches and 3¼ inches) are

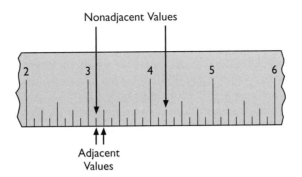

FIGURE 4.1
Adjacent and Non-adjacent Values

adjacent values. Any two points on the scale that have values intervening between them (for instance, 3⅛ inches and 4¼ inches) are *not* adjacent points. We could, of course, think of adjacent intervals larger than ⅛ of an inch. For example, adjacent 1-inch intervals could be considered, and the adjacent points would then be 1 inch, 2 inches, and so on.

Nominal Scales

On *nominal scales,* adjacent values have no inherent relationship. Nominal scales *name* values on the scale. For example, at the local ice cream shop, ice cream flavor is a variable. The specific values that this variable can take are names: chocolate, strawberry, tutti-frutti, mocha almond fudge, and others. The first flavor listed is no better than the second flavor listed. Banana sherbet is no better than orange sherbet (although many people may prefer one or the other). In education and psychology, we occasionally use nominal scales to describe attributes (for example, sex or eye color); geographic region in which a person resides (for example, the Pacific Northwest); educational classification (for example, learning disabled or emotionally disturbed); and so forth. However, few, if any, test scores are nominal.

Because values on a nominal scale represent names, the various mathematical operations cannot be performed with these values. For example, we cannot average banana and orange sherbet. Mathematically, all we can do with nominal scales is determine the frequency of each value (for example, how many times orange sherbet is chosen).

An occasionally confusing aspect of nominal scales is that numbers may be used as names. For example, numbers on athletic shirts identify players in the same way that social security numbers identify people. When numbers are used only to name people or objects, with these numbers having no inherent relationship to one another in terms of their adjacent values, the scale of measurement is a nominal scale. An obvious illustration of a nominal scale is the assignment of numbers to football players. The player who wears number 80 is not necessarily a better player than the player who wears number 70 or number 77; 80 is just a different player. Numbers 68 and 69, which are typically thought of as adjacent values, have no relationship to each other on a nominal scale; there is no implied rank ordering in the numbers worn on the shirts. It would not make any sense to add up shirt numbers to determine which athletic team is the best.

Ordinal Scales   *Ordinal scales* order things from better to worse or from worse to better. A scale may be ordinal whether or not numbers are used to designate locations on the scale. For example, locations on ordinal scales are sometimes designated by names. All adjectival comparisons are ordinal: good, better, best; tall, taller, tallest; poor, worse, worst; and so forth. Classroom teachers may use other adjectives (for example, novice, intermediate, and expert). Thus an ordinal scale may have as few as two or three adjectives as values, one of which is assigned to each individual being ranked. Such names always imply the quantitative relationship of higher or lower.

More frequently, ordinal scales use numbers to designate locations of the variable. Ordinal numbers (that is, first, second, third, and so on) designate locations; for example, ordinal numbers are used to indicate standing in the graduating class, a ranking of the top 20 football or basketball teams, and so forth. Thus ordinal values can be assigned all along the continuum (for example, class standing) or only in some parts of the continuum (for example, the top 20 teams); in the latter case, there are implicit losers, those not in the top 20.

A simple example of an ordinal scale is a ranking of persons from first to last on some trait or characteristic, such as weight or test scores. Suppose Ms. Smith administers a test to her arithmetic class, in which 25 students are enrolled. The test results are reported in Table 4.1. Column 1 gives the name of each student, and column 2 contains each child's raw score. Column 3 contains the ranking of the 25 students; the children are listed in decreasing rank order, from the student with the best performance to the student with the poorest performance. It is important to note that the difference between each student's raw score and the raw score of the immediately preceding student is not the same as the difference in rank for the two. Differences in adjacent ranks do not reflect the magnitude of differences in raw scores. The difficult concept to keep in mind is that, although the difference between rank scores (first, second, third, and so on) is 1 everywhere on the scale, the differences between the raw scores that correspond to the ranks are not necessarily equal.

Educators often use ordinal scales. As the chapter "Quantification of Test Performance" shows, many test scores are ordinal: age equivalents, grade equivalents, and percentiles. Ordinal scales have some interpretive value; however, they are not suitable for more complex interpretations that require some mathematical comparison (for example, calculating averages or differences between achievement in mathematics and achievement in reading).

Ratio Scales   *Ratio scales* have all the characteristics of ordinal scales and two additional ones. First, the magnitude of the difference between any two adjacent points on the scale is the same. For example, weight in pounds is measured on a ratio scale; the 1-pound difference between 15 and 16 pounds is the same as the 1-pound difference between 124 and 125 pounds. The second additional characteristic is that ratio scales have an absolute and logical zero. For instance, temperature on the Kelvin scale is a ratio scale. Absolute zero on that scale indicates the complete cessation of molecular action, or the absence of heat. The absolute zero of a ratio scale allows scores to be compared as ratios. For example, if John weighs 200

			Difference Between Score and Next Higher Score
Student	**Raw-Score Total**	**Rank**	
Bob	27	1	0
Lucy	26	2	1
Sam	22	3	4
Mary	20	4	2
Luis	18	5	2
Barbara	17	6	1
Carmen	16		
Jane	16	8	1
Charles J.	16		
Hector	14		
Virginia	14		
Frankie	14		
Sean	14	13	2
Joanne	14		
Jim	14		
John	14		
Charles B.	12		
Jing-Jen	12	18	2
Ron	12		
Carole	11	20	1
Bernice	10	21	1
Hugh	8	22	2
Lance	6	23	2
Ludwig	2	24	4
Harpo	1	25	1

TABLE 4.1   Ranking of Students in Ms. Smith's Arithmetic Class

pounds and Shawn weighs 100 pounds, John weighs twice as much as Shawn. Few, if any, educational or psychological tests give this type of score.

When ratio scales are used, all mathematical operations can be performed. We can add scores, square scores, create ratios of and differences between scores, and so forth. Thus ratio scales are potentially very useful. In education and psychology, ratio scales are associated almost exclusively with the measurement of physical characteristics (for example, height and weight) and some time-based measures (for example, times in a 100-meter dash).

Equal-Interval Scales   *Equal-interval scales* are ratio scales without an absolute and logical zero. Fahrenheit and Celsius temperature scales are equal-interval, not ratio, scales—neither zero Fahrenheit nor zero Celsius indicates an absolute absence of heat.

FIGURE 4.2
The Measurement of
Lines as a Function of
the Starting Point

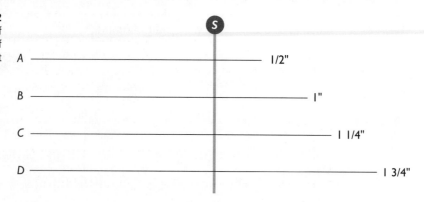

Classroom tests, such as Ms. Smith's arithmetic test shown in Table 4.1, also lack an absolute zero. Because a student gets no problem correct does not mean that the student knows absolutely nothing about arithmetic. Because equal-interval scales lack an absolute zero, we cannot construct ratios with data measured on these scales. For example, 64 degrees Fahrenheit is not considered "twice as hot" as 32 degrees Fahrenheit, and Sam does not know twice as much about arithmetic as Carole.

Consider the information in Figure 4.2. The differences among lines *A*, *B*, *C*, and *D* are readily measured. We can start measuring from any point, such as from the point where line *S* intersects lines *A*, *B*, *C*, and *D*. The portion of line *A* to the right of *S* is ½ inch long; that of line *B* to the right of *S* is 1 inch long; that of line *C* to the right of *S* is 1¼ inches long; and that of line *D* to the right of *S* is 1¾ inches long. The lines are measured on an equal-interval scale, and the differences among the lines would be the same no matter where the starting point *S* was located. However, because *S* is not a logical and absolute zero, we cannot make ratio comparisons among the lines. Although, when we began measuring from *S*, we found line *A* to measure ½ inch from *S* and line *B* to measure 1 inch from *S*, the whole of line *B* is obviously not twice as long as the whole of line *A*. In the same way that line *B* is not twice as long as line *A*, an IQ of 100 is not twice as large as an IQ of 50; IQ is not measured on a ratio scale.

In education and psychology, we often use equal-interval scales. As the chapter "Quantification of Test Performance" shows, all standard scores use equal-interval scales. Because we can add, subtract, multiply, and divide data measured on an equal-interval scale, these scales can be very useful when test givers make complex interpretations of test scores.

Distributions

Distributions of scores may be graphed to represent visually the relations among the scores in the group or set. In such graphs, the horizontal axis (*abscissa*) is the continuum on which the individuals are measured; the vertical axis (*ordinate*) is the frequency (that is, the number) or percentage of individuals earning any given score shown on the abscissa. Three types of graphs of distributions are common in education and psychology: *histograms,* polygrams, and curves. To illustrate these, we graph the examination scores already presented in Table 4.1. The scores earned on Ms. Smith's arithmetic examination can be grouped in 3-point intervals (that is, 1 to 3, 4 to 6, ... , 25 to 27). The grouped scores are presented as a histogram in the upper part of Figure 4.3. In the middle part of

FIGURE 4.3
Distribution of Ms. Smith's
Pupils on a Histogram, a
Polygram, and a Curve

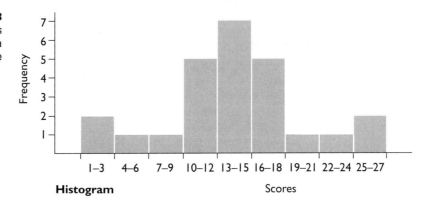

Histogram

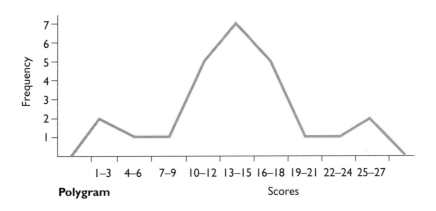

Polygram

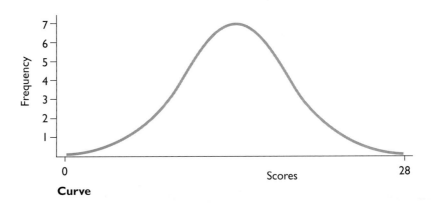

Curve

that figure, the same data are presented as a polygram; note that the midpoints of the intervals used in the histogram are connected in constructing the polygram. The lower part of Figure 4.3 shows a smoothed curve.

Curves are defined by four characteristics: mean, variance, skew, and kurtosis. The *mean* is the arithmetic average of the scores and is the balance point of the distribution. The variance describes the spread, or clustering, of scores in a distribution. Both of these characteristics are discussed in greater detail in later sections.

Skew refers to the symmetry of a distribution. The distribution of scores from Ms. Smith's exam is not skewed; the distribution is symmetrical. However, if Ms. Smith had given a very easy test on which many students earned very high scores and only a few students earned low scores, the distribution would have been skewed. In such a case, the distribution would have "tailed off" to the low end and would be termed a *negatively skewed distribution*. But if she had given a very hard test on which most of her students earned low scores and relatively few earned high scores, the distribution of scores would have tailed off to the higher end of the continuum. Such a distribution is termed a *positively skewed distribution*. Figure 4.4 shows an example of a positively skewed curve and a negatively skewed curve. The label assigned to a skewed distribution is determined by the direction of the tail of the distribution. Skewed distributions in which the tail is in the upper (higher-score) end are positively skewed, whereas those in which the tail slopes toward the lower end are negatively skewed.

Kurtosis, the fourth characteristic of curves, describes the peakedness of a curve, or the rate at which a curve rises. Distributions that are flat and rise slowly are termed *platykurtic curves.* (Platykurtic curves are flat, just as a plate or a plateau is flat.) Fast-rising curves are termed *leptokurtic curves.* Tests that do not "spread out" (or discriminate among) the scores of those taking the test are typically graphed as leptokurtic. Figure 4.5 illustrates a platykurtic and a leptokurtic curve.

The normal curve is a particular symmetrical curve. Many variables are distributed normally in nature; many are not. The only value of the normal curve lies in the fact that, for this curve, the proportion of cases that fall between any two points on the horizontal axis of the curve is known exactly.

FIGURE 4.4
Positive and Negative Skews

FIGURE 4.5
A Platykurtic Curve and a Leptokurtic Curve

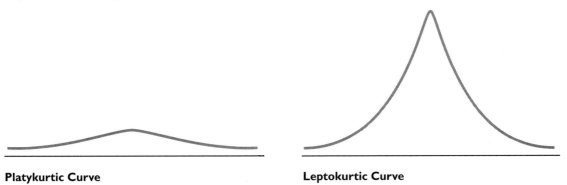

Platykurtic Curve   **Leptokurtic Curve**

Basic Notation

A number of symbols are used in statistics, and different authors use different symbols. Table 4.2 lists the symbols that we use in this book. The summation sign Σ means "add the following"; X denotes any score. The number of scores in a distribution is symbolized by N; n denotes the number of scores in a subset of a distribution; and f is used to denote the frequency of occurrence of a particular score. The arithmetic average (mean) of a distribution is denoted by $\bar{X}$. The variance of a distribution is symbolized by S^2, and the standard deviation, by S.

Measures of Central Tendency

A set of scores can be described by its average. The average gives us a general description of how the group as a whole performed. Actually, three different averages are used: mode, median, and mean. The *mode* is defined as the score most frequently obtained. A mode (if there is one) can be found for data on a nominal, ordinal, ratio, or equal-interval scale. Distributions may have two modes (if

---

TABLE 4.2	Commonly Used Statistical Symbols

Symbol	Meaning
Σ	Summation sign
X	Any score
N	Number of cases
n	Number in subset
f	Frequency
$\bar{X}$	Mean
S^2	Variance
S	Standard deviation

they do, they are called "bimodal distributions"), or they may have more than two. The mode of the distribution of raw scores obtained by Ms. Smith's class on the arithmetic test is readily apparent from an inspection of the data in Table 4.1 and the graphs in Figure 4.3. The mode of this distribution is 14; seven children earned this score.

The *median* is the score that divides the top 50 percent of test takers from the bottom 50 percent. It is that point on a scale above which 50 percent of the cases (people, *not* scores) occur and below which 50 percent of the cases occur. Medians can be found for data on ordinal, equal-interval, and ratio scales; they should not be used with nominal scales. The median score may or may not actually be earned by a student. For the set of scores 4, 5, 7, and 8, the median is 6, although no one earned a score of 6. For the set of scores 4, 5, 6, 7, and 8, the median is 6, and someone earned that score.

Online Study Center
General Resources

The *mean* is the arithmetic average of the scores in a distribution. It is the sum of the scores divided by the number of scores. The mean, like the median, may or may not be earned by any child in the distribution. Means should be computed only for data on ratio and equal-interval scales. The formula for computing the mean, using statistical notation, is given in Equation 4.1.

$$\bar{X} = \frac{\Sigma X}{N}$$

(4.1)

FIGURE 4.6
Relationships Among Mode, Median, and Mean for Symmetrical and Asymmetrical Distributions

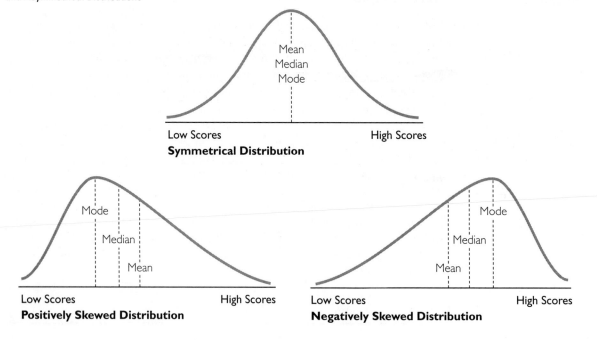

Using the scores obtained from Ms. Smith's arithmetic examination (Table 4.1), we find that the sum of the scores is 350 and that the number of scores is 25. The mean (arithmetic average), then, is 14. The mean was earned by seven children in the class.

The mode, median, and mean have particular relationships, depending on the symmetry (skew) of a distribution. As Figure 4.6 shows, in symmetrical "unimodal" (that is, having just one mode) distributions, the mode, median, and mean are at the same point. In positively skewed distributions, the median and mean are displaced toward the positive tail of the curve; the mode is a lower value than the median, and the median is a lower value than the mean. In negatively skewed distributions, the median and mean are displaced toward the negative tail of the curve; the mode is a higher value than the median, and the median is a higher value than the mean.

Measures of Dispersion

Although a mean tells us about a group's average performance, it does not tell us how close to the average people scored. For example, did everyone earn 92 percent correct on the weekly spelling test, or were the scores spread out from 0 to 100 percent? To describe how scores spread out, we use three indexes of dispersion: range, variance, and standard deviation. All three measures can be computed when the scale of measurement is ratio or equal interval, and none of the three can be computed when the scale of measurement is nominal. Range can be described with ordinal data (for example, "ratings ranged from excellent to poor"). The *range* is the distance between the extremes of a distribution, including those extremes; it is the highest score less the lowest score plus 1. On Ms. Smith's test (Table 4.1), it is 27 (27 = 27 − 1 + 1). The range is a relatively crude measure of dispersion because it is based on only two bits of information.

The variance and the standard deviation are the most important indexes of dispersion. The *variance* is a numerical index describing the dispersion of a set of scores around the mean of the distribution. Specifically, the variance (S^2) is the average squared distance of the scores from the mean. Because the variance is an average, it is not affected by the number of cases in the set or the distribution. Large sets of scores may have large or small variances; small sets of scores may have large or small variances. Also, because the variance is measured in terms of distance from the mean, it is not related to the actual value of the mean. Distributions with large means may have large or small variances; distributions with small means may have large or small variances. The variance of a distribution may be computed with Equation 4.2. The variance (S^2) equals the sum (Σ) of the square of each score less the mean [$(X - \bar{X})^2$] divided by the number of scores (N).

$$S^2 = \frac{\Sigma(X - \bar{X})^2}{N}$$

(4.2)

As an example, we use the scores from Ms. Smith's arithmetic test again to compute variance (see Table 4.3). Column B in Table 4.3 contains the score earned by each student. The first step in computing the variance is to find the mean. Therefore, the scores are added, and the sum (350) is divided by the number of scores (25). The mean in this example is 14. The next step is to subtract the mean from each score; this is done in column C of Table 4.3, which is labeled $X - \bar{X}$. Note that scores above the mean are positive, scores at the mean are zero, and scores below the mean are negative. The differences (column C) are then squared (multiplied by themselves); the squared differences are in column D, labeled $(X - \bar{X})^2$. Note that all numbers in this column are positive. The squared differences are then summed; in this example, the sum of all the squared distances of scores from the mean is 900. The variance equals the sum of all the squared distances of scores from the mean divided by the number of scores; in this case, the variance equals 900/25, or 36.

TABLE 4.3   Computation of the Variance of Ms. Smith's Arithmetic Test

Student (A)	Test Score (B)	$X - \bar{X}$ (C)	$(X - \bar{X})^2$ (D)
Bob	27	13	169
Lucy	26	12	144
Sam	22	8	64
Mary	20	6	36
Luis	18	4	16
Barbara	17	3	9
Carmen	16	2	4
Jane	16	2	4
Charles J.	16	2	4
Hector	14	0	0
Virginia	14	0	0
Frankie	14	0	0
Sean	14	0	0
Joanne	14	0	0
Jim	14	0	0
John	14	0	0
Charles B.	12	−2	4
Jing-Jen	12	−2	4
Ron	12	−2	4
Carole	11	−3	9
Bernice	10	−4	16
Hugh	8	−6	36
Lance	6	−8	64
Ludwig	2	−12	144
Harpo	1	−13	169
SUM	350	000	900

FIGURE 4.7
Scores on Three Scales,
Expressed in Standard-
Deviation Units

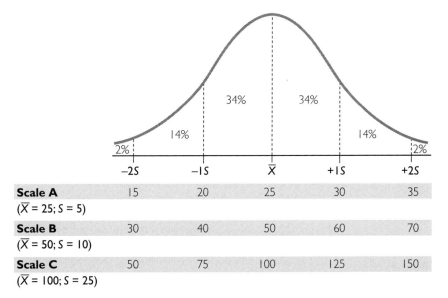

	−2S	−1S	$\overline{X}$	+1S	+2S
Scale A ($\overline{X} = 25; S = 5$)	15	20	25	30	35
Scale B ($\overline{X} = 50; S = 10$)	30	40	50	60	70
Scale C ($\overline{X} = 100; S = 25$)	50	75	100	125	150

The variance is very important in psychometric theory but has very limited application in score interpretation. However, its calculation is necessary for the computation of the standard deviation (S), which is very important in the interpretation of test scores. The *standard deviation* is the positive square root ($\sqrt{\ }$) of the variance.[1] Thus, in our example, because the variance is 36, the standard deviation is 6. In later chapters, the standard deviation will be used in other computations, such as standard scores and the standard error of measurement.

The standard deviation is used as a unit of measurement in much the same way that an inch or a ton is used as a unit of measurement. Scores are equal interval when they are measured in terms of standard deviation units from the mean. The advantage of measuring in standard deviations is that, when the distribution is normal, we know exactly what proportion of cases occurs between the mean and the particular standard deviation. As shown in Figure 4.7, approximately 34 percent of the cases in a normal distribution always occur between the mean and one standard deviation (S) either above or below the mean. Thus approximately 68 percent of all cases occur between one standard deviation below and one standard deviation above the mean (34% + 34% = 68%). Approximately 14 percent of the cases occur between one and two standard deviations below the mean or between one and two standard deviations above the mean. Thus about 48 percent of all cases occur between the mean and two standard deviations either above or below the mean (34% + 14% = 48%). About 96 percent of all cases occur between two standard deviations above and two standard deviations below the mean.

---

1. The square root of a particular number is the number that, when multiplied by itself, produces the particular number. For example, $\sqrt{144} = 12$, $\sqrt{25} = 5$, $\sqrt{4} = 2$.

Appendix 1 lists the proportion of cases in a normal distribution occurring between the mean and any standard deviation above or below the mean. As an example, if we enter Appendix 1 at 0.44 (that is 0.4 plus 0.04), we find the number .1700. This number means that 1,700/10,000, or 17 percent, of the cases in the normal curve occur between the mean and 0.44 standard deviation from the mean, either below or above the mean. Thus 33 percent of the cases fall below 0.44 standard deviation below the mean. (Half the cases, 50 percent, fall below the mean; 17 percent fall between $-0.44S$ and the mean; $50\% - 17\% = 33\%$.)

As shown by the positions and values for scales A, B, and C in Figure 4.7, it does not matter what the values of the mean and the standard deviation are. The relationship holds for various obtained values of the mean and the standard deviation. For Scale A, where the mean is 25 and the standard deviation is 5, 34 percent of the scores occur between the mean (25) and one standard deviation below the mean (20) or between the mean and one standard deviation above the mean (30). Similarly, for Scale B, where the mean is 50 and the standard deviation is 10, 34 percent of the cases occur between the mean (50) and one standard deviation below the mean (40) or between the mean and one standard deviation above the mean (60).

It is extremely important that those who use tests to make decisions about students be aware of the means and standard deviations of the tests they use. Most intelligence tests, for example, have a mean of 100 and a standard deviation of 15. If scores on those tests are normally distributed, we would expect approximately 68 percent of the school population to have IQs between 85 and 115. Some tests of intelligence have different standard deviations. Thus the meaning of a score depends on the mean and the standard deviation. This is an obvious point, yet it is often overlooked.

Correlation

Correlation quantifies relationships between variables. *Correlation coefficients* are numerical indexes of these relationships. They tell us the extent to which any two variables go together; that is, the extent to which changes in one variable are reflected by changes in the second variable. These coefficients are used in measurement to estimate both the reliability and the validity of a test. Correlation coefficients can range in value from .00 to *either* +1.00 or −1.00. The sign (+ or −) indicates the direction of the relationship; the number indicates the magnitude of the relationship. A correlation coefficient of .00 between two variables means that there is no relationship between the variables. The variables are independent; changes in one variable are not related to changes in the second variable. A correlation coefficient of either +1.00 or −1.00 indicates a perfect relationship between two variables. Thus, if you know a person's score on one variable, you can predict that person's score on the second variable without error. Correlation coefficients between .00 and 1.00 (or −1.00) allow some prediction, and the greater the coefficient is, the greater is its predictive power.

Correlation coefficients are very important in assessment. The chapter "Reliability" shows how correlations are used to estimate the amount of error associ-

---

TABLE 4.4	Scores Earned on Two Tests Administered by Ms. Smith to Her Arithmetic Class

Student	Raw Score, Test 1	Raw Score, Test 2
Bob	27	26
Lucy	26	22
Sam	22	20
Mary	20	27
Luis	18	14
Barbara	17	18
Carmen	16	16
Jane	16	17
Charles J.	16	16
Hector	14	14
Virginia	14	14
Frankie	14	16
Sean	14	14
Joanne	14	12
Jim	14	14
John	14	12
Charles B.	12	14
Jing-Jen	12	11
Ron	12	12
Carole	11	10
Bernice	10	14
Hugh	8	6
Lance	6	1
Ludwig	2	2
Harpo	1	8

ated with measurement. The chapter "Validity" shows how correlation coefficients are also used to estimate a test's validity.

The Pearson Product-Moment Correlation Coefficient

The most commonly used correlation coefficient is the *Pearson product-moment correlation coefficient* (*r*). This is an index of the straight-line (linear) relationship between two variables measured on an equal-interval scale. Suppose Ms. Smith administered a second exam to her arithmetic class. The results of the first exam (the data from Table 4.1) are reproduced in column 2 of Table 4.4; the results of the second exam are presented in column 3. (For the sake of simplicity, the example has been constructed so that the second test has the same mean and the same standard deviation as the first test—that is, 14 and 6, respectively.) The two scores for each student are plotted on a graph (termed a scattergram, or scatterplot) in Figure 4.8. The scatterplot contains 25 points, one point for each child. The figure indicates that there is a pronounced tendency for high scores on the first test to be associated with high scores on the second test. There is a positive relationship (correlation) between the first and second tests. The line drawn

FIGURE 4.8
Scatterplot of the Two
Tests Administered by
Ms. Smith

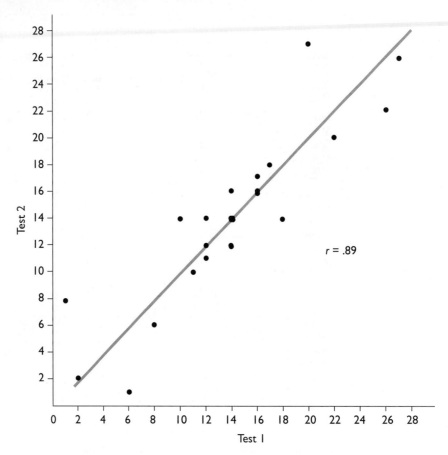

$r = .89$

through the scatterplot in Figure 4.8 is termed a regression line. When the points corresponding to each pair of scores cluster closely around the regression line, there is a high degree of relationship. The points from Table 4.4 do cluster closely around the regression line; there is a high correlation (specifically, .89) between the first and second tests.[2] If all the points fell directly on the regression line, there would be a perfect correlation (1.00).

Figure 4.9 shows six scatterplots of different degrees of relationship. In parts a and b, all points fall on the regression line, so the correlation between the variables is perfect. Part a has a correlation coefficient of +1.00; high scores on one test are associated with high scores on the other test. Part b has a correlation of −1.00; high scores on one test are associated with low scores on the other test

2. The correlation coefficient can be computed with the following formula, where X is a raw score on one measure, and Y is a raw score on a second measure.

$$r = \frac{N\Sigma XY - (\Sigma X)(\Sigma Y)}{\sqrt{N\Sigma X^2 - (\Sigma X)^2}\sqrt{N\Sigma Y^2 - (\Sigma Y)^2}}$$

FIGURE 4.9
Six Scatterplots of Different Degrees and Directions of Relationship

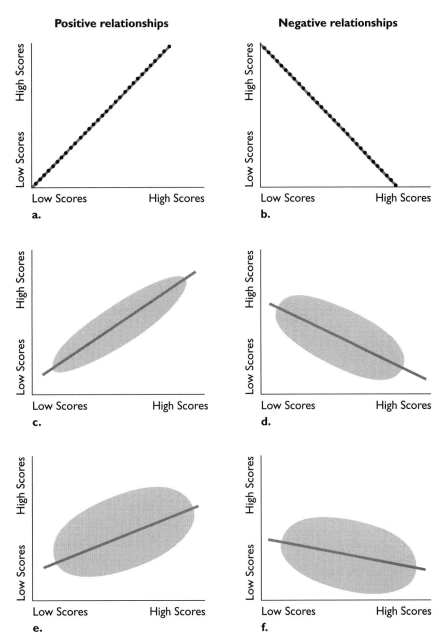

(this negative correlation is sometimes called an "inverse relationship"). Parts c and d show a high degree of positive and negative relationship, respectively. Note that the departures from the regression lines are associated with lower degrees of relationship. Parts e and f show scatterplots with a low degree of relationship. Note the wide departures from the regression lines.

Zero correlation can occur in three ways, as shown in Figure 4.10. First, if the scatterplot is essentially circular (part a), the correlation is .00. In such a case, there is no relationship between the two variables; each value of the first variable can be associated with any (and perhaps all) values of the second variable. Second, if either variable is constant (part b), the correlation is .00. For example, if a

FIGURE 4.10
Three Zero-Order
Linear Correlations

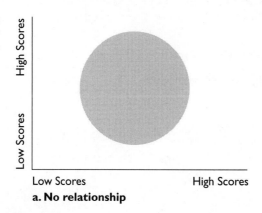

a. **No relationship**

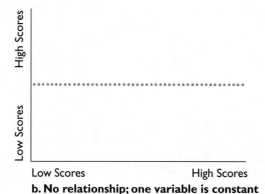

b. **No relationship; one variable is constant**

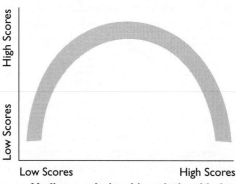

c. **No linear relationship; relationship is curvilinear**

researcher tried to correlate gender and reading achievement with a sample made up entirely of boys, the correlation would be zero because gender would have only one value (male); gender would be a constant, not a variable. Third, two variables can be related in a nonlinear way (part c). For example, willingness to take risks is related to age. Younger children and adults are less willing to take risks than are teenagers. Although there is a strong curvilinear relationship, the linear regression line would parallel one of the axes. Thus there is a curvilinear relationship, but the coefficient of linear correlation is approximately .00.

Pearson Family Correlation Coefficients

Test authors may report correlation coefficients by different names to indicate a variable's scale of measurement and whether one or both variables in the relationship are dichotomous (have only two values) or continuous (have many values). The most commonly reported coefficients are members of the Pearson family of correlation coefficients, meaning that they are all computed by computationally equivalent formulas. When both variables to be correlated are measured on an equal-interval or ratio scale (such as IQ and SAT verbal score), the correlation coefficient is called a Pearson product-moment correlation coefficient. The symbol for this statistic is r. When both variables to be correlated are measured on an ordinal scale (such as class standing and rank on the school's competency examination for seniors), the correlation coefficient is called a *Spearman rho;* the symbol for rho is ρ. Sometimes the variables to be correlated are dichotomous (for instance, male/female). When two dichotomous variables are correlated, the correlation coefficient is called a *phi coefficient;* the symbol for phi is ϕ. When one of the variables is dichotomous (right or wrong on a test question) and the other variable is continuous (total number correct on the test), the correlation coefficient is called a *point biserial correlation coefficient;* its symbol is r_{ptbis}. Although there are other kinds of Pearson family coefficients (such as *biserial rho*) and computationally different coefficients (such as *tetrachoric* and *biserial*), they are seldom reported in test manuals. (For an explanation of these correlation coefficients, visit the website for this text and click on your textbook.

Online Study Center
General Resources

Causality   No discussion of correlation is complete without a mention of causality. Correlation is a necessary but not a sufficient condition for causality. Two variables cannot be causally related unless they are correlated. However, the mere presence of a correlation does not establish causality. For any correlation coefficient between variables (A and B), there are four possible interpretations (the first depends on chance; the other three do not).

First, the variables may be correlated by chance. For example, the incidence of chicken pox in Egypt (A) may be highly correlated with the sale of Purina Puppy Chow in the state of Arizona (B). There is simply no logical or reasonable explanation for the correlation other than serendipity. (The probability of a correlation coefficient of a specific value occurring by chance can be determined; when a correlation coefficient is found to be "statistically significant" at the .05

level, a correlation of that magnitude occurs by chance only 5 times in 100.) Second, *A* can cause *B*; for example, burning buildings (*A*) cause firefighters to be present (*B*). Third, *B* can cause *A*; for example, Bradbury (1953) reports that firefighters (*B*) cause fires (*A*). Fourth, *C* can cause both *A* and *B*. For example, there actually is a positive relationship between shoe size and mental age. Clearly, big feet do not cause mental development (*A* does not cause *B*). Moreover, mental development does not cause big feet (*B* does not cause *A*). The most satisfactory explanation of the correlation is that maturation, a third variable (*C*), causes both *A* and *B:* As children grow older, they develop both mentally and physically.

Although the preceding examples illustrate obvious instances of inappropriate reasoning, in testing situations the errors or potential errors are not so clear. For example, IQ scores and scores on achievement tests are correlated. Some argue that intelligence causes achievement; others argue that achievement causes intelligence. Because there are at least four possible interpretations of correlational data—and because correlational data do not tell us which interpretation is true—we must never draw causal conclusions from such data alone.

SUMMARY

Descriptive statistics provide summary information about groups of individuals. Data can be obtained on one of four types of measurement scales: nominal, ordinal, ratio, and equal-interval scales. Collections of scores are termed *distributions*. Distributions are defined by four characteristics: mean, variance, skew, and kurtosis. Depending on the scale of measurement, three indexes may be used to indicate a distribution's central tendency: the mode (the most frequent score), the median (the score that separates the top 50 percent from the bottom 50 percent), and the mean (the arithmetic average). Depending on the scale of measurement, the dispersion of a distribution can be described by three indexes: the range of scores, the variance, and the standard deviation.

The quantification of the relationship between two variables is a correlation. When there is no relationship between variables, the correlation is zero. When there is a perfect relationship between variables, the correlation is one. A plus or a minus sign indicates the type of relationship, not the magnitude of the relationship. A positive correlation indicates that high scores on one variable are associated with high scores on the second variable. A negative correlation indicates an inverse relationship: High scores on one variable are associated with low scores on the other variable. There are several types of correlations that are often used in describing tests.

QUESTIONS FOR CHAPTER REVIEW

1. After all third-grade students in the state took an achievement test, statewide norms were developed. The superintendent of public instruction reviewed the test results and in a news conference voiced concern for the quality of education in

the state. The superintendent reported, "Half the third-grade children in this state performed below the state average." What is foolish about that statement?

2. What is the relationship among the mode, the median, and the mean in a normal distribution?

3. The following statements about Test A and Test B are true: Tests A and B measure the same behavior; Tests A and B have means of 100; Test A has a standard deviation of 15; and Test B has a standard deviation of 5.

   a. Following classroom instruction, the pupils in Mr. Radley's room earn an average score of 130 on Test A. Pupils in Ms. Purple's room earn an average score of 110 on Test B. On this basis, the local principal concludes that Mr. Radley's students learn more than Ms. Purple's. What is fallacious about this conclusion?

   b. Assuming that the pupils were equal prior to instruction, what conclusions could the principal legitimately make?

4. On the Stanford-Binet Intelligence Scale, Harry earns an IQ of 52, and Ralph earns an IQ of 104. Their teacher concludes that Ralph is twice as smart as Harry. Why is this conclusion wrong?

5. Discuss the relationship between correlation and causality.

6. In one state, the criteria for identifying a student as having mental retardation include, among other things, the requirement that the student have an IQ of 79 or less. The use of this criterion for IQ means that several different levels of eligibility are written into the state's rules. Explain why this is so.

PROBLEMS

1. Ms. Robbins administers a test to ten children in her class. The children earn the following scores: 14, 28, 49, 49, 49, 77, 84, 84, 91, and 105. For this distribution of scores, find the following:

   a. Mode

   b. Mean

   c. Range

   d. Variance and standard deviation

2. Mr. García administers a test to six children in his class. The children earn the following scores: 21, 27, 30, 54, 39, and 63. For these scores, find the following:

   a. Mean

   b. Range

   c. Variance and standard deviation

3. Ms. Shumway administers a test to six children in her nursery school program. The children earn the following scores: 23, 33, 38, 53, 78, and 93. Find the mean and standard deviation of these six scores.

4. Using Appendix 2, find the proportion of cases that occur

   a. between the mean and the following standard deviation units: $-1.5, +.37, +.08, +2.75$.

   b. between + and $-1.7S$, between + and $-0.55S$, and between + and $-2.1S$.

   c. above $-0.7S$, above $+1.3S$, and above $+1.9S$.

   d. below $-0.7S$, below $+1.3S$, and below $+1.9S$.

Answers

1. (a) 49; (b) 63; (c) 92; (d) 784 and 28

2. (a) 39; (b) 43; (c) 225 and 15

3. Mean = 53; standard deviation = 25

4. (a) .4332, .1443, .0319, .4970; (b) .9108, .4176, .9642; (c) .7580, .0968, .0287; (d) .2420, .9032, .9713

RESOURCES FOR FURTHER INVESTIGATION

Technology Resources

ASSESSMENT IN SPECIAL AND INCLUSIVE EDUCATION
education.college.hmco.com/students
This site contains additional exercises for practicing basic computations.

THE DATA AND STORY LIBRARY (DASL)
lib.stat.cmu.edu/DASL
DASL is a library on the Web that contains data files and stories to illustrate basic statistical concepts. Under List All Methods, the searcher can find stories about keywords, such as distribution, mean, median, and scatterplots.

HYPERSTAT ONLINE TEXTBOOK
davidmlane.com/hyperstat/index.html
Look here for further explanations about distributions
and data.

STATISTICAL HOME PAGE
members.aol.com/johnp71/javastat.html
This page links to over 300 other pages that perform
statistical calculations and contain other statistical resources.

SURFSTAT AUSTRALIA: AN ONLINE TEXT IN
INTRODUCTORY STATISTICS
**www.anu.edu.au/nceph/surfstat/surfstat-home/
surfstat.html**
This page contains information on summary and presentation of data, production of data, variation and
probability, and statistical inference.

INTRODUCTION TO DESCRIPTIVE STATISTICS
www.mste.uiuc.edu/hill/dstat/dstat.html
This website contains great examples of such statistics
as central tendency, variance, and standard deviation.

CHAPTER 5

Quantification of Test Performance

MOST BEHAVIORS OCCUR WITHOUT BEING SYSTEMATICALLY OBSERVED, QUANTIFIED, and evaluated, and the vast majority occur in situations that are not specifically structured to quantify and evaluate the behaviors. Assessment is an exception. Tests and systematic observations occur in structured, standardized situations. Tests require the presentation of standardized materials to an individual in a predetermined manner in order to evaluate that individual's responses, using predetermined criteria. Systematic observations require the use of predetermined definitions of behavior to be observed at predetermined times and settings.

How the individual's responses are quantified depends on the materials used, the intent of the test author, and the diagnostician's intention in choosing the procedure. If we were interested only in determining whether a student had learned a specific fact or concept (for example, "What is 3 + 5?"), we would make explicit the criteria for what constitutes a correct response and would classify the student's response as right or wrong without quantifying the result. If we were interested in determining whether a student had learned a finite set of facts (for example, the sums of all combinations of single-digit numbers), we could readily quantify a student's performance as the number or percentage of facts known. However, the assessment of every element (that is, every fact, concept, and skill) would require that all elements be specified. Therefore, this approach is generally reserved for the most essential information that a student must master.

More often, the information we wish to assess is not finite, and it is impractical or impossible to assess all the facts and relationships that might be tested. For example, it seems unlikely that anyone could make up a test to assess a student's knowledge of every aspect of all Shakespeare's plays; however, even if that were possible, administering all the possible questions to a student would be virtually impossible. Even when we cannot test much of the information on a topic, we still may want to estimate the amount of information students have learned. To do this, testers are forced to ask a few questions and to base their inferences about all the information, termed the *domain*, on student responses to the sample of questions.

When we sample a student's knowledge of an entire domain by assessing a smaller number of items, we assume that a student's performance on all the items in the domain can be accurately inferred from the performance on the sample of items. Particular items are important only as representatives of the domain; they have little individual importance. Moreover, we generally cannot infer the percentage correct on the entire domain directly from a test unless the items are representative of the domain, a condition that is seldom known on an a priori basis.

Scores Used in Norm-Referenced Assessment

When a large domain is assessed, a student's performance is typically interpreted by comparing it with the performances of a group of subjects of known demographic characteristics (age, gender, grade in school, and so on). This group is called a *normative sample,* or *norm group*. The comparison scores, called *derived scores,* are of two types: developmental scores and scores of relative standing.

Developmental Scores

Developmental Equivalents

Developmental equivalents are one type of derived (or transformed) score. The most common types of developmental equivalents are age equivalents (mental ages, for example) and grade equivalents. Suppose the average performance of 10-year-old children on an intelligence test was 27 correct answers. Further, suppose that Horace answered 27 questions correctly. Horace answered as many questions correctly as the average of 10-year-old children. He earns a mental age of 10 years. An *age equivalent* means that a child's raw score is the average (the median or mean) performance for that age group. Age equivalents are expressed in years and months; a hyphen is used in age scores (for example, 7-1 for 7 years, 1 month old). A *grade equivalent* means that a child's raw score is the average (the median or mean) performance for a particular grade. Grade equivalents are expressed in grades and tenths of grades; a decimal point is used in grade scores (for example, 7.1 for grade 7 1/10). Age-equivalent and grade-equivalent scores are interpreted as a performance equal to the average of X-year-olds and the average of Xth-graders' performance, respectively.

Suppose we gave a test to 1,000 children, 100 of each age (within two weeks of their birthday) from 5 to 14 years. For each 100 children at each age, there is a distribution with a mean. These hypothetical means are shown in Figure 5.1, connected by a curved line. As the figure shows, a raw score of 16 corresponds exactly to the average score earned by children in the 6-year-old distribution. Thus the child who earns a score of 16 has an age equivalent of 6 years, 0 months, or 6-0. A score of 36, by contrast, falls between the average of the 11-year-old distribution and the average of the 12-year-old distribution. A raw score of 36 would be estimated (interpolated) as an age score of 11-6; it would

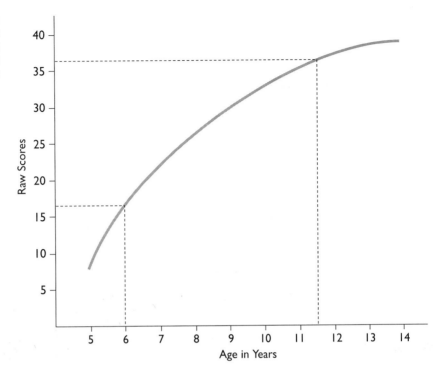

FIGURE 5.1

Mean Number Correct for Ten Age Groups: An Example of Arriving at Age-Equivalent Scores

be awarded a score between 11 and 12, despite the fact that no children between 11 and 12 years of age were tested. A score of 4 would fall below the average of the lowest age group, the 5-year-olds. If a child earned a raw score of 4, that child's age equivalent would be estimated (extrapolated) by continuing the curve in Figure 5.1. A raw score of 4 could be extrapolated to be the equivalent of an age score of 3-6, although no children that young were included in the sample. Similarly, a score greater than the average performance of the oldest children could also be extrapolated.

The interpretation of age and grade equivalents requires great care. Five problems occur in the use of developmental scores.

Problems with Developmental Scores

1. *Systematic misinterpretation.* Students who earn an age equivalent of 12-0 have merely answered as many questions correctly as the average for children 12 years of age. They have not necessarily performed as a 12-year-old child would; they may well have attacked the problems in a different way or demonstrated a different performance pattern from many 12-year-old students. Similarly, a second-grader and a ninth-grader may both earn grade equivalents of 4.0, but they probably have not performed identically. Thorndike and Hagen (1978) have suggested that it is more likely that the younger child has performed lower-level work with greater accuracy (for

instance, successfully answered 38 of the 45 problems attempted), whereas the older child has attempted more problems with less accuracy (for instance, successfully answered 38 of the 78 problems attempted).

2. *Need for interpolation and extrapolation.* Average age and grade scores are estimated for groups of children who are never tested. Consequently, a child can earn a grade equivalent of 3.2, although no children at grade 3.2 were in the norm group (for example, only children in the beginning and at the middle of third grade were in the norm group that was tested); or a child can earn a grade equivalent of 8.0, even though no children above the sixth grade were in the norm group that was tested.

3. *Promotion of typological thinking.* The average 12-0 pupil is a statistical abstraction surrounded by a family with 1.2 other children, 0.8 of a dog, and 2.3 automobiles; in other words, the average child does not exist. Average 12-0 children more accurately represent a range of performances, typically the middle 50 percent.

4. *Implication of a false standard of performance.* Educators expect a third-grader to perform at a third-grade level and a 9-year-old to perform at a 9-year-old level. However, the way equivalent scores are constructed ensures that 50 percent of any age or grade group will perform below age or grade level because half of the test takers earn scores below the median.

5. *Tendency for scales to be ordinal, not equal interval.* The line relating the number correct to the various ages is typically curved, with a flattening of the curve at higher ages or grades. Figure 5.1 is a typical developmental curve. Because the scales are ordinal and not based on equal-interval units, scores on these scales should not be added or multiplied in any computation.

Developmental Quotients

Before we try to interpret a developmental score (for example, a mental age), we must know the age of the person whose score is being calculated. Knowing developmental age as well as chronological age (CA) allows us to judge an individual's relative performance. Suppose that Ana earns a mental age (MA) of 120 months. If Ana is 8 years (96 months) old, her performance is above average. If she is 35 years old, however, it is below average. The relationship between developmental age and chronological age is often quantified as a developmental quotient. For example, a *ratio IQ* is

$$\text{IQ} = \text{MA (in months)} \times 100 \div \text{CA (in months)}$$

The *developmental age* is often interpreted as the level of functioning, whereas the developmental quotient is interpreted as the rate of development. In any such scheme, a third variable, chronological age, is always involved. Of the three variables, only chronological age and the developmental quotient are independent of each other (that is, uncorrelated). The developmental age is related to both of the other two variables. In the case of intelligence, the developmental age is far more closely associated with chronological age than it is with the developmental quotient (Kappauf, 1973). Developmental levels do not provide independent information. They only summarize data for age (or grade) and relative standing.

All the problems that apply to developmental levels also apply to developmental quotients. There is one additional problem that is particularly bothersome: The variance of developmental scores within different chronological age or grade groups may not be the same. This can cause two related problems. First, the same quotient may mean different things at different ages. For example, a developmental quotient of 120 at age 5 may mean that Billy performs better than 55 percent of 5-year-olds. However, a developmental quotient of 120 at age 11 may mean that Billy performs better than 53 or 58 percent (or some other percentage) of 11-year-olds. Second, different quotients at different ages can mean the same thing. For example, whereas a developmental quotient of 120 at age 5 may mean that Sally performs better than 55 percent of other 5-year-olds, a developmental quotient of 110 at age 10 could mean that Sally performs better than 55 percent of 10-year-olds. Thus different variances at different ages and grades render it impossible to interpret scores without knowing the variances.

Scores of Relative Standing

Unlike developmental scores, scores of relative standing use more information than the mean or median to interpret a person's test score. Moreover, when the same type of relative-standing score is used, the units of measurement are exactly the same. Thus we can compare the performances of different people even when they differ in age, and we can compare one person's scores on several different tests. This specificity of meaning is very useful. For example, it is not particularly helpful to know that George is 70 inches tall, Bridget is 6 feet 3 inches tall, Bruce is 1.93 meters tall, and Alexandra is 177.8 centimeters tall. To compare their heights, it is necessary to transform the heights into comparable units. In feet and inches, their heights are as follows: George, 5 feet 10 inches; Bridget, 6 feet 3 inches; Bruce, 6 feet 4 inches; and Alexandra, 5 feet 10 inches. Scores of relative standing put raw scores into comparable units, such as percentiles or standard scores.

Percentile Family

Percentile ranks (*percentiles*) can be used when the scale of measurement is ordinal or equal interval. They are derived scores indicating the percentage of people whose scores are at or below a given raw score. The percentage correct is *not* the same as the percentage of people scoring at or below a given score. Percentiles corresponding to particular scores can be computed by the following four-step sequence.

Online Study Center
General Resources

Computing Percentiles

1. Arrange the scores from the highest to the lowest (that is, best to worst).
2. Compute the percentage of people with scores below the score to which you wish to assign a percentile rank.

3. Compute the percentage of people with scores at the score to which you wish to assign a percentile rank.

4. Add the percentage of people with scores below the score to one half the percentage of people with scores at the score to obtain the percentile rank.

Table 5.1 gives a numerical example. Mr. Greenberg gave a test to his developmental reading class, which has an enrollment of 25 children. The scores are presented in column 1, and the number of children obtaining each score (the *frequency*) is shown in column 2. Column 3 gives the percentage of all 25 scores that each obtained score represents. Column 4 contains the percentage of all 25 scores that were below that particular score. In the last group of columns, the percentile rank is computed. Only one child scored 24; the one score is $\frac{1}{25}$ of the class, or 4 percent. No one scored lower than 24; so 0 percent ($\frac{0}{25}$) of the scores is below 24. The child who scored 24 received a percentile rank of 2—that is, 0 plus one half of 4. The next score obtained is 38, and again only one child received this score. Thus 4 percent of the total ($\frac{1}{25}$) scored at 38, and 4 percent of the total scored below 38. Therefore, the percentile rank corresponding to a score of 38 is 6—that is, 4 + ($\frac{1}{2}$)(4). Two children earned a score of 40, and two children scored below 40. Therefore, the percentile rank for a score of 40 is 12—that is, 8 + ($\frac{1}{2}$)(8). The same procedure is followed for every score obtained. The

---

TABLE 5.1 Computing Percentile Ranks for a Hypothetical Class of Twenty-Five

			Percentile Rank				
Score	Frequency	Percentage at the Score	Percentage Below the Score	+	Half of Percentage at the Score	=	Percentile
50	2	8	92	+	(1/2)(8)	=	96
49	0						
48	4	16	76	+	(1/2)(16)	=	84
47	0						
46	5	20	56	+	(1/2)(20)	=	66
45	5	20	36	+	(1/2)(20)	=	46
44	3	12	24	+	(1/2)(12)	=	30
43	2	8	16	+	(1/2)(8)	=	20
42	0	—					
41	0	—					
40	2	8	8	+	(1/2)(8)	=	12
39	0	—					
38	1	4	4	+	(1/2)(4)	=	6
.							
.							
.							
24	1	4	0	+	(1/2)(4)	=	2

best score in the class, 50, was obtained by two students. The percentile rank corresponding to the highest score in the class is 96.

The interpretation of percentile ranks is based on the percentage of people. The data from Table 5.1 provide a specific example. All students who score 48 on the test have a percentile rank of 84. These four students have scored as well as or better than 84 percent of their classmates on the test. Similarly, an individual who obtains a percentile rank of 21 on an intelligence test has scored as well as or better than 21 percent of the people in the group.

Because the percentile rank is computed using one half the percentage of those obtaining a particular score, it is not possible to have a percentile rank of either 0 or 100. Generally, percentile ranks contain decimals, so it is possible for a score to receive a percentile rank of 99.9 or 0.1. The fiftieth percentile rank is the median.

Deciles are bands of percentiles that are ten percentile ranks in width; each decile contains 10 percent of the norm group. The first decile contains percentile ranks from 0.1 to 9.9; the second decile contains percentile ranks from 10 to 19.9; the tenth decile contains percentile ranks from 90 to 99.9.

Quartiles are bands of percentiles that are 25 percentile ranks in width; each quartile contains 25 percent of the norm group. The first quartile contains percentile ranks from 0.1 to 24.9; the fourth quartile contains the ranks 75 to 99.9.

Standard Scores

A standardized distribution is a set of scores that have been transformed so that the mean and standard deviation of the set take predetermined (standard) values. The most basic standardized distribution is the *z*-distribution. A *z*-distribution has a predetermined mean of 0 and a predetermined standard deviation of 1. To transform raw scores (for example, the number correct on a test) to *z*-scores, the mean of the distribution is subtracted from each raw score; this operation sets the mean at 0. Next, the difference between the raw score and the mean is divided by the standard deviation; this operation sets the standard deviation at 1.

Standard score is the general name for any derived score that has been standardized. Although a distribution of scores can be standardized to produce any predetermined mean and standard deviation, there are five commonly used standard-score distributions: *z*-scores, *T*-scores, deviation IQs, normal-curve equivalents, and stanines.

z-Scores As just indicated, *z-scores* are standard scores, the distribution of which has a mean of 0 and a standard deviation of 1. Any raw score can be converted to a *z*-score by using Equation 5.1:

$$z = (X - \bar{X}) \div S \qquad (5.1)$$

A *z*-score equals the raw score less the mean of the distribution, divided by the standard deviation of the distribution. The *z*-scores are interpreted as standard deviation units. Thus a *z*-score of +1.5 means that the score is 1.5 standard deviations above the mean of the group. A *z*-score of −0.6 means that the score is 0.6 standard deviation below the mean. A z-score of 0 is the mean performance.

Because + and − signs have a tendency to get lost and decimals may be awkward in practical situations, z-scores often are transformed to other standard scores. The general formula for changing a z-score into a different standard score is given by Equation 5.2. In the equation, SS stands for any standard score, as does the subscript ss. Thus any standard score equals the mean of the distribution of standard scores ($\overline{X}_{ss}$) plus the product of the standard deviation of the distribution of standard scores (S_{ss}) multiplied by the z-score.

$$SS = \overline{X}_{ss} + (S_{ss})(z) \tag{5.2}$$

T-Scores   A *T-score* is a standard score with a mean of 50 and a standard deviation of 10. In Table 5.2, five z-scores are converted to T-scores. A T-score of 60 is 10 points above the mean (50). Because the standard deviation is 10, a T-score of 60 is always one standard deviation above the mean.

Deviation IQs   When it was first introduced, the IQ was defined as the ratio of mental age to chronological age, multiplied by 100. Statisticians soon found that MA has different variances and standard deviations at different chronological ages. Consequently, the same ratio IQ has different meanings at different ages— the same ratio IQ corresponds to different z-scores at different ages. To remedy that situation, MAs are converted to z-scores for each age group, and z-scores are converted to deviation IQs. *Deviation IQs* are standard scores with a mean of 100 and a standard deviation that is usually 15 but is occasionally 16. A z-score can be converted to a deviation IQ by using Equation 5.2. In Table 5.3, five z-scores are converted to deviation IQs with standard deviations of 15 (column 2) and 16 (column 3).

Normal-Curve Equivalents   *Normal-curve equivalents* are standard scores with a mean equal to 50 and a standard deviation equal to 21.06. Although the standard deviation may at first appear a bit strange, this scale divides the normal curve into 100 equal intervals.

Stanines   *Stanines* (short for *standard nines*) are standard-score bands that divide a distribution into nine parts. The first stanine includes all scores that are 1.75 standard deviations or more below the mean, and the ninth stanine includes

---

TABLE 5.2   Converting z-Scores to T-Scores

z-Score	T-Score = 50 + (10)(z)
z = +1.0	60 = 50 + (10)(+1.0)
z = −1.5	35 = 50 + (10)(−1.5)
z = −2.1	29 = 50 + (10)(−2.1)
z = +3.6	86 = 50 + (10)(+3.6)
z = 0.0	50 = 50 + (10)(0.0)

- -

TABLE 5.3	Converting z-Scores to Deviation IQs ($X = 100$)		
	z-Score (A)	IQ ($S = 15$) (B)	IQ ($S = 16$) (C)
	−2.00	70	68
	−1.00	85	84
	.00	100	100
	+1.00	115	116
	+2.00	130	132

all scores 1.75 or more standard deviations above the mean. The second through eighth stanines are each 0.5 standard deviation in width, with the fifth stanine ranging from 0.25 standard deviation below the mean to 0.25 standard deviation above the mean.

Advantages and Disadvantages of Standard Scores   Standard scores are frequently more difficult to interpret than percentile scores because the concepts of means and standard deviations are not widely understood by people without some statistical knowledge. Thus standard scores may be more difficult for students and their parents to understand. Aside from this disadvantage, standard scores offer all the advantages of percentiles plus an additional advantage: Because standard scores are equal interval, they can be combined (for example, added or averaged).[1]

Concluding Comments on Derived Scores

Test authors provide tables to convert raw scores into derived scores. Thus test users do not have to calculate derived scores. However, test users may wish to convert raw scores to other standard scores for which no conversion tables are provided. Because all standard scores are based on z-scores, standard scores have the same relationship to each other, regardless of a distribution's shape. Therefore, standard scores can be transformed into other standard scores readily, using the formulas provided earlier in this chapter. Standard scores can be converted to percentiles without conversion tables only when the distribution of scores is normal. In normal distributions, the relationship between percentiles

1. Standard scores also solve another subtle problem. When scores are combined in a total or composite, the elements of that composite (for example, 18 scores from weekly spelling tests that are combined to obtain a semester average) do not count the same (that is, they do not carry the same weight) unless they have equal variances. Tests that have larger variances contribute more to the composite than do tests with smaller variances. When each of the elements has been standardized into the same standard scores (for example, when each of the weekly spelling tests has been standardized as z-scores), the elements (that is, the weekly scores) will carry exactly the same weight when they are combined. Moreover, the only way a teacher can weight tests differentially is to standardize all the tests and then multiply by the weight. For example, if a teacher wished to count the second test as three times the first test, the scores on both tests would have to be standardized, and the scores on the second test would then be multiplied by three before the scores were combined.

and standard scores is known. Figure 5.2 compares various standard scores and percentiles for normal distributions. When the distribution of scores is not normal, conversion tables are necessary in order to convert percentiles to standard scores (or vice versa). These conversion tables are test-specific, so they can be provided only by a test author. Moreover, conversion tables are always required in order to convert developmental scores to scores of relative standing, even when the distribution of test scores is normal. If the only derived score available for a test is an age equivalent, then there is no way for a test user to convert raw scores to percentiles. However, age or grade equivalents can be converted back to raw scores, which can be converted to standard scores if the raw-score mean and standard deviation are provided.

The selection of the particular type of score to use and to report depends on the purpose of testing and the sophistication of the consumer. In our opinion, developmental scores should never be used. These scores are readily misinterpreted by both laypeople and professionals. In order to understand the precise meaning of developmental scores, the interpreter must generally know both the mean and the standard deviation, and then convert the developmental score to a more meaningful score, a score of relative standing. Various professional organizations (for example, the International Reading Association, the American Psychological Association, the National Council on Measurement in Education, and the Council for Exceptional Children) also hold very negative official opinions about developmental scores and quotients.

Standard scores are convenient for test authors. Their use allows an author to give equal weight to various test components or subtests. Their utility for the consumer is twofold. First, if the score distribution is normal, the consumer can readily convert standard scores to percentile ranks. Second, because standard

FIGURE 5.2
Relationship Among Selected Standard Scores, Percentiles, and the Normal Curve

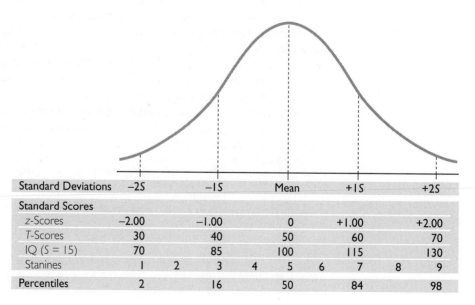

Standard Deviations	−2S		−1S		Mean		+1S		+2S
Standard Scores									
z-Scores	−2.00		−1.00		0		+1.00		+2.00
T-Scores	30		40		50		60		70
IQ (S = 15)	70		85		100		115		130
Stanines	1	2	3	4	5	6	7	8	9
Percentiles	2		16		50		84		98

scores are equal-interval scores, they are useful in analyzing strengths and weaknesses of individual students and in research.

We favor the use of percentiles. These unpretentious scores require the fewest assumptions for accurate interpretation. The scale of measurement need only be ordinal, although it is very appropriate to compute percentiles on equal-interval or ratio data. The distribution of scores need not be normal; percentiles can be computed for any shape of distribution. They are readily understood by professionals, parents, and students. Most important, however, is the fact that percentiles tell us nothing more than what any norm-referenced derived score can tell us—namely, an individual's relative standing in a group. Reporting scores in percentiles may remove some of the aura surrounding test scores, and it permits test results to be presented in terms users can understand.

Scores Used in Criterion-Referenced Assessment

Unlike norm-referenced scores, which compare a student's performance to the performances of other students, criterion-referenced scores compare a student's performance against an objective and absolute standard (criterion) of performance. Criterion-referenced measures are of two types: scores on single skills and scores on multiple skills.

Single-Skill Scores   The most basic score used in criterion-referenced assessment is pass-fail, right-wrong, or some variation on this theme. Usually, one option in this dichotomous scoring scheme is defined precisely, and the other option is scored by default. For example, a correct response to "1 + 2 = ?" might be defined as "3, written intelligibly and in the correct orientation"; a wrong response would be one that fails to meet one or more of the criteria for a correct response.

Single-skill scores may also be scored along a continuum that ranges from completely correct to completely incorrect. For example, a teacher might give partial credit for a response because the student used the correct algorithm to solve a mathematics problem, even though the student's answer was incorrect. Frequently, continuum scoring of single skills is used to show progress toward mastery of a skill. For example, in a daily-living or life-skills curriculum, a teacher might scale drinking from a cup without assistance in several ways. For instance, the teacher might observe frequency of proper drinking and scale it as usually, frequently, seldom, or never drinks from a cup without assistance. Alternatively, that teacher might scale drinking on the basis of assistance needed by a student (drinks from a cup without assistance, drinks from a cup with verbal prompts, drinks from a cup with physical guidance, or does not drink from a cup). Of course, each point on the continuum requires careful definition. However, having multiple points along a continuum can be useful when trying to document slow progress toward a goal.

Some newer types of assessment (for example, portfolio assessment and authentic assessment) appear to be similar to single-dimension, criterion-referenced assessment. These newer forms of assessment frequently scale performance from "novice" to "expert" on some dimension. However, the points along the continuum are frequently so subjective that they are virtually impossible to define or assess consistently. We view these types of assessments as scaled opinions about student performance, rather than meaningful assessments of student performance; therefore, we are reluctant to consider them within the category of criterion-referenced assessment.

Multiple-Skill Scores

When multiple skills (for example, addition facts), complex skills (for example, oral reading), or multiple observations of single skills are assessed, it is common to express the number of correct or incorrect responses as a function of the total number of responses (for example, percentage correct) or as a function of time (for example, the number of correct responses per minute). In this section, we refer to these two types of scores as percentages and rates. We realize that percentages are, indeed, rates, but the professional literature frequently refers to scores expressed in time units as rates and distinguishes these scores from percentages based on the number of opportunities. We use the professional jargon with the understanding that it is at odds with the usual meanings.

Percentage

Percentages are widely used in a variety of assessment contexts. For example, percentage correct is probably the score most frequently used by teachers in the assessment of academic skills; prevalence (the percentage of time a behavior occurs) is frequently used in systematic observation. Percentages are often the basis of other criterion-referenced scores. Three of the most commonly used derivative scores are accuracy, retention, and verbal labels for percentages (such as instructional level).

Accuracy   Accuracy refers to one of two different scores that define percentage correct. The first is based on the number of possible correct responses and is calculated by multiplying 100 times the ratio of the number of correct responses to the number of possible responses. For example, if Ben gets 25 correct answers on a 50-item test, he earns a score of 50 percent correct. The second type of percentage score is based on the number of attempted responses and is calculated by multiplying 100 times the ratio of the number of correct responses to the number of attempted responses. This form of percentage correct is most commonly used when a teacher intentionally uses an assessment procedure that precludes a student from responding to all items. (A situation in which there are more opportunities to respond than time to respond is termed a *free operant*. Free-operant situations arise in assessments that are timed to allow the opportunity for unlimited increases in rate.) For example, a teacher may ask a student to read orally for two minutes, but it may not be possible for that student (or any other student) to read the entire passage in the time allotted. Thus Benny may attempt 175 words in a 350-word passage in two minutes; if he reads 150 words correctly, his percentage correct would be about 86 percent—that is, 100 × (150/175).

Retention   *Retention* refers to the percentage of learned information that is recalled. Retention may also be termed recall, maintenance, or memory of what has been learned. Regardless of the label, it is calculated in the same way: Divide the number recalled by the number originally learned, and multiply that ratio by 100. For example, if Helen learned 40 sight vocabulary words and recalled 30 of them two weeks later, her retention would be 75 percent; that is, $100 \times (30/40)$. Because forgetting becomes more likely as the interval between the learning and the retention assessment increases, retention is usually qualified by the period of time between attainment of mastery and assessment of recall. Thus Helen's retention would be stated as 75 percent over a two-week period.

Verbal Labels for Percentages   Frequently, percentages are given verbal labels that are intended to facilitate instruction. The two most commonly used labels are "mastery" and "instructional level." *Mastery* divides the percentage continuum in two: Mastery is generally set at 90 percent correct, and nonmastery is less than 90 percent. The criterion of 90 percent for mastery is arbitrary, and in real life we sometimes set the skill level for mastery considerably higher. For example, we would probably want to define mastery of looking both ways before crossing a street as 100 percent correct.

Instructional level divides the percentage range into three segments: frustration, instructional, and independent levels. By convention, *frustration level* is usually defined as less than 85 percent correct, instructional level is defined as between 85 and 95 percent correct, and *independent level* is defined as above 95 percent correct. For example, in reading, students who decode more than 95 percent of the words should be able to read a passage without assistance; students who decode between 85 and 95 percent of the words in a passage should be able to read and comprehend that passage with assistance; students who cannot decode 85 percent of the words in a passage will probably have difficulty comprehending the material, even with assistance. (Students should not be given homework [independent practice] until they are at the independent level.)

Rate

Teachers often want their students to have a supply of information at their fingertips so that they can respond fluently (or automatically) without thinking. For example, teachers may want their students to recognize sight words without having to sound them out, recall addition facts without having to think about them, or supply Spanish words for their English equivalents. When fluency or automaticity is the desired level of performance, teachers may calculate the rate of correct response. *Rate* is defined as the number of correct responses within a specific time frame (for example, the number of words read correctly per minute). Criterion rates for successful performance are usually determined empirically. For example, readers with satisfactory comprehension usually read connected prose at rates of 100 or more words per minute (Mercer & Mercer, 1985). Readers interested in desired rates for a variety of academic skills are referred to Salvia and Hughes (1990).

A Word About Global Ratings

Teachers and psychologists sometimes make global ratings of pupil performance. These ratings may be used to rate an entire performance; for example, a teacher might give an entire essay a single rating. These ratings also may be used to rate specific dimensions of a performance; for example, a teacher might make separate ratings of three dimensions (spelling, capitalization, and content) of an essay. The ratings may be dichotomous (for example, pass-fail or satisfactory-unsatisfactory). More often, however, ratings are made on a continuum of several points that capture the range of good to bad performances. The dimensions to be rated and the points along the rating continuum are called *scoring rubrics*.

At times, ratings made with scoring rubrics may appear to be norm-referenced scores. For example, a teacher might rate a student's essay as advanced, comparable, or behind those of other students in the same grade. At other times, ratings made with scoring rubrics may sound like developmental scores. For example, a teacher might rate a student's essay as like that of a novice, emerging, or expert writer. At still other times, ratings may appear to be criterion-referenced scores. For example, a teacher might rate an essay as demonstrating (or not demonstrating) mastery in the correct use of punctuation marks.

Care must be taken in interpreting holistic or global ratings for at least three reasons. First, these ratings are not based on systematic analysis and quantification of performance; they are based on impressions of performance. As such, they are very susceptible to a host of extraneous influences. (This process, known as the halo effect, is well documented in psychological and educational research.) Second, there is little consistency among the ratings of even trained raters or for the same rater across several performances. Third, the ratings are ordinal and therefore cannot be added together or averaged.

SUMMARY

One method of interpreting student scores is to compare them with the scores of a group of students of known characteristics, called a norm group. Scores interpreted this way are called norm-referenced scores. Two types of norm-referenced comparisons can be made—across ages and within ages. Developmental scores (that is, age and grade equivalents) compare students' performances across age or grade groups. Within a group, comparisons can be made using sev-

eral different types of scores that have different characteristics. A developmental quotient (an age or grade equivalent divided by chronological age or actual grade placement, respectively) is the least desirable within-age comparison. Of greater value are standard scores (for example, z-scores, T-scores, and deviation IQs). Such scores have a predetermined mean and standard deviation that define them. In our view, the best derived scores for general use are percentile ranks.

A second method of interpreting student scores is to compare scores with an absolute standard of performance. Two types of criterion-referenced scores are commonly used: single-skill scores and multiple-skill scores. Single-skill scores are usually scored dichotomously (for example, pass-fail) but may be scaled on a continuum (for example, usually, frequently, never). Whether an instrument is scored dichotomously or along a continuum, the scoring criteria always should be expressed in precise and observable terms. Multiple skills (for example, weekly writing of spelling words) are scored as the percentage correct or as the number of correct responses in a specific period of time (for example, number of words read correctly per minute).

Finally, global ratings are occasionally used as scores. Although these scores may appear to be either norm-referenced or criterion-referenced scores, the bases for developing them are judgments that are seldom objective or precise.

QUESTIONS FOR CHAPTER REVIEW

1. Eleanore and Ahmad take an intelligence test. Eleanore obtains an MA of 3-5, and Ahmad obtains an MA of 12-2. The test had been standardized on 50 boys and girls at each of the following ages: 3-0 to 3-1, 4-0 to 4-1, 5-0 to 5-1, 6-0 to 6-1, and 7-0 to 7-1. The psychologist reports that Eleanore functions like a child age 3 years and 5 months, whereas Ahmad has the MA of a child 12 years and 2 months old. Identify five problems inherent in these interpretations.

2. Differentiate between a ratio IQ (developmental quotient) and a deviation IQ. Why is a deviation IQ preferable?

3. Shu-Yu earned a percentile rank of 83 on a kindergarten admission test. What is the statistical meaning of her score? To what decile does the score correspond? To what quartile does the score correspond?

4. Marvina takes a battery of standardized tests. The results are as follows:

   Test A: Mental age = 8-6

   Test B: Reading grade equivalent = 3.1

   Test C: Developmental age = 8-4

   Test D: Developmental quotient = 103

   Test E: Percentile rank = 56

What must the teacher do in order to interpret Marvina's performances on these five scales and compare the performances with one another?

5. Andrew earns a stanine of 1 on an intelligence test. To what z-scores, percentile ranks, and T-scores does his stanine score correspond?

6. Distinguish among frustration level, instructional level, and independent level. Why are these distinctions important?

7. Although scores are frequently reported as developmental scores, a number of problems are inherent in the use of these scores. Discuss three of these problems.

PROBLEMS

Turn back to Table 4.4, which shows the results of the two tests Ms. Smith gave to her arithmetic class. For test 1, make the following computations:

1. Compute the percentile rank for each student.

2. Compute each student's z-score.

3. Convert Bob's, Sam's, Sean's, and Carole's z-scores to T-scores.

4. Convert Lucy's, Carmen's, John's, and Ludwig's z-scores to deviation IQs with a mean of 100 and a standard deviation of 15.

Answers

1. 98, 94, 90, 86, 82, 78, 70, 70, 70, 50, 50, 50, 50, 50, 50, 50, 30, 30, 30, 22, 18, 14, 10, 6, 2
2. 2.17, 2.00, 1.33, 1.00, .67, .5, .33, .33, .33, 0, 0, 0, 0, 0, 0, 0, −.33, −.33, −.33, −.5, −.67, −1.00, −1.33, −2.00, −2.17
3. 72, 63, 50, 45
4. 130, 105, 100, 70

RESOURCES FOR FURTHER INVESTIGATION

Technology Resources

STATSOFT ELECTRONIC TEXTBOOK
www.statsoft.com/textbook/stathome.html
This is essentially an online textbook. By typing in keywords, one can search for information on terms and general statistical concepts. It is very well organized and extremely comprehensive.

INTRODUCTORY STATISTICS: CONCEPTS, MODELS, AND APPLICATIONS
psychstat.smsu.edu/sbk00.htm
A broad range of statistical topics is covered here, including *t*-tests and critical values. This website also includes a section on how to use a statistical calculator and a section with practice exercises.

COLLEGE OF EDUCATION, UNIVERSITY OF IOWA, TESTING PROGRAM
www.education.uiowa.edu/itp/itbs/ itbs_interp_score.htm
This site provides a comprehensive overview of all types of test scores and their interpretations. Included are the strengths and weaknesses of raw scores, percentages correct, grade equivalents, developmental standard scores, and percentile ranks.

CHAPTER 6

Norms

As discussed in the chapter "Quantification of Test Performance," derived scores (such as percentiles, standard scores, and developmental scores) compare a person's test performance with the performances of others on the same test. For example, if Kareem scored at the sixty-fifth percentile, we know he did equal to or better than 65 percent of the people with whom he is compared. The percentile rank tells us nothing, however, about the people with whom we compare Kareem's performance.

To understand a student's performance, we must also know the characteristics and abilities of the people with whom we compare a test taker, such as Kareem. In norm-referenced testing, we compare a test taker with a group of students tested by the test author; this group is usually called the norm group or *standardization sample*. Obviously, the meaning of a derived score is inextricably tied to the characteristics of the norm group. For example, suppose Kareem earned a percentile rank of 50 on an intelligence test. If the norm group comprised only students enrolled in programs for the mentally retarded, a score at the fiftieth percentile would indicate limited intellectual ability. However, if the norm group consisted of individuals enrolled in programs for the gifted, Kareem's score would indicate superior intellectual ability. In practice, only very specialized norms are based on individuals with very specific characteristics, such as mental retardation or giftedness. More typically, norm groups usually are based on people in general. In any case, "it is important that the reference populations be carefully and clearly described" (American Educational Research Association [AERA], American Psychological Association, & National Council on Measurement in Education, 1999, p. 51).[1]

---

1. In practice, it is also impossible to test the entire population because the membership of the population is constantly changing. Fortunately, the characteristics of a population can be accurately estimated from the characteristics of a representative sample.

Representativeness

Representativeness hinges on two questions: (1) Does the norm sample contain individuals with relevant characteristics and experiences? and (2) Are the characteristics and experiences present in the sample in the same proportion as they are in the population of reference?[2]

What makes a characteristic relevant depends on the construct being measured. Some characteristics have a clear logical and empirical relationship to a person's development, and several characteristics are important for any psychoeducational construct. Following are brief discussions of the most commonly considered developmental and sociocultural characteristics, as well as some other characteristics that have a demonstrated relationship to test performance.

Developmental Characteristics

Test performance may be directly related to a person's level of maturation. Therefore, a person's gender, age, and grade in school are important characteristics that are regularly considered by test authors.

Gender

Some biological differences between males and females have been well documented. Girls tend to physically develop faster than boys during the first year or two. Many more boys tend to have delayed maturation than do girls during the preschool and primary school years. After puberty, men tend to be bigger and stronger than women. Tests that directly or indirectly measure skills and abilities influenced by gender differences typically provide separate norms for males and females.

Age

We typically think of the range of ages for the norm groups as being one year. However, because we have known for more than 40 years that different psychological abilities develop at different rates (see Guilford, 1967, pp. 417–426), a one-year range may be inappropriate. When an ability or skill is developing rapidly (for example, locomotion in infants and toddlers), the age range of the norm group must be much less than one year. It would make no sense to conclude that a 3-month-old infant is motorically delayed when compared with a 1-year-old. Thus, on scales used to assess infants and young children, we often see norms in three-month ranges. Similarly, after an ability has matured, a one-year interval is unnecessary. If there are no meaningful differences in the distribution of 40-, 41-, 42-, and 43-year-olds, separate age norms for these groups are unnecessary. As a result, we often see norms in ten-year ranges on adult scales. Therefore, although one-year norms are most common, developmental theory and research can suggest norms of lesser or greater age ranges.

---

2. Characteristics expressed by less than 1 or 2 percent of the population may not be represented accurately.

Grade in School

All achievement tests and some intelligence tests measure learned facts, concepts, and behavior. Students of different ages are present in most grades, and grade in school bears a more direct relationship to what is taught in school than does age. Some 7-year-old children may not be enrolled in school; some may be in kindergarten, some in first grade, some in second, and some even in third. The academic proficiency of 7-year-olds can be expected to be more closely related to what they have been taught than to their age. Consequently, grade norms are more appropriate than are age norms for achievement tests used with students of school age.

Sociocultural Characteristics

In developing norms, test authors generally try to include males and females of all major ethnic, racial, and socioeconomic groups. On average, various groups differ somewhat in their performances on many achievement and ability tests. These differences are generally small, and many are growing smaller each year. Scientists and philosophers have long tried to understand why this might be so, and they have offered a number of explanations—genetics, environment, interactions between genes and environment. However, although trying to unravel the interactions among culture, genetics, and environment may be interesting scientifically and politically, such an endeavor is far beyond the scope of this text. What is important for our purposes is an understanding that these differences must be considered in developing norm groups.

First and foremost, norm groups should include persons with the same characteristics as those who will be tested (see AERA et al., 1999, p. 55). Including individuals from all groups is important for at least two reasons. First, to the extent that individuals from various backgrounds perform differently, test parameters (that is, means and variances) are likely to be biased. Second, because test authors frequently base their final selection of items on the performance of the norm group, exclusion of individuals from diverse backgrounds can bias test content.

Even though culture-related characteristics generally lack a direct theoretical relationship to the construct being measured, they are nonetheless relevant because they have an empirical relationship to that construct. For example, parental income is associated with school achievement. However, income per se makes little theoretical sense except as a marker for other variables that do have a clear relationship to achievement (access to nutritious foods and medical care, attendance at schools with better facilities, parenting styles, and so on). Following is a brief discussion of and rationale for the most commonly considered culture-related characteristics: gender, acculturation of parents, and race and cultural identity.

Gender

Males and females sometimes differ on their tested performances. Some of these differences can be appropriately attributed to differences in cultural expectations and experiences. Although gender-role expectations are changing, gender still may systematically limit the types of activities a child participates in because of modeling, peer pressure, or the responses of significant adults. We are also speculating about the causes of gender differences in other areas. For example, why do women tend to perform better on essay examinations whereas men tend to do better on multiple-choice tests?

Nevertheless, on most psychological and educational tests, gender differences are small, and the distributions of scores of males and females tend to overlap considerably. When gender differences are minor, norm groups clearly should contain the appropriate proportions of males (about 48 percent) and females (about 52 percent)—the proportion found in the general U.S. population. However, when gender differences are substantial, the correct course of action is unclear. Some favor separate norms for males and females. (Separate norms remove any differences in derived scores.[3]) Others favor norms containing proportional representation of both genders, which leaves one gender, on average, scoring lower than the other.

Acculturation of Parents

Acculturation is an imprecise concept that refers to an understanding of the language (including conventions and pragmatics), history, values, and social conventions of society at large. Nowhere are the complexities of acculturation more readily illustrated than in the area of language. Acculturation requires people to know more than standard American English; they must also know the appropriate contexts for various words and idioms, appropriate volume and distance between speaker and listener, appropriate posture to indicate respect, and so forth.

Because acculturation is a broad and somewhat diffuse construct, it is difficult to define or measure precisely. Typically, test authors use the educational or occupational attainment (socioeconomic status) of the parents as a general indication of the level of acculturation of the home. As it turns out, the socioeconomic status of a student's parents is strongly related to that student's scores on all sorts of tests—intelligence, achievement, adaptive behavior, social functioning, and so forth. The children of middle- and upper-class parents have tended to score higher on such tests (see Gottesman, 1968; Herrnstein & Murray, 1994). Whatever the reasons for class differences in child development, norm samples certainly must include all segments of society (in the same proportion as in the general population) in order to be representative.

Race and Cultural Identity

Race and cultural identity continue to be emotionally charged issues for U.S. society. The scientific and educational communities have often been insensitive and occasionally blatantly racist (for example, Down, 1866/1969). As recently as 1972, the Stanford-Binet Intelligence Scale excluded nonwhite individuals

---

3. The raw scores associated with particular derived scores (such as the fiftieth percentile) will be different, of course.

from the standardization sample. Although such overt discrimination is rare today, individuals of color still face subtle forms of discrimination and limited opportunities.

Race and culture are particularly relevant to our discussion of norms because persistent differences in *tested* achievement and intelligence remain among races and cultural groups, although these differences continue to narrow. Inclusion of individuals of all racial and cultural groups, both in field tests of items and in the standardization of a test, is important for two reasons. First, to the extent that individuals of different races undergo cultural experiences that differ even within a given social class and geographic region, norm samples that exclude (or underrepresent) one race are unrepresentative of the total population. Second, if individuals from various cultures are excluded from field tests of test items, item-difficulty estimates (*p*-values) and point biserial (item-total) correlations may be inaccurate, and the test's scaling may be in error. Thus, even if test designers could justify culturally homogeneous norms (and we are not saying that they could), the exclusion or underrepresentation of individuals of color in norm samples gives the appearance of bias.

Other Characteristics

Geography

As is readily apparent from any current test manual, there are differences in the attainment of individuals living in different geographic regions of the United States, and various psychoeducational tests reflect these regional differences. Most consistently, the average scores of individuals living in the southeastern part of the United States (excluding Florida) are often lower than the average scores of individuals living in other regions of the country. Moreover, community size, population density, and changes in population also have been related to academic and intellectual development.

There are several seemingly logical explanations for many of these relationships. For example, educational attainment is related to educational expenditures, and there are regional differences in the financial support of public education. Well-educated young adults tend to move away from communities with limited employment and cultural opportunities. When brighter and better-educated individuals leave a community, the average intellectual ability and educational attainment in that community go down, and the average ability and attainment of the communities to which the brighter individuals move go up. Regardless of the reasons for geographical differences, test norms should include individuals from all geographic regions, as well as from urban, suburban, and rural communities.

Intelligence

A representative sample of individuals in terms of their level of intellectual functioning is essential for standardizing an intelligence test—and most other kinds of tests. Intelligence is related to a number of variables that are considered in psychoeducational assessment. It is certainly related to achievement because most intelligence tests were actually developed to predict school success.

Correlations of achievement and intelligence are generally positive but decline as students age. For elementary school students, the correlation may be as high as .7, whereas for secondary school students the correlation drops to .5 to .6. The correlations continue to drop for college and graduate students (Atkinson, Atkinson, Smith, & Bem, 1993). Because language development and facility are often considered an indication of intellectual development, intelligence tests are often verbally oriented. Consequently, we also would expect to find substantial correlations between scores on tests of intelligence and scores on tests of linguistic or psycholinguistic ability. In addition, items thought to reflect perceptual ability appear on intelligence tests, and as early as 1941 Thurstone found various perceptual tasks to be a factor in intelligence. Thus intelligence must be considered in the development of norms for perceptual and perceptual-motor tests.

In the development of norms, it is essential to test the full range of intellectual ability. Limiting the sample to students enrolled in and attending school (usually general education classes) restricts the norms. Failure to consider individuals with mental retardation in standardization procedures introduces systematic bias into test norms by underestimating the population mean and standard deviation. (In the chapter "Making Accountability Decisions" we discuss the inclusion of students with disabilities in the assessment of educational outcomes.)

Technical Considerations

Finding People   Finding a broadly representative sample of people requires careful planning. Therefore, test authors or publishers usually develop sampling plans to try to locate potential participants with the needed characteristics. Sampling plans involve finding communities of specific sizes within geographic regions. Cluster sampling and selection of representative communities (or some combination of the two) are two common methods of choosing these communities. In cluster sampling, urban areas and the surrounding suburban and rural communities are selected. Such sampling plans have the advantage of requiring fewer testers and less travel. When a sampling plan calls for the selection of representative communities, a representative community is usually defined as one in which the mean demographic characteristics (such as educational level and income) of residents are approximately the same as the national or regional average. For example, in the 2000 U.S. Census, about 51 percent of the population was female, about 19 percent of the population lived in the Northeast region of the country, and about 25 percent of the population 25 years or older had a degree from a four-year college. A representative community in the Northeast region would be one in which about 51 percent was female, about 25 percent had earned a degree from a four-year institution, and so on.

Proportional Representation   Explicit in the preceding discussion of characteristics of people in a representative normative sample is the idea that various kinds of people should be included in the sample in the same proportion as they occur in the general population.

However, neither cluster sampling nor selection of representative communities guarantees that the participants as a group are representative of the population. Consequently, test authors may adjust norms to make them representative. One method of adjusting norms is to systematically oversample subjects (that is, to select many more subjects than are needed) and then to drop subjects until a representative sample has been achieved. Another method is to weight subjects within the normative sample differentially. Subjects with underrepresented characteristics may be counted as more than one subject, and subjects with overrepresented characteristics may be counted as fractions of persons. Both methods may be used. In such ways, norm samples can be manipulated to conform with population characteristics.

No matter how test norms are constructed, test authors should systematically compare the relevant characteristics of the population and their standardization samples. Although we frequently use the singular (that is, norm sample or group) when discussing norms, it is important to understand that tests have multiple normative samples. For example, an achievement test intended for use with students in kindergarten through twelfth grade has 13 norm groups (1 for each grade). If that achievement test has separate norms for males and females at each grade, then there are 26 norm groups. When we test a second-grade boy, we do not compare his performance with the performances of all students in the total norm sample. Rather, we compare the boy's performance with that of other second-graders (or of other second-grade boys if there are separate norms for boys and girls). Thus the preceding discussions of representativeness and the number of subjects apply to each specific comparison group within the norms—not to the aggregated or combined samples. Representativeness should be demonstrated for each comparison group. For example, Table 6.1 shows such a comparison for RISA (Salvia, Neisworth, & Schmidt, 1990), a norm-referenced adaptive behavior scale for use with adolescents between the ages of 12 and 19 years. Tables like these allow a test user to judge the representativeness of a test's norms.

Finally, the systematic development of representative norms is time consuming and expensive. Samples that are convenient, such as volunteers from all the parochial schools in a big city, reduce the time needed to locate subjects and are less expensive; however, they are unlikely to be representative, even when the number of subjects is impressively large.

Number of Subjects

The number of participants in a norm sample is important for several reasons. First, the number of subjects should be large enough to guarantee stability. If a sample is very small, another group of participants might have a different mean and standard deviation. Second, the number of participants should be large enough to represent infrequent characteristics. For example, if about 1 percent of the population is Native American, a sample of 25 or 50 people will be unlikely to contain even 1 Native American. Third, there should be enough subjects so that there can be a full range of derived scores. In practice, 100 participants in each age or grade are considered the minimum.

TABLE 6.1   Percentage of the 1980 U.S. Population and RISA-Weighted Norms by Selected Demographic Characteristics

		Age Groups							
	1980 *U.S.*	*12*	*13*	*14*	*15*	*16*	*17*	*18*	*19*
n		231	272	260	291	254	281	187	124
Sex									
Male	47.2	47.2	47.2	47.2	47.2	47.0	47.2	47.2	47.2
Female	52.8	52.8	52.8	52.8	52.8	53.0	52.8	52.8	52.8
Community									
Urban	73.7	73.6	73.5	73.7	73.7	73.7	73.7	73.7	73.7
Rural	26.3	26.4	26.5	26.3	26.3	26.3	26.3	26.3	26.3
Education									
Less than high school	29.2	29.3	29.2	29.3	29.3	29.1	29.2	29.2	29.3
High school graduate	36.5	36.6	36.4	36.5	36.4	36.3	36.6	36.3	36.2
Some college	15.3	15.2	15.6	15.2	15.3	15.7	15.3	15.5	15.3
College graduate or more		18.9	18.9	18.9	19.0	18.9	19.0	19.0	19.2
Region									
Northeast	21.7	21.4	21.5	21.9	21.8	21.5	21.8	20.7	21.5
North Central	26.0	26.5	25.6	25.9	25.8	26.0	26.1	26.0	26.0
South	33.3	33.2	33.9	33.3	33.4	33.0	33.3	33.1	33.5
West	19.0	18.8	18.9	18.9	19.0	19.5	18.9	20.2	19.0
Caucasian	79.6	79.8	75.9	65.1	78.1	78.4	66.8	73.0	66.7

SOURCE: Salvia, J., Neisworth, J., & Schmidt, M. (1990). *Examiner's manual: Responsibility and Independence Scale for Adolescents.* Allen, TX: DLM.

Smoothing of Norms

After the norm sample has been finalized, norm tables are prepared. Because of minor sampling fluctuations, even well-selected norm groups will show minor variations in distribution shape. Minor smoothing is believed to result in better estimates of derived scores, means, and standard deviations. For example, there might be a few outliers—scores at the extremes of a distribution that are not contiguous to the distribution of scores but are several points beyond what would be considered the highest or lowest score in a distribution. A test author might drop these outliers. Similarly, the progression of group means from age to age may not be consistent, or group variances may differ slightly from age to age for no apparent reason. As a result, test developers will often smooth these values to conform to a theoretical or empirically generated model of performance (for example, using predicted means rather than obtained means).

Smoothing is also done to remove unwanted fluctuations in the shapes of age or grade distributions by adjusting the relationship between standard scores and percentiles. Even when normal test distributions are expected on the basis of theory, the obtained distributions of scores are never completely normal. For example, several models of intelligence posit a normal distribution of scores; in practice, the distribution of test scores is skewed because of an excess of low-scoring individuals. Thus standard scores do not correspond to the percentile ranks that are expected in a normal distribution. In such cases, a test author may force standard scores into a normal distribution by assigning them to percentile ranks on the basis of the relationship between standard scores and percentiles found in normal distributions.

For example, a raw score corresponding to the eighty-fourth percentile will be assigned a *T*-score of 60, regardless of the calculated value. The process, called "area transformation," or normalizing a distribution, is discussed in detail in advanced measurement texts. When normal distributions are not expected, a test developer may remove minor inconsistencies in distribution shapes from age to age or grade to grade. To smooth out minor inconsistencies, test authors may average the percentile ranks associated with specific standard scores. For example, a *T*-score of 60 might be associated with percentile ranks of 72, 74, and 73 in 6-, 7-, and 8-year-old groups, respectively. These percentiles could be averaged, and *T*-scores of 60 in each of the age groups could be assigned a percentile rank of 73.

Age of Norms   For a norm sample to be representative, it must represent the current population. Levels of skill and ability change over time. Skilled athletes of today run faster, jump higher, and are stronger than the best athletes of a generation ago. Some of the improvement can be attributed to better training, but some also can be attributed to better nutrition and societal changes. Similarly, intellectual and educational performances have increased from generation to generation, although these increases are neither steady nor linear.

For example, on norm-referenced achievement tests, considerably more than half the students score above the average after the test has been in use for five to seven years. In such cases, the test norms are clearly dated, because only half the population can ever be above the median (Linn, Graue, & Sanders, 1990). While some increase in tested achievement can be attributed to teacher familiarity with test content (Linn et al., 1990), there is little doubt that some of the changes represent real improvement in achievement.

There are probably multiple causes for these increases. For example, during the late 1960s and 1970s, the social fabric of the United States changed substantially. The civil rights, women's, and right-to-education movements brought much-needed reform to the U.S. education system. The computer revolution forever changed the availability of information. Never before has there been so much knowledge accessible to so many people. Students of today know more than did the students of the 1990s. Students of today also probably know less than will the students of tomorrow.

The important point is that old norms tend to estimate a student's relative standing in the population erroneously because the old norms are too easy. The point at which norms become outdated will depend in part on the ability or skill being assessed. With this caution, it seems to us that 15 years is about the maximum useful life for norm samples used in ability testing; 7 years appears to be the maximum for norm life for achievement tests. Although test publishers should assure that up-to-date norms are readily available, test users ultimately are responsible for avoiding the inappropriate use of out-of-date norms (AERA et al., 1999, p. 59).

Normative Updates

Because the development of systematically standardized tests is so expensive, test publishers may update a test's norms more frequently than they revise the test. Normative updating can be done in two ways. First, a completely different set of norms may be systematically developed. Procedurally, this kind of update is identical to the development of any set of norms. Second, statistics based on a small representative sample can be used to adjust (or recalibrate) the old norms. The necessary statistics (for example, mean and standard deviation in classical test theory or difficulty, discrimination, and guessing parameters in item-response theory) can be accurately estimated from a small sample of individuals. The old norms are linearly transformed using the new statistics, and new tables are prepared to convert raw scores to standard scores. Moreover, if the distribution of scores is normal, new percentiles can be calculated based on their relationship with standard scores.

The difficulty with normative updates is that the content is unchanged. This is not a problem when content is timeless. However, if the content becomes easier (as is frequently the case with achievement tests), the new norms may not discriminate among high scorers. In addition, normative updates probably will not fix problems associated with reliability or validity (apart from normative considerations).

Relevance of Norms   Norms must provide comparisons that are relevant in terms of the purpose of assessment. National norms are the most appropriate if we are interested in knowing how a particular student is developing intellectually, perceptually, linguistically, or physically. In other circumstances, norms developed on a particular portion of the population may be meaningful. For example, if we wish to ascertain the degree to which Ramona has profited from her 12 years of schooling, norms developed for the particular school districts she attended are appropriate.

Local norms are usually more useful in retrospective interpretations of a student's performance than in predictive interpretations. In some cases, norms based on particular groups may be more relevant than those based on the population as a whole. Some devices are standardized on special populations (for example, the AAMR [American Association on Mental Retardation] Adaptive Behavior Scale was standardized on individuals with mental retardation). Aptitude tests are often standardized on individuals in specific trades or professions. The utility of special population norms is similar to the utility of local norms: They are likely to be more useful in retrospective comparisons than in future predictions. Unless we know how the special population corresponds to the general population, predictions may not be appropriate.

There are specific instances in which special population norms have been misused. Just because a person's performance is similar to that of a special population does not mean that the person belongs to or should belong to that population. When Mary earns the same score as a typical lawyer on a test of legal aptitude, her score does not mean that Mary is or should become a lawyer. The argument that she should contains a logical fallacy, an undistributed middle term. (According to this logic, if dogs eat meat and university professors eat meat, then dogs are or should be university professors—clearly not the case.)

Reasoning of this sort is often inferred when criterion groups are used in test standardization. Such inferences are valid if it can be demonstrated that only members of a particular group score in a particular manner. If some people who are not members of the particular group earn the same scores as members of that group, the relationship between group membership and scores should be quantified. For example, let us assume that 90 percent of youngsters with brain injury make unusual (perhaps rotated, distorted, or simplified) reproductions of geometric designs. Let us also assume that 3 percent of the total population is brain injured. If individuals without brain injury were the only ones who made normal drawings, we could say with certainty that anyone who makes normal drawings is not brain injured. However, because 10 percent of individuals with brain injuries make normal reproductions, we cannot be sure: 0.31 percent of the individuals who make normal drawings are brain injured. Moreover, in some instances the normal population makes deviant responses. Assume that 20 percent of the normal population and all brain-injured children make unusual drawings. If 3 percent of the population is brain injured, then 22.4 percent of the population will perform as brain-injured test takers do ([100% of 3%] + [20% of 97%] = 22.4%). A deviant performance on the test would mean only a 13 percent (0.03/0.224) chance that the person was brain injured.

Using Norms Correctly

The manuals accompanying commercially prepared tests usually contain a table that allows a tester to convert raw scores to various derived scores, such as percentile ranks, without tedious calculations. Occasionally, the tester is even confronted with several tables for converting raw scores. For example, it is not uncommon for the same manual to contain one set of tables for converting raw scores to percentile ranks on the basis of the age of the person tested and another set of tables for converting raw scores to percentile ranks on the basis of the school grade of the person tested. To select the appropriate table, the tester must determine the population to which the performance of the sample is inferred. This can be learned by examining how the norm group was selected. If the test author sampled by grades in school, then the population of reference is students in a particular grade; consequently, the grade tables should be used for converting raw scores to derived scores. Conversely, if the test author sampled by age, the age tables should be used because the population of reference is a particular age group.

Tests often lose their power to discriminate near the extremes of the distribution, and it may not be possible for a student to earn a score more than about 2.5 standard deviations from the mean. For example, a student might not be able to earn an IQ less than 50 even if no test items were passed. Because complete failure on a test provides little or no information about what a person can do, testers often administer tests based on a norm sample of people younger than the test taker. Although such a procedure may provide useful qualitative information, it cannot provide norm-referenced interpretations because the ages of the individuals in the norm group and the age of the person being tested are not the same.

Another serious error is committed when the tester uses a person's mental age to obtain derived scores from conversion tables set up on the basis of chronological age. We suppose the reasoning behind such practices is that if the person functions as an 8-year-old child intellectually, the use of conversion tables based on the performance of 8-year-old children can be justified. However, such practices are incorrect because the norms were not established by sampling persons by mental age. When assessing the reading skill of an adolescent or adult who performs below the first percentile, a tester has little need for further or more precise norm-referenced comparisons. The tester already knows that the person is not a good reader. If the examiner wants to ascertain which reading skills a person has or lacks, a criterion-referenced (norm-free) device will be more suitable. Sometimes the most appropriate use of norms is no use at all.

Concluding Comment: Caveat Emptor

If the test author recognizes that the test norms are inadequate, the test user should be explicitly cautioned (AERA et al., 1999). The inadequacies do not, however, disappear with the inclusion of a cautionary note; the test is still inadequate. Some may argue, incorrectly, that inadequate norms are better than no norms at all. However, inadequate norms do not allow meaningful and accurate inferences about performance. If poor norms are used, misinterpretations follow.

A joint committee of the American Educational Research Association, the American Psychological Association, and the National Council on Measurement in Education (1997) prepared a pamphlet, *Standards for Educational and Psychological Testing*, which outlines the standards to which test authors should adhere: "Norms that are presented should refer to clearly described groups. These groups should be the ones with whom users of the test will ordinarily wish to compare the people who are tested" (p. 33). The pamphlet states that the test author should report how the sample was selected and whether any bias was present in the sample. The author should also describe the sampling techniques and the resultant sample in sufficient detail for the test user to judge the utility of the norms. "Reports of norming studies should include the year in which normative data were collected, provide descriptive statistics, and describe the sampling design and participation rates in sufficient detail so that the study can be evaluated for appropriateness" (p. 33).

In the marketplace of testing, let the buyer beware.

SUMMARY

The primary purpose of norms is to compare a student's tested performance with the performance of other students. The group with which the student is compared is called a *norm group*. Norm groups must be representative of the target population on all relevant characteristics. Although special characteristics may be relevant for some specialized tests, many characteristics are relevant for most tests: student's age, school grade, gender, place of residence (geography), racial and cultural background, and general intellectual functioning, as well as the acculturation of the student's parents. These factors are important because most skills and abilities depend on (or are strongly related to) these factors. However, it is not enough simply to have the right kinds of people in the norms. The relevant characteristics must be represented in proportions that correspond to those in the target population.

To develop representative norms, test authors and publishers develop sampling plans to obtain enough individuals to prepare normative groups large enough to allow the use of derived scores. After a large number of individuals are tested, authors may adjust the norms to make them more representative. Thus they may drop subjects, differentially weight subjects, or smooth norms.

However, in evaluating a test's norms, users should consider not only whether the norms are generally representative, but also the age of the norms (that is, are the norms current?); the relevance of the norms (that is, is it appropriate to compare the performance of a specific test taker with the performances represented by the norm sample?); and the appropriate use of the norms (that is, are the inferences derived from the comparisons appropriate?).

QUESTIONS FOR CHAPTER REVIEW

1. How might the author of a test demonstrate that its normative sample is representative of the population of children attending school in the United States?

2. Read the manual of any achievement test. How were the individuals in the normative sample selected? Is the normative sample representative in terms of gender, ethnicity, and parental educational attainment? Were students with disabilities included in the norms? (If so, how did the test authors ensure that they would be included in the correct proportions?)

3. Discuss three approaches to tinkering with norms that you might use as a test developer to produce better norms.

PROJECT

Obtain a copy of the latest U.S. Census. Determine how well you and your classmates currently represent the general population. If you and your classmates were now 8 years old and attending the third grade in your local school system, how representative would you be of the general population?

RESOURCES FOR FURTHER INVESTIGATION

Print Resources

American Educational Research Association, American Psychological Association, & National Council on Measurement in Education. (1999). *Standards for educational and psychological testing*. Washington, DC: American Educational Research Association.

Cannell, J. J. (1988). Nationally normed elementary achievement testing in America's public schools: How all 50 states are above the national average. *Educational Measurement: Issues and Practice, 7*(2), 5–9.

Herrnstein, R., & Murray, C. (1996). *The bell curve: Intelligence and class structure in American life*. New York: The Free Press.

Linn, R., Graue, E., & Sanders, N. (1990). Comparing state and district test results to national norms: The validity of claims that "everyone is above average." *Educational Measurement: Issues and Practice, 9*(3), 5–14.

Salvia, J., Neisworth, J., & Schmidt, M. (1990). *Examiner's manual: Responsibility and Independence Scale for Adolescents.* Allen, TX: DLM.

Technology Resources

ABOUT THE NATIONAL COUNCIL ON MEASUREMENT IN EDUCATION (NCME)

www.ncme.org

The home page for the NCME provides information on the organization and links to other relevant measurement-related websites.

FAIRTEST: THE NATIONAL CENTER FOR FAIR AND OPEN TESTING

www.fairtest.org/facts/nratests.html

This page gives further information on norm-referenced tests and includes a position statement against their use by the National Center for Fair and Open Testing.

DEMOGRAPHIC CHARACTERISTICS OF AMERICAN CHILDREN

factfinder.census.gov/home/saff/main.html?_lang=en

This site provides a state-by-state summary of children's characteristics, including sex, race, and socioeconomic information.

CHAPTER 7

Reliability

WHEN WE ASSESS, WE ARE INTERESTED IN GENERALIZING WHAT WE SEE TODAY, UNDER one set of conditions, to other occasions and conditions. For example, if we cannot generalize from Linda's reading skills that are observed during testing to her skills in the classroom situation, then the test data are of little or no value. To the extent that we can generalize from a particular set of observations (a test, for example), those observations are reliable.

Reliability is a major consideration in evaluating an assessment procedure. For example, when we give a person an individually administered test, we would like to be able to generalize the results in three different ways. First, we would like to assume that similar, but different, test questions would give us the same results—we would like to be able to generalize to other test items in the same domain. Suppose Ms. Amig wanted to assess her kindergartners' recognition of upper- and lowercase letters of the English alphabet. She could assess the domain—all 52 upper- and lowercase letters—or she could sample from the domain. For example, she could ask each of her students to name the following letters: *A, h, j, L, q, r, u, V, w*. She would like to assume that her students would earn about the same score (say, percentage correct or percentile rank) whether they were tested on this sample, on the entire domain of letters, or on any other sample of letters (say, *b, E, k, m, s, T, U, x, Y, z*); she would like to be able to generalize from one sample of items to any and all other samples from the domain.

Second, we would like to assume that the behavior we see today would be seen tomorrow (or next week) if we were to test again—we would like to be able to generalize to similar times. Suppose Ms. Amig tests her pupils on Monday at 9:30 A.M. She would like to assume that the students would earn the same scores if they were tested Tuesday at 1:45 P.M.—or at any other time during the day or evening. There is a domain of times, as well as a domain of items. A test on any one occasion is a sample from the domain of all times. Ms. Amig would like to generalize the results found at one sample of time to the total domain (all times).

Third, we would like to assume that, if any other comparably qualified examiner were to give the test, the results would be the same—we would like to be able to generalize to similar testers. Suppose Ms. Amig listened to her students say the letters of the alphabet. It would not be very useful if she assigned Barney a score of 70 percent correct, whereas another teacher (or parent) who listened to Barney awarded a score of 50 percent correct or 90 percent correct for the same performance. Ms. Amig would like to assume that any other teacher (or parent) would score her students' responses in just the same way. Thus there are three kinds of reliability: (1) Reliability for generalizing to other test items is termed alternate-form reliability, or internal consistency; (2) reliability for generalizing to different times is called stability, or test-retest reliability; and (3) reliability for generalizing to different scorers is termed interrater or interscorer reliability.

An easy way to think of reliability is to think of any obtained score as consisting of two parts: true score and error. By definition, error is uncorrelated with true score and is essentially random. *Error* is best thought of as lack of generalizability that results from the failure to get a representative sample from the domain. For example, a sample of alphabet letters that consisted of *A, B, C, D,* and *E* would probably provide a much easier test than other samples of letters. A systematically easier sample would inflate the scores earned by Ms. Amig's students. Similarly, a sample made up of the most difficult letters would probably deflate the scores earned by her students. Thus error—failure to select a representative sample of items—can raise or lower scores. The average (mean) error in the long run is equal to zero. In the long run, across a large number of samples, the samples that raise scores are balanced by samples that lower scores. If Ms. Amig made up and administered all the possible four-letter tests, a student's mean performance would be that student's true score. There would be no error associated with that score. However, there would be a distribution of test scores around that mean; it would be a distribution of obtained test scores centered on the true score.

Another way to think of a *true score* is to view it as the score that a student would earn if the entire domain of items were assessed. On achievement tests dealing with beginning material and with certain types of behavioral observations, it is occasionally possible to assess an entire domain (for example, reading and writing the letters of the alphabet or knowing all the addition, subtraction, multiplication, and division facts). In such cases, the obtained score is a student's true score, and there is no need to estimate the test's item reliability. Opportunities to assess an entire domain are very limited, however, even in the primary grades. In more advanced curricula, it is often impossible to assess an entire achievement domain. Moreover, it is never possible to assess the entire domain when a hypothetical construct (such as intelligence or visual perception) is being assessed. Therefore, in these cases, item reliability should always be estimated.

The same argument can be made for reliability (generalization) over times and scores. If one time makes up the entire domain, then the student's performance at that time is the student's true score, although such a situation is difficult to imagine. Similarly, if evaluation by only one person makes up the entire domain, then the performance as assessed by that one person constitutes the entire domain, and the student's scores are true scores. Although such a situation is also difficult to imagine in the schools, personal evaluations are frequently all that matters outside of school. For example, your evaluation of the food at a restaurant is probably the only evaluation that is important in determining whether the food was good.

As you may recall from the discussion in the chapter "Assessment Processes and Concerns," people should always be concerned about error during assessment. Although there is always some degree of error, the important question is: How much error is attached to a particular score? Unfortunately, a direct answer to this question is not readily available. To estimate both the amount of error attached to a score and the amount of error in general, two statistics are needed: (1) a reliability coefficient for the particular generalization and (2) the standard error of measurement.

The Reliability Coefficient

The symbol used to denote a reliability coefficient is r with two identical subscripts (for example, r_{xx} or r_{aa}). The reliability coefficient is generally defined as the square of the correlation between obtained scores and true scores on a measure (r^2_{xt}), where x is the obtained score and t is the hypothetical true score. This quantity is identical to the ratio of the variance of true scores to the variance of obtained scores for a distribution. (The variance of obtained scores equals the variance of true scores plus the variance of error.) Accordingly, a *reliability coefficient* indicates the proportion of variability in a set of scores that reflects true differences among individuals. In the special case in which two equivalent forms of a test exist, the Pearson product-moment correlation coefficient between scores from the two forms is equal to the reliability coefficient for either form. These relationships are summarized in Equation 7.1, where x and x' are parallel measures, and S^2 is, of course, the variance.

$$r_{xx'} = r^2_{xt} = \frac{S^2_{\text{true scores}}}{S^2_{\text{obtained scores}}}$$

(7.1)

If there is relatively little error, the ratio of true-score variance to obtained-score variance approaches a reliability index of 1.00 (perfect reliability); if there is a relatively large amount of error, the ratio of true-score variance to obtained-score variance approaches .00 (total unreliability). (Although it is mathematically possible to obtain a negative reliability estimate, such an obtained estimate is theoretically meaningless.) Thus a test with a reliability coefficient of .90 has relatively less error of measurement and is more reliable than a test with a reliability coefficient of .50.

Different methods of estimating a reliability coefficient are used, depending on what generalization the test giver wishes to make. Test authors should always report the extent to which test givers can generalize to different times and the degree to which they can generalize to different samples of questions or items. If a test is difficult to score, the test author also should report the extent to which test givers can generalize to different scorers.

Generalizing to Different Times

Test-retest reliability is an index of stability over time. Educators are interested in many human traits and characteristics that, theoretically, change very little over time. For example, children diagnosed as colorblind at age 5 are expected to be diagnosed as colorblind at any time in their lives. Colorblindness is an inherited trait that cannot be corrected. Consequently, the trait should be perfectly stable. When an assessment identifies a student as colorblind on one occasion and not colorblind on a later occasion, the assessment is unreliable.

Other traits are less stable than color vision over a long period of time; they are developmental. For example, people's heights will increase from birth through adulthood. The increases are relatively slow and predictable. Consequently, measurement with a reliable ruler should indicate few changes in height over a one-month period. Radical changes in people's heights (especially decreases) over short periods of time would cause us to question the reliability of the measurement device. Most educational and psychological characteristics are conceptualized much as height is. For example, we expect reading achievement to increase with length of schooling but to be relatively stable over short periods of time, such as two weeks. Devices used to assess traits and characteristics must produce sufficiently consistent and stable results if those results are to have practical meaning for making educational decisions.

Estimating Stability

The procedure for obtaining a stability coefficient is fairly simple. A large number of students are tested. A short time later (preferably two weeks, but in practice, the time interval can vary from one day to several months), they are retested with the same device. The students' scores from the two administrations are then correlated. The obtained correlation coefficient is the *stability coefficient*.

Estimates of the amount of error derived from stability coefficients tend to be inflated. Any change in a student's true score that is attributable to maturation or learning is added to the error variance unless every student in the sample changes in the same way. Thus, if there is a "maturational spurt" between the two test administrations for only a few students, the change in the true score is incorporated into the error term. Similarly, if some of the students cannot answer some of the questions on the first administration of the test but learn the answers by the second administration, the learning (change in true score) is interpreted as error. The experience of taking the test once may also make answering the same questions the second time easier; the first test may sensitize the student to the second administration of the test. Generally, however, the closer together in time the test and retest are, the higher the reliability is, because within a shorter time span there is less chance of true scores changing.

Generalizing to Different Item Samples

There are two main approaches to estimating the extent to which we can generalize to different samples of items. The first approach requires that test authors develop two (or more) similar tests, called *alternate forms*; the second approach does not.

Alternate forms of a test are defined as two tests that (1) measure the same trait or skill to the same extent and (2) are standardized on the same population. Alternate forms offer essentially equivalent tests; sometimes, in fact, they are called "equivalent forms." A nonpsychometric example illustrates this equivalence. Each 12-inch ruler sold at a local variety store is thought to be the equivalent (or alternate form) of any other ruler. If you purchased a red ruler and a green ruler and measured several objects with both, you would expect a high correlation between the green measurements and the red measurements. This example is analogous to alternate-form reliability. There is one important difference, however: Alternate forms of tests do not contain the same items. Still, although the items are different, the means and variances for the two tests are assumed to be (or should be) the same. In the absence of error of measurement, any subject would be expected to earn the same score on both forms.

Estimating Alternate-Form Reliability

To estimate the reliability coefficient for two alternate forms (A and B) of a test, a large sample of students is tested with both forms. Half the subjects receive form A, then form B; the other half receive form B, then form A. Scores from the two forms are correlated. The resulting correlation coefficient is a reliability coefficient.

Estimates of reliability based on alternate forms are subject to one of the same constraints as stability coefficients: The more time that passes between the administration of the two (or more) forms, the greater is the likelihood of change in true scores. Alternate-form reliability estimates are less subject to a sensitization effect than are stability coefficients, because the subjects are not tested with the same items twice.

Estimating Internal Consistency

The second approach to estimating the extent to which we can generalize to different test items does not require that the authors develop more than one form of the test. This method of estimating a test's reliability, called *internal consistency*, is a little different.

Suppose we wanted to use this second method to estimate the reliability of a ten-item test. After the test was constructed, we would administer it to a sample of students (for example, 20 students). The results of this hypothetical test are presented in Table 7.1. If the ten individual test items all measure the same skill or ability, we can divide the test into two five-item tests, each measuring that same skill or ability. Thus, after the test is administered, we can create two alternate forms of the test, each containing one half of the total number of test items, or five items. We can then correlate the two sets of scores and obtain an estimate of the reliability of each of the two halves in the same way we would estimate

| TABLE 7.1 | | | | | | | | | | Hypothetical Performance of 20 Children on a Ten-Item Test | | | |

	Items										Totals		
Child	1	2	3	4	5	6	7	8	9	10	Total Test	Evens Correct	Odds Correct
1	+	+	+	−	+	−	−	−	+	−	5	1	4
2	+	+	+	+	−	+	+	+	−	+	8	5	3
3	+	+	−	+	+	+	+	−	+	+	8	4	4
4	+	+	+	+	+	+	+	+	−	+	9	5	4
5	+	+	+	+	+	+	+	+	+	−	9	4	5
6	+	+	−	+	−	+	+	+	+	+	8	5	3
7	+	+	+	+	+	−	+	−	+	+	8	3	5
8	+	+	+	−	+	+	+	+	+	+	9	4	5
9	+	+	+	+	+	+	−	+	+	+	9	5	4
10	+	+	+	+	+	−	+	+	+	+	9	4	5
11	+	+	+	+	+	−	+	−	−	−	6	2	4
12	+	+	−	+	+	+	+	+	+	+	9	5	4
13	+	+	+	−	−	+	−	+	−	−	5	3	2
14	+	+	+	+	+	+	+	−	+	+	9	4	5
15	+	+	−	+	+	−	−	−	−	−	4	2	2
16	+	+	+	+	+	+	+	+	+	+	10	5	5
17	+	−	+	−	−	−	−	−	−	−	2	0	2
18	+	−	+	+	+	+	+	+	+	+	9	4	5
19	+	+	+	+	−	+	+	+	+	+	9	5	4
20	+	−	−	−	−	+	−	+	−	−	3	2	1

the reliability of two alternate forms of a test. This procedure for estimating a test's reliability is called a *split-half reliability estimate*.

It should be apparent that there are many ways to divide a test into two equal-length tests. The aforementioned ten-item test can be divided into more than 100 different pairs of five-item tests. If the ten items in our full test are arranged in order of increasing difficulty, both halves should contain items from the beginning of the test (that is, easier items) and items from the end of the test (harder items). There are many ways of dividing such a test (for example, grouping items 1, 4, 5, 8, 9 and items 2, 3, 6, 7, 10). The most common way to divide a test is by odd-numbered and even-numbered items (see the columns labeled "Evens Correct" and "Odds Correct" in Table 7.1).

Odd-even division and the subsequent correlation of the two halves of a test are a common method for estimating a test's internal-consistency reliability, but this is not necessarily the best method. A more generalizable method of estimating internal consistency, called coefficient alpha, was developed by Cronbach (1951). *Coefficient alpha* is the average split-half correlation based on all possible divisions of a test into two parts. In practice, there is no need to compute all possible correlation coefficients; coefficient alpha, or r_{aa}, can be computed from the variances of individual test items and the variance of the total test score, as shown in Equation 7.2, where k is the number of items in the test.

$$r_{aa} = \frac{k}{k-1}\left(1 - \frac{\sum S^2_{items}}{S^2_{test}}\right)$$

(7.2)

Coefficient alpha can be used when test items are scored pass-fail or when more than one point is awarded for a correct response. An earlier, more restricted method of estimating a test's reliability, based on the average correlation between all possible split halves, was developed by Kuder and Richardson. This procedure, called *KR-20*, is coefficient alpha for dichotomously scored test items (that is, items that can be scored only right or wrong). Equation 7.2 can be used with dichotomous data; however, in this case, the resulting estimate of reliability is usually called a "KR-20 estimate" rather than "coefficient alpha." (Sometimes a test author will estimate KR-20 with a formula called KR-21.)

There are two major considerations in the use of internal-consistency estimates. First, this method should not be used for timed tests or tests that are not completed by all those being tested. Second, it provides no estimate of stability over time.

Generalizing to Different Scorers

There are two very different approaches to estimating the extent to which we can generalize to different scorers: a correlational approach and a percentage of agreement approach. The correlational approach is similar to the ways of estimating generalizability that we have just discussed. Two testers score a set of tests independently. Scores obtained by each tester for the set are then correlated. The resulting correlation coefficient is a reliability coefficient for scorers. For example, suppose that a psychologist (Ms. Jimenez) were interested in the distortion of body image in schoolchildren with emotional disturbance. Further, suppose she decided to assess distortion by evaluating the human-figure drawings of such children. Even with explicit criteria for what constitutes a distorted image, scoring of human-figure drawings is difficult. Would another, equally trained, tester—Mr. Torrance—arrive at the same conclusions as Ms. Jimenez? Can Ms. Jimenez's judgments be generalized to other testers and scorers?

To quantify the extent to which this type of generalization is possible, the two testers could evaluate the human-figure drawings made by a class of pupils with emotional disturbance. As shown in Table 7.2, there would be two ratings of distortion of body image for each drawing, and these two scores could be correlated. The resulting correlation coefficient ($\phi = .41$) would be an estimate of interscorer reliability or agreement.

Calculating Simple Agreement

The second approach to estimating generalizability to different scorers is prevalent in applied behavioral analysis. Instead of the correlation between two scorers' ratings, the percentage of agreement between raters is computed. Four indexes of percentage of agreement are used: simple agreement, point-to-point agreement, agreement for occurrence of the target behavior, and the kappa index of agreement. Simple agreement is calculated by dividing the smaller number of

----

| TABLE 7.2 | Judgment of Distorted Body Image in a Class of Children with Emotional Disturbance |

Child Number	Ms. Jimenez	Mr. Torrance
1	normal	normal
2	distorted	distorted
3	distorted	normal
4	normal	normal
5	normal	normal
6	distorted	distorted
7	distorted	distorted
8	distorted	normal
9	normal	normal
10	normal	distorted
11	distorted	distorted
12	normal	normal
13	normal	normal
14	normal	normal
15	distorted	distorted
16	normal	distorted
17	normal	normal
18	distorted	distorted
19	normal	distorted
20	normal	distorted

occurrences by the larger number of occurrences and multiplying the quotient by 100. As Table 7.2 shows, Ms. Jimenez observed eight distorted drawings, and Mr. Torrance observed ten distorted drawings. Their simple agreement is 80 percent; that is, (8/10)(100). This index may be quite misleading, however, because agreement for each observation is not considered. Thus it is possible (although not very likely) for two scorers to observe the same number of distorted drawings but to disagree with each other on which drawings are distorted. Therefore, the use of simple agreement should be restricted to those circumstances in which it is the only index that can be computed (for example, in assessing the latency of a response or the frequency of behavior under continuous observation).

Calculating Point-to-Point Agreement

A more precise way of computing percentage of agreement is to consider agreement for each data point. The computation of point-to-point agreement takes each data point into consideration (see Equation 7.3).

Percentage of point-to-point agreement =

$$\frac{(100)\text{number of agreements on occurrence and nonoccurrence}}{\text{number of observations}} \qquad (7.3)$$

TABLE 7.3	Summary of Agreements and Disagreements from Table 7.2		
	Ms. Jimenez Distorted Drawings	Ms. Jimenez Normal Drawings	
Mr. Torrance normal drawings	2	8	$\Sigma = 10$
Mr. Torrance distorted drawings	6	4	$\Sigma = 10$
	$\Sigma = 8$	$\Sigma = 12$	$N = 20$

The data from Table 7.2 are summarized in Table 7.3. The point-to-point agreement is computed by adding the frequency of agreement for occurrence (in this example, the occurrence of distorted drawings, $n = 6$) and the frequency of agreement for nonoccurrence (in this example, nonoccurrence is represented by normal drawings, $n = 8$), dividing this sum by the total number of observations, and multiplying the quotient by 100. Point-to-point agreement for the data in Table 7.3 is .70 [that is, $(14/20)(100)$].

Calculating Agreement for Occurrence

When the occurrences and nonoccurrences of a behavior differ substantially, point-to-point agreement overestimates the accuracy of the set of observations. In such cases, a more precise way of computing the percentage of agreement is to compute the percentage of agreement for the occurrence of the target behavior (see Equation 7.4).

$$\text{Percentage of agreement for occurrence} = \frac{(100)\text{number of agreements on occurrence}}{\text{number of observations} - \text{number of agreements on nonoccurrence}} \quad (7.4)$$

In this example, because Ms. Jimenez is interested in the occurrences of distorted body image, it might make better sense to look only at how well the two raters agree on the occurrence. The eight nonoccurrences (normal drawings) on which Ms. Jimenez and Mr. Torrance agree are not of interest and are ignored. The percentage of agreement for occurrence is 50 percent [that is, $(100)(6)/(20 - 8)$] calculated on the data in Table 7.3.

Calculating Kappa

Both the point-to-point agreement and the agreement of occurrence indexes can be affected systematically by chance agreement. Thus both indexes tend to overestimate agreement. Cohen (1960) developed a coefficient of agreement, called "kappa," which adjusts the proportion of agreement by removing the proportion of agreement that would occur by chance. Kappa values range from −1.00

(total disagreement) to +1.00 (total agreement); a value of 0 indicates chance agreement. Thus a positive index of agreement indicates agreement above what test givers would expect to find by chance. The computation of kappa is more complicated than the computation of other agreement indexes (see Equation 7.5, where P equals proportion).

$$Kappa = \frac{P_{occurrence} - P_{expected}}{1 - P_{expected}}$$

(7.5)

Because kappa is calculated more readily using proportions than using frequencies, the frequencies from Table 7.3 are displayed in Table 7.4 as proportions (that is, the frequency divided by the 20 total observations); the marginal frequencies (that is, Ms. Jimenez's and Mr. Torrance's proportions of normal and distorted drawings) are in parentheses.

The expected proportion of occurrence (that is, of distorted drawings) equals the product of the proportions of occurrence for each observer (in this example, .50 and .40); the expected proportion of nonoccurrence (that is, of normal drawings) equals the product of the proportions of nonoccurrence for each observer (in this example, .50 and .60). The expected proportion of agreement equals the sum of the expected proportion of agreement for occurrence and the expected proportion of agreement for nonoccurrence—in this example, .50 = (.50 × .40) + (.50 × .60). Substituting these values into Equation 7.5, we find that kappa equals .40; that is, (.40 + .30 − .20 − .30)/(1 − .20 − .30). Thus the ratings of drawings by Ms. Jimenez and Mr. Torrance demonstrate some agreement beyond what would be expected by chance; however, we should not have great confidence in their scoring.

Given the increased interest in subjective forms of assessment, such as portfolio assessment (see the chapter "Portfolio Assessment"), holistic scoring, and holistic observation, interscorer agreement takes on added importance. Unfortunately, we find that subjective assessments usually lack interscorer agreement.

TABLE 7.4   Proportions of Agreements and Disagreements from Table 7.2

	Ms. Jimenez Distorted Drawings	Ms. Jimenez Normal Drawings	Row Proportions
Mr. Torrance normal drawings	.10 (i.e., 2/20)	.40 (i.e., 8/20)	(.50)
Mr. Torrance distorted drawings	.30 (i.e., 6/20)	.20 (i.e., 4/20)	(.50)
Column proportions	(.40)	(.60)	

Factors Affecting Reliability

Several factors affect a test's reliability and can inflate or deflate reliability estimates: test length, test-retest interval, constriction or extension of range, guessing, and variation within the testing situation.

Test Length   As a general rule, the more items there are in a test, the more reliable the test is. Thus long tests tend to be more reliable than short tests. This fact is especially important in an internal-consistency estimate of reliability, because in this kind of estimate, the number of test items is reduced by 50 percent. Split-half estimates of reliability actually estimate the reliability of half the test. Therefore, such estimates are appropriately corrected by a formula developed by Spearman and Brown. As shown in Equation 7.6, the reliability of the total test is equal to twice the reliability as estimated by internal consistency divided by the sum of 1 plus the reliability estimate.

$$r_{xx} = \frac{2r_{\left(\frac{1}{2}\right)\left(\frac{1}{2}\right)}}{1 + r_{\left(\frac{1}{2}\right)\left(\frac{1}{2}\right)}}$$

(7.6)

For example, if a split-half estimate of internal consistency were computed for a test and found to be .80, the corrected estimated reliability would be .89.

$$\frac{(2)(.80)}{1+.80} = \frac{1.60}{1.80} = .89$$

A related issue is the number of effective items for each test taker. Tests are generally more reliable in the middle ranges of scores (for example, within $\pm 1.5S$). For a test to be effective at the extremes of a distribution, there must be both enough difficult items for very superior pupils and enough easy items for deficient pupils. Often, there are not enough very easy and very hard items on a test. Therefore, extremely high or extremely low scores tend to be less reliable than scores in the middle of a distribution.

Test-Retest Interval   As previously noted, a person's true abilities can and do change between two administrations of a test. The greater the amount of time between the two administrations, the more likely is the possibility that true scores will change. Thus, when employing stability or alternate-form estimates of reliability, test evaluators must pay close attention to the interval between tests. Generally, the shorter the interval is, the higher the estimated reliability is.

Constriction or Extension of Range   Constriction or extension of range refers to narrowing (constriction) or widening (extension) the range of ability of the people whose performances are used to estimate a test's reliability. When the range of ability of these people is less than the range of ability in the population, a test's reliability will be underestimated. The more constricted the range of ability is, the more biased (underestimated) the reliability coefficient will be.

FIGURE 7.1
Constricting the Range
of Test Scores and the
Resulting Reduction of
the Estimate of a Test's
Reliability

SOURCE: *Psychological
Testing*, 7e by Anastasi,
© 1997. Reprinted by
permission of Prentice-
Hall, Upper Saddle
River, NJ.

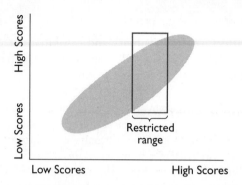

As Figure 7.1 shows, alternative forms of a test produce a strong positive correlation when the entire range of the test is used. However, within any restricted range of the test, as illustrated by the dark rectangular outline, the correlation may be very low. (Although it is possible to correct a correlation coefficient for restriction in range, it is generally unwise to do so.)

A related problem is that extension of range overestimates a test's reliability. Figure 7.2 illustrates correlations of scores on alternate-form tests given to students in the first, third, and fifth grades. The scatterplot for each grade, considered separately, indicates poor reliability. However, spelling test scores increase as a function of schooling; students in higher grades earn higher scores. When test authors combine the scores for several grades (or from several ages), poor correlations may be combined to produce a spuriously high correlation.

Guessing   Guessing is responding randomly to items. Even if a guess results in a correct response, it introduces error into a test score and into our interpretation of that score.

Variation Within the   The amount of error that the testing situation introduces into the results of test-
Testing Situation   ing can vary considerably. Children can misread or misunderstand the directions for a test, get a headache halfway through testing, lose their place on the answer

FIGURE 7.2
Extending the Range of
Test Scores and the Pos-
sible Spurious Increase in
the Estimate of a Test's
Reliability

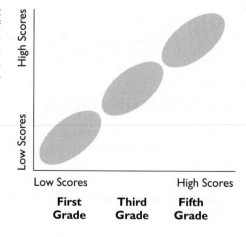

sheet, break the point of their pencil, or choose to watch a squirrel eat nuts on the windowsill of the classroom rather than take the test. All such situational variations introduce an indeterminate amount of error in testing and, in doing so, lower reliability.

Determining Which Reliability Method to Use

The first consideration in choosing a method of determining a test's reliability is the type of generalization we wish to make. We must select the method that goes with the type of generalization. For example, if we were interested in generalizing about the stability of a score or observation, the appropriate method would be test-retest correlations. It would be inappropriate to use interscorer agreement as an estimate of the extent to which we can generalize to different times. Additional considerations in selecting the reliability method to be used include the following.

Preferred Methods to Estimate Reliability

1. When one estimates stability, the convention is to retest after two weeks. There is nothing special about the two-week period, but if all test authors used the same interval, it would be easier to compare the relative stability of tests.

2. Many years ago, Nunnally (Nunnally & Bernstein, 1994; Nunnally, 1978) offered a hierarchy for estimating the extent to which we can generalize to similar test items. The first choice is to use alternate-form reliability with a two-week interval. (Again, there is nothing special about two weeks; it is just a convention.) If alternate forms are not available, divide the test into equivalent halves and administer the halves with a two-week interval, correcting the correlation by the Spearman-Brown formula given in Equation 7.6. When alternate forms are not available and subjects cannot be tested more than once, use coefficient alpha.

3. When estimating the extent to which we can generalize among different scorers, we prefer computing correlation coefficients rather than percentages of agreement. Correlation coefficients bear a direct relationship to other indicators of reliability and other uses of reliability coefficients; percentages of agreement do not. We also realize that current practice is to report percentages of agreement and not to bother with the other uses of the reliability coefficient. If percentage of agreement is to be used to estimate interscorer reliability, we feel that kappa should be used when possible.

Standard Error of Measurement

The *standard error of measurement (SEM)* is another index of test error. The SEM allows us to estimate the amount of each type of error associated with true scores. We can compute standard errors of measurement for scorers, times, and item samples. However, SEMs are usually computed only for stability and item samples.

Earlier, we discussed the generalization of performance on one sample of items to the domain. This process provides a convenient example for the interpretation of the SEM. Consider the alphabet recognition task again. There are many samples of ten-letter tests that could be developed. If we constructed 100 of these tests and tested just one kindergartner, we would probably find that the distribution of scores for that kindergartner was approximately normal. The mean of that distribution would be the student's true score. The distribution around the true score would be the result of imperfect samples of letters; some letter samples would overestimate the pupil's ability, and others would underestimate it. Thus the variance around the mean would be the result of error. The standard deviation of that distribution, the standard deviation of errors attributable to sampling, is the standard error of measurement.

When students are assessed with norm-referenced tests, they are typically tested only once. Therefore, we cannot generate a distribution similar to the one shown in Figure 7.3. Consequently, we do not know the test taker's true score or the variance of the measurement error that forms the distribution around that person's true score. By using what we know about the test's standard deviation and its reliability for items, we can estimate what that error distribution would be. However, when estimating the error distribution for one student, test users should understand that the SEM is an average; some standard errors will be greater than that average, and some will be less.

Equation 7.7 is the general formula for finding the SEM. The SEM equals the standard deviation of the obtained scores (S) multiplied by the square root of 1 minus the reliability coefficient ($\sqrt{1 - r_{xx}}$). The type of unit (IQ, raw score, and so forth) in which the standard deviation is expressed is the unit in which the SEM is expressed. Thus, if the test scores have been converted to T-scores, the standard deviation is in T-score units and is 10; the SEM is also in T-score units. Similarly, if the reliability coefficient is based on stability, then the SEM is for

FIGURE 7.3
The Standard Error of Measurement: The Standard Deviation of the Error Distribution Around a True Score for One Subject

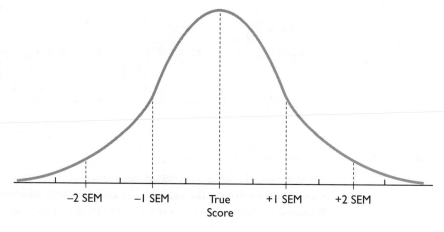

-2 SEM -1 SEM   True $+1$ SEM $+2$ SEM
                                    Score

TABLE 7.5	Relationship (Part A) Between Reliability Coefficient (r_{xx}) and SEM and (Part B) Between Standard Deviation (S) and SEM

	Part A			Part B	
S	r_{xx}	*SEM*	S	r_{xx}	*SEM*
10	.96	2	5	.91	1.5
10	.84	4	10	.91	3.0
10	.75	5	15	.91	4.5
10	.64	6	20	.91	6.0
10	.36	8	25	.91	7.5

times of testing. If the reliability coefficient is based on different scorers, then the SEM is for testers or scorers.

$$SEM = S\sqrt{1 - r_{xx}}$$
(7.7)

From Equation 7.7, it is apparent that, as the standard deviation increases, the SEM increases; and as the reliability coefficient decreases, the SEM increases. In Part A of Table 7.5, the same standard deviation (10) is used with different reliability coefficients. As reliability coefficients decrease, SEMs increase. When the reliability coefficient is .96, the SEM is 2; when the reliability coefficient is .64, the SEM is 6. In Part B of Table 7.5, different standard deviations are used with the same reliability coefficient (r_{xx} = .91). As standard deviations increase, SEMs increase.

Because measurement error is unavoidable, there is always some uncertainty about an individual's true score. The SEM provides information about the certainty or confidence with which a test score can be interpreted. When the SEM is relatively large, the uncertainty is large; we cannot be very sure of the individual's score. When the SEM is relatively small, the uncertainty is small; we can be more certain of the score.

Estimated True Scores

Unfortunately, we never know a subject's true score. Moreover, the obtained score on a test is not the best estimate of the true score. As mentioned in the previous discussion, true scores and errors are uncorrelated. However, obtained scores and errors are correlated. Scores above the test mean have more "lucky" error (error that raises the obtained score above the true score), whereas scores below the mean have more "unlucky" error (error that lowers the obtained score below the true score). An easy way to understand this effect is to think of a test on which a student guesses on half the test items. If all the guesses are correct, the student has been very lucky and earns a high grade. However, if all the guesses are incorrect, the student has been unlucky and earns a low grade. Thus obtained scores above or below the mean are often more discrepant from the

FIGURE 7.4
The Discrepancy Between Obtained Scores and True Scores for Reliable and Unreliable Tests

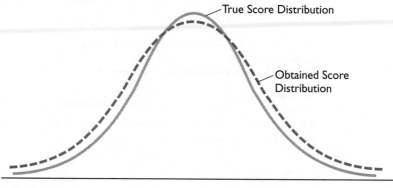

True Score Distribution

Obtained Score Distribution

Reliable Test

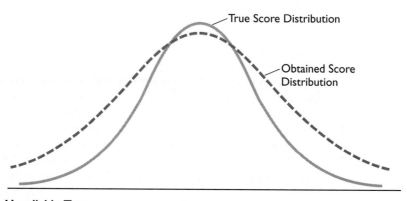

True Score Distribution

Obtained Score Distribution

Unreliable Test

true scores than are obtained scores closer to the mean. As Figure 7.4 illustrates, the less reliable the test is, the greater is the discrepancy between obtained scores and true scores. Nunnally (Nunnally & Bernstein, 1994; Nunnally, 1978) has provided an equation (Equation 7.8) for determining the estimated true score (X'). The estimated true score equals the test mean plus the product of the reliability coefficient and the difference between the obtained score and the group mean.

$$X' = \bar{X} + \left(r_{xx}\right)\left(X - \bar{X}\right) \tag{7.8}$$

The particular mean that is used has been the subject of some controversy. We believe that the preferred mean is the mean of the demographic group that best represents the particular child. Thus, if the student is Asian and resides in a middle-class urban area, the most appropriate mean would be the mean of same-age Asian students from middle socioeconomic backgrounds who live in urban areas. In the absence of means for particular students of particular backgrounds, we are forced to use the overall mean for the student's age. As mentioned earlier in this chapter, the choice of reliability coefficient depends on the type of generalization to be made.

The discrepancy between obtained scores and estimated true scores is a function of both the reliability of the obtained scores and the difference between the obtained score and the mean. Table 7.6 illustrates a general case in which the mean in each example is 100 and the obtained scores are 90, 75, and 50. The reliability coefficients are .90, .70, and .50.

When the reliability coefficient is constant, the further an obtained score is from the mean, the greater the discrepancy between the obtained score and the estimated true score. For example, when the obtained score is 90 and the estimated reliability is .90, the estimated true score is 91 [that is, 91 = 100 + (.90)(90 − 100)]. Thus the difference between the estimated true score and the obtained score is 1. However, when the obtained score is 50 and the reliability coefficient is .90, the estimated true score is 55 [that is, 100 + (.90)(50 − 100)]. Thus the difference between the estimated true score and the obtained score is 5.

When the reliability coefficient changes, less reliable measures produce larger differences between obtained and estimated true scores. For example, when the obtained score is 75 and the reliability coefficient is .90, the estimated true score is 77.5 [that is, 100 + (.90)(75 − 100)]. Thus the difference between the estimated true score and the obtained score is 2.5. However, when the reliability coefficient is .50, the estimated true score rises to 87.5 [that is, 100 + (.50)(75 − 100)]. Thus the difference between the estimated true score and the obtained score is 12.5.

When the obtained score is below the test mean and the reliability coefficient is less than 1.00, the estimated true score is always higher than the obtained score. Conversely, when the obtained score is above the test mean and the reliability coefficient is less than 1.00, the estimated true score is always lower than the obtained score. Note that Equation 7.8 does not give the true score, only the estimated true score.

TABLE 7.6   Estimated True Scores for Different Obtained Scores on Tests with Different Reliability Coefficients

Test Mean ($\bar{X}$)	Coefficient Reliability (r_{xx})	Obtained Score (X)	Estimated True Score (X')	Difference Between Estimated True Score and Observed Score
100	.90	90	91.0	+1.0
100	.90	75	77.5	+2.5
100	.90	50	55.0	+5.0
100	.70	90	93.0	+3.0
100	.70	75	82.5	+7.5
100	.70	50	65.0	+15.0
100	.50	90	95.0	+5.0
100	.50	75	87.5	+12.5
100	.50	50	75.0	+25.0

Confidence Intervals

Although we can never know a person's true score, we can estimate the likelihood that a person's true score will be found within a specified range of scores. This range is called a *confidence interval*. A 50 percent confidence interval is a range of values within which the true score will be found about 50 percent of the time. Of course, about 50 percent of the time, the true score will be outside the interval. A larger range—a wider confidence interval—could make us feel more certain that we have included the true score within the range. For example, 90 percent, 95 percent, and 99 percent confidence intervals can be constructed; with confidence intervals as certain as these, the chances of the true score's falling outside of the confidence interval are about 10 percent, 5 percent, and 1 percent, respectively.

There is some disagreement over how to construct confidence intervals (see Kubiszyn & Borich, 2003) or even whether to construct them at all (see Sabers, Feldt, & Reschly, 1988). In the following sections, we use the statistics recommended by Nunnally (Nunnally & Bernstein, 1994; Nunnally 1978): estimated true score and SEM. Others (for example, Kubiszyn & Borich, 2003) prefer to use the estimated true score and the standard error of estimation (which is the average standard deviation of true scores around an obtained score) rather than the SEM.[1] When test reliability is high, the difference between the two procedures is negligible.

Establishing Confidence Intervals for True Scores

The characteristics of a normal curve have already been discussed. We can apply the relationship between z-scores and areas under the normal curve to the normal distribution of error around a true score. We can use Equation 7.8 to estimate the mean of the distribution (the true score) and Equation 7.7 to estimate the standard deviation of the distribution (the SEM). With these two estimates, we can construct a confidence interval for the true score. Because 68 percent of all elements in a normal distribution fall within one standard deviation of the mean, there is about a 68 percent chance that the true score is within one SEM of the estimated true score. We can construct an interval with almost any degree of confidence except 100 percent confidence.

Table 7.7 shows the extreme area for the z-scores most commonly used in constructing confidence intervals. The extreme area is the proportion of cases in the tail of the curve—that is, the area from plus or minus two standard deviations to the end of the curve. The general formula for a confidence interval (c.i.) is given in Equation 7.9. The lower limit of the confidence interval equals the estimated true score less the product of the z-score associated with that level of confidence and the SEM. The upper limit of the confidence interval is the estimated true score plus the product of the z-score and the SEM.

1. The Standard Error of Estimate (SEE) is the product of the standard deviation of the dependent (or predicted variable, y) and the square root of 1 minus the square of the correlation between predictor (or independent, x) and predicted (or dependent, y) variables.

$$SEE_{est} = S_y \sqrt{1 - r_{xy}^2}$$

TABLE 7.7	Commonly Used z-Scores, Extreme Areas, and Area Included Between + and − z-Score Values

z-Score	Extreme Area	Area Between + and −
.67	25.0%	50%
1.00	16.0%	68%
1.64	5.0%	90%
1.96	2.5%	95%
2.33	1.0%	98%
2.57	.5%	99%

$$\text{Lower limit of c.i.} = X' - (z\text{-score})(\text{SEM})$$
$$\text{Upper limit of c.i.} = X' + (z\text{-score})(\text{SEM}) \qquad (7.9)$$

1. Select the degree of confidence—for example, 95 percent.

2. Find the z-score associated with that degree of confidence (for example, a 95 percent confidence interval is between z-scores of −1.96 and +1.96).

3. Multiply each z-score associated with the confidence interval (for example, 1.96 for 95 percent confidence) by the SEM.

4. Find the estimated true score.

5. Add the product of the z-score and the SEM to the estimated true score to obtain the upper limit of the confidence interval; subtract the product of the z-score and the SEM from the estimated true score to obtain the lower limit of the confidence interval.

For example, assume that a person's estimated true score is 75 and the SEM is 5. Further assume that you wish to be about 68 percent sure of constructing an interval that will contain the true score. Table 7.7 shows that a 68 percent degree of confidence is associated with a z-score of 1. Thus, about 68 percent of the time, the true score will be contained in the interval of 70 to 80 [that is, $75 - (1)(5)$ to $75 + (1)(5)$]; there is about a 16 percent chance that the true score is less than 70 and about a 16 percent chance that the true score is greater than 80. If you are unwilling to be wrong about 32 percent of the time, you must increase the width of the confidence interval. Thus, with the same true score (75) and SEM (5), if you wish 95 percent confidence, the size of the interval must be increased; it would have to range from 65 to 85 [that is, $75 - (1.96)(5)$ to $75 + (1.96)(5)$]. About 95 percent of the time, the true score will be contained within that interval; there is about a 2.5 percent chance that the true score is less than 65, and there is about a 2.5 percent chance that it is greater than 85.

Difference Scores

In many applied settings, we are interested in differences between two scores. For example, we might wish to know whether a student's reading achievement is commensurate with her intellectual ability, or we might want to know whether the achievement score obtained after instruction (that is, on a posttest) is greater than the achievement score obtained prior to instruction (that is, on a pretest). In many definitions of educational disorders (for example, learning disabilities), a "significant" discrepancy is a defining characteristic of the disorder. In other disorders (for example, mental retardation), significant discrepancies are not expected.

Because significant differences are used so frequently in special education, it is important for users of test information to understand the meaning of a "significant discrepancy." Salvia and Good (1982) have discussed three different meanings of the term significant difference: (1) reliable difference, (2) rare discrepancy or difference, and (3) educationally meaningful difference. The first meaning, a reliable difference, is the most pertinent to our discussion of reliability, although it is not the most important consideration in general. A difference is considered reliable when it is unlikely to have occurred by chance. Because every test score has some error associated with it, two test scores could appear discrepant because of chance or because of the measurement error associated with each test score. However, Salvia and Good point out that the fact that a difference is real does not mean that it is rare. A large proportion of students may show reliable discrepancies. Moreover, even if a difference is reliable and rare, it may not have educational implications.

Educators and psychologists are interested in meaningful differences. We can be sure that unreliable differences are not meaningful. (These differences are the result of chance.) Probably because only reliable differences can be meaningful and because too little emphasis has been placed on the rarity and meaningfulness of a difference, diagnosticians have relied heavily on a difference's reliability for interpretation.

Difference scores are usually less reliable than the scores on which the differences are based. The reliability of a difference between two scores (A and B) is a function of three things: (1) the reliability of test A, (2) the reliability of test B, and (3) the correlation between tests A and B. In addition, differences in norm groups can produce differences in obtained scores. For example, suppose that June was absolutely average in reading and intellectual ability. Further suppose that she was tested with an intelligence test normed on a sample of students somewhat lower in ability than the general population. June would earn an IQ above the mean. Suppose the test to measure reading was normed on a sample of students whose achievement was somewhat higher than that of the general population. June would earn a reading score somewhat lower than the mean. If the disparity in norms was sufficiently large, June might appear to have a significant discrepancy between her intellectual ability and her reading achievement. However, that discrepancy would be an artifact of inaccurate norms.

There are several approaches to evaluating the reliability of a difference. The following two methods are particularly useful but rest on different assumptions and combine the data in different ways (that is, use different formulas). One method uses a regression model and was originally described by Thorndike (1963). In this model, one score is presumed to cause the second score. For example, intelligence is believed to determine achievement. Therefore, intelligence is identified as an independent (or predictor) variable, and achievement is identified as the dependent (or predicted) variable. When the predicted score (for example, the predicted achievement score) differs from the achievement score that is actually obtained, a deficit exists. The reliability of a predicted difference is given by Equation 7.10.

$$\hat{D} = \frac{r_{bb} + (r_{aa})(r^2_{ab}) - 2r^2_{ab}}{1 - r^2_{ab}}$$

(7.10)

The reliability of a predicted difference ($\hat{D}$) is equal to the reliability of the dependent variable (r_{bb}) plus the product of the reliability of the independent variable and the square of the correlation between the independent variable and the dependent variable ($r_{aa}r^2_{ab}$) less twice the squared correlation between the independent and dependent variable ($2r^2_{ab}$). This value is divided by 1 minus the squared correlation between the independent and dependent variables ($1 - r^2_{ab}$). The standard deviation of predicted differences ($S_{\hat{D}}$), also called "standard error of the estimate" (SE_{est}), is given in Equation 7.11. The standard deviation of predicted differences ($S_{\hat{D}}$) is equal to the standard deviation of the dependent variable (S_b) multiplied by the square root of 1 minus the squared correlation between the independent and dependent variables ($\sqrt{1 - r^2_{ab}}$).

$$S_{\hat{D}} = S_b \sqrt{1 - r^2_{ab}}$$

(7.11)

The second method of evaluating the reliability of a difference was proposed by Stake and Wardrop (1971). In this method, one variable is not assumed to be the cause of the other; neither variable is identified as the independent variable. However, this method does require that both measures be in the same unit of measurement (for example, T-scores or IQs). The reliability of a difference in obtained scores is given in Equation 7.12. The reliability of an obtained difference (r_{dif}) equals the average reliability of the two tests [$\frac{1}{2}(r_{aa} + r_{bb})$] less the correlation between the two tests (r_{ab}); this difference is divided by 1 minus the correlation between the two tests ($1 - r_{ab}$).

$$r_{dif} = \frac{\frac{1}{2}(r_{aa} + r_{bb}) - r_{ab}}{1 - r_{ab}}$$

(7.12)

The standard deviation for obtained differences is given in Equation 7.13.

$$S_{dif} = \sqrt{S^2_a + S^2_b - 2r_{ab}S_aS_b}$$

(7.13)

The standard deviation of an obtained difference (S_{dif}) is equal to the square root of the sum of the variances of tests A and B ($S^2_a + S^2_b$) less twice the product of the correlation of A and B multiplied by the standard deviations of A and B ($2r_{ab}S_aS_b$).

The reliability and standard deviation of an obtained difference can be combined to estimate the SEM of the obtained difference (SEM$_{dif}$) using Equation 7.7. The standard deviation of the difference (S_{dif}; see Equation 7.13) is substituted for the test's standard deviation (S) in that equation; the reliability of the difference (r_{dif}; see Equation 7.12) is substituted for the test's reliability (r_{xx}) in the equation. These substitutions generate Equation 7.14.

$$\text{SEM}_{dif} = \sqrt{S^2_a + S^2_b - 2r_{ab}S_aS_b}\sqrt{1 - \frac{\frac{1}{2}\left(r_{aa}+r_{bb}\right)-r_{ab}}{1-r_{ab}}} \qquad (7.14)$$

The standard error of measurement of a difference (SEM$_{dif}$) describes the distribution of differences between obtained scores. To evaluate difference scores, the simplest method is to establish a level of confidence (for example, 95 percent) and find the z-score associated with that level of confidence (1.96). We then divide the obtained difference by the SEM of the difference. If the quotient exceeds the z-score associated with the level of confidence selected (1.96), the obtained difference is reliable. We can also estimate the true difference in the same manner as we estimate a true score on one test. In general, we assume that the group mean difference is 0.00. Thus the formula for estimating the true difference for a particular student simplifies to Equation 7.15.

$$\text{Estimated true difference} = (\text{obtained difference})(r_{dif}) \qquad (7.15)$$

Desirable Standards

It is important for test authors to present sufficient information in test manuals for the test user to be able to interpret test results accurately. For a test to be valid (that is, to measure what its authors claim it measures), it must be reliable. Although reliability is not the only condition that must be met, it is a necessary condition for validity. No test can measure what it purports to measure unless it is reliable. No score is interpretable unless it is reliable.

Therefore, test authors and publishers must present sufficient reliability data to allow the user to evaluate the reliability of the test scores that are to be interpreted. Thus reliability estimates should be presented for intermediate (for example, subtest) scores when they are to be interpreted. Moreover, reliability estimates should be reported for each age and grade. Furthermore, these indexes should be presented clearly in tabular form in one place. Test authors should not play hide-and-seek with reliability data. Test authors who recommend computing difference scores should provide, whenever possible, the reliability of the difference (r_{dif}) and the SEM of the difference (SEM$_{dif}$). Once test users have access to reliability data, they must judge the adequacy of the test.

How high must a test's reliability be before it can be used in applied settings? The answer depends on the use to which test data are put. A simple answer is to use the most reliable test available. However, that response may be misleading, for the "best" test may be too unreliable for any application (for example, its reliability may be only .45).

Choosing a Standard of Reliability

We recommend that the following two standards of reliability be used in applied settings:

1. *Group data.* If test scores are to be used for administrative purposes and are reported for groups of individuals, a reliability of .60 should probably be the minimum.

2. *Individual data.* If a test score is to be used to make a decision concerning an individual student, a much higher standard of reliability is demanded. When important educational decisions are to be made for a student, such as decisions about tracking and placement in a special class, the minimum standard should be .90. When the decision being made is a screening decision, such as a recommendation that a child receive further assessment, there is still a need for high reliability. For screening devices, we recommend a .80 standard.

Finally, we strongly recommend that confidence intervals be used when reporting test performance.

SUMMARY

Reliability refers to the ability to generalize from a sample to a domain. The domains to which we usually want to generalize are other times (stability or test-retest reliability), other scorers (interrater or interscorer reliability), and other items (alternate-form or internal-consistency reliability). Reliability coefficients may range from .00 (total lack of reliability) to 1.00 (total reliability); .90 is recommended as the minimum standard for tests used to make important educational decisions for students. Several factors affect reliability: the method used for calculating the reliability coefficient, the test length, the test-retest interval, constriction or extension of range, guessing, and variation within the testing situation.

In diagnostic work, the reliability coefficient has four major uses. It allows the user to estimate (1) the test's relative freedom from measurement error, (2) an individual subject's true score, (3) the standard error of measurement, and (4) confidence intervals for a subject's true score.

The discussion of estimated true scores, standard error of measurement, and confidence intervals can be extended to difference or discrepancy scores. The reliability of a difference score is affected by the reliability of the tests and by the correlation between the tests on which the difference is based. Differences in norm samples also affect difference scores, but this effect cannot be evaluated. Provided that the two tests are correlated, difference scores are less reliable than the average of the reliabilities of the tests on which the difference is based.

Although we have devoted an entire chapter to reliability, readers must bear in mind that reliability is important only insofar as it affects the validity of an assessment.

QUESTIONS FOR CHAPTER REVIEW

1. Why is it necessary for a test to be reliable?

2. Test A and test B have identical means and standard deviations. Test A has an SEM of 4.8; test B has an SEM of 16.3. Which test is more reliable and why?

3. What is the greatest limitation of reliability estimates based on test-retest correlation?

4. List and explain five factors that affect the estimated reliability of a test.

5. The SEM is the standard deviation of what? Illustrate your answer with a drawing.

6. Compare and contrast the two major approaches to estimating the extent to which we can generalize from different samples of items.

PROBLEMS

1. Mr. Treacher administers an intelligence test to his class. For this test, $\bar{X} = 100$, $S = 16$, and $r_{xx} = .75$. Five children earn the following scores: 68, 124, 84, 100, and 148. What are the estimated true scores for these children?

2. What is the SEM for the intelligence test in Problem 1?

3. What are the upper and lower boundaries of a symmetrical confidence interval of 95 percent for the first child in Problem 1?

4. What are the upper and lower boundaries of a symmetrical confidence interval of 50 percent for the child in Problem 1 who earns a score of 100?

5. Test A and test B have reliabilities of .90 and .80; the correlation between tests A and B is .50. What is the reliability of a difference between scores on test A and test B?

Answers

1. 76, 118, 88, 100, 136
2. 8
3. 92, 60
4. 105, 95
5. .70

PROJECT

Obtain the test manual for any standardized test. Remembering that it is the author's responsibility to prove reliability, check for a section on reliability. Check for evidence of each appropriate type of reliability. Are there reliability estimates for each subtest at each grade or age? Is the SEM provided? Which scores are stressed? Evaluate the adequacy of the test's reliability.

RESOURCES FOR FURTHER INVESTIGATION

Print Resources

American Educational Research Association, American Psychological Association, & National Council on Measurement in Education. (1999). *Standards for educational and psychological testing.* Washington, DC: American Educational Research Association.

Crocker, L., & Algina, J. (1986a). *Introduction to classical and modern test theory.* New York: Holt, Rinehart, and Winston. (Chapter 7: Procedures for estimating reliability.)

Technology Resources

HYPERSTAT ONLINE TEXTBOOK
davidmlane.com/hyperstat/index.html
Look here for further explanations about confidence intervals and hypothesis testing with standard errors.

SURFSTAT AUSTRALIA: AN ONLINE TEXT IN INTRODUCTORY STATISTICS
www.anu.edu.au/nceph/surfstat/surfstat-home/surfstat.html
This page contains information on summary and presentation of data, production of data, variation and probability, and statistical inference.

INDIANA UNIVERSITY, BLOOMINGTON, EVALUATION SERVICES AND TESTING
www.indiana.edu/~best/test_reliability.shtml
This page contains a description of how item sampling, item construction, test administration, test scoring, test difficulty, and various student factors affect test reliability. Suggestions to improve classroom tests are also provided.

CHAPTER 8

Validity

VALIDITY REFERS TO "THE DEGREE TO WHICH EVIDENCE AND THEORY SUPPORT THE interpretation of test scores entailed by proposed uses of tests" (American Educational Research Association [AERA], American Psychological Association, & National Council on Measurement in Education, 1999, p. 9). Validity is therefore the most fundamental consideration in developing and evaluating tests. The process of validation involves accumulating evidence to provide a sound scientific basis for the proposed score interpretations. It is the interpretations of test scores required by proposed uses that are evaluated, not just the test itself (AERA et al., 1999, p. 9). In a real sense, all questions of validity are local, asking whether the testing process leads to correct inferences about a specific person in a specific situation for a specific purpose.

Clearly, local inferences are a function of the purpose of testing and the type of test being used. For example, when using a test of reading achievement, the test giver is interested in drawing inferences about a student's skill in reading; for a test of intelligence, the inferences of interest center on a student's level of intellectual ability. Thus the type and the quality of a test generally relate to the validity of the inferences that can be drawn from it.

However, a test that leads to valid inferences in general or about most students may not yield valid inferences about a specific student. Two circumstances illustrate this. First, unless a student has been systematically acculturated in the values, behavior, and knowledge found in the public culture of the United States, a test that assumes such cultural information is unlikely to lead to appropriate inferences about that student. Consider, for example, the inappropriateness of administering a verbally loaded intelligence test to a recent U.S. immigrant. Correct inferences about this person's intellectual ability cannot be drawn from the testing because the intelligence test requires not only proficiency in English but also proficiency in U.S. culture and mores.

Second, unless a student has been systematically instructed in the content of an achievement test, a test assuming such academic instruction is unlikely to lead to appropriate inferences about that student's ability to profit from instruction. It would be inappropriate to administer a standardized test of written language (which counts misspelled words as errors) to a student who has been encouraged to use inventive spelling and reinforced for doing so. It is unlikely that the test results would lead to correct inferences about that student's ability to profit from systematic instruction in spelling.

Because it is impossible to validate all inferences that might be drawn from a test performance, test authors typically validate just the most common inferences. In so doing, they should consider each inference separately. Thus test users should expect some information about the degree to which each commonly encouraged inference has (or lacks) validity. Although the validity of each inference is based on all the information that accumulates over time, test authors are expected to provide some evidence of a test's validity for specific inferences at the time the test is offered for use.

It is impossible to validate every assessment because it is impossible to validate each inference within the context of every possible set of life circumstances. Therefore, test authors should validate the inferences for typical groups of students (that is, groups of students who are represented in the norm samples). Thus it is incumbent on the test author to demonstrate that the test leads to valid inferences for the kinds of individuals in the normative sample. Obviously, we would expect some variability (error) for individuals within groups.

Methods of Validating Test Inferences

The process of gathering information about the appropriateness of inferences is called validation. Several types of evidence can be considered (AERA et al., 1999, pp. 11–17).[1]

Evidence related to test content. Test content refers to "the themes, wording, and format of the items, tasks, or question on a test, as well as the guidelines for procedures regarding administration and scoring" (AERA et al., 1999, p. 11).

Evidence related to internal structure. Internal structure refers to the number of dimensions or components within a domain that are represented on the test. For example, if a test developer theorized that there were several components of intelligence, one would rightly expect the resulting test to contain several components of intelligence.

Evidence of the relationships between the test and other performances. The relationship to other performances refers to the accuracy with which test scores predict performance on the same type of test or other similar tests.

---

1. AERA et al. (1999) also recognizes evidence based on response processes that are usually described by test takers. This sort of evidence has not been widely accepted in special and inclusive education, perhaps because it can be so difficult to obtain reliably from children and individuals with disabilities. Therefore, we do not deal with response processes in this text.

Evidence of convergent and discriminant power. Convergent power refers to a test's ability to produce scores similar to those produced by other tests of the same ability or skills. Discriminant power refers to a test's ability to produce scores different from those produced by other tests of a different ability or skill.

Evidence of the consequences of testing. Tests are administered with the expectation that some benefit will be realized either to the test taker or to the organization requiring the test. In education, the possible benefits include the selection of efficacious instruction, materials, and placements. "A fundamental purpose of validation is to indicate whether these specific benefits are likely to be realized. Thus, in the case of a test used in a placement decision, the validation would be informed by evidence that alternative placements, in fact, are differentially beneficial to the persons and the institution" (AERA et al., 1999, p. 16).

Historically, the types of evidence under consideration have been categorized as follows: evidence of content validity, evidence of criterion-related validity, and evidence of construct validity. Indeed, most test authors still use these categories. Therefore, we use these three categories in our discussions of validity in this chapter. Specifically, we consider evidence related to test content as content validity; evidence of the relationships between the test and other performances as criterion-related validity; and evidence related to internal structure, evidence of convergent and discriminant power, and evidence of the consequences of testing as construct validity. (We have already discussed in preceding chapters other evidence of a test's validity—namely, the meaning of test scores, reliability, the adequacy of the test's standardization, and, when applicable, the test's norms.)

Content Validity
To judge a test's validity, those who assess students must have a clear understanding of the traits, abilities, or skills that are to be measured. Test authors must define what is to be measured before deciding how the measuring is to be done. The specific definition will depend on a test author's own definition of and assumptions about the domain to be measured, as well as scientific consensus.

Content validity is the extent to which a test's items actually represent the domain or universe to be measured. It is a major source of evidence for the validation of any educational or psychological test and many other forms of assessment (such as observations and ratings). Evidence of valid content is especially important in the measurement of achievement and adaptive behavior, and it is most easily understood in this context. A careful examination of a test's content is necessary; frequently, test developers rely on panels of experts for judgments about the appropriateness of test content. Whether test content is examined by experts or by those who use the tests, the examination is judgmental in nature and requires a clear definition of the domain or universe represented.

Therefore, in developing a test, a test developer must consider the purposes for which the test is going to be used and then specify adequately the universe of content that the test is intended to represent. If a test is to be used for making instructional decisions, it is important that there be agreement between the test and the specific instructional or curricular areas that the test is meant to cover. Assessors must make sure that the format and the response properties of the items or tasks that make up a test represent the universe of possible item and response types for the particular area being assessed.

Appropriateness of Included Items

In examining the appropriateness of the items included in a test, we must ask: Is this an appropriate test question, and does this test item really measure the domain or construct? Consider the four test items from a hypothetical primary (kindergarten through grade 2) arithmetic achievement test presented in Figure 8.1. The first item requires the student to read and add two single-digit numbers, the sum of which is less than 10. This seems to be an appropriate item for an elementary arithmetic achievement test. The second item requires the student to complete a geometric progression. Although this item is mathematical, the skills and knowledge required to complete the question correctly are not taught in any elementary school curriculum by the second grade. Therefore, the question should be rejected as an invalid item for an arithmetic achievement test to be used with children from kindergarten through the second grade. The third item likewise requires the student to read and add two single-digit numbers, the sum of which is less than 10. However, the question is written in Spanish. Although the content of the question is suitable (this is an elementary addition problem), the method of presentation requires language skills that most U.S. students do not have. Failure to complete the item correctly could be attributed either to the fact that the child does not know Spanish or to the fact that the child does not know that 3 + 2 = 5. Test givers should conclude that the item is not valid for an arithmetic test for children who do not read Spanish. The fourth item requires that the student select the correct form of the Latin verb *amare* ("to love"). Clearly, this is an inappropriate item for an arithmetic test and should be rejected as invalid.

In addition to making judgments about how appropriately an item fits within a domain, test developers often rely on point-biserial correlations be-

FIGURE 8.1
Sample Multiple-Choice Questions for a Primary-Grade (K–2) Arithmetic Achievement Test

1. Three and six are _____.

   a. 4
   b. 7
   c. 8
   d. 9

2. What number follows in this series?
   1, 2.5, 6.25, _____

   a. 10
   b. 12.5
   c. 15.625
   d. 18.50

3. ¿Cuántos son tres y dos?

   a. 3
   b. 4
   c. 5
   d. 6

4. Ille puer puellas _____.

   a. amo
   b. amat
   c. amamus
   d. amant

tween individual test items and the total score to make decisions about item appropriateness (see the chapter "Descriptive Statistics"). Items that do not correlate positively and at least moderately (.25 or .30 or more) with the total score are dropped. Retaining only items that have positive correlations with the total score ensures homogeneous test items and internally consistent (reliable) tests. Moreover, when test items are homogeneous, they are likely to be measuring the same skill or trait. Therefore, to obtain reliable tests, test developers are likely to drop items that do not statistically fit the domain.

When domains are not homogeneous, test authors can jeopardize validity by selecting items on the basis of point-biserial correlations to produce an internally consistent test. Therefore, it is generally a good idea to analyze the structure of a domain, either logically or statistically. When a domain comprises two or more homogeneous classes of test items, homogeneous subtests (representing each factor) can be developed using point-biserial correlations. In this way, the validity of the test can be heightened.

Completeness of Content

Test content must be examined to ascertain the completeness of the item sample. The validity of any elementary arithmetic test would be questioned if it included only problems requiring the addition of single-digit numbers with a sum less than 10. Educators would reasonably expect an arithmetic test to include a far broader sample of tasks (for example, addition of two- and three-digit numbers, subtraction, understanding of the process of addition, and so forth). Incomplete assessment of a domain usually results in an invalid appraisal.

How Content Is Measured

Content must be examined to ascertain how the test items assess content. The *how* of measurement is multifaceted. In one question in Figure 8.1, the student was expected to add two single-digit numbers, the sum of which was less than 10. However, test givers could evaluate a child's arithmetic skills in a variety of ways. The child might be required to recognize the correct answer in a multiple-choice array, supply the correct answer, demonstrate the addition process with manipulatives, apply the proper addition facts in a word problem, or analyze the condition under which the mathematical relationship obtains. How content is measured may affect the outcome.

This aspect of validity is currently being hotly debated by those favoring constructed responses such as extended answers, performances, or demonstrations. Current theory and research methods as they apply to trait or ability congruence under different methods of measurement are still emerging. Much of the current methodology grew out of Campbell and Fiske's (1959) early work and is beyond the scope of this text. There is, however, an emerging consensus that the methods used to assess student knowledge or ability should closely parallel those used in instruction.

Ensuring Content Validity

To ensure that a test has appropriate content, we can conceptualize its content precisely. One way to do this is by developing a table of specifications that maps the major areas of content and the desired ways of measuring that content. Although there are several approaches to content mapping, the procedures described by Bloom, Hastings, and Madaus (1971) in their classic text *Handbook of Formative and Summative Evaluation of Student Learning* are illustrative. They recommended that authors of achievement tests use a table of specifications to map the content to be tested. Such a table can be readily generalized to other types of tests. A table of specifications formally enumerates the particular contents of a test and the processes (or behaviors) it assesses.

"Content" refers to the particular domains or subdomains the test author wishes to assess. The task of test authors is to specify the content as precisely as possible in order to convey clearly what is being measured. The next step is to specify how the particular content objectives will be measured (the process by which the measurement will occur). Several types of measurement are possible; they range from knowledge objectives to evaluation objectives. The definitions used by Bloom (1956) and colleagues (Bloom et al., 1971) follow.

Measuring Content Objectives

1. Knowledge is the "recall or recognition of specific elements in a subject area" (Bloom et al., 1971, p. 41).

2. Comprehension is evaluated with three types of measurement: translation, interpretation, and extrapolation. Translation refers to rewording information or putting it into the learner's own words. Interpretation is evidenced "when a student can go beyond recognizing the separate parts of a communication and can see the interrelationships among the parts" (Bloom et al., 1971, p. 149). Interpretation also is evidenced when a student can differentiate the essentials of a message from unimportant elements. Extrapolation refers to the student's ability to go beyond literal comprehension and to make inferences about what the anticipated outcome of an action is or what will happen next.

3. Application is "the use of abstractions in particular and concrete situations. The abstractions may be in the form of general ideas, rules or procedures, or generalized methods. The abstractions may also be technical principles, ideas, and theories which must be remembered and applied" (Bloom, 1956, p. 205).

4. Analysis is "the breakdown of a communication into its constituent elements or parts such that the relative hierarchy of ideas is made clear and/or the relations between ideas expressed are made explicit. Such analyses are intended to clarify the communication, to indicate how the communication is organized, and the way in which it manages to convey its effects, as well as its basis and arrangements" (Bloom, 1956, p. 205).

5. Synthesis refers to "the putting together of elements and parts so as to form a whole. This involves the process of working with pieces, parts, elements, etc., and arranging and combining them in such a way as to constitute a pattern or structure not clearly there before" (Bloom, 1956, p. 206).

6. Evaluation means "the making of judgments about the value, for some purpose, of ideas, works, solutions, methods, material, etc. It involves the use of criteria as well as standards for appraising the extent to which particulars are accurate, effective, economical, or satisfying. The judgments may be quantitative or qualitative, and the criteria may be either those determined by the student or those which are given to him" (Bloom, 1956, p. 185).

To illustrate how a table of specifications can be used, let us assume that we wish to develop a test to assess the understanding of reliability demonstrated by beginning students. The first step is to enumerate the content areas of the domain. Using the chapter "Reliability" as a guide, we could assess the following areas: the reliability coefficient (its meaning, methods of estimating it, and factors affecting it); standard error of measurement (its meaning and computation); estimated true scores; confidence intervals (their meaning and computation); and difference scores. We might reasonably expect a test user to have a better understanding of the meaning of the reliability coefficient and the construction and interpretation of confidence intervals. Therefore, these content areas could be stressed.

The next step is to specify the processes by which the content areas are to be measured. We might expect beginning students to demonstrate understanding at the knowledge, comprehension, and application levels only. Therefore, the test might not contain items assessing analysis, synthesis, or evaluation. A table of specifications for this hypothetical test would resemble Table 8.1.

The number of questions used to assess each cell is given in the table. The table of specifications shows that, of the 28 questions in the test, 8 deal with the reliability coefficient and 9 deal with confidence intervals; 8 questions assess knowledge; 12 questions assess comprehension; and 8 assess application. Thus the hypothetical test assesses a student's understanding of reliability by emphasizing comprehension of the reliability coefficient and applications of confidence intervals.

TABLE 8.1	Specifications for a Hypothetical Reliability Test				
	Contents				
Processes	*Reliability Coefficient*	*Standard Error of Measurement*	*Estimated True Scores*	*Confidence Intervals*	*Difference Scores*
Knowledge	3 questions	2 questions	1 question	1 question	1 question
Comprehension	5 questions	2 questions	1 question	3 questions	1 question
Application	Not tested	2 questions	1 question	5 questions	Not tested
Analysis	Not tested	Not tested	Not tested	Not tested	Not tested
Synthesis	Not tested	Not tested	Not tested	Not tested	Not tested
Evaluation	Not tested	Not tested	Not tested	Not tested	Not tested

Extension to Other Forms of Assessment

The preceding discussion of content validity also applies to other forms of assessment. In systematic observation, the content of the observation protocol takes two forms. First, the contexts in which observation takes place can be considered an issue of content validity. For example, a behavior can occur in several contexts; thus a teacher might observe Harry to see the frequency of his hitting in class, at recess, during lunch, and so forth. Second, when states or traits are observed (for example, cooperation), the specific behaviors chosen to represent the state or trait are clearly issues of content validity. For example, taking turns, sharing toys, and using polite language (such as saying, "please") could be considered exemplars of cooperation.

In unstandardized assessment procedures, such as portfolio assessment, content validity is an especially critical issue. The contents of the portfolio—what is included and what is excluded—should accurately portray the student's work in the domain. The student's work should represent all important dimensions within the domain, and work not pertinent to the domain should be excluded from the assessment process (although such work may be kept in the student's portfolio).

Criterion-Related Validity

Criterion-related validity refers to the extent to which a person's performance on a criterion measure can be estimated from that person's performance on the assessment procedure being validated. This prediction is usually expressed as a correlation between the assessment procedure (for example, a test) and the criterion. The correlation coefficient is termed a *validity coefficient.*

Two types of criterion-related validity are commonly described: concurrent validity and predictive validity. These terms denote the time at which a person's performance on the criterion measure is obtained. *Concurrent criterion-related validity* refers to how accurately a person's current performance (for example, test score) estimates that person's performance on the criterion measure at the same time. *Predictive criterion-related validity* refers to how accurately a person's current performance (for example, test score) estimates that person's performance on the criterion measure at a later time. Thus concurrent and predictive criterion-related validity refer to the temporal sequence by which a person's performance on some criterion measure is estimated on the basis of that person's current assessment; concurrent and predictive validity differ in the time at which scores on the criterion measure are obtained.

The nature of the criterion measure is extremely important. The criterion itself must be valid if it is to be used to establish the validity of another measure. Let us investigate this point by looking briefly at two examples of criterion-related validation: the first, concurrent, and the second, predictive.

An Example of Concurrent Criterion-Related Validity

A basic concurrent criterion-related validity question is: Does a person's performance measured with a new or experimental test allow the accurate estimation of that person's performance on a criterion measure that has been widely accepted as valid? For example, if the Acme Ruler Company manufactures yard-sticks, how do we know that a person's height, as measured by an Acme yard-stick, is that person's true height? How do we know that the "Acme foot" is really a foot? The first step is to find a valid criterion measure.

The National Bureau of Standards maintains the standard foot (0.3048 meter), and this foot is the logical choice for a criterion measure. We can take several things to the bureau and measure them with both the Acme foot and the standard foot. If the two sets of measurements correspond closely (that is, are highly correlated and have very similar means and standard deviations), we can conclude that the Acme foot is a valid measure of length.

Similarly, if we are developing a test of achievement, we can ask: How does knowledge of a person's score on our achievement test allow the estimation of that person's score on a criterion measure? How do we know that our new test really measures achievement? Again, the first step is to find a valid criterion measure. However, there is no National Bureau of Standards for educational tests. Therefore, we must turn to a less-than-perfect criterion. There are two basic choices: (1) other achievement tests that are presumed to be valid and (2) judgments of achievement by teachers, parents, and the students themselves. We can, of course, use both tests and judgments. If our new test presents evidence of content validity and elicits test scores corresponding closely (correlating significantly) to judgments and scores from other achievement tests that are presumed to be valid, we can conclude that there is evidence for our new test's criterion-related validity.

An Example of Predictive Criterion-Related Validity

The basic predictive criterion-related validity question is: Does knowledge of a person's score allow an accurate estimation of that person's score on a criterion measure administered some time in the future? For example, if the Acme Ruler Company decides to diversify and manufacture tests of color vision, how do we know that a diagnosis of colorblindness made on the basis of the Acme test is accurate? How do we know that an Acme-based diagnosis will correspond to next month's diagnosis made by an ophthalmologist? We can test several children with the Acme test, schedule appointments with an ophthalmologist, and compare the Acme-based diagnoses with the ophthalmologist's diagnoses. If the Acme test accurately predicts the ophthalmologist's diagnoses, we can conclude that the Acme test is a valid measure of color vision.

Similarly, if we are developing a test to assess reading readiness, we can ask: Does knowledge of a student's score on our reading readiness test allow an accurate estimation of the student's actual readiness for subsequent instruction? How do we know that our test really assesses reading readiness? Again, the first step is to find a valid criterion measure. In this case, the student's initial progress in reading can be used. Reading progress can be assessed by a reading achievement test (presumed to be valid) or by teacher judgments of reading ability or reading readiness at the time reading instruction is actually begun. If our reading readiness test has content validity and corresponds closely with either later teacher judgments of readiness or validly assessed reading skill, we can conclude that ours is a valid test of reading readiness.

There are three important considerations when evaluating evidence of predictive criterion-related validity. First, the criterion measures should be carefully described and be valid themselves. Because the validity of the assessment inferences are established by their relationship to the inferences based on the criterion procedure, the criterion procedure is critical. Second, research reports that contain the evidence for validity should describe the statistical procedures used and the persons participating in the validation studies. Third, the authors should provide information about the degree to which the evidence can be generalized to other test takers, other criterion measures, and so forth.

Extension to Other Forms of Assessment

The preceding discussion of criterion-related validity also applies to other forms of assessment. For example, in systematic observation, some form of time sampling is often used. An observer might use momentary time sampling (see the chapter "Assessing Instructional Ecology") and record what a target pupil is doing every ten seconds. An appropriate question is: Does the sampling procedure affect the record of the student's performance? To investigate this question, assessors usually compare the data obtained when using continuous observation of target students with data from observations when using momentary time sampling. Similarly, if assessors wished to evaluate the criterion validity of portfolio assessment, an appropriate criterion would have to be selected (for example, all of a student's work—tests, work not included in the portfolio, and so forth). The score or scores assigned to the portfolio could then be compared with the score or scores based on the totality of student work during the marking period.

Construct Validity   *Construct validity* refers to the extent to which a procedure or test measures a theoretical trait or characteristic. Construct validity is especially important for measures of process, such as intelligence or scientific inquiry. To provide evidence of construct validity, a test author must rely on indirect evidence and inference. The definition of the construct and the theory from which the construct is derived allow us to make certain predictions that can be confirmed or disconfirmed. In a real sense, we do not validate inferences from tests or other assessment procedures; rather, we conduct experiments to demonstrate that the inferences are not valid. The continued inability to disconfirm the inferences in effect validates the inferences.

For example, intellectual ability is generally believed to be developmental. We could hypothesize that, if we were to conduct an investigation, intelligence test scores would be correlated with chronological age. If we found that a test of intelligence did not correlate with chronological age, this finding would cast serious doubt on the test as a measure of intelligence. (The experiment would disconfirm the test as a measure of intelligence.) However, the presence of a substantial correlation between chronological age and scores on the test does not confirm that the test is a measure of intelligence.[2] Gradually, the test developer accumulates evidence that the test continues to act in the way that it would if it were a valid measure of the construct. As the research evidence accumulates, the developer can make some claim to construct validity.

Several types of evidence are generally brought to bear in research on construct validity. For example, we often expect differences in the behavior of individuals with different levels of a trait or characteristic. Thus a test to assess learning ability should be able to differentiate between fast and slow learners. We can predict, therefore, that the individuals who learn more in a given amount of time have more learning ability; that is, they will have higher scores on a measure of learning ability. If children with IQs of 125 on test X learn more material in one week than do children with IQs of 100 on test X, there will be a failure to disconfirm the test as a valid measure of learning ability. This failure to disconfirm its validity offers some evidence for inferring that the test measures intelligence. Other examples of this type of research are numerous. We would expect tests of intelligence to predict school achievement, readiness tests to predict school achievement, and so forth.

Factors Affecting General Validity

Whenever an assessment procedure fails to measure what it purports to measure, validity is threatened. Consequently, any factor that results in measuring "something else" affects validity. Both unsystematic error (unreliability) and systematic error (bias) threaten validity.

Reliability Reliability sets the upper limit of a test's validity, so reliability is a necessary but not a sufficient condition for valid measurement. Thus all valid tests are reliable, unreliable tests are not valid, and reliable tests may or may not be valid. The validity of a particular procedure can never exceed the reliability of that procedure, because unreliable procedures measure error; valid procedures measure the traits they are designed to measure. The relationship between the reliability and the validity of any procedure is expressed in Equation 8.1. The empirically determined validity coefficient (r_{xy}) equals the correlation between true scores on the two variables ($r_{x(t)y(t)}$) multiplied by the square root of the product of the reliability coefficients of test X and test Y ($r_{xx}r_{yy}$).

$$r_{xy} = r_{x(t)y(t)} \sqrt{r_{xx}r_{yy}}$$

(8.1)

2. Many test authors systematically ensure that their tests will be correlated with age. Authors may use a positive correlation between age or grade and passing an item as a criterion for item inclusion. Some psychometricians advocate even more sophisticated methods—for example, item-characteristic curves (Thorndike, 1982)—to ensure that test scores are correlated with chronological age. Many other abilities besides intelligence correlate with chronological age—for example, achievement, perceptual abilities, and language skills.

Systematic Bias   *Method of Measurement*

The method used to measure a skill or trait is often believed to affect what score a child will receive. A true score can be considered a composite of trait variance and method-of-measurement variance (Campbell & Fiske, 1959). To take a classic example, Werner and Strauss (1941) conducted a series of experiments to ascertain the effect of brain injury on figure-background perception; all of their subjects were individuals with mental retardation. They presented stimulus items for a fraction of a second and asked their subjects to name what they saw. They found that individuals with brain injury responded to the background stimuli more often than did the individuals without brain injury. They concluded that brain injury results in a dysfunction in figure-ground perception. However, the method of testing and the trait to be tested (figure-ground perception) were confounded by the testing procedure. Rubin (1969) later demonstrated that, under different testing procedures, there were no differences between individuals with and without brain injury in figure-background perceptual responses. The differences between the findings of Werner and Strauss and those of Rubin are attributable to how figure-background perception was measured. It seems likely that Werner and Strauss were measuring perceptual speed because of their method of measurement. To the extent that trait or skill scores include variance attributable to the method of measurement, these scores may lack validity.

Enabling Behaviors

Enabling behaviors and knowledge are skills and facts that a person must rely on to demonstrate a target behavior or knowledge. For example, to demonstrate knowledge of causes of the American Civil War on an essay examination, a student must additionally be able to write. The student cannot produce the targeted behavior (the written answer) without the enabling behavior (writing).

Several behaviors are assumed in any testing situation. We must assume that the subject is fluent in the language in which the test is prepared and administered if there are any verbal components to the test directions or test responses. Yet, in many states with substantial Spanish-speaking populations, students whose primary language is not English are nonetheless tested in English. Intelligence testing in English of non–English-speaking children has been sufficiently commonplace that a group of parents brought suit against a school district (*Diana v. State Board of Education,* 1970). Students who are deaf are routinely given the Performance subtests of the Wechsler Adult Intelligence Scales (Baumgardner, 1993) even though they cannot hear the directions. Children with communication disorders often are required to respond orally to test questions. Such obvious limitations in or absences of enabling behaviors are frequently overlooked in testing situations, even though they invalidate the test's inferences for these students.

Differential Item Effectiveness

Test items should work the same way for various groups of students. Jensen (1980) has discussed several empirical ways to assess item effectiveness for different groups of test takers. First, we should expect that the relative difficulty of items is maintained across different groups. For example, the most difficult item for males should also be the most difficult item for females; the easiest item for whites should be the easiest item for nonwhites; and so forth. Second, the factor structure of a test should be identical for all groups of test takers. For example, if a test measures four independent factors for males, it should measure four factors for females, and so on. Third, the predictive validity should be the same for all groups of test takers. For example, if the correlation between an intelligence test and a reading achievement test is .80 for whites, the correlation between the two tests should also be .80 (+ or − sampling error) for nonwhites.

The most likely explanation for items having differential effectiveness for different groups of people is differential exposure to test content. Test items may not work in the same ways for students who experience different acculturation or academic instruction. For example, standardized achievement tests presume that the students who are taking the tests have been exposed to similar curricula. If teachers have not taught the content being tested, that content will be more difficult for their students (and inferences about the students' ability to profit from instruction will probably be incorrect).

Administration Errors

Unless a test is administered according to the standardized procedures, the inferences based on the test are invalid. Suppose Ms. Williams wishes to demonstrate how effective her teaching is by administering an intelligence test and an achievement test to her class. She allows the students five minutes less than the standardized time limits on the intelligence test and five minutes more on the standardized achievement test. The result is that the students earn higher achievement test scores (because they had too much time) and lower intelligence test scores (because they did not have enough time). The inference that less-intelligent students have learned more than anticipated is not valid.

Norms

Scores based on the performance of unrepresentative norms lead to incorrect estimates of relative standing in the general population. To the extent that the normative sample is systematically unrepresentative of the general population in either central tendency or variability, the differences based on such scores are incorrect and invalid.

Responsibility for Valid Assessment

The valid use of assessment procedures is the responsibility of both the author and the user of the assessment procedure.

> Evidence of validity should be presented for the major types of inferences for which the use of a test is recommended. A rationale should be provided to support the particular mix of evidence presented for the intended uses. . . . If validity for some common interpretation has not been investigated, that fact should be made clear, and potential users should be cautioned about making such interpretations. (AERA et al., 1999, p. 13)

SUMMARY

Validity is the only technical characteristic of an assessment procedure in which we are interested. All other technical considerations, such as reliability, are subsumed under the concept of validity and are analyzed separately to simplify the discussion of validity. We must know whether inferences derived from an assessment are accurate. Adequate norms, reliability, and lack of bias are all necessary conditions for validity. None—separately or in total—is sufficient to guarantee validity for a particular test taker.

Systematic evaluation of validity is based on several types of information. The content may be inspected to see whether each item is valid and to ensure that all aspects of the domain are represented. If a standard or criterion of known validity is available, the test should be compared against that standard. The construct validity of all tests should be examined.

Several factors affect the validity of inferences derived from tests: reliability, systematic bias, enabling behaviors, item selection, administration errors, and test norms. Problems with these factors can invalidate test inferences.

QUESTIONS FOR CHAPTER REVIEW

1. Why must test authors demonstrate validity for inferences based on their tests?

2. What is the relationship between reliability and validity?

3. How can a table of specifications assist in developing a valid test?

4. What is the difference between concurrent and predictive criterion-related validity?

5. Many test manuals contain no evidence of validity, but the tests are used in schools to make important educational decisions about children. Under what circumstances could such tests be used?

6. Kim Ngo, a recent arrival from a Vietnamese orphanage, speaks no English. When she enrolls in a U.S. school, her intelligence is assessed by a verbal test that has English directions and requires English responses. Kim performs poorly on the test, earning an IQ of 37. The tester concludes that Kim has severe mental retardation and recommends placement in a special class. What are two major errors in the interpretation of the test result?

7. Professor Johnson develops a test that he claims can be used to identify children who may have learning disabilities and will profit from perceptual-motor training. What must he do to demonstrate that his test is valid?

PROJECT

Obtain the test manual for any standardized test. Remembering that it is the author's responsibility to prove validity, evaluate the validity data. How does the author recommend using the test? What domains are measured, and how does the test author prove that these domains are measured? How were items chosen for the test? What types of validity data are provided? What assertions are made about particular uses of the test or certain scores? What data are provided to support these assertions?

RESOURCES FOR FURTHER INVESTIGATION

Print Resources

American Educational Research Association, American Psychological Association, & National Council on Measurement in Education. (1999). *Standards for educational and psychological testing*. Washington, DC: American Educational Research Association.

Crocker, L., & Algina, J. (1986b). *Introduction to classical and modern test theory*. New York: Holt, Rinehart, and Winston. (Chapter 10: Introduction to Validity.)

Jensen, A. R. (1980). *Bias in mental testing*. New York: The Free Press.

Messick, S. (1980). Test validity and the ethics of assessment. *American Psychologist, 35,* 1012–1027.

Messick, S. (1989). Meaning and values in test validation: The science and ethics of assessment. *Educational Researcher, 18*(2), 5–11.

Messick, S. (1993). Validity. In R. L. Linn (Ed.), *Educational measurement* (4th ed., pp. 13–103). New York: ACE/Macmillan.

Thorndike, R. L. (1997). *Measurement and evaluation in psychology and education* (6th ed.). Upper Saddle River, NJ: Prentice-Hall.

Technology Resources

NATIONAL CENTER FOR EDUCATION STATISTICS (NCES)
nces.ed.gov
This website offers an extensive set of statistical tables, charts, and studies produced by NCES to report the condition and progress of education.

ERIC DIGESTS
www.ericdigests.org/2000-3/validity.htm
This page covers traditional concepts of validity (content, criterion, and construct) and other modern concepts of reliability.

CHAPTER 9

Adapting Tests to Accommodate Students with Disabilities

OVER THE PAST DECADE THERE HAS BEEN INCREASED USE OF LARGE-SCALE ASSESSMENTS to make accountability decisions about students with disabilities. The requirement to include all students in statewide and district assessments has included a need for accommodations in assessments. Educators now must attend to the kinds of adaptations that can be made without compromising the technical adequacy of tests. In this chapter, we consider ways to enhance the participation of students with disabilities in assessments and the kinds of accommodations typically used with these students. We include recommendations for making accommodation decisions.

Why Be Concerned About Testing Adaptations?

Changes in Student Population

The diversity of students attending today's schools is mind boggling. When most people think of diversity, they think of race and ethnicity. Clearly, schools are becoming more racially and ethnically diverse. But they are becoming more diverse in other ways that concern assessment personnel. In large city school systems across the United States, students speak more than 50 different languages and dialects as their primary language. Diversity of language has created challenges in making instruction and assessment accessible to all students. Students enter school these days with a very diverse set of academic background experiences and opportunities. Within the same classroom, students often vary considerably in their academic skill development. A recent study we conducted illustrated this variation. When we tested sixth-graders in math, there was an 11-year range in skill development. Several students whom we tested were new immigrants from Somalia and lacked many very basic math skills. Others demonstrated advanced algebra skills. We learned that several had mothers who were software engineers for Honeywell Corporation, and they practiced solving quadratic equations in the evening for fun. A clear challenge for all educational professionals is the design of instruction that will accommodate this vast range in skill development and, similarly, the use of assessments that will capture the large range in student skills.

Since the mid-1970s, considerable attention has been focused on including all students in neighborhood schools and general education settings. Much attention has been focused on including students who are considered developmentally, physically, or behaviorally impaired. As federal and state officials make educational policies, they are now compelled to make them for all children and youth, including those with severe disabilities. Also, as policy makers attempt to develop practices that will result in improved educational results, they rely on data from district- and state-administered tests. However, relying on assessment data presents challenges. One set of challenges involves deciding whom to include in assessments and the kinds of changes that can be made to include students with disabilities. Another set of challenges arises as states and school districts try to move to new forms of assessment, such as performance tests or portfolio assessments, and try to have all students participate in those assessments.

Although it can be extremely challenging to assess the skills of such a diverse student population meaningfully, it is clear that all students need to be included in large-scale assessment programs. If students with disabilities are excluded from assessments, then the data on which policy decisions are made represent only part (perhaps 85 percent) of the school population. If students with disabilities are excluded from accountability systems, they may also be denied access to the general education curriculum. If data are going to be gathered on all students, then major decisions must be made regarding the kinds of data to be collected and how tests are to be modified or adapted to include students with disabilities. Historically, there has been widespread exclusion of students with disabilities from state and national testing (Thompson & Thurlow, 2001; McGrew, Thurlow, Shriner, & Spiegel, 1992). Participation in large-scale assessments is now recognized by many educators and parents as a critical element of equal opportunity and access to education. This is true for students with disabilities. Thurlow & Thompson (2004) report that all states now require participation of all students. Yet there is still variability in participation rates. It has been difficult to calculate participation rates, and now states have been revising their data management systems to enhance their ability to do so.

Changes in Educational Standards

Part of major efforts to reform or restructure schools has been a push to specify high standards for student achievement and an accompanying push to measure the extent to which students meet those high standards. It is expected that schools will include students with disabilities in assessments, especially assessments completed for accountability purposes.

State education agencies in nearly every state are engaging in critical analyses of the standards, objectives, outcomes, results, skills, or behaviors that they want students to demonstrate upon completion of school. Content area professional agencies, such as the National Council of Teachers of Mathematics and the National Science Foundation, have developed sets of standards in specific content areas, such as math, geography, and science. As they do so, they must decide the extent to which standards should be the same for students with and without disabilities. In the chapter "Making Accountability Decisions," you will learn about current state efforts to develop alternate achievement standards and modified achievement standards for students with disabilities. Development of standards is not enough. Groups that develop standards must develop ways of assessing the extent to which students are meeting the standards.

The Need for Accurate Measurement

It is critical that the assessment practices used for gathering information on individual students provide accurate information. Without accommodations, testing runs the risk of being unfair for students with disabilities. Some test formats make it harder for students with disabilities to understand what they are supposed to do or what the response requirements are. Because of their disabilities, some students find it impossible to respond in a way that can be evaluated accurately.

In this chapter, we first review the two major issues of who should participate in assessment and how assessments should be adapted to accommodate diverse students. In doing so, we focus more on group measurement activities than on individual appraisal. We then describe some major legal considerations in participation and accommodation. We also identify things that impede getting an accurate picture of students' skills. In the remainder of the chapter, we describe both current practice and best practice in (1) making decisions about how students ought to participate in assessments and (2) making accommodation decisions.

As you read this chapter, remember that the major objective of assessment is to benefit students. Assessment can do so either by enabling us to develop interventions that help a child achieve the objectives of schooling or by informing local, state, and national policy decisions that benefit all students, including individuals with disabilities.

The Twin Issues of Participation and Accommodation in Testing

Although many issues surround the assessment of students with disabilities, most of these can be grouped into two areas: participation and accommodation. In this section, we introduce these two issues. In later sections, we provide considerably more detail on them.

Participation

Educators use assessment information for many purposes. When screening, program evaluation, or accountability decisions are made, participation in testing is an issue. Too often, prior to testing, educators make assumptions that certain students should be excluded because "we already know how they would perform" or because "the students should not be subjected to the pain of participation" or because "they could not possibly respond correctly to the test items."

Moreover, data from large-scale (district, state, or national) assessments have major implications for educational funding, the reputations of districts (and teachers and administrators), and real estate values. Because it is widely believed that the participation of students with disabilities will lower the overall scores of schools, districts, or states, these students are often excluded from participation. To the extent that this belief is correct, exclusion of low-scoring students from large-scale assessments places districts that do include such students at a competitive disadvantage.

Current legislation explicitly states that national educational goals and standards are to apply to all students. If students with disabilities are not included in assessment, then a biased picture of local, state, or national performance is presented. As demonstrated in the chapter "Norms," exclusion of low-scoring students does inflate the mean and reduce the variance of scores. This bias can have major effects on scores that rank districts or states (for example, when districts within a state are assigned percentile ranks based on the tested performance of their students).

Accommodation   An accommodation is any change in testing materials or procedures that enables students to participate in assessments so that their abilities, rather than their disabilities, are assessed. There are four general types of accommodations:

- *Presentation* (for example, repeat directions, read aloud)
- *Response* (for example, mark answers in book, point to answers)
- *Setting* (for example, study carrel, separate room, special lighting)
- *Timing/schedule* (for example, extended time, frequent breaks, multiple days)

What legitimate changes can be made in assessment materials or procedures that still allow valid assessment results to be obtained? There is more concern about this than about the purpose and use of tests. Reschly (1993, p. 37) puts the issue well:

> My experience as a member of the state of Georgia Assessment Advisory Board (where state-wide educational assessment programs in Georgia and other states are reviewed) and the American Psychological Association Committee on Psychological Tests and Assessments (where various proposals for national literacy tests or assessment have been reviewed) indicates that assessment mechanics (e.g., item types), test content, and scaling typically dominate discussions at the expense of consideration of why the assessment is done, what will be assessed, what interpretation will result, how the results will be used, and what consequences will be established for good and poor performance.

Concern about accommodation applies to individual and large-scale assessments. The concerns are legal (Is an individual sufficiently disabled to require taking a modified test?), technical (To what extent can we adapt measures and still have technically adequate tests?), and political (Is it fair to give accommodations to some students, yet deny them to others?).

Factors Affecting Accurate Assessment

Five factors can impede getting an accurate picture of students' abilities and skills: (1) the students' ability to understand assessment stimuli; (2) the students' ability to respond to assessment stimuli; (3) the nature of the norm group; (4) the appropriateness of the level of the items (sufficient basal and ceiling items); and (5) the students' exposure to the curriculum being tested (opportunity to learn).

Ability to Understand Assessment Stimuli

Assessments are considered unfair if the test stimuli are in a format that, because of a disability, the student does not understand. For example, tests in print are considered unfair for students with severe visual impairments. Tests with oral directions are considered unfair for students with hearing impairments. In fact, because the law requires that students be assessed in their primary language and because the primary language of many deaf students is not English, written assessments in English are considered unfair and invalid for many deaf students. When students cannot understand test stimuli because of a sensory or mental limitation that is unrelated to what the test is targeted to measure, then accurate measurement of the targeted skills is hindered by the sensory or mental limitation. Such a test is invalid, and failure to provide an accommodation is illegal.

A major issue arises when tests with directions or stimuli in English are administered to students who primarily speak other languages. It often is assumed that the test giver can simply translate a test into another language, and then it can be used with students who speak that language. As we point out in the chapter "Testing Students with Limited English Proficiency," simply translating a test usually also changes its psychometric properties, because we cannot assume that the words and the concepts they represent are of equal difficulty in both languages. Suppose that a test requiring a student to read the word *cat* were translated into Spanish. *Cat* translates to *gato*. In English, the word contains two of the first three letters of the alphabet; in Spanish, it contains one of the first three letters. In English, the word is one syllable; in Spanish, it is two syllables.

The cultural relevance of the word may differ as well. If the referent for the word is a four-legged feline, cats may not have the same cultural familiarity. For example, are cats as commonly kept as household pets in Bolivia or in U.S. barrios as in Anglo-American homes? If the referent for the word is not a four-legged feline, there may be conceptual confusion. For example, the slang term *cool cat* may be meaningless within certain Spanish-speaking cultures.

Although the literal translation of a test is relatively easy, inferences cannot be drawn from scores on translated tests without first establishing the validity of these tests in the new language and culture. Usually, a translated test should be renormed within the particular culture, and new evidence for reliability and validity must be established.

Ability to Respond to Assessment Stimuli

All assessment measures require students to produce a response. For example, intelligence tests require verbal, motor (pointing or arranging), or written (including multiple-choice) responses. To the extent that physical or sensory limitations inhibit accurate responding, these test results are invalid. For example, some students with cerebral palsy may lack sufficient motor ability to arrange blocks. Others may have sufficient motor ability but have such slowed responses that timed tests are inappropriate estimates of their abilities. Yet others may be able to respond quickly but expend so much energy that they cannot sustain their efforts throughout the test. Not only are test results invalid in such instances, the use of such test results is proscribed by federal law.

Normative Comparisons

Norm-referenced tests are standardized on groups of individuals, and the performance of the person assessed is compared with the performance of the norm group. To the extent that the test was administered to the student differently than the way it was administered to the norm group, you must be very careful in interpreting the results. Adaptations of measures require changing either stimulus presentation or response requirements. The adaptation may make the test items easier or harder, and it may change the construct being measured. Although qualitative or criterion-referenced interpretations of such test performances are often acceptable, norm-referenced comparisons can be flawed. *Standards for Educational and Psychological Testing* (American Educational Research Association, American Psychological Association, & National Council on Measurement in Education, 1999), a joint publication of three professional associations, specifies that, when tests are adapted, it is important that there is validity evidence for the change that is made. Otherwise, it is important to describe the change when reporting the score and to use caution in score interpretation.

Appropriateness of the Level of the Items

In earlier chapters, we pointed out that tests are developed for students who are in specific age ranges or who have a particular range of skills. One issue to be decided regarding participation and accommodation is the extent to which a student can and should be given an *out-of-level test* (one intended for use with younger students). Assessors are tempted to give out-of-level tests when an age-appropriate test contains either an insufficient number of easy items or not enough easy items for the student being assessed. Of course, when out-of-level tests are given and norm-referenced interpretations are made, the students are compared with a group of students who differ from them. We have no idea how same-age or same-grade students would perform on the given test. Out-of-level testing may be appropriate to locate a student's current level of educational performance or to evaluate the effectiveness of instruction with a student who is instructed out of grade level. It is inappropriate for accountability purposes.

Exposure to the Curriculum Being Tested (Opportunity to Learn)

One of the issues of fairness raised by the general public is the administration of tests that contain material that students have not had an opportunity to learn. This same issue applies to the making of accommodation decisions. Students with sensory impairments have not had an opportunity to learn the content of test items that use verbal or auditory stimuli. Students receiving special education services who have not had adequate access to the general education curriculum have not had the same opportunity to master the general education curriculum.

To the extent that students have not had an opportunity to learn the content of the test (that is, they were absent when the content was taught, the content is not taught in the schools in which they were present, or the content was taught in ways that were not effective for the student), they probably will not perform well on the test. Their performance will reflect more a lack of opportunity to learn than limited skill and ability. Addressing this issue is especially challenging when students have been raised and educated in cultures that differ quite markedly from the culture of the test developer.

Environmental Considerations

Students should be tested in settings in which they can demonstrate maximal performance. If students cannot easily gain access to a testing setting, this may diminish their performance. Tests always should be given in settings that students with disabilities can access with ease. The settings should also be quiet enough to minimize distractibility. And because fatigue is an issue, tests should be given in multiple short sessions (broken up with breaks) so students do not become overly tired.

Legal Considerations

By law, students with disabilities have a right to be included in assessments, and accommodations in testing should be made in order to enable them to participate. This legal argument is derived largely from the Fourteenth Amendment to the U.S. Constitution (which guarantees the right to equal protection and to due process of law). The Individuals with Disabilities Education Act (IDEA) guarantees the right to education and to due process. Also, Section 504 of the Rehabilitation Act of 1973 indicates that it is illegal to exclude people from participation solely because of a disability.

The Americans with Disabilities Act of 1992 mandates that all individuals must have access to exams used to provide credentials or licenses. Agencies administering tests must provide either auxiliary aids or modifications to enable individuals with disabilities to participate in assessment, and these agencies may not charge the individual for costs incurred in making special provisions. Adaptations that may be provided include an architecturally accessible testing site, a distraction-free space, or an alternative location; test schedule variation or extended time; the use of a scribe, sign language interpreter, reader, or adaptive equipment; and modifications of the test presentation or response format.

The 1997 IDEA mandates that states include students with disabilities in their statewide assessment systems. The necessary accommodations are to be provided to enable students to participate. By July 2000, states were to have available alternate assessments. These are to be used by students who are unable to participate in the regular assessment even with accommodations. Alternate assessments are substitute ways of gathering data, often by means of portfolios or performance measures. The No Child Left Behind Act of 2001 included a requirement that states report annually on the performance and progress of all students, and this principle was reiterated in the 2004 reauthorization of the IDEA.

Recommendations for Making Participation Decisions

Students with disabilities routinely are included in testing to make screening and eligibility decisions. Our discussion of participation in testing is specific to participation in large-scale assessments. Elliott, Thurlow, and Ysseldyke (1996) indicate that states should have clear written guidelines for students' participation in assessments. They offer criteria for judging the adequacy of the guidelines. We reproduce these criteria below, modified to reflect the fact that school personnel must decide how students are to participate rather than whether they are to participate.

- The guidelines should include the premise that all students, including those with disabilities, are to participate in state or district accountability systems.
- Decisions about how students participate should be made by a person or group who knows the student.
- Decisions about how students participate should be based on the student's current level of functioning and learning characteristics.
- There should be a form listing variables to consider in making participation decisions.
- The kind of test a student is to take should be documented on his or her individualized education plan (IEP).
- Students must participate in an assessment if they receive any instruction on the content assessed, regardless of where instruction occurs.
- Decisions about how students participate should not be based on program setting, category of disability, or percentage of time spent in general education classrooms.
- Decisions about how students participate should allow some students to participate either in an alternate assessment or in part of a regular assessment.
- The guidelines should specify that only a small percentage of students with disabilities are allowed to participate in an alternate assessment (1 to 3 percent).
- Parents should understand the participation options and the implications of their child's not being included in an assessment or accountability system.
- Decisions about how students participate should be documented on the student's IEP.

Current Practice in Testing Accommodations

Practice in making test accommodations runs the gamut from permitting no adaptations and requiring that any students who are included in local, state, and national assessments take standard versions of tests being used, to allowing extensive alternative assessment procedures. Thurlow and Bolt (2001) have identified the kinds of accommodations states permit for their statewide assessments. These are listed in Table 9.1. Note that some of the accommodations involve changes in the way the test is presented, some are changes in response format, others are setting accommodations, and still others involve relaxing time constraints. Major testing organizations (such as the Educational Testing Service [ETS], the developers responsible for administration of the SAT and the Graduate Record Exam [GRE]; and the American College Testing Program, developers of the ACT) permit limited accommodations and require documentation of eligibility for accommodations. Reviewers from these testing programs examine individual requests for accommodations and decide which accommodations the student can use and still receive a valid score. Not all accommodations that students receive in school are considered valid among these testing programs.

Increasingly, states are permitting accommodations and aggregating the scores for students who receive them with all other students' test scores. Thurlow (2001) reports the results of a survey of state practices in permitting test accommodations. All states have written policies guiding the provision of assessment accommodations, yet the kinds of accommodations permitted in one state may be denied in a neighboring state.

| TABLE 9.1 | Most Frequently Allowed Accommodations in State Policies |

	Number of States Allowing Accommodation	
Accommodation	*With or Without Limitations*	*Without Limitations*
Individual administration	44	44
Dictate response to proctor/scribe	43	32
Small-group administration	41	41
Large print	40	38
Braille	38	33
Extended time	37	32
Interpreter for instructions	36	34
Read/reread/simplify/clarify directions	35	31
Computer/machine response	34	28
Read aloud	34	4
Mark answers test booklet	33	28
Testing with breaks	33	28

SOURCE: Thurlow, M. L., & Bolt, S. (2001). *Empirical support for accommodations most often allowed in state policy* (Synthesis Report 41). Minneapolis: University of Minnesota, National Center on Educational Outcomes.

Test publishers now are moving to build "universally designed assessments," which are assessments that are designed and developed from the beginning to be accessible and valid for the widest range of students, including students with disabilities and English-language learners. The concept of universal design is derived from work on making environments universally accessible (use of curb cutouts, access ramps to buildings, among others). Publishers work to

- provide very precise and explicit descriptions of what the test measures.
- eliminate items (such as color) that make use of accommodations impossible.
- field-test with a wide range of students, including those who use accommodations.

Recommendations for Making Accommodation Decisions

There are major debates about the kinds of accommodations that ought to be permitted in testing. There are also major arguments about the extent to which accommodations in testing destroy the technical adequacy of tests.

Making Decisions About Individuals

The issues in making accommodation decisions extend to more than screening and accountability. In fact, they play a major role in decisions about exceptionality, special need, eligibility, and instructional planning. We think there are some reasonable guidelines for best practice in making decisions about individuals.

- Conduct all assessments in the student's native language or mode of communication. The mode of communication is that normally used by the person (such as sign language, Braille, or oral communication). Loeding and Crittenden (1993, p. 19) point out that, for students who are deaf, the primary communication mode is either a visual-spatial, natural sign language used by members of the American Deaf Community called American Sign Language (ASL), or a manually coded form of English, such as Signed English, Pidgin Sign English, Seeing Essential English, Signing Exact English, or Sign-Supported Speech/English. Therefore, they argue, "traditional paper-and-pencil tests are inaccessible, invalid and inappropriate to the deaf student because the tests are written in English only."
- Make accommodations in format when the purpose of testing is not substantially impaired. It should be demonstrated that the accommodations assist the individual in responding but do not provide content assistance (for example, a scribe should record the response of the person being tested—not interpret what the person says, include his or her additional knowledge, and then record a response).
- With students who are deaf, use multimedia-based assessments that employ videodisk, CD-ROM, CD-1, or digital video interactive technology. A videodisk-based assessment designed for individuals with hearing impairments is

currently at the prototype stage and has been developed for a portion of the Scholastic Aptitude Test. The prototype makes both ASL and English-order signs available.

■ Make normative comparisons only with groups whose membership includes students with background sets of experiences and opportunities like those of the students being tested.

Making Decisions About Groups   Many recommendations can be implemented when collecting assessment data to make decisions about groups of students. Among these are the following, suggested by Thurlow, Elliott, and Ysseldyke (2003):

■ States and districts should have written guidelines for the use of accommodations in large-scale assessments used for accountability purposes.

■ Decisions about accommodations should be made by one or more persons who know the student, including the student's strengths and weaknesses.

■ Decision makers should consider the student's learning characteristics and the accommodations currently used during classroom instruction and classroom testing.

■ The student's category of disability or program setting does not influence the decision.

■ The goal is to ensure that accommodations have been used by the student prior to their use in an assessment—generally, in the classroom during instruction and in classroom testing situations. New accommodations should not be introduced for the district or statewide assessment.

■ The decision is made systematically, using a form that lists questions to answer or variables to consider in making the accommodation decision. Ideally, classroom data on the effects of accommodations are part of the information entered into decisions. Decisions and the reasons for them should be noted on the form.

■ Decisions about accommodations should be documented on the student's IEP.

■ Parents should be involved in the decision by either participating in the decision-making process or being given the analysis of the need for accommodations and by signing the form that indicates accommodations that are to be used.[1]

---

1. Adapted from Thurlow, Elliott, & Ysseldyke (2003), pp. 46–47, with permission.

SUMMARY

Education legislation mandates high standards for all students. It also mandates that all students, including those with disabilities and limited English proficiency, participate in assessments to ascertain the extent to which those high standards are being met. This chapter outlined recommendations for making decisions about how students should participate in assessments. We recommended that students with disabilities should be included in test development and should take tests, and that any reports of results of pupil performance should include reports on how students with disabilities performed.

To enable students with disabilities to participate in assessments, certain accommodations will be necessary. We outlined a set of recommendations for making accommodations in assessments. The most important principle to keep in mind is that assessment accommodation decisions should be made carefully, taking into consideration the student's individual needs, the test purpose, the accommodations the student receives during instruction, and the skills the test is intended to measure. Students should not, on the day of testing, suddenly be given accommodations they have never previously experienced.

QUESTIONS FOR CHAPTER REVIEW

1. What major factors have served as an impetus for increased participation of students with disabilities in large-scale state and national assessments?

2. We have recommended a set of practices for including students with disabilities in assessments. What can teachers and other school personnel do to ensure that participation happens?

3. Why is it important that there be an alignment between the classroom and assessment accommodations that a student receives?

PROJECT

Obtain several of the reports that ETS has provided on testing accommodations for the SAT and the GRE. Identify the criteria that ETS uses to decide whether an accommodation is appropriate. Examine the instructions accompanying these assessments to determine what documentation is needed in making these decisions.

RESOURCES FOR FURTHER INVESTIGATION

Print Resources

Bielinski, J., Ysseldyke, J. E., Bolt, S., Friedebach, M., & Friedebach, J. (2001). Prevalence of accommodations for students with disabilities participating in a statewide testing system. *Assessment for Effective Intervention, 26*(2), 21–28.

Elliott, J. L., Thurlow, M. L., & Ysseldyke, J. E. (1996). *Assessment guidelines that maximize the participation of students with disabilities in large-scale assessments.* Minneapolis: University of Minnesota, National Center on Educational Outcomes.

Thurlow, M. L., Elliott, J. L., & Ysseldyke, J. E. (2003). *Testing students with disabilities: Practical strategies for complying with district and state requirements.* Thousand Oaks, CA: Corwin Press.

Thurlow, M. L., House, A. L., Scott, D. L., & Ysseldyke, J. E. (2000). Students with disabilities in large-scale assessments: State participation and accommodation policies. *Journal of Special Education, 34*(3), 154–163.

Thurlow, M. L., & Thompson, S. (2004). *2003 state special education outcomes.* Minneapolis: University of Minnesota, National Center on Educational Outcomes.

Thurlow, M. L., & Ysseldyke, J. E. (2002). *Including students with disabilities in assessments.* Washington, DC: National Education Association.

Tindal, G., & Fuchs, L. (1999). *A summary of research on test changes: An empirical basis for determining testing accommodations.* Lexington, KY: University of Kentucky, Mid-South Regional Resource Center.

Ysseldyke, J. E., Thurlow, M. L., Bielinski, J., House, A., Moody, M., & Haigh, J. (2001). The relationship between instructional and assessment accommodations in an inclusive state accountability system. *Journal of Learning Disabilities, 34*(3), 212–220.

Technology Resources

FAIRNESS IN PERFORMANCE ASSESSMENT
www.uncg.edu/\\7,126\\ericcas2/assessment/diga25.html

This home page contains an article by Tony C. M. Lam about bias and fairness in assessment. The author describes the extent to which using performance assessment helps to minimize bias in testing.

SPECIAL EDUCATION RESOURCES
www.geocities.com/Wellesley/9641/sped.html

This home page offers suggestions for adapting tests to students with visual impairments or with severe disabilities.

ERIC CLEARINGHOUSE ON DISABILITIES AND GIFTED EDUCATION
ericec.org

From this website one can search the database for literature, information, and resources on education and development of individuals who are disabled and/or gifted. It includes links to the U.S. Department of Education and the federal regulations for the IDEA amendments of 1997.

NATIONAL CENTER ON EDUCATIONAL OUTCOMES
education.umn.edu/NCEO/accommodations/default.aspx

The website for the National Center on Educational Outcomes at the University of Minnesota includes this site, which is a searchable database on empirical research on the effects of testing accommodations.

STUDENTS WITH DISABILITIES AND STATEWIDE ASSESSMENT
www.dpi.state.wi.us/dpi/disea/een/index.html

This is the website for the Special Education Team of the Wisconsin Department of Public Instruction. It includes links to sites on students with disabilities and statewide assessment, and federal data collection, among others.

CHAPTER 10

Testing Students with Limited English Proficiency

THE ASSESSMENT OF STUDENTS WHO HAVE LIMITED ENGLISH PROFICIENCY (LEP) IS A particularly difficult task for educators and psychologists. The overwhelming majority of classroom and commercially prepared tests are administered in English. Students who do not speak or read English cannot access the content and respond verbally to these tests. For example, suppose Lupe does not understand English but is given an intelligence test; she might be asked, "What is a sled?" or "What is an orange?" She would not understand the questions, although she might be able to define these words. Similarly, she might respond, "¿Que?" and the examiner might not understand that she was asking, "What?" Obviously, this test is not valid for Lupe; it measures her proficiency in English, not her intelligence.

Testing students with limited English proficiency is not just about their knowing the language of a test. It is also about demographics and linguistic and cultural development. A student with limited English proficiency may speak some English. However, knowing enough English for some social conversation is not the same as knowing enough English for instruction or for the nuances of highly abstract concepts. Moreover, many students with limited English proficiency may come from a culture that is very different from the public culture of the United States. As a result, whenever a test item relies on a student's cultural knowledge to test some other area of achievement or aptitude, the test will necessarily be invalid because it will also test the student's knowledge of American culture. In this chapter, we discuss social, political, and demographic issues that complicate the assessment process, as well as how to assess students with limited English proficiency.

The Diversity of Students with Limited Proficiency in English

According to the 2000 census, large numbers of individuals do not speak English. Table 10.1 shows the 50 languages most frequently spoken by these individuals and the number of speakers of each of these languages. For 60 percent of these individuals, Spanish is the language of the home.

The number of different languages and the distribution of speakers of those languages cause problems for test makers and testers. First, because there are many languages with relatively few LEP speakers, it would be unprofitable for test publishers to develop and norm test versions in these languages. Second, it is unlikely that there would be many bilingual psychologists and teachers able to

TABLE 10.1   Fifty Most Frequently Spoken Languages Other Than English

Language	Number of Speakers 5 Years and Older	Language	Number of Speakers 5 Years and Older
Spanish	28,100,725	Mandarin	174,550
French / Fr. Creole	2,060,160	Miao, Hmong	168,065
Chinese	1,499,635	Dutch	150,485
German	1,382,615	Laotian	149,305
Tagalog	1,224,240	Panjabi	141,740
Vietnamese	1,009,625	Serbocroatian	130,100
Italian	1,008,370	Ukrainian	129,180
Korean	894,065	Bengali	128,820
Russian	706,240	Thai	120,465
Polish	667,415	Hungarian	117,975
Arabic	614,580	Romanian	114,840
Portuguese	563,835	Telugu	86,165
Japanese	477,995	Formosan	84,590
Greek	365,435	Tamil	83,965
Hindi	317,055	Pennsylvania Dutch	83,720
Persian	312,085	Amharic	82,070
Urdu	262,900	India, n.e.c.	80,240
Cantonese	259,750	Malayalam	79,855
Gujarathi	235,990	Albanian	79,515
Armenian	202,710	Ilocano	75,605
Hebrew	195,375	Turkish	74,130
Mon-Khmer, Cambodian	181,890	Czech	70,500
		Swedish	67,655
Kru, Ibo, Yoruba	179,275	Syriac	62,890
Yiddish	178,945	Croatian	58,390
Navaho	178,015		

SOURCE: Language Spoken at Home for the Citizen Population 18 Years and Over Who Speak English Less Than "Very Well" (STP194), 2000 Census of Population. Washington, DC: U.S. Bureau of the Census.

use foreign-language versions of those tests even if they were available. Finally, the students within the same language group might not be culturally homogeneous. For example, there are French speakers from Montreal and French speakers from Port-au-Prince; there are Russian speakers from Kazakhstan and Russian speakers from Belarus; and so forth. Students speaking the same language do not necessarily share a culture and a history.

Although the number of Spanish-speaking students with limited English proficiency is large enough to make it profitable for test publishers to develop Spanish-language versions of their tests, Spanish-speaking students are not a homogeneous group either. In the United States, about 66 percent of the Spanish speakers are of Mexican descent, about 14 percent are of Central or South American descent, about 9 percent are of Cuban descent, and about 4 percent are of Puerto Rican descent (Therrien & Ramirez, 2000).[1] Moreover, Spanish-speaking students of Mexican descent include those born in East Los Angeles and those who emigrated from Mexico; Spanish-speaking students of Puerto Rican descent include those born in New York City and those from San Juan. Spanish speakers from Central or South America may speak a Native American language (for example, Quechua) in addition to Spanish. Thus because students speak Spanish does not mean that they share a culture and a history with everyone else in the United States for whom Spanish is the first and primary language.

Finally, there are political and social differences among students with limited English proficiency, and these differences affect their learning of English and the culture of the United States. Regardless of the language they speak, how the students and their parents came to the United States has social and political implications. Some students are immigrants or the children of immigrants who intend to make the United States their new home. Some immigrants are simply seeking a better life in the United States, whereas others are fleeing repressive governments. Some have arrived at JFK or LAX by jet; others have negotiated the Straits of Florida on a raft to arrive in Miami. Some come with or join extended families; others come alone or with one parent.

Some parents of these students embrace the culture and ideals of the United States, and English is likely to eventually become their primary language educationally and socially. Other parents are short-term visitors to the country. For example, they may be the children of graduate students attending U.S. colleges and universities, of businesspeople working for foreign corporations, of diplomats, of individuals seeking political asylum—all of whom intend to return permanently to their homeland in the future. For these students, U.S. culture is more likely to be seen as something to understand rather than something to be embraced, and assimilation into U.S. culture may actually be disadvantageous. English is likely to be their temporary instructional language, whereas their first language is stressed in their home.

---

1. The figure of 9 percent excludes people living on the island of Puerto Rico.

Finally, some students are the descendants of people who were neither immigrants nor visitors, but who were living on lands captured or purchased by the U.S. government—for example, many Native Americans, Pacific Islanders, and Mexican Americans. These students and their parents can have attitudes toward English and U.S. culture that run the gamut from wanting to assimilate, to having multiple national or ethnic identities, to continuing resistance to the U.S. government by rejecting English and American culture.

U.S. policy toward individuals with limited English proficiency has evolved over the last 35 years. Prior to the mid-1960s, a number of practices were accepted that today would be considered illegal and repugnant. Voter registration in some states required potential voters to pass a literacy test, and these tests were sometimes used to disfranchise minority voters. Native American students were punished for speaking their first language during recess. One particularly offensive punishment was washing their mouths out with soap—as if their language consisted of dirty words. More pertinent to this text, students with limited English proficiency were routinely tested in English to ascertain whether they had mental retardation. When they could not pass the intelligence test in English, they were placed in segregated special education classes.

Today the United States officially celebrates the diversity of its citizenry, and we are a collage of ethnic music, dance, art, and food. Officially, the United States welcomes visitors and immigrants, but unofficially acceptance is neither all encompassing nor embraced by all citizens. For example, most Americans reject cultural practices that limit opportunities for women or that sexually mutilate girls.

In addition, although the state and federal governments champion diversity, it is the local communities that must pay for the services needed to make diversity workable. The federal government controls immigration, but local school districts must bear the added costs of educating students who have limited English proficiency.

In many ways, the debate about how to deal with LEP students is a debate about the very nature of who we are as a country. This debate lurks at the edges of discussions about assessing students with limited English proficiency. Although we acknowledge this debate, in this chapter we shall try, to the extent possible, to avoid the political and social issues surrounding the assessment of students with limited English proficiency. Instead, we first focus on legal and linguistic considerations in testing students with limited proficiency in English. Then we turn to approaches to testing these students. Finally, we discuss situational factors that can come into play when testing some students with limited English proficiency.

Legal Protections in Testing

Parents and their children with disabilities and limited proficiency in English have certain legal protections. These protections are designed to assure that students receive fair and appropriate assessments.

Protections for Students Being Assessed

The fundamental principle when assessing students with limited English proficiency is to assure that the assessment materials and procedures used actually assess students' target knowledge, skill, or ability, not their inability (or limited ability) to understand and use English. For example, suppose that Antonio cannot answer a word problem involving 2 two-digit addends and one extraneous fact (also a two-digit number). To what does the tester attribute Antonio's failure—lack of skill in adding numbers or inability to read English? Antonio must have sufficient knowledge of English in order for the tester to rule out his failure as a lack of proficiency in English.

Clearly, the intent of the Individuals with Disabilities Education Act (IDEA) and all other pertinent court decisions is to assess students' achievement and abilities unbiased by their limited proficiency in English. The principal rationale for protecting students with limited English proficiency during the assessment process can be found in the IDEA. As §300.532(a)(2) states, "Materials and procedures used to assess a child with limited English proficiency [must be] selected and administered to ensure that they measure the extent to which the child has a disability and needs special education, rather than measuring the child's English language skills." To accomplish this goal, tests must be selected and administered in such a way that they are not racially or culturally discriminatory. Indeed, to the extent feasible, tests and evaluation materials must be administered in the student's native language or other mode of communication. This principle is echoed in §300.534(b) of the IDEA, which forbids a student to be identified as in need of special educational services if the determining factor is limited proficiency in English.

However, it is important to note that, if the goal of assessment is to ascertain a student's current level of functioning in English, then it is appropriate to test the student in English. If the student cannot decode the words in a passage written in English, then the student cannot decode the passage written in English. If a student cannot comprehend the meaning of the individual words in a passage written in English, then the student cannot comprehend the meaning of that passage. The assessment has provided an indication of the student's current ability to use English.

Protections for Parents in the Assessment Process

Parents are the principal advocates for their children within the educational system, and the IDEA contains a number of protections for them as well, especially in terms of notice, participation, and consent. For example, §300.503(b) requires that parents receive prior notice if the school intends to initiate or change their child's identification as a student with a disability. That notice must "be provided in the native language of the parent or other mode of communication used by the parent, unless it is clearly not feasible to do so." Although notice is usually in written form, the IDEA also provides that interpreters be used if the native language or mode of communication of the parent is not written language. Parents must be given notice of their procedural safeguards. This notice must be in the parents' native language or other mode of communication if they do not understand English (§300.504[c]). Schools must take steps to make sure that the parents of a student with a disability have the opportunity to participate in team meetings. To that end, §300.345(e) requires the use of interpreters or other appropriate measures "for parents with deafness or whose native language is other than English." In those instances when parental consent is required (for example, to conduct an initial assessment of a student), that consent must be given in the parents' native language or mode of communication (§300.500[b][1]).

Linguistic Considerations

To assess students' knowledge, skills, or abilities rather than their proficiency in the language of the test, students must have sufficient fluency in the language of the test to allow valid assessment. Although this proposition is logical and quite easy to say, the hard part is in the doing.

Bilingual Students   "Bilingual" implies equal proficiency in two languages. Nevertheless, young children must learn which language to use with specific people. For example, they may be able to switch between English and Spanish with their siblings, speak only Spanish with their grandparents, and use only English with their older sister's husband, who still has not learned Spanish. Although children can switch between languages, sometimes in mid-sentence, they are seldom truly bilingual.

When students grow up in a home where two languages are spoken, they are seldom equally competent or comfortable in using both languages, regardless of the context or situation. These students tend to prefer one language or the other for specific situations or contexts. For example, Spanish may be spoken at home and in the neighborhood, whereas English is spoken at school. Moreover, when two languages are spoken in the home, the family may develop a hybrid language borrowing a little from each. For example, in Spanish *caro* means "dear," and *car* in English means "automobile." In some bilingual homes (and communities), *caro* comes to mean "automobile." These speakers may not be speaking "proper" Spanish or English, although they have no problem communicating.

These factors enormously complicate the testing of bilingual students. Some bilingual students may understand academic questions better in English, but the language in which they answer can vary. If the content was learned in English, they may be better able to answer in English. However, if the answer calls for a logical explanation or an integration of information, they may be better able to answer in their other language. Finally, it cannot be emphasized strongly enough that language dominance is not the same as language competence for testing purposes. Because a student knows more Spanish than English does not mean that the student knows enough Spanish to be tested in that language.

English as a Second Language

It is critical to distinguish between social/interpersonal uses of language and cognitive/academic uses. Students learning English as a second language usually need at least two years to develop social and interpersonal communication skills. However, they require five to six years to develop language sufficient for cognitive and academic proficiency (Cummins, 1984). Thus, after even three or four years of schooling, students who demonstrate few problems with English usage in social situations still probably lack sufficient language competence to be tested in English.

At least three factors can affect the time required for students to attain cognitive and academic sufficiency in English.

1. *Age.* Young children are programmed to learn language. Somewhere around 12 to 14 years of age, learning another language becomes much more difficult. Thus, all things being equal, one should expect younger students to acquire English faster than older students.

2. *Immersion in English.* The more contexts in which English is used, the faster will be its acquisition. Thus a student's learning of English as a second language will depend in part on the language the parents speak at home. If the native language is spoken at home, progress in English will be slower. This creates a dilemma for parents who want their children to learn (or remember) their first language and also learn English.

3. *Similarity to English.* Languages can vary along several dimensions. The phonology may be different. The 44 speech sounds of English may be the same or different from the speech sounds of other languages. For example, Xhosa (an African language) has three different click sounds; English has none. English lacks the sound equivalent of the Spanish *ñ*, the Portuguese *-nh*, and the Italian *-gn*. The orthography may be different. English uses the Latin alphabet. Other languages may use different alphabets (for example, Cyrillic) or no alphabet (Mandarin). English does not use diacritical marks; other languages do. The letter-sound correspondences may be different. The letter *h* is silent in Spanish but pronounced as an English *r* in one Brazilian dialect. The grammar may be different. Whereas English tends to be noun dominated, other languages tend to be verb dominated. Word order varies. Adjectives precede nouns in English, but they follow nouns in Spanish. The more language features the second language has in common with the first language, the easier it is to learn the second language.

Alternative Ways to Test Students with Limited English Proficiency

Four basic approaches have been used to test students whose English is sufficiently limited to make testing in English inappropriate: engaging in denial, using nonverbal tests, testing in the student's native language, and not testing at all. The strengths and weaknesses of each of these approaches are discussed.

Engage in Denial   A common procedure is to pretend that a student has sufficient proficiency to be tested in English. Denial is frequently accompanied by self-delusion or coercion. Self-delusion manifests itself when the tester talks with the student and believes that the student's adequate social language indicates sufficient academic language to be tested in English. Coercion is present when the tester's supervisor insists that the student be tested. Sometimes denial is only denial; in this case, the tester admits that the student's language may have somewhat limited his or her ability to take the test.

Use Nonverbal Tests   Several nonverbal tests are available for testing intelligence. This type of test is believed to reduce the effects of language and culture on the assessment of intellectual abilities. (Nonverbal tests do not, however, completely eliminate the effects of language and culture.) Some tests (see the chapter "Assessment of Intelligence: Individual Tests") do not require a student to speak—for example, the performance subscale of the third edition of the Wechsler Intelligence Scale for Children. However, these tests frequently have directions in English. Some tests (for example, the Comprehensive Test of Nonverbal Intelligence) allow testers to use either oral or pantomime directions. A few tests are exclusively nonverbal (for example, the Leiter International Performance Scale) and do not require language for directions or responses.

Because students' skills in language comprehension usually precede their skills in language production, performance tests with oral directions might be useful with some students. However, the testers should have objective evidence that a student sufficiently comprehends academic language for the test to be valid, and such evidence is generally not available. Tests that do not rely on oral directions or responses are more useful because they do not make any assumptions about students' language competence. However, other validity issues cloud the use of performance tests in the schools. For example, the nature of the tasks on nonverbal intelligence tests is usually less related to success in school than are the tasks on verbal intelligence tests.

Moreover, some cultural considerations are beyond the scope of directions and responses. For example, the very nature of testing may be more familiar in U.S. culture than in the cultures of other countries. When students are familiar with the testing process, they are likely to perform better. As another example, students from other cultures may respond differently to adults in authority, and these differences may alter estimates of their ability derived from tests. Thus, although performance and nonverbal tests may be a better option than verbal tests administered in English, they are not without problems.

Test in the Student's Native Language   There are several ways to test students using directions and materials in their native language. Commercial tests may have been developed in the student's native language. If such tests are not available, testers may locate a foreign-language version of the test. If foreign-language versions are not available, testers may be able to translate a test from English to the student's native language.

Use Commercially Translated Tests

Several tests are currently available in language versions other than English—most frequently, Spanish. These tests run the gamut from those that are translated, to those that are renormed, to those that are reformatted for another language and culture. The difference among these approaches is significant.

When tests are only translated, we can assume that the child understands the directions and the questions. However, the questions may be of different difficulty in U.S. culture and the English language for two reasons. First, the difficulty of the vocabulary can vary from language to language. For example, reading *cat* in English is different from reading *gato* in Spanish. *Cat* is a three-letter, one-syllable word containing two of the first three letters of the English alphabet; *gato* is a four-letter, two-syllable word with the first, seventh, fifteenth, and twentieth letters of the alphabet. The frequency of *cat* in each language is likely different, as is the popularity of cats as house pets.

The second reason that translated questions may be of different difficulty is that the difficulty of the content can vary from culture to culture because children from different cultures have not had the same opportunity to learn the information. For example, suppose we asked Spanish-speaking students from Venezuela, Cuba, and California who attended school in the United States to identify Simón Bolívar, Ernesto "Che" Guevara, and César Chávez. We could speculate that the three groups of students would probably identify the three men with different degrees of accuracy. The students from California would be most likely to recognize Chávez as an American labor organizer but less frequently recognize Bolívar and Guevara. Students from Venezuela would likely recognize Bolívar as a liberator of South America more often than would students from Cuba and the United States. Students from Cuba would be more likely to recognize Guevara as a revolutionary than would students from the other two countries. Thus the difficulty of test content is embedded in culture.

Also, when tests are translated, we cannot assume that the psychological demands made by test items remain the same. For example, an intelligence test might ask a child to define *peach*. A child from equatorial South America may never have eaten, seen, or heard of a peach, whereas U.S. students are quite likely to have seen and eaten peaches. For U.S. students, the psychological demand of identifying a peach is to recall the biological class and essential characteristics of something they have experienced. For South American children, the item measures their knowledge of an exotic fruit. For American children, the test would measure intelligence; for South American children, the test would measure achievement.

Some of the problems associated with a simple translation of a test can be circumvented if the test is renormed on the target population and items reordered in terms of their translated difficulties. For example, to use the Wechsler Intelligence Scale for Children, third edition, effectively with

Spanish-speaking Puerto Ricans, the test could be normed on a representative sample of Spanish-speaking Puerto Rican students. Based on the performance of the new normative sample, the items could be reordered as necessary. However, renorming and reordering do not reproduce the psychological demands made by test items in English.

Develop and Validate a Version of the Test for Each Cultural/Linguistic Group

Given the problems associated with translations, tests developed in the student's language and culture are clearly preferable to those that are not. For example, suppose one wished to develop a version of the Wechsler Intelligence Scale for Children *para los Niños de Cuba*. Test items could be developed within the Cuban American culture according to the general framework of the Wechsler scale. Specific items might or might not be the same. The new test would then need to be validated. For example, factor-analytic studies could be undertaken to ascertain whether the same four factors underlie the new test (that is, verbal comprehension, perceptual organization, freedom from distractibility, and processing speed).

Although they may be preferable, culture- and language-specific tests are not economically justifiable for test publishers except in the case of the very largest minorities—for example, Spanish-speaking students with quite a bit of U.S. acculturation. The cost of standardizing a test is sizable, and the market for intelligence tests in, for example, Hmong, Ilocano, or Gujarathi is far too small to offset the development costs. For Spanish-speaking students, many publishers offer both English and Spanish versions. Some of these are translations, others are adaptations, and still others are independent tests. Test users must be careful to assess the appropriateness of the Spanish version to make sure that it is culturally appropriate for the test taker.

Use an Interpreter

If the tester is fluent in the student's native language or if a qualified interpreter is available, it is possible (although undesirable) to administer tests that are interpreted for a student with limited English proficiency. Interpretations can occur on an as-needed basis. For example, the tester can translate or interpret directions or test content and answer questions in the student's native language. Although interpretation is an appealing, simple approach, it presents numerous problems. In addition to the problems associated with the commercial availability of translations, the accuracy of the interpretation is unknown.

Do Not Test   Not all educational decisions and not all assessments require testing. For students with limited English proficiency from a variety of cultures, testing is usually a bad idea. Most states include language in their laws or regulations specifying that students must be in school a minimum number of years before they can participate in the state testing program.

Making Entitlement Decisions Without Testing

Lack of progress in learning English is the most common reason students with limited English proficiency are referred to ascertain eligibility for special education (Figueroa, 1990). It seems that most teachers do not understand that it usually takes several years to acquire sufficient fluency to be fully functional academically and cognitively in English. However, the school cannot overlook the possibility that students with limited English proficiency are really handicapped beyond their English abilities.

Determination of disability can be made without psychological or educational testing. The determination of sensory or physical disability can be readily made with the use of interpreters. Students or their parents need little proficiency in English for professionals to determine if a student has a traumatic brain injury, other health impairments, or orthopedic, visual, or auditory disabilities. Disabilities based on impaired social function (such as emotional disturbance and autism) can be identified through direct observation of a student or interviews with family members (using interpreters if necessary), teachers, and so forth.

The appraisal of intellectual ability is required to identify students with mental retardation. When students have moderate to severe forms of mental retardation, it may be possible to determine that they have limited intellectual ability without ever testing. For example, direct observation may reveal that a student has not acquired language (either English or the native language), communicates only by pointing and making grunting noises, is not toilet trained, and engages in inappropriate play whether judged by standards of the primary culture or by standards of U.S. culture. The student's parents may recognize that the student is much slower than their other children and would be judged to have mental retardation in their native culture. In this case, parents may want special educational services for their child. In such a situation, identification would not be impeded by the student's (or parents') lack of English. However, students with mild mental retardation do not demonstrate such pronounced developmental delays; rather, their disability is relative and not easily separated from their limited proficiency in English.

The identification of students with specific learning disabilities seems impossible. The IDEA (§300.541) requires that an imperfect ability to listen, think, speak, read, write, spell, or do mathematical calculations be considered indicative of a specific learning disability only if the student has been "provided with learning experiences appropriate for the child's age and ability levels" and the discrepancy between ability and achievement is not the result of cultural disadvantage. Clearly, these conditions cannot be met for students with limited English proficiency, especially when the students are also culturally diverse.

Finally, limited English proficiency should not be considered a speech or language impairment. Although it is quite possible for a student with limited English to have a speech or language impairment, that impairment would also be present in the student's native language. Speakers of the student's native language, such as the student's parents, could verify the presence of stuttering, impaired articulation, or voice impairments; the identification of a language disorder would require a fluent speaker of the child's native language.

When it is not possible to determine whether a student has a disability, students with limited English proficiency who are experiencing academic difficulties still need to have services besides special education available. Districts should have programs in English as a second language (ESL) which could continue to help students after they have acquired social communication skills.

Other Considerations in Testing Students with Limited English Proficiency

Testing in English is not a problem if the purpose of testing is to ascertain a student's progress in learning English. However, when other types of tests are given, the performances of students with limited English proficiency must be interpreted with great care. Factors other than the skill or ability being assessed by the test may well affect a student's test performance.

Assessing Classroom Achievement

Interpreting the results of achievement in areas other than English is problematic. First, teachers must be especially sensitive to the distinction between achievement and attainment. Students with limited English proficiency, especially those not born in the United States, are unlikely to have learned the same things incidentally as have native-born English speakers. Rather, they are dependent on what they have been taught in school. Thus teachers must be very careful to test what they have taught.

Second, teachers should expect less fluency and greater latency of responses from students with limited English proficiency. It takes quite a while before students are able to think in English. Therefore, students who are still acquiring English will translate the English material into their native language, process the information, and then translate it back into English. Even when students have become somewhat fluent in English, low-frequency words, cultural references, or new concepts will require them to do background learning—that is, look up the word in English and native-language dictionaries, look up the cultural reference in an encyclopedia, and work through new concepts slowly.

Finally, teachers should allow students with limited English proficiency to demonstrate their understanding of the content of instruction in a variety of ways other than words. Paper-and-pencil tests and oral recitations are unlikely to be as valid as other, less language-based approaches for assessing student progress.

Cultural Considerations Affecting Testing

Cultural factors can complicate the testing of students. In some cultures, children are expected to speak minimally to adults or authority figures; elaboration or extensive verbal output may be seen as disrespectful. In some cultures, answering questions may be seen as self-aggrandizing, competitive, and immodest. These cultural values work against students in most testing situations.

Male-female relations are subject to cultural differences. Female students may be hesitant to speak to male teachers; male students (and their fathers) may not see female teachers as authority figures.

Children may be hesitant to speak to adults from other cultures, and testers may be reluctant to encourage or say no to children whose culture is unfamiliar. It is also well to remember that many French-speaking children with limited English proficiency may have fled the strife in Haiti or that many Spanish-speaking children with limited English proficiency may have fled repression in Cuba or civil strife in Peru, Nicaragua, El Salvador, or Colombia. These children may have been traumatized by the civil strife and therefore be wary of or frightened by strangers.

It may be difficult for an examiner to establish rapport with a student who has limited English proficiency. Some evidence suggests that children do better with examiners of the same race and cultural background (Fuchs & Fuchs, 1989).

Immigrant students and their families may have little experience with the types of testing done in U.S. schools. Consequently, these students may lack test-taking skills. Finally, doing well on tests may not be as valued within the first cultures of immigrant students.

SUMMARY

About 2 percent of U.S. schoolchildren lack sufficient knowledge of English to participate meaningfully in general education programs. When these students have or are thought to have disabilities, they have numerous legal protections that include being tested in their native language and not having their limited proficiency in English be the determining factor in special education placement. Moreover, when parents have limited English proficiency, they are entitled to various legal protections, such as notices and consent given in the parents' native language or mode of communication.

Students learning English as a second language usually need five to six years to develop language sufficient for cognitive and academic proficiency. However, three factors can affect the time required for students to attain cognitive and academic sufficiency in English: the age of the student, the student's immersion in English, and the similarity between English and the first language.

There are numerous approaches to testing students with limited English proficiency. A tester may engage in denial and use English-language tests—an inappropriate option. A tester may use nonverbal tests. A tester may use a commercially translated version of a test. A tester may use a test developed in the student's native language or culture. A tester who speaks the student's language may translate or interpret a test. Finally, a tester can seek alternatives to testing—for example, interviewing parents and teachers, conducting observations, and relying on medical findings.

When teachers can test students with limited English proficiency, they must understand that these students may not have acquired information incidentally as have native-born English speakers. Moreover, teachers should expect slower responses. Finally, teachers must be sensitive to potential cultural differences in the ways in which students respond to teachers.

QUESTIONS FOR CHAPTER REVIEW

1. For 30 minutes, watch a television station broadcasting in a language that you do not speak. Do you see any differences in the social aspects of communication (such as loudness, distance between speakers, facial expressions, and gestures)?

2. Read a recent magazine article about politics in the United States. List the references to people and events that are mentioned but not explained in the article. How would you explain who these people are or what the events were to a recent immigrant with limited proficiency in English?

3. What are the advantages and disadvantages of having immigrants or citizens who have limited proficiency in English or do not speak English at all?

4. Name three approaches to testing LEP students. What are the advantages and disadvantages of each approach?

PROJECT

Obtain a test that has a version for use with students speaking a language other than English. Ascertain if the authors treated all speakers of the test's language as culturally similar or how the authors accounted for potential cultural differences in test content. Evaluate if the reliability and validity of English and non-English versions are comparable.

RESOURCES FOR FURTHER INVESTIGATION

Print Resources

American Educational Research Association, American Psychological Association, & National Council on Measurement in Education. (1999). *Standards for educational and psychological testing* (pp. 91–100). Washington, DC: American Educational Research Association.

Bentz, J., & Pavri, S. (2000). Curriculum-based measurement in assessing bilingual students: A promising new direction. *Diagnostique, 25*(3), 229–248.

Gersten, R., & Baker, S. (2000). What we know about effective instructional practices for English-language learners. *Exceptional Children, 66*(4), 454–470.

Technology Resources

ASSESSMENT OF CULTURALLY AND LINGUISTICALLY DIVERSE STUDENTS
ericec.org/digests/e604.html
This page contains an article by Jane Burnette about the assessment of culturally and linguistically diverse students for special education eligibility.

ERIC CLEARINGHOUSE ON ASSESSMENT AND EVALUATION
www.ericae.net/faqs
This website provides balanced information concerning educational assessment. Go to Frequently Asked Questions (FAQs) under the Resources link to find information about bilingual special education assessment.

NATIONAL INFORMATION CENTER FOR CHILDREN AND YOUTH WITH DISABILITIES
www.kidsource.com/NICHCY/index.html
This is the home page for the National Information Center for Children and Youth with Disabilities. Under

Assessing Children for the Presence of a Disability, there is information about assessing students who are culturally or linguistically diverse.

RESOURCES ON LIMITED ENGLISH PROFICIENCY AND ENGLISH SKILLS
www.4teachers.org/profd/lep.shtml
High Plains Regional Technology in Education Consortium's website provides information for teachers on a variety of topics related to teaching children with limited English proficiency.

NO CHILD LEFT BEHIND
www.ed.gov/policy/elsec/leg/esea02/pg40.html
This site presents the legal requirements for educating students with limited English proficiency under No Child Left Behind, Title III, Part A, English Language Acquisition, Language Enhancement, and Academic Achievement Act.

PART 3

Assessment in Classrooms

The development of assessment has *never* been static, and its improvement has seldom been merely incremental. Scientific positivism was embraced by the mental-testing (such as intelligence tests) movement, and objective (scientific) tests gained widespread acceptance during the first half of the twentieth century. By the 1960s, however, experience with the use of norm-referenced, objectively scored tests suggested that they had a variety of technical shortcomings. A subsequent flurry of activity produced norm-referenced tests with greater reliability and substantially better norms. Nonetheless, educators frequently used these tests in inappropriate ways (for example, to plan and evaluate instruction).

As educators learned that these tests could not be used effectively to facilitate many classroom decisions, other assessment procedures were developed. Thus systematic observation procedures, so successful in experimental psychology, were adopted for classroom use. Similarly, there was renewed interest in the development of teacher-made tests. Although systematic observation and teacher-made tests were widely accepted and effectively used, many educators were still dissatisfied with the perceived limitations of these assessment techniques. During the late 1970s and 1980s, interest grew in assessing instruction and what went on in the classroom (rather than student abilities and skills). By the early 1990s, more subjective and qualitative approaches to assessment were advocated and tried.

Educational assessment may appear to have come full circle, but educators have gotten off at different points. Thus today there is no shortage of opinions about how classroom assessments ought to be conducted. Some educators still rely on norm-referenced achievement tests to plan and evaluate instruction; some rely on systematic observation; some rely on teacher-made tests and curriculum-based assessment; some rely on subjective and qualitative judgments to assess classroom learning; and some rely on a combination of approaches.

In Part 3 of this text, we discuss the approaches most likely to be used by classroom teachers. We do not consider these approaches to be informal or unstandardized. They are frequently formal: Students know that they are being assessed and that the assessments count for something. They are also frequently standardized: Students receive the same directions and tasks, and their responses are frequently scored using the same criteria. These approaches to assessment are used most frequently by classroom teachers, but we recognize that some specialists (such as school psychologists and speech and language therapists) may also use these approaches.

Part 3 begins with Chapter 11, on observation, which provides a general overview of basic considerations and good practice. The next chapter (12) deals with assessing the instructional ecology of classrooms. Chapter 13 provides an overview of objective and performance measures constructed by teachers. Chapter 14 provides an overview of an emerging, but controversial, approach to classroom assessment, using student portfolios.

server). These records should, at the minimum, contain a complete description of the behavior and the context in which it occurred.

In this chapter, we stress quantitative approaches to observation. (The chapter "Portfolio Assessment" offers more coverage of qualitative approaches.) Quantitative observation is distinguished by five characteristics: (1) The goal of observation is to measure (for example, count) specific behaviors; (2) the behaviors being observed have been precisely defined previously; (3) before observation, procedures for gathering objective and replicable information about the behavior are developed; (4) the times and places for observation are carefully selected and specified; and (5) the ways in which behavior will be quantified are specified prior to observation.

The major criticism of quantitative approaches is that they may oversimplify the meaning and interpretation of behavior. Despite this criticism, quantitative analysis of behavior has proved to be very useful in developing theory and practice related to the modification of human behavior. Assessment based on quantitative behavioral observation is a topic suitable for an entire text, and only a general overview of good practices for those who develop and use behavioral observations can be provided in this chapter; interested readers are referred to texts by Alberto and Troutman (1999), Salvia and Hughes (1990), and Shapiro and Kratochwill (2000), among others. Readers interested in the statistical bases of measurement procedures used in systematic observation may consult the text by Suen and Ary (1989). Finally, the procedures and concepts discussed in detail in preceding chapters are not explained again here.

Why Do Teachers Observe Behavior?

Humans are always monitoring external events, and the behavior of others is a primary target of our attention. Teachers are constantly monitoring themselves and their students. Sometimes they are just keeping an eye on things to make sure that their classrooms are safe and goal oriented, to anticipate disruptive or dangerous situations, or just to keep track of how things are going in a general sense. Often, teachers notice behavior or situations that seem important and require their attention: The fire alarm has sounded, Harvey has a knife, Betty is asleep, Jo is wandering around the classroom, and so forth. In other situations, often as a result of their general monitoring, teachers look for very specific behavior to observe: social behavior that should be reinforced, attention to task, performance of particular skills, and so forth. Information gained from observation can be used to make academic and social instructional decisions—for example, planning or evaluating instructional programs for individuals or groups of students.

General Considerations

Behavior that is to be analyzed quantitatively can be observed as it occurs (in real time) or by means of devices such as video or audio recorders that can replay, slow down, or speed up records of behavior displays after they have occurred. Observation can be enhanced with equipment (for example, a tele-scope), or it can occur with only the observer's unaided senses.

Observational systems can be classified along two dimensions: (1) obtrusive versus unobtrusive and (2) contrived versus naturalistic. These two dimensions are relatively independent and yield four combinations (such as obtrusive con-trived observation).

Obtrusive Versus Unobtrusive Observation

Observations are obtrusive when it is obvious that another person is observing and recording behavior; for example, the presence of a practicum supervisor in the back of the classroom makes it obvious to student teachers that they are being observed. The presence of observation equipment can signal that someone is observing; for example, a dark, late-model, four-door sedan idling on the side of the road with a radar gun protruding from the driver's window makes it obvi-ous to passing motorists that they are being observed. Something out of place in the environment can lead a person to believe that he or she is being observed; for example, a flickering light and noise coming from behind a mirror in a testing room can tell test takers that there is someone or something behind the mirror watching.

When observations are unobtrusive, the people being observed do not real-ize they are being watched. Observers may pretend that they are not observing or observe from hidden positions. They may use telescopes to watch from afar. They may use hidden cameras and microphones.

Unobtrusive observations are preferable for two reasons. First, people are reluctant to engage in certain types of behavior if another person is looking. Thus, when antisocial, offensive, or illegal behaviors are targeted for assess-ment, observation should be conducted surreptitiously. Behavior of these types tends not to occur if they are overtly monitored. For example, Billy is unlikely to steal Bob's lunch money when the teacher is looking, and Rodney is unlikely to spray-paint gang graffiti on the front doors of the school when other stu-dents are present.

Likewise, if people are being observed, they are reluctant to engage in highly personal behaviors in which they must expose private body parts. In these in-stances, the observer should obtain the permission of the person or the person's guardian before conducting such observations. Moreover, a same-sex observer who does not know the person being observed (and whom the person being ob-served does not know) should conduct the observations.

The second reason that unobtrusive observations are preferable is that the presence of an observer alters the observation situation. Observation can change the behavior of those in the observation situation. For example, when a principal sits in the back of a probationary teacher's classroom to conduct an annual evaluation, both the teacher's and the students' behavior may be affected by the principal's presence. Students may be better behaved or respond more enthusias-tically in the mistaken belief that the principal is there to watch them. The teacher may write on the chalkboard more frequently or give more positive rein-forcement than usual in the belief that the principal values those techniques. Ob-servation also can eliminate other types of behavior. For example, retail stores may mount closed-circuit TV cameras and video monitors in obvious places to let potential thieves know that they are being watched constantly and to try to discourage shoplifting.

When the target behavior is not antisocial, offensive, highly personal, or undesirable, obtrusive observation may be used provided the persons being observed have been desensitized to the observers or equipment. It is fortunate that most people quickly become desensitized to observers in their daily environment—especially if observers make themselves part of the surroundings by avoiding eye contact, not engaging in social interactions, remaining quiet and not moving around, and so forth. Observation and recording can become part of the everyday classroom routine. In any event, assessment should not begin until the persons to be observed are desensitized and are acting in their usual ways.

Contrived Versus Naturalistic Observation

Contrived observations occur when a situation is set up before a student is introduced into it. For example, a playroom may be set up with toys that encourage aggressive play (such as guns or punching-bag dolls) or with items that promote other types of behavior. A child may be given a book and told to go into the room and read or may simply be told to wait in the room. Other adults or children in the situation may be confederates of the observer and may be instructed to behave in particular ways. For example, an older child may be told not to share toys with the child who is the target of the observation, or an adult may be told to initiate a conversation on a specific topic with the target child.

In contrast, naturalistic observations occur in settings that are not contrived. For example, specific toys are not added to or removed from a playroom; the furniture is arranged as it always is arranged.

Defining Behavior

Behavior is usually defined in terms of its topography, its function, and its characteristics. The function that a behavior serves in the environment is not directly observable, whereas the characteristics and topography of behavior can be measured directly with varying degrees of accuracy.

Topography of Behavior

Behavioral topography refers to the way a behavior is performed. For example, suppose the behavior of interest is holding a pencil to write and that we are interested in Patty's topography for that behavior. The topography is readily observable: Patty holds the pencil at a 45-degree angle to the paper, grasped between her thumb and index finger; she supports the pencil with her middle finger; and so forth. Paul's topography for holding a pencil is quite different. Paul holds the pencil between his great toe and second toe so that the point of the pencil is toward the sole of his foot, and so forth.

Function of Behavior

The function of a behavior is the reason a person behaves as he or she does, or the purpose the behavior serves. Obviously, the reason for a behavior cannot be observed; it can only be inferred. Sometimes, a person may offer an explanation of a behavior's function—for example, "I was screaming to make him stop." We can accept the explanation of the behavior's function if it is consistent with the circumstances, or we can reject the explanation of the function when it is not consistent with the circumstances or is unreasonable. Other times, we can infer a behavior's function from its consequences. For example, Johnny stands screaming at the rear door of his house until his mother opens the door; then he runs into the back yard and stops screaming. We might infer that the function of Johnny's screaming is to have the door opened. Behavior typically serves one or more of five functions: (1) social attention or communication; (2) access to tangibles or preferred activities; (3) escape, delay, reduction, or avoidance of aversive tasks or activities; (4) escape or avoidance of other individuals; and (5) internal stimulation (Carr, 1994).

Measurable Characteristics of Behavior

The measurement of behavior, whether individual behavior or a category of behavior, is based on four characteristics: duration, latency, frequency, and amplitude. These characteristics can be measured directly (see Shapiro and Kratochwill, 2000).

Duration

Behaviors that have discrete beginnings and endings may be assessed in terms of their *duration*—that is, the length of time a behavior lasts. The duration of a behavior is usually standardized in two ways: average duration and total duration. For example, in computing average duration, suppose that Janice is out of her seat four times during a 30-minute activity and that the durations of the episodes are 1 minute, 3 minutes, 7 minutes, and 5 minutes. In this example, the average duration is 4 minutes—that is, (1 + 3 + 7 + 5)/4. To compute Janice's total duration, we add 1 + 3 + 7 + 5 to conclude that she was out of her seat a total of 16 minutes. Often, total duration is expressed as a rate by dividing the total occurrence by the length of an observation. This proportion of duration is often called the "prevalence of the behavior." In the preceding example, Janice's prevalence is .53 (that is, 16/30).

Latency

Latency refers to the length of time between a signal to perform and the beginning of the behavior. For example, a teacher might ask students to take out their books. Sam's latency for that task is the length of time between the teacher's request and Sam's placing his book on his desk. For latency to be assessed, the behavior must have a discrete beginning.

Frequency

For behaviors with discrete beginnings and endings, we often count *frequency*—that is, how often the behaviors occur. When the time periods during which the behavior is counted vary, frequencies are usually converted to rates. Using rate of behavior allows observers to compare the occurrence of behavior across different time periods and settings. For example, 3 episodes of out-of-seat behavior in 15 minutes may be converted to a rate of 12 per hour.

Alberto and Troutman (1999) suggest that frequency should not be used under two conditions: (1) when the behavior occurs at such a high rate that it cannot be counted accurately (for example, many stereotypic behaviors, such as foot tapping, can occur almost constantly) and (2) when the behavior occurs over a prolonged period of time (for example, cooperative play during a game of Monopoly).

Amplitude

Amplitude refers to the intensity of the behavior. In many settings, amplitude can be measured precisely (for example, with noise meters). However, in the classroom, it is usually measured with less precision. Often, amplitude is estimated by rating the behavior on a scale that crudely calibrates amplitude in terms of the behavior itself (for example, crying might be scaled as "whimpering," "sobbing," "crying," and "screaming"). Amplitude may also be calibrated in terms of its objective or subjective impact on others. For example, the objective impact of hitting might be scaled as "without apparent physical damage," "resulting in bruising," and "causing bleeding." More subjective behavior ratings estimate the internal impact on others; for example, a student's humming could be scaled as "does not disturb others," "disturbs students seated nearby," or "disturbs students in the adjoining classroom."

Selecting the Characteristic to Measure
The behavioral characteristic to be assessed should make sense; we should assess the most relevant aspect of behavior in a particular situation. For example, if Burl is wandering around the classroom during the reading period, observing the duration of that behavior makes more sense than observing the frequency, latency, or amplitude of the behavior. If Camilla's teacher is concerned about her loud utterances, amplitude may be the most salient characteristic to observe. If Molly is always slow to follow directions, observing her latency makes more sense than assessing the frequency or amplitude of her behavior. For most behaviors, however, frequency and duration are the characteristics measured.

Sampling Behavior

As with any assessment procedure, we can assess the entire domain if it is finite and convenient. If it is not, we can sample from the domain. As discussed in the chapters "Reliablity" and "Validity," observation samples include the contexts in which the behaviors occur, the times in which the behaviors occur, and the behaviors themselves.

Contexts
When specific behaviors become the targets of intervention, it is useful to measure the behavior in a variety of contexts. Usually, the sampling of contexts is purposeful rather than random. We might want to know, for example, how Jesse's behavior in the resource room differs from his behavior in the general

education classroom. Consistent or inconsistent performance across settings and contexts can provide useful information about what events might set the occasion for the behavior. Differences between the settings in which a behavior does and does not occur can provide potentially useful hypotheses about *setting events* (that is, environmental events that set the occasion for the performance of an action) and *discriminative stimuli* (that is, stimuli that are consistently present when a behavior is reinforced and that come to bring out behavior even in the absence of the original reinforcer).[1] Bringing behavior under the control of a discriminative stimulus is often an effective way of modifying it. For example, students might be taught to talk quietly (to use their "inside voice") when they are in the classroom or hallway.

Similarly, consistent or inconsistent performance across settings and contexts can provide useful information about how the consequences of a behavior are affecting that behavior. Some consequences of a behavior maintain, increase, or decrease behavior. Thus manipulating the consequences of a behavior can increase or decrease its occurrence. For example, assume that Joey's friends usually laugh and congratulate him when he makes a sexist remark and that Joey is reinforced by his friends' behavior. If his friends could be made to stop laughing and congratulating him, Joey would probably make fewer sexist remarks.

Times   With the exception of some criminal acts, few behaviors are noteworthy unless they happen more than once. Behavioral recurrence over time is termed *stability*, or *maintenance*. In a person's lifetime, there are almost an infinite number of times to exhibit a particular behavior. Moreover, it is probably impossible and certainly unnecessary to observe a person continuously during his or her entire life. Thus temporal sampling is always performed, and any single observation is merely a sample from the person's behavioral domain.

Time sampling always requires the establishment of blocks of time, termed *observation sessions*, in which observations will be made. A session might consist of a continuous period of time (for example, one school day). More often, sessions are discontinuous blocks of time (for example, every Monday for a semester). Observers can record behavior continuously within sessions, or they can sample within a session (that is, record discontinuously). Continuous observation requires the expenditure of more resources than does discontinuous observation. When the observation session is long (for example, when it spans several days), continuous sampling can be very expensive and is often intrusive.

Two options are commonly used to estimate behavior in very long observation sessions: the use of rating scales to make estimates and systematic observation to make more precise estimates. In the first option, rating scales can be used to obtain approximate estimates of the four characteristics of behavior. Following are some examples of such ratings:

1. Discriminative stimuli are not conditioned stimuli in the Pavlovian sense that they elicit reflexive behavior. Discriminative stimuli provide a signal to the individual to engage in a particular behavior because that behavior has been reinforced in the presence of that signal.

- *Duration.* A parent might be asked to rate how long Bernie typically watches TV each night—more than 3 hours, 2 to 3 hours, 1 to 2 hours, or less than 1 hour?

- *Latency.* A parent might be asked to rate how quickly Marisa usually responds to requests—immediately, quickly, slowly, or not at all (ignores requests)?

- *Frequency.* A parent might be asked to rate the frequency of a behavior. How often does Patsy usually pick up her toys—always, frequently, seldom, never?

- *Amplitude.* A parent might be asked to rate how much of a fuss Jessica usually makes at bedtime—screams, cries, begs to stay up, or goes to bed without fuss?

In the second observation option, duration and frequency are sampled systematically during prolonged observation intervals. Three different sampling plans have been advocated: whole-interval recording, partial-interval recording, and momentary time sampling.

Whole-Interval Recording

In *whole-interval recording,* an observation session is subdivided into intervals. Usually, observation intervals of equal length are spaced equally through the session, although the recording and observation intervals need not be the same length. In whole-interval recording, a behavior is scored as having occurred only when it occurs throughout the entire interval. Thus it is scored only if it is occurring when the interval begins and continues through the end of the interval.

Partial-Interval Recording

Partial-interval recording is quite similar to whole-interval recording. An observation session is subdivided into intervals, and the intervals in which the behavior occurs are noted. The difference between the whole-interval and partial-interval procedures is that, in partial-interval recording, an occurrence is scored if it occurs during any part of the interval. Thus, if a behavior begins before the interval begins and ends within the interval, an occurrence is scored; if a behavior starts after the beginning of the interval, an occurrence is scored; if two or more episodes of behavior begin and end within the interval, one occurrence is scored.

Momentary Time Sampling

Momentary time sampling is the most efficient sampling procedure. An observation session is subdivided into intervals. If a behavior is occurring at the last moment of the interval, an occurrence is recorded; if the behavior is not occurring at the last moment of the interval, a nonoccurrence is recorded.

Which Time-Sampling Procedure to Use

Salvia and Hughes (1990) have summarized a number of studies investigating the accuracy of these time-sampling procedures. Both whole-interval and partial-interval sampling procedures provide inaccurate estimates of duration and frequency.[2] Momentary time sampling provides an unbiased estimate of the proportion of time the behavior occurs but can underestimate the frequency of a behavior. The simplest and most accurate way to estimate frequency seems to be continuous recording with shorter observation sessions.

Behaviors   Teachers and psychologists may be interested in measurement of a particular behavior or a constellation of behaviors thought to represent a trait (for example, cooperation). When an observer views a target behavior as important in and of itself, only that specific behavior is observed. However, when a specific behavior is thought to be one element in a constellation of behaviors, other important behaviors within the constellation must also be observed in order to establish the content validity of the behavioral constellation. For example, if taking turns on a slide is viewed as one element of cooperation, we should also observe other behaviors indicative of cooperation (such as taking turns on other equipment, following the rules of games, working with others to attain a common goal, and so forth). Each of the behaviors in a behavioral constellation can be treated separately or aggregated for the purposes of observation and reporting.

Whether the behavior is important in and of itself or is representative of a larger constellation of behavior, it should be assessed in multiple contexts and at multiple times. For example, does Marc fail to take turns at the slide before school, during recess, and after school? Does the behavior manifest itself at home and at his neighborhood playground, as well as at school?

Targeting Behavior for Observation

Observations are usually conducted on two types of behavior. First, we regularly observe behavior that is desirable and that we are trying to increase. Behavior of this type includes all academic performances (for example, oral reading or science knowledge) and prosocial behavior (for example, cooperative behavior or polite language). Second, we regularly observe behavior that is undesirable or may indicate a disabling condition. These behaviors are harmful, stereotypic, inappropriately infrequent, or inappropriate at the times exhibited.

Harmful Behavior   Behavior that is self-injurious or physically dangerous to others is almost always targeted for intervention. Self-injurious behavior includes such actions as head banging, eye gouging, self-biting or self-hitting, smoking, and drug abuse. Potentially harmful behavior can include leaning back in a desk or being careless with reagents in a chemistry experiment. Behaviors harmful to others are those that

---

2. Suen and Ary (1989) have provided procedures whereby the sampled frequencies can be adjusted to provide accurate frequency estimates, and the error associated with estimates of prevalence can be readily determined for each sampling plan.

directly inflict injury (for example, hitting or stabbing) or are likely to injure others (for example, pushing other students on stairs or subway platforms, bullying, or verbally instigating physical altercations). Unusually aggressive behavior may also be targeted for intervention. Although most students will display aggressive behavior, some children go far beyond what can be considered typical or acceptable. These students may be described as hot-tempered, quick-tempered, or volatile. Overly aggressive behavior may be physical or verbal. In addition to the possibility of causing physical harm, high rates of aggressive behavior may isolate the aggressor socially.

Stereotypic Behavior

Stereotypic behavior, or stereotypies (for example, hand flapping, rocking, and certain verbalizations such as inappropriate shrieks), are outside the realm of culturally normative behavior. Such behavior calls attention to students and marks them as abnormal to trained psychologists or unusual to untrained observers. Stereotypic behaviors are often targeted for intervention.

Infrequent or Absent Desirable Behavior

Incompletely developed behavior, especially behavior related to physiological development (for example, walking), is often targeted for intervention. Intervention usually occurs when development of these behaviors will enable desirable functional skills or social acceptance. Shaping is usually used to develop absent behavior, whereas reinforcement is used to increase the frequency of behavior that is within a student's repertoire but exhibited at rates that are too low.

Normal Behavior Exhibited in Inappropriate Contexts

Many behaviors are appropriate in very specific contexts but are considered inappropriate or even abnormal when exhibited in other contexts. Usually, the problems caused by behavior in inappropriate contexts are attributed to lack of stimulus control. Behavior that is commonly called "private" falls into this category; elimination and sexual activity are two examples. The goal of intervention should be, not to get rid of these behaviors, but to confine them to socially appropriate conditions. Behavior that is often called "disruptive" also falls into this category. For example, running and yelling are very acceptable and normal when exhibited on the playground; they are disruptive in a classroom.

A teacher may decide on the basis of logic and experience that a particular behavior should be modified. For example, harmful behavior should not be tolerated in a classroom or school, and behavior that is a prerequisite for learning academic material must be developed. In other cases, a teacher may seek the advice of a colleague, supervisor, or parent about the desirability of intervention. For example, a teacher might not know whether certain behavior is typical of a student's culture. In yet other cases, a teacher might rely on the judgments of students or adults as to whether a particular behavior is troublesome or distracting for them. For example, are others bothered when Bob reads problems aloud during arithmetic tests? To ascertain whether a particular behavior bothers others, teachers can ask students directly, have them rate disturbing or distracting behavior, or perhaps use sociometric techniques to learn whether a student is being rejected or isolated because of his or her behavior. The sociometric technique is a method for evaluating the social acceptance of individual pupils and the social structure of a group: Students complete a form indicating their choice of companions for seating, work, or play. Teachers look at the number of times an individual student is chosen by others. They also look at who chooses whom.

For infrequent prosocial behavior or frequent disturbing behavior, a teacher may wish to get a better idea of the magnitude and pervasiveness of the problem before initiating a comprehensive observational analysis. Casual observation can provide information about the frequency and amplitude of the behavior; carefully noting the antecedents, consequences, and contexts may provide useful information about possible interventions if an intervention is warranted. If casual observations are made, anecdotal records of these casual observations should be maintained.

Conducting Systematic Observations

Preparation   Careful preparation is essential to obtaining accurate and valid observational data. Five steps should guide the preparation for systematic observation:

1. *Define target behaviors.* Target behaviors should be defined precisely in observable terms. References to internal processes (for example, understanding or appreciating) are avoided. It is also useful to anticipate potentially difficult discriminations and to include examples of instances and noninstances of the behavior. Therefore, instances should include subtle exhibitions of the target behavior, and noninstances should include related behaviors and behavior with similar topographies. The definition of the target behavior should include the characteristic of the behavior that will be measured (for example, frequency or latency).

2. *Select contexts.* The target behavior should be observed systematically in at least three contexts: the context in which the behavior was noted as troublesome (for example, in reading instruction), a similar context (for example, in math instruction), and a dissimilar context (for example, in physical education or recess).

3. *Select an observation schedule.* Two choices must be made, and these choices are related to the contexts for observation: session length and continuous versus discontinuous observation. In the schools, session length cannot exceed the period of time spanning a student's arrival and departure (including getting on and off the school bus, if appropriate). More often, session length is related to instructional periods or blocks of time within an instructional period (for example, 15 minutes in the middle of small-group reading instruction).

   The choice of continuous or discontinuous observation will depend on the resources available and the specific behaviors that are to be observed. When very-low-frequency behavior or behavior that must be stopped (for example, physical assaults) is observed, continuous recording is convenient and efficient. For other behavior, discontinuous observation is usually preferred, and momentary time sampling usually is the easiest and most accurate for teachers and psychologists to use.

When a discontinuous observation schedule is used, the observer requires some equipment to signal exactly when observation is to occur. The most common equipment is a portable audiocassette player and a tape with pure tones, recorded at the desired intervals. One student or several students in sequence may be observed. For example, three students can be observed in a series of five-second intervals. An audiotape would signal every five seconds. On the first signal, Henry would be observed; on the second signal, Joyce would be observed; on the third signal, Bruce would be observed; on the fourth signal, Henry would be observed again; and so forth.

4. *Develop recording procedures.* The recording of observations must also be planned. When a few students are observed for the occurrence of relatively infrequent behaviors, simple procedures can be used. The behaviors can be observed continuously and counted, using a tally sheet or a wrist counter. When time sampling is used, observations must be recorded for each time interval; thus some type of recording form is required. In the simplest form, the recording sheet contains identifying information (for example, name of target student, name of observer, date and time of observation session, observation interval length, and so forth) and two columns. The first column shows the time interval, and the second column contains places for the observer to indicate whether the behavior occurred during each interval. More complicated recording forms may be used for multiple behaviors and students. When multiple behaviors are observed, they are often given code numbers. For example, "out of seat" might be coded as 1; "in seat but off task" might be coded as 2; "in seat and on task" might be coded as 3; and "no opportunity to observe" might be coded as 4. Such codes should be included on the observation record form. Figure 11.1 shows a simple form on which to record multiple behaviors of students.

   Complex observational systems tend to be less accurate than simple ones. Complexity increases as a function of the number of different behaviors that are assessed and the number of individuals who are observed. Moreover, both the proportion of target individuals to total individuals and the proportion of target behaviors observed to the number of target behaviors to be recorded also have an impact on accuracy. The surest way to reduce inaccuracies in observations attributable to complexity is to keep things relatively simple.

5. *Select the means of observation.* The choice of human observers or electronic recorders will depend on the availability of resources. If electronic recorders are available and can be used in the desired environments and contexts, they may be appropriate when continuous observation is warranted. If other personnel are available, they can be trained to observe and record the target behaviors accurately. Training should include didactic instruction in defining the target behavior, the use of time sampling (if it is to be used), and the way in which to record behavior, as well as practice in using the observation system. Training is always continued until the desired level of accuracy is reached. Observers' accuracy is evaluated by comparing each observer's responses with those of the others or with a criterion rating

FIGURE 11.1
A Simple Recording Form
for Three Students and
Two Behaviors

Observer: *Mr. Kowalski*

Date: *2/15/02*

Times of observation: *10:15 to 11:00*

Observation interval: *10 sec*

Instructional activity: *Oral reading*

Students observed: Codes:

S1 = *Henry J.*   1 = out of seat
                                       2 = in seat but off task
S2 = *Bruce H.*   3 = in seat, on task
                                       4 = no opportunity to observe
S3 = *Joyce W.*

	S1	S2	S3
1	___	___	___
2	___	___	___
3	___	___	___
4	___	___	___
5	___	___	___
.			
.			
.			
179	___	___	___
180	___	___	___

(usually a previously scored videotape). Generally, very high agreement is required before anyone can assume that observers are ready to conduct observations independently. Ultimately, the decision of how to collect the data should also be based on efficiency. For example, if it takes longer to desensitize students to an obtrusive videorecorder than it takes to train observers, then human observers are preferred.

Data Gathering   As with any type of assessment information, two general sources of error can reduce the accuracy of observation: (1) random error can result in over- or underestimates of behavior, and (2) systematic error can bias the data in a consistent direction—for example, behavior may be systematically overcounted or undercounted. Careful preparation and systematic monitoring of the observation process can head off trouble. Before observation begins, human observers should make sure that they have an extra supply of recording forms, spare pens or pencils, and something to write on (for example, a clipboard or tabletop). When electronic recording is used, equipment should be checked before every observation session to make sure it is in good working condition. When portable equipment is employed, the observer should have extra batteries, signal tapes, or recording tapes available. Before beginning an observation, the observer can prepare a checklist of equipment and materials that will be used during the observation, and assemble everything that is needed for the observation session. Also, before the observation session, the observer should check out the setting to locate appropriate vantage points for equipment or furniture.

Random Error   Random errors in observation and recording usually affect observer agreement. Observers may change the criteria for the occurrence of a behavior, they may forget behavior codes, or they may use the recording forms incorrectly. Because changes in agreement can signal that something is wrong, the accuracy of observational data should be checked periodically. The usual procedure is to have two people observe and record on the same schedule in the same session. The two records are then compared, and an index of agreement (for example, kappa—see the chapter "Reliability") is computed. Poor agreement suggests the need for retraining or for revision of the observation procedures. To alleviate some of these problems, provide periodic retraining, and allow observers to keep the definitions and codes for target behaviors with them. Finally, when observers know that their accuracy is being systematically checked, they are usually more accurate. Thus observers should not be told when they are being observed and when they are not being observed. Observers should expect their observations to be checked.

One of the most vexing factors affecting the accuracy of observations is the incorrect recording of correctly observed behavior. Even when observers have applied the criterion for the occurrence of a behavior correctly, they may record their decision incorrectly. For example, if 1 is used to indicate occurrence and 0 (zero) is used to indicate nonoccurrence, the observer might accidentally record 0 for a behavior that has occurred. Inaccuracy can be attributed to three related factors.

Causes of Incorrect Recording

1. *Lack of familiarity with the recording system.* Observers definitely need practice in using a recording system when several behaviors or several students are to be observed. They also need practice when the target behaviors are difficult to define or when they are difficult to observe.

2. *Insufficient time to record.* Sufficient time must be allowed to record the occurrence of behavior. Problems can arise when using momentary time sampling if the observation intervals are spaced too closely (for example, one- or five-second intervals). Observers who are counting several different high-frequency behaviors may record inaccurately. Generally, inadequate opportunities for observers to record can be circumvented by electronic recording of the observation session; when observers can stop and replay segments of interest, they essentially have unlimited time to observe and record.

3. *Lack of concentration.* It may be hard for observers to remain alert for long periods of time (for example, one hour), especially if the target behavior occurs infrequently and is difficult to detect. Observers can reduce the time that they must maintain vigilance by either taking turns with several observers or recording observation sessions for later evaluation. Similarly, when it is difficult to maintain vigilance because the observational context is noisy, busy, or otherwise distracting, electronic recording may be useful in focusing on target subjects and eliminating ambient noise.

Unusual events and departures from the observation plan (for example, a missed observation interval) can be noted directly on the observation form. Finally, observation should begin and end at the planned times.

Systematic Error   Systematic errors are difficult to detect. To minimize error, four steps can be taken.

1. *Guard against unintended changes in the observation process.*[3] When assessment is carried out over extended periods of time, observers may talk to one another about the definitions that they are using or about how they cope with difficult discriminations. Consequently, one observer's departure from standardized procedures may spread to other observers. When the observers change together, modifications of the standard procedures and definitions will not be detected by examining interobserver agreement. Techniques for reducing changes in observers over time include keeping the scoring criteria available to observers, meeting with the observers on a regular basis to discuss difficulties encountered during observation, and providing periodic retraining.

   Surprisingly, even recording equipment can change over time. Audio signal tapes (used to indicate the moment a student should be observed) may stretch after repeated uses; a 10-second interval may become an 11-second interval. Similarly, the batteries in playback units can lose power, and signal tapes may play more slowly. Therefore, equipment should be cleaned periodically, and signal tapes should be checked for accuracy.

2. *Desensitize students.* The introduction of equipment or new adults into a classroom, as well as changes in teacher routines, can signal to students that observations are going on. Overt measurement can alter the target behavior or the topography of the behavior. Usually, the pupil change is temporary. For example, when Janey knows that she is being observed, she may be more accurate, deliberate, or compliant. However, as observation becomes a part of the daily routine, students' behavior usually returns to what is typical for them. This return to typical patterns of behavior functionally defines desensitization. The data generated from systematic observation should not be used until the students who are observed are no longer affected by the observation procedures and equipment or personnel. However, sometimes

3. Technically, general changes in the observation process over time are called "instrumentation problems."

the change in behavior is permanent. For example, if a teacher was watching for the extortion of lunch money, Robbie might wait until no observers were present or might demand the money in more subtle ways. In such cases, valid data would not be obtained through overt observation, and either different procedures would have to be developed or the observation would have to be abandoned.

3. *Minimize observer expectancies.* Sometimes, what an observer believes will happen affects what is seen and recorded. For example, if an observer expects an intervention to increase a behavior, that observer might unconsciously alter the criteria for evaluating that behavior or might evaluate approximations of the target behavior as having occurred. The more subtle or complex the target behavior is, the more susceptible it may be to expectation effects. The easiest way to avoid expectations during observations is for the observer to be blind to the purpose of the assessment. When video- or audiotapes are used to record behavior, the order in which they are evaluated can be randomized so that observers do not know what portion of an observation is being scored. When it is impossible or impractical to keep observers blind to the purpose, the importance of accurate observation should be stressed and such observation rewarded.

4. *Motivate observers.* Inaccurate observation is sometimes attributed to lack of motivation on the part of an observer. Motivation can be increased by providing rewards and feedback, stressing the importance of the observations, reducing the length of observation sessions, and not allowing observation sessions to become routine.

Data Summarization

Depending on the particular characteristic of behavior being measured, observational data may be summarized in different ways. When duration or frequency is the characteristic of interest, observations are usually summarized as rates (that is, the prevalence or the number of occurrences per minute or other time interval). Latency and amplitude should be summarized statistically by the mean and the standard deviation or by the median and the range. All counts and calculations should be checked for accuracy.

Criteria for Evaluating Observed Performances

Once accurate observational data have been collected and summarized, they must be interpreted. Some behavior can be judged on an a priori basis—for example, unsafe and harmful behavior. Most behavior is not evaluated simply by its presence, however. For example, knowing that the prevalence of Marie's out-of-seat behavior is 10 percent during instruction in content areas does not provide much information about whether that behavior should be decreased.

Behavior rates can be evaluated in several ways. Normative data may be available for some behavior, or, in some cases, data from behavior rating scales and tests can provide general guidelines. In the absence of such data, social comparisons can be made. In social comparison, a peer whose behavior is considered appropriate is observed. The peer's rate of behavior is then used as the standard against which to evaluate the target student's rate of behavior. The social tolerance for a behavior can also be used as a criterion. For example, the degree to which different rates of out-of-seat behavior disturb a teacher or peers can be assessed. Teachers and peers could be asked to rate how disturbing is the out-of-seat behavior of students who exhibit different rates of behavior. In a somewhat different vein, the contagion of the behavior to others can be a crucial consideration in teacher judgments of unacceptable behavior. Thus the effects of different rates of behavior can be assessed to see whether there is a threshold above which other students initiate undesirable behavior.

Determining a Behavior's Function

A behavior's function can be determined through a functional behavior assessment. This procedure requires complete descriptions of the target behaviors, including their characteristics (that is, duration, latency, frequency, or amplitude) and the contexts in which the behaviors occur. This procedure also requires gathering information about what happens prior to the behavior of interest in each context. An environmental event that occurs before the target behavior is called an antecedent. Antecedents can act as signals that a behavior will be reinforced (that is, be a discriminative stimulus), can change the effectiveness of reinforcers that follow the behavior (that is, be an establishing operation), or make the target behavior more likely to occur later in a different place (that is, be a setting event). (See Gresham, Watson, and Skinner [2001] for a more complete explanation of setting antecedent events.) Finally, functional behavior assessment requires an analysis of what happens after the behavior—the consequences of the behavior. A functional behavior assessment leads to hypotheses about the functions that a behavior serves.

Functional behavior analysis goes one step further. The hypothesis is tested experimentally to ascertain whether the behavior indeed serves the hypothesized function. Once the function is hypothesized or known, interventions can be used to develop other more acceptable behaviors to serve the same function.

SUMMARY

Behavioral observation is the process of gaining information visually, aurally, or sensorially. It can be used to assess any behavior or product of behavior; it cannot be used to assess events that are not observable (for example, thinking, feeling, or believing). Although behavior may be defined functionally or topographically, it is measured in terms of its duration, latency, frequency, and amplitude. Moreover, observers can assess the entire domain of behavior or can sample from the domain along three dimensions: contexts, times, and behaviors. Each dimension can provide important and useful information about the behavior and how it is maintained in the environment.

Three different sampling plans have been advocated for measuring the duration and frequency of behavior: whole-interval recording, partial-interval recording, and momentary time sampling. Of these three methods, momentary time sampling is the most useful and in general is the most accurate.

Observations are usually conducted on behavior that may require modification or behavior that may indicate a disability condition: harmful behavior, stereotypic behavior, infrequent or absent desirable behavior, or normal behavior shown in inappropriate contexts.

Systematic observations require as much care and precision as testing does in terms of preparation, data gathering, and data summarization. When observers are preparing to conduct systematic observations, they must (1) carefully define the target behaviors; (2) carefully select both the contexts in which observations will be conducted and the observation schedule; (3) thoughtfully develop the recording procedures; and (4) determine the means by which data will be collected (for example, using human observers).

When gathering data, the observer should minimize both random and systematic error. Random error is usually attributed to lack of familiarity with the recording system, to insufficient time to record, or to lack of concentration. Systematic error is usually attributed to unintended changes in the observation process, to failure to desensitize target students, to observer expectancies, or to unmotivated observers. Like all other assessment procedures, observations of student performances must be evaluated. Some behavior can be judged on an a priori basis—for example, unsafe and harmful behavior. Other behavior is evaluated on the basis of normative data, social comparison, or social tolerance.

Finally, the function that a behavior serves is often investigated through functional behavior analysis. This analysis requires the documentation of the antecedents and consequences of behavior, and the generation of hypotheses about the functions of the behavior.

QUESTIONS FOR CHAPTER REVIEW

1. Describe each of the four types of behavior that are frequently targeted for intervention.

2. Name four types of systematic errors that can occur during observation. What can an observer do to minimize these types of errors?

3. Name three types of random errors that can occur during observation. What can an observer do to minimize these types of errors?

4. Joey has been referred for assessment. His teacher reports that he seems to be lethargic all the time. A specific example provided by the teacher is that, when Joey's hand is raised and he is called on, it takes him much longer than any other child to begin giving his answer or asking his question. What type of observational data would you want to collect to check the teacher's informal observation?

5. A frustrating problem in observations is the occurrence of inaccurate coding of behavior that was correctly observed. Give an example of this problem, and list three ways to reduce the likelihood of its occurrence.

PROJECT

Read an article in which an observational study is reported. Identify the kind of data collected and how the data are summarized.

RESOURCES FOR FURTHER INVESTIGATION

Print Resources

Alberto, P. A., & Troutman, A. C. (1999). *Applied behavior analysis for teachers* (5th ed.). Upper Saddle River, NJ: Prentice-Hall.

Greenwood, C. R., Peterson, P., & Sideridis, G. (1995). Conceptual, methodological, and technological advances in classroom observational assessment. *Diagnostique, 20,* 73–99.

Gresham, F., Watson, T., & Skinner, C. (2001). Functional behavioral assessment: Principles, procedures, and future directions. *School Psychology Review, 30*(2), 156–172.

Hartmann, D. P. (Ed.). (1988). *Using observers to study behavior: New directions for methodology of social and behavioral science series,* No. 14 (pp. 5–20, Observer effects: Reactivity of direct observation, and pp. 21–36, Developing a behavior code). San Francisco: Jossey-Bass.

Shapiro, E. S., & Kratochwill, T. (Eds.). (2000). *Behavioral assessment in schools: Theory, research, and clinical foundations* (2nd ed.). New York: Guilford Press.

Technology Resources

BEHAVIORAL RECORDING
**maxweber.hunter.cuny.edu/pub/eres/
EDSPC715_MCINTYRE/BehRecord.html**
This site provides basic information about conducting student observations.

OBSERVING AND RECORDING STUDENT PERFORMANCE
para.unl.edu/para/observation/Intro.html
This website discusses the issues and techniques involved in gathering information about student behavior through observation. The five lessons presented include examples and practice activities.

BEHAVIORAL OBSERVATION AND PROGRAMMING
www.dpi.state.wi.us/dpi/een/bul00-01.html
This website provides information about functional behavioral assessment, conducting classroom observations, and developing intervention plans.

CHAPTER 12

Assessing Instructional Ecology

STUDENT ASSESSMENT CANNOT BE CONSIDERED COMPLETE WITHOUT AN ASSESSMENT of the student's instructional needs in the context of the classroom. This observation seems so obvious that few would disagree with it. Yet, in practice, most psychoeducational decisions for a student are made without careful, systematic analysis of the instructional ecology. In this chapter, we review systematic assessment of instructional environments. It is important to assess instructional environments because the quickest, most direct way to change student performance and educational results is to modify or adapt the environment in which students are taught.

Before teachers or assessors can modify instructional environments, they need to know a lot about the nature of the environments in which students are being taught. In this chapter, we first consider instructional ecology and the kinds of factors that are related to instructional results and then describe ways to gather data on (assess the presence or absence of) those factors.

What Is Instructional Ecology?

Ecology is the term we use to refer to mutual relationships between organisms and their environments. When we talk about *instructional ecology*, we are referring to the relationships between students and their instructional environments. Students' behavior and academic performance are influenced by the environments in which they are taught. Each student brings to instructional settings a set of individual characteristics and a learning history. Each student also responds differently to teachers' instructional efforts. There is a reciprocal relationship between students and instructional environments, and those who assess the instructional ecology are interested in that relationship.

The product of schooling (what students learn, or outcomes) is a function of (1) the content goals of the school, as expressed in scheduling and implementation of instruction; and (2) the instructional procedures employed by teachers, as

207

expressed in terms of their success in managing students' responses to academic tasks (Greenwood, Carta, Kamps, & Arreaga-Mayer, 1990). Those who engage in assessments of instructional environments evaluate, among other things, classroom structures, the amount of time allocated to instruction, the amount of time students are actively engaged in responding to instruction, the ways in which instructions are given for school tasks, the pacing of instruction, and the ways in which teachers use information about student performance to change or adapt instruction.

The Importance of Home-School Connections for Learning

Instructional results are a function of the interaction between individuals and instructional ecologies. However, the nature of this interaction is, in part, determined by the extent to which there is home support for the learning that occurs in school. Educational results are better when there is a strong collaborative relationship between homes and schools. When parents support teachers, supplement instruction in classrooms, and provide their children with an educative environment—and when teachers in turn support parents—results improve. Those who assess instructional ecologies have devised procedures for systematic assessment of home support for learning (Ysseldyke & Christenson, 2002).

Instructional results for students are enhanced when the level of expected performance held by key adults for the student is congruent across home and school, and when the adults believe the student can learn. Results are also enhanced when there are consistent structures and routines across home and school environments, and when there is mutual support, guidance, and positive communication. It is also critical that students get plenty of opportunities to learn, in both home and school environments, and that the environments in which they learn are positive, warm, and friendly. We think it is critical that those who assess students consider the extent to which youth-adult relationships are positive, as well as the extent to which parents and teachers model desired behaviors and a commitment to learning and working hard.

Factors That Contribute to Academic and Behavioral Problems in School

When educators are asked to indicate why students experience difficulty and fail in school, they give four categories of causes: students' deficits or disabilities, students' home and family problems, ineffective instruction, and unsuitable school organization. (Of course, educators also attribute success in school to these same four factors.) First, educators most often argue that school difficulties are caused by deficits, disorders, dysfunctions, or disabilities suffered by the student—for example, the child may have a brain injury, mental retardation, blindness, an emotional disability, or a learning disability. Second, educators contend that students who experience difficulty in school come from dysfunctional families, families in which there is little or no discipline, and home settings in which there is not an educative environment. Third, some educators argue that we know a great deal about the kinds of instructional practices that enhance student outcomes. When these factors are not present or are not present in ways that they should be, students experience academic and behavioral problems. Fourth, some of the difficulties that students experience in school may be due to the ways schools are organized, ways that just do not make sense for some students. In this chapter, our focus is on the third and fourth factors for success or failure. We consider ways in which the effectiveness of instruction and the suitability of school organization contribute to the results of schooling.

In the first part of this chapter, we review factors that are related to instructional results for students, and in the sections that follow, we review current practice in ecobehavioral assessment and functional assessment of instructional environments.

Carroll's Model of School Learning

More than 40 years ago, Carroll (1963) proposed a model of school learning that is the basis for most models of learning applied in schools today. Carroll's model is shown in Figure 12.1. According to Carroll, how much a student learns is a function of the amount of time the student actually spends learning, divided by the amount of time the student needs in order to learn what is being taught. The amount of time spent learning is influenced by "opportunity," which represents the time officially scheduled for learning and the time allocated by teachers and instructional programs, and by "perseverance," which represents the amount of time the student is willing to engage actively in learning, particularly when the task becomes more difficult and the student may be facing failure.

Carroll posits that the time needed for learning depends on the student's aptitude and ability to understand instruction, as well as on the quality of instruction. He defines *aptitude* as the amount of time needed to learn a task under optimal conditions. Carroll talks about aptitude as being task specific and speaks of students' "aptitude for learning this task" (Carroll, 1985, p. 63). "Ability to understand instruction" is seen as a function of the student's general intelligence and of how adequately tasks are explained. "Quality of instruction," in Carroll's model, is a function of the nature, objectives, content, and hierarchical structure of teacher-provided instruction and instructional materials. Quality of instruction varies as a function of the clarity of the task requirements, the adequacy of task presentation and of sequencing and pacing, and the degree to which the learner's unique needs have been considered during the instructional presentation. In Figure 12.1, we have shaded "Opportunity" and "Quality of instruction" because these are the factors we consider in detail in this chapter.

Algozzine and Ysseldyke's Model of Effective Instruction

Ysseldyke and Christenson (1987a) conducted a review of the literature on effective instruction. They identified student characteristics that were said or shown to be related to student outcomes. They also found environmental factors (school district conditions, within-school conditions, and general family characteristics) and instructional factors related to instructional outcomes.

The Ysseldyke and Christenson review served as the foundation for the development of the Algozzine-Ysseldyke Model of Effective Instruction. Algozzine

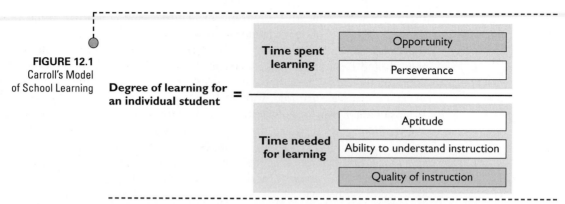

FIGURE 12.1
Carroll's Model
of School Learning

$$\text{Degree of learning for an individual student} = \frac{\text{Time spent learning}\ (\text{Opportunity} + \text{Perseverance})}{\text{Time needed for learning}\ (\text{Aptitude} + \text{Ability to understand instruction} + \text{Quality of instruction})}$$

SOURCE: From J. B. Carroll, "A Model of School Learning," *Teaching College Record*, v. 64, pp. 723–733. Copyright © 1963. Reprinted by permission of the publisher.

and Ysseldyke (1992) identify four components of effective instruction (planning, managing, delivering, and evaluating), the major principles of effective instruction for each component, and several strategies for putting principles into practice in classrooms. Whether they are instructing students who are gifted, are nondisabled, or have mild or severe disabilities, teachers must plan, manage, deliver, and evaluate instruction. The most recent version of the Algozzine-Ysseldyke model (Algozzine, Ysseldyke, & Elliott, 1997) is shown in Table 12.1 (pp. 212–214).

Planning Instruction

Effective instruction does not occur by chance. It must be planned. Instructional outcomes are enhanced by effective instructional planning for individual students. If all students in a class were at the same instructional level and if the goals and objectives of schooling were clearly defined and the same for all students, then instruction would consist of doing the same things with all students, being certain to do them in the right order and at the right time. However, students are not all alike, and the goals and objectives of instruction are not the same for all students. Schools are becoming increasingly diverse environments each year. This is why instructional planning is such an important part of teaching and assessment.

Outcomes are enhanced when teaching goals and teacher expectations for student performance and success are stated clearly and understood by the student. Those who plan instruction must (1) decide what to teach, (2) decide how to teach, and (3) communicate realistic expectations to individual learners.

Deciding What to Teach　Decisions about what to teach are enhanced by accurate assessment of student characteristics (such as skill levels or motivation), task characteristics (such as cognitive demands), and classroom characteristics (such as materials or instructional groupings). Using this information, effective teachers plan their instruction to produce logical lessons that best match student, task, and classroom characteristics to the instructional demands of the content they are teaching. The goal when deciding what to teach is to accurately determine the appropriate content to present, based on what is known about individual students and their learning needs and development. We can check on a school's performance in this area by looking at the extent to which school personnel have accurately diagnosed learner strengths and weaknesses, identified gaps between actual and expected levels of performance, considered the kinds of skills taught in the curriculum, sequenced the instruction in a logical way, and matched the student to the content of instruction at the right level.

Deciding How to Teach   Decisions must also be made about how to teach. It is difficult to know ahead of time the kinds of instructional practices that will be effective with individual students. Rather, teachers experiment with alternative teaching approaches until they identify the combination of approaches that works best in moving their students toward instructional goals. Educators can assess the extent to which there are clear instructional goals for individual students, the grouping structures are used appropriately, the instruction is paced appropriately, and the students' performance is monitored and used to plan subsequent instruction.

Communicating Realistic Expectations   The third principle of effective instructional planning is that results are enhanced when teachers communicate realistic expectations to students. Effective teachers set instructional goals and objectives that are realistic—neither too low nor too high. The goals and expectations must also be communicated clearly to the student. Outcomes are enhanced when students understand what they are expected to do. Note that failure to communicate goals and expectations can occur either because the teacher does not communicate clearly or because the child does not understand what is communicated.

Managing Instruction

Discipline is consistently identified as a concern in public and professional opinion polls about education. Classroom discipline and desirable instructional outcomes are enhanced by efficient, yet warm classroom management. Principles of effective classroom management include preparing for effective instruction, using time productively, and establishing a positive classroom environment. Appropriate discipline practices emerge when these principles are put into practice.

Preparing for Effective Instruction   Effective teachers establish classroom rules and communicate them early in the school year. They teach individual students to comply with rules, show students the consequences of either following or not following their rules, and handle rule infractions and other disruptions as quickly as possible after these occur. When teachers fail to establish and communicate classroom rules, instructional outcomes are diminished. In evaluating the instructional ecology, assessors take into account the extent to which rules have been communicated to the individual student, whether the student knows and understands the rules, and whether rule infractions by the student are handled immediately. Not all the onus is on the teacher; students can be taught to manage their own behavior.

Using Time Productively   Students achieve better instructional outcomes when they make effective use of their time. Teachers can modify the instructional environment to help students make good use of their time by establishing routines (for example, students know what to do when they are finished with their work), organizing physical space so that students are placed in settings that limit distractions, keeping students focused on academic work, allocating specific time to academic activities, and making sure that students understand task directions.

Establishing a Positive Classroom Environment   Students are more motivated to learn in environments in which they feel accepted. Assessors should take into account whether the classroom environment is both accepting of individual differences and supportive of students. Assessors should also look at the extent to which the student's teachers interact positively with him or her and encourage him or her to respond and participate in class.

Delivering Instruction

Instructional delivery is a complex process involving appropriate instructional matches, the clear presentation of lessons while following specific instructional procedures, the allocation of sufficient time for instructing individual learners, and providing sufficient opportunity for students to respond. Effective teachers use very specific strategies to present information, monitor presentations, and adjust presentations in light of student performance and progress. These strategies are listed in Table 12.1.

TABLE 12.1	The Algozzine-Ysseldyke Model of Effective Instruction	
Component	**Principle**	**Strategy**
Planning instruction	Decide what to teach.	Assess skill levels to identify gaps between actual and expected level of performance. Establish logical sequences of instruction. Consider contextual variables.
	Decide how to teach.	Set instructional goals. Establish performance standards. Choose instructional methods and materials. Establish grouping structures. Pace instruction appropriately. Monitor students' performance and use performance to plan instruction.
	Communicate realistic expectations.	Teach goals, objectives, and standards. Teach students to be active, involved learners. Teach students consequences of performance.

TABLE 12.1		The Algozzine-Ysseldyke Model of Effective Instruction (*cont.*)

Component	Principle	Strategy
Managing instruction	Prepare for instruction.	Set classroom rules. Communicate classroom rules. Teach rule compliance. Handle disruptions efficiently. Communicate consequences of behavior. Teach students to manage their own behavior.
	Use time productively.	Establish routines and procedures. Organize physical space. Give task directions. Keep transitions short. Allocate time to academic activities. Maintain academic focus.
	Establish positive classroom environment.	Make classrooms pleasant, friendly places. Accept individual differences. Keep interactions positive. Establish supportive, cooperative environment. Make students respond and participate.
Delivering instruction	Present instruction.	**For presenting content** Gain students' attention. Review prior skills or lessons. Provide organized, relevant lessons. Maintain students' attention. Interact positively with students. **For teaching thinking skills** Model thinking skills. Teach fact-finding skills. Teach divergent thinking. Teach learning strategies. **For motivating students** Show enthusiasm and interest. Help students value schoolwork. Use rewards effectively. Consider level and student interest. **For providing relevant practice** Develop automaticity. Vary opportunities for practice. Use seatwork effectively. Provide students with help. Use relevant tasks and varied materials. Assign the right amount of work. Vary methods during practice.

(continued)

TABLE 12.1   The Algozzine-Ysseldyke Model of Effective Instruction (*cont.*)

Component	Principle	Strategy
	Monitor instruction.	**For providing feedback** Give immediate, frequent, explicit feedback. Provide specific praise and encouragement. Model correct performance. Provide prompts and cues. Check student understanding. **For keeping students actively involved** Monitor performance regularly. Monitor performance during practice. Use peers to provide instruction. Provide opportunities for success. Limit opportunities for failure. Monitor engagement rates.
	Adjust instruction.	Adjust lessons to meet student needs. Provide many instructional options. Adjust pace.
Evaluating instruction	Monitor student understanding.	Check understanding of directions. Check process understanding. Monitor success rate.
	Monitor engaged time.	Check student participation. Teach students to monitor their own participation.
	Maintain records of student progress.	Teach students to chart their own progress. Regularly inform students of performance. Maintain records of student performance.
	Use data to make decisions.	Use data on student progress to decide when more services are warranted. Use student progress to make teaching decisions. Use student progress to make decisions about when to change service delivery.

SOURCE: Reprinted with permission from Algozzine, B. A., Ysseldyke, J. E., & Elliott, J. L. (1997). *Strategies and tactics for effective instruction* (2nd ed.). Longmont, CO: Sopris West.

Presenting Instruction   This requires decisions about content, how to teach thinking skills, how to motivate students, and how to provide relevant practice. When presenting content, effective teachers gain their students' attention, review previously covered material, provide organized lessons, introduce new material by relating it to known content whenever possible, and interact positively with their students. It is important to assess the extent to which these teaching actions are present in the instruction of individual students. When teaching thinking skills, effective teachers show students how to solve problems and give them alternative ways of finding answers. When motivating students, effective teachers focus on using internal as well as external sources of satisfaction. When providing relevant practice, effective teachers help students develop automatic responses. They also provide ample time and relevant, varied activities for guided and independent practice. The goal in presenting information is to teach students something they do not know.

Monitoring Instruction   This calls for decisions about how to provide feedback and how to keep students actively involved during delivery of instruction. When providing feedback, effective teachers provide immediate, frequent, explicit information that supports correct responses and provides models for improvement of incorrect responses. When keeping students actively involved, effective teachers regularly monitor responses during instructional presentations, use peers to enhance engagement, and provide ample, varied opportunities for supporting success and correcting failure. The goal in monitoring presentations is to ensure that students are learning the content as it was presented.

Adjusting Instruction   This relies on decisions about how to change instruction by modifying lessons, using alternative instructional options, and using differing levels of pace to meet the individual needs of students. Effective teachers teach skills until students master them, and they use information gathered during instructional presentations and practice sessions to decide when and how to modify their teaching so that all students can be successful. The goal in adjusting presentations is to make any changes needed to ensure that all students benefit from instruction.

Evaluating Instruction

Evaluation, an important part of teaching, is the means by which teachers decide whether the approach they are using is effective with individual students. Assessors must take into account the extent to which teachers monitor student understanding, monitor engaged time, keep records of student progress, and use evaluation data to make decisions. In checking on the ways in which teachers monitor student understanding, it is important to examine the extent to which they check whether or not students understand directions and understand the procedures to be followed in solving problems. Effective teachers regularly do this, and they also monitor the success rate experienced by individual students.

In evaluating instruction, assessors must also look at how teachers go about teaching students to monitor their own behavior and chart their own progress. They check for evidence that students are informed of how they are doing and that teachers are keeping records of student performance. Effective teachers use evaluation data to make decisions about students. Assessors will want to know how teachers use data to decide whether more services are warranted, whether and when to refer, and when to discontinue services.

Approaches to Gathering
Data on Instructional Ecology

In this chapter, we consider two approaches to gathering data on students' instructional environments or ecologies: ecobehavioral assessment and the Functional Assessment of Academic Behavior (FAAB). Ecobehavioral assessment is used to gather data on how students spend their time in school, looking specifically at opportunities to learn and academic engaged time. The Functional Assessment of Academic Behavior methodology developed by Ysseldyke and Christenson (2002) is used to systematically analyze the qualitative nature of the instruction that students receive in classroom and home environments.

Ecobehavioral Assessment   The term *ecobehavioral assessment* is used in educational assessment to describe observations of functional relationships (or interactions) between student behavior and its ecological contexts. The approach is used to identify interactions among student behavior, teacher behavior, time allocated to instruction, physical grouping structures, types of tasks being used, and instructional content. Ecobehavioral assessment thus enables educators to identify natural instructional conditions that are associated with academic success, behavioral competence, or challenging behaviors. Increasingly, ecobehavioral assessment is being used to develop and validate specific instructional procedures, develop a number of approaches to the reduction of challenging behaviors, improve understanding of the components of effective instruction (including the identification of instructional risk factors), and provide a better understanding of how the quality of instructional implementation affects student outcomes (Greenwood, Carta, & Atwater, 1991; Greenwood, Abbott, & Tapia, 2003). Ecobehavioral assessment is one way to gather data on the opportunity to learn, an important component of Carroll's model of school learning and the Algozzine-Ysseldyke Model of Effective Instruction.

Code for Instructional Structure and Student
Academic Response (CISSAR)

Ecobehavioral assessment approaches have been developed by Greenwood, Carta, Delquadri, Arreaga-Mayer, Utley, and their colleagues at the Juniper Gardens Children's Project in Kansas City, Kansas. The first version of the system, developed by Greenwood, Delquadri, and Hall (1978), was called the Code for Instructional Structure and Student Academic Response (abbreviated as CISSAR). Using this system, assessors can categorize ecobehavioral events into student behaviors, teacher behaviors, and ecology. The original system defined 19 student-behavioral codes that could be combined into three composite variables. The current CISSAR taxonomy is shown in Figure 12.2.

CISSAR uses momentary time sampling (ten-second intervals) over the entire school day. Observers record the ecology (specific activity, task used to control instruction, and class structure), teacher behavior (teacher position and actions), and student behavior (academic responses, competing responses, and task-management responses). After observational data have been recorded, the asses-

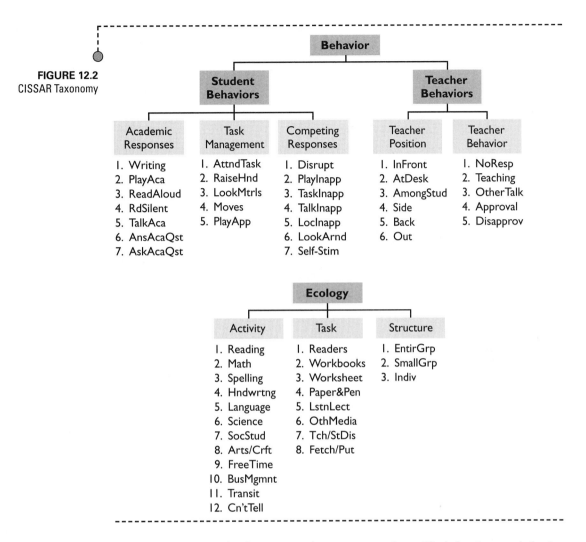

FIGURE 12.2
CISSAR Taxonomy

sor can determine the frequency of occurrence of specific behaviors and the interactions among behaviors and environmental stimuli.

Three derivatives of CISSAR have been developed since the late 1980s. One of these, Ecobehavioral System for Complex Assessments of Preschool Environments (ESCAPE), was developed for use with preschool children. Another, the mainstream version of CISSAR (MS-CISSAR), was designed to be used in observations of students with disabilities in general education classes. The MS-CISSAR taxonomy is shown in Figure 12.3. The third, Ecobehavioral System for the Contextual Recording of Interactional Bilingual Environments (ESCRIBE; Arreaga-Mayer, Carta, & Tapia, 1992), is designed for ecobehavioral assessment of bilingual students and classes for English-language learners. The four derivative ecobehavioral assessment systems (CISSAR, ESCAPE, MS-CISSAR, and ESCRIBE) have been combined in a new software program, Ecobehavioral Assessment System Software (EBASS).

Ecobehavioral Assessment System Software

EBASS (Greenwood, Carta, Kamps, & Delquadri, 1995) is an MS-DOS software system that enables school personnel to conduct systematic classroom observational assessments using laptop, notebook, or hand-held computers with at least one 720K floppy-disk drive. The EBASS package contains an assessment manual, a technical manual, computer software, and videotapes (to illustrate use of the system).

EBASS was designed specifically for school psychologists, but it may be used by other professionals responsible for assessment, teacher training, and program evaluation activities, including instructional staff in general and special education. Typical applications include assessments of individual students for the purpose of planning instructional interventions, evaluating individual pupil progress, and evaluating educational programs. Computerization allows computer-assisted training in instrument use, calibration of reliability checks, instrument modification (each of the three measures can be downsized into shorter measures), simple and complex data analyses, caseload management, and database capabilities.

Methodology   The classroom observer chooses whichever observational instrument is appropriate (ESCAPE, CISSAR, or MS-CISSAR) and goes into classrooms with a portable computer to gather data in ten-second intervals. The training package available with EBASS is used for teaching observers what to look for and how to code behaviors. The training system is self-instructional and includes short lessons, classroom video examples, computer exercises with feedback, and observational practice. It takes about eight to ten hours to learn any of the three instruments, and additional time is needed for practice in data collection.

Reports   Reports from an observation may be in one of two basic forms: (1) percentage occurrence for all events or (2) probabilities of student behavior given specific arrangements of the classroom ecology. These latter probabilities are called "conditional probabilities." The computer can generate reports based on a single observation, on observations sequenced by time of observation, and on observations pooled over time. The professional who uses EBASS is able to give the teacher information on academic engaged time, the occurrence of inappropriate behavior, and the occurrence of task management responses. The strength of EBASS is that it provides very precise information on the frequency of occurrence of specific kinds of behaviors (such as writing, playing inappropriately, waiting, and engaging in disruptive behavior) and on the kinds of contextual factors associated with the occurrence of each of the behaviors.

Examples of EBASS reports are shown in Tables 12.2 and 12.3. Table 12.2 illustrates the academic-response profile for an individual student. The student was observed for an entire day. He spent 11.94 percent of the day writing, 20.65 percent of the day reading silently, and so forth. The profile also shows that this student was responding to academic content 53.65 percent of the school day and making no academic response 49.35 percent of the day.

Table 12.3 shows a probability analysis for writing behavior and illustrates that there are important relationships between students' writing behavior and

FIGURE 12.3
MS-CISSAR Taxonomy

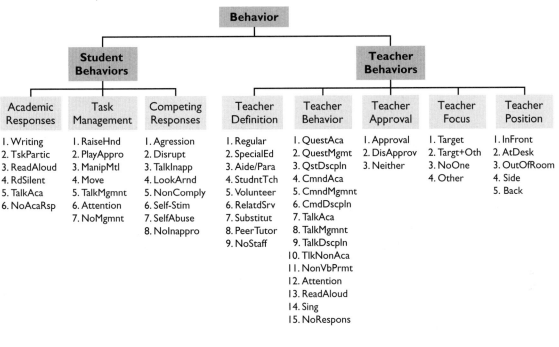

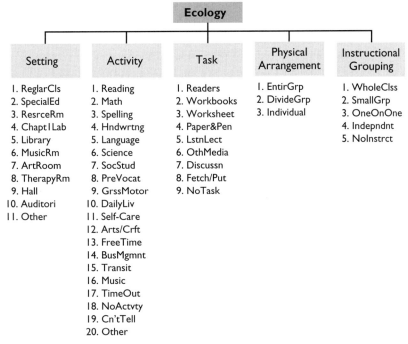

TABLE 12.2   **EBASS Academic Response Profile**

```
---------------------------------------------------------
CODES          FREQ        PERCENTAGE OCCURRENCE
------------------------------------------0--20--40--60--80--100
Writing         37       11.94%      |X
TskPartic       11        3.55%      |
ReadAloud       12        3.87%      |
RdSilent        64       20.65%      |XXX
TalkAca         29        9.35%      |X
---------------------------------------------------------
AcaRspComp     154       53.65%      |XXXXXXXX
NoAcaRsp       153       49.35%      |XXXXXXXX
Missing          4        1.29%      |
---------------------------------------------------------
TOTAL          310      100.00%      |
---------------------------------------------------------
Press ENTER to continue.
```

environmental conditions. The probability of outcome behaviors (writing), given context variables, is shown in the bottom half of Table 12.3. The probability of writing was .01 when readers were used, .27 when paper-and-pencil tasks were used, and .04 during discussion; this was in comparison with an unconditional probability of .15. The assessor would be able to tell the teacher that the probability of writing behavior decreased significantly when readers were used and increased significantly when paper-and-pencil tasks were used during reading. Discussion also reduced the probability of a writing response.

EBASS may also be used in making normative peer comparisons—comparisons of the behaviors of an individual student with the average of a peer group. Table 12.4 illustrates a normative peer comparison. It shows that the target student was looking around during 12 intervals (3.88 percent of the day) and talking inappropriately during eight intervals (2.59 percent of the day). The student's peers look around 3.29 percent of the time and talk inappropriately only 0.33 percent of the time. The difference in competing student and peer responses is also shown, and the magnitude of the differences has been computed. When D-STAT = 0, the student's performance is exactly like that of his or her peers.[1] The larger the D-STAT, the more different the student is from the peer group. Normative peer comparison data are very useful in making eligibility or exceptionality decisions.

Functional Assessment of Academic Behavior (FAAB)

We have said that, according to Carroll, the degree of learning achieved by an individual student is a function of time spent learning divided by time needed to learn. An important aspect of time needed to learn is the quality of instruction. We noted earlier that quality of instruction varies according to several factors,

1. D-STAT, or Difference Statistic, is an index of the discrepancy between the student's performance and that of his or her peers.

TABLE 12.3	EBASS Probability Analysis of Ecobehavioral Relations

```
--------<ECOLOGICAL MODEL>------------|---<OUTCOME Behavior>-----

      ACTIVITY AND TASK                ACADEMIC RESPONDING
                                     OUTCOME BEHAVIORS: Writing
-----------------------------------|------------------------
--<ECOLOGICAL MODEL>---|---<VALUES>        COND          SIGNIFI-
(at least 10% of data)   FREQ PCT    FREQ PROB Z-SCORE   CANCE
-----------------------  ---- ---    ---- ---- - -----   -----
Writing+Readers            75   30      1  0.01  -2.664    .01
Writing+Paper/Pen          71   29     19  0.27   2.295    .05
Writing+Discussn           56   22      2  0.04  -1.980    .05
Spelling+Paper/Pen         47   19     15  0.32   2.782    .01
-----------------------------------|------------------------
                                         UNCONDITIONAL
                                          PROBABILITY
                                   |------------------------
TOTAL SEQUENCES USED      249   80     37  0.15
TOTAL SEQUENCES RECORDED  310
-----------------------------------|------------------------
Press ENTER to continue.
```

```
                    Probability of Outcome Behaviors
ECOLOGICAL MODEL    0        0.1       0.2       0.3       0.4
     Values         |---------|---------|---------|---------|-

Writing+Readers     0.01XXXXXXXXXXXXX|
Writing+Paper/Pen                    |XXXXXXXXXXXXX0.27
Writing+Discussn    0.04XXXXXXXXXXX|
Spelling+Paper/Pen                   |XXXXXXXXXXXXXXXXXX0.32
                              0.15
                    (base probability level)
Press ENTER to continue.
```

including the clarity of task demands, adequacy of task presentation, and adequacy of pacing. The Algozzine-Ysseldyke Model of Effective Instruction includes a number of principles and strategies that, if present, will enhance the likelihood that students will achieve desired results. The Functional Assessment of Academic Behavior (Ysseldyke & Christenson, 2002) is designed for use in gathering data on the instructional needs, supportive conditions, and protective factors that promote learning for an individual student. An intervention tailored to the student's needs can be developed based on the extent to which components of effective instruction are present in a student's home and school environments.

In 1987 Ysseldyke and Christenson published The Instructional Environment Scale (TIES; Ysseldyke & Christenson, 1987b), the first comprehensive methodology enabling education professionals to systematically gather data on

----

TABLE 12.4   EBASS Normative Peer Comparison

```
COMPETING RESPONSE:  (Descriptive Comparison)
-----------------------------------------------------------------
CODES     TARGET PROFILE   INDEX PROFILE   DISCREPANCY PROFILE
--------|---------------|---------------|-----------------------
          Freq   Percent   Freq   Percent   Diff   DiffSq
          ----   -------   ----   -------   ----   ------
Agression    0    0.00      0     0.00      0.00    0.00
Disrupt      0    0.00      0     0.00      0.00    0.00
TalkInapp    8    2.59      1     0.33      2.26    5.11
LookArnd    12    3.88     10     3.29      0.59    0.35
NonComply    0    0.00      0     0.00      0.00    0.00
Self-Stim    0    0.00      7     2.30     -2.30    5.30
SelfAbuse    1    0.32      1     0.33     -0.01    0.00
NoInappro  285   92.23    274    90.13      2.10    4.42
Missing      3    0.97     11     3.62     -2.65    7.01
--------|---------------|---------------|-----------------------
TOTAL      309             304             9.9    22.188 SUM
                                                   4.71  D-STAT
-----------------------------------------------------------------
Press ENTER to continue.
```

```
COMPETING RESPONSE:  (Graphic Display)
-----------------------------------------------------------------
CODES       TARGET PROFILE    INDEX PROFILE   DISCREPANCY PROFILE
-----------|---------------|---------------|---------------------
Agression          |               |                 |
Disrupt            |               |                 |
TalkInapp     2.6%| _         0.3%| _         2.3%   | _
LookArnd      3.9%| _         3.3%| _         0.6%   | _
NonComply          |               |                 |
Self-Stim          |         2.3%| _        -2.3%   _ |
SelfAbuse     0.3%| _         0.3%| _        -0.0%   _ |
NoInappro    92.2%| ____     90.1%| ____      2.1%   | _
Missing       1.0%| _         3.6%| _        -2.6%   _ |
-----------|---------------|---------------|---------------------
TOTAL      100.0% (n=309) 100.0% (n=304)
-----------------------------------------------------------------
Press ENTER to continue.
```

----

the extent to which components of effective instruction are present in students' instructional environments at school. In 1993 TIES was updated and expanded as TIES-II, which included additional collection of information from the home environment. The focus of TIES-II was on how classroom and home environments can be manipulated to elicit more appropriate responses from the student. FAAB, published in 2002, represents a further expansion of the TIES system. FAAB examines the person-environment fit for learning over time and in this way can aid in enhancing the student's academic success. In addition to providing information on home and school environments, FAAB provides information on the degree of continuity across the student's home and school environments.

Based on the belief that student performance in school is a function of an interaction between the student and the learning (instructional) environment, FAAB provides a set of observational and interview forms, administration procedures, and an organizational structure that allow educators to both identify and address the instructional needs of individual students. The system is used to help professionals gather essential information on 12 instructional-environment components, five home-support-for-learning components, and six home–school-support-for-learning components. The components on which data are collected are listed and defined briefly in Table 12.5.

TABLE 12.5	Components of FAAB	
	Component	**Definition**
Instructional Environment Components	*Instructional match*	The student's needs are assessed accurately, and instruction is matched appropriately to the results of the instructional diagnosis.
	Instructional expectations	There are realistic, yet high, expectations for both the amount and the accuracy of work to be completed by the student, and these are communicated clearly to the student.
	Classroom environment	The classroom management techniques used are effective for the student; there is a positive, supportive classroom atmosphere; and time is used productively.
	Instructional presentation	Instruction is presented in a clear and effective manner; the directions contain sufficient information for the student to understand the kinds of behaviors or skills that are to be demonstrated; and the student's understanding is checked.
	Cognitive emphasis	Thinking skills and learning strategies for completing assignments are communicated explicitly to the student.
	Motivational strategies	Effective strategies for heightening student interest and effort are used with the student.
	Relevant practice	The student is given adequate opportunity to practice with appropriate materials and a high success rate; classroom tasks are clearly important to achieving instructional goals.
	Informed feedback	The student receives relatively immediate and specific information on performance or behavior; when the student makes mistakes, correction is provided.
	Academic engaged time	The student is actively engaged in responding to academic content; the teacher monitors the extent to which the student is actively engaged and redirects the student when the student is unengaged.
	Adaptive instruction	The curriculum is modified within reason to accommodate the student's unique and specific instructional needs.

(continued)

TABLE 12.5	Components of FAAB (*cont.*)	
	Component	**Definition**
	Progress evaluation	There is direct, frequent measurement of the student's progress toward completion of instructional objectives; data on the student's performance and progress are used to plan future instruction.
	Student understanding	The student demonstrates an accurate understanding of what is to be done and how it is to be done in the classroom.
Home-support-for-learning components	*Home expectations and attributions*	High, realistic expectations about schoolwork are communicated to the child, and the value of effort and working hard in school is emphasized.
	Discipline orientation	There is an authoritative, not permissive or authoritarian, approach to discipline, and the child is monitored and supervised by the parents.
	Home affective environment	The parent-child relationship is characterized by a healthy connectedness; it is generally positive and supportive.
	Parent participation	There is an educative home environment, and others participate in the child's schooling and learning, at home and/or at school.
	Structure for learning	Organization and daily routines facilitate the completion of schoolwork and support for the child's academic learning.
Home–school-support-for-learning components	*Shared standards and expectations*	The level of expected performance held by key adults for the student is congruent across home and school and reflects a belief that the student can learn.
	Consistent structure	The overall routine and monitoring provided by key adults for the student have been discussed and are congruent across home and school.
	Cross-setting opportunity to learn	The variety of learning options available to the youth during school hours and outside of school time (that is, home and community) supports the student's learning.
	Mutual support	The guidance provided by, the communication between, and the interest shown by adults to facilitate student progress in school is effective; it is what adults do on an ongoing basis to help the student learn and achieve.
	Positive, trusting relationship	The relationship is warm and friendly, the student receives praise and recognition, and the adult-youth relationship is positive and respectful. This component includes how adults in the home, in the school, and in the community work together to help the student be a learner.
	Modeling	Parents and teachers demonstrate to the student desired behaviors and commitment and value toward learning and working hard in daily life.

SOURCE: Reprinted with permission from Ysseldyke, J. E., & Christenson, S. L. (2002). *Functional assessment of academic behavior: Creating successful learning environments.* Longmont, CO: Sopris West.

FAAB is a flexible system that allows professionals to select the data collection tools they will use. Among the tools available for use is an instructional needs form, which is a checklist and free-response form to be completed by the teacher, indicating potential modifications in instruction that may be helpful for the student, as well as instructional strategies that have been found to be most effective. A checklist for parents can help identify parents' concerns about their child's school experiences. The assessor then uses an observation form to gather data in the classroom. Once that form is completed, the student is interviewed, after which the student interview form is completed. Similarly, teacher and parent interview forms are available to collect further information about both home and school environments. Once all of the data have been collected, the assessor completes the instructional environment checklist (either the regular or an annotated version), which involves rating the extent to which each of the 23 components of FAAB are present in the student's corresponding home and school environments. Assessors use the annotated version until they become familiar with the indicators of the components and then typically shift to using the short version. All ratings are qualitative judgments—judgments by a professional regarding the extent to which the factors are present.

The assessor meets with a team of professionals, including the teacher, to plan an instructional intervention for the student. FAAB outlines a detailed intervention planning and evaluation process. The FAAB manual includes an extensive set of interventions that may be selected and implemented once specific areas of need are identified.

SUMMARY

Learning happens when the learning environment is modified to facilitate an appropriate response from the student. Education and psychology have rich traditions of assessing students in order to identify causes of academic and behavioral difficulties and to develop interventions. More recently, the focus has shifted to the belief that the quickest way to close the gap between actual and desired student performance is to apply principles of effective instruction. Doing so requires identification of the extent to which the learner is getting an opportunity to learn and is willing to engage actively in learning, particularly when tasks become very difficult. It also requires identification of the extent to which components of effective instruction are present in a student's instructional environment and components of effective home support for learning are present in the home environment. In this chapter, we reviewed two systems—the Ecobehavioral Assessment System Software (EBASS) and Functional Assessment of Academic Behavior (FAAB).

EBASS is a computerized observational system designed to gather very specific information on student behavior in class. FAAB is a qualitative observation-and-interview system designed to provide more global judgments of the extent to which a student is exposed to effective instruction. Both systems are new ways of taking into account the interactions among students, tasks, and instructional methodologies that determine the extent to which a student achieves desired results. These systems provide a new way to look at complex interactions among individuals and contextual factors, and enable us to identify naturally occurring effective procedures in classrooms.

QUESTIONS FOR CHAPTER REVIEW

1. What is instructional ecology, and why is it important to take this into account in assessment?

2. Identify and describe the four components of effective instruction.

3. Select one component of the Algozzine-Ysseldyke Model of Effective Instruction and describe it in detail.

4. Describe the advantages and disadvantages of using both EBASS and FAAB for assessing instructional ecology.

PROJECT

Talk to a school psychologist about the assessment of the instructional ecology of a student referred for academic difficulties. Discuss both the need for this type of assessment and the extent to which the psychologist views it as relevant to his or her particular duties.

RESOURCES FOR FURTHER INVESTIGATION

Print Resources

Algozzine, B. A., Ysseldyke, J. E., & Elliot, J. L. (1997). *Strategies and tactics for effective instruction* (2nd ed.). Longmont, CO: Sopris West.

Arreaga-Mayer, C., Carta, J. J., & Tapia, Y. (1995). Ecobehavioral assessment: A new methodology for evaluating instruction for exceptional culturally and linguistically diverse students. In S. B. Garcia (Ed.), *Shaping the future: Defining effective services for exceptional culturally and linguistically diverse learners* (Monograph 1). Washington, DC: CEC-DDEL.

Arreaga-Mayer, C., Utley, C. A., Perdomo-Rivera, C., & Greenwood, C. R. (2003). Ecobehavioral assessment of instructional contexts in bilingual special education programs for English language learners at risk for developmental disabilties. *Focus on Autism and Other Developmental Disabilities, 18*(1), 28–40.

Elliott, J. L., Algozzine, B. A., & Ysseldyke, J. E. (1998). *Timesavers for educators.* Longmont, CO: Sopris West.

Greenwood, C. R., Carta, J. J., Kamps, D., & Delquadri, J. (1995). *Ecobehavioral Assessment System Software.* Kansas City, KS: Juniper Gardens Children's Center.

Greenwood, C. R., Carta, J. J., Kamps, D., Terry, B., & Delquadri, J. (1994). Development and validation of standard classroom observation systems for school practitioners: Ecobehavioral Assessment System Software (EBASS). *Exceptional Children, 61,* 197–210.

Greenwood, C. R., Horton, B. T., & Utley, C. A. (2002). Academic engagement: Current perspectives on research and practice. *School Psychology Review, 31*(3), 328–349.

Ysseldyke, J. E., & Christenson, S. L. (2002). *Functional assessment of academic behavior: Creating successful learning environments.* Longmont, CO: Sopris West.

Ysseldyke, J. E., Christenson, S. L., & Kovaleski, J. F. (1994). Identifying students' instructional needs in the context of classroom and home environments. *Teaching Exceptional Children, 26*(3), 37–41.

Technology Resources

THE JUNIPER GARDENS

www.jgcp.ku.edu

The home page for the Juniper Gardens Children's Project presents the background, purpose, and results of research on teaching and services for youth and children with disabilities in the Kansas City, Kansas, area.

ASSESSMENT

www.ncrel.org/ncrel/sdrs/areas/as0cont.htm

This page provides links to pages that examine critical issues in assessment, including integrating assessment and instruction in ways that support learning.

ERIC CLEARINGHOUSE ON ASSESSMENT AND EVALUATION

www.ericae.net

This website provides balanced information concerning educational assessment and resources to encourage responsible use of tests.

SOPRIS WEST

www.sopriswest.com

This is the website for Sopris West, publisher of materials used to help meet the needs of students at risk. Descriptions of products are available, including FAAB.

CHAPTER 13

Teacher-Made Tests of Achievement

MOST EVALUATIONS OF STUDENT ACHIEVEMENT ARE CONDUCTED BY TEACHERS WITH materials that they have developed themselves. Although the specific assessment practices that they actually use in their classrooms are not well documented, the professional literature suggests that assessment practices vary along a continuum from objective-analytic to subjective-holistic. When applied to assessment, the term *objective* carries two connotations. First, objective assessments are not influenced by emotion, conjecture, or personal prejudice; second, they are based on observable phenomena. (We recognize that complete objectivity may be difficult, if not impossible, to attain in some situations. However, greater objectivity is always better than lower objectivity.) The term *analytic* suggests an examination of the individual elements in a performance, although it does not preclude examining the whole performance, as well. The term *subjective* suggests that evaluations are limited to personal perceptions and are essentially unverifiable using external criteria. The term *holistic* implies attention only to performance as a whole, not to discrete elements of a performance.

Within an objective-analytic approach, teachers systematically assess both the key components of performance and the key elements within each component. Suppose, for example, that a teacher required students to conduct and document a scientific experiment in a lab book. The key components and elements the teacher might look for could include the following:

1. Follow each step in the scientific method.
   a. Make observations.
   b. Generate hypotheses.
   c. Develop procedures for collecting data.
   d. Collect data.
   e. Test hypotheses.

2. Follow each prescribed safety procedure.

   a. Wear safety glasses or goggles.

   b. Turn on hood fans.

   c. Keep caps on reagent bottles.

3. Write a description of the experiment.

   a. Use complete and grammatically correct sentences.

   b. Spell scientific terms correctly.

   c. Write in ink.

   d. Put the descriptions in lab notebooks.

After identifying the key elements in the task, the teacher then develops objective scoring standards to assess student performance. For example, the teacher can prepare a list of scientific terms that must be correctly spelled and deduct one point for each misspelled term (but not for each repeated misspelling of the same term). In this scenario, the scoring relies on both observable performance or products (the written spelling of scientific terms) and explicit criteria for a correct response applied to all students.

Within a subjective-holistic approach, the key components, key elements, and criteria for scoring need not be specified. At the extreme, this approach may be as simple as reading a product, getting an overall sense of correctness, and then awarding a grade based on that general impression. For example, a teacher might award an A to a report that contained no major errors or omissions. However, what constitutes a major error or omission could take into account any number of factors besides the student's actual performance. For example, a teacher might consider a student's performance history in awarding a grade. Thus a minor error committed by a student with a history of excellent work could be viewed more negatively than the same error committed by a student who had a history of poor work.

Subjective-holistic approaches frequently use scoring rubrics to guide teachers in reaching summary evaluations. A scoring rubric contains the important components (often called "dimensions") that should be considered in reaching an overall rating. For example, a teacher might rate the written description of a scientific experiment on three dimensions: following the scientific method, following safety procedures, and showing a high quality of written description. However, scoring rubrics do not enumerate the critical elements or provide objective criteria for rating performance on the dimensions. Rubrics can be as simple as a list of components that are awarded a summary grade (for example, following the scientific method = B, following safety procedures = A, and showing a high quality of written description = B–; overall grade = B). Dimensions within a rubric are sometimes scaled. For example, following the scientific method could be scaled from emerging to mastery. However, the scoring anchors (for example, emerging) are seldom objective.

We prefer an objective-analytic approach for three reasons. First, a student should earn the same score, no matter who does the scoring. An objective-analytic approach produces high interscorer reliability; a subjective-holistic approach does not. (In the chapter "Portfolio Assessment," the section on score reliability provides several references to the limited reliability of holistic scoring of writing samples.) Second, fairness and equity require that students be evaluated on the same dimensions with the same criteria. An objective-analytic approach applies the same criteria on the same dimensions to all students; a subjective-holistic approach celebrates different standards for different students. Third, students need to know what mistakes have been made or how to improve their performances. An objective-analytic approach provides this type of information; a subjective-holistic approach does not.

In addition, the use of objective-analytic methods is not merely a matter of personal preference. Federal regulations require that students with disabilities be evaluated using objective procedures. Thus special educators are usually trained in objective-analytic procedures. However, because general educators are usually trained in subjective-holistic approaches, the difference in paradigms can cause all sorts of problems when general and special educators work together to provide an education for all students in an inclusive classroom.

This chapter provides a general overview of objective-analytic practices for teachers who develop their own tests for classroom assessment in the core areas of reading, mathematics, spelling, and written language. Classroom assessment is a topic suitable for an entire text, and this chapter provides only a general overview of the formats for testing and the criteria for evaluating pupil performance. For more specific information on test construction, educational decision making, and managing assessment within the classroom, refer to texts such as those by Linn and Gronlund (2000) and Salvia and Hughes (1990). In addition, refer to other chapters in this text for discussion of various specific assessment procedures.

Why Do Teachers Assess Achievement?

Teachers regularly set aside time to assess their pupils for a variety of purposes. Most commonly, teachers make up tests to ascertain the extent to which their students have learned or are learning what has been taught or assigned. Knowledge about the extent to which students have mastered curricula allows teachers to make decisions on a variety of fronts—selection of current and future instructional objectives, placement of students in instructional groups, evaluation of the teachers' own instructional performances, and the necessity of referring students to other educational specialists for additional instructional services. Each of these decisions should be based on student achievement of instructional objectives.

When students have met their instructional objectives, it is time to move on to new or related objectives. Students who meet objectives so rapidly that they are being held back by slower peers can be grouped for enrichment activities or faster-paced instruction; slower students can be grouped so that they can learn necessary concepts to the point of mastery without impeding the progress of their faster-learning peers. When many students in a classroom fail to learn material, teachers should suspect that something is wrong with their materials, their techniques, or some other aspect of instruction. For example, the students may lack prerequisite concepts or skills, or the instruction may be too fast paced or poorly sequenced. Finally, when students lag far behind their peers in crucial curricular areas, teachers may seek outside help. For example, a student may be given Chapter I assistance (special remedial or compensatory instruction for students with difficulties who attend schools with large numbers of students from the lowest economic strata), be tutored, be placed in a slower educational track, or be referred to a child-study team to determine entitlement to receive other special educational services.

Advantages of Teacher-Made Tests

Often teacher-made tests are not held in high regard. For example, some measurement specialists (such as Thorndike & Hagen, 1978) list carefully prepared test items as an advantage of norm-referenced achievement tests. By implication, careful preparation of questions may not be a characteristic of teacher-made tests. In addition, adjectives such as "informal" or "unstandardized" may be used to describe teacher-made tests. As a group, however, teacher-made tests cannot be considered informal, because they are not given haphazardly or casually. They also cannot be considered unstandardized, because students usually receive the same materials and directions, and the same criteria usually are used in correcting student answers. Perhaps a better characterization of teacher-made tests is that they are not usually subject to public scrutiny and may be more variable than commercial tests in terms of their technical adequacy (that is, reliability and validity). However, these characterizations are themselves speculative.

Teacher-made tests can be better suited to evaluation of student achievement than are commercially prepared, norm-referenced achievement tests. The disadvantages of commercially prepared tests readily illustrate the two potential advantages of teacher-made tests: curriculum match and sensitivity.

First, commercially prepared tests are rarely designed to assess achievement within specific curricula (see, for example, Crocker, Miller, & Franks, 1989). Rather, these tests are intentionally constructed to have general applicability so that they can be used with students in almost any curriculum. This intentional generality is in sharp contrast to the development of distinctive curricula. It has become increasingly clear that various curriculum series differ from one another in the particular educational objectives covered, the performance level expected of students, and the sequence of objectives; for example, DISTAR mathematics differs from Scott, Foresman mathematics (Shriner & Salvia, 1988). Even within the same curriculum series, teachers modify instruction to provide enrichment or remedial instruction. Thus two teachers using the same curriculum series may offer different instruction. Although teachers may not construct tests that match the curriculum, they are in the best position to know precisely what has been taught and what level of performance is expected from students. Consequently, they are the only ones who can match testing to instruction.

Second, the overwhelming majority of commercially prepared, norm-referenced tests are intended, first and foremost, to discriminate efficiently among test takers. Developers of norm-referenced tests try to strike a balance between including the minimum number of test items to allow reliable discrimination and including enough items to ensure content validity. This practice results in relatively insensitive tests that are unable to discriminate small changes in pupil performance. For example, to produce a reliable, norm-referenced test, it may be unnecessary to discriminate students who know the single-digit addition facts with 2s, 4s, and 6s from those who also know them with 3s, 5s, and 7s. However, when instruction on all single-digit addends is provided, teachers probably will want to know, for example, which students have not yet mastered the 4s (and which of the 4s), so that they can provide further instruction as needed. Moreover, once students have mastered the 4s, the change in their skill level should be observable from changes in test performance.

In short, teachers need tests that are sensitive to small changes in knowledge. Norm-referenced tests are not well suited to this purpose, not only because they contain relatively few relevant items, but also because they seldom are published in multiple forms.[1] Teachers who are concerned with pupil mastery of specific concepts and skills are in a position to test a narrow range of objectives directly and frequently.

Testing Formats Used by Teachers

When a teacher wants either to compare the performance of several students on a skill or set of skills, or to assess pupil performance over time, the assessment must be standardized. Otherwise, observed differences could be reasonably attributed to differences in testing procedures. To be standardized, tests must use consistent directions, criteria for scoring, and procedures (for example, time allowed to complete a test). Almost any test can be standardized if it results in observable behavior or a permanent product (for example, a student's written response).

When a teacher wants to use a test to assess the extent to which a pupil has mastered a skill or a set of skills, then it is important that the competencies to be demonstrated are specified clearly. Teachers will need to know the objectives, standards, or outcomes that they expect students to work toward mastering, and they will need to specify the level of performance that is acceptable.

Test formats can be classified along two dimensions: (1) the modality through which the item is presented—test items usually require a student to look at or to listen to the question, although other modalities may be substituted, depending on the particulars of a situation or on characteristics of students—and (2) the modality through which a student responds—test items usually require an oral or written response, although pointing responses are frequently used with

---

1. Teachers assess frequently to detect changes in student achievement. However, frequent testing with exactly the same test usually produces a practice effect. Unless there are multiple forms for a test, student learning may be confused with practice effect.

students who are nonverbal. Teachers may use "see–write," "see–say," "hear–write," and "hear–say" to specify the testing modality dimensions.

In addition, "write" formats can be of two types. *Selection formats* require students to indicate their choice from an array of possible answers (usually termed "response options"). True-false, multiple-choice, and matching are the three common selection formats. However, they are not the only ones possible; for example, students may be required to circle incorrectly spelled words or words that should be capitalized in text. Formats requiring students to select the correct answer can be used to assess much more than the recognition of information, although they are certainly useful for that purpose. They can also be used to assess students' understanding, their ability to draw inferences, and their correct application of principles. Selection questions are not usually well suited for assessing achievement at the levels of analysis, synthesis, and evaluation. (See the chapter "Validity" for a discussion of these types of assessment.)

Supply formats require a student to produce a written or an oral response. This response can be as restricted as the answer to a computation problem or a one-word response to the question "When did the potato famine begin in Ireland?" Often, the response to supply questions is more involved and can require a student to produce a sentence, a paragraph, or several pages.

As a general rule, supply questions can be prepared fairly quickly, but scoring them may be very time consuming. Even when one-word responses or numbers are requested, teachers may have difficulty finding the response on a student's test paper, deciphering the handwriting, or correctly applying criteria for awarding points. In contrast, selection formats usually require a considerable amount of time to prepare, but once prepared, the tests can be scored quickly and by almost anyone.

The particular formats teachers choose are influenced by the purposes for testing and the characteristics of the test takers. Testing formats are essentially bottom up or top down. Bottom-up formats assess the mastery of specific objectives to allow generalizations about student competence in a particular domain. Top-down formats survey general competence in a domain and assess in greater depth those topics for which mastery is incomplete. For day-to-day monitoring of instruction and selecting short-term instructional objectives, we favor bottom-up assessment. With this type of assessment, a teacher can be relatively sure that specific objectives have been mastered and that he or she is not spending needless instructional time teaching students what they already know. For determining starting places for instruction with new students and for assessing maintenance and generalization of previously learned material, we favor top-down assessment. Generally, this approach should be more efficient in terms of teachers' and students' time because broader survey tests can cover a lot of material in a short period of time.

With students who are able to read and write independently, see–write formats are generally more efficient for both individual students and groups. When testing individual students, teachers or teacher aides can give the testing materials to the students and can proceed with other activities while the students are completing the test. Moreover, when students write their responses, a teacher can defer correcting the examinations until a convenient time.

See–say formats are also useful. Teacher aides or other students can listen to the test takers' responses and can correct them on the spot or record them for later evaluation. Moreover, many teachers have access to electronic equipment that can greatly facilitate the use of see–say formats (for example, tape recorders or digital video recorders).

The hear–write format is especially useful with selection formats for younger students and students who cannot read independently. This format can also be used for testing groups of students and is routinely used in the assessment of spelling when students are required to write words from dictation. With other content, teachers can give directions and read the test questions aloud, and students can mark their responses. The primary difficulty with a hear–write format with groups of students is the pacing of test items; teachers must allot sufficient time between items for slower-responding students to make their selections.

Hear–say formats are most suitable for assessing individual students who do not write independently or who write at such slow speeds that their written responses are unrepresentative of what they know. Even with this format, teachers need not preside over the assessment; other students or a teacher aide can administer, record, and perhaps evaluate the student's responses.

Considerations in Preparing Tests

Teachers need to build skills in developing tests that are fair, reliable, and valid. The following kinds of considerations are important in developing or preparing tests.

Selecting Specific Areas of the Curriculum

Tests are samples of behavior. When narrow skills are being assessed (for example, spelling words from dictation), either all the components of the domain should be tested (in this case, all the assigned spelling words), or a representative sample should be selected and assessed. The qualifier "representative" implies that an appropriate number of easy and difficult words—and of words from the beginning, middle, and end of the assignment—will be selected. When more complex domains are assessed, teachers should concentrate on the more important facts or relationships and avoid the trivial.

Writing Relevant Questions

Teachers must select and use enough questions to allow valid inferences about students' mastery of all the material taught in class. Nothing offends test takers quite as much as a test's failure to cover material they have studied and know, except perhaps their own failure to guess what content a teacher believes to be important enough to test. In addition, fairness demands that the way in which the question is asked be familiar and expected by the student. For example, if students were to take a test on the addition of single-digit integers, it would be a bad idea to test them using a missing-addend format (for example, "4 + __ = 7") unless that format had been specifically taught and was expected by the students.

Organizing and Sequencing Items

The organization of a test is a function of many factors. When a teacher wants a student to complete all the items and to indicate mastery of content (a power test), then it is best to intersperse easy and difficult items. When the desire is to measure automaticity or the number of items that can be completed within a specific time period (a timed test), it is best to organize items from easy to difficult. Pages of test questions or problems to be solved should not be cluttered.

Developing Formats for Presentation and Response Modes

Different response formats can be used within the same test, although it is generally a good idea to group together questions with the same format. Regardless of the format used, the primary consideration is that the test questions be a fair sample of the material being assessed.

Writing Directions for Administration

Regardless of question format, the directions should indicate clearly what a student is to do—for example, "Circle the correct option," "Choose the best answer," "Match each item in column b to one item in column a," and so forth. Also, teachers should explain what, if any, materials may be used by students; any time limits; any unusual scoring procedures (for example, penalties for guessing); and point values when the students are mature enough to be given questions that have different point values.

Developing Systematic Procedures for Scoring Responses

As discussed in the opening paragraphs of this chapter, teachers must have predetermined and systematic criteria for scoring responses. However, if a teacher discovers an error or omission in criteria, the criteria should be modified. Obviously, previously scored responses must be rescored with the revised criteria.

Establishing Criteria to Interpret Student Performance

Teachers should specify in advance the criteria they will use for assigning grades or weighting assignments. For example, they may want to specify that students who earn a certain number of points on a test will earn a specific grade, or they may want to assign grades on the basis of the class distribution of performance. In either case, they must specify what it takes to earn certain grades or how assignments will be evaluated and weighted.

Response Formats

Selection Formats

Three types of selection formats are commonly used: multiple-choice, matching, and true-false. Of the three, multiple-choice questions are clearly the most useful.

Multiple-Choice Questions

Multiple-choice questions are the most difficult to prepare. These questions have two parts: (1) a *stem* that contains the question and (2) a response set that contains both the correct answer, termed the *keyed response,* and one or more incorrect options, termed *distractors.* In preparing multiple-choice questions, teachers should generally follow these guidelines:

- Keep the response options short and of approximately equal length. Students quickly learn that longer options tend to be correct.

- Keep material that is common to all options in the stem. For example, if the first word in each option is "the," it should be put into the stem and removed from the options.

- Avoid grammatical tip-offs. Students can discard grammatically incorrect options. For example, when the correct answer must be plural, alert students will disregard singular options; when the correct answer must be a noun, students will disregard options that are verbs.

- Avoid implausible options. In the best questions, distractors should be attractive to students who do not know the answer. Common errors and misconceptions are often good distractors.

- Make sure that one and only one option is correct. Students should not have to read their teacher's mind to guess which wrong answer is the least wrong or which right answer is the most correct.

- Avoid interdependent questions. Generally, it is bad practice to make the selection of the correct option dependent on getting a prior question correct.

- Vary the position of the correct response in the options. Students will recognize patterns of correct options (for example, when the correct answers to a sequence of questions are a, b, c, d, a, b, c, d) or a teacher's preference for a specific position (usually c).

- Avoid options that indicate multiple correct options (for example, "all the above" or "both a and b are correct"). These options often simplify the question.

- Avoid similar incorrect options. Students who can eliminate one of the two similar options can readily dismiss the other one. For example, if citrus fruit is wrong, lemon must be wrong.

- Avoid using the same words and examples that were used in the students' texts or in class presentations.

- Make sure that one question does not provide information that can be used to answer another question. For example, teachers should not introduce one question with "In 1492, Columbus landed in the Western" and then ask another question requesting the year in which Columbus arrived in the Western Hemisphere.

When appropriate, teachers can make multiple-choice questions more challenging by asking students to recognize an instance of a rule or concept, by requiring students to recall and use material that is not present in the question, or by increasing the number of options. (For younger children, three options are generally difficult enough. Older students can be expected to answer questions with four or five options.) In no case should teachers deliberately mislead or trick students.

Matching Questions

Matching questions are a variant of multiple-choice questions in which a set of stems is simultaneously associated with a set of options. Generally, the content of matching questions is limited to simple factual associations (Gronlund, 1985). Teachers usually prepare matching questions so that there are as many options as stems, and an option can be associated only once with a stem in the set. Although we do not recommend their use, there are other possibilities: more options than stems, selection of all correct options for one stem, and multiple use of an option.[2] These additional possibilities increase the difficulty of the question set considerably.

In general, we prefer multiple-choice questions over matching questions. Almost any matching question can be written as a series of multiple-choice questions in which the same or similar options are used. Of course, the correct response will change. However, teachers wishing to use matching questions should consider the following guidelines:

- Each set of matching items should have some dimension in common (for example, explorers and dates of discovery). This makes preparation easier for the teacher and provides the student with some insight into the relationship required to select the correct option.

- Keep the length of the stems approximately the same, and keep the length and grammar used in the options equivalent. At best, mixing grammatical forms will eliminate some options for some questions; at worst, it will provide the correct answer to several questions.

- Make sure that one and only one option is correct for each stem.

- Vary the sequence of correct responses when more than one matching question is asked.

- Avoid using the same words and examples that were used in the students' texts or in class presentations.

It is easier for a student when questions and options are presented in two columns. When there is a difference in the length of the items in each column, the longer item should be used as the stem. Stems should be placed on the left and options on the right, rather than stems above with options below them. Moreover, all the elements of the question should be kept on one page. Finally, teachers often allow students to draw lines to connect questions and options. Although this has the obvious advantage of helping students keep track of where their answers should be placed, erasures or scratch-outs can be a headache to the person who corrects the test. There is a commercially available product (Learning Wrap Ups) that has cards printed with stems and answers, and a shoelace with which to "lace" stems to correct answers. The correct lacing pattern is printed on the back, so it is self-correcting. Teachers could make such cards fairly easily, as an alternative to trying to correct tests with lots of erasures.

2. Scoring for these options is complicated. Generally, separate errors are counted for selecting an incorrect option and failing to select a correct option. Thus the number of errors can be very large.

True-False Statements

In most cases, true-false statements should simply not be used. Their utility lies primarily in assessing knowledge of factual information, which can be better assessed with other formats. Effective true-false items are difficult to prepare. Because guessing the correct answer is so likely—it happens 50 percent of the time—the reliability of true-false tests is generally low. As a result, they may well have limited validity. Nonetheless, if a teacher chooses to use this format, a few suggestions should be followed:

- Avoid specific determiners such as "all," "never," "always," and so on.
- Avoid sweeping generalizations. Such statements tend to be true, but students can often think of minor exceptions. Thus there is a problem in the criterion for evaluating the truthfulness of the question. Attempts to avoid the problem by adding restrictive conditions (for example, "with minor exceptions") either render the question obviously true or leave a student trying to guess what the restrictive condition means.
- Avoid convoluted sentences. Tests should assess knowledge of content, not a student's ability to comprehend difficult prose.
- Keep true and false statements approximately the same length. As is the case with longer options on multiple-choice questions, longer true-false statements tend to be true.
- Balance the number of true and false statements. If a student recognizes that there are more of one type of statement than of the other, the odds of guessing the correct answer will exceed 50 percent.

Special Considerations for Students with Disabilities

In developing and using items that employ a selection format, teachers must pay attention to individual differences among students, particularly to disabilities that might interfere with performance. For example, students who have skill deficits in remembering things for short periods of time, or who do not attend well to verbally or visually presented information, may have difficulty with multiple-choice items. Students who have difficulty figuring out the organization of visually presented material will have difficulty with matching items.

Supply Formats It is useful to distinguish between items requiring a student to write one- or two-word responses (such as fill-in questions) and those requiring more extended responses (such as essay questions). Both types of items require careful delineation of what constitutes a correct response (that is, criteria for scoring). It is generally best for teachers to prepare criteria for a correct response at the time they prepare the question. In that way, they can ensure that the question is written in such a way as to elicit the correct types of answers—or at least not to mislead students—and perhaps save time when correcting exams. (If teachers change criteria for a correct response after they have scored a few questions, they should rescore all previously scored questions with the revised criteria.)

Fill-In Questions

Aside from mathematics problems that require students to calculate an answer and writing spelling words from dictation, fill-in questions require a student to complete a statement by adding a concept or fact—for example, "_____ arrived in America in 1492." Fill-ins are useful in assessing knowledge and comprehension objectives; they are not useful in assessing application, analysis, synthesis, or evaluation objectives. Teachers preparing fill-in questions should follow these guidelines:

■ Keep each sentence short. Generally, the less superfluous information in an item, the clearer the question will be to the student and the less likely it will be that one question will cue another.

■ If a two-word answer is required, teachers should use two blanks to indicate this in the sentence.

■ Avoid sentences with multiple blanks. For example, the item "In the year _____, _____ discovered _____." is so vague that practically any date, name, and event can be inserted correctly, even ones that are irrelevant to the content; for example, "In the year 1999, Henry discovered girls."

■ Keep the size of all blanks consistent and large enough to accommodate readily the longest answer. The size of the blank should not provide a clue about the length of the correct word.

The most problematic aspect of fill-in questions is the necessity of developing an appropriate response bank of acceptable answers. Often, some student errors may consist of a partially correct response; teachers must decide which answers will receive partial credit, full credit, and no credit. For example, a question may anticipate "Columbus" as the correct response, but a student might write "that Italian dude who was looking for the shortcut to India for the Spanish king and queen." In deciding how far afield to go in crediting unanticipated responses, teachers should look over test questions carefully to see whether the student's answer comes from information presented in another question (for example, "The Spanish monarch employed an Italian sailor to find a shorter route to").

Extended Responses

Essay questions are most useful in assessing comprehension, application, analysis, synthesis, and evaluation objectives. There are two major problems associated with extended response questions. First, teachers are generally able to sample only a limited amount of information because answers may take a long time for students to write. Second, extended essay responses are the most difficult type of answer to score. To avoid subjectivity and inconsistency, teachers should use a scoring key that assigns specific point values for each element in the ideal or criterion answer. In most cases, spelling and grammatical errors should not be deducted from the point total. Moreover, bonus points should not be awarded for particularly detailed responses; many good students will provide a complete answer to one question and spend any extra time working on questions that are more difficult for them.

Finally, teachers should be prepared to deal with responses in which a student tries to bluff a correct answer. Rather than leave a question unanswered, some students may answer a related question that was not asked, or they may structure their response so that they can omit important information that they cannot remember or never knew. Sometimes they will even write a poem or a treatise on why the question asked is unimportant or irrelevant. Therefore, teachers must be very specific about how they will award points, stick to their criteria unless they discover that something is wrong with them, and not give credit to creative bluffs.

Teachers should also be very precise in the directions that they give so that students will not have to guess what responses their teachers will credit. Following are a number of verbs (and their meanings) that are commonly used in essay questions. It is often worthwhile to explain these terms in the test directions to make sure that students know what kind of answer is desired.

- *Describe, define,* and *identify* mean to give the meaning, essential characteristics, or place within a taxonomy.
- *List* means to enumerate and implies that complete sentences and paragraphs are not required unless specifically requested.
- *Discuss* requires more than a description, definition, or identification; a student is expected to draw implications and elucidate relationships.
- *Explain* means to analyze and make clear or comprehensible a concept, event, principle, relationship, or so forth; thus *explain* requires going beyond a definition to describe the hows or whys.
- *Compare* means to identify and explain similarities between two or among more things.
- *Contrast* means to identify and explain differences between two or among more things.
- *Evaluate* means to give the value of something and implies an enumeration and explanation of assets and liabilities, pros and cons.

Finally, unless students know the questions in advance, teachers should allow students sufficient time for planning and rereading answers. For example, if teachers believe that 10 minutes are necessary to write an extended essay to answer a question that requires original thinking, they might allow 20 minutes for the question. The less fluent the students are, the greater is the proportion of time that should be allotted.

Special Considerations in Assessing Students with Disabilities

In developing items that employ a supply format, teachers must pay attention to individual differences among learners, particularly to disabilities that may interfere with performance. For example, students who write very slowly can be expected to have difficulty with fill-in or essay questions. Students who have considerable difficulty expressing themselves in writing will probably have difficulty completing or performing well on essay examinations. Remember, it is important to assess the skills that students have, not the effects of disability conditions.

Assessment in Core Achievement Areas

The assessment procedures used by teachers are a function of the content being taught, the criterion to which content is to be learned (such as 80 percent mastery), and the characteristics of the students. With primary-level curricula in core areas, teachers usually want more than knowledge from their students; they want the material learned so well that correct responses are automatic. For example, teachers do not want their students to think about forming the letter *a*, sounding out the word *the*, or using number lines to solve simple addition problems such as "3 + 5 = "; they want their students to respond immediately and correctly. Even in intermediate-level materials, teachers seek highly proficient responding from their students, whether that performance involves performing two-digit multiplication, reading short stories, writing short stories, or writing spelling words from dictation. However, teachers in all grades, but especially in secondary schools, are also interested in their students' understanding of vast amounts of information about their social, cultural, and physical worlds, as well as their acquisition and application of critical-thinking skills. The assessment of skills taught to high degrees of proficiency is quite different from the assessment of understanding and critical-thinking skills.

In the sections that follow, core achievement areas are discussed in terms of three important attributes: the skills and information to be learned within the major strands of most curricula, the assessment of skills to be learned to proficiency, and the assessment of understanding of information and concepts. Critical-thinking skills are usually embedded within content areas and are assessed in the same ways as understanding of information is assessed—with written multiple-choice and extended-essay questions.

Reading   Reading is usually divided into decoding skills and comprehension. The specific behaviors included in each of these subdomains will depend on the particular curriculum and its sequencing.

Beginning Skills

Beginning decoding relies on students' ability to analyze and manipulate sounds and syllables in words (Stanovich, 2000). Instruction in beginning reading can include letter recognition, letter-sound correspondences, sight vocabulary, phonics, and, in some curricula, morphology. Automaticity is the goal for the skills to be learned. See–say (for example, "What letter is this?") and hear–say (for example, "What sound does the letter make?") formats are regularly used for both instruction and assessment. During students' acquisition of specific skills, teachers should first stress the accuracy of student responses. Generally, this concern translates into allowing a moment or two for students to think about their responses. A generally accepted criterion for completion for early learning is 90 percent correct. As soon as accuracy has been attained (and sometimes before), teachers change their criteria from accurate responses to fast and accurate responses. For see–say formats, fluent students will need no thinking time for simple material; for example, they should be able to respond as rapidly as teachers can change stimuli to questions such as "What is this letter?" Once students accurately decode letters and letter combinations fluently, the emphasis shifts to fluency or the automatic retrieval of words. Fluency is a combination of speed and accuracy and is widely viewed as a fundamental prerequisite for reading comprehension (National Institute of Child Health and Human Development, 2000a, 2000b).

For beginners, reading comprehension is usually assessed in one of three ways: by assessing students' retelling, their responses to comprehension questions, or their rate of oral reading. The most direct method is to have students retell what they have read without access to the reading passage. Retold passages may be scored on the basis of the number of words recalled. Fuchs, Fuchs, and Maxwell (1988) have offered two relatively simple scoring procedures that appear to offer valid indications of comprehension. Retelling may be conducted orally or in writing. With students who have relatively undeveloped writing skills, retelling should be oral when it is used to assess comprehension, but it may be in writing as a practice or drill activity. Teachers can listen to students retell, or students can retell using tape recorders so that their efforts can be evaluated later.

A second common method of assessing comprehension is to ask students questions about what they have read. Questions should address main ideas, important relationships, and relevant details. Questions may be in supply or selection formats, and either hear–say or see–write formats can be used conveniently. As with retelling, teachers should concentrate their efforts on the gist of the passage.

A third convenient, although indirect, method of assessing reading comprehension is to assess the rate of oral reading. One of the earliest attempts to explain the relationship between rate of oral reading and comprehension was offered by LaBerge and Samuels (1974), who noted that poor decoding skills created a bottleneck that impeded the flow of information, thus impeding comprehension. The relationship makes theoretical sense: Slow readers must expend their energy decoding words (for example, attending to letters, remembering letter-sound associations, blending sounds, or searching for context cues), rather than concentrating on the meaning of what is written. Not only is the relationship between reading fluency and comprehension logical; empirical research also supports this relationship (Freeland, Skinner, Jackson, McDaniel, & Smith, 2002; National Institute of Child Health and Human Development, 2000a, 2000b; Sindelar, Monda, & O'Shea, 1990).

Therefore, teachers probably should concentrate on the rate of oral reading regularly with beginning readers. To assess reading rate, teachers should have students read for two minutes from appropriate materials. The reading passage should include familiar vocabulary, syntax, and content; the passage must be longer than the amount any student can read in the two-minute period. Teachers have their own copy of the passage on which to note errors. The number of words read correctly and the number of errors made in two minutes are each divided by two to calculate the rate per minute. Mercer and Mercer (1985) suggest a rate of 80 words per minute (with two or fewer errors) as a desirable goal for reading words from lists and a rate of 100 words per minute (with two or fewer errors) for words in text. See the chapter "Assessment of Reading" for a more complete discussion of errors in oral reading.

Advanced Skills

Students who have already mastered basic sight vocabulary and decoding skills generally read silently. Emphasis for these students shifts, and new demands are made. Decoding moves from oral reading to silent reading with subvocalization (that is, saying the words and phrases to themselves) to visual scanning without subvocalization; thus the reading rates of some students may exceed 1,000 words per minute. Scanning for main ideas and information may also be taught systematically. The demands for reading comprehension may go well beyond the literal comprehension of a passage; summarizing, drawing inferences, recognizing and understanding symbolism, sarcasm, irony, and so forth may be systematically taught. For these advanced students, the gist of a passage is usually more important than the details. Teachers of more advanced students may wish to score retold passages on the basis of main ideas, important relationships, and details recalled correctly, and the number of errors (that is, ideas, relationships, and details omitted plus the insertion of material not included in the passage). In such cases, the different types of information can be weighted differently, or the use of comprehension strategies (for example, summarization) can be encouraged. However, read–write assessment formats using multiple-choice and extended-essay questions are more commonly used.

Informal Reading Inventories

When making decisions about referral or initial placement in a reading curriculum, teachers often develop *informal reading inventories (IRIs),* which assess decoding and reading comprehension over a wide range of skill levels within the specific reading curricula used in a classroom. Thus they are top-down assessments that span several levels of difficulty.

IRIs are given to locate the reading levels at which a student reads independently, requires instruction, and is frustrated. Techniques for developing IRIs and the criteria used to define independent, instructional, and frustration reading levels vary. Teachers should use a series of graded reading passages that range from below a student's actual placement to a year or two above the actual placement. If a reading series prepared for several grade levels is used, passages can be selected from the beginning, middle, and end of each grade. Students begin reading the easiest material and continue reading until they can decode less than 85 percent of the words. Salvia and Hughes (1990) recommend an accuracy rate of

95 percent for independent reading and consider 85 to 95 percent accuracy the level at which a student requires instruction.

Mathematics Eight major components are usually considered in comprehensive mathematics curricula: readiness skills, vocabulary and concepts, numeration, whole-number operations, fractions and decimals, ratios and percentages, measurement, and geometry (Salvia & Hughes, 1990). At any grade level, the specific skills and concepts included in each of these subdomains will depend on the particular curriculum and its sequencing. Mathematics curricula usually contain both problem sets that require only computations and word problems that require selection and application of the correct algorithm as well as computation. The difficulty of application problems goes well beyond the difficulty of the computation involved and is related to three factors: (1) the number of steps involved in the solution (for example, a student might have to add and then multiply; Caldwell & Goldin, 1979); (2) the amount of extraneous information (Englert, Cullata, & Horn, 1987); and (3) whether the mathematical operation is directly implied by the vocabulary used in the problem (for example, words such as *and* or *more* imply addition, whereas words such as *each* may imply division; see Bachor, Stacy, & Freeze, 1986). Although reading level is popularly believed to affect the difficulty of word problems, its effect has not been clearly established (see Bachor, 1990; Paul, Nibbelink, & Hoover, 1986).

Beginning Skills

The whole-number operations of addition, subtraction, multiplication, and division are the core of the elementary mathematics curriculum. Readiness for beginning students includes such basics as classification, one-to-one correspondence, and counting. Vocabulary and concepts are generally restricted to quantitative words (for example, *same, equal, larger*) and spatial concepts (for example, left, above, next to). Numeration deals with writing and identifying numerals, counting, ordering, and so forth.

See–write is probably the most frequently used assessment format for mathematical skills, although see–say formats are not uncommon. For content associated with readiness, vocabulary and concepts, numeration, and applications, matching formats are commonly used. Accuracy is stressed, and 90 to 95 percent correct is commonly used as the criterion. For computation, accuracy and fluency are stressed in beginning mathematics; teachers do not stop their instruction when students respond accurately, but they continue instruction to build automaticity. Consequently, a teacher may accept somewhat lower rates of accuracy (that is, 80 percent).

When working toward fluency, teachers usually use probes. *Probes* are small samples of behavior. For example, in assessment of skill in addition of single-digit numbers, a student might be given only five single-digit addition problems. Perhaps the most useful criterion for math probes assessing computation is the number of correct digits (in an answer) written per minute, not the number of correct answers per minute. The actual criterion rate will depend on the operation, the type of material (for example, addition facts versus addition of two-digit numbers with regrouping), and the characteristics of the particular students. Students with motor difficulties may be held to a lower criterion or assessed with see–say formats. For see–write formats, students may be expected to write answers to addition and subtraction problems at rates between 50 and 80 digits per minute, and to write answers to simple multiplication and division problems at rates between 40 and 50 digits per minute (Salvia & Hughes, 1990).

Advanced Skills

The more advanced mathematical skills (that is, fractions, decimals, ratios, percentages, and geometry) build on whole-number operations. These skills are taught to levels of comprehension and application. Unlike those for beginning skills, assessment formats are almost exclusively see–write, and accuracy is stressed over fluency, except for a few facts such as "H equals 0.5 equals 50 percent." Teachers must take into account the extent to which specific student disabilities will interfere with performance of advanced skills. For example, difficulties in sequencing of information and in comprehension may interfere with students' performance on items that require problem solving and comprehension of mathematical concepts.

Spelling   Although spelling is considered by many to be a component of written language, in elementary school it is generally taught as a separate subject. Therefore, we treat it separately in this chapter.

Spelling is the production of letters in the correct sequence to form a word. The specific words that are assigned as spelling words may come from several sources: spelling curricula, word lists, content areas, or a student's own written work. In high school and college, students are expected to use dictionaries and to spell correctly any word they use. Between that point and fourth grade or so, spelling words are typically assigned, and students are left to their own devices to learn them. In the first three grades, spelling is usually taught systematically using phonics, morphology, rote memorization, or some combination of the three approaches.

Teachers may assess mastery of the prespelling rules associated with the particular approach they are teaching. For example, when a phonics approach is used, students may have to demonstrate mastery of writing the letters associated with specific vowels, consonants, consonant blends, diphthongs, and digraphs. Teachers assess mastery of spelling in at least four ways:

1. *Recognition response.* The teacher provides students with lists of alternative spellings of words (usually three or four alternatives) and reads a word to the student. The student must select the correct spelling of the dictated word from the alternatives. Emphasis is on accuracy.

2. *Spelling dictated single words.* Teachers dictate words, and students write them down. Although teachers often give a spelling word and then use it in a sentence, students find the task easier if just the spelling word is given

(Horn, 1967). Moreover, the findings from 1988 research suggest that a seven-second interval between words is sufficient (Shinn, Tindall, & Stein, 1988).

3. *Spelling words in context.* Students write paragraphs using words given by the teacher. This approach is as much a measure of written expression as of spelling. The teacher can also use this approach in instruction of written language by asking students to write paragraphs and counting the number of words spelled correctly.

4. *Students' self-monitoring of errors.* Some teachers teach students to monitor their own performance by finding and correcting spelling errors in the daily assignments they complete.

Written Language   Written language is no doubt the most complex and difficult domain for teachers to assess. Assessment differs widely for beginners and advanced students. Once the preliminary skills of letter formation and rudimentary spelling have been mastered, written-language curricula usually stress both content and style (that is, grammar, mechanics, and diction).

Beginning Skills

The most basic instruction in written language is *penmanship*, in which the formation and spacing of uppercase (capital) and lowercase printed and cursive letters are taught. Early instruction stresses accuracy, and criteria are generally qualitative. After accuracy has been attained, teachers may provide extended practice to move students toward automaticity. If this is done, teachers will evaluate performance on the basis of students' rates of writing letters. Target rates are usually in the range of 80 to 100 letters per minute for students without motor handicaps.

Once students can fluently write letters and words, teachers focus on teaching students to write content. For beginners, content generation is often reduced to generation of words in meaningful sequence. Teachers may use story starters (that is, pictures or a few words that act as stimuli) to prompt student writing. When the allotted time for writing is over, teachers count the number of words or divide the number of words by the time to obtain a measure of rate. Although this sounds relatively easy, decisions as to what constitutes a word must be made. For example, one-letter words are seldom counted.

Teachers also use the percentage of correct words to assess content production. To be considered correct, the word must be spelled correctly, be capitalized if appropriate, be grammatically correct, and be followed by the correct punctuation (Isaacson, 1988). Criteria for an acceptable percentage of correct words are still the subject of discussion. For now, social comparison, by which one student's writing output is compared with the output of students whose writing is judged acceptable, can provide teachers with rough approximations. Teaching usually boils down to focusing on capitalization, simple punctuation, and basic grammar (for example, subject-verb agreement). Teachers may also use multiple-choice or fill-in tests to assess comprehension of grammatical conventions or rules.

Advanced Skills

Comprehension and application of advanced grammar and mechanics can be tested readily with multiple-choice or fill-in questions. Thus this aspect of written language can be assessed systematically and objectively. The evaluation of content generation by advanced students is far more difficult than counting correct words. Teachers may consider the quality of ideas, the sequencing of ideas, the coherence of ideas, and consideration of the reading audience. In practice, teachers use holistic judgments of content (Cooper, 1977). In addition, they may point out errors in style or indicate topics that might benefit from greater elaboration or clarification. Objective scoring of any of these attributes is very difficult, and extended scoring keys and practice are necessary to obtain reliable judgments, if they are ever attained. More objective scoring systems for content require computer analysis and at this time are beyond the resources of most classroom teachers.

Potential Sources of Difficulty in the Use of Teacher-Made Tests

To be useful, teacher-made tests must avoid three pitfalls: (1) relying on a single summative assessment, (2) using nonstandardized testing procedures, and (3) using technically inadequate assessment procedures. The first two are easily avoided; avoiding the third is more difficult.

First, teachers should not rely solely on a single summative assessment to evaluate student achievement after a course of instruction. Such assessments do not provide teachers with information they can use to plan and modify sequences of instruction. Moreover, minor technical inadequacies can be magnified when a single summative measure is used. Rather, teachers should test progress toward educational objectives at least two or three times a week. Frequent testing is most important when instruction is aimed at developing automatic or fluent responses in students. Although fluency is most commonly associated with primary curricula, it is not restricted to reading, writing, and arithmetic. For example, instruction in foreign languages, sports, and music often is aimed at automaticity.

Second, teachers should use standardized testing procedures. To conduct frequent assessments that are meaningful, the tests that are used to assess the same objectives must be equivalent. Therefore, the content must be equivalent from test to test; moreover, test directions, kinds of cues or hints, testing formats, criteria for correct responses, and type of score (for example, rates or percentage correct) must be the same.

Third, teachers should develop technically adequate assessment procedures. Two aspects of this adequacy are especially important: content validity and reliability. The tests must have content validity. There should seldom be problems with content validity when direct performances are used. For example, the materials used in finding a student's rate of oral reading should have content validity when they come from that student's reading materials; tests used to assess mastery of addition facts will have content validity because they assess the facts that have been taught. A problem with content validity is more likely when teachers use tests to assess achievement outside of the tool subjects (that is, other than reading, math, and language arts).

Although only teachers can develop tests that truly mirror instruction, teachers must not only know what has been taught but also prepare devices that test what has been taught. About the only way to guarantee that an assessment covers the content is to develop tables of specifications for the content of instruction and testing. However, test items geared to specific content may still be ineffective (see the chapter "Validity").

Careful preparation in and of itself cannot guarantee the validity of one question or set of questions. The only way a teacher can know that the questions are good is to field-test the questions and make revisions based on the field-test results. Realistically speaking, teachers do not have time for field-testing and revision prior to giving a test. Therefore, teachers must usually give a test and then delete or discount poor items. The poor items can be edited and the revised questions used the next time the examination is needed. In this way, the responses from one group of students become a field test for a subsequent group of students. When teachers use this approach, they should not return tests to students because students may pass questions down from year to year.

The tests must also be reliable. Interscorer agreement is a major concern for any test using a supply format but is especially important when extended responses are evaluated. Agreement can be increased by developing precise scoring guides for all questions of this type and by sticking with the criteria. Interscorer agreement should not be a problem for tests using selection or restricted fill-in formats. For selection and fill-in tests, internal consistency is of primary concern. Unfortunately, very few people can prepare a set of homogeneous test questions the first time. However, at the same time that they revise poor items, teachers can delete or revise items to increase a test's homogeneity (that is, delete or revise items that have correlations with the total score of .25 or less). Additional items can also be prepared for the next test.

SUMMARY

Teachers assess during instruction in order to monitor pupil progress. They need to engage in careful monitoring so that they can modify instruction, correct errors early, and maintain appropriate instructional pacing. Teachers also assess at the end of an instructional sequence to evaluate what their students have learned, assign grades, and select future instructional objectives. Because teacher-made tests are seldom subject to public scrutiny, many test theorists have doubts about their technical adequacy. However, teacher-made tests have several advantages over professionally prepared tests. Most important are (1) the ability of teachers to tailor their tests' content to the content of their teaching and (2) the potential to include many more pertinent test items, thereby allowing teachers to make finer discriminations.

Tests require students to select or supply responses to stimuli. The stimuli are usually auditory or visual, and student responses are usually vocal or written. For testing in core academic areas (that is, reading, mathematics, spelling, and written language), testing formats will vary, depending on the criteria that teachers use to evaluate learning and the level at which objectives are prepared. When fluent responses are sought by teachers, student performances in reading, math, and spelling are directly evaluated by supply formats. Selection formats (multiple-choice and matching) are useful in assessing instructional objectives prepared at the levels of knowledge, comprehension, and application. They are not well suited to higher-level objectives. Supply formats (fill-in or extended essay) have varying utility. Fill-in questions can be used in much the same way as questions prepared in selection formats. Extended essays can be used to assess objectives prepared at any level higher than knowledge, although they are probably best reserved for objectives stressing analysis, synthesis, and evaluation. Teacher-made tests are most useful when they are administered during and after instruction, are carefully standardized, have content validity, and are reliable.

QUESTIONS FOR CHAPTER REVIEW

1. Explain the advantages and disadvantages of multiple-choice, matching, and true-false questions.

2. Explain the advantages and disadvantages of teacher-made tests.

3. List four of the eight major components that are usually considered in comprehensive mathematics curricula.

4. Why is written language the most complex and difficult domain for teachers to assess?

5. Describe bottom-up and top-down formats as used in teacher-made tests, and indicate when it would be appropriate to use each format.

PROJECT

Interview a teacher about tests that he or she has developed and used. Attempt to find out how the teacher decides what to test and how to test. Write a brief report on these answers. Then compare your interviewed teacher's responses with the responses of other teachers interviewed by your classmates. Are similar procedures used by different teachers?

RESOURCES FOR FURTHER INVESTIGATION

Print Resources

Bangert-Drowns, R., & Others. (1991). Effects of frequent classroom testing. *Journal of Educational Research, 85*(2), 89–99.

Doggett, R., Edwards, R., & Moore, J. (2001). An approach to functional assessment in general education classroom settings. *School Psychology Review, 30*(3), 313–328.

Griswold, P. (1990). Assessing relevance and reliability to improve the quality of teacher-made tests. *NASSP Bulletin, 74*(523), 18–24.

Salvia, J., & Hughes, C. (1990). *Curriculum-based assessment: Testing what is taught.* New York: Macmillan. (Chapter 4: Development of appropriate assessment procedures: Collection and summarization of results.)

Tindal, G. A., & Marston, D. B. (1990). *Classroom-based assessment: Evaluating instructional outcomes.* Columbus, OH: Merrill. (Chapter 15: Individual-referenced evaluation.)

Technology Resources

THE TEACHERS NETWORK
www.teachnet.org
This website is sponsored by IMPACT II—The Teachers Network, a nonprofit organization that supports teachers with innovative ideas. It provides a resource of classroom projects available for a wide range of subject areas.

ALTERNATIVES TO STANDARDIZED TESTS
www.ericdigests.org/pre-927/tests.htm
This ERIC document looks at alternatives to standardized tests, including teacher-made tests and criterion-referenced tests.

CHAPTER 14

Portfolio Assessment

EDUCATORS CONTINUE TO LOOK FOR ALTERNATIVES TO OBJECTIVE, ANALYTIC, AND quantitative forms of assessment such as those discussed in the chapter "Assessing Instructional Ecology." By objective, we mean both uninfluenced by emotion or personal bias and based on observable phenomena. Objective tests have predetermined criteria for evaluating observable responses by procedures that are applied to all test takers in the same ways. By analytic, we mean that the elements or parts of a performance can be evaluated separately. By quantitative, we mean capable of being measured either as present or absent or as present in varying degrees.

Subjective, qualitative, and holistic approaches to judging student work have received considerable attention in recent years. By subjective, we mean that evaluations are based on personal perceptions that cannot be evaluated by external and objective criteria. By qualitative, we mean the value of a characteristic or property without regard for the amount of that characteristic or property. By holistic, we mean a focus on the entire performance without regard for individual components that make up that performance. Subjective assessments have been closely associated with constructivist approaches to teaching, as well as with the alternate, or authentic, assessment movement. Such approaches rely on holistic methods to evaluate student products for evidence of such higher-order skills as synthesis and evaluation. In this chapter, we address the assessment of student learning through the use of portfolios, an integral part of alternative assessment. But first, let us look at criticisms and misuse of norm-referenced tests as a way to understand the best use of both types of assessment.

Addressing Criticisms of Norm-Referenced Tests

Much of the professional literature on alternative assessment discusses what is wrong with objective and quantitative testing. Critics argue that educators overly rely on norm-referenced achievement tests to assess students' ability to profit from instruction and to guide instruction. They also argue that norm-referenced tests determine educational goals. Finally, some even argue that subjective and qualitative approaches to assessment are superior to objective quantitative methods for assessing important educational outcomes. In this section, we discuss these concerns.

Can Norm-Referenced Tests Assess a Student's Ability to Profit from Instruction?

We have argued in this and previous editions that when norm-referenced (or any other type of) achievement tests do not correspond to a student's curriculum, educators cannot infer that low scores indicate the student's failure to profit from instruction. Test scores that students earn on norm-referenced achievement tests are related to the degree of curricular match (Good & Salvia, 1989). Students earn higher scores when tests match what has been taught and lower scores when tests do not reflect the curriculum. Considerable research suggests that norm-referenced achievement tests do not correspond well to specific curricula, especially in mathematics and reading (see, for example, the chapters "Assessment of Academic Achievement with Multiple-Skill Devices" and "Assessment of Reading"). Thus a low test score, in and of itself, does not necessarily suggest a student's failure to profit from instruction.

For a variety of reasons, norm-referenced achievement tests are not suitable for guiding day-to-day instruction. First, these tests are specifically designed to produce stable scores. In practice, the stability of scores makes these tests insensitive to small but important changes in student learning. Thus students who are developing slowly may show no gains in tested performance. For these students, standardized, norm-referenced tests may not be valid measures of progress.

Second, the results of group-administered, machine-scored tests are frequently unavailable to teachers until weeks after administration. Thus, by the time a teacher knows the scores, they may not be pertinent to students' current levels of functioning. Moreover, when only test scores are reported, teachers have no opportunity to analyze errors or ascertain patterns of strength and weakness within an academic area (for example, decoding in reading); scores are aggregations of strengths and weaknesses.

Third, even when a teacher administers and scores a norm-referenced achievement test, there are problems. Most norm-referenced tests do not contain enough test items to allow judgments about a student's understanding or mastery of specific elements of the curriculum that can guide instructional decision making. Test authors include enough items to assure general content validity, to discriminate among test takers, and to provide reliable scores. Their intent is not to provide enough items for fine-grain analyses.

Fourth, tests assess knowledge about a subject, not ability to acquire such knowledge. Thus group-administered achievement tests are unlikely to be useful to teachers in making day-to-day instructional decisions—and we know of no professional educators or test authors who would claim that these tests are suitable for this purpose.

Should Norm-Referenced Tests Determine the Curriculum?

Some critics of objective quantitative tests believe that these tests determine curriculum rather than assess progress in curricula determined by other means. This criticism can be readily dismissed because instructional goals are determined by the state and norm-referenced tests are developed to assess what states believe are important educational outcomes. However, this criticism contains a more serious accusation: The format of a test determines how learning occurs. Thus, according to some critics, tests with select formats (for example, multiple-choice questions) lead curricula away from contextualized information upon which students reflect critically. Consequently, tests restrict the development of higher-order thinking skills (Camp, 1993; Hacker & Hathaway, 1991).

In addition, many contend that educational reform goes hand in hand with reforms in assessment. For example, Fredricksen and Collins have written that a "systematically valid test is one that induces in the education system curricular and instructional changes that foster the development of cognitive skills that the test is designed to measure" (1989, p. 27). But the relationship of educational reform to the assessment of student skill in reading, writing, and solving mathematical problems is unclear.

Are Subjective and Qualitative Assessments Better Than Norm-Referenced Tests?

Some proponents of alternative assessment believe that more subjective and qualitative approaches are better for assessing many important educational outcomes (for example, writing for specific audiences or using the scientific method). Many teachers already use such methods to assess student performance in music, art, photography, drafting, writing, wood shop, and so forth. Teachers also draw inferences and make judgments in more concrete domains. For example, teachers examine student computations to judge whether pupils used correct mathematical algorithms. Thus subjective and qualitative judgments can provide valuable additional information for use in educational decision making.

However, today the role of qualitative and subjective appraisals has broadened and, in some circles, is replacing more objective and quantitative assessment procedures. Dwyer (1993) notes an increased tolerance for subjectivity and a valuing of human judgment and intuition over precise decision rules and logical operations. Some advocate that student work be assessed more within the context of who students are. For example, Gitomer (1993) notes the belief that the more assessors know about students, the more accurate their judgments are.

Yet subjective appraisals present some serious problems for those charged with conducting educational and psychological evaluations. For good reason, examiners and teachers historically have aspired to be objective, impartial, and disinterested appraisers. As Bennett points out, human judgment "seems to be distrusted because it has so often been a historical companion to bias" (1993, p. 17). Bennett's observation is particularly apropos in special education, where disability labels have long been known to bias and distort subjective evaluations (see, for example, Salvia & Meisel, 1980). This inherent weakness in subjective evaluation partly explains the emphasis that interscorer reliability (see the chapter "Reliability") has received in professional literature, as well as the legal mandates for objective criteria for evaluating the progress of students with disabilities.[1]

---

1. As one example, federal regulations require individualized education plans (IEPs) to contain "appropriate objective criteria . . . for determining whether the short-term instructional objectives are being achieved" (34 CFR §300.46(a)(5)).

Portfolio Assessment

Proponents of portfolio assessment often cite the fact that *portfolios* are used in many fields and disciplines. Indeed, they have played an integral part in the evaluation process in fields such as art, music, photography, journalism, commercial arts, and modeling (Winograd & Gaskins, 1992). Collecting a variety of products in a portfolio has allowed artists and craftspeople to show the range and depth of their creative accomplishment; they show what a person has done, and they imply what a person is capable of doing. In these contexts, where judgments of quality are personal and subjective, a portfolio allows potential employers or customers to decide for themselves whether they like an artisan's work.

The use of work samples is also neither new nor innovative in U.S. classrooms. We are all familiar with student work displayed in classrooms. Teachers frequently show parents samples of their children's work on back-to-school nights. These samples are tangible proof for students, parents, and building visitors of what pupils create—stories, poems, drawings, and mechanical devices.

However, the use of portfolios is no longer confined to school subjects in which creative activities are taught and evaluated. Columba and Dolgos (1995) have described three types of portfolios that are being used in more traditional academic areas, such as reading, mathematics, and science, to document student effort, growth, and achievement.

▪ *Showcase portfolios* are intended to show a student's best and most representative work. Like artisan portfolios, these portfolios are intended to show a student's breadth of talent.

▪ *Teacher-student portfolios* are intended to facilitate communication during the development and revision of projects. They are working portfolios.

▪ *Assessment portfolios* are used for holistic assessments. The contents of these portfolios are scored, rated, or otherwise evaluated.

Portfolio assessment projects have been initiated statewide in some states (for example, in Vermont, Kentucky, and California) and are recognized as an assessment option in others (for example, in Pennsylvania). Some educators believe portfolio assessment is useful in special education. For example, Salend (1998) asserts that portfolios help teachers make decisions and recommendations about instructional and educational programs and mastery of IEP goals.

Portfolio Assessment Defined

Although different authors stress different components of portfolio assessment (for example, Arter & Spandel, 1992; Camp, 1993; Dwyer, 1993; Gelfer & Perkins, 1998; Grace & Shores, 1992; Katz & Johnson-Kuby, 1996; Kearns, Kleinert, Clayton, Burdge, & Williams, 1998; Salend, 1998), these six elements are generally highlighted in the literature advocating this form of assessment:

1. *Targets valued outcomes for assessment.* Generally, valued outcomes include those that require higher levels of understanding (that is, analysis, synthesis,

and evaluation), those that require applying specific processes or strategies to reach answers, and those that are complex and challenging.

2. *Uses tasks that mirror work in the real world.* Authentic assessments require students to solve the types of problems found in the real world. These problems may be ill structured (open ended), require significant amounts of student time to solve, or require students to integrate knowledge and skills, rather than treat them as discrete entities.

3. *Encourages cooperation among learners and between teacher and student.* Outcomes to be assessed should include products or performances created by groups of students, as well as by individual students.

4. *Uses multiple dimensions to evaluate student work.* In portfolio assessment, teachers should evaluate more than content knowledge. They should also consider content-specific strategies, methods of inquiry, and work processes that are essential components of student learning.

5. *Encourages student reflection.* Students should think critically about what they and their peers have created or accomplished, and they should strive to improve their products. Thus teachers should encourage students to revise and polish their work, rather than turning in a one-shot test, essay, or project.

6. *Integrates assessment and instruction.* Assessment must serve instructional purposes from which it is inseparable. Thus assessment should do more than provide accurate information about student performance on a continuous basis; it should also motivate students and facilitate teaching.

Issues and Concerns to Be Resolved

The use of portfolios, either as an addition to other assessment procedures or as a replacement for other forms of assessment done by teachers, has considerable intuitive appeal. However, portfolio assessment is a new approach, and assessment specialists still need to resolve issues related to the assembling and scoring of portfolios, veracity of items included, bias, instructional utility, efficiency, and use in actual practice.

Assembling Portfolios
What goes into a portfolio is of fundamental concern because educational decisions will be based, at least in part, on these student products. Teachers have been urged to structure portfolios according to the type of decision that they will make. Yet the literature on portfolio assessment offers little practical guidance about the types of decisions teachers should be making, the characteristics (for example, amount) of the content used for specific decisions, or criteria to guide decision making about any of the following: grading, identification and remediation of a student's academic weaknesses, instructional improvement and staff development, eligibility for entitlement programs (such as special education), assessment of educational outcomes, and educational reform. This absence of theory and empirical research to guide practice in portfolio assessment stands in

stark contrast to the situation for other approaches to classroom assessment (for example, curriculum-based assessment).

Portfolio assessment has developed largely outside the field of special education. A consequence, perhaps, is that many of the decisions made on behalf of students in special education do not appear to have been considered. Similarly, advocates of portfolio assessment do not appear to have considered the processes and criteria on which these decisions are based. Many decisions in special education rely, at least in part, on interstudent comparisons. For example, a student may be referred for prereferral intervention on the bases of both failing to meet standards of performance and being substantially behind other students in class; a boy with a learning disability might be mainstreamed when his achievement is commensurate with that of a nondisabled student in the classroom. Because the content of portfolios is not standardized from student to student, interstudent comparisons based on portfolio assessment are extremely difficult. Thus portfolios, in the form advocated by most supporters, are unlikely to gain widespread acceptance in special education.[2]

If portfolios replace tests, educators will need to address some issues of record maintenance. Portfolios can be maintained for a specific marking period, a semester, a year, or a career. When portfolios are used to make long-term decisions (such as determining eligibility, documenting attainment of outcomes required for graduation, and documenting the provision of high-quality education), some guidelines for maintenance of records will have to be established (see the chapter "Legal and Ethical Considerations in Assessment"). Storage and retrieval of portfolios may present problems even with digital technology. Although it is possible to maintain electronic copies of portfolios on compact disc, the costs are currently prohibitive.

Specific Content Issues

Portfolio Content

Portfolios should be tailored for a specific purpose. Without a predetermined purpose, a portfolio is just a pile of papers or projects placed in a folder or, increasingly, stored electronically (Stiggins, 1997). Depending on its purpose, a portfolio might include all or some classroom assignments, a list of books that have been read, journal entries, completed projects, self-evaluations, students' reflections on their work, and so forth, accumulated over the course of an academic year, semester, or marking period (Polin, 1991). More likely, a portfolio might be dedicated to a single project. For example, a portfolio for a story might include outlines, drafts, revisions, and final copy (see, for example, Katz & Johnson-Kuby, 1996). When portfolios contain everything students have created during a year, their contents become more variable, but teachers spend no time deciding what to include. However, teachers will spend more time in evaluations if they evaluate all products in their students' portfolios.

---

2. We note that many advocates of portfolio assessment (as well as advocates of other alternative forms of assessment) oppose interstudent comparisons on philosophical grounds (see, for example, National Council of Teachers of Mathematics, 1993).

Student Participation in Content Selection   Collaboration and consultation of students and teachers are integral to the creation of portfolios. The guidelines for student participation suggested in the professional literature tend to be inconsistent or even incompatible. For example, some advocate having students select products they think are particularly good; others advocate having students select products they do not like. Moreover, some educators believe that what students select and the rationales for their selections are as important as the pieces themselves (Arter & Spandel, 1992; Frazier & Paulson, 1992; Hebert, 1992; Paulson, Paulson, & Meyer, 1991; Wolf, 1989). The diagnostic and instructional implications of including products chosen because students like or dislike them are unknown. For example, it is not established that products that a student likes lead to the same decisions as products that the student dislikes; we do not know if there are interactions between student criteria for selection and the quality of various decisions that are made in the schools. Finally, we can locate no evidence to suggest that students, let alone students with cognitive disabilities, can determine what content is pertinent to the multitude of decisions that teachers make.

Quality of Student Work   Conflicting advice is offered in the literature about what student work to include. In the absence of research, we can only speculate about the usefulness of different criteria for including student work in portfolios. Some advocate including the student's best work. Best-work portfolios show what a student is capable of producing; they are likely to be the most useful in assessing a student's attainment of specific educational goals or outcomes. However, these portfolios fail to provide information about the variability of student work and the quality of typical work. Others advocate including a student's typical work in the portfolio. Although typical-work portfolios may be the most useful in making decisions, they do not provide information about the variability of student work or about the best and worst of a student's work. Finally, some recommend including a range of quality in a student's portfolio. Such portfolios provide the most information, but they may not be pertinent to some decisions.

Sufficient Information for Decision Making   It is axiomatic that accurate and valid information is the basis for good educational decision making. The psychometric theories on which achievement tests are based allow users to estimate a student's true score on the domain of interest. When these tests do not contain enough items to draw reliable inferences about a student's true score, test authors can estimate (with the Spearman-Brown formula) the number of additional items needed to make their tests reliable.

Psychometricians have yet to develop the necessary theories to allow similar estimation of true scores from portfolios. Most would agree that portfolios should contain enough products to allow reliable appraisal, but at this time it is unclear how educators are to know what the minimum number of pieces should be. The bromide "the more, the better" is no doubt correct but fails to address the issue of threshold of adequacy. Additionally, the more pieces included in a portfolio, the more time is required for assessment. Therefore, when efficiency is a consideration, portfolios should not contain more products than are needed to make reliable decisions.

Many who write about portfolios urge teachers to base their assessments on untimed, extended projects (see, for example, Camp, 1993). Such projects require multiple collections of skills that vary considerably across tasks; successful products depend on context-situated skills, as well as knowledge of the context itself (Bennett, 1993, p. 9). Thus generalizations from one constructed response or performance to other constructed responses are problematic. Teachers cannot assume that, because a child performed poorly (or well) on one project, other performances will be similarly poor (or good). It is important that educational decisions be based on more than one pertinent product in a student's portfolio, but when individual products in a portfolio require extended time to create, it is unlikely that multiple products will be available.

Specific Scoring Issues

The majority of articles on portfolio assessment elaborate on the importance of scoring and evaluation systems, and the philosophical bases for establishing criteria for judging a portfolio's merit; little attention is devoted to the specifics of scoring student work. Evaluation processes are loosely defined, if they are explained at all (Arter & Spandel, 1992; Polin, 1991). Yet the scoring of projects and of constructed responses is neither simple nor straightforward.

The joint committee of the American Educational Research Association (AERA), American Psychological Association, and National Council for Measurement in Education has offered guidance that is useful in scoring portfolios:

> The criteria used for scoring test takers' performance on extended-response items should be documented. This documentation is especially important for performance assessments, such as scorable portfolios and essays, where the criteria for scoring may not be obvious. . . . The completeness and clarity of the test specifications, including the definition of the domain, are essential in developing the scoring criteria. The test developer needs to provide a clear description of how the test scores are intended to be interpreted to help ensure the appropriateness of the scoring procedures. (1999, p. 46; emphasis removed)

Score Interpretation

Meaning of Evaluative Descriptions   Whether products are evaluated for the presence or absence of specific attributes or on some dimension, interpretation of the resulting scores is likely to present some problems. Consider a science project described by Shavelson, Baxter, and Pine (1991). A teacher asks students to determine which of three paper towels holds the most water. If the students saturate and weigh the towels, the care with which they weigh the towels can be evaluated on a 3-point scale (that is, yes, no, or a little sloppy). However, the meanings of yes, no, and a little sloppy are undefined.

Instead, consider the evaluation of a student's written-language project in which various elements are scored as novice, apprentice, proficient, and distinguished. These terms are likely to lack meaning to anyone unfamiliar with the context-specific meanings developed by a teacher in the classroom. Indeed, we find no evidence to suggest that teacher (or student) ratings of portfolio products are meaningful to anyone outside the classroom or school. Thus parents and policy makers may find them less useful than other types of descriptions or scores.

Generalizability of Scores   Generalizability of scores presents two problems. First, we know very little about the number of products necessary to estimate a student's ability accurately. For example, Shavelson, Gao, and Baxter (1991) found that from 8 to 20 performances were needed to estimate a student's problem-solving ability in mathematics and science accurately. Yet such estimates will probably vary by the content area (that is, physics, general science, algebra), the specific curriculum, and the grade level at which the material is taught. Second, there is some evidence that evaluation context (context can refer to a specific domain, such as history or mathematics) affects student performance (for example, see Gearhart, Herman, Baker, & Whittaker, 1992). What students are asked to do and the circumstances under which they are asked to perform will affect the outcome and, necessarily, inferences about what students have learned and what they are capable of doing.

Lack of Interstudent Comparisons   Although advocates of portfolio assessment often eschew interstudent comparisons, these comparisons are invariably part of the information needed to qualify students for special services. In schools where interindividual comparisons are based on portfolios with variable contents, making valid comparisons will be a formidable undertaking. In schools where interindividual comparisons are avoided, portfolio assessment is unlikely to provide useful information for a variety of special education decisions.

Student Reflections   The role of student reflections, often suggested for inclusion in portfolio assessment, is unclear. Although student reflections and self-evaluations may be motivational, it remains to be demonstrated how these reflections facilitate or contribute to assessments of academic or behavioral development. Because student ratings can be influenced by a desire to please the teacher, these ratings may not be independent (or particularly meaningful).

Score Aggregation

Portfolio ratings are aggregated both within individual pieces and across pieces in a portfolio. When one piece of student work is evaluated on several dimensions and then given a summary rating, the summary rating represents an aggregate of the ratings of the component dimensions. For example, suppose a teacher was evaluating a student's accomplishment as a writer. Further suppose that the student's performance varied on the six characteristics of that dimension. Each characteristic would be rated on a 6-point Likert scale along a continuum ranging from inadequate performance to outstanding performance. Having rated each characteristic, how would the teacher determine the overall rating? If the rating scale was ordinal, scores from the characteristics should not be added or averaged. If the scores were assumed to be equal-interval, should they be weighted equally? Unless the scores from characteristics were converted to z-scores before weighting, they would be weighted by their variance.

When the summary scores from several pieces are aggregated to arrive at a portfolio score, there are additional problems. Portfolios are intended to include a variety of work. For example, a writing portfolio may consist of poetry, reactions to short stories or news items, journal entries, drafts of extended pieces of prose, and so forth. Insofar as different scoring rubrics are used for different types of writing, summary ratings will be based on different considerations. Thus the summary ratings will compare apples and oranges, and interpretation of these aggregates will be very challenging.

To illustrate, consider the following scenario. A teacher wishes to make a decision about a student's literacy progress over the course of a semester, using the student's portfolio as the basis of the decision. The portfolio contains the following 17 items produced during the semester:

- A videotape of the student's classroom presentation on Harriet Tubman (a project prepared during the first nine weeks of the semester)
- One group paper about dinosaurs and some drawings (a project prepared during the last nine weeks of the semester)
- Six biweekly journal entries, completed at home, giving personal reactions to poems read during the first six weeks of the semester
- Three weekly journal entries, completed in school, giving personal reactions to short stories read in class during the middle six weeks of the semester
- Six weekly journal entries, completed at home and in school, giving personal reactions to articles appearing in a student newspaper (completed during the last six weeks of the semester)

Further assume that the teacher uses scoring rubrics to judge 20 characteristics associated and that each score can range from 1 to 6. How does the teacher combine the scores? Does the teacher aggregate scores from journal entries with group projects? Does the teacher combine scores across different reading materials (that is, poetry, short stories, and articles from the student newspaper)? How would a teacher incorporate judgments on progress over time, as the materials and tasks vary systematically over the semester? One thing is certain: Different aggregation procedures will yield different summary evaluations.

Guidelines for aggregating ratings are seldom provided to teachers, and there is no evidence that teachers (or students) who invent their own guidelines apply them consistently. Thus the meanings of summary ratings of individual pieces and of the portfolio as a whole are likely to be idiosyncratic and inconsistently applied.

Score Reliability

Without clear and objective scoring rubrics to guide the evaluation of multiple skills and complex attributes, portfolio assessment is prone to unreliable scoring. Moreover, the products that students construct or create and that are put into portfolios are, by their very nature, difficult to score consistently, whether individual pieces in a portfolio are evaluated separately or aggregated. Part of the difficulty lies in subjective scoring. As Dwyer (1993) notes, efforts at educational reform, and particularly reform of assessment, have celebrated subjectivity: There are "clear indications that [reformers'] orientation includes increasing tolerance for subjectivity, and a valuing of human judgment—and even intuition—over precise decision rules and logical operations" (p. 269). However, precise decision rules and logical operations bring consistency to scoring.

What happens without precise scoring rules is well documented. The research literature on evaluating written language is the most extensive, although written language is difficult to score under any system. In several studies dealing with holistic scoring of writing samples, Breland and colleagues found interscorer agreement ranging from .52 to .65 (Breland, 1983; Breland, Camp, Jones, Morris, & Rock, 1987). In the National Assessment of Educational Progress's portfolio study (Educational Testing Service, 1990), interscorer agreement was computed for ratings of three types of writing (narrative, informative, and persuasive) on a 6-point scale. Interscorer reliabilities ranged from .76 to .89, probably because the scorers had received intensive training just before evaluating the portfolios.

Consistent scoring of student writing is even more difficult when students can select topics and genres. As Dorans and Schmitt (1993, p. 135) note, "To the extent that a constructed-response item is unconstrained and examinees are free to produce any response they wish, the test scorer has a difficult and challenging task of extracting information from examinee responses. To date the psychometrics for dealing with this unconstrained response type have lagged behind the development and administration of these items." As Breland and colleagues (Breland, 1983; Breland et al., 1987) have found, interscorer agreement drops from the range of .52 to .65 to a range of .36 to .46 when the writing tasks vary.

Experience in evaluating writing portfolios in Vermont also reflects this tendency. Camp (1993) noted that writing teachers received considerable training before scoring portfolios:

> The criteria for evaluating the portfolios were developed by a statewide committee of writing teachers and applied to sample portfolios by fourth- and eighth-grade teachers in regional meetings throughout the state. They were refined as a result of these experiences. The five portfolio criteria focus on characteristics of writing that are sufficiently generic to be observable in pieces written for different purposes and audiences: clarity of purpose; organization of ideas or information; use of specific detail; personal expression or voice; and appropriate usage, mechanics, and grammar. In the process of applying the portfolio criteria and examining them in relation to the design for the portfolio, the teachers begin to internalize the criteria and to refine their understanding of the portfolio's purpose. (pp. 201–202)

These portfolios were assessed using 4-point scales. "Depending on the grade and subject, the average correlation between raters (across the five or seven scales) ranged from .33 to .43" (Koretz, 1993, p. 2).

Similar findings have been reported in other content areas. For example, in a study dealing with scoring science notebooks, Baxter, Shavelson, Goldman, and Pine (1992) found similarly low interscorer agreement (.66), although direct observations were more reliable. Consistent problems have also been noted in the scoring of mathematics portfolios (Koretz, Klein, McCaffrey, & Stecher, 1993). Thus the evidence to date suggests that level of agreement when teachers score portfolios, especially when the portfolios contain constructed responses, is likely to be below the generally accepted criterion for reliable assessment (.90).

Although research dealing with consistent scoring of portfolios by students is lacking, some indirect evidence is available. Gordon (1990) found that teachers' criteria for judging good stories were often quite different from the criteria used by students. Thus, to the extent that students' evaluations are included in assessment, systematic variation will be introduced. Also, because the literature on portfolio assessment fails to address special training for students who self-evaluate, it is likely that students' criteria and scoring will produce more error than is produced by teachers specifically trained in scoring performances and constructed performances.

Finally, research on behavioral observation, in which definitions of target behaviors are considerably more precise and objective, strongly suggests that, as the complexity of observation increases, interscorer agreement decreases (Salvia & Hunt, 1984). Consistent monitoring of and feedback about accuracy can reduce or prevent drifting of criteria, which contributes to lack of reliability (Salvia & Hunt, 1984). These issues remain unaddressed by advocates of portfolio assessment.

In summary, the very nature of portfolio assessment makes reliable scoring extremely difficult. Thus different teachers should be expected to award different scores to the same piece of work or portfolio. As Bennett has noted, constructed responses "by their very nature will produce less reliable scores. Lower reliability will make the measurement of new constructs relatively inaccurate, limiting the ability to generalize performance beyond the administered tasks and the specific raters grading them" (1993, p. 9). Although advocates of portfolio assessment have downplayed or ignored these problems, the problems have not gone away and will not go away until scoring procedures, as well as procedures for training scorers, are improved.

Veracity of Products

Teachers must determine that their students actually created the products in their portfolios (Gearhart, Herman, Baker, & Whittaker, 1993). For example, how does a teacher know whether students completed the work or handed in someone else's work under their own name? Did a parent, sibling, or friend do the homework? Similarly, if a student revises a paper based on the teacher's formal review of a draft, is the revision considered the student's work or the teacher's? Teachers will need some way to authenticate or weigh the student's contribution to each product. The easiest solution is to use only work completed in class, but this criterion severely restricts a teacher's options.

Bias

Many advocates of portfolio assessment seem to believe that, if subjective appraisal replaced objective assessment in the schools, prejudice and bias would be somehow reduced.[3] Assertions that subjectively scored portfolios are less biased

3. Problems with biased scoring standards are tacitly recognized when moderation is used to overcome different internal criteria and biases in subjective ratings. However, moderation assumes that most of the judges are free of bias.

appear to be based on ignorance of or cavalier disregard of a substantial research literature. As noted in the chapter "Assessment Processes and Concerns," researchers have repeatedly shown the susceptibility of subjective decision making to stereotypes associated with race, ethnicity, social class, and gender. Especially pertinent to those working with students with disabilities is the substantial research literature demonstrating that subjective teacher evaluations are quite susceptible to the biasing effects of disability labels (such as mental retardation). Thus all the relevant research seems to argue against subjective methods of appraisal when more objective methods are available. Snow (1993) has pointed out that bias can be determined objectively and eliminated from objectively scored tests. At this juncture, we cannot say the same of portfolio assessment.

Of course, assessment procedures may be biased in ways other than through their scoring. In addition to content considerations, test format may produce systematic advantage (or disadvantage) for some groups. For example, students of different ethnicities vary in their willingness to attempt open-ended types of questions (Koretz, Lewis, Skewes-Cox, & Burstein, 1992). Snow (1993) has summarized other relevant findings:

- Extended responses (for example, essay questions) produce greater anxiety in students; objective formats seem to help more anxious students.
- The less structured the instruction is (a condition associated with portfolio assessment), the greater is the effect of a student's intelligence. Structure facilitates learning for students with lower ability.
- Women do better on tests requiring constructed responses.

Instructional Utility   Portfolios supposedly have two instructional advantages. First, portfolios are favored because they are believed to promote higher-order thinking skills. This belief has yet to be supported empirically. Baker, O'Neil, Jr., and Linn's 1993 summary of the state of affairs in assessing extended student performances (the preferred form of material to be included in portfolios) remains true today:

> Advocates of performance-based assessment have been remarkably remiss in providing clear-cut conceptual frameworks for their efforts. Many rather loosely link their exemplars to measurement of higher order thinking without documenting the cognitive processes that students use. Neither explicit frameworks for generating assessments nor detailed descriptions of student learning are offered. Most of the arguments in favor of performance-based assessment, therefore, are based on single instances, essentially hand-crafted exercises whose virtues are assumed because they have been developed by teachers or because they are thought to model good instructional practice. (p. 1211)

Later in the same article, they also point out that the

> student's instructional experiences (and the nature of practice on the task) can subvert intentions to measure higher order thinking. With repeated instructional exposure, nominally higher order tasks, such as constructing analyses of a drama or a geometric proof, can be transformed into rote tasks, a fact that may

go undetected without collateral information about instructional processes. (p. 1211)

Similarly, Snow (1993) has noted that, when students expect essay examinations, they try to learn how text authors have structured the material, as well as the content. Thus students do not tend to construct their own structure; instead, they try to memorize someone else's.

Second, portfolios are favored because they are believed to facilitate instructional decision making. Clearly, student products accumulated in portfolios are instructionally relevant. Unlike the empirical validity associated with other forms of alternative assessment (for example, curriculum-based assessment), however, the evidence supporting the role of portfolios, apart from bold and unsupported assertions or testimonials from teachers, remains largely intuitive or unreported. The research that is reported suggests that the relationship of student performance to instructional decision making is neither a simple nor a straightforward matter. For example, Fleischer (1997) found that teachers who were given writing samples collected over an entire year were inconsistent in their recognition of achievement problems and their ability to judge educational progress. Moreover, because portfolio assessment has developed largely outside of special education, it may not be well suited for some of the decisions that must be made in these contexts. These decisions are discussed in detail in the chapters "Instructional Decision Making" and "Outcomes-Based Accountability Assessment," but a few examples illustrate this context.

Concerns Regarding Portfolio Assessment for Students with Disabilities

▪ How are portfolio contents related to the criterion used to decide whether a student is making satisfactory progress?

▪ How are portfolio contents related to the criterion used to decide whether a student should be referred to ascertain eligibility for special education?

▪ How are portfolio contents related to decisions to alter instruction when a student is not making satisfactory progress?

▪ How can a student's portfolio be used to make decisions about inclusion?

▪ How can a student's portfolio be used to determine current instructional levels?

▪ How can a student's portfolio be used to determine rates of acquisition and retention?

Besides the issues of scoring and bias, which clearly impinge on classroom decision making, there are two additional indications that portfolios may lack instructional utility: insensitivity to change and infrequency of assessment. One potentially serious issue is sensitivity to change. For any classroom assessment to be useful, it must be sufficiently sensitive to small but important student changes. We find no empirical evidence for the ability of portfolio scoring systems to detect important changes in student development (unlike the empirical validity associated with other forms of alternative assessment). If portfolio scoring systems do not detect important changes, then teachers cannot gauge the effectiveness of their instruction over relatively short periods of time. Indeed, as Linn and Baker (1993, p. 8) have noted, global scores "would not help teachers to improve teaching and learning. They would function like a qualitative stanine."

A second potentially serious issue is the frequency with which assessments can be conducted. Unlike other forms of assessment, which rely on one- or two-minute probes to assess student progress, portfolios frequently contain extended projects. Teachers may find it difficult to use extended projects to adjust instruction on a daily or weekly basis. Thus students who are not progressing satisfactorily may experience prolonged periods of failure before their difficulties become apparent to their teachers.

Efficiency   Efficiency is always an issue in assessment. Two issues are especially pertinent when considering portfolio assessment: (1) time and money, and (2) additional training needs.

Time and Money

The first issue is the actual time devoted to assessment activities. In those models of portfolio assessment in which assessment is the shared responsibility of both teacher and student and in which assessment occurs during conferences, the instructional value of the evaluation may be worth the added time that must be invested. However, this remains an empirical question.

The evaluation of an extended project is, by its very nature, labor intensive. Yet to produce generalizable estimates of student ability and learning, teachers must have several projects. According to the estimates offered by Shavelson, Gao, and Baxter (1991), teachers will need from 8 to 20 projects to evaluate each student's ability in mathematics and science. Clearly, this is a substantial investment of teacher time; the impact of this time investment on instruction remains unclear. However, educators should expect some reasonable tradeoff between depth of coverage and breadth of coverage. Thus, in those classrooms where portfolios are used to collect extended projects, there is likely to be narrowed curricular content.

In those models of portfolio assessment using moderation, inordinate amounts of time could be diverted from teaching. Consider the use of portfolio assessment to assign semester grades in English at the secondary level, where teachers have five classes of 25 or 30 students each. If three teachers score each portfolio, each teacher would be required to evaluate between 375 and 450 portfolios, instead of 125 to 150 without moderation. Even highly dedicated teachers might find this prospect burdensome.

An issue related to time is cost. Because portfolio assessment is labor intensive and requires considerable teacher time, cost can be a factor. Moreover, when high-stakes scores are moderated, the costs can soar (Nuttall, 1992).

Additional Training

The second issue is training. Even when given considerable training in methods of subjective appraisal, raters typically produce unreliable ratings. Yet, even assuming for the sake of argument that the current amounts of training were adequate, additional training to maintain high levels of agreement in portfolio assessment will be necessary. Retraining requires a considerable investment of time and resources. To date, advocates of portfolio assessment have infrequently considered the costs of training, retraining, and maintenance of scoring standards.

Use of Portfolios in Practice

In practice, portfolio assessment falls far short of even the modest standards recommended by portfolio advocates. In 1993 Calfee and Perfumo conducted a national survey seeking information about portfolio practices and visited several schools and classrooms where portfolios were used. Their findings suggest a state of anarchy in which inconsistent practice was the rule. They found the following:

■ No clear indication of how achievement was measured

■ No guidelines to help teachers analyze, score, or grade portfolios

■ Use of normative rather than developmental procedures

■ An absence of procedures to establish reliability

■ An absence of procedures to establish validity

In their surveys and site visits, they found that the popularity of portfolios appeared to be a local reaction to external control—the perception seemed to be that the rebels do portfolios (p. 536).

Improving Portfolio-Assessment Practices

Those who wish to use portfolios for assessment purposes should give serious consideration to the assembly and evaluation of portfolios. Greater objectivity, less complexity, more scorer training, and greater comparability of portfolio contents are the keys to better practice.

Collection of Student Products

The content of a portfolio should be tailored to the purpose of assessment, but teachers seldom know at the beginning of the year all the decisions they will have to make throughout the year. For example, they may not know that Mary will be referred to the school assistance team late in the first semester. Because retrieval of papers and projects can be difficult (and live performances are unretrievable if not recorded), it is probably a good idea to collect all potentially useful student work into the portfolios. Teachers can then assemble decision-specific portfolios.

Teachers can be sure that certain types of decisions (for example, grading) will be made during a semester or year. In these cases, teachers should carefully plan the semester's activities to ensure that there will be enough products at appropriate times in the term to make anticipated decisions. If teachers intend to assess progress, they should plan to include in portfolios comparable products from throughout the term. Teachers should also include the criteria for scoring each type of product in the portfolio so that these criteria remain consistent over time.

Using portfolios to make high-stakes decisions requires considerably more structure. For meaningful comparisons of a student's progress over time or for comparisons of students, portfolios must have comparable content. For example, it is very difficult for a teacher to judge student progress in writing from diverse products such as a poem, observations from a science walk, a letter, and a story; it is similarly difficult for teachers to compare the progress of two students when one student's portfolio contains persuasive prose and the other student's portfolio contains haiku. The products themselves are not comparable. Generally, the more comparable the products are, the less prone to error are the assessments.

Objective Scoring of Portfolios

Since the 1950s, a substantial research literature on consistent rating and scoring has developed. The scoring of portfolios requires essentially the same processes as are used for conducting systematic observations. Specifically, careful preparation is necessary for the scoring of portfolios to be reliable and valid. Criteria should be specified clearly to allow different scorers to agree on whether specific target outcomes have occurred; references to internal process should be minimized (see the chapter "Assessing Behavior Through Observation"). Finally, consistent scoring requires instances and noninstances of what meets criteria.

Unfortunately, current practices in portfolio assessment contradict most of what we have learned from research. To be minimally acceptable, portfolio scoring schemes must be sufficiently objective to withstand parent and student disagreement with scores (and grades) and potential court challenges about fairness (Davis & Felknor, 1994). Historically, subjective scoring systems have failed to meet minimum standards. The obvious alternative is more objective scoring systems. One place to start objectifying scoring is to anchor scales in observable and objective characteristics of a performance or product. Without observable anchors, scale values such as novice performance, strong performance, and evidence of serious effort have no objective referents and are likely to defy consistent judging. A second way to increase consistency is to simplify scoring rubrics. Indeed, Koretz (1993) mentioned scoring rubrics that were too complex or unclear as a possible cause of the unreliable evaluations found in the initial Vermont portfolio studies.

Training and Retraining of Scorers

Even when clear scoring standards have been developed, educators should not assume that teachers will apply the scoring standards consistently without training. The scoring of constructed responses (for example, essays) is very difficult. Therefore, teachers should be provided with direct and systematic instruction until they are able to score portfolios consistently. In addition to helping scorers achieve consistency, training has the added benefit of uncovering scoring criteria that are unclear. Moreover, inconsistent scoring following training strongly suggests that the scoring criteria should be revised. Thus training acts as a field test for scoring criteria and procedures.

Training should not end once teachers have mastered the scoring system. There is a strong tendency for scorers to lose their accuracy over time. For example, with experience, a teacher may develop idiosyncratic scoring rules or may stop using some scoring criteria. Thus scoring criteria drift. To maintain consistency over time, scorers require periodic retraining.

Concluding Comments

Currently, there appears to be more conviction than empirical support for the use of portfolios. The lack of empirical support can be partly attributed to a rejection of quantitative methods and an empirical orientation; many advocates of portfolio assessment staunchly believe in the superiority of qualitative approaches to assessment. Thus the published literature created by these advocates consists essentially of testimonials about what is wrong with tests of all kinds (but especially objectively scored tests), rejection of quantitative methods of assessing students, and advice about constructing portfolios. Even given the most optimistic interpretation of the validity of portfolio assessment, we believe that the current literature provides an insufficient basis for acceptance of portfolio assessment on any basis other than experimental. More pessimistically, we concur with Siegler's (1989, p. 15) observation that "if cognitive assessment techniques contain biases that jeopardize the validity of their outcomes, the time does not seem ripe to advocate their use in classrooms." At this time, portfolios offer great research opportunities. Yet educators must also remember the requirements of the Buckley amendment (see the chapter "Legal and Ethical Considerations in Assessment"), which mandates informed consent before students can participate in research. We conclude with Dwyer's (1993) observation about assessment:

> It is the unfortunate tendency, in education as well as in other complex systems, for bad practice to drive out good. This tendency means that for innovative as well as traditional assessment systems, we must anticipate ways in which the system is likely to be debased. Safeguards against bad practice, to the extent that such practices can be reasonably anticipated, must be designed into the assessment system. Also implied is an obligation, as part of on-going validation, to ensure the integrity of the system. (p. 287)

SUMMARY

Interest in portfolio assessment stems from general concern about the validity and utility of norm-referenced achievement tests, the potential negative effects that standardized tests may have on learning, dissatisfaction in some circles with objective appraisal, and the belief that reform in the area of assessment can drive or support broader efforts in educational reform. Six elements define portfolio assessment: targeting valued outcomes for assessment, using tasks that mirror work in the real world, encouraging cooperation among learners and between teacher and student, using multiple dimensions to evaluate student work, encouraging student reflection, and integrating assessment and instruction.

Depending on its purpose, the contents of a portfolio can vary considerably. Despite an initial surge of interest in the use of portfolios, several concerns and limitations have not been systematically addressed: selecting the criteria for including work in a student's portfolio, determining the nature of student participation in content selection, ensuring sufficient content generated by a student to reach valid decisions, and finding a way to make portfolio assessment more reliable, with consistency of scoring and breadth of sampling of student performances. In addition, there are concerns about biased scoring, instructional utility, and efficiency. Portfolio assessment will remain difficult and expensive for schools, and educators who wish to pursue this alternative should give serious attention to how portfolios are assembled and evaluated. Objectivity, less complexity, and comparability are the keys to better practice.

QUESTIONS FOR CHAPTER REVIEW

1. Why is interscorer agreement important in portfolio assessment?

2. How might a scoring rubric be developed to increase objective scoring of portfolios?

3. How might portfolios of students with disabilities be used to determine the students' eligibility for special educational services?

4. Identify and discuss assumptions made in norm-referenced assessment and in portfolio assessment that are in direct opposition to each other.

PROJECT

Review the educational literature about portfolio assessment. For each article presenting empirical data, give a rating (good, neutral, poor) of the demonstrated value of portfolio assessment with students with disabilities.

RESOURCES FOR FURTHER INVESTIGATION

Print Resources

Black, L., Daiker, D. A., Sommers, J., & Stygall, G. (Eds.). (1994). *New directions in portfolio assessment: Reflective practice, critical theory, and large-scale scoring.* Portsmouth, NH: Boynton/Cook.

Fleischer, K. (1997). The effects of structured rating paradigms on the reliability of teacher ratings of written language samples over time. Unpublished doctoral dissertation, Pennsylvania State University, University Park, PA.

Gillespie, C. S., Ford, K. L., Gillespie, R. D., & Leavell, A. G. (1996). Portfolio assessment: Some questions, some answers, some recommendations. *Journal of Adolescent & Adult Literacy, 39,* 480–491.

Kampfer, S., Horvath, L., Kleinert, H., & Kearns, J. (2001). Teachers' perceptions of one state's alternative assessment: Implications for practice and preparation. *Exceptional Children, 67*(3), 361–374.

Supovitz, J., & Brennan, R. (1997). Mirror, mirror on the wall, which is the fairest test of all? An examination of the equitability of portfolio assessment relative to standardized tests. *Harvard Educational Review, 67*(3), 472–506.

Ysseldyke, J., & Olsen, K. (1999). Putting alternative assessments into practice: What to measure and possible sources of data. *Exceptional Children, 65*(2), 175–185.

Technology Resources

DESIGNING ONLINE PORTFOLIOS
64.233.161.104/search?q=cache:sJ2Aoo3VPUUJ :jite.org/documents/Vol3/v3p065-081-127.pdf+ Portfolio+Assessment&hl=en&start=53
This paper outlines the main findings of research about the value of online portfolio systems.

PORTFOLIOS IN MATHEMATICS EDUCATION
www.ericdigests.org/2000-2/portfolio.htm
This site gives an overview of math portfolios and provides tips and further resources.

ELECTRONIC PORTFOLIOS IN K–12 CLASSROOMS
www.nea.org/lessons/tt040614.html
This site provides general information about how and why to develop electronic portfolios in elementary and secondary classrooms.

PART **4**

Assessment Using Formal Measures

Part 4 deals with tests and scales used for making decisions entitling students to special education services. The chapters in Part 4 describe the most common domains in which assessment of processes (or abilities) and products are conducted. With the exceptions of "How to Evaluate a Test" and "Assessment of Intelligence: An Overview," each chapter in this part focuses on a different process or skill domain and opens with an explanation of why the domain is assessed. We next provide a general overview of the components of the domain (that is, the behaviors that are usually assessed) and then discuss the more commonly used tests within the domain. Each chapter concludes with some suggestions for coping with problems in assessing the domain and a general summary of chapter content.

The criteria we used in selecting and reviewing specific tests warrant some discussion. First, in selecting tests, we could not, and did not, include all the available measures for each domain. Rather, we tried to select representative and commonly used devices in each area. We moved some reviews that were included in previous editions of this textbook to the website for the book.

Online Study Center
General Resources

And, as new tests become available, we will review them and include the reviews on the website. Readers interested in tests not reviewed in this book may want to consult the website first, then consult books devoted entirely to test reviews, such as *Tests: A Comprehensive Reference for Assessments in Psychology, Education, and Business* (Sweetland & Keyser, 1991) or Buros's *Mental Measurements Yearbooks.*

Second, in evaluating the technical adequacy of each test, we restricted our evaluation to information in the test manuals. There were two reasons for this decision: (1) As stated in the *Standards for Educational and Psychological Testing* (AERA et al., 1999), test authors are responsible for providing all necessary technical information in their test manuals. The test authors must have some basis for claiming that their tests are valid. Therefore, we searched the manuals for technical information that supports the test authors' contentions. (2) An attempt to include the vast body of research literature on commonly used tests would have resulted in a multivolume opus that would be impossible to publish as a current work. Entire books have been written on the subject of using and interpreting single tests.

In reviewing each test, we always use the same format. We describe the general format of the test and the specific behaviors that the test is designed to sample; these descriptions allow the reader to evaluate the extent to which specific tests sample the domain. Next, we describe the kinds of scores that the test provides for the practitioner; this gives information about the meaning and interpretation of those scores. Subsequently, we examine the standardization sample for each test; this enables the reader to judge—recalling the discussion in the chapter "Norms"—the adequacy of the norm group and to evaluate the appropriateness of each test for use with specific populations of students. After that, we evaluate the evidence of reliability for each test, using the standards set forth in the chapter "Reliability." Then we examine evidence of validity for each device, evaluating the adequacy of the evidence in light of the standards set forth in the chapter "Validity." Finally, we give a summary of each test.

We urge our readers to examine the research on tests in which they might be interested. Test users are ultimately responsible for test selection and interpretation. Thus, if you are considering using a particular test that has incomplete or inadequate technical characteristics, it is your responsibility to demonstrate its validity. Current research may provide the support you need to demonstrate the validity of your assessment. Therefore, we urge our readers to go beyond our reviews.

CHAPTER 15

How to Evaluate a Test

THE FIRST STEP IN EVALUATING A TEST IS TO PICK A TEST TO EVALUATE. OFTEN, teachers want to evaluate a test that is currently used in their school or office, or they are just curious about a specific test. Other times, they may need to select a test. When educators need to find a test to use, it is usually necessary to conduct a preview of the available tests in the domain of interest (for instance, individually administered reading tests). Current publishers' catalogues or a reference work (for example, *Tests: A Comprehensive Reference for Assessments in Psychology, Education, and Business* [Maddox, 2003]) can generally produce quick and accurate results. It is cumbersome and time consuming, but one can also go to specific publishers' websites (such as Harcourt's Education to see what tests they have in a domain of interest. In this phase, one should check the publication date of the test to make sure it is sufficiently current to consider. Generally, tests that were published 15 or more years ago are dated and should not be used unless absolutely necessary. However, they may be the only tests available to assess a specific domain, or newer tests may lack adequate norms, reliability, or validity. It is also a good idea to contact the publisher to make sure that the most recent version of a test is being considered. It is a waste of time to evaluate a test that is not the latest edition or one that will be replaced shortly by a newer version.

Regardless of how a test is chosen for evaluation, the second step is to acquire all of the relevant materials. Usually this means contacting a test publisher and obtaining a specimen kit and any supplementary manuals that are available. Sometimes publishers will give or lend specimen kits; sometimes these must be purchased. There are restrictions on purchasing (or even receiving review copies of) some kinds of tests. For example, one must be licensed in order to review most intelligence tests.[1]

---

1. Students in training can expect their programs to maintain a supply of tests.

Tests are not sold only by the company that owns the copyright; the same test kit may be sold by several publishers. Usually, however, the company that owns the copyright on a test is more willing to provide a specimen kit. Test users must determine whether a test will result in accurate and appropriate inferences about the specific students who will be assessed. This and other books can evaluate tests only in terms of their general usefulness. There are so many idiosyncratic student characteristics and life circumstances that it is impossible to consider a test's usefulness with all possible combinations of characteristics and circumstances.

In evaluating the general accuracy and appropriateness of inferences drawn from students' test performances, we rely on *Standards for Educational and Psychological Testing* recommended by the American Educational Research Association (AERA), American Psychological Association, and National Council on Measurement in Education (1999). The standards provide guidelines about the kinds of evidence that should be used to evaluate a test's usefulness. However, examination should go beyond checking to see whether specific information relating to important standards is provided; users should also consider the quality of the evidence presented. Evaluating the evidence presented in test materials requires a "prove or show me" mind set. Test authors must demonstrate to potential users that their tests provide accurate educational and psychological information which can be used properly to draw inferences about students. One should not count on test authors' admitting that their test was poorly normed because there was no money to pay testers or that their test was unreliable because they developed too few test items. Test authors tend to put the best face on their tests, so one should evaluate tests critically.

How Do We Review a Test?

A user's first job is to locate the evidence presented by the author. Occasionally one finds neatly organized test manuals that have useful chapter titles, subsections, and indexes, so that one can readily find a section (such as reliability), turn to the beginning of the section, and locate the evidence being sought. When a manual lacks chapters or headings, one just begins reading and making notes, adding headings if necessary. Even when a test manual is organized carefully, one often must extract the evidence from large tables or appendices.

When test materials are not well organized or use idiosyncratic terminology, locating the evidence is more difficult. In such instances, users need to assemble all the materials. Because all of them often must be open at once, a large workspace is needed. Also, for most of us, test materials are not spellbinding. Thus the workspace in which the evaluation is conducted should not be conducive to nodding off.

It is also usually a good idea to use several sheets of paper (or computer files) for note taking, establishing different locations for each topic: purposes, materials, and procedures; norms and scores; reliability; and validity. It really does not matter much where one starts, except that the validity and usefulness of inferences based on test scores are better left until last.

Test Purposes   The search begins by finding the uses that the author recommends for a test. For example, the authors of the Gray Oral Reading Tests (Wiederholt & Bryant, 2001, p. 4) state that their test is intended to (1) help identify students who are significantly below their peers in oral reading proficiency; (2) aid in determining particular kinds of reading strengths and weaknesses; (3) document students' progress in reading as a consequence of special intervention programs; and (4) be used in research of the abilities of school children. Thus, in evaluating the Gray Oral or any other test, users should look for evidence that the test can be used effectively for the purposes intended by the test authors.

Test Content and Testing Procedures

Test Content

Next, one considers the test's content. The adequacy and usefulness of test interpretations depend on the rigor with which the purposes of the test and the domain represented by the test have been defined and explicated (AERA et al., 1999, p. 43.)

Some test manuals contain extensive descriptions of the domains they assess. Other manuals merely name the domains, and those names can imply a far broader assessment than the test content actually provides. For example, the Wide Range Achievement Test 3 claims to measure reading. However, cursory examination of the test's content reveals that the test assesses only letter recognition, letter naming, and saying words in isolation. It does not assess accuracy and fluency of reading-connected discourse (such as prose), nor does it assess comprehension. For tests with incomplete or inadequate descriptions of the domain being sampled, it is necessary to examine the content carefully.

Testing Procedures

Users should also examine testing procedures. Some tests use very tight testing procedures which specify exactly how test materials are to be presented, how test questions are to be asked, if and when questions can be restated or rephrased, and how and when students can be asked to explain or elaborate on their answers. Other tests use loose testing procedures, with flexible directions and procedures. In either case, the directions and procedures should contain sufficient detail for test takers to respond to a task in the manner that the author intended (AERA et al., 1999, p. 47). When test authors provide adaptations and accommodations for students who lack the enabling skills to take the test in the intended manner, the author should provide evidence that the adaptations and accommodations produce scores with the same meaning as those produced by nonadapted, nonaccommodated procedures. Generally, the more flexible the materials and directions are, the more valid test results will be for students with severe disabilities. For example, the Scales of Independent Behavior—Revised can be administered to any respondent who is thoroughly familiar with the person being assessed.

It is also necessary to examine how test content is tested. Specifically, one should look for evidence that the test's content and scoring procedures represent the defined domain (AERA et al., 1999, p. 45). Evidence may include any of the following, alone or in combination:

- Comparisons of tested content with some external standard (For example, the National Council of Teachers of Mathematics has explicated extensive standards for what and how mathematical knowledge should be tested.)
- Comparisons of tested content with the content tested by other accepted tests
- Expert opinion
- Reasoned rationale for the inclusion and exclusion of test content as well as assessment procedures

Scores   When evaluating a test's scores, test users should first consider the types of derived scores available on a test. This should be the most straightforward aspect of gathering and evaluating evidence about a test. Information about the types of scores might be found in several places: in a section on scoring the test, in a description of the norms, in a separate section on scores, in a section on interpreting scores, on the scoring form, or in norm tables.

Next, one must consider whether the types of scores lead to correct inferences about students. For example, norm-referenced scores lead to inferences about a student's relative standing on the skills or abilities tested. Such scores are appropriate when a student is being compared with other students—for example, when trying to determine whether a student is lagging significantly behind peers. Such scores are not appropriate when trying to determine whether a student has acquired specific information (for example, knows the meaning of various traffic signs) or skills (for example, can read material at grade level fluently). On the other hand, knowing that a student can perform accurately and fluently with grade-level material provides no information about how that performance compares with the performance of other similarly situated students.[2]

If test authors use unique kinds of scores (or even scores that they create), it is their responsibility to define the scores. For example, the authors of the Woodcock-Johnson Psychoeducational Battery created a "W-Score" as one unit of analysis. They define the score and give examples of how to use it. One should always look at whether the explanations are obtuse, whether they assume a great deal of technical knowledge that standard users cannot be expected to have (such as teacher knowledge of Rasch item calibrating procedures), or whether the derivation and use of scores are clear.

Norms   Whenever a student's score is interpreted by comparing it with scores earned by a reference population (such as scores earned by other test takers who comprise the normative sample), the reference population must be clearly and carefully described (AERA et al., 1999, p. 51). For example, whenever a student's perfor-

2. We repeat the warning that grade equivalents do not indicate the level of materials at which a student should be instructed. A grade equivalent of 3.0 does not indicate that a student is accurate or fluent in 3.0 materials. More likely, 3.0 materials are far too difficult for a student with a grade equivalent of 3.0.

mance is converted to a percentile or some other derived score, it is essential that those students who make up the normative sample be of sufficient number and relevant characteristics.

In evaluating a test's norms, one must first figure out the groups with which students' performances are actually compared. For example, in developing test norms, several thousand students may actually have been tested. However, the scores of all those students will probably not be used to derive a score for a student. Scores might be dropped for any one of several reasons, including the following:

- Demographic data are missing (for example, a student's gender or age might not be noted).

- A student failed to complete the test, or an examiner inadvertently failed to administer all items.

- A student failed to conform to criteria for inclusion in the norm group (for example, he or she may have been too old or too young).

- A score may be an outlier (for example, a fifth-grader may correctly answer all of the questions that could be given to an adult).

Thus the number of students initially tested will not be the same as the number of students in the norm group.[3]

Most often, a student's score was never intended to be compared with the scores of all the students in the normative sample. Rather, a student's score is usually compared to the scores of same-age (or same-grade) students; sometimes it is compared to scores of same-age (or -grade) and same-sex students. To ascertain to whom a student's score is compared, one usually needs only to inspect a manual's conversion tables or to read their description in the manual.

However, good norms are based on far more than just the age (or grade) and gender of students. Norms must be generally representative of all students of that age or in that grade. Thus we would expect students from major racial and ethnic groups (that is, Caucasian Americans, African Americans, Asian Americans, and Hispanic Americans) to be included. We would also expect students from across the United States, as well as students from urban, suburban, and rural communities, to be included. Finally, we would expect students from all socioeconomic classes to be included. Moreover, we would expect that the proportions of students from each of these groups would be approximately the same as the proportions found in the general population.

The first bit of evidence to look for is a detailed description of the composition of each separate norm group. Students from different demographic groups may undergo different acculturation and have different life opportunities that influence their development. Therefore, one would want to see that all groups are represented in each norm group. Thus users should look for a systematic comparison of the proportion of students with each characteristic to the general population for

---

3. The difference between the number of students tested and the number of students actually used in the norms is of relevance only when such a large number of students is dropped that the validity of the norming process is called into question.

each separate norm group. For example, when the scores of nine-year-old girls are compared with those of nine-year-old girls in general, one looks for evidence (1) that the nine-year-old girls in the norm group consist of the correct proportions of Caucasian Americans, African Americans, and Asian Americans; (2) that the norm group contains the correct proportion of Hispanic students; (3) that the norm group contains the correct proportion of students from each region of the country and each type of community; and so forth. Because some authors do not use weighting procedures, we do not expect perfect congruence with the population proportions. However, when the majority group's proportion differs by 5 percent or more from its proportion in the general population, we believe the norms may have problems. (We recognize that this is an arbitrary criterion, but it seems generally reasonable to us.)

Reliability   For every score that is recommended for interpretation, a test author must provide evidence of reliability. First, "every score" means all domain and norm comparison scores. *Domain scores* are scores for each domain or subdomain that can be interpreted appropriately. For example, an author of an achievement test might recommend interpreting scores for reading, written language, and mathematics; one author might recommend interpreting scores for oral reading and reading comprehension, whereas another author might use oral reading and reading comprehension as intermediate calculations that should not be interpreted. *Norm comparison* means each normative group to which a person's score could be compared (for example, a reading score for third-grade girls, for second-grade boys, or for all fifth-graders). Thus, if an author provides whole-year norms for students (boys and girls combined) in the first through third grades in reading and mathematics, there should be reliability information for 6 scores; that is, 3 grades multiplied by 2 subject matter areas. If there were whole-year norms for students in the first through the twelfth grades in 3 subject matter areas, there would be 36 recommended scores; that is, 12 grades multiplied by 3 subject matter areas. In practice, it is not unusual to see reliability information for 100 or more domain-by-age (or -grade) scores.[4]

As we have already learned, reliability is not a unitary concept. It refers to the consistency with which a test samples items from a domain (that is, item reliability); it refers to the stability of scores over time (that is, test-retest reliability); and it refers to the consistency with which testers score responses (that is, interscorer agreement). Information about a test's item reliability as well as its stability estimates must be presented; these indices are necessary for all tests. Information about interscorer reliability is required only when scoring is difficult or not highly objective. Thus we expect to see estimates of item reliability and stability (and perhaps interscorer agreement) for each domain or subdomain by norm-group combination. Thus, if there are normative comparisons for reading

---

4. Note that information about reliability coefficients applies to any type of score (for example, standard scores, raw scores, and so forth). Information about standard errors of measurement is specific to each type of score.

and mathematics for students in the first through third grades, and item reliability and stability were estimated, there would be 12 reliability estimates: 6 estimates of item reliability for reading and mathematics at each grade, and 6 estimates of stability for reading and mathematics at each grade.

Given modern computer technology, there is really no excuse for failing to provide all estimates of internal consistency (for instance, KR-20 or coefficient alpha). Collecting evidence of a test's stability is far more expensive and time consuming. Thus we often find incomplete stability data. This can occur in a couple of ways. One way is for authors to report an average stability by using standard scores from a sample that represents the entire age or grade range of the test.[5] Although this procedure gives an idea of the test's stability in general, it provides no information about the stability of scores at a particular age or grade. Another way in which authors incompletely report stability data is to provide data for selected ages (or age ranges) that span a test's age range. For example, if a test was intended for students in kindergarten through sixth grade, an author might report stability only for the first, third, and fifth grades.

It is not enough, however, for a test merely to contain the necessary reliability estimates. Each and every reliability estimate should be sufficient for each and every purpose for which the test was intended. Thus tests (and subtests) used in making important educational decisions for students should have reliability estimates of .90 or higher. And each test (and subtest) must have sufficient reliability for each age or grade at which it is used. For example, if a reading test is highly reliable for all grades except second grade, it would not be suitable for use with second-graders.

Finally, when test scoring is less than completely objective, evidence for interscorer agreement must be provided. Failure to report this type of evidence severely limits the utility of a test.

Validity   The evaluation of a test's general validity can be the most complicated aspect of test evaluation. Strictly speaking, a test found lacking in its content, procedures, scores, norms, or reliability cannot yield valid inferences. Regardless of the domains they assess, all tests should present convincing evidence of general validity. General validity refers to evidence that a test measures what its authors claim that it measures. If a test author claims a test measures reading skill, then we would expect evidence that the test indeed measures reading skill. This type of evidence can take several forms.

■ *Content validity.* The evidence for content validity can often be found in the section of a manual detailing how the test was developed. This section should explain the criteria for item development, the process used to prepare items, how the item was field-tested, and the criteria used to revise, reject, and include items.

5. Using raw scores would overestimate the test's stability if raw scores were correlated with age or grade.

▪ *Criterion-related validity.* Evidence for criterion-related validity usually consists of concurrent or predictive correlations with other well-accepted tests. The reported correlations should be logical. For example, the reading subtest on test 1 should correlate with the reading subtest on test 2, and it should correlate more highly than with subtests in different domains of test 2. The magnitude of the correlations is a matter of judgment. Generally, correlations should be high enough that it is clear that the two tests (or subtests) are measuring the same ability or skill.

▪ *Factor structure.* If authors claim that their test measures several different skills or abilities (such as verbal ability, nonverbal reasoning, perceptual speed, and freedom from distractibility), we would expect to find empirical evidence from factor analyses supporting the four-factor interpretation.

▪ *Freedom from bias.* If a test is intended to be used generally, we would expect to see evidence that test scores and interpretations are not biased against certain groups (women, students of color, students with disabilities, and so forth). Evidence of freedom from bias generally begins with expert judgments about the lack of bias in a test's content or administration. Evidence may also include comparisons of factor structures or criterion-related validity correlations for minority and majority students. Finally, evidence may consist of advanced statistical analyses. For example, partial correlations between minority status and success on individual test items, holding total score constant, are frequently used to show the extent of bias in test items.

Test authors should also present evidence that their test leads to valid inferences for each specific purpose for which they recommend the test be used. For example, if test authors claim their test can be used to identify students with learning disabilities, we would expect to see evidence that use of the test leads to correct inferences about the presence of a disability. When these inferences rely on the use of cutoff scores, there should be evidence that the specific cutoff scores are valid.

Some achievement test authors claim that their test is useful in planning instruction. Evidence for a standardized test's utility in planning instruction would consist of data showing how a test score or profile can be used to find instructional starting points—and the accuracy of those starting points. Similarly, some achievement test authors claim that their test is useful in monitoring students' progress. Evidence for this inference would consist of data showing that the test (or subtest) can detect small changes in a student's mastery of the curriculum. In our experience, test authors never relate the content of their tests to specific curricula, and they never relate their tests' derived scores to placement in a specific curriculum. Thus one rarely finds evidence to support such claims.

Making a Summative Evaluation

In reaching an overall evaluation of a test, it is a good idea to remember that it is the test authors' responsibility to convince potential test users of the usefulness of their test. However, once you use a test, you—not the test author—become responsible for test-based inferences.

Test-based inferences can be correct only when a test is properly normed, yields reliable scores, and has evidence of its general validity. If evidence for any one of these components is lacking or insufficient (for example, the norms are inadequate or the scores are unreliable), then the inferences cannot be trusted.

Having found that a test is generally useful, it is still necessary to determine whether it is appropriate to use with the specific students you intend to test. Of course, a test that is not generally useful will not be useful with a specific student.

SUMMARY

Once a test has been selected for review and all relevant materials have been obtained, test users must determine if a test will result in accurate and appropriate inferences about the specific students who will be assessed. When we evaluate a test, we begin by finding the uses which the author recommends for a test. Then we look for evidence that the test can be used effectively for the purposes intended by the test authors. The first type of evidence we generally consider is a test's content and the testing procedures. Next, we examine the types of derived scores available on a test and if the scores lead to correct inferences about students. Norm-referenced scores require appropriate norms that are fully described in terms of race, ethnicity, gender, place of residence, and socioeconomic status. We examine how and where norm samples are located. Next, we usually look for evidence of item reliability, stability, and (when appropriate) scorer agreement for each score recommended for interpretation by the test author. All reliability estimates should be sufficient for every purpose for which the test was intended. Next, we look for general evidence of content validity, criterion-related validity, construct validity (paying particular attention to factor structure and freedom from bias). Finally, we consider the evidence in its totality to reach a judgment about a test's validity for each purpose recommended by the test's author.

QUESTIONS FOR CHAPTER REVIEW

1. Tests should be reliable enough for the purposes for which they are intended. What kind of reliability information should be available for a diagnostic test of oral reading?

2. In considering the use of any standardized achievement test, what information about a test's norms should teachers look for?

3. What are some of the types of information one could expect to find in a section on the content validity of a mathematics test?

PROJECT

Without consulting the review in this text, review one standardized norm-referenced test that is reviewed in this text. Compare your summary with the text's summary. If your summary differs from the text's review, reconcile the differences.

RESOURCES FOR FURTHER INVESTIGATION

Print Resources

Maddox, T. (Ed.). (2003). *Tests: A comprehensive reference for assessments in psychology, education, and business* (5th ed.). Austin, TX: Pro-Ed.

Buros Institute in Lincoln. *The mental measurements yearbook*. Lincoln, NE: University of Nebraska Press.

Technology Resources

QUESTIONS TO ASK WHEN EVALUATING TESTS
pareonline.net/getvn.asp?v=4&n=2
In this article from the online journal *Practical Assessment, Research and Evaluation,* Lawrence Rudner considers several important questions that can be asked about various test characteristics: coverage and use, samples used to research and norm the test, reliability, various types of reliability, test administration, reporting test results, and test and item bias.

ERIC TEST REVIEW LOCATOR SEARCH
searcheric.org
More than 100,000 documents published in ERIC since 1993 can be downloaded free of charge. Simply type in the name of the test in the Find box to obtain the titles and abstracts of relevant articles.

CHAPTER 16

Assessment of Intelligence: An Overview

NO OTHER AREA OF ASSESSMENT HAS GENERATED AS MUCH ATTENTION, CONTRO-versy, and debate as the testing of what we call "intelligence." For centuries, philosophers, psychologists, educators, and laypeople have debated the meaning of intelligence. Numerous definitions of the term *intelligence* have been proposed, with each definition serving as a stimulus for counterdefinitions and counterproposals. Several theories have been advanced to describe and explain intelligence and its development, such as Cattell-Horn, Gardner, Kaufman, Sternberg, and Guilford (Flanagan & Harrison, 2005). The extent to which intelligence is genetically or environmentally determined has been of special concern. Genetic determinists, environmental determinists, and interactionists have all observed differences in the intelligence test performances of different populations of children.

Both the interpretation of group differences in intelligence measurements and the practice of testing the intelligence of schoolchildren have been topics of recurrent controversy and debate, aired in professional journals, in the popular press, and on television. In some instances, the courts have acted to curtail or halt intelligence assessment in the public schools; in others, the courts have defined what composes intelligence assessment. Debate and controversy have flourished about whether intelligence tests should be given, what they measure, and how different levels of performance attained by different populations are to be explained.

No one, however, has seen a specific thing called "intelligence." Rather, we observe differences in the ways people behave—either differences in everyday behavior in a variety of situations or differences in responses to standard stimuli or sets of stimuli; then we attribute those differences to something we describe as intelligence. In this sense, intelligence is an inferred entity, a term or construct we use to explain differences in present behavior and to predict differences in future behavior.

We have repeatedly stressed the fact that all tests, including intelligence tests, assess samples of behavior. Regardless of how an individual's performance on any given test is viewed and interpreted, intelligence tests—and the items on those tests—simply sample behaviors. A variety of different kinds of behavior samplings are used to assess intelligence; in most cases, the kinds of behaviors sampled reflect a test author's conception of intelligence. The behavior samples are combined in different ways by different authors, usually on the basis of the ways in which they view the concept of intelligence. In this chapter, we review the kinds of behaviors sampled by intelligence tests, with particular emphasis on the psychological demands of different test items, as a function of pupil characteristics. We also describe several ways in which intelligence theorists and test authors have conceptualized the structure of intelligence.

Intelligence Tests as Samples of Behavior

There is a hypothetical domain of items that could be used to assess intelligence. In practice, it is impossible to administer every item in the domain to a student whose intelligence we want to assess. The darker screened areas in Figure 16.1 represent different items in the domain of behaviors that could be used to assess intelligence. No two tests evaluate identical samples of behavior; some tests overlap in the kinds of behaviors they sample, and others do not. Figure 16.1 shows that tests A and D sample different behaviors. Both tests assess some behaviors sampled by test E. None of the tests sample all the possible behaviors in the domain.

The characterization of behaviors sampled by intelligence tests is complex. Some persons have argued, for example, that intelligence tests assess a student's capacity to profit from instruction, whereas others argue that such tests assess merely what has been learned; some have characterized intelligence tests as either verbal or nonverbal; some characterize intelligence tests as either culturally

FIGURE 16.1
Intelligence Tests as Samples of Behavior from a Larger Domain of Behaviors

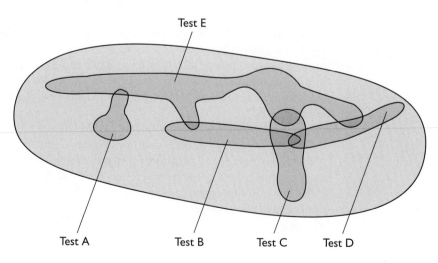

biased or culturally fair. In actuality, nearly any contention regarding what intelligence tests measure can be supported. The relative merit of competing opinions, theories, and contentions is primarily a function of the interaction between the characteristics of an individual and the psychological demands of items in an intelligence test. It is also a function of the stimulus and response requirements of the items.

There are many kinds of nonverbal behavior samples. A test might require children (1) to point to objects in response to directions read by the examiner, (2) to build block towers, (3) to manipulate colored blocks in order to reproduce a design, or (4) to copy symbols or designs on paper. Similarly, there are many kinds of verbal behavior samples. We could, for example, ask students factual questions, such as "Who wrote *The Adventures of Huckleberry Finn?*" We could ask them to define words or to identify similarities and differences in words or objects. We could ask them to state actions that they would take in specific social situations or to repeat sequences of digits. Test items may be presented orally, or the test takers may have to read the items.

Similar behaviors may be assessed in different ways. In assessing vocabulary, for example, the examiner may ask pupils to define words, to name pictures, to select a synonym of a stimulus word, or to point to pictures depicting words read by the examiner. All four kinds of assessments are called "vocabulary tests," yet they sample different behaviors. The psychological demands of the items change with the ways the behavior is assessed.

In evaluating the performance of individuals on intelligence tests, teachers, administrators, counselors, and diagnostic specialists must go beyond test names and scores to look at the kinds of behaviors sampled on the test. They must be willing to question the ways test stimuli are presented, to question the response requirements, and to evaluate the psychological demands placed on the individual.

The Effect of Pupil Characteristics on Assessment of Intelligence

Acculturation is the most important characteristic to consider in evaluating performance on intelligence tests. Acculturation refers to an individual's particular set of background experiences and opportunities to learn in both formal and informal educational settings. This, in turn, depends on the experiences available in the person's environment (that is, culture) and the length of time the person has had to assimilate those experiences. The culture in which an individual lives and the length of time that the person has lived in that culture effectively determine the psychological demands presented by a test item. Simply knowing the kind of behavior sampled by a test is not enough, for the same test item may create different psychological demands for different people.

Suppose, for example, that we assess intelligence by asking children to tell how hail and sleet are alike. Children may fail the item for very different reasons. Mitch, for example, does not know what hail and sleet are, so he stands little chance of telling how hail and sleet are alike; he will fail the item simply because he does not know the meanings of the words. Marcie may know what hail is and what sleet is, but she fails the item because she is unable to integrate these two words into a conceptual category (precipitation). The psychological demand of the item changes as a function of the children's acculturation. For the child who has not learned the meanings of the words, the item assesses vocabulary. For the child who knows the meanings of the words, the item is a generalization task.

In considering how individuals perform on intelligence tests, we need to know how acculturation affects test performance. Items on intelligence tests range along a continuum, from items that sample fundamental psychological behaviors that are relatively unaffected by the test taker's learning history to items that sample primarily learned behavior. To determine exactly what is being assessed, we need to know the essential background of the student. Consider for a moment the following item:

> Jeff went walking in the forest. He saw a porcupine that he tried to take home for a pet. It got away from him, but when he got home, his father took him to the doctor. Why?

For a student who knows what a porcupine is, that a porcupine has quills, and that quills are sharp, the item can assess comprehension, abstract reasoning, and problem-solving skill. The student who does not know any of that information may very well fail the item. In this case, failure is due not to an inability to comprehend or solve the problem but to a deficiency in background experience.

Similarly, we could ask a child to identify the seasons of the year. The experiences available in children's environments are reflected in the way they respond to this item. Children from central Illinois, who experience four discernibly different climatic conditions, may well respond, "summer, fall, winter, and spring." Children from central Pennsylvania, who also experience four discernibly different climatic conditions but who live in an environment where hunting is prevalent, might respond, "buck season, doe season, rabbit season, and squirrel season." Within specific cultures, both responses are logical and appropriate; only one is scored as correct.

Items on intelligence tests also sample different behaviors as a function of the age of the child assessed. Age and acculturation are positively related; older children in general have had more opportunities to acquire the skills assessed by intelligence tests. The performances of 5-year-old children on an item requiring them to tell how a cardinal, a blue jay, and a swallow are alike are almost entirely a function of their knowledge of the word meanings. Most college students know the meanings of the three words; for them, the item assesses primarily their ability to identify similarities and to integrate words or objects into a conceptual category. As children get older, they have increasing opportunities to acquire the elements of the collective intelligence of a culture.

The interaction between acculturation and the behavior sampled determines the psychological demands of an intelligence test item. For this reason, it is impossible to define exactly what intelligence tests assess. Identical test items place different psychological demands on different children. Thirteen kinds of behaviors sampled by intelligence tests are described in the next section of this chapter. For the sake of illustration, let us assume that there are only three discrete sets of background experiences, which we identify as *m*. (This is a very conservative estimate; there are probably many times this number in the United States alone.) To further simplify our example, let us consider only the 13 kinds of behaviors sampled by intelligence tests, identified as *n,* rather than the millions of items that could be used to sample each of the 13 kinds. Even with these very restrictive conditions, there are still $(mn)!/m!n!$ possible interactions between behavior samples and types of acculturation, or $(3 \times 13)!/3!13!$. (The exclamation marks are mathematical symbols for "factorial"; for example, 3! is $3 \times 2 \times 1 = 6$.) This very restrictive estimate produces more than 1.35×10^{32} interactions. No wonder there is controversy about what intelligence tests measure! They measure more things than we can conceive of, and they measure different things for different children.

Used appropriately, intelligence tests can provide information that can lead to the enhancement of both individual opportunity and protection of the rights of students. Used inappropriately, they can restrict opportunity and rights. The chapters "Assessment of Intelligence: Individual Tests" and "Assessment of Intelligence: Group Tests" review commonly used individually administered and group-administered intelligence tests, with particular reference to the kinds of behaviors sampled by those tests and to their technical adequacy.

Behaviors Sampled by Intelligence Tests

Regardless of the interpretation of measured intelligence, it is a fact that intelligence tests simply sample behaviors. This section describes the kinds of behaviors sampled, including discrimination, generalization, motor behavior, general knowledge, vocabulary, induction, comprehension, sequencing, detail recognition, analogical reasoning, pattern completion, abstract reasoning, and memory.

Discrimination   Intelligence test items that sample skill in discrimination usually present a variety of stimuli and ask the student to find the one that differs from all the others. Figural, symbolic, or semantic discrimination may be assessed. Figure 16.2 illustrates items assessing discrimination: Items a and b assess discrimination of figures; items c and d assess symbolic discrimination; items e and f assess semantic discrimination. In each case, the student must identify the item that differs from the others. The psychological demand of the items differs, however, depending on the student's age and particular set of background experiences.

Generalization   Items assessing generalization present a stimulus and ask the student to identify which of several response possibilities goes with the stimulus. Again, the content of the items may be figural, symbolic, or semantic; the difficulty may range from simple matching to a more difficult type of classification. Figure 16.3 illustrates several items assessing generalization. In each case, the student is given a stimulus element and is required to identify the one that is like it or that goes with it.

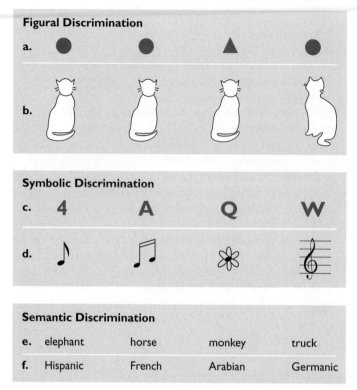

Motor Behavior

Many items on intelligence tests require a motor response. The intellectual level of very young children, for example, is often assessed by items requiring them to throw objects, walk, follow moving objects with their eyes, demonstrate a pincer grasp in picking up objects, build block towers, and place geometric forms in a recessed-form board. Most motor items at higher age levels are actually visual-motor items. The student may be required to copy geometric designs, trace paths through a maze, or reconstruct designs from memory. Obviously, because motor responses can be required for items assessing understanding and conceptualization, many items assess motor behavior at the same time that they assess other behaviors.

General Knowledge

Items on intelligence tests sometimes require a student to answer specific factual questions, such as "In what direction would you travel if you were to go from Poland to Argentina?" and "What is the cube root of 8?" Essentially, such items are like the kinds of items in achievement tests; they assess primarily what has been learned.

Vocabulary

Many different kinds of test items are used to assess vocabulary. In some cases, the student must name pictures, and in others, she or he must point to objects in response to words read by the examiner. Some vocabulary items require the stu-

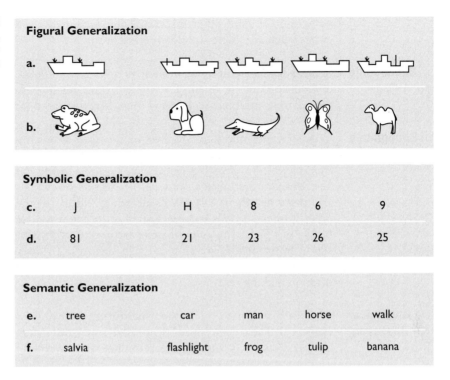

FIGURE 16.3
Items That Assess Figural, Symbolic, and Semantic Generalization

dent to produce oral definitions of words, whereas others call for reading a definition and selecting one of several words to match the definition. Some tests score a student's definitions of words as simply pass or fail; others use a weighted scoring system to reflect the degree of abstraction used in defining words. The Wechsler Intelligence Scale for Children–IV, for example, assigns 0 points to incorrect definitions, 1 point to definitions that are descriptive (an orange is round) or functional (an orange is to eat), and 2 points to more abstract definitions (an orange is a citrus fruit).

Induction   Induction items present a series of examples and require the student to induce a governing principle. For example, the student is given a magnet and several different cloth, wooden, and metal objects, and is asked to try to pick up the objects with the magnet. After several trials, the student is asked to state a rule or principle about the kinds of objects that magnets can pick up.

Comprehension   There are three kinds of items used to assess comprehension: items related to directions, to printed material, and to societal customs and mores. In some instances, the examiner presents a specific situation and asks what actions the student would take (for example, "What would you do if you saw a train approaching a washed-out bridge?"). In other cases, the examiner reads paragraphs to a student and then asks specific questions about the content of the paragraphs. In still other instances, the student is asked questions about social mores, such as, "Why should we keep promises?"

Sequencing

Items assessing sequencing consist of a series of stimuli that have a progressive relationship among them. The student must identify a response that continues the relationship. Four sequencing items are illustrated in Figure 16.4.

Detail Recognition

In general, not many tests or test items assess detail recognition. Those that do evaluate the completeness and detail with which a student solves problems. For example, certain drawing tests, such as the Goodenough-Harris Draw-a-Person Test, evaluate a student's drawing of a person on the basis of inclusion of detail. The more details in a student's drawing, the more credit the student earns. In other instances, items require a student to count the blocks in pictured piles of blocks in which some of the blocks are not directly visible, to copy geometric designs, or to identify missing parts in pictures. To do so correctly, the student must attend to detail in the stimulus drawings and must reflect this attention to detail in making responses.

Analogical Reasoning

"A is to B as C is to __" is the usual form for analogies. Element A is related to element B. The student must identify the response having the same relationship to element C as B has to A. Figure 16.5 illustrates several different analogy items.

Pattern Completion

Some tests and test items require a student to select from several possibilities the missing part of a pattern or matrix. Figures 16.6 and 16.7 illustrate two different completion items. The item in Figure 16.6 requires identification of a missing part in a pattern. The item in Figure 16.7 calls for identification of the response that completes the matrix by continuing both the triangle, circle, rectangle sequence and the solid, striped, and clear sequence.

Abstract Reasoning

A variety of items on intelligence tests sample abstract reasoning ability. The Stanford-Binet Intelligence Scale, for example, presents absurd verbal statements

FIGURE 16.4
Items That Assess
Sequencing Skill

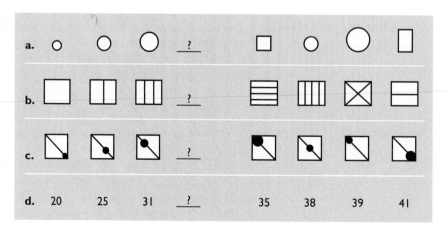

FIGURE 16.5
Analogy Items

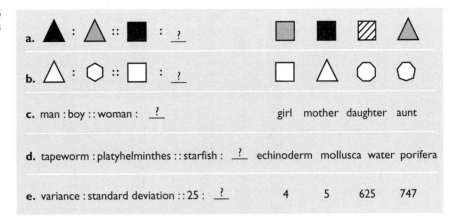

and pictures and asks the student to identify the absurdity. It also includes a series of proverbs, the essential meanings of which the student must state. In the Stanford-Binet and other scales, arithmetic reasoning problems are often thought to assess abstract reasoning.

Memory   Several different kinds of tasks assess memory: repetition of sequences of digits presented orally, reproduction of geometric designs from memory, verbatim repetition of sentences, and reconstruction of the essential meaning of paragraphs or stories. Simply saying that an item assesses memory is too simplistic. We need to ask: Memory for what? The psychological demand of a memory task changes

FIGURE 16.6
A Pattern Completion Item

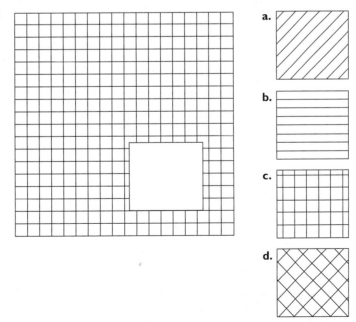

FIGURE 16.7
A Matrix Completion Item

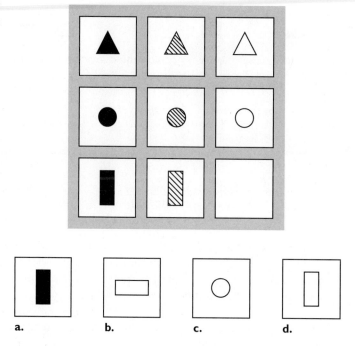

a.   b.   c.   d.

in relation to both the method of assessment and the meaningfulness of the material to be recalled.

Factors Underlying Intelligence Test Behaviors

Early in the study of intelligence, it became apparent that the behaviors used to assess intelligence were highly related to one another. Charles Spearman, an early-twentieth-century psychologist, demonstrated that a single statistical factor could explain the high degree of intercorrelation among the behaviors. He named this single factor *general intelligence* (*g*). Although he noted that performance on different tasks was influenced by other specific intelligence factors, he argued that knowing a person's level of *g* could greatly improve predictions of performance on a variety of tasks. Today, nearly every intelligence test allows for the calculation of an overall test score that is frequently considered indicative of an individual's level of *g* in comparison to same-age peers.

Later it became clear that different factor structures would emerge depending on the variables analyzed and the statistical procedures used. Thurstone proposed an alternative interpretation of the correlations among intelligence test behaviors. He conducted factor analyses of several tests of intelligence and perception, and concluded the existence of seven different intelligences that he called "primary mental abilities." These included the following: verbal comprehension, word fluency, number, space, associative memory, perceptual speed, and reasoning. Although Thurstone recognized that these different abilities were often positively correlated, he emphasized multiplicity rather than unity within the construct of intelligence. This approach to interpreting intellectual performance was further expanded by Raymond Cattell and his associates. Cattell suggested the existence of two primary intelligence factors: fluid intelligence (*gf*) and crystallized intelligence (*gc*). *Fluid intelligence* refers to the efficiency with which an individual learns and completes various tasks. This type of intelligence increases as a person ages until early adulthood and then decreases somewhat steadily over time. *Crystallized intelligence* represents the knowledge and skill one acquires over time, and increases steadily throughout one's life. Several current tests of intelligence provide separate composite scores for behaviors that are representative of fluid and crystallized intelligence. The fluid intelligence score might represent performance on tasks such as memorizing and later recalling names of symbols, or recalling unrelated words presented in a particular sequence. A crystallized intelligence score might represent performance on items that measure vocabulary or general knowledge. James Horn and John Carroll have expanded on this theory to include additional intelligence factors, now called the Cattell-Horn-Carroll theory (CHC theory). These factors include general memory and learning, broad visual perception, broad auditory perception, broad retrieval ability, broad cognitive speediness, and decision/reaction time/speed. This is the theory on which the Woodcock-Johnson Test of Cognitive Abilities–III is based. Descriptions of several factors based on CHC theory are included in Table 16.1.

Commonly Interpreted Factors on Intelligence Tests

Educational professionals will encounter many different terms that describe various intelligence test factors, clusters, indexes, and processes. We describe several common (and overlapping) terms in Table 16.1.

Assessment of Processing Deficits

People have become more and more intrigued with the possibility of identifying specific cognitive processing deficits that contribute to a student's academic difficulties. Some current conceptualizations of learning disabilities include cognitive processing deficits as a defining characteristic. Test developers have begun to develop specific tests that are intended to measure particular weaknesses that students might have in processing information. For instance, there is now a supplemental instrument to the Wechsler Intelligence Scale for Children–IV (WISC-IV) called the WISC-IV Integrated. This supplemental material, which includes a variety of additional subtests that allow for the comparison of student performance across a variety of conditions, is intended to facilitate the identification of specific processing deficits. The Woodcock-Johnson Test of Cognitive Abilities–III (WJ-III) includes a related vehicle for test score interpretation, whereby one can analyze student performance according to an information processing model.

TABLE 16.1   Common Intelligence Test Terms, Associated Theorists and Tests, and Examples of Associated Behaviors Sampled

Term	Definition	Theorist*	Test	Example of a Behavior Sampled	Source of Information Obtained
Attention	Alertness	Das, Naglieri	CAS, WJ-III	When given a target figure and many distracting stimuli, the individual must quickly select those that are identical to the target figure.	assess.nelson.com/test-ind/cas.html
Auditory perception/processing	Ability to analyze, manipulate, and discriminate sounds	Cattell, Horn, Carroll	WJ-III	When given a set of pictures, and listening to a recording in which a spoken word is presented along with noise distractions, the individual must select the picture that goes with the spoken word.	WJ-III Examiner's Manual
Cognitive efficiency/speediness	Ability to process information quickly and automatically	Carroll	WJ-III	When given several figures, the individual must quickly select the two that are most alike.	WJ-III Examiner's Manual
Cognitive fluency	Speed in completing cognitive tasks		WJ-III	When given a set of pictures, the individual must quickly say the names of the pictures.	WJ-III Examiner's Manual
Comprehension knowledge	Term used on the WJ-III to describe crystallized intelligence	Cattell, Horn, Carroll	WJ-III	When shown various pictures, the individual must provide the names for the pictures.	WJ-III Examiner's Manual
Executive processing	Use of higher-level thinking strategies to organize thought and behavior		WJ-III	When given a maze to complete, the individual must complete the maze correctly without mistakes on the first try.	WJ-III Examiner's Manual
Fluid reasoning/intelligence	Efficiency with which an individual learns and completes various tasks	Cattell, Horn, Carroll	WJ-III	When given a set of simple relationships or rules among symbols, the individual must apply the rules to correctly identify missing links within increasingly complicated patterns.	WJ-III Examiner's Manual
Long-term retrieval/delayed recall	Ability to store and easily recall information at a much later point in time	Cattell, Horn, Carroll	WJ-III	Two days after an individual was taught the words associated with certain symbols, the symbol is presented and the individual must recall the associated words.	WJ-III Examiner's Manual
Perceptual reasoning	Ability to identify and form patterns		WISC-IV	When given a pattern and various colored blocks, the individual must form the blocks in the shape of the given pattern.	WISC-IV Technical and Interpretive Manual
Planning	Ability to identify effective strategies to reach a particular goal	Das, Naglieri	CAS	When given multiple numbers, the individual must select the two that are the same.	assess.nelson.com/test-ind/cas.html

Term	Definition	Theorists*	Test	Task description	Reference
Processing speed	Ability to quickly complete tasks that require limited complex thought	Cattell, Horn, Carroll	WJ-III, WISC-IV	The individual is presented with a key for converting numbers to symbols and must quickly write down the associated symbols for numbers that are presented.	WISC-IV Technical and Interpretive Manual
Quantitative knowledge	Mathematical knowledge and achievement	Cattell, Horn	WJ-III	The individual must answer math word problems correctly.	WJ-III Examiner's Manual
Short-term memory or working memory	Ability to quickly store and then immediately retrieve information within a short period of time	Cattell, Horn	WISC-IV, WJ-III	The examiner says several numbers, and the individual must repeat them accurately and in the same order.	WISC-IV Technical and Interpretive Manual
Simultaneous processing	Extent to which one can integrate pieces of information into a complete pattern	Das, Naglieri	CAS	When asked a question verbally and presented with figures, the individual must pick the figure that answers the question.	assess.nelson.com/test-ind/cas.html
Speed of lexical access	Fluency with which one can recall pronunciations of words, word parts, and letters	Carroll	WJ-III	When given many pictures, the individual must say the picture names as quickly as possible.	WJ-III Examiner's Manual
Successive processing	Extent to which one can recall things presented in a particular order	Das, Naglieri	CAS	When given a set of words, the individual must repeat them back in the same order.	assess.nelson.com/test-ind/cas.html
Thinking ability	Composite cluster within the WJ-III that is comprised of performance on several less-automatic cognitive tasks		WJ-III	Includes tasks associated with long-term retrieval, visual-spatial thinking, auditory processing, and fluid reasoning (see task examples for these terms in this table)	WJ-III Technical Manual
Verbal ability	Composite cluster within the WJ-III that is comprised of language tasks		WJ-III	Includes tasks associated with comprehension/knowledge (see task example for this term above)	WJ-III Technical Manual
Verbal comprehension	"Verbal abilities utilizing reasoning, comprehension, and conceptualization" (p. 6)		WISC-IV	The individual must verbally express how two things are similar.	WISC-IV Technical and Interpretive Manual
Visual perception/processing	Integrating and interpreting visual information	Cattell, Horn, Carroll	**	When presented only part of an image, the individual must identify what the entire image is.	WJ-III Examiner's Manual
Visual-spatial thinking	Ability to store and manipulate visual images in one's mind		WJ-III	A picture is briefly shown and removed; the individual must then select the originally shown picture from a set of additional pictures.	WJ-III Technical and Interpretive Manual

*There are often many theorists, researchers, and tests associated with a given intelligence term; we provide here just one or two individuals who were key in defining these terms and tests that involve measurement of behaviors associated with these terms.
**No test specifically includes this as an index or factor, but it is a factor in CHC theory and is associated with many tasks included on intelligence tests.
WJ-III is the Woodcock-Johnson Test of Cognitive Abilities–III.
WISC-IV is the Wechsler Intelligence Scale for Children–IV.
CAS is the Cognitive Assessment System.

Dilemmas in Current Practice

The practice of assessing children's intelligence is currently marked by controversy. Intelligence tests assess simply samples of behavior, and different intelligence tests sample different behaviors. For that reason, it is wrong to speak of a person's IQ. Instead, we can refer only to a person's IQ on a specific test. An IQ on the Stanford-Binet Intelligence Scale is not derived from the same samples of behavior as an IQ on any other intelligence test. Because the behavior samples are different for different tests, educators and others must always ask, "IQ on what test?"

This should also be considered when interpreting factor scores for different intelligence tests. Just as the measurement of overall intelligence varies across tests, factor structures and the behaviors that comprise factors differ across tests. Although authors of intelligence tests may include similar factor names, these factors may represent different behaviors across different tests. It is helpful to understand that, for the most part, the particular kinds of items and subtests found on an intelligence test are a matter of the way in which a test author defines intelligence and thinks about the kinds of behaviors that represent it.

When interpreting intelligence test scores, it is best to avoid making judgments that involve a high level of inference (judgments that suggest that the score represents much more than the specific behaviors sampled). Always remember that these factor, index, and cluster scores represent merely student performance on certain sampled behaviors and that the quality of measurement can be affected by a whole host of unique student characteristics that need to be taken into consideration.

Authors' Viewpoint

Interpreting a student's performance on intelligence tests must be done with great caution. First, it is important to note that factor scores tend to be less reliable than total (or *g*) scores because they have fewer items. Second, the same test may make different psychological demands on various test takers, depending on their ages and acculturation. Test results mean different things for different students. It is imperative that we be especially aware of the relationship between a person's acculturation and the acculturation of the norm group with which that person is compared.

We think it is also important to note that many of the behaviors sampled on intelligence tests are more indicative of actual achievement than ability to achieve. For instance, quantitative reasoning (a factor commonly included in intelligence tests) typically involves measuring a student's math knowledge and skill. Students who have had more opportunities to learn and achieve are likely to perform better on intelligence tests than those who have had less exposure to information, even if they both have the same overall potential to learn. Intelligence tests, as they are currently available, are by no means a pure representation of a student's ability to learn.

SUMMARY

Many different kinds of behaviors are sampled by intelligence tests. This chapter has described 13 kinds: discrimination, generalization, motor behavior, general knowledge, vocabulary, induction, comprehension, sequencing, detail recognition, analogical reasoning, pattern completion, abstract reasoning, and memory. Intelligence test performance is often summarized according to various factors that are believed to represent the underlying structure of intelligence. Guidelines for interpreting the results of intelligence tests are provided.

QUESTIONS FOR CHAPTER REVIEW

1. Describe at least three kinds of behaviors sampled by intelligence tests.

2. Using the categorization of behavior samplings described in this chapter, identify the kind or kinds of behaviors sampled by the following test items:
   a. How many legs does an octopus have?
   b. In what way are *first* and *last* alike?
   c. Find the one that is different: (1) table (2) bed (3) pillow (4) chair
   d. Who wrote *Macbeth*?
   e. Window is to sill as door is to ____. (1) knob (2) entrance (3) threshold (4) pane
   f. Define *hieroglyphic*.
   g. Identify the one that comes next: 3, 6, 9, ____. (1) 12 (2) 11 (3) 18 (4) 15

3. What role does acculturation play in the assessment of intelligence? How is acculturation related to age?

4. Compare and contrast the behaviors of sequencing, pattern completion, and memory.

5. What are some general theories that have guided intelligence test development and interpretation?

6. Name three important things to remember when interpreting intelligence test results.

PROJECT

Examine your own state's special education regulations and guidelines, or examine criteria used in a local school district, to determine whether specific intelligence tests are required or recommended. If specific tests are required or recommended, are data provided on the technical adequacy of those tests?

RESOURCES FOR FURTHER INVESTIGATION

Print Resources

Carroll, J. B., & Horn, J. L. (1981). On the scientific basis of ability testing. *American Psychologist, 36,* 1012–1020.

Flanagan, D. P., & Harrison, P. L. (2005). *Contemporary intellectual assessment: Theories, tests, and issues* (2nd ed.). New York: Guilford Press.

Keith, T. Z. (1994). Intelligence *is* important, intelligence *is* complex. *School Psychology Quarterly, 9,* 209–221.

Technology Resources

APA NEWS RELEASE: APA TASK FORCE EXAMINES THE KNOWNS AND UNKNOWNS OF INTELLIGENCE
www.apa.org/releases/intell.html
This news release includes the results of the American Psychological Association (APA) task force that examined the concept of intelligence and how it can be measured.

INSTITUTE FOR APPLIED PSYCHOMETRICS
www.iapsych.com
This website includes information and documents related to the application of the Cattell-Horn-Carroll theory of cognitive abilities to the development of intelligence tests.

TRADITIONAL INTELLIGENCE IN EDUCATION
www.edwebproject.org/edref.mi.intro.html
The theory of multiple intelligences is presented as an alternative view of traditional intelligence. Look here to find out more information about the theory and its implications for education.

HUMAN INTELLIGENCE: HISTORICAL INFLUENCES, CURRENT CONTROVERSIES, TEACHING RESOURCES
www.indiana.edu/~intell/
This website includes biographies of intelligence theorists and summaries of current controversies in intelligence testing.

CHAPTER 17

Assessment of Intelligence: Individual Tests

IN THE CHAPTER "ASSESSMENT OF INTELLIGENCE: AN OVERVIEW," WE DISCUSSED THE various kinds of behaviors sampled by intelligence tests and indicated that different tests sample different behaviors. In this chapter, we review the most commonly used individually administered intelligence tests, with special reference to the kinds of behaviors they sample and to their technical adequacy.

Although some individual intelligence tests may be appropriately administered by teachers, counselors, or other specialists, the intelligence tests on which school personnel rely most heavily must be given by psychologists. All intelligence tests yield scores of relative standing (and some still provide developmental scores) that provide information about a test taker's performance relative to the performances of other similar test takers. This comparative information is usually critical in reaching a decision about a student's eligibility for special educational services. However, other aspects of a test taker's performance (for example, the psychological implications of a low score), as well as interpretations of a student's behavior during testing, require much greater understanding of cognitive development if the interpretations are to be appropriate. As mentioned previously, one of the basic assumptions underlying psychoeducational assessment is that the person who uses a test should be adequately trained to administer, score, and interpret it. The correct administration, scoring, and interpretation of individual intelligence tests are complex. Despite the claims of test developers, we believe that intelligence tests should be used only by licensed or certified psychologists who have received specific training in their use.

In this chapter, we review commonly used measures of global intelligence: the Wechsler Preschool and Primary Scale of Intelligence–III (WPPSI-III), the Woodcock-Johnson Psychoeducational Battery–III (WJ-III), the Stanford-Binet Intelligence Scale, Fifth Edition (SB5), and the Wechsler Intelligence Scale for Children–IV (WISC-IV). Additional global intelligence tests are reviewed on the website for this textbook. Global intelligence tests reviewed there include the Detroit Tests of Learning Aptitude–4 (DTLA-4), the Cognitive Assessment System

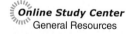
Online Study Center
General Resources

(CAS), the Wechsler Adult Intelligence Scale–III (WAIS-III), and the Kaufman Assessment of Basic Competencies (K-ABC). In general, these tests sample the 13 different kinds of behavior described in "Assessment of Intelligence: An Overview." We conclude the chapter with a discussion of more specialized tests: the Comprehensive Test of Nonverbal Intelligence (CTONI), the Leiter International Performance Scale–Revised (Leiter–R), the Test of Nonverbal Intelligence–3 (TONI-3), the Universal Nonverbal Intelligence Test (UNIT), the Naglieri Nonverbal Ability Test (NNAT), and the Peabody Picture Vocabulary Test–Revised (PPVT-III). We include reviews of additional specialized tests on the website for this book. These include the Comprehensive Test of Nonverbal Intelligence, the Universal Nonverbal Intelligence Test, the Naglieri Nonverbal Ability Test, and the Pictorial Test of Intelligence–2. The Woodcock-Johnson Psychoeducational Battery–III is a two-part test. It consists of a Cognitive Battery and an Achievement Battery. Rather than review half the test here and half in the chapter on individual tests, we review the entire test in this chapter.

In previous editions of *Assessment,* other individually administered intelligence tests were also reviewed: the McCarthy Scales of Children's Abilities, the Quick Test and the Full-Range Picture Vocabulary Test, the Blind Learning Aptitude Test, the Detroit Tests of Learning Aptitude–Primary 2, the Slosson Intelligence Test, and the Nebraska Test of Learning Aptitude. The norms for most of these tests are now so old that use of the tests should be discouraged.

Why Do We Give Individual Intelligence Tests?

Individually administered intelligence tests are most frequently used for making exceptionality, eligibility, and educational placement decisions. State special education eligibility guidelines and criteria typically specify that the collection of data about intellectual functioning must be included in the decision-making process for eligibility and placement decisions, and that these data must come from individual intellectual evaluation by a certified school psychologist.

Diagnostic Systems

In the late 1970s, test publishers began to develop diagnostic systems: measures that sample behaviors from several domains. Diagnostic systems were designed to provide a comprehensive testing instrument to link students' learning abilities to their school achievement in one continuous system of measurement. Teachers can use these interrelated findings as the basis for instructional planning. Diagnostic systems offer two major advantages: accurate comparison of scores and convenience. The first advantage is technical. The same normative sample provides derived scores for all measures in the various domains assessed in the diagnostic system. As you recall from the chapter "Norms," differences between test scores may be a function of differences in normative samples. Thus, if an intelligence test shows that Masayuki's IQ is 115 and his standard score on an achievement test is 106 (mean = 100; standard deviation = 15), part of the difference between 115 and 106 may be attributable to differences in the norms of the two tests. Diagnostic systems provide more accurate comparisons of a person's performances in different domains because the derived scores in the different domains are based on the same norm group.

The second advantage of diagnostic systems is that they may be more convenient for the assessor to use than several tests of single domains. For example, the time it takes to administer tests may be reduced because redundancies in several domains may be lessened. In addition, it may take assessors less time to put together the necessary materials for testing.

General Intelligence Tests

Wechsler Preschool and Primary Scale of Intelligence

The Wechsler Preschool and Primary Scale of Intelligence–III (WPPSI-III; Psychological Corporation, 2002) is an individually administered clinical instrument for assessing the intelligence of children ages 2 years 6 months through 7 years 3 months. It is a revision of the earlier WPPSI (Wechsler, 1967) and the WPPSI-R (Wechsler, 1989). The test provides composite IQs in Verbal and Performance domains, and a full-scale IQ. The test differs from earlier editions in that efforts were made to enhance measures of fluid reasoning and to incorporate measures of processing speed. In addition, efforts were made to simplify instructions to the child, add teaching items and prompts, revise the scoring criteria, reduce the effects of speed on performance, reduce the confounding effects of expressive language development, and update test materials.

There are two tests within one for the WPPSI-III. There is one scale for children ages 2-6 to 3-11 and another for those ages 4-0 to 7-3. There are three types of subtests in the WPPSI: core, supplemental, and optional. Some subtests are core for one of the age groups and supplemental for the other. The core subtests must be administered if one is to obtain a verbal IQ, performance IQ, and full-scale IQ. The supplemental subtests can be used in place of core subtests, but administration of all core and supplemental subtests allows users to derive additional composite scores (a Processing Speed Quotient for ages 4-0 to 7-3; or a General Language Composite for ages 2-6 to 3-11). The test differs for children above and below age 4, with different subtest batteries for each of these age bands. For the younger children, the core verbal subtests are Receptive Vocabulary and Information, and the core performance subtests are Block Design and Object Assembly. There is one supplemental subtest, Picture Naming, which can be either substituted for the Receptive Vocabulary subtest or used along with the other verbal subtests to compute a General Language Composite IQ.

There are three core verbal subtests, three core performance subtests, and one processing speed subtest for use with children older than 4-0. The core subtests for the verbal scale are Information, Vocabulary, and Word Reasoning. The core performance subtests are Block Design, Matrix Reasoning, and Picture Concepts. The processing speed subtest is called Coding. Behaviors sampled by the subtests are described below.

Verbal Subtests

Information　This subtest assesses ability to answer specific factual questions and is a core subtest for all ages of children who take the WPPSI-III. The content is learned, and the test is said to be a measure of crystallized intelligence. Six of the items are picture items; the remaining 28 are verbal.

Vocabulary　This core subtest for children older than 4 measures ability to define words. Five of the items are pictures; the remaining 20 are verbal.

Word Reasoning　This core subtest for children older than 4 measures the child's ability to identify a common concept being described in a series of increasingly specific clues. It is thought to measure comprehension, identification of analogies, generalization, and verbal abstraction.

Receptive Vocabulary　This subtest is core for children 2-6 to 3-11 and optional for children older than 4-0. The child is required to identify which of four pictures best represents a word spoken by the examiner.

Picture Naming　This subtest is supplemental for ages 2-6 to 3-11 and an optional verbal subtest for ages 4-0 to 7-3. The child is required to name a picture that is displayed in a stimulus book.

Comprehension　This subtest is supplemental for ages 4-0 to 7-3. The child must answer questions based on his or her understanding of general principles and social situations. The child is asked questions like "Why is it important to wear mittens when it is cold outside?"

Similarities　This subtest is supplemental for children ages 4-0 to 7-3. The child is read an incomplete sentence containing two concepts that share a common characteristic. The child is asked to complete the sentence by providing a response that reflects the shared characteristic. For example, the child may be asked "Green and blue are both _____."

Performance Subtests

Block Design　Children must manipulate blocks to reproduce a visually presented stimulus design. The test is untimed.

Object Assembly　The child is provided with a set of puzzle pieces and allowed 90 seconds to put them together into a whole.

Matrix Reasoning　The child is shown an incomplete matrix and selects the missing piece from four to five response options.

Picture Concepts　The child is presented with two or three rows of pictures and chooses one picture from each row to form a group with a common characteristic (for example, two fruits).

Picture Completion　The child is shown a picture with an important part missing. He or she must point to or name the missing part.

Processing Speed Subtests

Coding   The child is given a key showing symbols and shapes that correspond. The child must copy symbols that represent geometric shapes.

Symbol Search   The child is given a group of symbols along with a target symbol. Children are given 120 seconds to find and mark the target symbols that are in the group.

Scores

Recall that the WPPSI-III includes three kinds of subtests: core, supplemental, and optional. Core subtests are used to compute a verbal, performance, and full-scale IQ. Users can give supplemental subtests in addition to core subtests and obtain a Processing Speed Quotient for children ages 4-0 to 7-3 or a General Language Composite for children younger than 4-0. The IQs have a mean of 100 and a standard deviation of 15. Scaled scores may be obtained for each subtest and reflect performance relative to one's age group. They have a mean of 10 and a standard deviation of 3.

Norms

Development of the WPPSI included both an item tryout phase and a standardization phase. The national tryout included 424 children. In addition, data were collected from a number of special groups and an oversample of African American children and Hispanic children.

   The WPPSI-III was standardized on 1,700 children ages 2-6 to 7-3 and also on a sample of children from special groups. An additional sample of children was given several cognitive measures in a concurrent validity study. Children excluded from the norm sample included any with uncorrected visual or hearing impairment, those who did not speak English, those with upper extremity disability that impaired motor movement, those admitted to hospitals or institutions, those currently taking medications that might depress test performance, and those diagnosed with illnesses that might depress test performance. The standardization sample included 200 children at each of the 6-month age intervals in the sample with 100 children 7-0 to 7-3. The sample was stratified on the basis of age, gender, race/ethnicity, parent education level, and geographic region. No cross-tabs are reported in the manual, so although the sample is said to be representative, we have no way of knowing whether males and females from various ethnic/racial groups were distributed in a representative manner across regions.

Reliability

Split-half coefficients are reported on the norm sample as evidence of internal consistency. Reliability coefficients for the composite scales range from .89 to .96, and reliabilities for the subtests range from .75 to .95, with most being above .88. Reliabilities for special groups (such as gifted and talented students,

students who are mildly retarded, and LEP students) are generally higher than for the entire sample of students.

Evidence for test-retest stability was obtained by testing 157 children over a time interval ranging from 14 to 50 days. Nearly all reliability coefficients exceeded .80. The exception here is for the Block Design, Symbol Search, and Object Assembly subtests. Two of these (Symbol Search and Object Assembly) are time limited. Test-retest stability for the composite scores is consistently above .80. The composites are sufficiently reliable for use in making important decisions, although this cannot be said for the subtests.

Validity

The authors report four kinds of validity evidence: based on test content, on response processes, on internal structure, and on relations with other measures. They argue that there is evidence based on test content because the items tap a broad range of cognitive domains, including verbal reasoning, concept formation, sequential processing, auditory comprehension, cognitive flexibility, and so forth. These domains were drawn from a review of the literature, and the team of authors developed items that they thought measured the domains.

Evidence based on response processes again was largely judgmental. The authors provide theoretical justification for all of the WPPSI-III subtests, and they indicate that they examined frequently occurring incorrect responses to determine whether they were plausible. Finally, the authors tested the limits for the test by asking children to explain how they solved problems.

The authors argue that there is evidence for validity based on internal structure. They report that "research using the Wechsler scales has provided strong evidence of validity" and that "the nature of this evidence has evolved in line with advances in intelligence theory and assessment, as well as in the fields of neuropsychology and cognitive development" (p. 71). They go on to explain how they have changed their thinking about the names of some subtests or factors and whether they belong in the test. They added factors because the literature indicated that additional factors were involved in intelligence. They report the results of studies of intercorrelations among the subtests and of exploratory and confirmatory factor analysis.

The fourth kind of evidence cited as indicative of the validity of the WPPSI-III is evidence based on relationships with other variables. They looked at relationships between the WPPSI-III and external measures including WPPSI-R, WISC-III, DAS, Wechsler Individual Achievement Test–II (WIAT-II), and CMS. All of the measures were developed by the Psychological Corporation. Intercorrelations were about as would be expected.

Summary

The WPPSI-III is actually two scales in one: one designed for children between 2-6 and 3-11 years of age, the other for children 4-0 to 7-3. Verbal, performance, and full-scale IQs can be obtained for both age levels. In addition, users can obtain a General Language Composite IQ for children ages 2-6 to 7-3 and a

Processing Speed Quotient for ages 4-0 to 7-3. The test was standardized on a sample of students who match the U.S. Census, but data on cross-tabs are not reported. There is good evidence for the reliability and validity of the composite scores, but limited evidence to support use of the subtest scores in making eligibility or instructional planning decisions.

Wechsler Intelligence Scale for Children–IV

The WISC-IV[1] (Wechsler, 2003) is the latest version of the Wechsler Intelligence Scale for Children (WISC) and is designed to assess the cognitive ability and problem-solving processes of individuals ranging in age from 6 years 0 months to 16 years 11 months.

Developed by David Wechsler in 1949, the WISC adapted the 11 subtests found in the original Wechsler Scale, the Wechsler-Bellevue Intelligence Scale (1939), for use with children, and added the Mazes subtest. In 1974 the Wechsler Intelligence Scale for Children–Revised (WISC-R) was developed. This revision retained the 12 subtests found in the original WISC but altered the age range from 5–15 years to 6–16 years. The Wechsler Intelligence Scale for Children–III (WISC-III) was developed in 1991. This scale retained the 12 subtests and added a new subtest, Symbol Search. Previous editions of the WISC provided verbal IQ, performance IQ, and full-scale IQ scores. The WISC-III maintained this tradition but introduced four new index scores: Verbal Comprehension (VCI), Perceptual Organization (POI), Freedom from Distractibility (FDI), and Processing Speed (PSI).

The WISC-IV provides a new scoring framework while still maintaining the theory of intelligence underlying the previous scales. This theory was summarized by Wechsler when he stated that "intelligence is the overall capacity of an individual to understand and cope with the world around him" (Wechsler, 1974, p. 5). The definition is consistent with his original one, in which he stated that intelligence is "the capacity of the individual to act purposefully, to think rationally, and to deal effectively with his or her environment" (1974, p. 3).

Based on the premise that intelligence is both global (characterizing an individual's behavior as a whole) and specific (composed of distinct elements) (Wechsler, 2004, p. 2), the WISC-IV measures overall global intelligence, as well as discrete domains of cognitive functioning.

The WISC-IV presents a new scoring framework. Unlike its predecessors, it does not provide verbal and performance IQ scores. However, it maintains both the full-scale IQ (FSIQ) as a measure of general intellectual functioning and the four index scores as measures of specific cognitive domains. The WISC-IV developed new terminology for the four index scores in order to more accurately reflect the cognitive abilities measured by the subtest composition of each index. The four indexes are the Verbal Comprehension Index (VCI), the Perceptual

---

[1] The WISC-IV is also available as the WISC-IV Integrated (Kaplan, Fein, Kramer, Morris, Delis, & Maerlender, 2004). The WISC-IV Integrated is composed of the Core and Supplemental subtests of the WISC-IV plus 16 additional process-oriented subtests. The WISC-IV Integrated is a clinical instrument that, in our opinion, has limited application to school settings. The process-oriented subtests of the WISC-IV Integrated do not have sufficient reliability to be used to make decisions in school settings. The 16 process-oriented subtests are *in addition to* the core and supplemental subtests, and they never can be substituted for core or supplemental subtests.

Reasoning Index (PRI), the Working Memory Index (WMI), and the Processing Speed Index (PSI). A description of the subtests that comprise each index is provided below. Subtests can be categorized as either core or supplemental. Core subtests provide composite scores. Supplemental subtests (indicated by italics) provide additional clinical information and can be used as substitutes for core subtests. Those familiar with the WISC-III will note that, in the WISC-IV revisions, three subtests have been dropped, ten subtests have been retained, and five subtests have been added (indicated with an asterisk).

Subtests   *Verbal Comprehension Subtests*

Similarities   This subtest requires identification of similarities or commonalities in superficially unrelated verbal stimuli.

Vocabulary   Items on this subtest assess ability to define words. Beginning items require individuals to name picture objects. Later items require individuals to verbally define words that are read aloud by the examiner.

Comprehension   This subtest assesses ability to comprehend verbal directions or to understand specific customs and mores. The examinee is asked questions such as "Why is it important to wear boots after a large snowfall?"

Information   This subtest assesses ability to answer specific factual questions. The content is learned; it consists of information that a person is expected to have acquired in both formal and informal educational settings. The examinee is asked questions such as "Which fast food franchise is represented by the symbol of golden arches?"

*Word Reasoning**   In this subtest, individuals are presented with a clue or a series of clues and must identify the common concept that each clue or group of clues describes. It is thought to measure comprehension, identification of analogies, generalization, and verbal abstraction. A sample item for this scale is "This has a long handle and is used with water to clean the floor" (mop). When partially correct responses are given, additional clues are provided.

Perceptual Reasoning Subtests

Block Design   In this subtest, individuals are given a specified amount of time to manipulate blocks in order to reproduce a stimulus design that is presented visually.

Picture Concepts   In this subtest, an individual is shown two or three rows of pictures and must choose one picture from each row in order to form a group that shares a common characteristic. For example, an individual would choose the picture of the horse in row 1 and the picture of the mouse in row 2 because they are both animals. This is basically a picture classification task.

Matrix Reasoning   In this subtest, children must select the missing portion of an incomplete matrix given five response options. Matrices range from 2×2 to

3×3. The last item differs from this general form, requiring individuals to identify the fifth square in a row of six.

Picture Completion   This subtest assesses the ability to identify missing parts in pictures within a specified time limit.

Working Memory Subtests

Digit Span   This subtest assesses immediate recall of orally presented digits. In Digit Span Forward, children repeat numbers in the same order that they were presented aloud by the examiner. In Digit Span Backward, children repeat numbers in the reverse of the order that they were presented by the examiner.

Letter-Number Sequencing*   This subtest assesses an individual's ability to recall and mentally manipulate a series of numbers and letters that are orally presented to them. After hearing a random sequence of numbers and letters, individuals must first repeat the numbers in ascending order and then repeat the letters in alphabetical order.

Arithmetic   This subtest assesses ability to solve problems requiring the application of arithmetic operations. In this subtest, children must mentally solve problems presented orally within a specified time limit.

Processing Speed Subtests

Coding   This subtest assesses the ability to associate symbols with either geometric shapes or numbers and to copy these symbols onto paper within a specified time limit.

Symbol Search   This subtest consists of a series of paired groups of symbols, each pair including a target group and a search group. The child scans the two groups and indicates whether the target symbols appear in the search group within a specified time limit.

*Cancellation**   In this subtest, individuals are presented with first a random and then a structured arrangement of pictures. For both arrangements, individuals must mark the target pictures within the specified time limit.

Scores

Subtest raw scores obtained on the WISC-IV are transformed to scaled scores with a mean of 10 and a standard deviation of 3. The scaled scores for three Verbal Comprehension subtests, three Perceptual Reasoning subtests, two Working Memory subtests, two Processing Speed subtests, and all ten subtests are added and then transformed to obtain the composite VCI, PRI, WMI, PSI, and FSIQ scores, respectively. IQs for Wechsler scales are deviation IQs with a mean of 100 and a standard deviation of 15. Tables are provided for converting the subtest scaled scores and composite scores to percentile ranks and confidence intervals. Raw scores may also be transformed to test ages that represent the average performance on each of the subtests by individuals of specific ages. Seven process scores can also be derived. Process scores "are designed to provide more detailed information on the cognitive abilities that contribute to a child's subtest performance" (Wechsler, 2004, p. 107). The WISC-IV provides for subtest, index, and process score discrepancy comparisons. Tables provide the difference scores needed in order to be considered statistically significant at the .15 and .05 confidence level for each age group, and information on the percentage of children in the standardization sample who obtained the same or a greater discrepancy between scores.

The WISC-IV employs a differential scoring system for some of the subtests. Responses for the Digit Span, Picture Concepts, Letter-Number Sequencing, Matrix Reasoning, Picture Completion, Information, and Word Reasoning subtests are scored pass-fail. A weighted scoring system is used for the Similarities, Vocabulary, and Comprehension subtests. Incorrect responses receive a score of 0, lower-level or lower-quality responses are assigned a score of 1, and more abstract responses are assigned a score of 2. The remainder of the subtests are timed. Individuals who complete the tasks in shorter periods of time receive more credit. These differential weightings of responses must be given special consideration, especially when the timed tests are used with children who demonstrate motor impairments that interfere with the speed of response.

Norms

The WISC-IV was standardized on 2,200 children ages 6-0 to 16-11. This age range was divided into 11 whole-year groups: (for example 6-0 to 6-11). All groups had 200 participants. The standardization group was stratified on the basis of age, sex, race/ethnicity (whites, African Americans, Hispanics, Asians, and others), parent education level (based on number of years and degree held), and geographic region (Northeast, South, Midwest, and West), according to 2000 U.S. Census information. A representative sample of children from the special group studies (such as children with learning disorders, children identified as gifted, children with attention deficit hyperactivity disorder, and so on) conducted during the national tryout were included in the normative sample (approximately 5.7 percent), in order to accurately represent the population of children enrolled in school. Extensive tables in the manual are used to compare sample data with census data. These tables are stratified across the following characteristics: (1) age, race/ethnicity, and parent education level; (2) age, sex, and parent education level; (3) age, sex, and race/ethnicity; and (4) age, race/ethnicity, and geographic region. Overall, the samples appear representative of the U.S. population of children across the stratified variables.

Reliability

Because the Coding, Symbol Search, and Cancellation subtests are timed, reliability estimates for these subtests are based on test-retest coefficients. However, split-half reliability coefficient alphas corrected by the Spearman-Brown formula are reported for all the remaining subtest and composite scores. Moreover, standard errors of measurement (SEM) are reported for all scores. Scores are reported for each age group and as an average across all age groups. As would be expected, subtest reliabilities (overall averages range from .79 to .90; age levels range from .72 to .94) are lower than index reliabilities (overall averages range from .88 to .94; age levels range from .81 to .95). Reliabilities for the full-scale IQ are excellent, with age-level coefficient alphas ranging from .96 to .97.

Test-retest stability data were collected on a sample of 243 children. These data were calculated for five age groups (6 to 7, 8 to 9, 10 to 11, 12 to 13, and 14 to 16) using Pearson's product-moment correlation. Scores for the overall sample were calculated using Fisher's z-transformation. Stability coefficients[2] are provided for each subtest, process, index, and IQ. Stability coefficients for the FSIQ among these five groups ranged from .91 to .96. Process stabilities ranged from .64 to .83. Index stabilities ranged from .84 (Working Memory, ages 8 to 9) to .95 (Verbal Comprehension, ages 14 to 16), and subtest stability correlations ranged from .71 (Picture Concepts, ages 6 to 7; Cancellation, ages 8 to 9) to .95 (Vocabulary, ages 14 to 16).

The full-scale IQ and index scores are reliable enough to be used to make important educational decisions. The subtests and process indicators are not sufficiently reliable to be used in making these important decisions.

Validity

The authors present evidence for validity based on four areas: test content, response processes, internal structure, and relationship to other variables. In terms of test content, they emphasize the extensive revision process, based on comprehensive literature and expert reviews, which was used to select items and subtests that would adequately sample the domains of intellectual functioning they sought to measure.

Evidence for appropriate response processes (child's cognitive process during subtest task) is based on (1) prior research that supports retained subtests and (2) literature reviews, expert opinion, and empirical examinations that support the new subtests. Furthermore, during development, the authors engaged in empirical (for instance, response frequencies conducted to identify incorrect answers that occurred frequently) and qualitative (for instance, directly questioned students regarding their use of problem-solving strategies) examination of response processes and made adjustments accordingly.

In terms of internal structure, evidence of convergent and discriminant validity is provided based on the correlations between subtests using Fisher's z-transformation. All subtests were found to significantly correlate with one another, as would be expected considering that they all presumably measure g (general intelligence). Moreover, subtests that contribute to the same index score (VC, PR, WM, or PS) were generally found to highly correlate with one another.

Further evidence of internal structure is presented through both exploratory and confirmatory factor analysis. Exploratory factor analysis was conducted on

---

[2] Stability coefficients provided are based on corrected correlations.

two samples. Support for the four-factor structure and the stability of index scores across samples was found in cross-validation analysis. Moreover, confirmatory factor analysis using structural equation modeling and three goodness-of-fit measures confirmed that the four-factor model provided the best fit for the data.

In terms of relationships with other variables, evidence is provided based on correlations between WISC-IV and other Wechsler measures. The WISC-IV FSIQ score was correlated with the full-scale IQ or achievement measures from other Wechsler scales. The correlations are as follows: Wechsler Intelligence Scale for Children–III (WISC-III), $r = .89$; Wechsler Preschool and Primary Scale of Intelligence–III (WPPSI-III), $r = .89$; Wechsler Adult Intelligence Scale–III (WAIS-III), $r = .89$; Wechsler Abbreviated Scale of Intelligence (WASI), $r = .83$ (with FSIQ-4 measure) and $r = .86$ (with FSIQ-2 measure); and Wechsler Individual Achievement Test–II (WIAT-II), $r = .87$. Correlations were made with a set of specific intellectual measures, such as the Children's Memory Scale (CMS), Gifted Rating Scale–School Form (GRS-S), BarOn Emotional Quotient Inventory: Youth Edition (BarOn EQ), Adaptive Behavior Assessment System–II–Parent Form (ABAS-II-P), and Adaptive Behavior Assessment System–II–Teacher Form (ABAS-II-T). Correlations were very low (ranging from –.01 to .72). There is no evidence of the predictive validity of the WISC-IV.

The authors conclude by presenting special group studies that they conducted during standardization in order to examine the clinical utility of the WISC-IV. They note the following four limitations to these studies: (1) random selection was not used; (2) diagnoses might have been based on different criteria due to the various clinical settings from which participants were selected; (3) small sample sizes that covered only a portion of the WISC-IV age range were used; and (4) only group performance is reported. The authors caution that these studies provide examples but are not fully representative of the diagnostic categories. The studies were conducted with children identified as intellectually gifted and children with mild to moderate mental retardation, learning disorders, learning disorders and attention deficit hyperactivity disorder (ADHD), ADHD, expressive language disorder, mixed receptive-expressive language disorder, traumatic brain injury, autistic disorder, Asperger's syndrome, and motor impairment.

Summary

The WISC-IV is a widely used individually administered intelligence test that assesses individuals ranging in age from 6 years 0 months to 16 years 11 months. Evidence for the reliability of the scales is good. Reliabilities are much lower for subtests, so subtest scores should not be used in making placement or instructional planning decisions. Evidence for validity, as presented in the manual, is based on four areas: test content, response processes, internal structure, and relationship to other variables. Evidence for validity is limited.

The WISC-IV is of limited usefulness in making educational decisions. The WISC-IV Integrated adds 16 process-oriented subtests to explain poor performance on WISC-IV subtests that have limited reliability. The process-oriented subtests are even less reliable than the WISC-IV core and supplemental subtests. Those who use the WISC-IV in educational settings would do well not to go beyond using the full-scale and four domain scores in making decisions about students.

Woodcock-Johnson Psychoeducational Battery–III: Tests of Cognitive Abilities and Tests of Achievement

The Woodcock-Johnson Psychoeducational Battery–III (WJ-III; Woodcock, Mc-Grew, & Mather, 2001) is an individually administered, norm-referenced assessment system for the measurement of general intellectual ability, specific cognitive abilities, scholastic aptitudes, oral language, and achievement. The battery is intended for use from preschool to geriatric ages. The complete set of WJ-III test materials includes four easels for presenting the stimulus items: one for the standard battery cognitive tests, one for the extended battery cognitive tests, one for the standard achievement battery, and one for the extended achievement battery. Other materials include examiner's manuals for the cognitive and achievement tests, one technical manual, test records, and subject response booklets.

The WJ-III contains several modifications. The Tests of Cognitive Abilities (WJ-III-COG) were revised to reflect more current theory and research on intelligence, and several clusters have been added to the battery. New clusters were added to the Tests of Achievement (WJ-III-ACH) to assess several specific types of learning disabilities. Finally, a new procedure was added to ascertain intraindividual differences. The procedure allows professionals to compute discrepancies between cognitive and achievement scores within any specific domain.

WJ-III Tests of Cognitive Abilities

The 20 subtests of WJ-III-COG are based on the Cattell-Horn-Carroll theory of cognitive abilities (CHC theory). General Intellectual Ability is intended to represent the common ability underlying all intellectual performance. A Brief Intellectual Ability score is also available for screening purposes.

The primary interpretive scores on the WJ-III-COG are based on the broad cognitive clusters. Examiners are urged to note significant score differences among the tests comprising each broad ability to learn how the narrow abilities contribute. The broad and narrow abilities measured by the WJ-III-COG are presented in Table 17.1.

The standard WJ-III-COG subtests shown in Table 17.1 can be combined to create additional clusters: Verbal Ability, Thinking Ability, Cognitive Efficiency, Phonemic Awareness, and Working Memory. If the supplemental subtests are also administered, additional clusters can be created: Broad Attention, Cognitive Fluency, and Executive Processes.

Comprehension–Knowledge (Gc) assesses a person's acquired knowledge, the ability to communicate one's knowledge (especially verbally), and the ability to reason using two subtests: Verbal Comprehension (measuring lexical knowledge and language development) and General Information.

TABLE 17.1	Broad and Narrow Abilities Measured by the WJ-III Tests of Cognitive Abilities

	WJ-III Tests of Cognitive Abilities	
Broad CHC Factor	**Standard Battery Test** *Primary Narrow Abilities Measured*	**Extended Battery Test** *Primary Narrow Abilities Measured*
Comprehension–Knowledge (Gc)	Test 1: Verbal Comprehension *Lexical knowledge* *Language development*	Test 11: General Information *General (verbal) information*
Long-Term Retrieval (Glr)	Test 2: Visual-Auditory Learning *Associative memory* Test 10: Visual-Auditory Learning—Delayed *Associative memory*	Test 12: Retrieval Fluency *Ideational fluency*
Visual-Spatial Thinking (Gv)	Test 3: Spatial Relations *Visualization* *Spatial relations*	Test 13: Picture Recognition *Visual memory* Test 19: Planning *Deductive reasoning* *Spatial scanning*
Auditory Processing (Ga)	Test 4: Sound Blending *Phonetic coding: synthesis* Test 8: Incomplete Words *Phonetic coding: analysis*	Test 14: Auditory Attention *Speech-sound discrimination* *Resistance to auditory stimulus distortion*
Fluid Reasoning (Gf)	Test 5: Concept Formation *Induction*	Test 15: Analysis–Synthesis *Sequential reasoning* Test 19: Planning *Deductive reasoning* *Spatial scanning*
Processing Speed (Gs)	Test 6: Visual Matching *Perceptual speed*	Test 16: Decision Speed *Semantic processing speed* Test 18: Rapid Picture Naming *Naming facility* Test 20: Pair Cancellation *Attention and concentration*
Short-Term Memory (Gsm)	Test 7: Numbers Reversed *Working memory* Test 9: Auditory Working Memory *Working memory*	Test 17: Memory for Words *Memory span*

SOURCE: Copyright © 2001 by the Riverside Publishing Company. Reproduced from the *WJ III Technical Manual* by Kevin S. McGrew and Richard W. Woodcock with permission of the publisher.

Long-Term Retrieval (Glr) assesses a person's ability to retrieve information from memory fluently. Two subtests are included: *Visual-Auditory Learning* (measuring associative memory) and *Retrieval Fluency* (measuring ideational fluency).

Visual-Spatial Thinking (Gv) assesses a person's ability to think with visual patterns with two subtests: *Spatial Relations* (measuring visualization) and *Picture Recognition* (a visual memory task).

Auditory Processing (Ga) assesses a person's ability to analyze, synthesize, and discriminate speech and other auditory stimuli with two subtests: *Sound Blending* and *Auditory Attention* (measuring one's understanding of distorted or masked speech).

Fluid Reasoning (Gf) assesses a person's ability to reason and solve problems using unfamiliar information or novel procedures. The *Gf* cluster includes two subtests: *Concept Formation* (assessing induction) and *Analysis–Synthesis* (assessing sequential reasoning).

Processing Speed (Gs) assesses a person's ability to perform automatic cognitive tasks. Two subtests are included: *Visual Matching* (a measure of perceptual speed) and *Decision Speed* (a measure of semantic processing speed).

Short-Term Memory (Gsm) is assessed by two subtests: *Numbers Reversed* and *Memory for Words*.

WJ-III Tests of Achievement

Several new subtests have been added to the WJ-III-ACH. As shown in Table 17.2, the WJ-III-ACH now contains 22 tests that can be combined to form several clusters. The subtests and clusters from the standard battery can be combined to form scores for broad areas in reading, mathematics, and writing.

The *Oral Expression* cluster assesses linguistic competency and semantic expression with two subtests: *Story Recall* (measuring listening skills) and *Picture Vocabulary*.

The *Listening Comprehension* cluster assesses listening comprehension with two subtests: *Understanding Directions* and *Oral Comprehension*.

The *Basic Reading Skills* cluster assesses sight vocabulary and phonological awareness with two subtests: *Letter–Word Identification* and *Word Attack* (measuring one's skill in applying phonic and structural analysis skills to nonwords).

The *Reading Comprehension* cluster assesses reading comprehension and reasoning with two subtests: *Passage Comprehension* and *Reading Vocabulary*.

The *Phoneme/Grapheme Knowledge* cluster assesses knowledge of sound/symbol relationships.

TABLE 17.2   Broad and Narrow Abilities Measured by the WJ-III Tests of Achievement

	WJ-III Tests of Achievement	
Broad CHC Factor	**Standard Battery Test** *Primary Narrow Abilities Measured*	**Extended Battery Test** *Primary Narrow Abilities Measured*
Reading–Writing (*Grw*)	Test 1: Letter–Word Identification *Reading decoding*	Test 13: Word Attack *Reading decoding* *Phonetic coding: analysis and synthesis*

TABLE 17.2	Broad and Narrow Abilities Measured by the WJ-III Tests of Achievement (*cont.*)

	Test 2:	Reading Fluency	Test 17:	Reading Vocabulary
		Reading speed		*Language development/ comprehension*
	Test 9:	Passage Comprehension	Test 16:	Editing
		Reading comprehension		*Language development*
		Lexical knowledge		*English usage*
	Test 7:	Spelling	Test 22:	Punctuation and Capitalization
		Spelling		*English usage*
	Test 8:	Writing Fluency		
		Writing ability		
	Test 11:	Writing Samples		
		Writing ability		
Mathematics (*Gq*)	Test 5:	Calculation	Test 18:	Quantitative Concepts
		Mathematics achievement		*Knowledge of mathematics*
	Test 6:	Math Fluency		*Quantitative reasoning*
		Mathematics achievement		
		Numerical facility		
	Test 10:	Applied Problems		
		Quantitative reasoning		
		Mathematics achievement		
		Knowledge of mathematics		
Comprehension Knowledge (*Gc*)	Test 3:	Story Recall	Test 14:	Picture Vocabulary
		Language development		*Language development*
		Listening ability		*Lexical knowledge*
	Test 4:	Understanding Directions	Test 15:	Oral Comprehension
		Listening ability		*Listening ability*
		Language development	Test 19:	Academic Knowledge
				General information
				Science information
				Cultural information
				Geography achievement
Auditory Processing (*Ga*)			Test 13:	Word Attack
				Reading decoding
				Phonetic coding: analysis and synthesis
			Test 20:	Spelling of Sounds
				Spelling
				Phonetic coding: analysis
			Test 21:	Sound Awareness
				Phonetic coding: analysis
				Phonetic coding: synthesis
Long-Term Retrieval (*Glr*)	Test 12:	Story Recall—Delayed		
		Meaningful memory		

The *Math Calculation Skills* cluster assesses computational skills and automaticity with basic math facts using two subtests: *Calculation* and *Math Fluency*.

The *Math Reasoning* cluster assesses mathematical problem solving and vocabulary with two subtests: *Applied Problems* (measuring skill in solving word problems) and *Quantitative Concepts* (measuring mathematical knowledge and reasoning).

The *Written Expression* cluster assesses writing skills and fluency with two subtests: *Writing Samples* and *Writing Fluency*.

Scores

The WJ-III must be scored by a computer program, a change that eliminates complex hand-scoring procedures. Age norms (age 2 to over 90) and grade norms (from kindergarten to first-year graduate school) are included. Although WJ-III age and grade equivalents are not extrapolated, they still imply a false standard and promote typological thinking. (See the chapter "Quantification of Test Performance" for a discussion of these issues.) A variety of other derived scores are also available: percentile ranks, standard scores, and Relative Proficiency Indexes. Scores can also be reported in 68 percent, 90 percent, or 95 percent confidence bands around the standard score. Discrepancy scores (predicted differences) are also available. Finally, each Test Record contains a seven-category Test Session Observation Checklist to rate a student's conversational proficiency, cooperation, activity, attention and concentration, self-confidence, care in responding, and response to difficult tasks.

Norms

WJ-III norms are based on the performances of 8,818 individuals living in more than 100 geographically and economically diverse communities in the United States. Individuals were randomly selected within a stratified sampling design that controlled for ten specific community and individual variables. The preschool sample includes 1,143 children from 2 to 5 years of age (not enrolled in kindergarten). The K–12 sample is composed of 4,784 students. The college/university sample is based on 1,165 students. The adult sample includes 1,843 individuals. An oversampling plan was employed to ensure that the resultant norms would match, as closely as possible, the 1995 statistics from the U.S. Department of Commerce, Bureau of the Census.

Reliability

The *WJ-III Technical Manual* (McGrew & Woodcock, 2001) contains extensive information on the reliability of the WJ-III. The precision of each test and cluster score is reported in terms of the standard error of measurement (SEM). SEMs are provided for the W and standard score at each age level. The precision with which relative standing in a group can be indicated (rather than the precision of the underlying scores) is reported for each test and cluster by the reliability coefficient. The reliability of the various WJ-III aptitude-achievement discrepancy scores, as well as the intracognitive, intraachievement, and intraindividual discrepancy scores are also reported. Odd-even correlations, corrected by the Spearman-Brown formulas, were used to estimate reliability for each untimed test.

Some human traits are more stable than others; consequently, some WJ-III tests that precisely measure important, but less stable, human traits show reliabilities in the .80s. However, in the WJ-III, individual tests are combined to provide clusters for educational decision making. All reliabilities for the broad cognitive and achievement clusters exceed .90.

Validity

Careful item selection is consistent with claims for the content validity of both the Tests of Cognitive Ability and the Tests of Achievement. All items retained had to fit the Rasch measurement model as well as other criteria, including bias and sensitivity.

The evidence for validity based on internal structure comes from studies using a broad age range of individuals.

Factor-analytic studies support the presence of seven CHC factors of cognitive ability, and several domains of academic achievement. To augment evidence of validity based on internal structure, the authors examined the intercorrelations among tests within each battery. As expected, tests assessing the same broad cognitive ability or achievement area usually correlated more highly with each other than with tests assessing different cognitive abilities or areas of achievement.

For the Tests of Cognitive Ability, evidence of validity based on relations with other measures is provided. Scores were compared with performances on other intellectual measures appropriate for individuals at the ages tested. The criterion measures included the Wechsler Intelligence Scale for Children–III, the Differential Ability Scale, the Universal Nonverbal Intelligence Test, and the Leiter–R. The correlations between the WJ-III General Intellectual Ability score and the WISC-III Full-Scale IQ range from .69 to .73.

For the Tests of Achievement, scores were compared with other appropriate achievement measures (for example, the Wechsler Individual Achievement Tests, Kaufman Tests of Educational Achievement, and Wide Range Achievement Test–III). The pattern and magnitude of correlations suggests that the WJ-III-ACH is measuring skills similar to those measured by other achievement tests.

Summary

The WJ-III consists of two batteries: the WJ-III Tests of Cognitive Abilities and the WJ-III Tests of Achievement. These batteries provide a comprehensive system for measuring general intellectual ability, specific cognitive abilities, scholastic aptitude, oral language, and achievement over a broad age range. There are 20 cognitive tests and 22 achievement tests. A variety of scores are available for the tests and are combined to form clusters for interpretive purposes. A wide variety of derived scores are available. The WJ-III's norms, reliability, and validity appear adequate.

The Stanford-Binet Intelligence Scale, Fifth Edition (SB5; Roid, 2003), is the latest version of the scale originally developed by Alfred Binet in 1905 and revised for American children by Terman and Merrill (1916, 1937). In 1960 a third version of the scale combined the best items from earlier forms into one form (L-M) and provided new norms with deviation IQs. In 1972 the scale was renormed, but the items were unchanged. In the fourth edition (Thorndike, Hagen, & Sattler, 1986), the authors sought to bring the SB up to date by basing the scale on a hierarchical model of intelligence and assessing four areas of cognitive ability: Verbal Reasoning, Abstract/Visual Reasoning, Quantitative Reasoning, and Short-Term Memory.

The fifth edition maintains continuity with the past while also making use of advances in the field of psychometrics. The author drew on item response theory (Rasch, 1980) in creating the routing, subtest, and functional levels. Like the fourth edition, the fifth edition is based on the hierarchical model of intelligence, recognizing a global *g* factor and several broad factors that comprise *g*. However, SB5 differs from the fourth edition in a number of ways. SB5 adds a fifth factor. Moreover, SB5 requires fewer verbal responses from the examinee, with half of the subtests requiring either limited or no verbal response. The SB5 also includes items that measure very low and very high functioning, and has been extended to measure cognitive abilities across the entire lifespan.

The SB5 is an individually administered, norm-referenced measure of cognitive abilities that can be given to persons between the ages of 2 and over 85 years. A total of ten subtests are grouped into the following five factors: Fluid Reasoning (FR), Knowledge (KN), Quantitative Reasoning (QR), Visual-Spatial Processing (VS), and Working Memory (WM). Two subtests, one verbal and one nonverbal, are used to measure functioning in each of these five areas. The five nonverbal subtests together comprise a nonverbal domain; likewise, the five verbal subtests together comprise a verbal domain.

Administration of the scale begins with two routing subtests: the nonverbal Fluid Reasoning subtest and the verbal Knowledge subtest. The nonverbal FR subtest score determines the level at which the examinee begins the remaining nonverbal subtests, and the verbal KN subtest score determines the level at which the examinee begins the remaining verbal subtests. Examiners may choose to administer only one of the domains (verbal or nonverbal) if it is deemed the most appropriate assessment strategy for a particular individual. A description of the subtest activities used to sample behaviors in each area is provided below.

Fluid Reasoning

Subtests in this area measure an individual's ability to problem solve using inductive and deductive reasoning.

Nonverbal Subtest
Object Series/Matrices (routing subtest; no levels). Early items require an individual to identify geometric objects and to complete patterns or simple matrices composed of geometric shapes or animals. Later items are composed entirely of multiple-choice matrix completion problems. For these items, indi-

viduals must decide which piece completes each matrix based on the underlying rules or relationships among pieces. Items involve both 2 × 2 matrices and 3 × 3 matrices, with most of the 2 × 2 matrices occurring early in the subtest.

Verbal Subtests

Early Reasoning (Levels 2–3). Early items require the examinee to describe what is occurring in a picture, with particular attention to the cause and effect of the events shown. In later items, individuals must sort and classify picture chips into categories. Test takers are given 30 chips and asked to sort them into as many groups of 3 as they can within a five-minute time limit.

Verbal Absurdities (Level 4). This subtest presents individuals with statements that are silly or impossible and requires them to identify the absurdity in the statement.

Verbal Analogies (Levels 5–6). The test taker is presented with verbal analogies (A is to B as C is to D) that are missing two key components ("What is to B as C is to what?"), and the test taker must complete them.

Knowledge

Subtests in this area assess general knowledge that a person has accumulated through school, home, work, or other life experiences.

Nonverbal Subtests

Procedural Knowledge (Levels 2–3). This activity assesses an individual's knowledge about common actions and objects. Test takers demonstrate this knowledge through nonverbal actions. Test takers are given instructions such as "Show me how you would throw a ball" or are shown a picture of an ice cream cone, with the question "Show me what you do with this."

Picture Absurdities (Levels 4–6). This activity presents individuals with pictures that are silly or impossible and requires them to explain why the pictures are absurd. For instance, test takers might be shown a picture of the continental United States from which Florida is missing.

Verbal Subtest

Vocabulary (routing subtest; no levels). This subtest assesses an individual's knowledge of concepts and language. In early items, individuals are asked to identify objects or actions presented in a picture format. In later items, test takers are asked to orally define increasingly difficult words that are presented both orally and visually.

Quantitative Reasoning

Subtests in this area assess a person's numerical problem-solving abilities. Activities focus on the application of problem-solving skills rather than the use of specific mathematical principles learned in school.

Nonverbal Subtest

Quantitative Reasoning (Levels 2–6). In this subtest, individuals are asked to solve increasingly difficult quantitative problems. Early items focus on the examinee's understanding of initial mathematical concepts (for instance, concepts such as bigger or more, early counting abilities, and identification of numbers). Later items focus on arithmetic and algebraic skills, including the ability to identify geometric and numerical patterns. Moreover, some items require the test taker to identify functional concepts or relationships that are presented in pictures and apply those concepts or relationships when solving specific problems. In this nonverbal subtest, problems are presented with concrete objects or as illustrations, with later problems presented in multiple-choice format.

Verbal Subtest

Quantitative Reasoning (Levels 2–6). In this subtest, individuals must complete mathematical tasks and solve mathematical problems that become increasingly more difficult. Early tasks focus on number identification, counting, and basic addition and subtraction skills. Later items introduce the test taker to increasingly difficult word problems that are presented orally and/or visually.

Visual-Spatial Processing

Subtests in this area assess a person's "ability to see patterns, relationships, spatial orientations, or the gestalt whole among diverse pieces of a visual display" (p. 137 of Examiner's Manual).

Nonverbal Subtests

Form Board (Levels 1–2). This activity requires an individual to complete patterns by moving geometric forms into the appropriate place on a three-hole form board. In later items, test takers must first combine pieces to make the geometric forms and then put them in the correct place.

Form Patterns (Levels 3–6). Individuals are shown increasingly complex geometric designs that resemble humans and animals. They are given geometric pieces and asked to arrange the pieces so that they copy the design within a given time limit.

Verbal Subtest

Position and Direction (Levels 2–6). In early items, individuals are asked to place a block in the appropriate position on a picture when given spatial directions, such as "on," "bottom," "highest," "in front of," "south of." In later items, individuals are asked to direct people in a picture to a destination, using directional phrases, such as "right," "south," "east"; determine the final direction they are facing after imagining themselves making a series of turns; and solve visual-spatial story problems.

Working Memory

Subtests in this area assess processes that are associated with short-term memory.

Nonverbal Subtests

Delayed Response (Level 1). This activity assesses an individual's ability to sort visual information in short-term memory. A toy duck or car is hidden under one of two or three cups. Depending on the difficulty level of the item, the cups are kept in their original position, reversed in view of the test taker, or hidden behind a screen. After a brief delay (three seconds), the individual is asked to identify the cup in which the object is hidden.

Block Span (Levels 2–6). This subtest similarly assesses short-term memory processing abilities. The examiner lays out green blocks and taps them using another green block. The test taker is asked to repeat the tapping sequence. As items get increasingly difficult, another row of four blocks is added.

Verbal Subtests

Memory for Sentences (Levels 2–3). In this activity, the examiner reads a sentence, and the test taker must repeat the sentence verbatim. The sentences become longer throughout the subtest.

Last Word (Levels 4–6). In this activity, the examiner asks the test taker a series of questions. After answering the questions, the examinee is asked to remember the last word in each sentence. When the series of questions is complete, the test taker is asked to repeat the last word of each question in the order they were asked. The questions become increasingly more complex, and the series of questions becomes longer as the test progresses.

Scores

Raw scores for each subtest are converted into standard scores, with a mean of 10 and a standard deviation of 3. These scores are combined and converted into nine composite standard scores, each of which has a mean of 100 and a standard deviation of 15. There are factor index scores and four IQ scores. The verbal subtests combine to yield a standard verbal IQ (VIQ) score. The nonverbal subtests combine to yield a standard nonverbal IQ (NVIQ) score. Overall, the combination of all subtest scores yields the full-scale IQ (FSIQ) score. An Abbreviated Battery IQ (ABIQ) can also be obtained through a combination of scores on the two routing subtests. The author explains that the ABIQ is useful for screening purposes or as a global estimate of cognitive level. However, the author cautions that it "should not be used as the primary measure when making irreversible decisions" and "should never be used as the sole criterion for consequential decisions that affect the examinees' lives" (p. 127 in Examiner's Manual). Extensive tables are provided for conversions. Tables are also provided for obtaining confidence intervals (90 and 95 percent), converting composite scores into percentile ranks, and converting raw scores into Change Sensitive Scores (CSS) and related age equivalents. CSS are based on item response theory and allow for a criterion-referenced interpretation of test performance.

Norms

The normative sample is comprised of 4,800 subjects, ages 2 to over 85. These individuals were tested over a 12-month period in 2001 and 2002. Primary sites from all four major census regions in the United States were chosen in order to standardize the SB5. The census areas were targeted in two ways: examiners were solicited and provided with training, and full-time examiners were recruited and hired. The primary sites included schools, day care centers, and senior centers. The normative sample is compared to the U.S. population (according to the 2001 census) across the following stratification variables: age; sex; race/ethnicity (white or Anglo-American, black or African American, Hispanic, Asian, and others [includes individuals of mixed origin, American Indians, Alaskan Natives, and Native Hawaiians or Other Pacific Islanders]); geographic region; and socioeconomic level. Educational attainment was used as the indicator of socioeconomic level, with children under 18 years old being measured based on the years of education completed by parents or guardians. In general, the norms appear representative of the 2001 U.S. population across these characteristics. The author contends that differences in the ethnic composition of the elderly age groups represent real differences that exist in the U.S. population, and the lower percentages of males over 80 represented are due to factors such as differential life expectancies for females and the lower percentage of elderly males in ethnic minorities. Tables provided in the technical manual show cross-tabulations for a variety of the variables; these correspond reasonably well to those for the U.S. population. Although included in the validity studies, persons were excluded from the normative sample if they had severe medical conditions, limited English language proficiency, severe sensory or communication deficits, or severe behavioral or emotional disturbance, or were officially enrolled in special education for more than 50 percent of the day.

Reliability

Reliability coefficient alphas and SEMs are reported for each subtest, factor index, and IQ score at each age level (23 age ranges provided) and as an average across all age levels. As would be expected, subtest reliabilities are lower than composite reliabilities: they range from .72 to .96 for age ranges, with 52 out of 230 being equal to or greater than .90. The reliabilities for factor indexes range from .84 to .96, with 62 out of 115 being equal to or greater than .90. Reliabilities for the NVIQ range from .93 to .97, and those for the VIQ range from .94 to .97. Reliabilities for the FSIQ range from .97 to .98. The ABIQ coefficient alphas range from .85 to .96, with 18 out of 23 being equal to or greater than .90.

Test-retest data were available for four age groups: 2 to 5 years ($n = 96$), 6 to 20 years ($n = 87$), 21 to 59 years ($n = 81$), and 60 years and over ($n = 92$). Stability coefficients[3] are provided for each subtest, factor index, and IQ score. Stability coefficients for the FSIQ among these four groups ranged from .93 to .95. VIQ and NVIQ stability coefficients ranged from .89 to .95, and ABIQ stabili-

---

[3] Stability coefficients provided are based on corrected correlations.

ties ranged from .84 to .88. Factor index stabilities ranged from .79 (Working Memory, ages 21 to 59) to .95 (Knowledge, ages 60 and over), and subtest stability correlations ranged from .66 (Nonverbal Working Memory, ages 21 to 59) to .93 (Verbal Knowledge, ages 21 to 59).

Subtests and factor indexes should be interpreted with caution because some of the age-level reliabilities do not exceed .90. When making decisions, the manual should be consulted to determine the reliability for the age level and subtest or factor index of interest. Moreover, the manual should also be referenced for age-level ABIQ reliabilities. The NVIQ, VIQ, and FSIQ reliabilities all exceed .90. Test-retest data are adequate.

Validity

Validity Evidence Based on Content   The author argues that evidence for content validity is provided by professional judgment, coverage of important constructs, and empirical item analyses. First, the author explains that, throughout the development of the SB5, numerous researchers, experts in assessment, and examiners provided feedback about item appropriateness and the potential for bias. Next, because SB5 is based on the Cattell-Horn-Carroll (CHC) theory of intelligence, experts in this theory rated the items according to the CHC factor being measured. Based on expert opinion and factor analyses, the two-domain and five-factor SB5 design was created and used as a template throughout SB5 development. Finally, content validity was examined through empirical item analysis, such as item discrimination, percentage correct at successive age levels, model-data-fit statistics, and differential item functioning (DIF). Items with poor fit statistics were typically dropped.

Validity Evidence Based on Relations with External Criteria   Evidence for validity is provided based on demonstrated relationships with several external measures. In one study, 104 subjects between the ages of 3 and 20 were given both the SB5 and the SB4 within one to ten days apart. The Composite Standard Age Score (SAS) of SB4 correlated with the SB5 full-scale IQ ($r = .90$). In another study, 80 children between the ages of 3 and 19 years were given both the SB5 and an older SB (form L-M). The correlation for FSIQ was .85. The SB5 was also correlated with the three versions of the Wechsler intelligence scales. In the first Wechsler study, 71 children between the ages of 3 and 5 years were given both the Wechsler Preschool and Primary Scale of Intelligence–Revised (WIPPSI-R) and the SB5. An FSIQ correlation of .83 was found. The correlation of SB5 with the Wechsler Intelligence Scale for Children–III (WISC-III) ($n = 66$; age range 6 to 16) was .84. The SB5 had a correlation of .82 with the Wechsler Adult Intelligence Scale–III ($n = 87$; ages 16 to 84). In another study ($n = 145$; ages 4 to 11), a correlation of .78 was found between SB5 FSIQ and the General Intellectual Ability (GIA) score from the Woodcock-Johnson Tests of Cognitive Abilities–III (WJ-III).

Evidence for predictive validity is provided through an examination of the relationship between SB5 and achievement test scores. However, the manual provides no information about elapsed time between the administration of each test.

In one study (n = 472; ages 6 to 19), correlations ranged from .50 to .84 when WJ-III Tests of Achievement cluster scores were compared to SB5 factor indexes and IQ scores. When SB5 was compared to the Wechsler Individual Achievement Test (n = 80; ages 6 to 15), a correlation of .80 was found between the SB5 FSIQ and the WIAT Total Achievement score. A higher correlation (r = .83) was found between the SB5 VIQ and the WIAT Total Achievement score. Special studies were also conducted of students (n = 29) with deafness or hard-of-hearing conditions. Scores on the SB5 were compared to scores on the Universal Nonverbal Intelligence Test (UNIT); r = .57 when nonverbal SB5 IQ compares to UNIT full-scale IQ. Another study compared preschool children designated as developmentally disabled or in programs for mental retardation across SB5 scores and the Scales of Independent Behavior–Revised. Full-scale IQ correlations were .59. These studies provide additional support for the SB5's validity with these populations.

Studies also examined the performance of examinees previously identified as individuals with giftedness, mental retardation, developmental delay, autism, limited English language competency, speech or language disorders, learning disabilities, attention deficit disorder, severe emotional disturbance, and orthopedic or motor conditions. As was expected, students classified as gifted received higher than average FSIQs (mean FSIQ = 123.7); students classified as learning disabled received lower than average FSIQs (LD in math, mean FSIQ = 85.6; LD in reading, mean FSIQ = 84.1; LD in writing, mean FSIQ = 94.9); and students classified as mentally retarded received the lowest FSIQs (mean FSIQ = 56.5).

The author provides evidence for validity based on the internal structure of the test. He explains the SB5 within the context of current theoretical formulations about intelligence, justifying the development of a scale that assesses g, a general factor. The selection of items and factors are explained within a Cattell-Horn-Carroll theoretical framework. The author offers evidence for validity based on internal structure in a number of ways: (1) Because intellectual abilities are developmental in nature, it is expected that performance on the SB5 would follow certain developmental patterns (age trends). Mean raw scores on the SB5 increase until late adolescence or middle adult age and then show a gradual decline in the elderly. (2) The author explains that most of the subtests have principal component loadings above .70 on g, which indicates that they are good measures of g. None falls below the .50 level. (3) Confirmatory factor analysis was conducted in order to confirm the two domains and five factors of the test. Loadings confirmed a verbal and a nonverbal domain. Furthermore, goodness-of-fit statistics and cross-battery, confirmatory factor analysis confirmed the five-factor model as the best fit for the various subtest scores.

Summary

The fifth edition of the Stanford-Binet Intelligence Scale improves on previous editions by providing the current edition with a strong psychometric foundation. Improving on the fourth edition, SB5 includes five factors, items measuring greater extremes of cognitive functioning, more nonverbal content, and a standardization sample that allows for the measurement of cognitive abilities across the full lifespan. SB5 manuals provide the technical data needed to evaluate the adequacy of its reliability, showing it to be a reliable scale. Although the standardization sample appears representative of the U.S. population for a number of relevant variables, certain groups of students were systematically excluded from the sample. Evidence of reliability is mixed. Reliability coefficients for verbal, nonverbal, and full-scale IQs are high, but many subtest reliabilities are too low to be used in making important decisions. The test has good test-retest reliability. There is good evidence for the validity of the test, but limited evidence of validity, of course, for subtests that do not have adequate reliability.

Nonverbal Intelligence Tests

A number of nonverbal tests are among the most widely used tests for assessment of intelligence. Some are designed to measure intelligence broadly; others are called "picture-vocabulary tests." Before we describe an individual picture-vocabulary test, we believe it is important to state what these devices measure. The tests are not measures of intelligence per se; rather, they measure only one aspect of intelligence: receptive vocabulary. In picture-vocabulary tests, pictures are presented to the test taker, who is asked to identify those pictures that correspond to words read by the examiner. Some authors of picture-vocabulary measures state that the tests measure receptive vocabulary; others equate receptive vocabulary with intelligence and claim that their tests assess intelligence. Because the tests measure only one aspect of intelligence, they should not be used to make eligibility decisions. Some commonly used picture-vocabulary tests were reviewed in earlier editions of this textbook. They have not been updated for so long that they are no longer useful. We review only one picture-vocabulary test (the Peabody Picture Vocabulary Test–III) in this section of the chapter. Other measures used to assess receptive vocabulary are reviewed in the chapter "Assessment of Language."

Leiter International Performance Scale–Revised

The Leiter International Performance Scale–Revised (Leiter–R; Roid & Miller, 1997) is a new revision of the Leiter International Performance Scale (LIPS) and the Arthur Adaptation of the Leiter International Performance Scale (AALIPS). The LIPS, first published in 1929, was one of the original nonverbal measures of intelligence and has been used for more than 65 years. Arthur renormed the test in 1950, although the items remained unchanged. Both the LIPS and the AALIPS used wooden blocks that were manipulated by children to match sequences of figures and pictures depicted on a wooden frame that would hold the reordered blocks. The Leiter–R is a nonverbal measure of intelligence requiring no speaking or writing on the part of either the examiner or the test taker. For this reason, the test has been very popular for use with students with hearing impairments, cerebral palsy, communication disorders, and non–English-language backgrounds. Because the test's authors regularly claim that the measure is culture free, it is popular for use with students whose acculturation differs from that of public school students from the dominant culture.

Subtests

The Leiter–R is now available with stimulus items in easel format, and with lightweight, laminated response cards rather than wooden blocks (see Figure 17.1). The test is now in color rather than in the black-and-white format of earlier versions. The test is used with individuals 2-0 to 20-11 years of age; there is no indication of how long it takes to give the Leiter–R. The test measures intellectual performance in four domains: Reasoning, Visualization, Memory, and Attention. It includes the following 20 subtests.

Reasoning

Classification. This subtest assesses skill in categorization of objects or geometric designs.

Sequencing. This test measures skill in identifying the stimulus that comes next in a sequence.

Repeated Patterns. Students must identify which of several stimuli fill in missing parts in repeated sequences of pictures or figures.

Design Analogies. Students must identify geometric shapes that complete matrix analogies.

Visualization (Spatial)

Matching. Testees must match response cards to easel pictures.

Figure-Ground. Students must identify designs embedded in complex backgrounds.

Form Completion. Students are given randomly displayed parts of designs and must select the whole design from several alternatives.

Picture Context. Students must use visual-context clues to identify a part of a picture that has been removed from a larger picture.

Paper Folding. This test measures skill in viewing an unfolded object in two dimensions and then matching it to a picture of the whole object.

Figure Rotation. Students must identify rotated pictures of original nonrotated objects.

Memory

Immediate Recognition. Students are shown five pictures or figures for five seconds, and after these items are removed and re-presented, students must identify the one item that is missing.

Delayed Recognition. After a 20-minute delay, students must identify the objects presented in the Immediate Recognition subtest.

Associated Pairs. Students are shown pairs of objects for five to ten seconds, and after the objects are removed, students must make meaningful associations for each pair.

Delayed Pairs. This is a 20-minute-delay measure of the items in the Associated Pairs subtest.

Forward Memory. Students must remember pictured objects to which the examiner points and must repeat the sequence in which the examiner points to the objects.

Reversed Memory. The examiner points to pictures or figures in order, and the student must point to the same pictures in reverse order.

Spatial Memory. The student is shown increasingly complex stimulus displays, arranged in matrix format, and the student must then place cards in order on a blank matrix display.

Visual Coding. This is a nonverbal task requiring matching of pictures and geometric objects to numbers.

Attention

Attention Sustained. Students are given large numbers of stimuli and must identify those that are alike. They mark all squares containing a geometric shape. There are three parallel forms of increasing difficulty for ages 2 to 5, 6 to 10, and 11 to 21.

FIGURE 17.1
Materials for Leiter International Performance Scale–Revised

SOURCE: Copyright © The Stoelting Company, 620 Wheat Lane, Wood Dale, Illinois 60191. All rights reserved. Reproduction by permission.

Attention Divided. Students must divide attention between a moving display of pictures and the sorting of playing cards.

Scores

Several scores are available for the Leiter–R, including full-scale IQ, brief screening IQ, brief attention deficit hyperactivity disorder, screening score, brief gifted screening score, and scaled scores for the Reasoning, Visualization, Memory, and Attention subtests. In addition, scaled scores can be obtained for each subtest, and all scaled scores can be converted to age- and grade-equivalent scores.

Norms

Restandardization of the Leiter–R took place between 1993 and 1995. The test was tried out by 60 field researchers on 550 so-called typical children, of whom 325 either had communication disorders or cognitive impairments, or spoke English as a second language. Based on the performance of these students, 17 subtests were retained, and items were redesigned. The final version of the test was standardized on 1,800 children considered "normal" and 725 children and adolescents designated as clinical/atypical, stratified on the basis of gender, race, parent educational level, and geographic region, using data from the 1993 census. The authors show that the percentages in various gender, race, and other categories closely match the 1993 census data, but no cross-tabulations are presented.

Reliability

The authors provide extensive information about the reliability of the Leiter, and for each kind of reliability they provide a good description of the sample. Internal-consistency reliability coefficients are provided for the Visualization/Reasoning Battery, the Attention/Memory Battery, and the Attention/Memory Battery Special Diagnostic Scales. Fewer than half the coefficients are above .80. Reliabilities are also provided for IQ and composite scores. Most of these exceed .80. The subtests have limited application in making important decisions about individuals. IQs and composite scores are more reliable for this purpose. Evidence is also provided for test-retest reliability. Coefficients are high for composites and (except above age 11) low for subtests.

Validity

Evidence of validity based on test content is illustrated by mapping of the test to theoretical models of intelligence presented by Gustafson (1984) and by Carroll (1993). Evidence of criterion-related validity was based on the performance of diagnostic groups. Representative mainstream students earned an average brief IQ of 101, students with severe hearing impairments averaged 94, students with severe cognitive disabilities averaged 56, students who were gifted and talented averaged 115, and students who were not native English speakers averaged 95.

In addition, the Leiter brief IQ correlated .83 with full-scale IQs on the WISC-III and the original Leiter.

Evidence of validity based on internal structure consisted of completion of factor analyses showing a match between the scale and the theoretical model that guided its development. In addition, the authors argue that demonstration of comparable performance across several racial groups is evidence of construct validity.

Evidence of validity based on relations with other measures is very limited. As noted above, there is a high correlation between performance on the Leiter–R and the WISC-III. The author indicates further that additional analyses of relations to external measures are being conducted. To date, these are not reported in the manual.

Summary

The Leiter–R is a measure of intelligence that requires no verbalization on the part of the examiner or the examinee. The test measures intellectual skill development in four domains. The test is adequately standardized, and there is good evidence that IQs and composite scores are reliable. Reliabilities of subtests are too low for use in making diagnostic decisions about individuals. Evidence for the validity of the Leiter–R is extremely limited.

Test of Nonverbal Intelligence–3

The Test of Nonverbal Intelligence–3 (TONI-3; Brown, Sherbenou, & Johnsen, 1997) is the third edition of a test that was first published in 1982 and revised in 1990. The test is an individually administered measure of the aptitude of children and adults who require a language-free, motor-reduced, or culture-reduced test of abstract/figural problem solving. The test includes pantomimed directions and requires no verbal response by the examinee. So, the authors describe the TONI-3 as a language-free measure, one that in its content, instructional format, and response format requires no reading, writing, speaking, or listening. It is designed to be used in both screening and diagnosis with individuals between 5-0 and 85-11 years of age. The test is untimed and takes about 15 minutes to administer.

There are two forms of the TONI-3; each has 45 items (10 less than the TONI-2). All TONI-3 items require test takers to solve problems by identifying relationships among abstract figures. The subject must point to the one response among several alternatives that best fits a missing part in a pattern or matrix. There are five types of problem-solving items: simple matching, analogies, classification, intersections, and progressions. The test items shown in Figure 17.2 are examples of the kinds of items used in the TONI-3. The authors claim that the test is particularly useful with "subjects whose test performance may be confounded by language and motor impairments arising from such conditions as aphasia, hearing impairments, lack of proficiency with spoken or written English, cerebral palsy, stroke, head trauma, and lack of familiarity with the culture of the United States" (Brown et al., 1997, p. 32).

FIGURE 17.2
Representative Items from the TONI-3

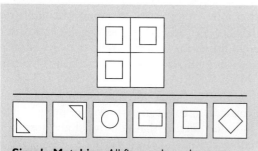

Simple Matching. All figures share the same number of critical attributes. No differences exist among the figures in the stimulus.

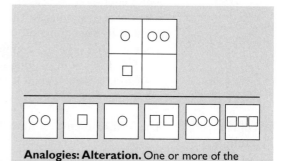

Analogies: Subtraction. Figures change by subtracting one or more attributes.

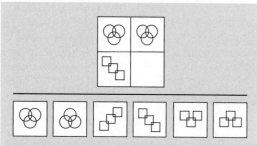

Analogies. The relationship among the figures in one of the rows or columns is the same as the relationship among the figures in the other rows and columns. The relationship varies in the following ways: *Matching.* No differences exist among figures.

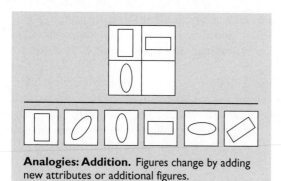

Analogies: Alteration. One or more of the attributes of a figure are changed or altered.

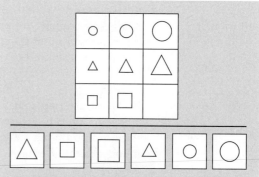

Analogies: Addition. Figures change by adding new attributes or additional figures.

Analogies: Progressions. The same change continues between or among figures.

FIGURE 17.2
(Continued)

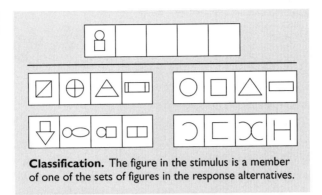

Classification. The figure in the stimulus is a member of one of the sets of figures in the response alternatives.

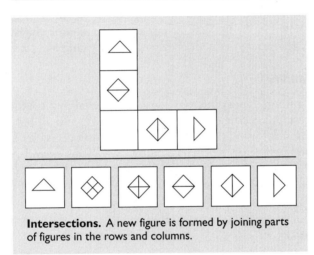

Intersections. A new figure is formed by joining parts of figures in the rows and columns.

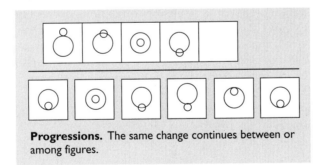

Progressions. The same change continues between or among figures.

SOURCE: From Test of Non-Verbal Intelligence–3 (TONI-3). Copyright © 1997 by Pro-Ed. Reprinted by permission of the publisher.

Scores

Two kinds of scores—percentile ranks and TONI quotients—may be obtained. TONI quotients are standard scores with a mean of 100 and a standard deviation of 15.

Norms

The authors developed a set of new norms for this third edition of the TONI. The TONI-3 was standardized on a sample of 3,451 people residing in 28 states. The authors selected six primary standardization sites, using data on geographic regions reported in the U.S. Census. A total of 2,060 individuals were tested at these sites. The remaining standardization sample was chosen by contacting professionals who had purchased earlier versions of the test. Cross-tabulations are shown in the manual for age and other sample characteristics, but not for the other characteristics with one another (for example, race by geographic region).

Reliability

The authors report internal-consistency reliability coefficients for both forms of the test. All coefficients equal or exceed .89, and all but four are in the .90s, the criterion for using the test to make important decisions about individuals. Correlations between performance on the two forms exceed .80, and means and standard deviations on the two forms are nearly identical at all age intervals. One-week test-retest stability reliabilities exceeded .90 for a group of 170 individuals between 13 and 40 years of age.

Validity

Evidence for validity is limited to evidence based on relations to other measures. The authors report the results of correlations of the TONI-3 with scores on the CTONI, WISC-III, and WAIS-R (now the WAIS-III). Correlations were within expected ranges. Surprisingly, the correlations between the TONI-3 and the WISC-III were about the same for verbal and nonverbal scales of the WISC-III. This was not true for the WAIS-R, where correlations with the nonverbal scale significantly exceeded those for the verbal scale.

Summary

The TONI-3 is an individually administered, nonverbal measure of problem-solving ability. This third edition was renormed. Evidence for the reliability of the test is good, but evidence for validity is limited to demonstrations of reasonable relationships with external measures.

Peabody Picture Vocabulary Test–III   The Peabody Picture Vocabulary Test–III (PPVT-III; Dunn & Dunn, 1997) is an individually administered, norm-referenced test of listening comprehension for the spoken word in standard English. The authors of the PPVT-III identify two uses for the test: "The PPVT-III is designed as a measure of an examinee's receptive (hearing) vocabulary acquisition, and the PPVT-III serves as a screening test of verbal ability, or as one element in a comprehensive test battery of cognitive processes" (Dunn & Dunn, 1997, p. 2).

The PPVT-III is a revision of the Peabody Picture Vocabulary Test, which originally appeared in 1959 and later in 1981. Many of the features of the earlier editions were retained in the third edition. For example, the test still consists of two parallel forms, is used with a wide age range of examinees, is untimed, requires no reading by the examinee, and includes training items. New features of the third edition include an increase to 204 items in each form of the test, an extension of national norms to ages 2½ years to over 90, modernized content, and new packaging. There are two forms of the PPVT-III (IIIA and IIIB). Each has a separate test kit, which contains an examiner's manual, performance records, and a norms booklet. Each test kit includes four training items and 17 sets of picture plates. In a separate publication, *Technical References to the Peabody Picture Vocabulary Test, Third Edition* (Williams & Wang, 1997), considerable detail is given about development of the test, standardization, reliability, and validity.

The PPVT-III is administered in easel format, with the examiner showing the test taker a series of plates on which four pictures are drawn. The examiner reads a stimulus word for each plate, and the person being tested points to the picture that best represents the stimulus word. The PPVT-III is an untimed *power test*, and it usually takes about 15 minutes to administer. There are 17 sets of items, and those sets that are too easy or too difficult are not administered. On average, the test involves 5 sets of 12 items each, or 60 test items out of 204 (30 percent). The authors provide recommended start items, based on the age of the examinee.

Scores

The student's raw score is the number of pictures correctly identified between the basal and the ceiling items. The test employs a multiple-choice format. The basal is the lowest set administered in which the respondent makes one or no errors. The ceiling is the highest set in which the examinee makes eight or more errors. Raw scores are obtained by subtracting the total number of errors from the ceiling item. Two types of derived scores can be obtained: deviation-type scores (standard scores, percentiles, stanines, and normal-curve equivalents) and developmental scores (age scores). Procedures are included in the manual for calculating confidence intervals for obtained scores.

Norms

The development of the PPVT-III began with an item tryout program in 1994. A total of 908 persons (ages 2½ to 21) were tested at 73 sites, using 480 items. Of the 480 items, 242 were retained from the PPVT-R, and 238 new items were created. Both traditional item analysis and Rasch-Wright latent-trait methods were used to select final items for the two forms of the test.[4] As a result of the national tryout, 75 items were dropped from the item pool.

[4] For a general description of Rasch scaling and item-response theory, visit the website for this text.

The PPVT-R was standardized on a representative national sample of 3,726 individuals. An effort was made to include 100 individuals at each half-year interval from ages 2½ to 7 years, 100 at each year interval from ages 7 to 14, 150 at each two-year interval from ages 15 to 24, and 125 at each ten-year interval from ages 31 to 60. An effort was made to include an additional 100 people over 61 years of age. A table is included in the manual showing the actual numbers of individuals at each age level included in the standardization.

The standardization sample for the PPVT-III was selected by recruiting examiners in each of four geographic areas. Test coordinators at a total of 268 sites in the four regions selected the subjects to participate in the standardization. They sent questionnaires to parents of individuals between 2½ and 24 years of age, and they received returned questionnaires from more than 8,000 parents. The parents indicated the child's age, gender, and ethnicity/race, and their own (the parents') educational level. The questionnaires were sent to the publisher, and examiners were given lists of individuals to assess. The sample was selected on the basis of 1994 census data. Extensive numbers of tables are included in the manual, showing sample breakdown by geographic region, race, ethnicity, age, and parent or examinee educational level. Sample proportions match census proportions very well.

Reliability

Extensive reliability data are provided in the technical manual for the PPVT-III. There is also a separate section on the equivalency of the PPVT-R and the PPVT-III. Three kinds of reliability data are reported for the PPVT-III: coefficient alpha and split-half indexes of internal consistency; immediate test-retest reliability using alternative forms; and delayed test-retest reliability (8 to 203 days' delay) using alternative forms. Coefficient alpha reliabilities range from .92 to .98, with a median of .95 for each form. Split-half reliability coefficients range from .86 to .97, with a median of .94 for both forms. Alternative-forms reliabilities range from .88 to .96, with a median of .94, and test-retest reliabilities for four age samples (2-6 to 5-11, 6-0 to 10-11, 12-0 to 17-11, and 26-0 to 57-11) range from .91 to .93. Reliabilities for the PPVT-III are exceptionally high.

Validity

Extensive information is provided on the validity of the PPVT-III based on relations with external measures. Four studies are reported in which scores on the PPVT-III are compared with performance on measures of oral vocabulary and cognitive ability. The studies were carried out in conjunction with standardization of the test, which facilitated selection of representative samples of subjects. Correlations with the WISC-III, Kaufman Adolescent and Adult Intelligence Test, and Kaufman Brief Intelligence Test (Kaufman & Kaufman, 1990) are reported. The correlations are higher with verbal than with performance measures, and they are within expected ranges. Correlations with a measure of oral language (Oral and Written Language Scales) are reported. Again, correlations are within an expected range.

The authors include studies of the performance on the PPVT-III of seven special populations: students with speech impairment, language delay, language impairment, mental retardation, learning disability in reading, and hearing impairment, and also gifted students. Individuals who participated in the studies were matched (on the basis of gender, age, race/ethnicity, socioeconomic status, and geographic region) with individuals in the standardization sample. Results of the seven studies were as would be expected and show the value of the PPVT-III in differentiating representatives of special populations from other individuals.

Summary

The PPVT-III is an individually administered, norm-referenced measure of receptive vocabulary. The test is well developed and adequately standardized. Data in the technical manual indicate adequate reliability and validity for screening purposes. Overall, the technical characteristics of this scale far surpass those of other picture-vocabulary tests. If used properly and with the awareness that it samples only receptive vocabulary, the PPVT-III can serve as a useful screening device.

Dilemmas in Current Practice

The biggest difficulty encountered in trying to use individual intelligence tests is a problem of definition. What is intelligence? We noted in the chapter "Assessment of Intelligence: An Overview" that intelligence is an inferred construct. No one has seen a thing called "intelligence." Yet there are many tests of this thing that no one has seen, and assessors are regularly required to assess it. Most of the definitions of conditions that indicate need or eligibility for special education include reference to cognitive functioning, intelligence, or capability. Students who have mental retardation are said to have too little of it; students who are gifted have more than most. Students with learning disabilities are said to have average intelligence but fail to demonstrate school performance commensurate with the amount that they have.

Authors' Viewpoint
Those who assess intelligence—and most diagnostic personnel are required to do so—must recognize that they can only infer intelligence from a sample of behavior derived through testing. Assessors must pay special attention to the kinds of behaviors sampled by intelligence tests. Two considerations are especially important. First, intelligence tests are usually administered for the purpose of making a prediction about future academic performance. In selecting an intelligence test, test

givers must always ask, "What is the relationship between the kinds of behavior sampled by the test and the kinds of behavior I am trying to predict?" The closer the relationship is, the better is the prediction. It is wise to try to select tests that sample behaviors that are related as closely as possible to the behaviors to be predicted.

Second, test givers must always consider what behaviors or attributes are being assessed by intelligence test items. In particular, when different kinds of intelligence tests are used to assess students with disabilities, it is very important to be aware of the stimulus and response demands of the items. The descriptions of the kinds of behaviors sampled by intelligence tests that were provided in the previous chapter should be helpful. When we assess students' intelligence, we want the test results to reflect intelligence, not sensory dysfunction.

It is important to remember that intelligence is not a fixed thing that we measure. Rather, it is an inferred entity, one that is understood best by evaluating the ways in which individuals who have different kinds of acculturation perform several different kinds of tasks. Intelligence tests differ markedly; individuals differ markedly. Evaluations of the intelligence of an individual must be understood as a function of the interaction between the skills and characteristics the individual brings to a test setting and the behaviors sampled by the test.

SUMMARY

In this chapter, we have reviewed individually administered intelligence tests that are commonly used or that offer new approaches to assessment. The kinds of behaviors sampled differ among the various measures of intelligence because test authors have differing theories of intelligence. Thus it is critical for test users to go beyond global scores and consider the actual behavior sampled by tests.

QUESTIONS FOR CHAPTER REVIEW

1. Why is it more appropriate to use an individual test than a group test to assess intelligence?

2. The Cognitive Battery of the WJ-III and the Wechsler Intelligence Scale for Children–IV are two intelligence tests frequently used with school-age children. Identify similarities and differences in the domains of behavior sampled by these two tests.

3. Explain why it is more appropriate to use the WISC-III for making placement decisions than to use tests such as the Peabody Picture Vocabulary Test–III.

4. You have just joined a school system and have been asked to become involved in the triennial review process for a 10-year-old youngster with a learning disability. Your supervisor asks your opinion about using the Peabody Picture Vocabulary Test in the test battery. How would you respond?

5. What is there about the scoring of the Woodcock-Johnson Psychoeducational Battery–III that might lead educators to suggest the need for information about interscorer agreement?

PROJECTS

1. Using information found in the text, write a summary for three individually administered tests used in the assessment of intelligence. When you have finished, compare your summary with the text summary. Then go to the *Mental Measurements Yearbook,* and compare and contrast your summaries with the reviews of the tests you selected. If your summary is different, has the reviewer used different information and different standards?

2. Assume that you wish to use one of the systems reviewed in this text. Which system would be your first choice? Why? Compare your answer with a classmate's answer. Reconcile any differences.

RESOURCES FOR FURTHER INVESTIGATION

Print Resources

Carroll, J. G. (1993). *Human cognitive abilities: A survey of factor-analytic studies.* New York: Cambridge University Press.

Gustafson, J. E. (1984). A unifying model for the structure of intellectual abilities. *Intelligence, 8,* 179–203.

Kamphaus, R. W. (1994). *Clinical assessment of children's intelligence.* Boston: Allyn & Bacon.

Technology Resources

ASSESSMENT AND GUIDANCE
assess.nelson.com/nelson/assess/a-ind.html
Here is a list of several tests of assessment, including the Woodcock-Johnson Psychoeducational Battery–Revised, with links to detailed product information.

PRO-ED CATALOGUE INFORMATION FOR PRODUCTS
www.proedinc.com
Find product and ordering information about the Detroit Tests of Learning Aptitude (Fourth Edition, Adult Edition, and Primary Edition) and the Test of Nonverbal Intelligence–3.

PSYCHOLOGICAL CORPORATION
www.psychcorp.com
Under Psychological Assessment and Intervention there is information on the various Wechsler scales of intelligence, as well as information on other tests of assessment.

RIVERSIDE PUBLISHING
www.riverpub.com
Go to Products and Services; under Clinical and Special Needs you will find information on the Das-Naglieri Cognitive Assessment System and the Universal Nonverbal Intelligence Test.

AGS ONLINE PRODUCTS AND SERVICES
www.agsnet.com
Look for product and ordering information about the instruments available from American Guidance Services (AGS). Search by product title for the Peabody Picture Vocabulary Test–III and the Kaufmann Brief Intelligence Test.

CHAPTER 18

Assessment of Intelligence: Group Tests

GROUP INTELLIGENCE TESTS DIFFER FROM ONE ANOTHER IN THREE WAYS: IN FORMAT, in the kinds of scores they provide, and in their emphasis on speed versus power. First, whereas some group tests consist of a single battery to be administered in one sitting, others contain a number of subscales or subtests and are administered in two or more sittings. Second, some provide IQs or mental ages based on a global performance; others provide the same kinds of scores but differentiate them into subscale scores (for example, verbal, performance, and total; language, nonlanguage, and total). Third, some group intelligence tests are *speed tests*, which are timed, and others are power tests, which are untimed.

Why Do We Administer Group Intelligence Tests?

Group intelligence tests are used for one of two purposes: as screening devices for individual students or as sources of descriptive information about groups of students. Most often, they are routinely administered as screening devices to identify those students who differ enough from average to warrant further assessment. In these cases, the tests' merit is that teachers can administer them relatively quickly to large numbers of students. The tests suffer from the same limitations as any group test: They can be made to yield qualitative information only with difficulty, and they require students to sit still for about 20 minutes, to mark with a pencil, and, often, to read.

Group intelligence tests are also used to provide descriptive information about the level of capability of students in a classroom, a district, or even a state. They are, on occasion, used to track students, in place of or in addition to achievement tests. When used in this way, the tests set expectations; they are thought to indicate the level of achievement to be expected in individual classrooms or districts.

Over the past 15 years it has become increasingly common for school districts to drop the practice of group intelligence testing. When administrators are asked why they are doing so, they cite (1) the limited relevance of knowing about students' capability, as opposed to knowing about the subject matter skills (such as for reading and math) that students do and do not have; (2) the difficulty teachers experience in trying to use the test results for instructional purposes; and (3) the cost of a schoolwide intellectual screening program. At the same time, many school districts continue to use these measures as an index of the capability of the students in their schools. In this chapter, we review the two most commonly used group intelligence tests: the Cognitive Abilities Test (CogAT) and the Otis-Lennon School Ability Test, Eighth Edition (OLSAT 8).

Specific Group Tests of Intelligence

Cognitive Abilities Test

The Cognitive Abilities Test (Lohman & Hagen, 2001) is a further development of the Lorge-Thorndike Intelligence Tests, which first appeared in 1954. The Iowa Tests of Basic Skills, the Tests of Achievement and Proficiency, and the CogAT compose the Riverside Basic Skills Assessment Program. We suggest three uses of the CogAT: (1) to guide adaptations to instruction, (2) to provide a measure of cognitive development, and (3) to identify students with discrepant achievement and ability levels.

There are eleven levels of the CogAT. Levels K, 1, and 2 make up the primary battery; Levels A through H constitute the multilevel battery; and Levels K through 2 are appropriate for kindergarten, first-grade, second-grade, and third-grade students who demonstrate slower cognitive development. The other eight levels of the test contain items that range from easy third-grade items on Level A to very difficult items at the twelfth-grade level (Level H). The inclusion of eight levels of the test in a single multilevel battery allows teachers to administer levels of difficulty appropriate to the ability of their students. The scales increase in difficulty in very small steps. For students who attain little more than chance-level performance, the next easier level of the scale may be administered; for those who get nearly every item correct, the next more difficult level may be administered. Sample items are provided to students for each subtest.

Levels K, 1, and 2 are designed for assessing the extent to which the child has developed the ability to reason inductively, to solve problems, to comprehend verbal statements, to scan pictorial and figural stimuli to obtain either specific or general information, to compare stimuli and detect similarities and differences in relative size, to classify or order familiar objects, and to use quantitative and special relationships and concepts, as well as for assessing the child's store of general information and concepts. All items in these levels are read to students and have picture answer choices. These levels are administered in three sessions and are estimated to take from 35 to 40 minutes each.

The multilevel battery of the CogAT was constructed to provide a variety of tasks that require the student to discover and use relationships to solve problems. The tasks use verbal, numerical, and nonverbal symbols. Teachers read directions and sample items; the student completes the rest of the test individually. It is administered in three sessions, each of which requires 45 to 50 minutes of administration time.

Although all levels include separate batteries—verbal, quantitative, and non-verbal—the subtests included in the two levels differ. The various subtests are described here.

Verbal Battery—Levels K, 1, and 2

Oral Vocabulary   The examiner reads a word or phrase aloud, and the student must mark the picture that illustrates it.

Verbal Reasoning   Students are asked to make inferences, transformations, and judgments or to remember sequences in response to common situations.

Quantitative Battery—Levels K, 1, and 2

Quantitative Concepts   The examiner asks the child to solve simple story problems or to solve a series problem based on a mathematical principle. All the problems can be solved by using counting strategies that the majority of children develop before entering kindergarten.

Relational Concepts   The examiner asks the child to mark the picture illustrating a particular relational concept (for example, biggest, tallest, or beside) read aloud by the examiner.

Nonverbal Battery—Levels K, 1, and 2

Matrices   The student must select from among four response choices the one that best completes a stimulus figure.

Figure Classification   The child is shown three figures that are alike in some way and must select from four response possibilities the one figure that is like the three stimulus figures.

Verbal Battery—Levels A through H

Sentence Completion   The student reads a sentence with a missing word and must select the response word that most appropriately fills the blank.

Verbal Classification   The student is given three or four words that are members of a conceptual category and must identify which response word best fits into the same category as the stimulus words.

Verbal Analogies   The student must complete verbal analogies of the form A is to B as C is to __.

Quantitative Battery—Levels A through H

Quantitative Relations   The student must make judgments about relative sizes or amounts of material. Given two quantities (for example, $2 + 4$ and 2×4), the student must identify which one is greater.

Number Series   Given a series of numbers that have a progressive relationship to one another, the student must select the number that best completes the relationship.

Equation Building   The student must construct correct equations using numbers and symbols for mathematical operations.

Nonverbal Battery—Levels A through H

Figure Classification   Given three figures that are alike in some way, the student must identify the response figure that best fits into the same conceptual category.

Figure Analogies   The student must deduce the relationship between a pair of figures and must then select the last element of a second pair so that it accurately completes the analogy.

Figure Analysis   The student must deduce the relationship between a pair of figures and must then select the last element of a second pair so that it accurately completes the analogy.

Scores

Four scores are provided for each level of the CogAT, one for each battery (verbal, quantitative, and nonverbal) and a composite. Scores are not obtained for subtests within each battery. Among the scores available for each battery are raw scores, standard age scores (mean = 100; standard deviation = 15), national grade and age percentile ranks, and grade and age stanines. A raw score for a particular level corresponds to a Universal Scale Score, which can provide a continuous measure of cognitive development over time. Fall, midyear, and spring normative scores are each available.

Norms

The CogAT was standardized concurrently with the Iowa Tests of Basic Skills (Hoover, Dunbar, & Frisbie, 2001) and the Iowa Tests of Educational Development (Forsyth, Ansley, Feldt, & Alnot, 2002). These measures were standardized on a carefully selected stratified national sample of about 180,000 students. All public school districts in the United States were stratified first on the basis of geographic region and then on the basis of size of enrollment. Districts were then stratified according to socioeconomic status (SES) within the district, based on the percentage of students in the district falling below the federal government's poverty guideline. One district was randomly selected to participate from each geographic region by enrollment and by SES category. Once data were collected, weighting procedures were used to ensure that the sample was appropriately representative of the population on each of the characteristics described (SES, enrollment size, and geographic region). In addition to the public school norm sample, norms are provided for Catholic schools and for private non-Catholic schools, as well as for special populations, such as large-city and high- and low-socioeconomic school districts.

Reliability

Data on internal-consistency reliability are reported for the verbal, quantitative, and nonverbal batteries. Reliabilities for Level K range from .85 to .89; Level 1 reliabilities range from .87 to .93; Level 2 reliabilities range from .86 to .92; reliabilities for Levels A through H range from .93 to .95. Composite score reliabilities range from .94 to .98. No other reliability data are reported in the manual.

Validity

Rationale for item selection and evidence of limited bias are displayed in the manual; however, no other data on the validity of the CogAT are provided.

Summary

The CogAT consists of three batteries (verbal, quantitative, and nonverbal) designed to measure the intelligence of students in kindergarten through grade 12. The procedures used in standardizing this test are exemplary. Evidence for internal-consistency reliability is good, but there are no data on other forms of reliability. There are currently very limited data on the validity of the CogAT.

Otis-Lennon School Ability Test, Eighth Edition

The eighth edition of the Otis-Lennon School Ability Test (OLSAT 8; Harcourt Educational Measurement, 2003) is the latest in a series of intelligence tests that date back to 1918. The original Otis test, developed by Arthur Otis, was called the Otis Group Intelligence Test. Later Otis developed the Otis Self-Administering Tests of Mental Ability and the Otis Quick-Scoring Mental Ability Tests. Otis then worked with Roger Lennon to revise the test, and it was called the Otis-Lennon Mental Ability Test, and in subsequent editions, the Otis-Lennon School Ability Test (OLSAT). The OLSAT 8 requires a student to perform tasks such as detecting similarities and differences, solving analogies and matrices, classifying, and determining sequence as a measure of those verbal and nonverbal skills that are most closely related to school achievement. The test is designed to assess "the examinees' ability to cope with school learning tasks, to suggest their possible placement for school learning functions, and to evaluate their achievement in relation to the talents they bring to school learning situations" (Harcourt Educational Measurement, 2003, p. 5).

Seven levels of the OLSAT 8 (designated A through G) are used to assess the abilities of students in grades K–12. There are separate tests for each grade from K to 3, one test for grades 4 through 5, one for grades 6 through 8, and one for the high school grades. At levels A and B (kindergarten and first grade), the entire test is dictated. Level C (second grade) contains two self-administered subtests, with the remainder of the test dictated. All other levels (D through G) are self-administered.

Subtests

The 21 different types of items that compose the OLSAT 8 fall into five clusters: Verbal Comprehension, Verbal Reasoning, Pictorial Reasoning, Figural Reasoning, and Quantitative Reasoning. The clusters, in turn, make up the verbal and nonverbal scales. Behaviors sampled by subtests in the clusters are as follows.

Verbal Comprehension   Items in this cluster assess knowledge of vocabulary, skill in identifying relationships among words, ability to derive meaning from words, and skill in identifying subtle differences between similar words and phrases. Subtests in the Verbal Comprehension Cluster include Following Directions, Antonyms, Sentence Completion, and Sentence Arrangement.

Verbal Reasoning   Items in this cluster assess skill in inferring relationships among words, including verbal math problems; in making verbal classification; and in identifying similarities and differences between words. Subtests included in the Verbal Reasoning Cluster include Aural Reasoning, Arithmetic Reasoning, Logical Selection, Word/Letter Matrix, Verbal Analogies, Verbal Classification, and Inference.

Pictorial Reasoning   All items in this cluster use pictures and require students to classify pictures, complete sequences, and solve analogies. Subtests in this cluster include Picture Classification, Picture Analogies, and Picture Series.

Figural Reasoning   Items in this cluster assess skill in using geometric figures to identify analogies and to complete matrices and sequences. Subtests in this cluster include Figural Classification, Picture Analogies, and Picture Series.

Quantitative Reasoning   Items in this cluster assess reasoning, completion of sequences, and completion of matrices using numbers. Subtests in the Quantitative Reasoning Cluster include Number Series, Numeric Inferences, and Number Matrix.

Scores

Raw scores earned on verbal, nonverbal, and total test sections of the OLSAT 8 may be converted to one or more derived scores: scaled scores, school ability indexes (with a mean of 100 and a standard deviation of 16), percentile ranks, stanines, or normal-curve equivalents (NCEs).

Norms

The OLSAT 8 is made up of items from the OLSAT 6, OLSAT 7, and an unspecified number of new items. Items from the OLSAT 6 and new items were submitted to an item tryout with 40,000 students in 2001. Items used from the OLSAT 7 were considered new enough not to need item tryout. All items were then submitted to bias review, and based on expert opinion, those considered biased were eliminated from the test. The OLSAT 8 was then standardized in both spring and fall of 2002. The spring standardization sample consisted of 275,500 students from 725 school districts; the fall standardization used 135,000 students. The sampling of students took into account socioeconomic status, region of the country, environment (urban or rural), and ethnicity. There was no specific stratification on the basis of age, grade, or gender. The sampling distribution is reported, but cross-tabulations are not. The sample is not a stratified sample; for example, we do not know how many students from the Northeast were from urban environments. A quick inspection of the list of "districts" participating in the standardization revealed that a very large number of districts were actually individual private or parochial schools. The authors include norms for performance by age and norms for performance by grade.

The OLSAT 8 was standardized concurrently with the Stanford Achievement Test 10 (SAT 10). Those who use this combination of ability and achievement tests will have the advantage of using tests standardized on the same population. As we noted in the chapter "Norms," this is better than using tests standardized on different populations.

Reliability

At each level, KR-20s are reported for cluster scores for each age and grade. All reliability coefficients exceed .80. There are no data on test stability over time.

Validity

The authors of the OLSAT 8 argue that they made judgments about test content when they selected items and that users must do the same. Evidence for content validity is presented in the form of high correlations between the OLSAT 8 and the OLSAT 7. Evidence for internal structure validity consists of showing that the verbal and nonverbal subtests are highly intercorrelated. The other form of validity evidence is demonstration of relationships to external variables. The authors report that the verbal and nonverbal scales are highly intercorrelated, and argue that the relationship between the OLSAT 8 and the Stanford Achievement Test (SAT) parallels the "known relationship between ability and achievement" (Harcourt Educational Measurement, 2003, p. 39). Most correlations are in the .70s except at grades 9 through 12. At these "higher" levels, the correlations are far more modest.

Summary

The OLSAT 8 is a quickly administered group test of intelligence for which there is reasonable evidence of internal consistency. There is no evidence of stability over time. Evidence for validity is limited. The authors do not report the stratification of the standardization sample.

Dilemmas in Current Practice

A number of specific limitations are inherent in the construction and use of group intelligence tests. The first limitation is that most tests have many levels designed for use in specific grades (for example, Level A for kindergarten through third grade, Level B for third through sixth grade). Tests are typically standardized by grade, but students of different ages are enrolled in the same grade, and students of the same age are enrolled in different grades. Further, students with disabilities are often in ungraded programs. Test authors then use interpolation and extrapolation to compute mental ages for students based on grade sampling. In earlier discussions, an age score was defined as the average score earned by individuals of a given age. Let us now consider a problem.

Problem

Suppose that an intelligence test has a Level Q, which is designed to measure the intelligence of students in grades 6 through 9. As is typical of group intelligence tests, the test is standardized on students in grades 6 through 9, students who range in age from approximately 10 or 11 to 14 or 15 years. Norms are based on this age range. The test is later administered to Stanley, age 10-8, who earns a mental age of 7-3.

How can this be? Stanley, who is 10 years, 8 months old, could not possibly earn the same score as is typically earned on the test by students who are 7 years, 3 months old, because no students 7 years and 3 months old were included in the normative sample. The score is based on an extrapolation, its first limitation.

The second limitation is that most group intelligence tests, although standardized on large numbers of students, often are not standardized on representative populations. Most are standardized on school districts, not on individual students. An effort is made to select representative districts, but these may not necessarily include a representative population of individuals. Yet the normative tables for group intelligence tests typically provide scores for individuals, not for groups.

The third limitation is that most group intelligence tests are standardized on volunteer samples. In the process of standardizing the test, representative districts are selected and are asked to participate. Districts that refuse, for any of a number of reasons, are replaced by what are believed to be comparable districts. This process of replacement may introduce bias into the standardization.

A final limitation is that, when tests are standardized in public schools, those students who are excluded from school are also excluded from the standardization population. Students who have severe mental retardation, are severely disturbed, or have dropped out of school are excluded from the norms. Similarly, most authors of group intelligence tests do not describe the extent to which they included students enrolled in special education classes in their standardization samples. Exclusion of students with low IQs biases the norms; the range of performance of the standardization group is reduced, and the standard deviation is decreased. It is extremely important for the authors of group tests to provide tables in test manuals illustrating the composition of the standardization sample. Such tables should include descriptions of the kinds of individuals on whom a test was standardized, rather than descriptions of districts.

Authors' Viewpoint

In spite of their limitations and problems, group intelligence tests are still used. Those who use the tests must recognize that the tests are sampling behaviors and must be aware of the behaviors sampled by the tests. School personnel give group intelligence tests to predict future performance, usually future achievement. It is wise, therefore, to use group intelligence tests and group achievement tests that have been standardized on the same population. We recommend that school personnel first select the group achievement test to be used and then choose the group intelligence test that has been standardized on the same population. The following pairs of tests have been standardized on identical groups of students: the OLSAT 8 and the Stanford Achievement Test 10; the CogAT and the Iowa Tests of Basic Skills; and the CogAT and the Tests of Achievement and Proficiency.

SUMMARY

Group intelligence tests are used primarily as screening devices; they are designed to identify those whose intellectual development deviates significantly enough from normal to warrant individual intellectual assessment. Many different group intelligence tests are currently used in the schools. A review of the most commonly used group tests illustrates the many kinds of behaviors sampled in the assessment of intelligence. When teachers evaluate students' performances on group intelligence tests, they must go beyond obtained scores to look at the kinds of behaviors sampled by the tests. When selecting group intelligence tests, teachers must evaluate the extent to which specific tests are standardized on samples of students with whom they want to compare their pupils and the extent to which the tests are technically adequate for their own purposes.

QUESTIONS FOR CHAPTER REVIEW

1. Obtain a copy of any group intelligence test, and identify the domains of behaviors sampled by at least ten items. Use the domains described in the chapter "Assessment of Intelligence: An Overview."

2. Identify at least four major factors that a teacher must consider when administering a group intelligence test to students.

3. Suppose you had to decide which group intelligence test to give in your school. What factors would you consider in selecting a test? Which test might you select? Justify your answer.

4. You have just been hired as a classroom teacher. On your first day, you were told that one of your students had recently been evaluated and identified as having a learning disability. The school psychologist provides you with her test results, and you note that the youngster had difficulty with generalization, spatial relationships, and sentence-completion subtests. With what classroom activities might this youngster have difficulty?

PROJECT

Using information found in the text, write a summary for one of the group intelligence tests. Upon completion, compare your summary with the text summary. Then go to the *Mental Measurements Yearbook*, and compare and contrast your summary with the review of the test you selected. If your summary is different, has the reviewer used different information and different standards?

RESOURCES FOR FURTHER INVESTIGATION

Technology Resources

RIVERSIDE PUBLISHING
www.riverpub.com
Go to Products and Services, and then, under Educational Assessments in the index of products, you will find information on the Cognitive Abilities Test.

HARCOURT EDUCATIONAL MEASUREMENT
www.harcourtassessment.com
Here you will find information on the Otis-Lennon School Ability Test, Eighth Edition.

CHAPTER 19

Assessment of Sensory Acuity

THE FIRST THING TO CHECK WHEN A CHILD IS HAVING ACADEMIC OR SOCIAL DIFFICULTIES is whether that child is adequately and properly receiving environmental information. In efforts to identify why children experience difficulties, too often we overlook the obvious in search of the subtle. Vision and hearing difficulties interfere with the educational progress of a significant number of schoolchildren.

The teacher's role in assessment of sensory acuity is twofold. First, the teacher must be aware of behaviors that may indicate sensory difficulties and thus must have at least an embryonic knowledge of the kinds of sensory difficulties that children experience. Second, the teacher must know the instructional implications of sensory difficulties. Communication with vision specialists (teachers of students with visual impairments, ophthalmologists, optometrists, and orientation and mobility specialists) and hearing specialists (teachers of students with hearing impairments, audiologists, speech and language pathologists, and otolaryngologists) is the most effective way to gain such information. The teacher must have basic knowledge about procedures used for assessing sensory acuity in order to comprehend and use data from specialists. This chapter provides basic knowledge about the kinds of vision and hearing difficulties pupils experience, as well as an overview of procedures and devices used to assess sensory acuity.

Why Do We Assess Sensory Acuity?

Difficulties in seeing or hearing are among the most obvious reasons that students experience academic and behavioral difficulties in school. They also generally are the kinds of difficulties most easily corrected or compensated for. The link between sensory difficulties and academic problems is easy to appreciate. The fact that sensory difficulties may cause behavioral problems, although not so obvious, has also been established.

Visual Difficulties

Types of Visual Impairment

There are three ways in which vision may be limited: (1) Visual acuity may be limited; (2) the field of vision may be restricted; or (3) color vision may be imperfect. The first two are the most significant. *Visual acuity* refers to the clarity or sharpness with which a person sees. The method of measuring visual acuity is derived from the use of the Snellen Wall Chart. A person is described as having normal vision (20/20 in both eyes) if, at 20 feet from the chart, that person is able to distinguish letters that an average person can distinguish at 20 feet. A rating of 20/200 means that the person can distinguish letters at 20 feet that the average person can distinguish at 200 feet. Conversely, 20/10 vision means the person is able to distinguish letters at 20 feet that the average person can distinguish only at 10 feet. The former demonstrates limited vision, whereas the latter demonstrates better-than-average visual acuity.

A person's field of vision may be restricted in either of two ways. First, a person may demonstrate normal central visual acuity with a restricted peripheral field; this is usually referred to as *tunnel vision.* Second, a person may have a *scotoma,* a blind or dark spot in the visual field. If the spot occurs in the middle of the eye, it may result in central vision impairment, particularly if both eyes are impaired.

Color vision is determined by the discrimination of three qualities of color: hue (such as red versus green), saturation (that is, pure versus muddied colors), and brightness (that is, vibrant versus dull reflection of light). The essential difference between people who have colorblindness and those who do not is that hues that appear different to normal persons look the same to a colorblind person. Colorblind persons frequently do not know that they are colorblind unless they have been tested and told so. Colorblindness is not usually an all-or-nothing condition. Most colorblindness is partial; the person has difficulty distinguishing certain colors, usually red and green. Total colorblindness is extremely rare. Colorblindness is an inherited trait found in about 1 out of 12 males and about 1 out of 200 females. There is no cure for colorblindness, but the condition is not usually regarded as a disability.

Impaired Visual Acuity

Blindness may be either congenital or acquired. Congenital blindness or blindness acquired prior to age 5 years has the most serious educational implications. Few people are totally blind. Many can perceive at least some light (versus total darkness) and some objects; any perception of light or of objects helps with mobility. Blindness, for legal purposes, is defined as

> central visual activity of 20/200 or less in the better eye, with correcting glasses, or central visual acuity of more than 20/200 if there is a field defect in which the peripheral field has contracted to such an extent that the widest diameter of visual field subtends an angular distance no greater than 20 degrees [tunnel vision]. (Hurlin, 1962, p. 8)

According to Taylor (cited in Barraga, 1976, p. 13; italics added):

The term *visually handicapped* is being used widely at present to denote the total group of children who have impairments in the structure or functioning of the visual sense organ—the eye—irrespective of the nature and extent of the impairment. The term has gained acceptance because the impairment causes a limitation that, even with the best possible correction, interferes with incidental or normal learning through the sense of vision.

When we deal with children, we are concerned primarily with the educational implications of reduced acuity. Educational needs resulting from low acuity lead to students' being declared eligible for special education services. Barraga (1976, p. 14) differentiates among three categories of visual disabilities:

Blind. This term [is] used to refer to children who have only light perception without projection, or those who are totally without the sense of vision. . . . Educationally, the blind child is one who learns through Braille and related media without the use of vision . . . , although perception of light may be present and useful in orientation and movement.

Low vision. Children who have limitations in distance vision but are able to see objects and materials when they are within a few inches or at a maximum of a few feet away are another subgroup. Most low-vision children will be able to use their vision for many school learning activities, a few for visual reading perhaps, whereas others may need to use tactual materials and possibly even Braille to supplement printed and other visual materials. . . .

Visually limited. This term refers to children who in some way are limited in their use of vision under average circumstances. They may have difficulty seeing learning materials without special lighting, or they may be unable to see distant objects unless the objects are moving, or they need to wear prescriptive lenses or use optical aids and special materials to function visually. Visually limited children will be considered for all educational purposes and under all circumstances as seeing children.

Estimates of the number of school-age children who experience some form of visual difficulties range from 5 to 33 percent. Obviously, estimates differ as a function of the definition used and the screening devices employed.

Teachers must be consistently on the lookout for symptoms and signs of visual difficulty. When children complain of symptoms such as frequent headaches, dizziness, sensitivity to light, or blurred vision, efforts must be made to evaluate the extent to which they are seeing properly. Obvious signs of possible visual difficulty include crossed eyes or turned-out eyes (strabismus); red, swollen, or encrusted eyelids; constant rapid movement of the eyes; watery eyes or discharges from the eye; and haziness in the pupils. These symptoms and signs should receive special attention in the form of referral for vision screening (U.S. Public Health Service, 1971).

Certain behaviors also may indicate visual difficulties. According to the U.S. Public Health Service (1971), behaviors indicative of potential visual difficulties include holding books unusually close to or far from the eyes while reading; frequent blinking, squinting, or rubbing of the eyes; abnormal tilting or turning of the head; inattention during blackboard lessons; poor alignment of letters in written work; unusual choice of colors in artwork; confusion of certain letters of the alphabet in reading (*o*'s and *a*'s, *e*'s and *c*'s, *b*'s and *h*'s, *n*'s and *r*'s); inability or reluctance to participate in games requiring distance vision or visual accuracy; and irritability when doing close work.

Vision Screening and Assessment

Schools conduct vision screening, whereas vision testing is done clinically by ophthalmologists and optometrists. When youngsters experience learning difficulties or when routine vision screening indicates visual difficulties, the child is referred for a clinical vision exam. If the clinical exam indicates 20/20 vision, no additional visual assessment needs to be done by educational personnel. Similarly, if visual acuity is limited but can be corrected by glasses, no visual assessments need be conducted by education personnel. However, if vision is 20/70 or less with best correction or if there is a limited visual field, educational personnel must ensure that a clinical low-vision exam, functional-vision assessment, or learning-media assessment is conducted. The purpose of these tests is intervention planning.

Most schools now have vision-screening programs, but the effectiveness of these programs varies. Two fundamentally different kinds of tests are used: those that screen only central visual acuity at a distance, and those that assess both central visual acuity and a number of other visual capabilities. Most preschool screening programs also include screening for amblyopia, often called "lazy eye."

Basic Screening   The standard Snellen Wall Chart is the most commonly used screening test to assess visual acuity. The test consists simply of a wall chart of standard-sized letters that a child is asked to read at a distance of 20 feet. The test provides limited information about vision, assessing only central visual acuity at a distance of 20 feet. Specific difficulties may be encountered in using the test with some school-age children. First, children may be unable to read the letters or to discriminate between letters such as *F* and *P*. Second, children can often memorize the letters ahead of time. Third, the letters of the alphabet differ in legibility, which leads to guessing. The practical criterion for referral using this test is acuity of 20/40 or less in either eye for children in kindergarten through third grade, and 20/30 or less in either eye for older children and juveniles (National Society for the Prevention of Blindness, 1961).

An adaptation of the Snellen Wall Chart, the Snellen E Test, is the most commonly used test with preschool children and those who are unable to read. The letter *E* is presented with its arms facing in one of four directions, and the person being tested is asked either to name the direction, to point, or to hold up a letter *E* to match the stimulus. Again, this test assesses only central visual acuity at a distance.

Both of the Snellen tests fail to identify students with near-vision problems, the kinds of problems that are often the most critical to reading. They also miss physical difficulties and problems in the internal structure of the eye (such as the retina). Some schools use the Keystone Telebinocular, a device that assesses 14 different visual skills. Visual functioning is assessed at both a near point (16 inches) and a far point (20 inches). The distances are produced optically, and children remain seated in front of the instrument throughout testing.

Clinical Low-Vision Exams

More and more, educators are recognizing the limitations of assessing visual acuity with traditional measures. They note that low-vision students with similar ratings on measures of acuity vary considerably in their actual classroom functioning. For example, some children have vision but are unable to use it spontaneously. Others can use their vision in certain situations (for example, during one-to-one instruction in a controlled setting) but not for incidental learning. Still other students choose, consciously or unconsciously, not to use their vision (Corn, 1983). Corn (1983) outlines a theoretical model that can be used to think about vision and to assist professionals in eliciting vision behaviors or maximizing function in individuals with low vision. She points out that low vision results from differing visual disabilities (that is, retinal acuity, retinal field, or cortical brain functions) and that these interact with other individual differences (such as cognition and physical makeup, including motor development and health), as well as with environmental factors (such as poor lighting or highly complex visual field), to influence visual functioning. She illustrates why so much of the assessment of students with visual impairments is individualized and clinical. In essence, educators use whatever methods they can to try to elicit visual behaviors in students who are not demonstrating them spontaneously. (For example, they might use a penlight, and if that did not work, they might use a large white dot on a television screen, to try to elicit a response to light.) Also, educators assess the extent to which educational adaptations (such as large print) optimize the functioning of students with low vision.

Functional-Vision Assessment

A significant effort is under way to develop in-school measures of residual vision and of functional vision. Unfortunately, most of the assessment procedures available are informal, nonstandardized sets of procedures or are more formal standardized procedures that are still under development (and have been for a very long time). Researchers at the University of Minnesota have been working on the Minnesota Functional Vision Assessment (Knowlton, 1988). They have produced eight subtests, each designed to assess an aspect of functional vision: acuity, binocular coordination, contrast, color, motion, functional fields, accommodation, and illusion. This assessment instrument is for use in the general education environment.

Others have been working on assessment of functional vision. Jose, Smith, and Shane (1988) outline a set of procedures for gathering information on the following aspects of functional vision: pupillary response, muscle imbalance (the tendency for the eyes to deviate), blink reflex, eye preference, central and peripheral fields, visual field preference, tracking ability, responses to lights and to objects (reaching for or shifting attention to them), scanning ability, matching, ability to follow moving objects, imitation, object concept (response to objects and pictures), and object permanence. Langley and DuBose (1989) provide a set of procedures for functional-vision testing and a checklist for diagnostic personnel to use in evaluating responses to visual stimuli, responses to objects on the basis of their size and distance, integration of visual and cognitive processing, and integration of visual and motor processing.

Learning-Media Assessment

Learning-media assessment is an objective process of systematically selecting learning and literacy media for students with visual impairments. Koening and Holbrook (1993), at the Texas School for the Blind and Visually Impaired, have developed this informal assessment method for gathering data on general learning media and literacy media. General learning media include instructional materials (such as rulers, worksheets, and pictures) and instructional methods (such as demonstration and modeling). Literacy media are the tools for reading and writing.

Koening and Holbrook (1993) indicate that three types of information are gathered on the student in learning-media assessment:

1. The efficiency with which the student gathers information from various sensory channels

2. The types of learning media the student uses or will use to accomplish learning tasks

3. The literacy media the student will use for reading and writing

Braille Assessment Inventory (BAI)

In Minnesota, teachers of students with visual impairments have been developing the Braille Assessment Inventory (BAI; Sharpe, McNear, & McGrew, 1996). This is an empirically based scale to be used by child study teams that are charged with the task of designing interventions for students with visual impairments. The scale is used to decide the appropriateness of Braille instruction for students who are blind and visually impaired. Composed of 43 items grouped into five scales, the test is used to decide whether students should begin or continue to receive Braille instruction. The BAI was developed by a national sample of teachers of students who were blind or visually impaired. The three subscales of this measure are object recognition, visual orientation, and tactual orientation. Behaviors measured by the subscales are as follows:

Object recognition. A measure of the student's skill in recognizing objects, people, and letters at varying distances

Visual orientation. A measure of functional vision in skills such as the student's using and reading printed materials and reading her or his own handwriting, as well as a means of detecting signs of visual fatigue

Tactual orientation. A measure of a student's skill in discriminating symbols and objects, in using tactual materials, and in perceiving various objects

The scoring of this measure is functional. It is recommended that students who obtain raw scores greater than 96 be taught using print materials. For those who score lower than 85, Braille instruction is recommended, whereas for those who earn scores between 86 and 95, the preferred mode of instruction is not certain. Reliability of this scale (based on interrater reliability computation) exceeds .90.

Hearing Difficulties[1]

Signs of Hearing Loss
Early detection of hearing problems in preschool and school-age children is imperative, so that appropriate remedial or compensatory procedures can be instituted. Children with hearing problems characteristically fail to pay attention, provide wrong answers to simple questions, frequently ask to have words or sentences repeated, and hear better in quiet conditions and when watching the teacher's face. Such children often function below their educational potential, are withdrawn, or exhibit behavior problems. Children who are repeatedly sick, having frequent earaches, colds or other upper respiratory infections, allergies, or fluid draining from their ears, may also have a concomitant hearing problem. Further, children who do not speak clearly or who show other types of speech or language problems, and children who fail to discriminate between sounds or words with similar vowels but different consonants, may also have hearing problems. Finally, some preschool and school-age children are more at risk for hearing problems, including children with craniofacial anomalies such as cleft palate or Down syndrome; children from a lower socioeconomic class; Native Americans and Eskimos, who may not be receiving appropriate and routine health care (Northern & Downs, 1991, pp. 22–24); and children with mental retardation or severe disabilities who cannot express that they have trouble hearing.

Any child, regardless of age, who has one or more of the aforementioned hearing-loss symptoms and any child at risk for hearing loss should be referred for a hearing test. Depending on the school system, the hearing test may be given by the school nurse, a speech-language pathologist, a hearing therapist, an audiologist, or a trained technician. In a preschool setting, support personnel for assessing hearing problems may not be available. Children in such a setting should be referred to their family physician or directly to a hearing specialist.

If a hearing problem is detected or if the child is difficult to test, making the results questionable, the child should be referred to a physician specializing in disorders of the ear, called an "otologist" or an "otolaryngologist," or to a specialist in hearing evaluation and rehabilitation, called an "audiologist." The otologist and the audiologist often work together as a team. An otologist has expertise in physical examination of the ears and in diagnosing and treating ear disorders. If a child has a correctable hearing loss, the otologist can provide the appropriate treatment (such as drug therapy or surgery). The audiologist has expertise in hearing assessment and rehabilitation. If a child has an educationally significant and noncorrectable hearing loss, the audiologist can prescribe, fit, and monitor the use of hearing aids. Further, the audiologist can make recommendations to

---

[1] This section was written especially for this book by Dr. Tom Frank, Professor of Audiology, Department of Communication Disorders, College of Health and Human Development, The Pennsylvania State University.

teachers, hearing therapists, speech-language pathologists, and parents concerning the child's hearing ability in different listening environments.

Modes of Hearing

The sensation of hearing can be initiated through two modes: air conduction and bone conduction. Air-conduction hearing occurs when the sense of hearing is initiated by an airborne sound that enters the outer ear, passes through the middle and inner ear and the brainstem, and is processed in the central auditory system. The vast majority of our everyday hearing experiences occur by air conduction—for example, listening to a teacher's voice or a television. To test hearing, air-conduction signals can be transmitted to the ear via either a loudspeaker or, more commonly, an earphone placed on the outer ear.

Bone-conduction hearing occurs when the head is mechanically vibrated, so that the sense of hearing is initiated in the inner ear, with little or no participation of the outer or middle ear. Hearing by bone conduction occurs when we listen to ourselves speak. To test hearing by bone conduction, signals are transmitted to the ear via a small vibrator, commonly placed behind the outer ear on the mastoid bone. It is very important to note that normal hearing by air conduction depends on the normal functioning of the outer, middle, and inner ear and the neural pathways, whereas normal hearing by bone conduction depends solely on the normal functioning of the inner ear and neural pathways.

Hearing-screening tests initiate the sense of hearing using the air-conduction mode of hearing. Diagnostic hearing tests, which require the measurement of hearing thresholds, initiate the sense of hearing by both air and bone conduction. This is done to define the type and severity of a hearing loss, the severity of a hearing loss being generally defined as the average air-conduction hearing thresholds. Hearing screening, hearing-threshold testing, and other types of hearing tests are conducted with an electronic instrument known as an audiometer.

Types of Screening and Assessment

The identification of preschool and school-age children with hearing problems usually falls within the realm of a hearing-screening program, which may also be called a "hearing conservation program," a "hearing-loss identification program," or "identification audiometry." All states have laws requiring hearing screening of school-age children. Unfortunately, hearing screening for many children in preschool programs is not mandated by state or federal laws. Therefore, many preschool children who have educationally significant hearing losses are not being identified and may become educationally delayed. Hearing-screening programs generally have three components: the actual hearing screening, follow-up hearing-threshold tests for those who fail the screening, and referral for those diagnosed with hearing impairment.

Hearing Screening

The primary purpose of hearing screening in a school situation is to identify children with educationally significant hearing problems. Experience has indicated that teachers and parents may not be able to identify a child with an educationally significant hearing loss. Further, teachers and parents sometimes identify a normal child as having hearing loss. Thus, subjective estimates of a child's hearing ability are not always reliable, and more objective testing must be conducted. This is the purpose of hearing screening.

Hearing screening should be conducted for one child at a time. Screening a large number of children individually is more effective in identifying children with hearing problems and in the long run is more cost effective than screening groups of children.

Typically, hearing-screening guidelines require that hearing screening include (1) a case history and visual inspection of the outer ear, the ear canal, and the eardrum; (2) pure-tone hearing screening; and (3) tympanometry (discussed later in this chapter). Hearing should be screened annually for children functioning at a developmental level of 3 years through third grade and for high-risk children regardless of grade. High-risk children are those who have repeated a grade; require special education; are new to the school; are absent during the hearing screening; have failed previous hearing screenings; have speech, language, or communication problems; are suspected of having a hearing impairment or have a medical problem associated with hearing impairment (for example, chronic earaches or allergies); or are involved in coursework in which they are around loud noise (such as band, woodworking, and auto repair).

The case history and visual inspection of the ear must be done by a qualified individual, such as a school nurse, speech-language pathologist, or audiologist. If a child has a significant case history for ear problems or if inspection of the ear reveals abnormalities (such as wax blocking the ear canal, fluid draining from the middle ear, or an eardrum perforation), the child is removed from the screening and should be referred for medical evaluation or treatment. Even though the case history and ear inspection should be the first step in hearing screening, this step is often bypassed, and hearing screening using air-conducted pure tones becomes the first step.

When pure-tone hearing screening is conducted, the child is instructed to respond, even if the tone is very soft, by raising his or her hand. Older children may use a response button. Some preschool and younger school-age children must be taught or conditioned to respond. The tester then places earphones directly over the child's ears, making sure that there is no hair in between the earphone and the opening to the ear canal, that eyeglasses have been removed, and that earrings are removed if they cause a problem. The child should be seated so that he or she cannot see the examiner. Because earphones are employed, the child's entire auditory system is being stimulated; that is, the child's hearing is being tested by air conduction.

Typically for hearing screening, the frequencies 500, 1,000, 2,000, and 4,000 Hz are presented at a hearing level (HL) of 20 dB. However, if tympanometry screening is also conducted, screening at 500 Hz can be excluded. The choice of frequencies relates to the fact that hearing sounds in the range of 500 to 4,000 Hz is crucial for understanding speech, and 20 dB HL is the upper range of normal hearing for children. Many states have regulations pertaining to hearing screening that also specify hearing-screening frequencies and hearing levels. Needless to say, all hearing testing should be done in a very quiet room, separated not only acoustically but also by distance from noisy parts of the school. If hearing testing is done in the presence of excessive external noise, the noise will cover up, or mask, a pure tone. Consequently, many children who have normal hearing will fail the hearing screening because the external noise will prevent them from hearing the pure tone, especially at lower pitches.

A frequent criterion for failing is the failure to respond at the hearing-screening level at any frequency in either ear. However, state hearing-screening regulations may have different criteria for failure. Regardless of the failure criteria, all failures should be retested immediately, after the child is given a more careful set of instructions.

Hearing-Threshold Testing

Children who fail both the initial hearing screening and the repeat screening should receive a more detailed hearing test and be referred to an audiologist or an otologist. The more detailed test is known as the pure-tone threshold test, or pure-tone audiometry. The purpose of this test is to determine the child's hearing thresholds for different-frequency pure tones in each ear. For this testing, hearing is measured using both earphones (air conduction) and a bone vibrator (bone conduction). Bone conduction should never be assessed in a school setting, because many variables may influence the results. A hearing threshold is usually defined as the lowest hearing level at which the child responds to a minimum of two out of three pure tones.

In some situations, hearing thresholds must be obtained for one ear while a noise signal is directed to the other ear. This is called "masking," and the resultant hearing threshold for the ear being tested is called a "masked threshold." Masking is necessary so that the ear not being tested does not respond and the true hearing threshold of the test ear can be obtained. Masked thresholds should be obtained only by an audiologist or otologist.

The hearing-threshold levels obtained as a result of the pure-tone threshold test can be expressed numerically. However, it is more common to plot the hearing thresholds on a graph termed an *audiogram,* as shown in Figure 19.1. On the audiogram, frequency in Hz is shown along the top, in octave and half-octave intervals from 125 to 8,000 Hz. Hearing level in dB is shown along the side of the audiogram, from −10 to 120 dB in 10-dB steps. The symbols plotted on the audiogram correspond to the hearing threshold for each ear at each frequency tested, using earphones (air conduction) or a bone vibrator (bone conduction) when the thresholds were unmasked or masked. Each audiogram contains an adjacent legend that defines the meaning of the symbols used on it. An audiogram legend is shown in Figure 19.2. A circle indicates an unmasked air-conduction threshold for the right ear, and an X indicates an unmasked air-conduction threshold for the left ear. It is also common practice to mark thresh-

FIGURE 19.1
Audiogram Showing
Frequency in Hertz (Hz)
(top) and Hearing Level in
Decibels (dB) (side)
Average normal hearing is
0 dB HL at each frequency,
and the normal range is from
−10 to 20 dB, regardless of
frequency.

SOURCE: "Guidelines
for Audiometric Sym-
bols," Figure 1. *ASHA,*
32, 25–30, 1990.
Reprinted by permission
of the American Speech-
Language-Hearing
Association.

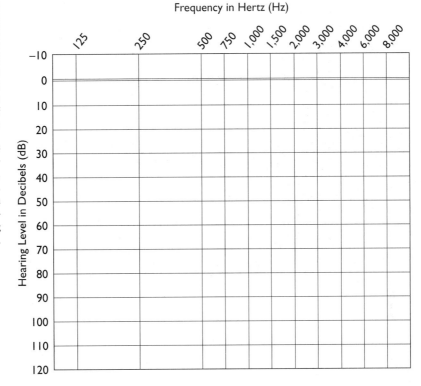

olds for the right ear in red and for the left ear in blue. The criteria for failing a pure-tone threshold test are generally the same as for the hearing screening.

Tympanometry Screening

Even though the pure-tone air-conduction screening and the threshold test are commonly used to identify children with educationally significant hearing loss, they have a number of drawbacks. Both the amount of external noise in the test environment and the rapport between the child and the examiner influence the results. Also, some children with normal hearing may fail these tests because they are immature or inattentive, or because they do not understand the instructions. Moreover, some children may pass these tests but have a minor hearing problem or a fluctuating hearing loss, usually due to abnormal conditions of the middle ear. Consequently, several school systems and states have initiated another type of screening test, used alone or in conjunction with pure-tone screening. This test, known as tympanometry, is the third step in the guidelines for hearing screening. Tympanometry has also been called "impedance audiometry," "admittance audiometry," "oto-admittance," "middle-ear screening," and "tympanometric screening." Tympanometry can be defined as a method for detecting

FIGURE 19.2
Audiogram Legend Showing the Meaning of Symbols Plotted on an Audiogram
This legend shows the symbols for air-conduction unmasked and masked thresholds, and for bone-conduction unmasked and masked thresholds when a bone vibrator is placed on the mastoid bone behind the ear. There are many other symbols that can be used to plot hearing thresholds. The symbols shown in this figure are the most commonly used.

SOURCE: Adapted from "Guidelines for Audiometric Symbols," Table 1. *ASHA*, 32, 25–30, 1990. Reprinted by permission of the American Speech-Language-Hearing Association.

Audiogram Legend			
Modality	Ear		
	Left	Unspecified	Right
Air Conduction—Earphones			
Unmasked	X		O
Masked	☐		△
Bone Conduction—Mastoid			
Unmasked	>	⊓	<
Masked	]		[

normal, as well as abnormal, conditions of the eardrum and middle ear. Overall, tympanometry screening is designed to detect abnormal conditions, not to detect educationally significant hearing losses. Disorders of the middle ear are the most frequent cause of educationally significant hearing loss in children, especially for preschool and young school-age children.

Tympanometry is done using an instrument known as a middle-ear screener, tympanogram screener, middle-ear analyzer, or impedance or admittance meter. Middle-ear screening instruments are automatic, so the procedure takes less than ten seconds per ear.

The results of tympanometry are plotted on a graph known as a tympanogram, which shows eardrum movement on the y-axis, as a function of air pressure in the ear canal on the x-axis. Figure 19.3 shows tympanograms for a normal middle ear and for middle ears that have various pathologic conditions.

Children who fail tympanometry (that is, have abnormal tympanograms) but pass the pure-tone air-conduction screening should be rescreened (with both a pure-tone test and tympanometry) in four to six weeks. If they fail either rescreening procedure, they should be referred for additional testing and diagnosis. However, depending on the type of tympanogram, an immediate referral for further diagnosis or treatment should be made.

It is important to recognize that screening for middle-ear disorders is not the same as screening for hearing loss; a child could have a middle-ear disorder but pass the pure-tone screening. To differentiate, note that the primary goal of pure-tone screening is to identify children with educationally significant hearing loss, whereas the primary goal of tympanometry screening is to identify children with middle-ear disorders. Even though some states require only pure-tone screening, it is in the best health interests of preschool and school-age children to have both a pure-tone and a tympanometry (middle-ear) screening in the same session. Further, criteria for failure and consequential referral should include the screening

FIGURE 19.3

Tympanogram Configurations for a Normal Middle Ear (a) and for Middle Ears Having a Pathologic Condition (b–e)

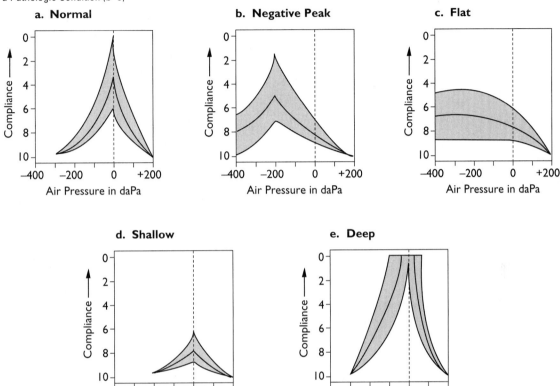

Each tympanogram shows eardrum mobility, called "compliance," on the *y*-axis, air pressure on the *x*-axis, and a shaded area used for interpreting the tympanogram. Tympanogram (a) is normal. Tympanogram (b) is called "negative peak" and is observed in children having negative pressure in their middle ear. Tympanogram (c) is called "flat" and is commonly observed in children having middle-ear fluid. Tympanogram (d) is called "shallow" and is observed when the middle ear is stiffer than normal but does not contain fluid. Tympanogram (e) is called "deep" and is observed in children who have a flaccid eardrum or disarticulation of the middle-ear bones.

SOURCE: From F. H. Bess and L. E. Humes, *Audiology: The Fundamentals*, 1st edition, Copyright Williams and Wilkins, 1990. Reprinted by permission of Lippincott Williams & Wilkins.

results for both air-conduction hearing (pure-tone screening) and middle-ear disorders (tympanometry).

Other Types of Hearing Testing

In addition to tympanometry and pure-tone audiometry, audiologists conduct several other hearing and middle-ear-function tests. These tests aid in diagnosis and hearing-aid fitting and are beyond the scope of this section. However, there are two important and routine tests that employ speech as the test signal. One test, known as a speech recognition threshold (SRT), is used to determine a hearing threshold for speech. The other test, known as a word recognition score (WRS), is used to determine word recognition ability. (Word recognition tests were once known as "speech discrimination" or "speech intelligibility" tests.) Generally, both the SRT and the WRS are obtained both via earphones for each ear separately and via a loudspeaker located in an audiometric test booth. When testing is done via the loudspeaker, only the better-hearing ear responds. In cases in which each ear hears at the same level, the advantage of binaural (both-ears) hearing, compared with monaural (one-ear) hearing, can usually be demonstrated.

The SRT is determined by having the child repeat back or point to printed bisyllabic words (for example, hot dog, baseball, snowman), spoken with a spondaic stress pattern (that is, equal stress on both syllables) while the hearing level is varied. The SRT is defined as the lowest hearing level at which the child responds to 50 percent of the words. The SRT is used to check the validity of the air-conducted pure-tone hearing thresholds, to provide an estimate of the child's threshold for speech, and to adjust and fit hearing aids.

A WRS is usually determined by having the child repeat back or point to printed words when the words are presented at a hearing level loud enough to produce maximum recognition. A WRS is simply the percentage of words correctly heard. A WRS can also be determined by presenting the words through a loudspeaker at a hearing level corresponding to the level of normal conversational speech. This testing is very important for estimating the child's hearing handicap for speech. For example, if a child had a WRS of 90 percent in his or her better-hearing ear when speech was presented loud enough to be heard but had a WRS of only 20 percent when speech was presented at a normal level, the child would be very educationally handicapped for hearing speech. This result would also indicate that, if speech were made louder through the use of hearing aids or if the hearing loss were medically corrected to normal, the child's WRS would increase from 20 percent to about 90 percent, drastically decreasing the educational significance of the child's hearing loss.

Types of Hearing Loss

As noted previously, the sense of hearing can be stimulated by both air and bone conduction. When hearing thresholds are obtained for both air- and bone-conducted pure tones, the type of hearing loss can be defined.

Normal hearing for preschool and school-age children is usually defined within a range around 0 dB HL, from −10 to 20 dB HL. The audiogram in Figure 19.4 shows the air-conduction thresholds for a 6-year-old girl with normal hearing in each ear, from 250 to 8,000 Hz. Note that the right- and left-ear air-conduction symbols show about average normal hearing (0 dB HL) and lie within the normal range of −10 to 20 dB HL. In this case, bone-conduction thresholds were not measured because the child had normal air-conduction hearing.

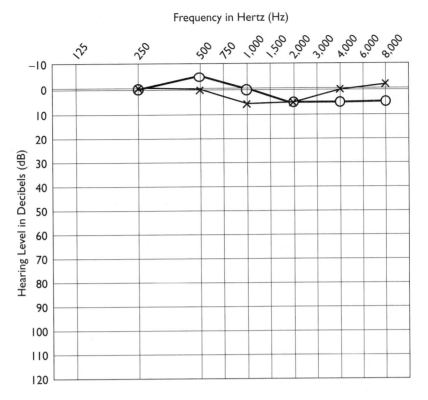

FIGURE 19.4
Audiogram for a 6-Year-
Old Girl Having Normal
Air-Conduction Hearing
in Each Ear from 250
to 8,000 Hz

Conductive Hearing Loss

If a child has a hearing loss caused by an abnormal condition or pathology in the outer ear, such as an excessive buildup of wax (cerumen) in the ear canal, or an abnormal condition of the middle ear, such as fluid in the middle ear (otitis media) or a perforation in the eardrum, bone-conduction hearing will be normal, because the inner ear is not affected. However, the child's hearing by air conduction will be abnormal, because the dysfunction is due to a pathology in the outer or middle ear or both. This type of hearing loss, evidenced by normal bone-conduction but abnormal air-conduction hearing, is known as a *conductive hearing loss*, because the pathology has affected the sound-conducting mechanisms of the outer or middle ear or both. The audiogram in Figure 19.5 shows the air- and bone-conduction thresholds of a 5-year-old girl with a mild, bilateral (both ears), conductive hearing loss due to middle-ear fluid. Note that the bone-conduction masked thresholds are normal, but the air-conduction thresholds are abnormal (> 20 dB HL). This child failed the pure-tone screening and threshold test and had an abnormal tympanogram. She was classified as having an educationally significant hearing loss in each ear and was referred to an otologist for treatment. After the middle-ear fluid problem was resolved by medication, her air-conduction hearing and tympanogram returned to normal.

FIGURE 19.5
Audiogram for a 5-Year-Old Girl Having a Mild, Bilateral (Both Ears), Conductive Hearing Loss Due to Middle-Ear Fluid in Each Middle Ear

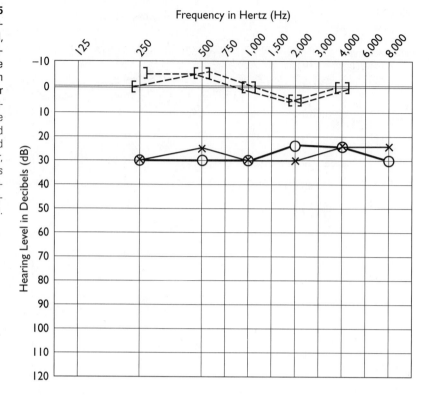

FIGURE 19.5
Audiogram for a 5-Year-Old Girl Having a Mild, Bilateral (Both Ears), Conductive Hearing Loss Due to Middle-Ear Fluid in Each Middle Ear
Note that her bone-conduction thresholds were normal and were obtained when masking was directed to the nontest ear. However, her air-conduction thresholds were abnormal and demonstrated an educationally significant hearing loss.

The most common type of hearing problem in preschool and school-age children is a conductive hearing loss due to the presence of middle-ear fluid. This condition is commonly known as otitis media with effusion (fluid) and can have several causes. However, almost all the causes are related to dysfunction of the Eustachian tube. Some children have many episodes of otitis media and earaches, especially in early childhood. These children might be categorized as being otitis media prone. Hearing loss due to otitis media is usually mild to moderate in degree; may fluctuate, with more hearing loss on some days than on others; and is usually temporary, lasting until the fluid dissipates and the eardrum and middle ear return to normal. Generally, otitis media is treated by drug therapy. If this is not successful, the fluid can be removed surgically. This is done by making an incision in the lower part of the eardrum, removing the fluid, and then placing a small plastic tube in the eardrum incision. This surgical procedure is known as a myringotomy with tubal insertion. The small tube, called a "pressure-equalization (PE) tube," temporarily takes over the function of the Eustachian tube by allowing air to enter the middle-ear space. A PE tube usually works its way out of the eardrum over time and can be removed, if necessary.

Educators are starting to identify the associations among otitis media, speech and language development, attention, and learning ability. Many researchers (Feagans, Sanyal, Henderson, Collier, & Appelbaum, 1986; Friel-Patti & Finitzo, 1990; Northern & Downs, 1991, pp. 18–28) have suggested that children who have chronic otitis media have more speech and language, attention, and learning problems than children who do not suffer middle-ear disease. After appropriate treatment for conductive hearing loss, hearing ability can almost always be restored to normal. When this is not possible, if the hearing loss is educationally significant, the use of hearing aids should be seriously considered. However, children with long-standing conductive hearing loss probably will need additional instruction to make up for what they missed when their hearing loss was present.

Sensorineural Hearing Loss

If a child has a hearing loss due to a dysfunction of the inner ear, both bone- and air-conduction hearing will be equally abnormal. This type of loss (abnormal bone- and equally abnormal air-conduction hearing) is known as a *sensorineural hearing loss* (also called "cochlear" or "neurosensory hearing loss"). There are many causes of sensorineural hearing loss, such as noise exposure, inheritance, ototoxic drugs, mumps, measles, and head trauma. The audiogram in Figure 19.6 is for a 7-year-old boy with a mild to moderate, bilateral, high-frequency sensorineural hearing loss, probably due to a very high fever in infancy. Note that, for the higher frequencies, the bone- and air-conduction thresholds are equally abnormal (> 20 dB HL). This child failed the pure-tone screening and

FIGURE 19.6
Audiogram for a 7-Year-Old Boy Having a Mild to Moderate, Bilateral, High-Frequency Sensorineural Hearing Loss
Note that his air- and bone-conduction thresholds were equally abnormal for the higher pitches.

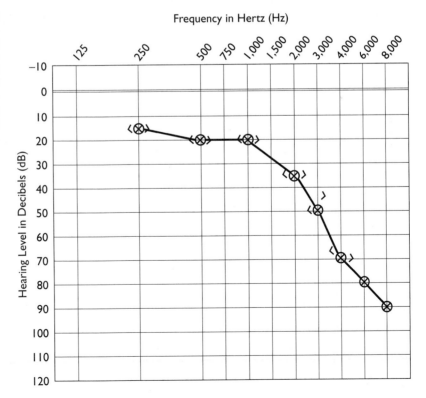

threshold test and was classified as having an educationally significant hearing loss in each ear. Because the child's hearing loss was not due to an outer- or middle-ear problem, he passed the middle-ear screening (with a normal tympanogram). The child was referred to an audiologist and otologist, and was fitted with a behind-the-ear hearing aid for each ear.

An educationally significant moderate or more severe sensorineural hearing loss will almost always be detected before a child enters preschool. On the other hand, other problems—such as educationally significant sensorineural hearing losses in just one ear (unilateral), bilateral losses in the very high frequencies, or bilateral and very mild losses in all frequencies—are usually detected by hearing screening when a child enters kindergarten or first grade. At present, a sensorineural hearing loss will not respond to medical or surgical treatment. For the vast majority of children with sensorineural hearing loss, hearing aids are very helpful.

Mixed Hearing Loss

A hearing loss can also be a combination of conductive and sensorineural hearing loss. This type is known as a *mixed hearing loss* (abnormal bone- and even more abnormal air-conduction hearing). For example, a mixed loss could arise if a child had a problem both with the middle ear (due to middle-ear fluid) and with the inner ear (hair-cell dysfunction due to a very high fever). Generally, mixed hearing losses in children are the result of a pathology that creates a conductive loss on top of an existing sensorineural hearing loss. An otologist can usually alleviate the conductive part of the hearing loss through medical or surgical treatment. However, in some cases, the conductive part of the mixed loss cannot be corrected. If a mixed hearing loss is educationally significant following medical or surgical treatment, the use of hearing aids is warranted.

Central Auditory Hearing Loss

Another type of hearing problem can occur in preschool and school-age children with either normal hearing or hearing loss. This type of hearing problem is related to the function and processing capabilities of the central auditory system and is generally termed a central auditory processing dysfunction or central auditory hearing loss. Children who have a central auditory processing dysfunction generally pass hearing screenings, threshold tests, and tympanometry because they have normal air-conduction hearing and middle-ear function. Further, they respond to whispers or speech spoken at a normal level when there is little background noise. However, these children may have difficulty understanding speech against a noisy background, as would occur in a classroom, and have problems with short- and long-term auditory memory, auditory sequential memory, sounding out of words (phonetics), or reading comprehension. A central auditory processing problem can be educationally very significant and frustrating not only to the child but also to the teacher and parents. Any child who passes a hearing screening but is still suspected of having a hearing problem should be considered a candidate for central auditory processing testing. Testing for central auditory processing also should be considered for children with a reading or visual perception problem.

Several standardized tests have been developed for the sole purpose of determining a child's central auditory processing ability. Some of these tests can be administered by a school psychologist, a speech-language pathologist, or an audiologist. Testing for central auditory processing is very complex, and the results are often difficult to interpret. Children suspected of having a central auditory processing problem should be evaluated by a team of professionals representing many disciplines. If a central auditory problem is diagnosed, new teaching and learning strategies may need to be developed to reduce the educational significance of the problem. These strategies can be provided by special education teachers, speech-language pathologists, or school psychologists.

Severity of Hearing Loss

Besides providing a way to judge the type of hearing loss, a pure-tone threshold test provides valuable information regarding the severity of hearing loss for individual frequencies and frequency regions. This information is very important for fitting students' hearing aids and for helping students to understand speech. There are many ways to calculate hearing-loss severity and many classification schemes to categorize it. The most common method for determining severity is based on the average better-ear air-conduction hearing threshold. This is calculated by determining the lowest air-conduction hearing threshold, regardless of ear, at 500, 1,000, and 2,000 Hz, and then determining the average hearing level. This measure is usually referred to as the better-ear three-frequency average. The frequencies of 500, 1,000, and 2,000 Hz—termed the speech frequencies—were chosen because several speech sounds needed for understanding speech occur between 500 to 2,000 Hz. (However, it is important to realize that many speech sounds also needed for understanding speech are located in frequencies higher than 2,000 Hz. These speech sounds include many of the voiceless consonants, such as *f, s,* and *sh.*)

The average hearing loss can be described or classified in reference to a severity category and in relation to hearing and understanding speech. Figure 19.7 shows an audiogram that classifies hearing impairment by both severity and handicap for hearing speech. For example, a child with an average hearing loss of 35 dB would be classified as having a mild hearing loss and would have difficulty hearing whispered or faint speech. A child with a hearing loss of 80 dB would be classified as having a severe hearing impairment and could understand only shouted or amplified speech.

Speech Understanding and Hearing Loss

Recall that children with a conductive hearing loss have a normal inner ear. Such children can perceive speech normally if it is loud enough to overcome the hearing loss. The effect of a 30- to 40-dB conductive hearing loss can be simulated by wearing a tight-fitting earplug in each ear. If you had such a loss, you would be able to hear normal conversational speech but at a very reduced level. You would have to strain to understand what was said and would not be able to hear people talking at a distance. In addition, you might not be able to hear yourself talk or hear whispers. Imagine what it is like for a child to sit in a classroom all

FIGURE 19.7
Classification of the
Severity of Hearing
Impairment in Relation
to Hearing Handicap
for Speech Recognition,
Shown on an Audiogram

SOURCE: From F. H.
Bess and L. E. Humes,
*Audiology: The Funda-
mentals,* 1st edition,
Copyright Williams and
Wilkins, 1990. Reprinted
by permission of Lippin-
cott Williams & Wilkins.

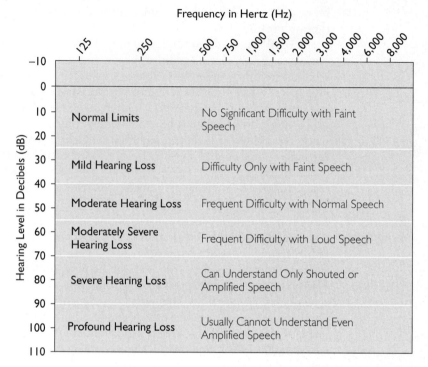

day every day, perhaps for months, without being able to hear and understand everything that is being said!

Children with a sensorineural hearing loss have abnormal function of the inner ear, and the severity of the hearing loss usually increases as the sound frequency increases. These children often report that they can hear someone talking, but they cannot always understand what is said, sometimes even with the use of hearing aids. This occurs because the child can hear low-frequency vowel sounds, which carry the power of speech, but cannot hear the high-frequency consonant sounds, which carry the intelligibility of speech. It is difficult to simulate the effects of a sensorineural hearing loss. However, try listening to a radio station when your radio is slightly mistuned, then turn down the level and increase the bass. You will notice that you can hear speech but not understand what is being said.

Children who have sensorineural hearing loss have extreme difficulty hearing in a noisy environment. In most classrooms, the teacher's voice is only about 6 to 10 dB louder than the background noise. Research has clearly demonstrated that, if the teacher's voice is about 15 to 20 dB louder than the classroom noise, children with sensorineural loss—and, for that matter, normal-hearing children—will have better speech understanding. In other words, improving the signal-to-noise ratio (teacher's voice to classroom noise) will improve speech understanding for all children in the classroom.

There are many ways to improve the signal-to-noise ratio. One way is for the teacher simply to talk louder. Another way is to reduce the level of classroom noise by fitting the classroom with carpeting, acoustic ceiling tile, and window drapes. An audiologist can recommend additional ways to improve the signal-to-noise ratio so as to increase speech understanding. Research has also demonstrated that a child with sensorineural hearing loss will have improved understanding for speech when speech is more distinctly articulated, spoken directly to the child, and spoken at a slightly slower rate.

Dilemmas in Current Practice

The accurate assessment of sensory acuity poses fewer difficulties than other kinds of assessment. Those who assess vision or hearing acuity are assessing relatively stable human characteristics, for the most part. There are well-accepted objective standards of performance for making decisions about the nature and extent of vision or hearing difficulties. With the exception of color vision, the relationship between sensory difficulties and performance in the curriculum is well understood and established. Also, there are known treatments (corrective lenses or hearing aids) for most mild vision or hearing problems. There are also methods for coping with severe vision or hearing problems.

Problem
The major dilemma in assessment of sensory acuity is that, with the exception of routine screening, assessment is done by people outside the school. Students who have serious vision problems are assessed by optometrists or ophthalmologists. Those who have serious hearing problems are assessed by audiologists or ear, nose, and throat specialists. Communication between specialists outside the school and school personnel may be difficult—specialists may not be familiar with the curriculum, understand the educational relevance of their diagnoses, or take the necessary time to speak with school personnel about their findings for individual children. Difficulty may also arise when school personnel do not understand the vocabulary used by those who assess vision and hearing problems.

Authors' Viewpoint
Problems are most effectively overcome when there is very good communication and ongoing interaction among school personnel and out-of-school specialists.

SUMMARY

Vision and hearing difficulties can have a significant effect on the performance of children in educational environments. School personnel can more readily decide how to intervene when they have a basic overview of the kinds of vision and hearing difficulties children experience and of the procedures used to assess sensory acuity. Screening tests of both visual and auditory acuity must be individually administered. This chapter reviewed individually administered screening tests that are appropriate and reasonably effective.

The actual diagnosis of sensory difficulties must be completed by specialists: ophthalmologists, optometrists, audiologists, and otologists. Teachers of students who are visually impaired, deaf, and hard of hearing are very helpful in facilitating communication with such specialists.

QUESTIONS FOR CHAPTER REVIEW

1. Identify several characteristics (behaviors) a student might demonstrate that would make you question whether that individual is seeing adequately.

2. Identify several characteristics (behaviors) a student might demonstrate that would make you question whether that individual is hearing adequately.

3. After a complete visual examination, the doctor reported that "Paolo demonstrates 20/20 corrected vision, and the visual field subtends an angular distance of 15 degrees." Glasses were prescribed. Translate the report into nontechnical terms. Will Paolo's vision have any implications for instructional procedures?

4. Thela's hearing test, administered in November, showed a 35-dB loss on a pure-tone audiometric sweep in the speech range. In December, she was assessed using the Wechsler Intelligence Scale for Children–III and the Test of Adolescent Language, and scored very poorly on subtests requiring auditory reception. In April, the audiologist reported a 10-dB loss in the speech range. In July (and following several months of intensive remediation), Thela was reevaluated in the school and performed substantially better on both intelligence measures and tests of oral language. What conclusions can be drawn about Thela's performance?

PROJECT

Contact your local school district and find out what provisions are made for educating students with sensory disorders. What factors determine when the child will be sent to a special school for the blind or the deaf?

RESOURCES FOR FURTHER INVESTIGATION

Print Resources

Bess, F. H., & Hall, J. W. (1992). *Screening children for auditory function*. Nashville, TN: Bill Wilkerson Center Press.

Chase, J. B. (1985). Assessment of the visually impaired. *Diagnostique, 10,* 144–160.

Sharpe, M., McNear, D., & McGrew, K. (1996). *Braille assessment inventory*. Columbia, MO: Hawthorne Educational Services.

Technology Resources

AMERICAN COUNCIL OF THE BLIND
www.acb.org
The American Council of the Blind's home page provides general information about the council and resources and information about blindness.

COLOR BLINDNESS
www.aph.org
The official site of the American Printing House for the Blind provides employment information, APHB products, media production, information on cortical visual impairment, accessible testing, and so forth.

AMERICAN PRINTING HOUSE FOR THE BLIND
www.vischeck.com/vischeck/vischeckURL.php
Use this website to see what a person with color blindness sees when looking at colorful materials.

NATIONAL ASSOCIATION OF THE DEAF
www.nad.org
This website of the National Association of the Deaf contains links to a large resource of information for those interested in knowing more about deafness.

GALLAUDET RESEARCH INSTITUTE
gri.gallaudet.edu/index.php
The Gallaudet Research Institute (GRI) researchers gather and analyze data that educators need about the demographic and academic characteristics of deaf and hard-of-hearing populations.

CHAPTER 20

Assessment of Perceptual and Perceptual-Motor Skills

PERCEPTION IS THE PROCESS OF ACQUIRING, INTERPRETING, AND ORGANIZING SENSORY information. Experience, learning, cognitive ability, and personality all influence how one interprets and organizes that sensory information. Perceptual-motor skills refer to the production of motor behavior that is dependent on sensory information.

Educators and psychologists recognize that adequate perception and perceptual-motor skills are important in and of themselves. Thus perception and perceptual-motor tasks are regularly incorporated in tests of intelligence. For example, the Perceptual Organization portion of the Wechsler Intelligence Scale for Children–IV requires visual discrimination, attention to visual detail, sequencing, spatial and nonverbal problem solving, part-to-whole relationships, visual motor coordination, and concentration. Many perceptual and perceptual-motor skills (especially those involving vision, audition, and proprioception) are necessary for school success. For example, the ability to sense how one's body is moving and to correct one's movements based on those sensations is important in athletic and artistic (for example, dancing) endeavors; the ability to coordinate visual information with motor performance is essential in writing and drawing.

Psychologists have long been interested in perceptual distortions and perceptual-motor difficulties for at least two reasons. First, various groups of individuals with disabilities demonstrate distorted perceptions. Some individuals with diagnosed psychoses show distortions in visual, auditory, and olfactory perceptions. Many individuals known to have sustained brain damage have great difficulty writing and copying, regularly reverse letters and other symbols, have distortions in figure-ground perception, and show deficits in attention and focus. Moreover, some educators and psychologists believe that learning and behavior invariably build on and evolve out of early perceptual-motor integration, and any failures in early learning will adversely affect later learning. Thus some professionals in the 1960s and 1980s sought to remediate learning disabilities by first remediating perceptual-motor problems (Barsch, 1966; Doman et al., 1967; Kephart, 1971), visual-perceptual problems (Frostig, 1968), psycholinguistic problems (Kirk & Kirk, 1971), or sensory integration (Johnson & Myklebust, 1967; Ayers, 1981). Although many of these approaches were recognized as lacking merits (see, for example, Ysseldyke & Salvia, 1974) and have subsequently been abandoned because of a lack of evidence of their efficacy, some (such as sensory integration) persist today. Recently, professional interest in process deficits and learning disabilities has gained renewed interest and resulted in much better assessment procedures.

Why Do We Assess Perceptual-Motor Skills?

Perceptual and perceptual-motor skills are assessed for four reasons. In the schools, these tests are used to screen students who may need instruction to remediate or ameliorate perceptual problems before they interfere with school learning. Second, they are also used to assess perceptual and perceptual-motor problems in students who are already experiencing school learning problems. If such students also demonstrate poor perceptual-motor performance, they may also receive special instruction aimed at improving their perceptual abilities. Third, perceptual-motor tests are also often used in assessments to determine a student's eligibility for special education. Students thought to be learning disabled are often given these tests to ascertain whether perceptual problems coexist with learning problems. Moreover, in some states, there is a specific category of "perceptually handicapped"; tests of perceptual-motor skills would likely be used in eligibility decisions for this category. Finally, perceptual-motor tests are often used by clinical psychologists as an adjunct in the diagnosis of brain injury or emotional disturbance.

Specific Tests of Perceptual-Motor Skills

Bender Visual Motor Gestalt Test, Second Edition

The second edition of the Bender Visual Motor Gestalt Test (BVMGT-2; Brannigan & Decker, 2003) is the latest iteration of the test originally developed by Lauretta Bender in 1938. The current version of the BVMGT is a norm-referenced, individually administered test intended to assess the visual-motor integration skills of individuals between the ages of 4 and over 85 years. The BVMGT-2 consists of a copying test and three supplementary subtests. The copying test requires test takers to reproduce designs presented individually on stimulus cards that remain in view. There are two sets of designs, with 13 designs for children under 8 years of age and 12 designs for test takers 8 years of age and older. The two sets have 8 designs that are common to both sets. The test is untimed. The three supplementary tests are a design recall subtest, a motor subtest, and a perception subtest.

Recalling designs. After the designs and the stimulus materials have been copied and removed from sight, test takers are asked to draw as many of designs as they can remember. The subtest is untimed.

Motor test. This test consists of four test items, and each item contains three figures. Test takers are required to connect dots in each figure without lifting their pencil, erasing, or tilting their paper. Four minutes are allowed to complete the subtest.

Perception test. This test consists of ten items that require a test taker to match a design in a multiple-choice array to a stimulus design. Four minutes are allowed to complete the task.

Scores

Each copied and recalled design is scored holistically on a 5-point scale: 0 = no resemblance to the stimulus; 1 = slight or vague resemblance to the stimulus; 2 = some or moderate resemblance to the stimulus; 3 = strong or close resemblance to the stimulus; and 4 = nearly perfect. Examples of each score are presented for each design in the test manual. Each figure on the motor subtest and each item on the perception subtest are scored pass or fail. Raw scores from the copying and recall subtests can be converted to standard scores (mean = 100; standard deviation = 15) and percentiles; 90 percent and 95 percent confidence intervals are available for standard scores. Percentiles are available for the motor and perception subtests.

Norms

The normative sample consists of 4,000 individuals between 4 and over 85 years of age. Individuals with limited English proficiency, severe sensory or communication deficits, traumatic brain injury, and severe behavioral or emotional disorders were excluded from the normative sample. Students placed in special education for more than 50 percent of the school day were also excluded from the normative sample. About 5 percent of the school-age population was included in regular education classrooms. Thus the normative sample systematically underrepresents the proportion of students with disabilities, the population with whom the BVMGT-2 is intended to be used. For students of preschool and school age, the norms appear generally representative in terms of race/ethnicity, educational level of parents, and geographic region for each age group.

Reliability

Corrected split-half correlations were used to estimate the internal consistency of the copying test. For the 14 coefficients for students between 4 and 20 years of age, only four were less than .90, and they were in the .80s. Thus the BVMGT-2 usually has sufficient reliability for use in making important educational decisions.

Stability of the copying and recall tests was estimated by test-retest using the standard scores of 213 individuals in four age groups. There were 39 students in the 5- to 7-year-old group and 62 students in the 8- to 17-year-old group. The obtained correlation for the younger group was .77, and the correlation for the older group was .76. Thus the BVMGT-2 is insufficiently stable to use in making important educational decisions.

Interscorer agreement was assessed in two ways. Five experienced scorers scored 30 protocols independently. Correlations among scorers for copied designs ranged from .83 to .94; correlations for recalled designs were adequate, ranging from .94 to .97. The agreement between the scoring of 60 protocols by one experienced and one inexperienced scorer was also examined. The correlation for copied designs was .85, whereas the correlation for recalled designs was .92. Thus the scoring of copied designs may not consistently have sufficient reliability for use in making important educational decisions on behalf of students.

No reliability data of any kind are presented for the motor or perception subtests.

Validity

Evidence for the internal validity of the copying test of the BVMGT-2 comes from three sources. First, the items were carefully developed to assess the ability to reproduce designs. Second, factor analysis of test items using the normative sample suggests that a single factor underlies copying test performance. Third, copying test performance varies with age in expected ways: It increases sharply around age 7, continues to increase, though less rapidly, to about age 15, where it plateaus until around age 40, where it begins to decline. No evidence of content validity is presented for the recall, motor, or perception subtests.

Criterion-related validity was examined in several studies. In one study, the Koppitz[1] scoring system was compared to the system used by the BVMGT-2. The responses of 76 individuals from the normative sample were scored using the two systems. The obtained correlation between scores for the copied designs was .70; the correlation between the Koppitz score for copied designs and the BVMGT-2 score for recalled designs was .49. Another study examined the relationship between the BVMGT-2 and the Beery-Buktenica Developmental Test of Visual-Motor Integration (DTVMI) with 75 individuals between the ages of 4 and 17. The obtained correlation between the copying score on the BVMGT-2 and the DTVMI was .55, whereas the obtained correlation between the recall score and the DTVMI was .32.

Other studies examined the relationship between copying and recall on the BVMGT-2 and academic achievement. Obtained correlations with the Woodcock-Johnson Psychoeducational Battery, Achievement Battery–III for the copying test ranged from .22 (with Basic Reading) to .43 (with Math Reasoning), and obtained correlations for the recall subtest ranged from .21 (with Basic Reading) to .38 (with Broad Math). Obtained correlations with the Wechsler Individual Achievement Test–II for the copying test ranged from .18 (with Oral Language)

---

[1] Koppitz developed a scoring system and norms for the original Bender VMGT in 1963. Her scoring system became the standard way to score the test in school and clinical settings.

to .42 (with Written Language), and the obtained correlations for the recall sub-test ranged from .18 (with Written Language) to .32 (with Math).

The relationship between BVMGT-2 scores and IQs was also examined. In one study, the Stanford-Binet Intelligence Scale, Fifth Edition, was used as the criterion measure. Obtained correlations for the copying test ranged from .47 with verbal IQ to .51 with nonverbal IQ; obtained correlations for the recall subtest ranged from .44 with verbal IQ to .47 with nonverbal IQ. In another study, copying and recall scores were correlated with IQs from the WISC-III. Obtained correlations for the copying test ranged from .31 with Verbal IQ to .62 with Performance IQ; obtained correlations for the recall subtest ranged from .16 with VIQ to .32 with PIQ. A third study with the WAIS-III had similar findings.

Finally, evidence is presented for differential performance by groups of individuals with disabilities. The mean of individuals with mental retardation, learning disabilities in reading, learning disabilities in math, learning disabilities in written language, autism, and attention deficit hyperactivity disorder are all significantly lower than the mean of nondisabled individuals on both the copying and the recall tests. Gifted students earn significantly higher scores on the copying and recall tests.

No evidence of validity is presented for motor or perception subtests.

Summary

The BVMGT-2 is a norm-referenced, individually administered test intended to assess an individual's ability to copy and recall geometric designs as well as to connect dots and perform match to sample tasks with such designs. The norms for school-age persons appear generally representative, although they exclude some of the very individuals with whom the test is intended to be used. No reliability data of any kind are presented for the motor or perception subtests. The copying test appears generally to have adequate internal consistency, but there is no information about the internal consistency of the recall subtest. The copying and recall tests have poor stability and may have inadequate interscorer agreement. Evidence for the content validity of the copying test is adequate, but the correlations to establish criterion-related validity are too low to be compelling. Although the copying and recall tests of the BVMGT-2 can discriminate groups of individuals known to have disabilities, no evidence is presented regarding these tests' accuracy in categorizing undiagnosed individuals. Reliability and validity evidence for the motor and perception subtests are absent; these subtests should not be used in educational decision making and are of unknown value in clinical situations.

Developmental Test of Visual Perception, Second Edition (DTVP-2)

The second edition of the Developmental Test of Visual Perception (DTVP-2; Hammill, Pearson, & Voress, 1993) is an individually administered, norm-referenced test designed for use with children between the ages of 4 and 10 years. The second edition of the DTVP is different in several ways from the first edition, published in the 1960s. Two new composite scores have been added (motor-reduced perception and visual-motor integration), the age range of the test has been extended to age 10 years, and the technical characteristics (and their reporting) have been substantially improved.

Subtests

Requiring 30 to 60 minutes to administer, the DTVP-2 has eight subtests, all of which have demonstration items.

Eye-Hand Coordination   Four items require children to draw a line on a band that progressively narrows and curves from item 1 to item 4. Each band is segmented, and the child receives a point for each segment in which performance is acceptable. Thus, although there are only four items, the child may earn up to 52 points for staying on the band and not picking up the pencil.

Position in Space   Twenty-five items require children to match a figure from an array containing the same figure in three to five different rotations.

Copying   Twenty items require a child to copy a sample figure of increasing difficulty in a 1.75-inch box. Each drawing is awarded 0, 1, or 2 points on the basis of clear scoring standards.

Figure-Ground   Eighteen items require children to identify two or more figures embedded in a stimulus composed of overlapping and overdrawn figures. Each item is scored pass (1) or fail (0). For example, in item 10 of this subtest, the child must find all of the figures shown in the boxed area that are included in the stimulus drawing at the top of the item.

Spatial Relations   Ten items require children to connect some dots in an array of dots so as to reproduce a stimulus pattern.

Visual Closure   In these 20 items, children are shown a stimulus picture and are required to select (from a multiple-choice array) the option that could match the stimulus picture if that option were completed. The child does not need to draw the stimulus from the option but needs only to recognize the one option that could be completed.

Visual-Motor Speed   On this timed subtest, children are shown four stimuli: large circle, small circle, large square, and small square. The large circle contains two parallel horizontal lines, and the small square contains two diagonal lines connecting opposite corners. Below these stimuli are 128 figures (32 large circles, 32 small circles, and so on, in random order) that do not contain the internal lines. Children must add the lines to as many other appropriate figures as they can in one minute. One point is awarded for each figure correctly completed without drawing outside the figure.

Form Constancy   The 20 items in this subtest each contain a stimulus (a geometric form) and an array of response options. For each item, children are required to identify the two options that are the same shape as the stimulus. However, correct response options may differ from the stimulus in size, rotation, color, or shading.

Scores

All subtests except Visual-Motor Speed have ceiling rules. Subtest raw scores may be converted to age equivalents, percentiles, and normalized standard scores (mean = 10; standard deviation = 3). Subtest standard scores can be summed and converted to three different composite standard scores (each with a mean of 100 and standard deviation of 15): general visual perception quotient (based on all eight subtests); motor-reduced visual perception quotient (based on the four subtests that require only a pointing response); and visual-motor integration quotient (based on the four subtests that require drawing).

Norms

To obtain a normative sample, the authors of the DTVP-2 asked those who had purchased other Pro-Ed perceptual-motor tests to test children in their immediate geographic vicinity. The resulting sample of 1,972 children from 12 states appears representative of the United States (1990 census) in terms of race, ethnicity, gender, residence (urban/rural), geographic area, and handedness. Approximately 3 percent of the sample were children with disabilities. The number of children at each age appears to be more than sufficient, except for 4-year-olds.[2]

Reliability

Alphas for individual subtests range from .80 (Figure-Ground at three ages) to .97 (Spatial Relations at two ages). Of the 56 subtest-by-age alphas, 30 are in the .80s, and 20 equal or exceed .90. Thus individual subtests generally do not have sufficient reliability for making important educational decisions for individual students. The alphas of the three composites are all excellent, ranging from .43 to .98. Similar patterns of results were found for stability. Eighty-eight students, ranging in age from 4 through 10 years, were tested and retested two weeks later.[3] Reliabilities for subtests range from .71 to .86; stabilities for the composites range from .89 to .95. Thus the composites are quite stable. Finally, interscorer agreement, estimated from the protocols of 88 students, is excellent for subtests and composites.

Validity

The selection of specific subtests is based on classic research and theory in visual perception, and careful and thoughtful item development closely approximates the theoretical constructs on which the subtests are based. Thus there is a strong

---

[2] Raw scores are converted to derived scores by six-month intervals. For example, the scores of children from 4-0 through 4-5 are converted using one table; scores of children from 4-6 through 4-11 are converted using a different table. The number of children in whole-year groups (for example, 4-0 through 4-11) is reported, not the number of children in each half-year group. Nonetheless, assuming even a 60 percent–40 percent division of children into the two age subgroups, all age subgroups would have at least 100 children, except for the 4-year-old subgroups, each of which would have around 50 students.

[3] The authors report stabilities with the effects of age correctly controlled.

rationale for the DTVP-2's content validity. Strong evidence of criterion-related validity is also presented in the manual. DTVP-2 scores were correlated with scores from the Motor-Free Visual Perception Test (MFVPT) and the Developmental Test of Visual-Motor Integration (VMI; a test that requires copying, discussed in the following section). The correlations between the DTVP-2 subtests and these measures range from .27 to .95. As should occur, DTVP-2 subtests that have a motor component generally correlate more highly with the VMI, whereas subtests without a perceptual component generally correlate more highly with the MFVPT. This pattern is even more pronounced for the composite scores of the DTVP-2.

Some evidence of construct validity is provided by the DTVP-2's relationship with age (as should be expected). More compelling are the results of factor-analytic studies suggesting that two related factors, approximately the same as motor-reduced visual perception and visual-motor integration, underlie the test. In addition, the DTVP-2 appears to differentiate between groups of children known to be normal and those known to be below average in visual-perceptual ability. Finally, the DTVP-2 has low correlations with cognitive measures, which supports the notion that visual perception is a discrete ability.

Summary

The revised Developmental Test of Visual Perception is an individually administered, norm-referenced test suitable for use with children between the ages of 4 and 10 years. The DTVP-2 has eight subtests: (1) Eye-Hand Coordination, (2) Position in Space, (3) Copying, (4) Figure-Ground, (5) Spatial Relations, (6) Visual Closure, (7) Visual-Motor Speed, and (8) Form Constancy. Raw scores can be converted to age equivalents, percentiles, or normalized standard scores; subtest standard scores can be combined to form three composite scores: general visual perception quotient, motor-reduced visual perception quotient, and visual-motor integration quotient. The second edition of the DTVP represents a significant improvement over the first edition in all technical aspects. The norms appear representative, the test is internally consistent and stable, and the test has good interscorer reliability. The considerable amount of information presented by the authors strongly suggests that the DTVP-2 is a valid measure of visual perception.

Developmental Test of Visual-Motor Integration (Beery VMI)

The Developmental Test of Visual-Motor Integration (Beery VMI; Beery & Beery, 2004) is a set of geometric forms to be copied with paper and pencil. The authors contend that the set of forms is arranged in a developmental sequence from easy to more difficult. The Beery VMI is designed to assess the extent to which individuals can integrate their visual and motor abilities. The authors state that the primary purpose of the Beery VMI is to "help identify, through early screening, significant difficulties that some children have integrating, or coordinating, their visual-perceptual and motor (finger and hand movement) abilities" (p. 9). Beery defines visual-motor integration as the degree to which visual perception and finger-hand movements are well coordinated (2004, p. 12). He indicates that, if a child performs poorly on the Beery VMI, it could be because he or she has adequate visual-perceptual and motor-coordination abilities but has not yet learned to integrate, or coordinate, these two domains. Two supplemental tests, the Beery VMI Visual Perception Test and the Beery VMI Motor Coordination Test, are provided to enable users to attempt to sort out the relative contribution of visual and motor difficulties to poor performance on measures of visual-motor integration.

There are two versions of the Beery VMI. The full Beery VMI is intended for use with individuals from age 2 years to adult. It contains all 30 VMI forms, including the initial 3 that are both imitated and copied directly. The short Beery VMI contains 21 items and is intended for use with children age 2 to 7 years. Items for the supplemental tests are identical to items for the full VMI. The VMI may be administered individually or to groups. The test can be administered and scored by a classroom teacher and usually takes about 15 minutes. Scoring is relatively easy, because the designs are scored pass-fail, and individual protocols can be scored in a few minutes.

Scores

The manual for the Beery VMI includes two pages of scoring information for each of the 30 designs. The child's reproduction of each design is scored pass-fail, and criteria for successful performance are clearly articulated. A raw score for the total test is obtained by adding the number of reproductions copied correctly before the test taker has three consecutive failures. Normative tables provided in the manual allow the examiner to convert the total raw score to a developmental age equivalent, grade equivalent, standard score, scaled score, stanine, or percentile.

Norms

The Beery VMI was standardized in the United States five times since its initial development in 1967. The test was originally standardized on 1,030 children in rural, urban, and suburban Illinois. In 1981 the test was cross-validated with samples of children "from various ethnic and income groups in California" (Beery, 1982, p. 10). In 1988 the test was again cross-validated with an unspecified group of students "from several Eastern, Northern and Southern states" (Beery, 1989, p. 10). The 1988 norm sample is not representative of the U.S. population with respect to ethnicity and residence of the students. The Beery VMI and its supplemental tests were normed in 2003 on 2,512 children from 2 to 18 years of age, selected from five major sections of the United States. The sample was selected by contacting school psychologists and learning-disabilities specialists chosen at random from membership lists for major professional organizations. Those who indicated a willingness to participate tested the subjects. A total of 23 child care, preschool, private, and public schools participated. Although the norms collectively were representative of the U.S. population, cross-tabulations are shown only for age by gender, ethnicity, socioeconomic status, and geographic region. Thus we do not know whether, for example, all the African American students were from middle-SES families, from the East, and so on.

Reliability

The authors report the results of studies of internal consistency on an unspecified sample of individuals. Internal consistency ranges from .76 to .91, with an average of .85. Interscorer reliability is .92 for the Beery VMI, .98 for the Beery visual supplement, and .93 for the motor supplement. Test-retest reliability was assessed by administering the Beery VMI to 122 children between the ages of 6 and 10 years, in general education public school classrooms. The sample is not further defined. Test-retest reliability is .87 for the Beery VMI, .84 for the visual supplement, and .83 for the motor supplement. The Beery VMI has adequate reliability for screening purposes.

Validity

The authors contend that the Beery VMI has good content validity because of the way in which the items were selected. Evidence for validity based on internal structure comes from comparing results of performance on the Beery VMI to performance on the copying subtest of the Developmental Test of Visual Perception–2 and the drawing subtest of the Wide Range Assessment of Visual-Motor Abilities. The sample is described only as 122 students attending public schools. Correlations were moderate.

The authors provide evidence for validity based on internal structure by (1) generating a set of hypotheses about what performance on the test would look like if it were measuring what is intended and (2) providing answers to the hypotheses. They show that the abilities measured by the Beery VMI are developmental, that they are related to one another, and that the supplements measure a part, but not the whole, of the abilities measured by the Beery VMI. They also show that performance on the Beery VMI is related more closely to nonverbal than to verbal aspects of intelligence, that performance on the test correlates moderately with performance on academic achievement tests, and that test performance is related to disabling conditions.

Summary

The Beery VMI is designed to assess the integration of visual and motor skills by asking a child to copy geometric designs. As is the case with other such tests, the behavior sampling is limited, although the 30 items on the VMI certainly provide a larger sample of behavior than is provided by the 9 items on the BVMGT. The VMI has relatively high reliability and validity in comparison with other measures of perceptual-motor skills.

Test of Visual-Motor Integration (TVMI)

The Test of Visual-Motor Integration (TVMI; Hammill, Pearson, & Voress, 1996) measures the ability to relate visual stimuli to motor responses in an accurate, appropriate manner. The test is intended for use with children and adolescents aged 4 to 17 years, and takes about 15 to 30 minutes to administer. The authors identify four uses of this test: "(a) to document the presence and degree of visual-motor difficulties in individual children, (b) to identify candidates for referral, (c) to verify the effectiveness of intervention programs, and (d) to serve as a research tool" (1996, p. 3).

The 30 TVMI items each require a student to copy a design. The number of items administered depends on the student's age and proficiency in copying designs. For students younger than 11 years, the test is always started with the first design and continued until the student scores a 0 on three items in a row. Students over 11 years of age begin with item 13 and continue until they earn a score of 0 on three items in a row.

Scores

Students earn scores of 0, 1, 2, or 3, depending on the quality of their copies of designs. Examples of how to score the test are included in the manual. Raw scores on the TVMI can be transformed to age equivalents, percentiles, and standard scores.

Norms

The TVMI was standardized on 2,478 children in 13 states. Data were collected in 1992 and 1995. Students were tested by 14 examiners, and the sample was stratified for age only. Tables in the manual compare the makeup of the standardization sample to that of the 1990 census on gender, urban/rural residence, race, geographic region, ethnicity, income, educational attainment of parents, and age. There are cross-tabulations for age only, so we do not know, for example, where the males came from.

Reliability

The authors report the internal-consistency reliability of the TVMI, based on the performance of the entire norm sample. The internal-consistency coefficient is .91. Test-retest reliability is based on the performance of 88 students, ages 4 through 10 years, attending a private school in Austin, Texas. The students are not described. The test-retest coefficient is .80. Interscorer reliability was established by having two people score 40 protocols. A coefficient of .96 was attained.

Validity

There are two important validity questions: Does this test measure visual-motor integration? Does it predict performance in school? In selecting the content for this test, the authors picked designs from other measures of visual-motor integration. To establish criterion-related validity, they gave it to a limited sample of students. The TVMI, MFVPT, and VMI were given to 99 "students with various neurologic impairments and autism" attending a private school in Pennsylvania. The group is not described further. The TVMI correlates .67 with the MFVPT and .95 with the VMI.

In providing evidence of construct validity, the authors argue and demonstrate that the test should (1) correlate more highly with age for younger than for older students, (2) show a low relationship to measures of school achievement,

(3) correlate moderately well with broad-based measures of intelligence, and (4) differentiate groups of people known to be average and below average in visual integration ability. Evidence is based on the performance of limited samples. The TVMI does measure the same skills as other measures of visual-motor integration, but performance on the test does not predict performance in school.

Summary

In the TVMI, students are asked to copy geometric designs. The sample of behavior is limited to 30 items (6 more than on the VMI). Evidence of reliability and validity is very limited.

Dilemmas in Current Practice

The assessment of perceptual-motor skills is a difficult undertaking. Without an adequate definition of perceptual-motor skills and with few technically adequate tests to rely on, the assessor is in a bind. Usually, the best way to cope with these problems is not to test. If assessments cannot be done properly or are not educationally necessary, they should not be conducted. Assessment of perceptual-motor skills usually falls into this category. We encourage those who are concerned about development of perceptual-motor skills to engage in direct systematic observation in the natural environment in which these skills actually occur. After all, when students cannot print legibly, we do not need to know that they have difficulty copying geometric designs.

Authors' Viewpoint

At the onset, it is important to realize that, when test authors write about perceptual-motor skills, they are talking only about a very small subset of those skills—visual perception and fine hand movements. These tests do not address auditory or proprioceptive perception, and they do not address gross motor skills or fine motor

skills other than manual ones. It is also important to recognize that much of the theoretical importance of perceptual-motor assessment is not well founded. First, the specific mechanisms by which perceptual-motor development affects reading are seldom specified and never validated. Thus theorists may opine that perceptual-motor skills are necessary for reading, but they do not specify what those skills are and how they affect reading. Other than focusing on print material and turning pages, the motor component of reading is unclear. Second, it is based on an incorrect interpretation of the correlation between achievement and perceptual-motor skills. For example, it is well established that poor readers also tend to have poorly developed perceptual-motor skills. However, it is not poor perceptual-motor skills that cause poor reading. Rather, it is poor reading that causes poor perceptual-motor skills. Perceptual-motor skills improve with practice, and learning academics provides that practice. Thus good readers of material written in English typically develop good left-to-right tracking because they practice tracking from left to right as they read.

SUMMARY

Educational personnel typically assess perceptual-motor skills for prevention, remediation, or differential diagnosis. First, the preventive use of perceptual-motor tests to identify children who demonstrate perceptual-motor difficulties is based on the assumption that, without special perceptual-motor training, these children will experience academic difficulties. Second, tests are used to try to ascertain whether perceptual-motor difficulties are already causing academic difficulties and must therefore be remediated. Third, perceptual-motor tests are used diagnostically to identify brain injury or emotional difficulties.

In this chapter, we reviewed the most commonly used perceptual-motor tests. Most lack the reliability needed in making important instructional decisions. Likewise, they lack demonstrated validity; we simply cannot say with much certainty that the tests measure what they purport to measure.

The practice of perceptual-motor assessment is linked directly to perceptual-motor training or remediation. There is an appalling lack of empirical evidence to support the claim that specific perceptual-motor training facilitates the acquisition of academic skills or improves the chances of academic success. Perceptual-motor training will improve perceptual-motor functioning. When the purpose of perceptual-motor assessment is to identify specific important perceptual and motor behaviors that children have not yet mastered, some of the devices reviewed in this chapter may provide useful information; performance on individual items will indicate the extent to which specific skills (for example, walking along a straight line) have been mastered. There is no support for the use of perceptual-motor tests in planning programs designed to facilitate academic learning or to remediate academic difficulties.

QUESTIONS FOR CHAPTER REVIEW

1. Identify the major difficulties in conducting perceptual-motor skill assessment.

2. Discuss the rationale for using perceptual-motor tests. Discuss the degree to which the rationale is supported by research.

3. Assume that you have to assess a student's perceptual-motor skills. How would you go about doing this in a way that would be appropriate?

4. Homer, age 6-3, takes two visual-perceptual-motor tests, the Developmental Test of Visual Perception–2 and the Developmental Test of Visual-Motor Integration. On the DTVP-2, he earns a developmental age of 5-6, and on the VMI, he earns a developmental age of 7-4. Give two different explanations for the discrepancy between the scores.

5. Performance on the Bender Visual Motor Gestalt Test–2 is used as a criterion in the differential identification of children as brain injured, perceptually handicapped, or emotionally disturbed. Why must the examiner use caution in interpreting and using test results for these purposes?

PROJECT

Using information found in the text, write a summary for one test used in the assessment of perceptual-motor skills. Upon completion, compare your summary with the text summary. Then go to the most recent edition of the *Mental Measurements Yearbook*, and compare and contrast your summary with the review of the test you selected. If your summary differs from the review, did the reviewer use information and standards different from those that you used?

RESOURCES FOR FURTHER INVESTIGATION

Print Resources

Arter, J., & Jenkins, J. R. (1979). Differential diagnosis—prescriptive teaching: A critical appraisal. *Review of Educational Research, 49,* 517–556.

Koppitz, E. M. (1975). *The Bender-Gestalt Test for Young Children. Volume II: Research and application, 1963–1973.* New York: Grune & Stratton.

Hammill, D., Pearson, N., & Voress, J. (1996). *Test of Visual-Motor Integration.* Austin, TX: Pro-Ed.

Mann, L. (1971). Perceptual training revisited: The training of nothing at all. *Rehabilitation Literature, 32,* 322–335.

Technology Resources

HISTORICAL PERSPECTIVE ON THE ROLE OF PERCEPTION IN THE CONCEPTUALIZATION OF LEARNING DISABILITIES
www.nrcld.org/html/information/articles/ldsummit/hallahan3.html

This site provides an excellent historical perspective on the role played by perception in early formulations of learning disability.

WHY SENSORY INTEGRATION DISORDER IS A DUBIOUS DIAGNOSIS
www.quackwatch.org/01QuackeryRelatedTopics/sid.html

This site documents the lack of well-designed scientific studies to demonstrate that sensory integration disorder is a disorder, and whether the treatments currently prescribed are effective or necessary. Numerous references are provided.

CHAPTER 21

Assessment of Academic Achievement with Multiple-Skill Devices

ACHIEVEMENT TESTS ARE THE MOST FREQUENTLY USED TESTS IN EDUCATIONAL SETTINGS. Multiple-skill achievement tests evaluate knowledge and understanding in several curricular areas, such as reading and math. These tests are intended to assess the extent to which students have profited from schooling and other life experiences, compared with other students of the same age or grade. Consequently, most achievement tests are norm referenced, although some are criterion-referenced or performance measures. Norm-referenced, criterion-referenced, and performance tests are designed in consultation with subject-matter experts and are believed to reflect national curricula and national curricular trends in general.

Achievement tests can be classified along several dimensions; perhaps the most important one describes their specificity and density of content. Diagnostic achievement tests have dense content; they have many more items to assess specific skills and concepts, and allow finer analyses to pinpoint specific strengths and weaknesses in academic development. Tests with fewer items per skill allow comparisons among test takers but do not have enough items to pinpoint students' strengths and weaknesses. These tests may still be useful for estimating a student's current general level of functioning in comparison with other students, and they estimate the extent to which an individual has acquired the skills and concepts that other students of the same age have acquired.

Another important dimension is the number of students who can be tested at once. Achievement tests are designed to be given to groups of students or to individual students. Generally, group tests require students to read and either write or mark answers; individually administered tests may require an examiner to read questions to a student and may allow students to respond orally. The primary advantage of individually administered tests is that they afford examiners the opportunity to observe students working and solving problems. Therefore, examiners can glean valuable qualitative information in addition to the quantitative information that scores provide. Finally, a group test may be appropriately given to one student at a time, but individual tests should not be given to a group of students.

Table 21.1 shows the different categories of achievement tests. The Stanford Achievement Test (SAT), for example, is both a norm-referenced and a criterion-referenced (objective-referenced), group-administered screening test that samples skill development in many content areas. The Stanford Diagnostic Reading Test (SDRT), detailed in the chapter "Assessment of Reading," is both a norm-referenced, group-administered test and a criterion-referenced, individually administered diagnostic test that samples skill development strengths and weaknesses in the single skill of reading. The SDRT is intended to provide a classroom teacher with a more detailed analysis of students' strengths and weaknesses in reading, which may be of assistance in program planning and evaluation.

The most obvious advantage of multiple-skill achievement tests is that they can provide teachers with data showing the extent to which their pupils have acquired information and skills. By using group-administered, multiple-skill batteries, teachers can obtain a considerable amount of information in a relatively short time.

TABLE 21.1	Categories of Achievement Tests			
	Norm Referenced		**Criterion Referenced**	
	Single Skill	*Multiple Skill*	*Single Skill*	*Multiple Skill*
Group-Administered Screening Devices	Gates-MacGinitie*	California Achievement Tests* Metropolitan Achievement Tests (Survey Battery) Stanford Achievement Test Series Terra Nova–2	None	California Achievement Tests* Iowa Tests of Basic Skills Metropolitan Achievement Tests (Instructional Batteries) Stanford Achievement Test Series
Individually Administered Screening Devices	Test of Mathematical Abilities–2*	Kaufman Test of Educational Achievement* Peabody Individual Achievement Test Wide Range Achievement Test 3 Woodcock-Johnson Psychoeducational Battery–III Kaufman Assessment Battery for Children* Wechsler Individual Achievement Test–II	None	

TABLE 21.1	Categories of Achievement Tests (*cont.*)			
	Norm Referenced		**Criterion Referenced**	
	Single Skill	*Multiple Skill*	*Single Skill*	*Multiple Skill*
Group-Administered Diagnostic Devices	Group Reading Assessment and Diagnostic Evaluation Group Mathematics Assessment and Diagnostic Evaluation Stanford Diagnostic Reading Test–4* Stanford Diagnostic Mathematics Test	None		None
Individually Administered Diagnostic Devices	Gray Oral Reading Test–4 Gates-McKillop-Horowitz Reading Diagnostic Tests* Woodcock Reading Mastery Tests–Revised Test of Written Language–3 Test of Written Spelling–4 Test of Reading Comprehension–3* Formal Reading Inventory* STAR Reading STAR Math Test of Language Development–I:3 Test of Language Development–P:3 Test of Adolescent Language–2*	Diagnostic Achievement Battery–3*	Key Math* Stanford Diagnostic Reading Test–4* Standardized Reading Inventory *	

*An asterisk indicates a test reviewed on the web but not included in this book.

Considerations for Selecting a Test

In selecting a multiple-skill achievement test, teachers must consider four factors: content validity, stimulus-response modes, the standards used in his or her state, and relevant norms. First, teachers must evaluate evidence for content validity, the most important kind of validity for achievement tests. Many multiple-skill tests have general content validity: The tests measure important concepts and skills that are generally part of most curricula. This validity makes their content suitable for assessing general attainment. However, if a test is to be used to assess the extent to which students have profited from school instruction—that is, to measure student achievement—more than general content validity is required: The test must match the instruction provided. Tests that do not match instruction lack content validity, and decisions based on such tests should be restricted. When making decisions about content validity for students with disabilities, educators must consider the extent to which the student has had an opportunity to learn the content of the test. Many students with disabilities are assigned to a curriculum (often a functional curriculum) that differs from the curriculum to which nondisabled students are exposed.

Second, educators who use achievement tests for students with disabilities need to consider whether the stimulus-response modes of subtests may be exceptionally difficult for students with physical or motor problems. Tests that are timed may be inappropriately difficult for students whose reading or motor difficulties cause them to take more time on specific tasks. (Many of these issues were described in greater detail in the chapter "Adapting Tests to Accommodate Students with Disabilities.")

Third, educators must consider the state education standards for the state in which they work. In doing so, they should examine the extent to which the achievement test they select measures the content of their state standards.

Fourth, educational professionals must evaluate the adequacy of each test's norms by asking whether the normative group is composed of the kinds of individuals with whom they wish to compare their students. If a test is used to estimate general attainment, a representative sample of students from across the nation is preferred. However, if a test is used to estimate achievement in a school system, local norms are probably better. Finally, teachers should examine the extent to which a total test and its components have the reliability necessary for making decisions about what students have learned.

Why Do We Assess Academic Achievement?

The very term *screening device* reflects the major purpose of achievement tests. These tests are used most often to screen students, to identify those who demonstrate low-level, average, or high-level attainment in comparison with their peers. Achievement tests provide a global estimate of academic skill development and may be used to identify individual students for whom educational intervention is necessary, either in the form of remediation (for those who demonstrate relatively low-level skill development) or in the form of academic enrichment (for those who exhibit exceptionally high-level skill development). However, screening tests have limited behavior samples and lower requirements for reliability. Therefore, students who are identified with screening tests should be further assessed with diagnostic tests to verify their need for educational intervention.

Although multiple-skill, group-administered achievement tests are usually considered to be screening devices, they are occasionally used in eligibility or entitlement decisions. In principle, such use is generally inappropriate, although it may be justifiable and even desirable when the group tests (for example, the

Stanford Achievement Test Series or the Metropolitan Achievement Tests) contain behavior samples that are more complete than those contained in some individually administered tests of achievement used for placement (such as the Wide Range Achievement Test 3 [WRAT3]). Use of an achievement test with a better behavior sample is desirable if the tester goes beyond the scores earned to examine performance on specific test items.

Multiple-skill achievement tests may also be used for progress evaluation. Most school districts have routine testing programs at various grade levels to evaluate the extent to which pupils in their schools are progressing in comparison with state standards. Scores on achievement tests provide communities, school boards, and parents with an index of the quality of schooling. Schools and the teachers within those schools are often subject to question when pupils fail to demonstrate expected progress.

Finally, achievement tests are used to evaluate the relative effectiveness of alternative curricula. For instance, Brown School may choose to use the Scott, Foresman Reading Series in third grade, whereas Green School decides to use the Lippincott Reading Program. If school personnel can assume that children were at relatively comparable reading levels when they entered the third grade, then achievement tests may be administered at the end of the year to ascertain the relative effectiveness of the Scott, Foresman and the Lippincott programs. Educators must, of course, avoid many assumptions in such evaluations (for example, that the quality of individual teachers and the instructional environment are comparable in the two schools) and many research pitfalls if comparative evaluation is to have meaning.

Specific Tests of Academic Achievement

The remainder of this chapter addresses specific multiple-skill devices and examines six popular group-administered, multiple-skill batteries: the California Achievement Tests (CAT/6); the Iowa Tests of Basic Skills; the Metropolitan Achievement Tests, Eighth Edition (MAT8); the Stanford Achievement Test Series; the Terra Nova, Second Edition; two individually administered, multiple-skill batteries (the Peabody Individual Achievement Test–Revised–Normative Update [PIAT-R-NU] and the Wide Range Achievement Test 3 [WRAT3]); and one individually administered, norm-referenced measure that is co-normed with intelligence tests (the Wechsler Individual Achievement Test, Second Edition [WIAT-2]). Later chapters discuss both screening and diagnostic tests that are devoted to specific content areas, such as reading and mathematics. In the chapter "Assessment of Intelligence: Individual Tests," we included the Achievement Battery of the Woodcock-Johnson Psychoeducational Battery–III.

Iowa Tests of Basic Skills

There are four forms of the Iowa Tests of Basic Skills (ITBS): Forms K and L, first published in 1994; Form M, published in 1996; and Form A, published in 2001. Our review focuses on Form A. Table 21.2 lists the names of the subtests that make up the ITBS at each grade level. Form A is published in a complete battery booklet (which includes from 5 to 15 subtests, depending on the level);

TABLE 21.2 Testing Levels, Batteries, and Times for the ITBS, Form A

Level	Battery	Time
5	Complete	2:00
6	Complete	2:43
7	Complete	4:25
	Core	3:05
	Survey	1:25
8	Complete	4:25
	Core	3:05
	Survey	1:25
9	Complete	6:11
	Core	4:16
	Survey	1:30
10–14	Complete	5:26
	Core	3:31
	Survey	1:30

in machine-scorable complete, core, and survey battery booklets for Level 9 (grade 3); in a core battery for Levels 7 and 8; and in a survey battery booklet (3 subtests) for Levels 7–8 (grades 1–2) and Levels 10–14 (grades 4–8). Testing times are shown in Table 21.2. Note that the survey battery takes about 1½ hours to administer, whereas the complete battery can take more than 6 hours to administer.

The ITBS was designed to provide information about individual student competence in the basic school subject-matter areas. The authors state three main purposes of the test: (1) to obtain information for supporting instructional decisions, (2) to report individual progress to students and parents, and (3) to evaluate the progress of groups of students. The authors of the ITBS stress the fact that the test was designed to measure critical-thinking skills (often referred to as higher-order thinking skills) that are more complex than the recall of factual material. The test is designed to assess the complex skills involved in interpretation, inference, classification, analysis, and making comparisons. Following are the subtests of the ITBS and the skills they assess.

Subtests

Vocabulary   At Levels 5 and 6, this standalone subtest measures students' listening vocabulary. Reading vocabulary is assessed at Levels 7 and 8. At the highest levels, students' skills in identifying words in context are assessed.

Word Analysis   This subtest is available only at the levels of the test intended for use in kindergarten through fourth grade. At the lower levels, the subtest provides information about skill development in letter recognition and letter-sound correspondence. At the higher levels, this subtest assesses students' knowledge of letter-sound relationships and includes more complicated word-building tasks.

Reading/Reading Comprehension   At Level 6, this subtest assesses word recognition, word attack, and literal and inferential comprehension. At higher levels, the subtest assesses skill development in constructing factual meaning (understanding factual information and deducing the literal meaning of words or phrases); constructing inferential/interpretive meaning (drawing conclusions, making inferences or deducing meaning, inferring feelings, interpreting nonliteral language); and analyzing and generalizing passage meaning (determining main ideas, identifying author's viewpoint, analyzing style and structure). This subtest is divided into two sections in order to reduce student fatigue.

Listening   This subtest, included at Levels 5–9, assesses skill in comprehending literal meaning and inferential meaning, following directions, sustaining listening, predicting outcomes, and understanding visual and sequential relationships.

Language   At Levels 5 and 6, this subtest measures students' understanding of prepositions, singular versus plural words, comparative versus superlative modifiers, spatial-directional language, verb tense, and operational language. At Levels 7 and 8, students correct spelling, punctuation, capitalization, and usage errors in written passages that teachers read aloud. At Levels 9–14, spelling, capitalization, punctuation, and usage and written expression are assessed separately. In the Spelling, Punctuation, and Capitalization sections, students must read and identify corresponding errors in written sentences. In the Usage and Expression section, students must identify errors in usage, indicate the most appropriate ways to organize and express ideas, and understand appropriate placement of particular sentences in a paragraph (beginning, transitional, and ending sentences).

Mathematics   At Levels 5 and 6, this subtest measures student understanding of basic math concepts (number properties and operations, geometry, measurement, problem solving). Three kinds of math tests are included at Levels 7–14. The first assesses knowledge of mathematical concepts, the second requires students to solve written problems and interpret data, and the third requires students to solve computational problems. At lower levels of the test, the directions are read to students; at higher levels, students must read the directions themselves. The content of this subtest was heavily influenced by the math standards published by the NCTM.

Social Studies   This subtest, available for Levels 7–14, includes an assessment of students' factual and conceptual knowledge and understanding of social studies, as well as their ability to evaluate facts and concepts in economics, geography, history, political science, sociology, anthropology, and related social sciences.

Science   This subtest, available for Levels 7–14, assesses students' factual and conceptual knowledge and understanding of science, as well as their ability to evaluate facts and concepts in the content areas of life science, earth and space science, and physical science.

Sources of Information   At Levels 7 and 8, this is a single subtest that assesses student skills in using tables of contents, maps, and alphabetizing. At Levels

9–14, this area is divided into two subtests: Maps and Diagrams measures students' skills in reading maps, charts, and diagrams; and Reference Materials requires students to demonstrate knowledge of how to alphabetize, read tables of contents, and use an index, dictionary, encyclopedia, and other general reference materials.

Tests of Achievement and Proficiency

The Tests of Achievement and Proficiency (TAP) are available only in Form M. This form of the test is a 1995 updated-norms version of forms originally standardized in 1992. The test is appropriate for use with students in grades 9–12 and is available in two booklet formats: a complete battery and a survey battery. The complete battery takes 4 hours, 35 minutes, to administer, whereas the survey battery takes 1 hour, 40 minutes. The authors indicate five purposes for administering the TAP: (1) identifying skill-development strengths and weaknesses for both individuals and classes, (2) monitoring student progress, (3) deciding which secondary school courses students should take, (4) providing a basis for progress reports to parents, and (5) evaluating programs and curricula. The subtests of the TAP and the skills they assess follow.

Subtests

Vocabulary   This subtest assesses students' working vocabulary, free of contextual cues. The student identifies synonyms of words drawn from the content of secondary school curricula in science, math, and so forth.

Written Expression   This subtest emphasizes complete written composition and assesses the skills necessary for expressing ideas in writing. It includes questions on spelling, sentence structure, and the correct use of pronoun references, and measures students' skill in writing letters, reports, and anecdotes, and in analyzing sentences and paragraphs.

Reading Comprehension   This subtest assesses students' skill in constructing three kinds of meaning from prose: factual meaning, interpretive meaning, and evaluative meaning. The content of the reading selections is general, from literature, from science, and from social studies.

Information Processing   This subtest assesses the extent to which students can read and use various types of maps, charts, and graphs, and use references to locate information.

Mathematics   Two types of mathematics tests are included in the TAP. The first measures both the understanding of mathematical principles and the use of basic mathematics in managing the quantitative aspects of everyday living. The second, optional test assesses computational skills.

Social Studies   This subtest assesses students' knowledge of issues and problems associated with interactions both among people and between people and the environment.

Science This subtest measures problem solving and the interpretation of scientific information. Content is drawn from the life sciences and from the earth and space sciences.

Iowa Tests of Educational Development

The Iowa Tests of Educational Development (ITED) is a norm-referenced and curriculum-referenced test intended for use with students in grades 9–12. It is available in Forms A, K, L, and M. This review focuses on Form A, which was published in 2001. This form has two batteries: a complete battery and a core battery. Subtests included in the complete battery include those listed in this review of the ITED, plus Science, Social Studies, and Sources of Information subtests. The core battery does not include the Social Studies, Science, or Sources of Information sections. All test questions are in multiple-choice format. An optional questionnaire, included in both batteries, is designed to assess students' educational and occupational interests and goals. The complete battery takes 4 hours, 20 minutes, to administer, whereas the core battery takes 2 hours, 40 minutes. The authors indicate three main purposes for the ITED: (1) to provide information to support instructional decisions, (2) to evaluate progress of groups of students, and (3) to report individual progress to students and parents. Subtests included in the complete battery and the behaviors they sample follow.

Subtests

Vocabulary In this measure of general vocabulary development, the words are those encountered in general communication rather than content-specific words. They are presented in phrases, and students must identify synonyms.

Reading Comprehension The test measures students' ability to derive meaning from a variety of materials (poems, fiction, nonfiction, science, and social studies articles). It assesses student construction of factual, nonliteral, and inferential meaning. In addition, items are included that measure student competence in drawing generalizations about themes and ideas, and in recognizing literary techniques and tone.

Spelling In this 30-item test, students must indicate which of four presented words is misspelled; in some cases, all choices are correctly spelled, so students must then indicate that there are no mistakes in that item.

Language: Revising Written Materials This subtest measures students' skills in recognizing correct and effective use of Standard American English in writing. Students are required to edit and revise prose.

Math Concepts and Problem Solving This subtest measures problem-solving skills, rather than computational ability. Based on the NCTM standards, this subtest measures problem-solving skills based on realistic situations.

Math Computation This subtest measures students' ability to add, subtract, multiply, and divide, as well as to manipulate variables and understand exponents and square roots.

Analysis of Social Studies Materials This subtest requires students to respond to multiple-choice questions by evaluating and analyzing social studies information. The kinds of behaviors assessed include making inferences or predictions, distinguishing facts from opinions, recognizing an author's purpose, and judging the adequacy of information for reaching conclusions.

Analysis of Science Materials This subtest requires students to evaluate and analyze science information. Behaviors assessed include making inferences or predictions based on observed data; defining the problem in a scientific experiment; distinguishing among hypotheses, assumptions, data, and conclusions; and selecting the best evidence for answering a question.

Sources of Information This subtest measures students' ability to use important sources of information. One of the difficulties the authors encountered in building this subtest was the fact that different schools use different computerized periodical guides. Therefore, students are asked more general questions about search procedures that would be relevant to a variety of reference systems.

Scores

The ITBS, TAP, and ITED provide eight types of scores: raw scores, percentage correct scores, developmental standard scores, grade equivalents, national percentile ranks, local percentile ranks, stanines, and normal-curve equivalents. The developmental standard score provides an estimate of a student's location on an academic achievement continuum. The median standard score for each grade is computed and placed along the continuum of scores. The standard score can then be interpreted, based on the typical performance of students in each grade. For example, the developmental standard score for students in grade 1 is 150, and the median score for students in grade 7 is 239. The ITBS, TAP, and ITED can be hand scored or machine scored. A data management system is available that aids in organizing, reporting, and using test data.

Norms

The TAP was standardized on a different population of students than the ITBS and ITED. The TAP was standardized in 1992 concurrently with earlier forms of the ITBS, ITED, and Cognitive Abilities Test (CogAT) (Thorndike & Hagen, 1994). The ITBS and ITED were standardized concurrently in 2000 with the CogAT (Lohman & Hagan, 2001). ITBS Form A, ITED Form A, and CogAT Form 6 were standardized on a carefully selected stratified national sample of about 170,000 students (the CogAT manual states that there were 180,000 students). In the standardization of all of these tests, all public school districts in the United States were stratified, first on the basis of geographic region and then on the basis of size of enrollment. Districts were then stratified on the basis of socioeconomic status, using the percentage of students in the district falling below the federal government's poverty guideline. Within each socioeconomic stratum, one district was randomly selected to participate. Data provided in the test manuals show the breakdown of the sample by district size, region of the country, and district socioeconomic status.

In addition to the public school norm sample, norms are provided for Catholic schools and for private non-Catholic schools. Catholic schools were selected on the basis of geographic region and size of the diocesan school system of which they were members. Private non-Catholic schools were selected on the basis of region. There are several sets of norms—national, interpolated, local, large city, Catholic/private school, high socioeconomic, and low socioeconomic—so that student performance can be compared with that of various groups. Both fall and spring norms are provided.

Reliability

Internal-consistency reliability data for the TAP are based on the performance of students in the 1992 standardization sample. All reliability coefficients exceeded .80, and the authors report that internal-consistency reliability studies were conducted on the 1996 norms and that all reliabilities exceeded .80. There are no data on the test-retest reliability of the TAP.

Internal-consistency reliability data for the ITBS and ITED are based on the performance of the spring 2000 standardization sample. Because major areas of the tests (for example, reading total and mathematics total) are most often used in norm-referenced interpretation, these are the reliabilities of greatest concern. Reliabilities for the ITBS raw scores range from .64 to .89 at Levels 5 and 6, and from .66 to .93 for the other levels of the test. At Level 5, the Word Analysis subtest is the only subtest with reliability that is sufficient for the test to be used in making screening decisions about individuals (that is, the reliabilities for this subtest exceed .80). At Level 6, only the Word Analysis, Mathematics, and Reading subtests have reliabilities high enough for the tests to be used in making screening decisions about individuals. At Levels 7 and 8, the reliabilities of the Listening, Mathematics Concepts, Social Studies, and Science subtests are too low for these tests to be used in making screening decisions about individuals. At Level 9, the Listening test is too low for making such decisions.

Data on internal-consistency reliability of the ITED are also based on the performance of the spring 2000 standardization sample. The reliability coefficients for the ITED raw scores all exceed .80. There are no data on the stability of raw scores on the ITBS or ITED.

Validity

The authors of the ITBS, TAP, and ITED attempted to ensure content validity by following a number of steps in the development of the tests. Curriculum guides, textbooks, teachers, and administrators were consulted in the writing of the items. Items were tried out on a national sample of students in each grade. Potential items were reviewed by experts for content fit and item bias. Item selection was based on the performance of the sample and judgments made by the panel of experts. Remember that the data for the TAP are based on performance in the 1992 standardization, whereas those on the ITBS and ITED are based on year 2000 studies. There is no evidence for validity of the ITBS or ITED based on internal structure or relations to other measures.

Summary

The ITBS, TAP, and ITED are a comprehensive battery designed to assess broad critical-thinking skills in grades K–12. Development and standardization of the ITBS and ITED appear exemplary. The TAP standardization was completed in 1992, and updated norms were developed in 1995. Reliability is variable. Test users should check the manuals to ascertain the reliability for the grades and subtests they are considering. There are no data on the long-term stability (test-retest reliability) of the ITBS, the TAP, or the ITED. Users must judge the content validity of these tests for their particular use. There are no data on the validity of the ITBS, TAP, and ITED based on either internal structure or relations with external measures. Those who want to use a consistent series from K–12 would best select the ITBS/ITED combination, as these are both standardized on the same population in 2000. The TAP is a 1992 test, renormed in 1995. Given the datedness of the norms and the limited evidence for the validity of these measures, there are better achievement tests to use.

Metropolitan Achievement Tests

The Metropolitan Achievement Tests, Eighth Edition (MAT8; Harcourt Educational Measurement, 2002) are standardized group achievement tests designed to measure student achievement in reading, language arts, mathematics, science, and social studies. The tests have been completely revised to address recent changes in school curricula. Leading textbooks, curriculum guidelines, and standards described by national professional organizations were analyzed to create test specifications and blueprints. The MAT8 includes 13 levels, spanning kindergarten through twelfth grade. Two levels were created for kindergarten, one level for each grade between grades 1 and 10, and one combined level for grades 11–12. Depending on the test level, the complete battery requires from 1 hour, 30 minutes, to 4 hours, 35 minutes, to administer. An additional short form of the test has been developed. Besides the five content areas, the MAT8 assesses research skills and thinking skills. The subtests of the MAT8 are described next.

Subtests

Sounds and Print   This subtest, which is administered at only the first five levels of the test, measures phonemic awareness, letter and word recognition, concepts of print, and sentence reading.

Reading Vocabulary   This subtest, which must be read by students, assesses skills in deriving meaning from words in context. Strategies for understanding words, as well as word knowledge, are measured.

Reading Comprehension   This subtest assesses students' initial understanding, interpretation, and reflective thinking in regard to a variety of reading selections.

Open-Ended Reading   In this subtest, students read a passage and answer nine open-ended questions about the passage. These questions require students to describe main ideas, understand relationships in the passage, and make judgments about the passage.

Mathematics   This subtest appears at the preprimer and primer levels, as well as at the most advanced levels. The questions assess student knowledge of mathematics, the ability to solve problems, and math communication and reasoning skills. The NCTM standards were used in the development of the mathematics test.

Mathematics Concepts and Problem Solving   This subtest comprises the following five clusters: Number and Operations; Patterns, Relationships, and Algebra; Geometry and Measurement; Data, Statistics, and Probability; and Problem Solving. Students must apply mathematical strategies to problems and evaluate the results.

Mathematics Computation   This subtest requires students to demonstrate addition, subtraction, multiplication, and division skills. Many of the items are presented in context so that students must identify which operation is necessary.

Open-Ended Mathematics   In this subtest, students answer nine open-ended questions corresponding to a particular theme. The questions require student demonstration of mathematical communication, reasoning, and problem solving.

Language   In this subtest, development in listening-vocabulary and listening-comprehension skills is measured at the lower levels of the test. For other levels, students' prewriting, composing, and editing skills are assessed.

Spelling   In this subtest, students must identify misspelled words in the context of written sentences.

Open-Ended Writing   This subtest measures six widely recognized features of good writing: ideas and development; organization, unity, and coherence; word choice; sentences; grammar and usage; and mechanics. Students provide written responses to picture prompts.

Science   This subtest assesses students' knowledge of basic science facts and concepts derived from physical, earth and space, and life sciences. Also assessed are inquiry skills and skill in critical analysis.

Social Studies   This subtest assesses knowledge and comprehension of facts and concepts from the areas of history, geography, political science, economics, and culture.

Scores

Raw scores and several types of derived scores can be obtained for subtests and components of the MAT8. Derived scores include scaled scores, individual and group percentile ranks and stanines, grade equivalents, normal-curve equivalents, content-cluster performance categories, p-values, and performance indicators and standards. Achievement-ability comparisons can be determined if students are given the Otis-Lennon School Ability Test (OLSAT).

Scaled scores allow for determining progress across time over different levels of the test. Content-cluster performance indicators are used to describe each student's performance on each content cluster of the MAT8 relative to the performance of a nationwide sample of students at the same grade level. *P*-values indicate group performance on particular items and help identify specific items that were particularly difficult for a group of students when compared to the national sample. Performance indicators range from 0 to 3; can be provided for item, cluster, or total scores; and describe performance on open-ended sections of the test. Performance standards describe student performance according to levels teachers have determined are necessary to demonstrate competence in a given area. Obtained scores fit into one of four levels: level 1 = below basic, level 2 = basic, level 3 = proficient, and level 4 = advanced.

The MAT8 may be hand scored or submitted to the publisher for computerized scoring. The scoring service may be used to obtain class summary reports, norm-referenced analyses for classes and for individual pupils, and criterion-referenced analyses for classes and individuals.

Norms

The MAT8 was standardized during the fall and spring of the 1999–2000 school year. The fall standardization sample consisted of 80,000 students; the spring sample consisted of 60,000 students. The authors state that the sample was stratified originally by socioeconomic status, community type (urban, suburban, or rural), and ethnicity, and then was statistically weighted to match the 1990 and 1995 Census of Population and Housing, and the National Center on Educational Statistics (1997–1998). This weighted estimate took into account these characteristics as well as geographic region and school type (public, Catholic, or private).

Reliability

Two forms of internal-consistency reliability data were computed: KR-20 and KR-21 coefficients. Subtest coefficients generally exceeded .80 across the 13 levels of the test, although several reliabilities dropped below the .80 mark. Reading comprehension reliabilities tended to be relatively higher than other reliabilities. Test-retest reliabilities were provided and ranged from .43 to .91 across levels and subtests. The test appears to be adequate for group reporting and screening but should not be used to make placement or instructional decisions about individuals.

Validity

Although the content validity of an achievement test must ultimately be determined by the user, the authors of the MAT8 rigorously attempted to match the test with current school curricula. An effort also was made to eliminate cultural bias from the test items, mostly by asking individuals from different cultural groups to review the items. Evidence for validity of the MAT based on internal structure is limited to an illustration that growth occurs across levels of the test and that items can discriminate across grade levels. Evidence of validity based on relations to other measures is extremely limited.

Summary

The MAT8 is a norm-referenced and criterion-referenced achievement test designed for use in grades K–12. The test was adequately standardized and is reliable for group reporting and screening purposes. The test was redesigned to match current school curricula. Judgments about content validity must be made by users, who must consider the extent to which the test samples what they teach. Evidence for validity based on other indices is extremely limited.

Stanford Achievement Test Series (SESAT, SAT, TASK) — Three separate measures are included in the Stanford Achievement Test Series, Tenth Edition (SAT-10; Harcourt Assessment, 2004), which is a test series that samples skill development in several different academic areas. The series includes the following: the Stanford Early School Achievement Test (SESAT), the Stanford Achievement Test (SAT), and the Test of Academic Skills (TASK). The SESAT has two levels and is intended for use in the assessment of kindergartners and first graders. There are eight levels of the SAT, seven of which are typically administered to first through seventh graders, and one that is administered to eighth and ninth graders; these eight levels are arranged according to primary, intermediate, and advanced categories. The TASK is intended for students in the ninth through twelfth grades.

All levels of the test are group administered. The test is both norm referenced and criterion referenced, and all items are presented in a multiple-choice format. The grades at which each subtest is administered, as well the number of items and administration time associated with each subtest, are listed in Table 21.3. Although the extended version of the test is the focus of this review, an abbreviated version of the test is available that consists of a subset of items from the full-length test. Total administration time for the full-length test typically ranges from 2 hours, 15 minutes, to 5 hours, 30 minutes. Administration time for the abbreviated format ranges from 1 hour, 41 minutes, to 3 hours, 54 minutes.

Subtests

The following section describes the subtests of the Stanford series and the associated behaviors that are sampled.

Sounds and Letters This subtest, included only in SESAT 1 and 2, assesses the following early reading skills: matching two words that begin or end with the same sound, recognizing letters, and matching letters to sounds.

TABLE 21.3 Subtests Included at Various Levels of the SAT-10

Test Levels	S1 (K.0–K.5)	S2 (K.5–1.5)	P1 (1.5–2.5)	P2 (2.5–3.5)	P3 (3.5–4.5)	I1 (4.5–5.5)	I2 (5.5–6.5)	I3 (6.5–7.5)	A1 (7.5–8.5)	A2 (8.5–9.9)	T1 (9.0–9.9)	T2 (10.0–10.9)	T3 (11.0–12.9)
Sounds and Letters	X	X											
Word Study Skills			X	X	X	X							
Word Reading	X	X	X										
Sentence Reading		X	X										
Reading Vocabulary				X	X	X	X	X	X	X	X	X	X
Reading Comprehension			X	X	X	X	X	X	X	X	X	X	X
Mathematics	X	X											
Mathematics Problem Solving			X	X	X	X	X	X	X	X	X	X	X
Mathematics Procedures			X	X	X	X	X	X	X	X			
Language			X	X	X	X	X	X	X	X	X	X	X
Spelling			X	X	X	X	X	X	X	X	X	X	X
Listening to Words and Stories	X	X											
Listening			X	X	X	X	X	X	X	X			
Environment	X	X	X	X									
Science					X	X	X	X	X	X	X	X	X
Social Science					X	X	X	X	X	X	X	X	X
Testing Time	2:15	2:50	5:25	4:55	5:30	5:30	5:10	5:10	5:10	5:10	3:50	3:50	3:50

Word Reading   This subtest, available only at the SESAT and Primary 1 levels, measures students' abilities to recognize words by identifying the printed word for a given illustration or a spoken word.

Sentence Reading   This subtest, used at the SESAT 2 and Primary 1 levels, assesses students' abilities to comprehend single, simple sentences.

Word Study Skills   This subtest, used in the Primary 1 through Intermediate 1 levels, measures students' skills in decoding words and identifying relationships between sounds and spellings.

Reading Vocabulary   This subtest assesses a student's vocabulary knowledge and acquisition strategies. Items focus on measuring student knowledge of synonyms (general word knowledge), multiple-meaning words (defined based on the context), and using context clues (students must rely on other parts of the sentence in order to define an unknown word).

Reading Comprehension   At the Primary 1 level, this subtest assesses students' abilities to identify a picture described by a two-sentence story that is read, complete sentences in short reading passages using the cloze format, and answer more general questions about a passage. At the Primary 2 level and beyond, students read textual, functional, or recreational passages. These passages are followed by multiple-choice test items that assess important reading processes such as initial understanding, interpretation, critical analysis, and the use of reading strategies.

Mathematics   The Primary 1 through Advanced 2 levels include two mathematics subtests: Mathematics Problem Solving and Mathematics Procedures. The single subtest Mathematics is used at the SESAT and TASK levels. The Mathematics and Mathematics Problem-Solving Test both assess mathematical problem-solving processes. Calculators are allowed for some levels. Mathematics Procedures focuses on the application of math computation procedures; calculators are not allowed for this subtest. The math subtests were developed in alignment with the National Council of Teachers of Mathematics standards for school mathematics (NCTM, 2000).

Language   This subtest is available in two formats: traditional Language and Comprehensive Language. Traditional Language assesses students' abilities in mechanics and expression. Comprehensive Language assesses proficiency "through techniques that support actual instruction including prewriting, composing, and editing processes" (Harcourt Assessment, 2004, p. 65).

Spelling   In this subtest, students are presented with a sentence in which three words are underlined. Students must decide which word is misspelled. At higher levels, students are presented with a fourth "no mistake" option.

Environment   This is a teacher-dictated subtest that measures kindergarten through second-grade student understanding of natural and social science concepts.

Science   This subtest measures students' understanding of "life sciences, physical sciences, Earth and space sciences, and the nature of science" (Harcourt

Assessment, 2004, p. 66), with a focus on student knowledge of unifying themes in science rather than specific vocabulary. Test items assess students' processing of science information and their science inquiry skills. In developing this subtest, the authors aligned item content with the standards and skills emphasized in the National Science Education Standards, *Benchmarks for Science Literacy,* and *Science for All Americans* (American Association for the Advancement of Science, 1987, 1993).

Social Science   This subtest measures students' skill development in history, geography, political science, and economics, as well as students' abilities to interpret data presented through maps, charts, or political cartoons. The authors state that this subtest "primarily measures students' thinking skills" (Harcourt Assessment, 2004, p. 68), requiring students to use both acquired knowledge and processing skills in order to interpret associated data.

Listening   This subtest is used at the SESAT 1 through Advanced levels and is composed of both a listening vocabulary and a listening comprehension section. In the listening vocabulary section, a sentence is read to the class, and students must answer a question about the meaning of one of the words in the sentence. In the listening comprehension section, literary, informational, and functional passages are read to students. Older students (grade 3 and above) are encouraged to take notes as the tester reads the material. This section measures students' initial understanding as well as their ability to interpret and analyze the material.

Special Editions

There are three special editions of the Stanford Achievement Test. The Braille edition can be used to assess blind or partially sighted students. Harcourt also provides a large-print edition (with content identical to the regular edition but containing adjusted graphics) for students who are visually impaired. There is also an edition for assessing students who are deaf and hearing impaired. This edition includes screening tests and special norms for students who are deaf and hearing impaired that were gathered by the Gallaudet Research Institute and the Harcourt Educational Measurement Research Group.

The *Technical Data Report* manual provides additional information on the accommodations that are considered "standard" and "nonstandard" for the test.

Scores

A variety of transformed scores are obtained for the Stanford series: stanines, grade-equivalent scores, percentiles, and various standard scores. The tests may be scored by hand or submitted to the publisher for machine scoring. When protocols are submitted to the publisher's scoring service, the publisher can provide record sheets for individual students, forms for reporting test results to parents, item analyses, class profiles, profiles comparing individual achievement with individual capability, analyses of each student's attainment of specific objectives, local norms, and so forth.

Performance scores can also be obtained. Performance standards were developed through the expert judgment of national panels of educators in each content area. Performance is scored as Below Basic, Basic, Proficient, and Advanced. These standards have been linked to the performance standards developed for the SAT-9.

Norms

The tenth edition of the Stanford Achievement Test Series was standardized simultaneously with the OLSAT 8 in both the spring and fall of 2002. Separate norms are thus provided for schools in which students must be tested at these varying times of the year. Standardizing the series along with the OLSAT 8 enabled the authors to account for the ability levels of the students in the standardization population and also to develop a set of tables for comparison of ability to achievement.

Sample selection was based on several variables, including socioeconomic status, community type (urban, suburban, rural), public/nonpublic-school status, and ethnicity. Students from all but two states and the District of Columbia were included. Student scores were weighted to best match the aforementioned demographic characteristics of the U.S. population. For the most part, the fall and spring standardization samples appear to adequately represent characteristics of the U.S. population, although there are a few examples of overrepresentation within a particular standardization sample (for instance, underrepresentation of students from the Northeast and from urban areas in the fall standardization sample). Approximately 250,000 students participated in the spring standardization, and 110,000 students participated in the fall standardization.

Cross-tabulations are not shown, so we do not know, for example, the number of eighth graders from urban areas.

Reliability

Reliability data for the SESAT, SAT, and TASK consist of KR-20 internal-consistency coefficients and alternate-forms reliability coefficients for each level of the test according to the fall and spring standardization data separately. KR-20 coefficients for subtests from the full-length test (Forms A and B) ranged from .69 to .97, with only 25 of the over 400 coefficients below .80. KR-20 coefficients for the abbreviated test (Forms A and B) ranged from .59 to .96. Alternate-forms reliability estimates (Forms A and B) ranged from .63 to .93.

Extensive tables listing reliability coefficients and standard errors of measurement are included in the technical manual. With only a few exceptions, the scores for subtests are reliable enough for group decision making and reporting.

Validity

The validity evidence provided for the Stanford series rests primarily on item development procedures. In developing the Stanford 10 items, the authors reviewed recent editions of textbooks, analyzed current curricula and instructional standards, and consulted professional organizations. Originally, pools of new test items were written by trained writers experienced in the different content areas. These items were then submitted to a group of content experts to establish content accuracy and alignment with standards, levels, and processes. Measurement experts examined and edited the items, and the items were reviewed for writing clarity by general editors.

Following this process, an item tryout program was conducted in order to choose items for the final test. Of interest during the item tryout were issues relating to item format, question difficulty, item sensitivity, progressive difficulty of items, and test length. Teachers in tryout samples provided feedback on the clarity of the item layout, appropriateness, and artwork. Following the tryout program, test items were reviewed for bias by a culturally diverse panel of prominent members of the educational community. Furthermore, all items were analyzed using Mantel-Haenszel procedures to determine differential item functioning between majority and minority groups. Data from the item tryout were also analyzed using traditional item analysis and Rasch model techniques to inform final decisions about item inclusion. Information on correlations with the SAT-9 are provided and are generally in the .60-to-.90 range for corresponding subtests and total scores. Correlations with the OLSAT 8 were generally much lower, as expected.

Summary

The Stanford Achievement Test Series is composed of the SESAT, the SAT, and the TASK. The tests provide a comprehensive continuous assessment of skill development in a variety of areas. Standardization, reliability, and validity are adequate for screening purposes.

Terra Nova, Second Edition

The Terra Nova, Second Edition (CTB/McGraw-Hill, 2002), is a group-administered, multiple-skill battery that provides norm-referenced and objective-mastery scores. It provides alternate forms (Forms C and D) that are parallel to and can be used interchangeably with the original forms of the Terra Nova (Forms A and B; CTB/McGraw-Hill, 1997). The test, also referred to as Nova/CAT6, includes selected-response items (multiple-choice) and extended open-ended items. The Terra Nova, Second Edition, is available in multiple formats called Terra Nova Complete Battery, Terra Nova Survey Battery, and Terra Nova Multiple Assessment. For each battery, users may administer the basic test, consisting of four subtests, or the basic test plus supplemental tests. All items in the survey and complete battery are selected-response items; selected-response items and open-ended items are included in the multiple assessment. There are 13 levels of the test, one level per grade (K–12); the two most advanced levels can be administered to either grade 11 or grade 12. Subtests included in the three batteries, grade levels, and testing times are shown in Table 21.4.

Subtests

Reading/Language Arts   Skills assessed in this subtest include listening comprehension; basic understanding; text analysis, including drawing conclusions; eval-

TABLE 21.4	Terra Nova, Second Edition, Subtests, Grade Levels, and Testing Times		
Battery	**Subtests**	**Grade Levels**	**Testing Time**
Complete	Reading/		
	Language Arts	K–12	1:35 @ K
	Mathematics	K–12	2:40 @ grade 1
	Science	1–12	3:05 @ grade 2
	Social Studies	1–12	3:40 @ grade 3
			4:10 @ grades 4–12
Complete with	Word Analysis	1–3	3:30 @ grade 1
Supplemental Tests	Vocabulary	1–12	4:25 @ grade 2
	Language Mechanics	2–12	5:00 @ grade 3
	Spelling	2–12	5:15 @ grades 4–12
	Mathematics		
	Computation	1–12	
Survey	Reading/		
	Language Arts	2–12	2:15 @ grade 2
	Mathematics	2–12	2:25 @ grade 3
	Science	2–12	2:50 @ grades 4–12
	Social Studies	2–12	
Survey with	Word Analysis	2–3	3:35 @ grade 2
Supplemental Tests	Vocabulary	2–12	3:45 @ grade 3
	Language Mechanics	2–12	3:55 @ grades 4–12
	Spelling	2–12	
	Mathematics		
	Computation	2–12	
Multiple Assessments	Reading/		
	Language Arts	1–12	4:00 @ grade 1
	Mathematics	1–12	4:20 @ grade 2
	Science	1–12	4:45 @ grade 3
	Social Studies	1–12	5:35 @ grades 4–12
Multiple Assessment	Word Analysis	1–3	4:50 @ grade 1
with Supplemental	Vocabulary	1–12	5:40 @ grade 2
Tests	Language Mechanics	2–12	6:05 @ grade 3
	Spelling	2–12	6:40 @ grades 4–12
	Mathematics		
	Computation	1–12	

uation; identification of reading strategies; knowledge of sound-symbol and structural relationships in letters, words, and signs; understanding of sentence structure, including punctuation and capitalization; sentence writing and connected prose writing; and editing skills.

Mathematics Measured skills include number recognition and number relations, computation and estimation, basic mathematics operations, measurement, geometry, data analysis, statistics and probability, algebra and math functions, problem solving and reasoning, and math vocabulary and terminology.

Science   Skills assessed include understanding of the fundamental concepts of scientific inquiry; understanding of fundamental concepts and principles of physical science, life science, and earth and space science; understanding of how technology and science interact; and the history and nature of science.

Social Studies   Geography, cultural perspectives, history, civics, government, and economics are tested.

Word Analysis   A measure of word skill consists of recognizing consonants, blends, digraphs, sight words, vowels, contractions and compounds, roots, and affixes.

Vocabulary   This subtest is an assessment of skill in understanding word meanings and relationships, including the use of context to infer words missing from passages.

Language Mechanics   The appropriate use of capitalization and punctuation in writing conventions is assessed.

Spelling   Students identify the correct spelling of words presented in sentences and paragraphs.

Mathematics Computation   Skills assessed in this subtest include addition, subtraction, multiplication, and division; use of decimals, fractions, and percents; and algebraic operations.

Norms

The standardization sample for the Terra Nova, Second Edition, represents a stratified random sample of students. Students from public, Catholic, and private non-Catholic schools were included. Public schools were stratified by region, community type, and socioeconomic status; Catholic and private non-Catholic schools were stratified by region and community type. Over 114,000 students participated in the fall standardization, and nearly 150,000 students participated in the spring standardization. A unique feature of the norm sample is that it includes students with individualized education plans (IEPs) who were tested with the accommodations specified on their IEPs. Student scores were weighted to appropriately represent national proportions of individuals from specific school types (public, Catholic, private non-Catholic), community types, geographic regions, socioeconomic statuses, and ethnicities as reported by Quality Education Data (2001) and the U.S. Census Bureau (1999).

Scores

Those who use the Terra Nova, Second Edition, may receive a variety of reports. The Individual Profile Report provides the teacher with specific information about student strengths and weaknesses in both norm-referenced and criterion-referenced terms. Teachers can quickly identify their students' instructional needs. The Home Report gives parents information about student performance, and the Performance Level Summary Report gives educators standards-based information about academic achievement. Administrators receive summary information about student performance in the form of an Evaluation Summary, and school board members can get data in the form of a Board Report. For all reports, norm-referenced scores are in the form of national percentiles, and standards-referenced scores indicate relative standing on specific objectives.

Reliability

Internal-consistency coefficients for the Terra Nova, Second Edition, Survey Plus, Complete Battery Plus, and Multiple Assessments Plus are shown in the test manual. Internal-consistency coefficients range from .67 to .91 for subtests of the survey battery, .64 to .94 for the complete battery, and .67 to .93 for the multiple assessments. There are no data on test-retest reliability or on alternate-form reliability. Reliabilities of some of the separate subtests are too low for use in making decisions about individuals.

Validity

There is limited evidence for the validity of the Terra Nova, Second Edition, batteries. The authors indicate that they ensured validity based on test content by anchoring the test to curricula used in schools. They describe procedures used to limit the number of items that were biased by gender or ethnicity. The authors attempt to provide evidence of validity based on relations to external measures by correlating performance on the Terra Nova, Second Edition, with performance on InView (CTB/McGraw-Hill, 2001), a recently developed test of cognitive skills. Yet our examination of tables in the manual indicated that correlations between measures of cognitive skills (as measured by InView) and achievement are about the same as correlations among Terra Nova, Second Edition, subtests. It could be argued that the test is a measure of cognition as much as of achievement.

Summary

The Terra Nova, Second Edition, is one of several multiple-skill achievement batteries available to schools and districts. Those who must make a decision about which test to use should carefully examine the match between their curriculum and the various tests. There is less evidence for the technical adequacy of the Terra Nova, Second Edition, than for that of other comparable achievement batteries.

Peabody Individual Achievement Test–Revised– Normative Update (PIAT-R-NU)

The most recent edition of the Peabody Individual Achievement Test (PIAT; Markwardt, 1998) is not a new edition of the test but a normative update of the 1989 edition of the PIAT-R. The test is an individually administered, norm-referenced instrument designed to provide a wide-ranging screening measure of academic achievement in six content areas. It can be used with students in kindergarten through twelfth grade. PIAT-R test materials are contained in four easel kits, one for each volume of the test. Easel-kit volumes present stimulus materials to the student at eye level; the examiner's instructions are placed on the reverse side. The student can see one side of the response plate, whereas the examiner can see both sides. The test is recommended by the author for use in individual evaluation, guidance, admissions and transfers, grouping of students, progress evaluation, and personnel selection.

The original PIAT (Dunn & Markwardt, 1970) included five subtests. The PIAT-R added a written expression subtest. The 1989 edition updated the content of the test. The 1998 edition is identical to the 1989 edition. Behaviors sampled by the six subtests of the PIAT-R-NU follow.

Subtests

Mathematics   This subtest contains 100 multiple-choice items, ranging from items that assess such early skills as matching, discriminating, and recognizing numerals to items that assess advanced concepts in geometry and trigonometry. The test is a measure of the student's knowledge and application of math concepts and facts.

Reading Recognition   This subtest contains 100 items, ranging in difficulty from preschool level through high school level. Items assess skill development in matching letters, naming capital and lowercase letters, and recognizing words in isolation.

Reading Comprehension   This subtest contains 81 multiple-choice items assessing skill development in understanding what is read. After reading a sentence, the student must indicate comprehension by choosing the correct picture out of a group of four.

Spelling   This subtest consists of 100 items sampling behaviors from kindergarten level through high school level. Initial items assess the student's ability to distinguish a printed letter of the alphabet from pictured objects and to associate letter symbols with speech sounds. More difficult items assess the student's ability to identify, from a response bank of four words, the correct spelling of a word read aloud by the examiner.

General Information   This subtest consists of 100 questions presented orally, which the student must answer orally. Items assess the extent to which the student has learned facts in social studies, science, sports, and the fine arts.

Written Expression   This subtest assesses written-language skills at two levels. Level I, appropriate for students in kindergarten and first grade, is a measure of prewriting skills, such as skill in copying and writing letters, words, and sentences from dictation. At Level II, the student writes a story in response to a picture prompt.

Scores

All but one of the PIAT-R-NU subtests are scored in the same way: The student's response to each item is rated pass-fail. On these five subtests, raw scores are converted to grade and age equivalents, grade- and age-based standard scores, percentile ranks, normal-curve equivalents, and stanines. The Written Expression subtest is scored differently than the other subtests. The examiner uses a set of scoring criteria included in an appendix in the test manual. At Level I, the examiner scores the student's writing of his or her name and then scores 18 items pass-fail. For the more difficult items at Level I, the student must earn a specified number of subcredits to pass the item. Methods for assigning subcredits are specified clearly in the manual. At Level II, the student generates a free response, and the assessor examines the response for certain specified characteristics. For example, the student is given credit for each letter correctly capitalized, each correct punctuation, and absence of inappropriate words. Scores earned on the Written Expression subtest include grade-based stanines and developmental scaled scores (with mean = 8 and standard deviation = 3).

Three composite scores are used to summarize student performance on the PIAT-R-NU: total reading, total test, and written language. Total reading is described as an overall measure of "reading ability" and is obtained by combining scores on Reading Recognition and Reading Comprehension. The total test score is obtained by combining performance on the General Information, Reading Recognition, Reading Comprehension, Mathematics, and Spelling subtests. A third composite score, the written-language composite score, is optional and is obtained by combining performance on the Spelling and Written Expression subtests.

Norms

The 1989 edition of the PIAT-R was standardized on 1,563 students in kindergarten through grade 12. The 1998 normative update was completed in conjunction with normative updating of the Kaufman Test of Educational Achievement, the Key Math–Revised, and the Woodcock Reading Mastery Tests–Revised. The sample for the normative updates was 3,184 students in kindergarten through grade 12. A stratified multistage sampling procedure was used to ensure selection of a nationally representative group at each grade level. Students in the norm group did not all take each of the five tests. Rather, one fifth of the students took each test, along with portions of each of the other tests. Thus the norm groups for the brief and comprehensive forms consist of about 600 students. There are as few as 91 students at three-year age ranges. Because multiple measures were given to each student, the authors could use linking and equating to increase the size of the norm sample.

Approximately ten years separate the data collection periods for the original PIAT norms and the updated norms. Changes during that time in curriculum and educational practice, in population demographics, and in the general cultural environment may have affected levels of academic achievement.

Reliability

All data on the reliability of the PIAT-R-NU are for the original PIAT-R. The performance of students on the two measures has changed, so the authors should have conducted a few reliability studies on students in the late 1990s. Generalizations from the reliability of the original PIAT-R to reliability of the PIAT-R-NU are suspect.

Validity

All data on validity of the PIAT-R-NU are for the original PIAT-R. The performance of students on the two measures has changed, so the authors should have conducted a few validity studies on students in the late 1990s. Generalizations from the validity of the original PIAT-R to the validity of the PIAT-R-NU are suspect. This is especially true for measures of validity based on relations with external measures where the measures (for example, the Wide Range Achievement Test or the Peabody Picture Vocabulary Test) have been revised.

Summary

The PIAT-R is an individually administered achievement test that was renormed in 1998. Reliability and validity information is based on studies of the 1989 edition of the test. As with any achievement test, the most crucial concern is content validity. Users must be sensitive to the correspondence of the content of the PIAT-R to a student's curriculum. The test is essentially a 1970 test that was revised and renormed in 1989 and then renormed again in 1998. Data on reliability and validity are based on the earlier version of the scale, which of course has gone unchanged. The practice of updating norms without gathering data on continued technical adequacy is a dubious practice.

Wide Range Achievement Test 3

The Wide Range Achievement Test 3 (WRAT3; Wilkinson, 1993) is designed to measure the "codes which are needed to learn the basic skills of reading, writing, spelling and arithmetic" (p. 10). The author states that an attempt was made to eliminate the effect of comprehension. This was done to enable diagnosticians to determine whether an academic problem is caused by an inability to learn specific codes or by an inability to derive meaning from the codes.

The WRAT3 is a single-level, individually administered test that can be used with individuals aged 5 to 75 years. Two forms were developed; these can be either used individually or combined to give a more comprehensive evaluation. The author suggests using the alternative forms for pre- and posttesting situations. The test contains three subtests.

Subtests

Reading   This subtest assesses skill in letter recognition, letter naming, and pronunciation of words in isolation.

Spelling   This subtest assesses students' skills in copying marks onto paper, writing their names, and writing single words from dictation.

Arithmetic This subtest assesses skills in counting, reading numerals, solving problems presented orally, and performing written composition of arithmetic problems.

Scores

Six kinds of scores can be derived from the WRAT3: raw, absolute, standard, grade equivalent, percentile, and normal-curve equivalent. The absolute score provides an interval-based estimate of an individual's performance level, which can be used to make comparisons across scales or between individuals. The standard scores have a mean of 100 and a standard deviation of 15. A profile analysis form is provided, which can be used to compare WRAT3 scores with intelligence test scores; it gives a picture of the degree of difficulty of the items passed by the test taker.

Norms

The WRAT3 was standardized on 4,443 individuals. The sample was stratified and counterbalanced by age, regional residence, gender, and ethnicity, based on 1990 U.S. Census data. The author controlled for socioeconomic level based on the occupational category of the individual or of his or her caregiver. The author states that a minimum of four states per region were used, but the total number of states and settings (rural, urban, suburban) is not reported.

Reliability

The WRAT3 appears to be internally consistent. Three forms of internal consistency were provided. Coefficient alphas for each of the 23 age groups were computed for each form. The median coefficient alphas for the individual forms ranged from .85 to .91. The combined-form coefficients all exceeded .90. Alternate-forms correlations were also computed. The median correlations for the Reading, Spelling, and Arithmetic subtests are .92, .93, and .89, respectively. Rasch Person Separation indexes, a form of internal consistency, ranged from .98 to .99. The stability of the WRAT3 appears to be more than adequate. Corrected test-retest reliability coefficients for a sample of 142 individuals between the ages of 6 and 16 years were all greater than .91.

Validity

The author argues that, because the Rasch Item Separation indexes are all 1.00, the test has content validity. However, information is not provided regarding the match between the WRAT3 content and that of a typical curriculum; therefore the content validity is questionable. Several forms of support for validity based on internal structure are provided. The mean scores of the subtests increase with age, which is in accordance with the developmental nature of basic academic skills. Moderate correlations exist between the WRAT3 and two measures of intelligence: the Wechsler Intelligence Scale for Children–III (WISC-III) and the Wechsler Adult Intelligence Scale–Revised (WAIS-R). Moderate correlations were found between the WRAT3 and three standardized group achievement tests: the California Achievement Test–Form E, the California Test of Basic Skills–4, and the Stanford Achievement Test. The WRAT3 was able to discriminate among 222 general and special education students. The test was able to group students labeled gifted, learning disabled, educable, mentally retarded, and general education with 68 percent success.

Summary

The WRAT3 is an individually administered achievement test designed to assess the basic academic skills necessary in reading, spelling, and arithmetic. The test is well standardized and has adequate reliability. There are two forms of the test. Data on standardization are incomplete. The test has sufficient reliability to be used in making decisions about individuals. Several forms of evidence for validity based on internal structure are provided in the manual that accompanies the test, but the test's content validity is questionable.

Wechsler Individual Achievement Test, Second Edition

The Wechsler Individual Achievement Test, Second Edition (WIAT-2; Psychological Corporation, 2001), is an individually administered, norm-referenced achievement test designed to be used with students in grades pre-K through 12 who are between the ages of 4 and 19 years. A supplemental manual is available that provides norms for adults through 85 years of age. The first edition (WIAT) was conormed with the Wechsler series of intelligence tests: the Wechsler Preschool and Primary Scale on Intelligence–Revised (WPPSI-R), the WISC-III, and the WAIS-R. The WIAT-2 was linked to the WPPSI-R, the WISC-III, and the WAIS-III through a sample of 1,069 individuals who took the WIAT-2 and the age-appropriate intelligence test. The authors contend that this linking of ability and achievement tests provides more reliable estimates of a student's aptitude-achievement discrepancy.

The test's authors created subtests that parallel and, they argue, comprehensively cover the seven areas of learning disability specified in Public Law 94-142: basic reading skills, reading comprehension, mathematics reasoning, mathematics calculation, listening comprehension, oral expression, and written expression. These seven domains, plus spelling and pseudoword (a combination of letters that can be pronounced but is not an English word) decoding, compose the nine subtests of the WIAT-2. The WIAT-2 can be completed in approximately 45 minutes for very young children (pre-K and K), 90 minutes for grades 1 through 6, and 1½ to 2 hours for grades 7 through 16. The behaviors sampled by the WIAT-2 subtests are described in Table 21.5.

Scores

Eight types of scores—standard, percentile rank, age equivalent, grade equivalent, normal-curve equivalent, stanine, quartile, and decile—can be derived from each of the subtests and five composites. The mathematics, oral language, and written language composites are each based on two subtests; the reading composite is based on three subtests. The total composite is based on all the subtests.

TABLE 21.5	Description of the WIAT-2 Composites and Subtests

Composite	Subtest	Description
Reading	Word Reading	Assess prereading (phonological awareness) and decoding skills. • Name the letters of the alphabet. • Identify and generate rhyming words. • Identify the beginning and ending sounds of words. • Match sounds with letters and letter blends. • Read aloud from a graded word list.
	Reading Comprehension	Reflect reading instruction in the classroom. • Match a written word with its representative picture. • Read passages and answer content questions. • Read short sentences aloud and respond to comprehension questions.
	Pseudoword Decoding	Assess the ability to apply phonetic decoding skills. • Read aloud a list of nonsense words designed to mimic the phonetic structure of words in the English language.
Mathematics	Numerical Operations	Evaluate the ability to identify and write numbers. • Count using 1:1 correspondence. • Solve written calculation problems. • Solve simple equations involving all basic operations (addition, subtraction, multiplication, and division).
	Math Reasoning	Assess the ability to reason mathematically. • Count. • Identify geometric shapes. • Solve single- and multistep word problems. • Interpret graphs. • Identify mathematical patterns. • Solve problems related to statistics and probability.
Written Language	Spelling	Evaluate the ability to spell. • Write dictated letters, letter blends, and words.
	Written Expression	Measure the examinee's writing skills at all levels of language. • Write the alphabet (timed). • Demonstrate written word fluency. • Combine and generate sentences. • Produce a rough draft paragraph (grades 3–8) or a persuasive essay (grades 7–16).
Oral Language	Listening Comprehension	Measure the ability to listen for details. • Select the picture that matches a word or sentence. • Generate a word that matches a picture and oral description.
	Oral Expression	Reflect a broad range of oral language activities. • Demonstrate verbal word fluency. • Repeat sentences verbatim. • Generate stories from visual clues. • Generate directions from visual or verbal clues.

The standard score, which has a mean of 100 and a standard deviation of 15, can be computed by age or grade. Quartile scores represent corresponding quarters of the distribution; decile scores represent corresponding tenths of the distribution (that is, a decile score of 1 represents the first tenth, or the bottom 10 percent, of the distribution). Ability-achievement discrepancy scores based on the WIAT-2 standard scores and one of the three Wechsler ability tests (WPPSI-R, WISC-III, or WAIS-III) are also provided. The test authors provide two methods of computing discrepancy scores—simple difference and predicted achievement—and provide information regarding the limitations of each approach.

Norms

The WIAT-2 was standardized on 3,600 children for the grade-based sample (K–12) and on 2,950 children for the age-based sample (ages 4 to 19); 2,171 students were included in both samples. A sample of 1,069 children was used to link the WIAT-2 with the WPPSI-R, the WISC-III, and the WAIS-III. The information collected from the linking studies was used to develop the ability-achievement discrepancy statistics. The sample selection was based on 1998 U.S. Census data. The sample was randomly selected and stratified by age, grade, gender, race/ethnicity, geographic region, and parent education. Economic status was not used as a stratification variable. Demographic information on race/ethnicity, gender, geographic region, and parent education is disaggregated by age and grade. Crosstabulations of parent education level by ethnicity are also provided.

Reliability

Three forms of reliability data were calculated for the WIAT-2. Split-half reliability coefficients based on age and grade subtest scores generally exceed .80. Numerical Operations, Written Expression, Listening Comprehension, and Oral Expression fall below .80 for certain ages and grades. The split-half coefficients for the four composites are all greater than .80, with two of the four composites exceeding .90 at all age and grade levels (Reading and Written Expression). A sample of 297 students ages 6 to 19 was selected to determine the test-retest reliability of the WIAT-2. The subtest reliabilities are all above .80; coefficients are provided according to three age groups (6 to 9 years, 10 to 12 years, and 13 to 19 years). Interrater agreement was calculated among 2,180 examinee responses for three subtests that require subjective scoring. The correlation between raters for Reading Comprehension ranges from .94 to .98. The interrater agreement for Oral Expression ranges from .91 to .99. The interrater agreement for Written Expression ranges from .71 to .94.

Validity

The WIAT-2 has evidence for validity based on test content, internal structure, and relations with other measures. Expert judgment and empirical item analyses were used to establish the content validity of the instrument. Experts analyzed the extent to which the items measured specific curriculum objectives. Empirical item analyses were used to eliminate poorly constructed items in order to prevent bias. The validity based on the internal structure of the WIAT-2 was documented through analysis of subtest intercorrelations, correlations with ability measures, and expected developmental differences across age and grade groups.

Several forms of support for validity based on relations with external criteria are provided. There are many moderate correlations between WIAT-2 subtests and subtests from the Wide Range Achievement Test, Third Edition; the Differential Ability Scales; and the Peabody Picture Vocabulary Test, Third Edition. The WIAT-2 also correlated as would be expected with subtests of several group-administered achievement tests, including the Stanford Achievement Test, Ninth Edition, and the Metropolitan Achievement Tests, Eighth Edition. The correlation between the WIAT-2 and school grades was generally low, but this is no different from what would be expected, given the low reliability of school grades.

Summary

The WIAT-2 is an individually administered achievement test that is linked to the Wechsler series of intelligence tests. The subtests are designed to measure the seven areas of learning disability defined in Public Law 94-142. The test has an adequate standardization sample and appears to be reliable and valid. Two methods and statistical tables for computing ability-achievement discrepancies are provided, along with a description of the limitations of each method.

Dilemmas in Current Practice

Problem

Two limitations affect the use of achievement tests as screening devices: the match of the test to the content of the curriculum and the fact that the tests are group administered. Unless the content assessed by an achievement test reflects the content of the curriculum, the results are meaningless. Students will not have had a formal opportunity to learn the material tested. When students are tested on material they have not been taught or tested in ways other than those by which they are taught, the test results will not reflect their actual skills. Jenkins and Pany (1978) compared the contents of four reading achievement tests with the contents of five commercial reading series at grades 1 and 2. Their major concern was the extent to which students might earn different scores on different tests of reading achievement simply as a function of the degree of overlap in content between tests and curricula. Jenkins and Pany calculated the grade scores that would be earned by students who had mastered the words taught in the re-

spective curricula and who had correctly read those words on the four tests. Grade scores are shown in Table 21.6. It is clear that different curricula result in different performances on different tests.

Authors' Viewpoint

The data produced by Jenkins and Pany are now over 25 years old. Yet the table is still the best visual illustration of test-curriculum overlap. Shapiro and Derr (1987) showed that the degree of overlap between what is taught and what is tested varied considerably across tests and curricula. Also, Good and Salvia (1989) demonstrated significant differences in test performance for the same students on different reading tests. They indicate the significance of the test-curriculum overlap issue, stating:

Curriculum bias is undesirable because it severely limits the interpretation of a student's test score. For example, it is unclear whether a student's reading score of 78 reflects deficient reading skills or the selection of a test with poor content validity for the pupil's curriculum. (p. 56)

TABLE 21.6 Grade-Equivalent Scores Obtained by Matching Specific Reading Test Words to Standardized Reading Test Words

Curriculum	PIAT	MAT Word Knowledge	Word Analysis	SDRT	WRAT
Bank Street Reading Series					
Grade 1	1.5	1.0	1.1	1.8	2.0
Grade 2	2.8	2.5	1.2	2.9	2.7
Keys to Reading					
Grade 1	2.0	1.4	1.2	2.2	2.2
Grade 2	3.3	1.9	1.0	3.0	3.0
Reading 360					
Grade 1	1.5	1.0	1.0	1.4	1.7
Grade 2	2.2	2.1	1.0	2.7	2.3
SRA Reading Program					
Grade 1	1.5	1.2	1.3	1.0	2.1
Grade 2	3.1	2.5	1.4	2.9	3.5
Sullivan Associates Programmed Reading					
Grade 1	1.8	1.4	1.2	1.1	2.0
Grade 2	2.2	2.4	1.1	2.5	2.5

SOURCE: Grade-Equivalent Scores Obtained by Matching Specific Reading Test Words to Standardized Reading Test Words. From "Standardized Achievement Tests: How Useful for Special Education?" by J. Jenkins & D. Pany, *Exceptional Children, 44,* (1978), 450. Copyright 1978 by The Council for Exceptional Children. Reprinted with permission.

Getting the Most Out of an Achievement Test

The achievement tests described in this chapter provide the teacher with global scores in areas such as word meaning and work-study skills. Although global scores can help in screening children, they generally lack the specificity to help in planning individualized instructional programs. The fact that Emily earned a standard score of 85 on the Mathematics Computation subtest of the ITBS does not tell us what math skills Emily has. In addition, a teacher cannot rely on test names as an indication of what is measured by a specific test. For example, a reading score of 115 on the WRAT3 tells a teacher nothing about reading comprehension or rate of oral reading.

A teacher must look at any screening test (or at any test, for that matter) in terms of the behaviors sampled by that test. Here is a case in point. Suppose Richard earned a standard score of 70 on a spelling subtest. What do we know about Richard? We know that Richard earned enough raw-score points to place him 2 standard deviations below the mean of students in his grade. That is all we know without going beyond the score and looking at the kinds of behaviors sampled by the test. The test title tells us only that the test measures skill development in spelling. However, we still do not know what Richard did to earn a score of 70.

First, we need to ask, "What is the nature of the behaviors sampled by the test?" Spelling tests can be of several kinds. Richard may have been asked to write a word read by his teacher, as is the case in the Spelling subtest of the WRAT3. Such a behavior sampling demands that he recall the correct spelling of a word and actually produce that correct spelling in writing. On the other hand, Richard's score of 70 may have been earned on a spelling test that asked him just to recognize the correct spelling of a word. For example, the Spelling subtest of the PIAT-R presents the student with four alternative spellings of a word (for example, empti, empty, impty, emity), and the teacher asks a child to point to the word *empty*. Such an item demands recognition and pointing, rather than recall and production. Thus we need to look first at the nature of the behaviors sampled by the test.

Second, we must look at the specific items a student passes or fails. This requires going back to the original test protocol to analyze the specific nature of skill development in a given area. We need to ask, "What kinds of items did the child fail?" and then look for consistent patterns among the failures. In trying to identify the nature of spelling errors, we need to know "Does the student consistently demonstrate errors in spelling words with long vowels? with silent *e*'s? with specific consonant blends?" and so on. The search is for specific patterns of errors, and we try to ascertain the student's relative degree of consistency in making certain errors. Of course, finding error patterns requires that the test content be sufficiently dense to allow a student to make the same error at least two times.

Similar procedures are followed with any screening device. Quite obviously, the information achieved is not nearly as specific as the information obtained from diagnostic tests. Administration of an achievement test that is a screening test gives the classroom teacher a general idea of where to start with any additional diagnostic assessment.

SUMMARY

Screening devices used for assessing academic achievement provide a global picture of a student's skill development in academic content areas. Screening tests must be selected on the basis of the kinds of behavior each test samples, the adequacy of its norms, its reliability, and its validity. When selecting an achievement test or when evaluating the results of a student's performance on an achievement test, the classroom teacher needs to take into careful consideration not only the technical characteristics of the test, but also the extent to which the behaviors sampled represent the goals and objectives of the student's curriculum. The teacher can adapt certain techniques for administering group tests and for getting the most mileage out of the results of group tests.

QUESTIONS FOR CHAPTER REVIEW

1. Identify at least four important considerations in selecting a specific achievement test for use with the third graders in your local school system.

2. Describe the major advantages and disadvantages of group-administered, multiple-skill achievement tests.

3. A new student is assessed in September using the WRAT3. Her achievement-test scores (using the PIAT-3) are forwarded from her previous school and place her in the ninetieth percentile overall. However, the latest assessment places her only in the seventy-seventh percentile. Give three possible explanations for this discrepancy.

4. Ms. Epstein decides to assess the achievement of her fifth-grade pupils. She believes that they are unusually "slow" learners and estimates that, in general, they are functioning on about a third-grade level. She decides to use Primary Level III of the SAT. What difficulties will she face?

5. Mr. Fitzpatrick has used the results of a group-administered achievement test to make a placement decision concerning John. What facts about group-administered achievement tests has Mr. Fitzpatrick failed to attend to? Under what conditions could he use an achievement test designed to be administered to a group?

PROJECT

Assume that you wish to use one of the tests reviewed in this text as a screening test for achievement. What test would be your first choice? Why? Compare your answer with a classmate's answer. Reconcile your differences.

RESOURCES FOR FURTHER INVESTIGATION

Print Resources

Feldt, L. S., Forsyth, R. A., Ansley, T. N., & Alnot, S. D. (1996). *Iowa Tests of Educational Development.* Chicago: Riverside Publishing Company.

Good, R. H., & Salvia, J. A. (1989). Curriculum bias in published norm-referenced reading tests: Demonstrable effects. *School Psychology Review, 17*(1), 51–60.

Harcourt Brace Educational Measurement (1996a). *Stanford Achievement Test* (9th ed.). San Antonio, TX: Psychological Corporation.

Harcourt Brace Educational Measurement (1996c). *Stanford Early School Achievement Test.* San Antonio, TX: Psychological Corporation.

Harcourt Brace Educational Measurement (1996d). *Test of Academic Skills.* San Antonio, TX: Psychological Corporation.

Hoover, H. D., Hieronymus, A. N., Frisbie, D. A., & Dunbar, S. B. (2001). *Iowa Tests of Basic Skills.* Chicago: Riverside Publishing Company.

Scannell, D. P. (1996). *Tests of Achievement and Proficiency.* Chicago: Riverside Publishing Company.

Shapiro, E. S., & Derr, T. (1987). An examination of overlap between reading curricula and standardized reading tests. *Journal of Special Education, 21*(2), 59–67.

Woodcock, R., McGrew, K., & Werder, J. (1994). *Mini-Battery of Achievement.* Chicago: Riverside Publishing Company.

Technology Resources

AGS ONLINE PRODUCTS AND SERVICES
www.agsnet.com
Look for product and ordering information about the instruments available from American Guidance Services (AGS). Search by product title to find information about the Kaufman Test of Educational Achievement and the Peabody Individual Achievement Test–Revised.

PRO-ED CATALOGUE INFORMATION FOR PRODUCTS
www.proedinc.com
Find product and ordering information about the Diagnostic Achievement Battery–2 and the Diagnostic Achievement Test for Adolescents–3.

RIVERSIDE PUBLISHING
www.riverpub.com
Go to product categories. Under educational assessments in the Achievement index, you will find information on the Iowa Tests of Basic Skills, the Tests of Achievement and Proficiency, and the Iowa Tests of Educational Development, as well as other tests of academic achievement.

CHAPTER 22

Assessment of Reading

IN THE PREVIOUS CHAPTER, WE DESCRIBED MULTIPLE-SKILL ACHIEVEMENT TESTS, which provide global information about a student's achievements. Often, school personnel need more specific information. In this chapter, we give detailed descriptions of the kinds of behaviors sampled by reading tests and then describe commonly used reading tests, both norm-referenced (comparative) and criterion-referenced (performance) measures.

Why Do We Assess Reading?

Reading is one of the most fundamental skills that students learn. For poor readers, life in school is likely to be difficult even with appropriate curricular and testing accommodations and adaptations, and life after school is likely to have constrained opportunities and less personal independence and satisfaction. Moreover, students who have not learned to read fluently by the end of third grade are unlikely ever to read fluently (Adams, 1990). For these reasons, students' development of reading skills is closely monitored in order to identify those with problems early enough to enable remediation.

Diagnostic tests are used primarily to improve two educational decisions. First, they are administered to children who are experiencing difficulty in learning to read. In this case, tests identify a student's strengths and weaknesses so that educators can plan appropriate interventions. Second, they are given to ascertain a student's initial or continuing eligibility for special services. Tests given for this purpose are used to compare a student's achievement with the achievement of other students. Diagnostic reading tests may also be administered to evaluate the effects of instruction. However, this use of diagnostic reading tests is generally unwise. Individually administered tests are an inefficient way to evaluate instructional effectiveness for large groups of students; group survey tests are generally more appropriate for this purpose. Diagnostic tests are generally too insensitive to identify small but important gains by individual students. Teachers should monitor students' daily or weekly progress with direct performance measures (such as having a student read aloud currently used materials to ascertain accuracy [percentage correct] and fluency [rate of correct words per minute]).

The Ways in Which Reading Is Taught

For about 150 years, educators have been divided (sometimes acrimoniously) over the issue of teaching the language code (letters and sounds). Some educators favor a "look–say" (or whole-word) approach, in which students learn whole words and practice them by reading appropriate stories and other passages. Proponents of this approach stress the meaning of the words and usually believe that students learn the code incidentally (or with a little coaching). Finally, proponents of this approach offer the opinion (contradicted by empirical research) that drilling children in letters and sounds destroys their motivation to read. Other educators favor systematically teaching the language code: how letters represent sounds and how sounds and letters are combined to form words—both spoken and written. Proponents of this approach argue that specifically and systematically teaching phonics produces more skillful readers more easily; they also argue that reading failure destroys motivation to read.

For the first hundred years or so of the debate, observations of reading were too crude to indicate more than that the reader looked at print and said the printed words (or answered questions about the content conveyed by those printed words). Consequently, theoreticians speculated about the processes occurring inside the reader, and the speculations of advocates of whole-word instruction dominated the debate until the 1950s. Thereafter, phonics instruction (systematically teaching beginning readers the relationships among the alphabetic code, phonemes, and words) increasingly became part of prereading and reading instruction. Some of that increased emphasis on phonics may be attributable to *Why Johnny Can't Read* (Flesch, 1955), a book vigorously advocating phonics instruction; more importantly, the growing body of empirical evidence increasingly showed phonics instruction's effectiveness. By 1967, there was substantial evidence that systematic instruction in phonics produced better readers and that the effect of phonics instruction was greater for children of low ability or from disadvantaged backgrounds. With phonics instruction, beginning readers had better word recognition, better reading comprehension, and better reading vocabulary (Bond & Dykstra, 1967; Chall, 1967). Subsequent empirical evidence leads to the same conclusions (Rayner, Foorman, Perfetti, Pesetsky, & Seidenberg, 2001; National Institute of Child Health and Human Development, 2000a, 2000b; Adams, 1990; Foorman, Francis, Fletcher, Schatschneider, & Mehta, 1998; Pflaum, Walberg, Karegianes, & Rasher, 1980; Stanovich, 1986).

While some scholars were demonstrating the efficacy of phonics instruction, others began unraveling the ways in which beginners learn to read. Today that process is much clearer than it was even in the 1970s. Armbruster and Osborn

(2001) have provided an excellent summary of the processes involved in early reading. First, beginning readers must understand how words are made up of sounds before they need to read. This process, called "phonemic awareness," is the ability to recognize and manipulate phonemes, which are the spoken sounds that affect the meaning of a communication. Phonemic awareness can be taught if it has not already developed before reading instruction begins. Second, beginning readers must associate graphemes (alphabet letters) with phonemes. Beginning readers learn these associations best through explicit phonics instruction. Third, beginning readers must read fluently in order to comprehend what they are reading.

After students become fluent decoders, they read more difficult material. This material often contains advanced vocabulary that students must learn. It contains more complex sentence structure, more condensed and abstract ideas, and perhaps less literal and more inferential meaning. Finally, more difficult material frequently requires that readers read with the purpose of understanding what they are reading.

While learning more about how students begin to read, scholars also learned that some long-held beliefs were not valid. For example, it is incorrect to say that poor readers read letter by letter, but skilled readers read entire words and phrases as a unit. Actually, skilled readers read letter by letter and word by word, but they do it so quickly that they appear to be reading words and phrases (see, for example, Snow, Burns, & Griffin, 1998). It is also incorrect to say that good readers rely heavily on context cues to identify words (Share & Stanovich, 1995). Good readers do use context cues to verify their decoding accuracy. Poor readers rely on them heavily, however, probably because they lack skill in more appropriate word-attack skills (see, for example, Briggs & Underwood, 1984).

Today, despite clear evidence indicating the essential role of phonics in reading and strong indications of the superiority of reading programs with direct instruction in phonics (Foorman et al., 1998), some professionals continue to reject phonics instruction. Perhaps this may explain why most students who are referred for psychological assessment are referred because of reading problems and why most of these students have problems changing the symbols (that is, alphabet letters) into sounds and words. The obvious connection between phonics instruction and beginning reading has not escaped the notice of many parents, however. They have become eager consumers of educational materials (such as "Hooked on Phonics" and "The Phonics Game") and private tutoring (for example, instruction at a Sylvan Learning Center).

Educators' views of how students learn to read and how students should be taught will determine their beliefs about reading assessment. Thus diagnostic testing in reading is caught between the opposing camps. If the test includes an assessment of the skills needed to decode text, it is attacked by those who reject analytic approaches to reading. If the test does not include an assessment of decoding skills, it is attacked by those who know the importance of those skills in beginning reading.

Skills Assessed by Diagnostic Reading Tests

Reading is a complex process that changes as readers develop. Beginning readers rely heavily on a complex set of decoding skills that can be assessed holistically by having a student read orally and assessing his or her accuracy and fluency. Decoding skills may also be measured analytically by having students apply these skills in isolation (for example, using phonics to read nonsense words). Once fluency in decoding has been attained, readers are expected to go beyond the comprehension of simple language and simple ideas to the process of understanding and evaluating what is written. Advanced readers rely on different skills (that is, linguistic competence and abstract reasoning) and different facts (that is, vocabulary, prior knowledge and experience, and beliefs). Comprehension may be assessed by having a student read a passage that deals with an esoteric topic and is filled with abstract concepts and difficult vocabulary; moreover, the sentences in that passage may have complicated grammar with minimal redundancy.

Assessment of Oral Reading Skills

A number of tests and subtests are designed to assess the accuracy or fluency of a student's oral reading. Oral reading tests consist of a series of graded paragraphs that are read sequentially by a student. The examiner notes reading errors and behaviors that characterize the student's oral reading. The Gray Oral Reading Test, Third Edition (GORT-3), was specifically designed to assess oral reading; other commonly used tests (for example, the Stanford Diagnostic Reading Test 4 [SDRT4]) include oral reading subtests. (In earlier editions we also reviewed the Gilmore Oral Reading Test, the Gates-McKillop-Horowitz Reading Diagnostic Tests, the Formal Reading Inventory, and the Durrell Analysis of Reading Difficulty. For these reviews, visit the website for this text.)

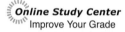
Online Study Center
Improve Your Grade

Errors and Miscues

Rate and fluency of oral reading are based on correct reading. Therefore, it is necessary to define what constitutes an error. Different oral reading tests record different behaviors as errors (also sometimes called miscues). Following are descriptions of commonly recorded errors.

Teacher Pronunciation or Aid If a student either hesitates for a time without making an audible effort to pronounce a word or appears to be attempting for ten seconds to pronounce the word, the examiner pronounces the word and records an error.

Hesitation The student hesitates for two or more seconds before pronouncing a word.

Gross Mispronunciation of a Word A gross mispronunciation is recorded when the pupil's pronunciation of a word bears so little resemblance to the proper pronunciation that the examiner must be looking at the word to recognize it. An example of gross mispronunciation is reading "encounter" as "actors."

Partial Mispronunciation of a Word A partial mispronunciation can be one of several different kinds of errors. The examiner may have to pronounce part of a word for the student (an aid); the student may phonetically mispronounce specific letters (for example, by reading "red" as "reed"); or the student may omit part of a word, insert elements of words, or make errors in syllabication, accent, or inversion.

Omission of a Word or Group of Words   Omissions consist of skipping individual words or groups of words.

Insertion of a Word or Group of Words   Insertions consist of the student's putting one or more words into the sentence being read. The student may, for example, read "the dog" as "the mean dog."

Substitution of One Meaningful Word for Another   Substitutions consist of the replacement of one or more words in the passage by one or more different meaningful words. The student might read "dense" as "depress." Students often replace entire sequences of words with others, as illustrated by the replacement of "he is his own mechanic" with "he sat on his own machine." Some oral reading tests require that examiners record the specific kind of substitution error. Substitutions are classified as meaning similarity (the words have similar meanings), function similarity (the two words have syntactically similar functions), graphic/phoneme similarity (the words look or sound alike), or a combination of the preceding.

Repetition   Repetition occurs when students repeat words or groups of words while attempting to read sentences or paragraphs. In some cases, if a student repeats a group of words to correct an error, the original error is not recorded, but a repetition error is. In other cases, such behaviors are recorded simply as spontaneous self-corrections.

Inversion, or Changing of Word Order   Errors of inversion are recorded when the child changes the order of words appearing in a sentence; for example, "house the" is an inversion.

Nonerrors

Examiners may note characteristics of a student's oral reading that are not counted as errors. Self-corrections are not counted as errors. Disregarded punctuation marks (for example, failing to pause for a comma or to inflect vocally to indicate a question mark) are not counted as errors. Repetitions and hesitations due to speech handicaps (for example, stuttering or stammering) are not counted as errors. Dialectic accents are not counted as mispronunciations. Examiners may also note various characteristics of a student's oral reading that are problematic (although not errors) or that may have contributed to a student's errors. Commonly noted indicators include poor posture, inappropriate head movement, finger pointing, loss of place, lack of expression (for example, word-by-word reading, lack of phrasing, or monotone voice), and strained voice.

Assessment of Reading Comprehension   Diagnostic tests assess five different types of reading comprehension.

1. *Literal comprehension* entails understanding the information that is explicit in the reading material.

2. *Inferential comprehension* means interpreting, synthesizing, or extending the information that is explicit in the reading material.

3. *Critical comprehension* requires analyzing, evaluating, and making judgments about the material read.

4. *Affective comprehension* involves a reader's personal and emotional responses to the reading material.

5. *Lexical comprehension* means knowing the meaning of key vocabulary words.

In our opinion, the best way to assess reading comprehension is to give readers access to the material and have them restate or paraphrase what they have read.

Poor comprehension has many causes. The most common is poor decoding, which affects comprehension in two ways. First, if a student cannot convert the symbols to words, he or she cannot comprehend the message conveyed by those words. The second issue is more subtle. If a student expends all of his or her mental resources on sounding out the words, he or she will have no resources left to process their meaning. For that reason, increasing reading fluency frequently eliminates problems in comprehension.

Another problem is that students may not know how to read for comprehension (Taylor, Harris, Pearson, & Garcia, 1995). They may not actively focus on the meaning of what they read or know how to monitor their comprehension (for example, by asking themselves questions about what they have read or whether they understand what they have read). Students may not know how to foster comprehension (for example, by summarizing material, determining the main ideas and supporting facts, and integrating material with previous knowledge). Finally, individual characteristics can interact with the assessment of reading comprehension. For example, in an assessment of literal comprehension, a reader's memory capacity can affect comprehension scores unless the reader has access to the passage while answering questions about it or retelling its gist. Inferential comprehension depends on more than reading; it also depends on a reader's ability to see relationships (a defining element of intelligence) and on background information and experiences.

Assessment of Word-Attack Skills

Word-attack, or word analysis, skills are those used to derive the pronunciation or meaning of a word through phonic analysis, structural analysis, or context cues. Phonic analysis is the use of letter-sound correspondences and sound blending to identify words. Structural analysis is a process of breaking words into morphemes, or meaningful units. Words contain free morphemes (such as *farm, book,* and *land*) and bound morphemes (such as *-ed, -s,* and *-er*).

Because lack of word-attack skills is the principal reason that students have trouble reading, a variety of subtests of commonly used diagnostic reading tests specifically assess these skills. Subtests that assess word-attack skills range from such basic assessments as analysis of skill in associating letters with sounds to tests of syllabication and blending. Generally, for subtests that assess skill in as-

FIGURE 22.1
An Item That Assesses
Blending Skill

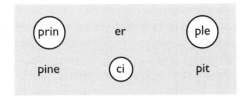

sociating letters with sounds, the examiner reads a word aloud, and the student must identify the consonant-vowel-consonant cluster or digraph that has the same sound as the beginning, middle, or ending letters of the word. Syllabication subtests present polysyllabic words, and the student must either divide the word orally into syllables or circle specific syllables.

Blending subtests, on the other hand, are of three types. In the first method, the examiner may read syllables out loud ("wa-ter-mel-on," for example) and ask the student to pronounce the word. In the second type of subtest, the student may be asked to read word parts and to pronounce whole words. In the third method, the student may be presented with alternative beginning, middle, and ending sounds and asked to produce a word. Figure 22.1 illustrates the third method, used with the Stanford Diagnostic Reading Test 4.

Assessment of Word Recognition Skills

Subtests of diagnostic reading tests that assess a pupil's word recognition skills are designed to ascertain what many educators call "sight vocabulary." A student learns the correct pronunciation of letters and words through a variety of experiences. The more a student is exposed to specific words and the more familiar those words become to the student, the more readily he or she recognizes those words and is able to pronounce them correctly. Well-known words require very little reliance on word-attack skills. Most readers of this book immediately recognize the word *hemorrhage* and do not have to employ phonetic skills to pronounce it. On the other hand, a word such as *nephrocystanastomosis* is not a part of the sight vocabulary for most of us. Such words slow us down; we must use phonetics to analyze them.

Word recognition subtests form a major part of most diagnostic reading tests. Some tests use paper tachistoscopes to expose words for brief periods of time (usually one-half second). Students who recognize many words are said to have good sight vocabularies or good word-recognition skills. Other subtests assess letter recognition, recognition of words in isolation, and recognition of words in context.

Assessment of Rate of Reading

Reading rate is generally played down in the diagnostic assessment of reading difficulties. There are, however, some exceptions. Two levels of the Stanford Diagnostic Reading Test have subtests to assess rate of reading. On the other hand, tests such as the Gray Oral Reading Test, Fourth Edition (GORT-4), are timed, with time affecting the score a pupil receives. A pupil who reads a passage on the GORT-4 slowly but makes no errors in reading may earn a lower score than a rapid reader who makes one or two errors in reading.

Assessment of Other Reading and Reading-Related Behaviors

A variety of subtests that fit none of the aforementioned categories are included in diagnostic reading tests as either major or supplementary subtests. Examples of such tests include oral vocabulary, spelling, handwriting, and auditory discrimination. In most cases, such subtests are included simply to provide the examiner with additional diagnostic information.

Oral Reading Tests

Gray Oral Reading Test, Fourth Edition (GORT-4)

The Gray Oral Reading Test, Fourth Edition (GORT-4), is the third revision of the Gray Oral Reading Test by Wiederholt and Bryant (2001). The GORT-4 remains an individually administered, norm-referenced measure of oral reading and comprehension. Each of the two forms (A and B) of the GORT-4 contains 14 reading passages of increasing difficulty. Students are required to read paragraphs orally and to respond to five comprehension questions for each passage that are read by the examiner. The test is intended for use with students between the ages of 6-0 and 18-11. Specific basal and ceiling rules are used to limit time, which typically ranges from 15 to 45 minutes.

The authors of the GORT-4 state four purposes of the test:

> (a) to help identify those students who are significantly below their peers in oral reading proficiency and who may profit from supplemental help; (b) to aid in determining the particular kinds of reading strengths and weaknesses that individual students possess; (c) to document students' progress in reading as a consequence of special intervention programs; and (d) to serve as a measurement device in investigations where researchers are studying the abilities of school-age students. (Wiederholt & Bryant, 2001, p. 4)

In the manual, the authors go into considerable detail in describing the development of the oral reading passages for the GORT-4 and how the comprehension questions for each passage were written to assess literal, inferential, critical, and affective comprehension. However, except for one reading passage added to each form of the GORT-4, the most recent version of the GORT is identical in every way to the GORT-3 and to the Gray Oral Reading Test–Revised (GORT-R), which are in turn identical to Forms B and D of the Formal Reading Inventory (Wiederholt, 1986). Modifications to the previous edition of the test (GORT-3) include an updated norm sample, the addition of a lower-level passage on each form, and new reliability and validity information.

Scores

The examiner (1) records the number of seconds that the student needed to read the passage aloud and (2) tallies the number of deviations from the text (that is, any deviation from print is scored as an oral reading miscue, unless the deviation is the result of normal speech variations). At the bottom of the test protocol is a matrix. The top row of the matrix has a six-point scale (0 to 5); the next row of the matrix has six time ranges corresponding to the six-point scale. The examiner awards points (0 to 5) for the speed and accuracy with which the passage is read. For each passage, the sum of the rate and accuracy scores is called the "fluency score." A comprehension score is determined from the number of multiple-choice comprehension questions answered correctly (0 to 5). The rate, accuracy, passage, and comprehension scores for the stories read are then summed to yield total scores for rate, accuracy, fluency, and comprehension. From these total scores, corresponding age and grade equivalents, percentiles, and standard scores (mean = 10, standard deviation = 3) can be found in various tables in the manual. The passage and comprehension standard scores are added and then transformed into a standard score called the "oral reading quotient," which has a mean of 100 and a standard deviation of 15. The examiner can also record both the number and kinds of miscues using a separate worksheet. Then the number can be converted into a percentage.

Norms

The GORT-4 was standardized on 1,677 students from 28 states. The norms appear to be representative of the school-age population as reported by the U.S. Census Bureau (1997) in terms of gender, ethnicity, geographical region, various disability statuses, family income and education level, and race; however, slightly higher proportions of white students and students of urban residence were identified in the sample. The sample was additionally stratified according to 13 age intervals for all of the aforementioned variables, with the exception of residence and disability status. No further cross-tabulations are provided in the manual.

Reliability

The internal consistency for five scores (rate, accuracy, passage, comprehension, and oral reading quotient) at 13 ages (6 years to 18 years) was estimated from the performances of all students in the normative sample. The 104 alphas for subtests ranged from .87 to .98; 89 of the 104 coefficients equaled or exceeded .90. Alpha for the oral reading quotient equaled or exceeded .94 at all ages. Test-retest reliability correlation coefficients were determined for both forms. In addition, reliability between the alternate forms allows the estimation of both error due to content sampling and error due to instability. These coefficients ranged from .78 to .95. Overall, the oral reading quotient of the GORT-4 appears sufficiently reliable for making important decisions for individual students; use of other scores for this purpose will depend on the age of the student and the particular score.

Validity

The manual fails to provide evidence of the GORT-4's validity for any purpose other than to document students' progress in reading as a consequence of special intervention programs. Two studies using the GORT-R and one using the GORT-3 demonstrated that significant differences in scores were obtained following implementation of interventions. The authors argue that the test has good content validity because of the procedures used in test construction. Specifically, they argue that the reading passages were written with "close attention to the structure of sentences, the logical connections between sentences and clauses, and the coherence of topics" (Wiederholt & Bryant, 2001, p. 73). They also describe item-level analyses that were conducted in order to eliminate biased items. Results indicated that there were no items demonstrating substantial gender, race, or ethnic bias.

With two exceptions, the criterion-related validity of the GORT-4 is based on studies previously reported for the GORT-R and GORT-3. Relying on the validity of a previous edition is often problematic; in this case, however, this reliance is appropriate because the content of the test has been only slightly changed. Early test versions were correlated with various reading subtests and total scores from the Test of Word Reading Efficiency; Iowa Test of Educational Development; California Achievement Test, Fifth Edition; Gray Oral Reading Tests–Diagnostic; Diagnostic Achievement Battery, Second Edition; Woodcock Reading Mastery Tests–Revised; and Wide Range Achievement Test–Revised. The GORT-4 was correlated with various subtests of the Gray Diagnostic Reading Tests, Second Edition, and the Gray Silent Reading Tests (GSRT). Median correlations for all of these studies for the rate, accuracy, fluency, and comprehension scores ranged from .45 (comprehension) to .75 (accuracy). Median correlation for the oral reading quotient among these studies was .63.

The authors examined the construct validity of the GORT-4 by showing that GORT-4 scores increase with age and are appropriately correlated with measures of spoken and written language and measures of intelligence. Evidence is also provided that the GORT-4 distinguishes groups of students identified as having reading deficits from groups of students without deficits.

Summary

The GORT-4 is an individually administered, norm-referenced measure of oral reading and comprehension for use with students between the ages of 6-0 and 18-11. Multiple scores are derived from a student's reading (rate, accuracy, and rate plus accuracy); a single score is derived for comprehension; and a composite score based on rate, accuracy, and comprehension can be calculated. The standardization sample used for the GORT-4 appears to be generally representative of the U.S. population in terms of gender, place of residence, race, ethnicity, geographic region, and socioeconomic status (SES). Overall, the oral reading quotient of the GORT-4 appears sufficiently reliable for making important decisions for individual students; use of other scores for this purpose will depend on the age of the student and the particular score. The GORT-4 appears to have satisfactory validity.

Diagnostic Reading Tests

Woodcock Diagnostic Reading Battery (WDRB) The Woodcock Diagnostic Reading Battery (WDRB; Woodcock, 1997) is a set of individually administered tests used to measure ten aspects of reading achievement and a set of closely related abilities. The ten subtests for this test are identical to ten subtests contained in the cognitive and achievement batteries of the

FIGURE 22.2
The Reading
Performance Model

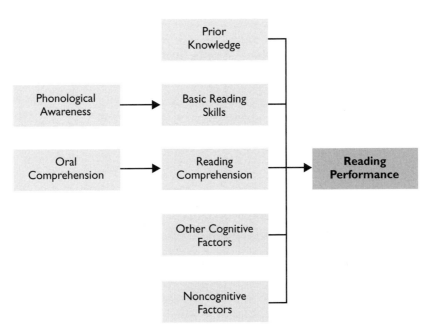

Woodcock-Johnson Psychoeducational Battery–Revised (Woodcock & Johnson, 1989). In that sense, this is not a new test, but rather one formed by combining some of the parts of a more extensive cognitive and achievement battery.

The WDRB is based on a model of reading performance illustrated in Figure 22.2. Woodcock views reading performance as a result of a combination of prior knowledge, basic reading skills, reading comprehension, other cognitive factors, and noncognitive factors. Basic reading skills are seen as the direct result of the application of phonological awareness skills, and reading comprehension is de-rived from application of oral comprehension.

The WDRB is used with individuals between 5 and 90 years of age. It is used to diagnose strengths and weaknesses in five areas: basic reading skills, reading comprehension, phonological awareness, oral language comprehension, and reading aptitude. The author claims that the test is useful in making eligibility decisions and provides a method for computing an ability-achievement discrep-ancy in reading. The test is also designed for use in instructional planning, progress monitoring, and research.

Subtests

The ten subtests of the WDRB are combined to provide cluster scores in seven areas. The tests and the ways in which they are combined into clusters are illus-trated in Figure 22.3. The subtests and the behaviors they sample follow.

Letter-Word Identification   Items in this subtest include those measuring ability to match photographic representations of words (rebuses) with actual pictures of objects, and items that assess letter and word recognition.

FIGURE 22.3
WDRB Selective Testing Table

SOURCE: Copyright © 1997 by The Riverside Publishing Company. Reproduced from *Woodcock Diagnostic Reading Battery, Examiner's Manual,* by Richard W. Woodcock with permission of the publisher. All rights reserved.

	TESTS	Reading: Total Reading	Reading: Broad Reading	Reading: Basic Reading Skills	Reading: Reading Comprehension	Related Abilities: Phonological Awareness	Related Abilities: Oral Comprehension	Related Abilities: Reading Aptitude
Reading	1. Letter-Word Identification	●	●	●				
Reading	2. Word Attack	●		●				
Reading	3. Reading Vocabulary	●			●			
Reading	4. Passage Comprehension	●	●		●			
Related Abilities	5. Incomplete Words					●		
Related Abilities	6. Sound Blending					●		●
Related Abilities	7. Oral Vocabulary						●	●
Related Abilities	8. Listening Comprehension						●	
Related Abilities	9. Memory for Sentences							●
Related Abilities	10. Visual Matching							●

Word Attack This measure of phonic and structural analysis requires students to pronounce nonwords or unfamiliar words.

Reading Vocabulary This subtest measures students' skill in gaining meaning from the words they read. Both synonyms and antonyms are included.

Passage Comprehension Students read phrases or short passages and either point to pictures that illustrate what they read or identify missing words in the phrases or short passages.

Incomplete Words This subtest has words with one or more missing phonemes that the individual must identify.

Sound Blending This is a measure of the individual's skill in synthesizing syllables into words.

Oral Vocabulary The individual gives synonyms or antonyms in response to stimulus words read by the examiner.

Listening Comprehension This is an oral cloze test; the individual listens to a passage and supplies the last word.

Memory for Sentences   This subtest consists of phrases and sentences that are presented individually on audiotape and must be repeated by the individual.

Visual Matching   This subtest consists of 70 sets of numbers; each set consists of six numbers that range from single digits to three-digit numbers. The individual's score is based on the number of sets that are matched correctly within three minutes.

Subtest Clusters   The ten subtests are combined into the following clusters: total reading, broad reading, basic reading skills, reading comprehension, phonological awareness, oral comprehension, and reading aptitude. The WDRB is available in easel format, with stimulus pictures or words facing the individual being tested and test directions facing the examiner. An audiotape is provided for use in administering some of the subtests.

Scores

Scores are available for each subtest and cluster. Raw scores may be converted to standard scores, percentile ranks, *W*-scores, age equivalents, grade equivalents, relative performance indexes, and cluster difference scores. RPIs are expressed as ratios of percentage of success relative to peers. An RPI of 60/90 indicates that the individual achieves 60 percent success on a task on which peers achieve 90 percent success. Percentile ranks and standard scores are peer-comparison scores. RPIs are descriptions of proficiency or quality of performance, whereas age and grade equivalents describe developmental level.

Norms

The norms for the WDRB are a subset of the norms for the Woodcock-Johnson Psychoeducational Battery. The sample comprised 6,026 individuals who were assessed during 1986 to 1988. The sample was drawn from 100 geographically diverse settings, stratified on the basis of ten community and subject variables: census region, community size, gender, race, Hispanic/non-Hispanic, funding of college or university, education of adults, occupational status of adults (employed/unemployed), and occupation of adults (white collar, blue collar/farm, service). The sample is representative of the U.S. Census.

Reliability

Data on both internal-consistency and test-retest reliability are reported in the manual for the WDRB. Table 22.1 lists the median internal-consistency reliabilities for students ages 5 to 18 years and for adults. Test-retest reliabilities are based on the performance of 504 students and range from .62 (Incomplete Words) to .92 (Letter-Word Identification). With the exception of those for the Incomplete Words subtest, reliabilities look sufficiently high to use the test for making decisions about individuals.

TABLE 22.1	Median Reliabilities for WDRB Subtests and Clusters	

Subtests	Median Reliability in 5–18 Age Range	Median Reliability in Adults
Letter-Word Identification	.94	.95
Word Attack	.91	.90
Reading Vocabulary	.92	.93
Passage Comprehension	.88	.92
Incomplete Words	.72	.87
Sound Blending	.86	.91
Oral Vocabulary	.88	.92
Listening Comprehension	.80	.83
Memory for Sentences	.86	.88
Visual Matching	.78	.84
Clusters		
Total Reading	.98	.98
Broad Reading	.95	.96
Basic Reading Skills	.96	.96
Reading Comprehension	.95	.96
Phonological Awareness	.88	.93
Oral Comprehension	.91	.95
Reading Aptitude	.93	.96

Validity

Extensive evidence on validity is presented in the manual. In supporting content validity, Woodcock shows how reading skills to sample, from simple to complex, were selected and matches these to a model of reading. In supporting concurrent validity, he illustrates appropriately high correlations with the Peabody Individual Achievement Test, Basic Academic Skills Individual Screener, Kaufman Assessment Battery for Children, Kaufman Test of Education Achievement, Wide Range Achievement Test–Revised, Stanford-Binet Intelligence Scale, and Wechsler Intelligence Scale for Children–Revised. Also, good evidence for construct validity is provided.

Summary

The WDRB is a test that was built by pulling a subset of tests from the Woodcock-Johnson Psychoeducational Battery–Revised. In that sense, the test is not new. The strength of this measure is that it puts in one place the reading subtests and clusters from the Woodcock-Johnson. The test is used to measure behaviors in ten subtests and clusters, and it is intended to be used for diagnostic and instructional planning purposes. The test is among the best-normed diagnostic reading tests, and there is good evidence for its reliability and validity.

Group Reading Assessment and Diagnostic Evaluation (GRADE)

The Group Reading Assessment and Diagnostic Evaluation (GRADE; Williams, 2001) is a norm-referenced test of reading achievement that can be administered individually or in a group. It is designed to be used for students between the ages of 4 years (preschool) and 18 years (twelfth grade). There are 11 test levels, each with two forms (A and B). These include separate levels across each grade for prekindergarten through sixth grade, a middle school level (M), and two high school levels (H and A). Although the test is untimed, the author estimates that older students should be able to complete the assessment in one hour, whereas younger children may require up to 90 minutes. The manual provides both fall and spring norms to help in tracking progress over a school year. The following five test applications are discussed by the author: (1) placement and planning, (2) understanding the reading skills of students, (3) testing on level and out of level (which may allow more appropriate information on a child's strengths and weaknesses to be obtained among children at the margins), (4) monitoring growth, and (5) research.

Subtests

Five components of reading are assessed: prereading, reading readiness, vocabulary, comprehension, and oral language. Different subtests are used to assess these components at different levels.

Prereading Component

Picture Matching. For each of the 10 items in this subtest, a student must mark the one picture in the four-picture array that is the same as the stimulus picture.

Picture Differences. For each of the 8 items in this subtest, a student must mark the one picture in the four-picture array that is different from the other pictures.

Verbal Concepts. For each of the 10 items in this subtest, a student must mark the one picture in the four-picture array that is described by the examiner. For each of the 10 items in this subtest, a student must mark the one picture in the four-picture array that does not belong with the other pictures.

Reading Readiness

Sound Matching. For each of the 12 items in this subtest, a student must mark the one picture in the four-picture array that has the same beginning (or ending) sound as a stimulus word. Students are told what words the pictures represent.

Rhyming. For each of the 14 items in this subtest, a student must mark the one picture in the four-picture array that rhymes with a stimulus word. Students are again told what words the pictures represent.

Print Awareness. For each of the 4 items in this subtest, a student must mark the one picture in the four-picture array that has the following print elements: letters, words, sentences, capital letters, and punctuation.

Letter Recognition. For each of the 11 items in this subtest, a student is given a five-letter array and must mark the capital or lowercase letter read by the examiner.

Same and Different Words. For each of the 9 items in this subtest, a student must mark the one word in the four-word array that is either the same as or different from the stimulus word.

Phoneme-Grapheme Correspondence. For each of the 16 items in this subtest, a student must mark the one letter in the four-word array that is the same as the beginning (or ending) sound of a word read by the examiner.

Vocabulary

Word Reading. The subtest contains 10 to 30 items, depending on the level. For each item in this subtest, a student is given a four-word array and must mark the word read by the examiner.

Word Meaning. For each of the 27 items in this subtest, a student must mark the one picture in the four-picture array that represents a written stimulus word.

Vocabulary. This subtest contains 30 to 40 items, depending on the test level. Students are presented a short written phrase or sentence that has one word bolded. A student must mark the one word in the four- or five-word array that has the same meaning as the bolded word.

Comprehension

Sentence Comprehension. For each of the 19 cloze items in this subtest, a student must choose the one word in the four- or five-word array that best fits in the blank.

Passage Comprehension. The number of reading passages and items for this subtest varies by test level. A student must read a passage and answer several multiple-choice questions about the passage. Questions are of four types: questioning, clarifying, summarizing, and predicting.

Oral Language

Listening Comprehension. In this 17- or 18-item subtest, the test administrator reads aloud a sentence. A student must choose which of four pictures represents what was read. Items require students to comprehend basic words, understand grammar structure, make inferences, understand idioms, and comprehend other nonliteral statements.

Scores

Subtest raw scores can be converted into stanines. Depending on the level administered, certain subtest raw scores can be added to produce composite scores. Similarly, each level has a different set of subtest raw scores that are added in computing the total test raw score. Composite and total test raw scores can be converted to unweighted standard scores (mean of 100, standard deviation of 15), stanines, percentiles, normal-curve equivalents, grade equivalents, and growth scale values.[1] Conversion tables provide both fall and spring normative scores. For students who are very skilled or very unskilled readers in comparison to their same-grade peers, out-of-level tests may be administered. Appropriate normative tables are available for some out-of-level tests in the teacher's scoring and interpretive manuals. Other out-of-level normative scores are reported only in the scoring and reporting software.

Norms

The GRADE standardization sample included 16,408 students in the spring sample and 17,024 in the fall sample. Numbers of students tested in each grade ranged from 808 (seventh grade, spring) to 2,995 (kindergarten, spring). Gender characteristics of the sample were presented by grade level, and roughly equal numbers of males and females were represented in each grade and season level (fall and spring). Geographic region characteristics were presented without disaggregating results by grade and were compared to the population data as reported by the U.S. Census Bureau (1998). Southern states were slightly over-represented, whereas western states were slightly underrepresented in both the fall and spring norm samples. Information on community type was also presented for the entire fall and spring norm samples; the samples are appropriately representative of urban, suburban, and rural communities. Information on students receiving free lunch was also provided. Information on race was also compared to the percentages reported by the U.S. Census Bureau (1998) and appeared representative of the population. It is important to note, again, that this information was not reported by grade level. Finally, the authors report that special education students were included in the sample but do not provide the number included.

Reliability

Total test coefficient alphas were calculated as measures of internal consistency for each form of the test, for each season of administration (fall and spring). These ranged from .89 to .98. Coefficient alphas were also computed for various subtests and subtest combinations (for example, Picture Matching and Picture Differences were combined into a Visual Skills category at the preschool and kindergarten levels). These were calculated for each GRADE level, form, and season of administration; several reliabilities were calculated for out-of-level tests (for example, separate alpha coefficients were computed for preschoolers and kindergartners taking the kindergarten-level test). These subtest-subtest

---

[1] Because growth scale values include all levels on the same scale, these scores make it possible to track a student's reading growth when the student has been given different GRADE levels over the years. It is important to note, however, that particular skills measured on the test vary from level to level, so growth scale values may not represent the same skills at different years.

combination coefficients ranged from .45 (Listening Comprehension, Form B, eleventh grade, spring administration) to .97 (Listening Comprehension, Form A, preschool, fall administration). Of the 350 coefficients calculated, 99 met or exceeded .90. The Comprehension Composite was found to be the most reliable composite score across levels. Listening Comprehension had consistently low coefficients from the first-grade level to the highest level (Level A), and thus are not included in calculating the total test raw scores for these levels. Alternate-form reliability was determined across a sample of 696 students (students were included at each grade level). Average time between testing ranged from 8 days to 32.2 days. Correlation coefficients ranged from .81 (eleventh grade) to .94 (preschool and third grade). Test-retest reliability was determined from a sample of 816 students. The average interval between testing ranged from 3.5 days (eighth-grade students taking Form A of Level M) to 42 days (fifth-grade students taking Form A of Level 5). Test-retest correlation coefficients ranged from .77 (fifth-grade students taking Form A of Level 5) to .98 (fourth-grade students taking Form A of Level 4). Reliability data were not provided on growth scale values.

Validity

The author presents three types of validity: content, criterion-related, and construct validity. Rationale is provided for why particular item formats and subtests were included at particular ages, and what skills each subtest is intended to measure. Also, a comprehensive item tryout was conducted on a sample of children across the nation. Information from this tryout informed item revision procedures. Statistical tests and qualitative investigations of item bias were also conducted during the tryout. Finally, teachers were surveyed, and this information was used in modifying content and administration procedures (although specific information on this survey is not provided). Criterion-related validity provided by the author included correlations of the GRADE total test standard score with five other measures of reading achievement: the total reading standard score of the Iowa Test of Basic Skills, the California Achievement Test total reading score, the Gates-MacGinitie Reading Tests total score, the Peabody Individual Achievement Test–Revised (PIAT-R) scores (General Information, Reading Recognition, Reading Comprehension, and Total Reading subtests), and the Terra Nova. Each of these correlation studies was conducted with somewhat limited samples of elementary and middle school students. Coefficients ranged from .61 (GRADE total test score correlated with PIAT-R General Information among 30 fifth-grade students) to .90 (GRADE total test score correlated with Gates total reading score for 177 first-, second-, and sixth-grade students). Finally, construct validity was addressed by showing that the GRADE scores were correlated with age. Also, scores for students with dyslexia ($N = 242$) and learning disabilities in reading ($N = 191$) were compared with scores for students included in the standardization sample that were matched on GRADE level, form taken, gender, and race/ethnicity, but who were not receiving special education services. As a group, students with dyslexia performed significantly below the matched control group. Similarly, students with learning disabilities in reading performed significantly below the matched control group.

Summary

The GRADE is a standardized, norm-referenced test of reading achievement that can be group administered. It can be used with children of a variety of ages (4 to 18 years) and provides a "growth scale value" score that can be used to track growth in reading achievement over several years. Different subtests and skills are tested, depending on the grade level tested; 11 forms corresponding to 11 GRADE levels are included. Although the norm sample is large, certain demographic information on the students in the sample is not provided, and in some cases, groups of students are over- or underrepresented. Total test score reliability data are strong. However, other subtest-subtest composite reliability data do not support the use of these particular scores for decision-making purposes, although the validity data provided in the manual suggest that this test is a useful measure of reading skills.

Measures of Reading Comprehension

Test of Silent Word Reading Fluency (TOSWRF)

The Test of Silent Word Reading Fluency (TOSWRF; Mather, Hammill, Allen, & Roberts, 2004) is a group or individually administered, norm-referenced test designed to screen poor readers and to monitor reading development in children ages 6-6 to 17-11 years of age. The TOSWRF includes two equivalent forms (A and B), each of which requires approximately 10 minutes to administer. Students are presented with rows of letter strings made up of words that are not separated by spaces (for example, bluenowcat). Students are instructed to divide the string of letters into words by drawing a line between words (for example, blue/now/cat). Students have three minutes to identify as many words as they can.

Scores

Clear scoring procedures and a sufficient number of examples make scoring ambiguous responses easy. The TOSWRF uses a basal rule to speed scoring. The raw score is the sum of the number of correctly divided words above the basal plus the number of words below the basal. If both forms are administered, a composite score is obtained. Raw scores are transformed to standard scores with a mean of 100 and a standard deviation of 15, as well as percentile ranks, age-equivalent scores, and grade-equivalent scores.

Norms

The TOSWRF was standardized on a sample of 3,592 children between the ages 6-6 and 17-11. Norm groups are in three-month intervals between 6-6 and 7-11, six-month intervals from 8-0 to 11-11, and one-year intervals from 12-0 on. The individual norm groups range in size from 119 to 460. Overall, the sample is representative in terms of geographic residence, gender, race, Hispanic status, and educational attainment of the parents. Except for geographic region, individual norm groups are also representative on these characteristics.

Reliability

To estimate alternate-form reliability, the norm sample was divided into two groups. The first group was tested with Form A before Form B; the second group was tested with Form B before Form A. All scores were then converted to standard scores and correlated. The estimated reliability for 6- and 7-year-olds exceeds .90, and the estimated reliability for 8- through 16-year-olds was in the .80s. The reliability of the composite (if both forms were given) would equal or exceed .90 for students between the ages of 6 and 16. The estimated reliability of 17-year-olds, although less than .80 for the single forms and less than .90 for the composite, is sufficient for screening purposes. Alternate-form estimates were also obtained for several subgroups (specifically, males, females, blacks, whites, Hispanics, poor readers, and seven exceptionalities). TOSWRF was sufficiently reliable to use for screening with any of these groups.

Test-retest data were collected on five groups of students using both forms. Estimated stabilities (corrected for constricted range) exceed .90 for the elementary group, two middle school groups, and one high school group; the estimated stability for the second group of high school students was .74.

In general, the best estimate of reliability comes from alternate-form correlations with two weeks between test administrations. This procedure allows the simultaneous estimation of error associated with item and time sampling. Reliability estimates were calculated with five groups, as was done with test-retest estimates. Corrected correlations for the elementary sample, two middle school samples, and one high school sample exceeded .90. The correlation for one high school sample appeared anomalous, .73.

Finally, interscorer correlation between two independent scorers scoring identical protocols was .99 for both forms.

Validity

The TOSWRF's general validity is based on its content- and criterion-related indices. Its content validity rests in part on the research demonstrating that timed word strings without spaces have been used successfully to measure word identification speed and in part on the careful selection of progressively more difficult words used in word strings.

The TOSWRF correlates highly with the Sight Word Efficiency and the Phonemic Decoding Efficiency subtests of the Test of Word Reading Efficiency; the Reading Comprehension subtest of the Stanford Achievement Test Series, Ninth Edition; Oral Reading Fluency passages 1 through 3 on the Dynamic Indicators of Basic Early Literacy Skill, Fifth Edition; the Word Identification subtest of the Woodcock Reading Mastery Tests–Revised–Normative Update; and the Letter-Word Identifications and Passage Comprehension subtests from the Woodcock-Johnson Psychoeducational Battery–Revised Tests of Achievement.

In addition, TOSWRF scores are quite developmental (correlating strongly with age). The test discriminates between average and below-average readers, and students with language disorders and poor readers on average earn scores below the mean. Finally, TOSWRF scores correlate with other measures of school success (for example, Skills Cluster, Broad Reading, Broad Math, and Broad Knowledge on the Woodcock-Johnson Psychoeducational Battery–Revised Tests of Achievement), as well as general intellectual functioning as measured by the Wechsler Intelligence Scale for Children, Third Edition.

Summary

The TOSWRF is a group- or individually administered, norm-referenced test designed to assess the silent word-reading fluency of students from 6-6 to 17-11 years of age. Its norms appear representative of the U.S. population across geographic area, gender, race, ethnicity, educational attainment of parents, and exceptionality status within age groups. Reliabilities frequently are generally excellent for a screening measure, and when both forms are administered, it is sufficiently reliable to use in making important educational decisions for students. The TOSWRF manual presents good evidence of validity.

Test of Reading Comprehension–3 (TORC-3)

The Test of Reading Comprehension–3 (TORC-3; Brown, Hammill, & Wiederholt, 1995) is an individually administered, norm-referenced measure of students' understanding of written language. The authors of the TORC identify four purposes for using the test:

> (1) to identify students whose scores are significantly below their peers and who might need interventions designed to improve reading comprehension, (2) to determine relative strengths and weaknesses in areas of reading comprehension, (3) to document student progress in reading comprehension, and (4) [to aid] in research. (p. 8)

Changes were made in the third edition of this test to address concerns that we and others had raised regarding earlier editions. Specifically, we had raised concerns about the way the norm sample was stratified, the description of the sample, and the validity. In developing this third edition, the authors collected all new normative information, stratified the norm sample by age (but not by other student characteristics), reported on studies of gender and race bias, provided new test-retest reliability data, and provided updated and expanded information on criterion-related and content validity. The content of the test remains as in the first edition.

The TORC-3 may be given to individuals, groups of three to five students, or entire classes. It is appropriate for use with students ages 7-0 to 17-11. In developing the TORC-3, the authors set out (1) to construct a measure of comprehension of written language that was independent of any instructional program; (2) to use multiple formats or styles to assess reading comprehension; (3) to minimize the likelihood of obtaining correct responses solely as a result of general information, memorization, or guessing; (4) to use a silent rather than an oral reading format; and (5) to avoid overuse of vocabulary from any specific content area. For the most part, they were successful. The authors clearly state that any results obtained from this measure are to be treated as instructional hypotheses to be confirmed through more individualized, behaviorally focused strategies.

Subtests

The TORC-3 is made up of eight subtests. Four are combined to form a general reading comprehension core, three are measures of content-specific vocabularies, and one is a measure of the student's skill in reading directions in schoolwork. Following is a brief description of each subtest.

General Vocabulary   The student is required to read three stimulus words that are related in some way and then to select from four response words the two that are related to the three stimulus words.

Syntactic Similarities   The student is given five sentences and must select the two that are most closely related in meaning.

Paragraph Reading   The student is required to read paragraphs and then answer five multiple-choice questions for each paragraph. The questions differ in their demands: One question requires the selection of a "best title" for the paragraph, two require the literal recall of story details, one requires the inference of meaning, and one requires a negative inference.

Sentence Sequencing   Each item consists of five randomly ordered sentences, which the student must order in such a way that they make a meaningful story.

Mathematics Vocabulary   The format of this subtest is identical to that of the General Vocabulary subtest. The words are taken from recent mathematics textbooks.

Social Studies Vocabulary   The format of this subtest is identical to that of the General Vocabulary subtest. The words are taken from recent social studies textbooks.

Science Vocabulary   The format of this subtest is identical to that of the General Vocabulary subtest. The words are taken from recent science textbooks.

Reading the Directions of Schoolwork   This subtest is designed for younger and remedial readers. The student must read a set of directions and then implement the instructions on an answer sheet.

Subtest Items   The TORC-3 contains a relatively limited number of items for a measure spanning a ten-year age range. Six of the subtests contain 25 items each, the Sentence Sequencing subtest contains 10 items, and the Paragraph Reading subtest contains 6 reading passages, each of which is followed by 5 questions. Item selection was based on the performance of 120 elementary school students in grades 2 through 6 in one school district in Austin, Texas. The authors used the performance of these students to reduce the test from an initial 358 items to the 190 items that make up the test.

Scores

Raw scores, percentiles, and standard scores may be obtained for each subtest. In addition, an overall reading comprehension quotient may be calculated. Standard scores have a mean of 10 and a standard deviation of 3. The reading comprehension quotient is obtained by adding the standard scores for the General Vocabulary, Syntactic Similarities, Paragraph Reading, and Sentence Sequencing subtests. These four subtests compose the general reading comprehension score. The reading comprehension quotient has a mean of 100 and a standard deviation of 15.

The authors provide grade-equivalent scores for the TORC-3 but appropriately caution readers about their use. They indicate that the reason for including grade scores is because they are required in many state education agencies and local education agencies. Throughout the manual, they warn users about the limitations and potential misuse of grade scores.

Norms

The TORC-3 was standardized on a sample of 1,962 students from 19 states. The norm population was selected in two ways. First, the authors picked one or two cities from each of four U.S. Census regions and used a test coordinator in each city to coordinate the collection of data on a total of 950 students. They do not specify the reason for the selection of the specific city within each region. Second, people who had purchased reading tests from the publisher were contacted and asked to assess 20 students each. Fifty-one people volunteered, and they collectively tested 1,012 students. The authors provide a table showing the gender, residence (urban versus rural), race, ethnicity, geographic region, and disabling condition of students in the norm sample, and they contrast these data with census information. They provide stratification information for age with some variables (such as 12-year-old females) but not with other variables (such as number of African American students who were from urban environments or number of males from the South). These data are necessary to make judgments concerning the representativeness of the norm group.

Reliability

The authors of the TORC-3 provide data on three kinds of reliability: internal consistency, test-retest, and interscorer. Internal-consistency coefficients were computed for each of the individual subtests at each age. Eighty-nine percent of those coefficients exceed .90, and all but one of the coefficients exceed the desirable standard of .80.

Validity

The authors have not done a convincing job of demonstrating that the TORC-3 is, indeed, a measure of reading comprehension. First, the rationale for inclusion of the eight subtests as measures of reading comprehension is not convincing. This is especially true for the subtests that measure content-specific vocabulary in mathematics, social studies, and science. The authors report that they selected vocabulary for these subtests by sampling textbooks in science, social studies, and math. Yet the textbooks sampled were all published prior to 1978. It is our contention that textbooks in these subject areas have changed in the more than 20 years since the authors sampled them.

The results of six criterion-related validity studies reported by the authors raise some major questions. The investigations were conducted with very specific samples (for example, 54 boys and girls attending second and third grade in Norman, Oklahoma; 28 adolescent girls attending a residential treatment center in Austin, Texas). Sample size ranged from 28 to 94, and performance on the TORC-3 was correlated with performance on other measures of reading, intelligence, mathematics, and language arts. The measures are all old and no longer published. Correlations of TORC-3 subtests with measures of intelligence and measures of mathematics achievement were as high as correlations with other measures of reading, language arts, and reading comprehension.

Summary

The Test of Reading Comprehension–3 is a norm-referenced measure designed to provide an evaluation of students' comprehension of written language. In addition to a reading comprehension quotient, which is based on pupil performance on four subtests, the test provides users with an assessment of pupil performance in content-specific vocabulary and in following the directions of schoolwork. There is some question about the adequacy of the norms. In general, TORC-3 appears sufficiently reliable for making important individual decisions about students, but the extent to which the test measures reading comprehension is uncertain.

Criterion-Referenced Testing in Reading

The tests we have discussed to this point are norm-referenced tests, which are designed to compare individuals with their peers. Criterion-referenced diagnostic testing in reading is a practice that dates from the late 1960s. Criterion-referenced diagnostic reading tests are designed to analyze systematically an individual's strengths and weaknesses without comparing that individual with others. The principal objective of criterion-referenced tests is to assess the specific skills a pupil has, to determine those skills the pupil does not have, and to relate the assessment to curricular content. Criterion-referenced assessment is tied to instructional objectives, and individual items are designed to assess mastery of specific objectives.

Although all criterion-referenced reading tests are based on task analyses of reading, the particular skills assessed and their sequences differ from test to test, because different authors view reading in different ways and see the sequence of development of reading skills differently. For this reason, it is especially important with criterion-referenced tests (as with norm-referenced tests) that teachers pay special attention to the behaviors and sequences of behaviors sampled by the tests.

Because normative comparisons are not made in criterion-referenced assessment, no derived scores are calculated. For that reason, many authors of criterion-referenced tests downplay the importance of reliability for their scales. Nonetheless, reliable assessment is important in criterion-referenced tests. Although we are not concerned with the consistency of derived scores, we are concerned with the consistency of responses to items when all items in the domain are assessed. If a different pattern of item scores is obtained each time an individual takes the test, we begin to question the reliability of the device. Because criterion-referenced devices generally contain relatively limited samples of behavior, it is important that test authors report the consistency with which their tests assess each specific behavior. Test authors can and should report test-retest reliabilities for each item. It is important to note the consistency with which the test samples the domain of possible test items when the domain is not exhausted. When alternative forms of a criterion-referenced test are available, the authors should report correlations between performances on the two forms.

Dynamic Indicators of Basic Early Literacy Skills, Sixth Edition (DIBELS)

The Dynamic Indicators of Basic Early Literacy Skills, Sixth Edition (DIBELS; Good & Kaminski, undated), is intended to screen and monitor progress in beginning reading three times each year, beginning in kindergarten and continuing through third grade. The DIBELS consists of seven individually administered tests assessing phonological awareness, alphabetic understanding, and fluency with connected text. The DIBELS has English and Spanish versions, is available on the Internet (at dibels.uoregon.edu), and materials can be downloaded without charge.

There are two measures of phonological awareness. Initial Sounds Fluency[2] (ISF) assesses the skill of preschoolers through mid-kindergartners in identifying and producing the initial sound of a given word. Students must select from an array of pictures named by the examiner the one picture that begins with a specific sound. Then students are asked to give the beginning sound of the previously named pictures. Phonemic Segmentation Fluency[3] (PSF) assesses the skill of mid-kindergartners through students at the end of first grade in segmenting words into phonemes. Students must produce the individual phonemes of words read by the examiner. In this task, examiners orally present words consisting of three to four phonemes, and students must verbally produce the individual phonemes that comprise the word.

There are two measures of alphabetic understanding. Letter Naming Fluency[4] (LNF) assesses the skill of beginning kindergartners through beginning first graders in naming upper- and lowercase letters in one minute. Nonsense Word Fluency[5] (NWF) assesses the knowledge of mid-kindergartners through students at the end of first grade of letter-sound correspondences as well their ability to blend letters using their most common sound to form nonsense words.

Fluency is measured by three tests. Oral Reading Fluency[6] (ORF) assesses the skill of students from the mid-first grade through the end of second grade in

---

[2] Developed by Roland H. Good III, Deborah Laimon, Ruth A. Kaminski, and Sylvia Smith.
[3] Developed by Roland H. Good III, Ruth Kaminski, and Sylvia Smith.
[4] Developed by Ruth A. Kaminski and Roland H. Good III.
[5] Developed by Roland H. Good III and Ruth A. Kaminski.
[6] Developed by Roland H. Good III, Ruth A. Kaminski, and Sheila Dill.

reading aloud connected text in grade-level material for one minute. Retell Fluency (RTF) is administered to check reading comprehension. Students retell everything they can remember from the Oral Reading Fluency passage, and the number of words used in the student's retell are tabulated. Word Use Fluency (WUF) assesses the ability of students from the beginning of kindergarten through third grade to correctly use specific words in sentences.

Scores

Except for Word Use Fluency, which uses the number correct, student performances are converted to the number of correct responses per minute. Subtest scores are converted by grade placement to three ranges: students who are at risk for achieving early literacy benchmarks, at some risk for achieving those goals, and at low risk of achieving those goals.

Norms

DIBELS tests are designed to provide local normative comparisons. As a result, the normative, or comparison, sample is representative because it is the group to which scores are compared; the comparisons are current because the local districts provide the normative information.

Reliability

Alternate-form methods must be used to estimate the item sample reliability of timed tests. However, when there are weeks between administration of the forms, error associated with time is added to error associated with item sampling. This appears to be the case for DIBELS tests. Combined item-stability estimates range from .72 (Initial Sounds Fluency) to .94 for Oral Reading Fluency. When multiple tests (three seems sufficient) are given, estimated reliability exceeds .90. No estimates of item-sample reliability are presented for Retell Fluency or Word Use Fluency.

Validity

The DIBELS's general validity rests on the content- and criterion-related validity. The content is directly based on current empirical research that stresses the importance of fluency in basic skill areas: phonemic awareness, alphabetic principle, and reading fluency. Fluency on each subtest is well documented in the research literature as essential to success in learning to read. Benchmark goals and timelines are based on research reviews.

In addition, numerous studies indicate that each subtest correlates well with established reading measures. For example, Letter Naming Fluency correlates .70 with the Readiness Cluster and .65 with the Reading Cluster of the Woodcock-Johnson Psychoeducational Battery–Revised; it correlates .77 with the Metropolitan Readiness Test. Oral Reading Fluency correlates .36 with the Reading Cluster of the Woodcock-Johnson. Phonemic Segmentation Fluency correlates .54 with the Woodcock-Johnson Readiness Cluster and .65 with the Metropolitan Readiness Test. Correlations between Nonsense Word Fluency and the Woodcock-Johnson Readiness Cluster ranges from .36 to .59, depending on the student's grade; the correlation with the Total Reading Cluster is .66. Oral Reading Fluency correlations with various reading measures range from .52 to .91.

Summary

The DIBELS consists of seven individually administered tests assessing phonological awareness, alphabetic understanding, and fluency. Single tests are generally sufficient for screening purposes; however, three or four tests must be administered for there to be sufficient reliability for making important educational decisions for individual students. Evidence for content validity is excellent, and criterion-related validity is good.

STAR Early Literacy Computer-Adaptive Diagnostic Assessment

STAR Early Literacy is a criterion-referenced test designed to provide quick and accurate estimates of the early literacy skills of children in kindergarten through third grade. A computer-adaptive process is used to match test items to the student's ability and performance level; students have up to 90 seconds to answer each item. The specific items that students receive depend on how well they perform on previous items. Each test is uniquely tailored to the individual student. Because students can be tested more than ten times in one year without concern for previous item exposure, the test is suitable for monitoring student progress.

Items on STAR Early Literacy measure literacy skills in seven domains: General Readiness (understanding word boundaries, length, patterns, shapes, and numbers); Phonemic Awareness (the ability to identify sounds in words); Phonics (the ability to pronounce letter and letter group sounds); Graphophonemic Knowledge (understanding the relationship between letters and sounds); Structural Analysis (understanding the relationship between words and word parts); Vocabulary (ability to identify common words and understand antonyms and synonyms); and Reading and Listening Comprehension (ability to read and understand text). Students answer a minimum of two items in each of these domains. All of the items have audio instructions and include three answer choices, with one choice being correct.

Scores

Raw scores are converted to scaled scores that range from 300 to 900 and are intended to roughly indicate the typical age of similarly performing students; for example, 300 is a performance of a 3-year-old, and 900 is a performance of a 9-year-old. Students are classified as emergent, transitional, or probable readers based on the scaled score. Domain and skill scores are also calculated and represent an estimated percentage of all the items in the test bank for the given domain or skill that the student would be likely to answer correctly.

Norms

Calibration and pilot studies were conducted based on preliminary versions of the test. The technical manual provides comparisons of various sample characteristics with those of the population; however, very few of the population characteristics were appropriately represented in the samples. Approximate percentile ranks can be obtained for each grade level based on data from these studies.

Reliability

Alternate-form stability was estimated using 9,000 students who had participated in the pilot study. The test-retest interval was several days. These reliability estimates ranged from .63 at prekindergarten to .70 at first grade. Item reliabilities were also estimated using conditional standard errors. These reliability estimates were .85 for each grade except for kindergarten, which was .77. The test's reliability is sufficient for making screening decisions for students.

Validity

Correlations between STAR Early Literacy and performance on a number of standardized reading and early achievement tests are listed in an extensive table in the manual. Comparison tests included the Gates-McGinitie Reading Test, the Iowa Test of Basic Skills, the Metropolitan Readiness Test, the Terra Nova, and STAR Reading, among others. Averages of these correlations were calculated and ranged from .57 to .64 for the different grade levels. Prekindergarten students were not included in these studies. The authors present evidence of construct validity by showing that the scale scores increased with age and grade level in the pilot study sample data.

Summary

STAR Early Literacy is a criterion-referenced, computer-adaptive test of early reading skills that gives teachers information about students' instructional levels and their areas of strength and weakness in seven domains. Norms used in calibrating items appear less than representative, and evidence for reliability is adequate. The evidence for validity is adequate.

Standardized Test for the Assessment of Reading (S.T.A.R.)

The Standardized Test for the Assessment of Reading (S.T.A.R.; Advantage Learning Systems, 1997) is designed to provide teachers with quick and accurate estimates of students' instructional reading levels and estimates of their reading levels relative to national norms. The test is administered using computer software, so the specific test items each student receives are determined by his or her responses to previous test items. Using computer-adaptive procedures, a branching formula matches test items to student ability and performance level. The test uses a vocabulary-in-context format in which students must identify the best choice for a missing word in a single-context sentence. Correct answers fit both the semantics and the syntax of the sentence. All incorrect answers either fit the syntax of the sentence or relate to the meaning of something in the sentence.

Scores

Users of S.T.A.R. may obtain grade equivalents, percentile ranks, normal-curve equivalents, and scaled scores. In addition, they may obtain information about the zone of proximal development, an index of the low and high ends of the range at which students can read. The software used to administer the test provides the information, and scores are obtained immediately.

Norms

Items for S.T.A.R. were developed using 13,846 students from 59 schools. The development sample was stratified on the basis of gender, grade, geographic region, district socioeconomic status, school type, and district enrollment. The primary unit of selection was school rather than students. Tables in the manual contrast sample characteristics with national population characteristics. For the most part, sample characteristics approximate population characteristics. Notable exceptions include an underrepresentation of students from the Northeast (9 percent versus 20 percent in the population) and of schools with small (less than 2,500) and large (more than 25,000) enrollments.

S.T.A.R. was standardized on 42,000 students from 171 schools. The standardization sample was stratified on the basis of geographic region, school system and per-grade district enrollment, and socioeconomic status. Sample characteristics very closely approximate population characteristics. Students from all geographic regions, socioeconomic levels, and school sizes were selected in proportion to their presence in the population. Normative tables in the manual describe the close approximation of the sample to the U.S. population.

Reliability

S.T.A.R. is a computer-adaptive test that offers a virtually unlimited number of test forms, so traditional methods of conducting reliability analyses do not apply. The authors instead conducted reliability analyses using a test-retest methodology with alternative forms. Reliability was tested using both scaled scores and instructional reading levels. A total of 34,446 students were tested twice with S.T.A.R., each taking the second test an average of five days after the first. Test-retest reliabilities ranged from .85 to .95 for scaled scores, and from .79 to .91 for instructional reading level.

Validity

Performance on S.T.A.R. was correlated with performance on a number of different standardized measures of reading skills administered to those in the standardization group. An extensive table in the manual reports these results. Comparison tests included the California Achievement Test, Comprehensive Test of Basic Skills, Degrees of Reading Power, Gates-MacGinitie, Iowa Test of Basic

Skills, Metropolitan Achievement Test, Stanford Achievement Test, and several custom-built state tests (Connecticut, Texas, Indiana, Tennessee, Kentucky, North Carolina, and New York). Performance on S.T.A.R. is related closely to performance on the other measures of reading.

Summary

S.T.A.R. is a norm-referenced, computer-adaptive reading test that provides teachers with information about students' instructional levels as well as their level of performance relative to a national sample. S.T.A.R. enables users to sample a wide range of reading behaviors in a relatively limited period of time. The test was standardized on a large and representative group of students. Evidence for reliability and validity is satisfactory. The test should be very useful to those who want immediate scoring and information about appropriate student instructional level.

The Test of Phonological Awareness, Second Edition: Plus (TOPA 2+)

The Test of Phonological Awareness, Second Edition: Plus (TOPA 2+; Torgesen & Bryant, 2004) is a norm-referenced device intended to identify students who need supplemental services in phonemic awareness and letter-sound correspondence. The TOPA 2+ can be administered individually or to groups of students between the ages of 5 and 8 years to assess phonological awareness and letter-sound correspondences.

Two forms are available: the Kindergarten form and the Early Elementary form for students in the first or second grades. The Kindergarten form has two subtests. The first, Phonological Awareness, has two parts, each consisting of 10 items. In the first part, students must select from a three-choice array the word that begins with the same sound as the stimulus word read by the examiner. In the second part, students must select from a three-choice array the word that begins with a different sound. The second subtest, Letter Sounds, consists of 15 items requiring students to mark the letter in a letter array that corresponds to a specific phoneme. The Early Elementary form also has two subtests. The first, Phonological Awareness, also has two parts, each consisting of 10 items. In the first part, students must select from a three-choice array the word that ends with the same sound as the stimulus word read by the examiner. In the second part, students must select from a three-choice array the word that ends with a different sound. The second subtest, Letter Sounds, requires students to spell 18 nonsense words that vary in length from two to five phonemes.

Scores

The number correct on each subtest is summed, and sums can be converted to percentiles and a variety of standard scores.

Norms

Separate norms for the Kindergarten form are in four 6-month age intervals (that is, 5-0 through 5-5, 5-6 through 5-11, 6-0 through 6-5, and 6-6 through

6-11). Separate norms for the Early Elementary form are 12-month age groups (that is, 6-0 through 6-11, 7-0 through 7-11, and 8-0 through 8-11).

The TOPA 2+ was standardized on a total of 2,085 students, 1,035 of whom were in the Kindergarten form and the remaining 1,050 of whom were in the Early Elementary form. Norms for each form at each age are representative of the U.S. population in 2001 in terms of geographic regions, gender, race, ethnicity, and family income. Parents without a college education are slightly underrepresented.

Reliability

Coefficient alpha was calculated for each subtest at each age. For the Kindergarten form, only Letter Sounds for 6-year-olds fell below .90; that subtest reliability was .88. For the Early Elementary form, all alphas were between .80 and .87. Additionally, alphas were calculated separately for males and females, whites, blacks, Hispanics, and students with language or learning disabilities. These alphas ranged from .82 to .91.

Test-retest correlations were used to estimate stabilities. For the Kindergarten form, 51 students were retested within about a two-week interval. Stability for Phonological Awareness was .87, and stability for Letter Sounds was .85. For the Early Elementary form, 88 students were retested within about a two-week interval. Stability for Phonological Awareness was .81, and stability for Letter Sounds was .84.

Finally, interscorer agreement was evaluated by having two trained examiners each score 50 tests. On the Kindergarten form, interscorer agreement for Phonological Awareness was .98 and for Letter Sounds was .99. On the Early Elementary form, interscorer agreement for Phonological Awareness was .98 and for Letter Sounds was .98.

Overall, care should be taken when interpreting the results of the TOPA 2+. The internal consistency is sufficient for screening and in some cases for use in making important educational decisions for students.

Validity

Evidence for the general validity of the TOPA 2+ comes from several sources. First, the contents of scales were carefully developed to represent phonemic awareness and knowledge of letter-sound correspondence. For example, the words in the phonological awareness subscales come from the 2,500 most frequently used words in first graders' oral language, and all consonant phonemes had a median age of customary articulation no later than 3.5 years of age. Next, the TOPA 2+ correlates well with another scale measuring similar skills and abilities (Dynamic Indicators of Basic Early Literacy Skills) and with teacher judgments of students' reading abilities. Evidence for differentiated validity comes from the scales' ability to distinguish students with language and learning disabilities from those without such problems. Other indices of validity include absence of bias against males or females, whites, African Americans, and Hispanics.

Summary

The TOPA 2+ assesses phonemic awareness using beginning and ending sounds and letter-sound correspondence at the kindergarten and early elementary levels. The norms appear representative and are well described. Coefficient alpha for phonemic awareness is generally good for kindergartners, but only suitable for screening students in the early elementary grades and for letter-sound correspondence for all students. Stability was estimated in the .80s, but interscorer agreement was excellent. Overall, care should be taken when interpreting the results of the TOPA 2+. Evidence for validity is adequate.

Comprehensive Test of Phonological Processing (CTOPP)

The Comprehensive Test of Phonological Processing (CTOPP; Wagner, Torgesen, & Rashotte, 1999) is an individually administered, norm-referenced test that is appropriately used with individuals ranging in age from 5 to 25 years. In addition to use in research, the CTOPP is intended for identifying individual strengths and weaknesses in phonological processing, for diagnosing individuals who lag significantly behind their peers in phonological skills, and for documenting development of these skills.

Subtests

The CTOPP is composed of 13 subtests in three areas of phonology: phonological awareness, phonological memory, and rapid naming. As shown in Table 22.2, the required and supplemental subtests differ for two age groups: children 5 and 6 years of age and individuals 7 years of age and older.

Elision   This subtest measures the ability to delete sounds from spoken words in order to create new words. Test takers repeat a word read by the examiner and then say the word again without a particular sound. For example, "Say 'cold.' Now say 'cold' without saying *k*."

Blending Words   This subtest measures the ability to synthesize sounds into words. Test takers listen to syllables and then say what word the syllables make. For example, "can-dy" requires a response of "candy."

Sound Matching   This subtest measures the ability to discriminate words with the same beginning or ending sounds by having test takers point to a drawing depicting a word that starts (or ends) with the same sound as a stimulus word.

Blending Nonwords   This subtest measures the ability to synthesize sounds into units like words by requiring test takers to listen to separate sounds and then blend them into a nonsense word. For example, "flib-bo" is "flibbo."

Segmenting Nonwords   This subtest measures the ability to separate the sounds in nonwords by having test takers listen to a nonsense word (like "flibbo"), repeat the word, then repeat the nonsense word one syllable at a time ("flib-bo").

Memory for Digits   This subtest measures the ability to recall a sequence of numbers by having test takers repeat a series of digits in the same order as presented. The digit sequences range in length from two to eight.

| TABLE 22.2 | CTOPP Subtests by Age and Phonological Process |

Subtest	Age Group	
	5–6	7–21
Phonological Awareness		
Elision	C[a]	C
Blending Words	C	C
Sound Matching	C	
Blending Nonwords[b]	S	S
Segmenting Nonwords[b]		S
Phonological Memory		
Memory for Digits	C	C
Nonword Repetition	C	C
Rapid Naming		
Rapid Color Naming	C	S[c]
Rapid Object Naming	C	S[c]
Rapid Digit Naming		C
Rapid Letter Naming		C
Additional Diagnostic Subtests		
Phoneme Reversal		S
Segmenting Words		S

[a]C indicates that the subtest is used in the composite, and S indicates that the subtest is supplemental.
[b]Subtest is part of the Alternate Phonological Awareness composite.
[c]Subtest is part of the Alternate Rapid Naming composite.

Nonword Repetition This subtest measures the ability to recall nonwords by having test takers listen to a stimulus composed of 3 to 15 sounds and then repeat it.

Rapid Color Naming This subtest measures the ability to recall and fluently say the names of colors by having test takers name blocks printed in one of six different colors. The blocks are arranged in two matrices, each on a separate page. Each matrix consists of four rows and nine columns of randomly arranged colors. The score is the number of seconds needed to name the colors of the 72 blocks.

Rapid Object Naming This subtest measures the ability to recall and fluently say the names of familiar objects by having test takers name drawings of them. The drawings are arranged in two matrices, each on a separate page. Each matrix consists of four rows and nine columns of randomly arranged drawings. The score is the number of seconds needed to name the 72 objects.

Rapid Digit Naming This subtest measures the ability to recall and fluently say the names of numbers by having test takers say the names of six different integers. The integers are arranged in two matrices, each on a separate page. Each matrix consists of four rows and nine columns of randomly arranged integers. The score is the number of seconds needed to name the 72 integers.

Rapid Letter Naming This subtest measures the ability to recall and fluently say the names of letters by having test takers say the names of six different letters. The letters are arranged in two matrices, each on a separate page. Each matrix consists of four rows and nine columns of randomly arranged letters, and the score is the number of seconds needed to name the 72 letters.

Phoneme Reversal This subtest measures the ability to say phonemes in reverse order to create a meaningful word by having test takers listen to a nonword, repeat the nonword, and then reorder the sounds to form a word. For example, a child might hear "o-g" and be required to make the word "go" from the two sounds.

Segmenting Words This subtest measures the ability to separate the sounds in words by having test takers listen to a word (like "it"), repeat the word, then repeat the word one phoneme at a time ("i-t").

Scores

Subtest raw scores can be converted to percentiles, standard scores with a mean of 10 and standard deviation of 3, and age and grade equivalents. In addition, selected subtests can be combined to form composites. As shown in Table 22.2, the subtests used to form the three usual composites (that is, Phonological Awareness, Phonological Memory, and Rapid Naming) differ for students of different ages. Two alternative composites are also available for older test takers (Alternate Phonological Awareness and Alternate Rapid Naming). Composites can be converted to percentiles and to standard scores with a mean of 100 and a standard deviation of 15.

Norms

The CTOPP was normed on 1,656 individuals residing in 30 states. The sampling plan consists of three poorly described strategies to locate individuals. The authors present data to show that the standardization sample has approximately the same proportions of individuals as the U.S. population in 1997. However, there are two problems. First, there is no discussion of the criteria used for categorization into urban/rural resident, ethnic group, or race. Second, the data presented do not correspond to the specific normative comparisons. Separate norms tables are provided for individuals in whole-year groups (that is, for individuals from 5 years 0 months to 5 years 11 months, and so on) except for persons aged 18 through 24. However, the data describing the norms are presented in two-year intervals, and no data are presented for the normative groups for individuals aged 18 through 24.

Reliability

Coefficient alpha was used to estimate the reliability of item samples for all untimed subtests. The authors state on page 68 of the manual that they estimated the reliability of item samples for the timed tests (that is, Rapid Color Naming, Rapid Object Naming, Rapid Digit Naming, and Rapid Letter Naming) by alternate-form procedures. Although not explained in the manual, the procedures do not appear to be the usual alternate-form method of estimating reliability, because the test has no alternate forms. The reported estimates of item reliability for the individual subtests are generally too low to be used in making decisions on behalf of individual children. Of the 165 subtest by age group estimates, only 34 (almost 21 percent) equal or exceed .90, and 42 (about 25 percent) are less than .80. Estimates of the reliability of item samples for composites vary by age. For 5- and 6-year-olds, the reliability of Phonological Awareness equals or exceeds .95; the other composites are less than .90. For older individuals, reliability estimates equal or exceed .90 for 8 of the 12 age groups on the Phonological Awareness composite and for 9 of the 12 age groups on the Rapid Naming composite; on the Phonological Memory composite, the highest estimated item reliability is .86. Reliability estimates equal or exceed .90 for 9 of the 12 age groups on the Alternate Phonological Awareness composite and for 1 of the 12 age groups on the Alternate Rapid Naming composite.

Stability of CTOPP scores was estimated using 91 Floridians who were tested within a two-week period. For children 5 to 7 years of age, only the Phonological Memory composite has a test-retest correlation equaling or exceeding .90. Rapid Digit Naming and Rapid Letter Naming also had stabilities over .90, but these subtests are not given to children in this age range, and no norm tables are available to convert raw scores. For individuals 8 to 17 years of age, only Rapid Object Naming and the Alternate Rapid Naming composite have a test-retest correlation of .90 or more. Finally, for the 18-and-older group, Rapid Digit Naming, the Phonological Memory composite, and the Alternate Rapid Naming composite have test-retest correlations of .90 or more.

To investigate the interscorer reliability, two individuals independently scored 30 completed protocols (that is, answered forms) for 5- and 6-year-olds and 30 completed protocols for individuals 7 through 24. All 60 protocols were selected randomly from the normative sample. The scorers summed the number correct and converted the raw scores to standard scores. Correlations between scores were uniformly high, equaling or exceeding .95. However, the scorers apparently did not evaluate the students' actual responses to ascertain whether they were correct or incorrect. Thus the high coefficients reflect only the degree to which adults can apply ceiling rules, sum correct responses, and look up scores.

Validity

The three aspects of phonological processing were selected by the authors because of their relationship to academic achievement (especially in reading and mathematics) and the comprehension of oral and written language, and because of their implication in learning disability. The behaviors used to assess the three aspects of phonological processing are based on experimental tasks.

Several studies demonstrating the CTOPP's criterion-related predictive validity are reported in the test manual. Illustrative is one study that used the three composites to predict decoding scores on the Woodcock Reading Mastery Tests–Revised administered one year later. The correlations with decoding scores are impressive for kindergartners and first graders: $r = .71$ and $.80$ for Phonological Awareness, $r = .66$ and $.70$ for Rapid Naming, and $r = .42$ and $.52$ for Phonological Memory. Overall, there is considerable evidence that the CTOPP predicts decoding.

Evidence for the CTOPP's construct validity comes from several sources. Confirmatory factor analyses support the test's organization and conceptual model. Scores on most subtests increase with age, supporting the developmental nature of the skills being assessed. Students with independently identified speech disabilities, language disabilities, or learning disabilities earn lower scores than nondisabled students. CTOPP scores show neither racial, ethnic, nor gender bias. Finally, CTOPP scores appear to be sensitive to intervention; that is, improved skills following intervention are reflected in increased test scores.

Summary

The Comprehensive Test of Phonological Processing is an individually administered, norm-referenced test intended to assess phonological awareness, phonological memory, and rapid naming. Different combinations of the 13 subtests are used to assess these abilities for test takers of different ages. The number of individuals in the CTOPP normative sample (1,656) is adequate, and the overall sample appears representative of the nation. However, questions about the representativeness of the sample remain because the sampling plan is poorly described, and the data presented in the manual do not correspond to the actual normative comparisons. Except for Phonological Awareness, reliability estimates are generally too low for making decisions concerning individuals. There is strong evidence for the CTOPP's validity.

Dilemmas in Current Practice

There are five major problems in the diagnostic assessment of reading strengths and weaknesses. The first is the problem of curriculum match. Students enrolled in different reading curricula have different opportunities to learn specific skills. Reading series differ in the skills that are taught, in the emphasis placed on different skills, in the sequence in which skills are taught, and in the time at which skills are taught. Tests differ in the skills they assess. Thus it can be expected that pupils studying different curricula will perform differently on the same reading test. It can also be expected that

pupils studying the same curriculum will perform differently on different reading tests. Diagnostic personnel must be very careful to examine the match between skills taught in the student's curriculum and skills tested. Most teacher's manuals for reading series include a listing of the skills taught at each level in the series. Many authors of diagnostic reading tests now include in test manuals a list of the objectives measured by the test. At the very least, assessors should carefully examine the extent to which the test measures what has been taught. Ideally, assessors would select specific parts of tests to

Dilemmas in Current Practice (*continued*)

measure exactly what has been taught. To the extent that there is a difference between what has been taught and what is tested, the test is not a valid measure.

The second problem is also a test-curriculum match problem. Most reading instruction now takes place in general education classrooms, using the content of typical reading textbooks. This is true for developmental reading instruction, remedial reading instruction, and the teaching of reading to students with disabilities. Most diagnostic reading tests measure student skill-development competence in isolation. Also, they do not include assessments of the comprehension strategies, such as the metacognitive strategies that are now part of reading instruction.

A third problem is the selection of tests that are appropriate for making different kinds of educational decisions. We noted that there are different types of diagnostic reading tests. In making classification decisions, educators must administer tests individually. They may either use an individually administered test or give a group test to one individual. For making instructional planning decisions, the most precise and helpful information will be obtained by giving individually administered criterion-referenced measures. Educators can, of course, systematically analyze pupil performance on a norm-referenced test, but the approach is difficult and time consuming. It may also be futile because norm-referenced tests usually do not contain enough items on which to base a diagnosis.

When evaluating individual pupil progress, assessors must consider carefully the kinds of comparisons they want to make. If they want to compare pupils with same-age peers, norm-referenced measures are useful. If, on the other hand, they want to know the extent to which individual pupils are mastering curriculum objectives, criterion-referenced measures are the tests of choice.

The fourth problem in the assessment of reading strengths and weaknesses is that there are few technically adequate tests. We have noted that, for many norm-referenced reading tests, there is no adequate description of the groups on which the tests were standardized. Other tests were inadequately standardized. There is no evidence of the reliability or validity of many diagnostic reading tests. The reliability of other tests is not sufficient to allow valid decisions about individuals. Diagnostic personnel should refrain from using technically inadequate measures. At the very least, they must operate with full awareness of the technical limitations of the devices they use.

The fifth problem is one of generalization. Assessors are faced with the difficult task of describing or predicting pupil performance in reading. Yet reading itself is difficult to describe, being a complex behavior composed of numerous subskills. Those who engage in reading diagnosis will do well to describe pupil performance in terms of specific skills or subskills (such as recognition of words in isolation, listening comprehension, and specific word-attack skills). They should also limit their predictions to making statements about probable performance of specific reading behaviors, not probable performance in reading.

SUMMARY

In this chapter, we have reviewed the kinds of behaviors sampled by diagnostic reading tests. Several specific norm-referenced and criterion-referenced tests have been evaluated in terms of the kinds of behaviors they sample and their technical adequacy. Most of the norm-referenced devices clearly lack the technical characteristics necessary for use in making specific instructional decisions. Many do not present evidence of reliability and validity. In fact, some tests present the assessor with numerous normative tables for interpreting test data without describing the nature of the normative population.

The criterion-referenced test described in this chapter is designed to pinpoint skill-development strengths and weaknesses, provide teachers with instructional objectives, and direct teachers to materials that help teach to those objectives. We do not yet have sufficient empirical evidence to judge the extent to which criterion-referenced tests meet their stated objectives. Teachers need to judge for their own purposes the sequences of the behavior samplings and the sequences of behaviors sampled. The systems still contain many rough spots that need to be smoothed out.

How, then, do teachers and diagnostic specialists assess skill development in reading and prescribe developmental, corrective, or remedial programs? Reliance on scores provided by diagnostic reading tests is indeed precarious. Teachers and diagnostic specialists must rely on the qualitative information obtained in testing. Some tests provide checklists of observed difficulties, which may be of considerable help in identifying an individual pupil's reading characteristics. Also, teachers and diagnostic specialists must rely on data they obtain by watching students read texts and by asking students questions about the reading strategies the students use.

In assessing reading strengths and weaknesses, teachers must first ask themselves what kinds of behaviors they want to assess. Specific subtests of larger batteries can then be used to assess those behaviors. Teachers should choose the subtests that are technically most accurate. Interpretation must be in terms of behaviors sampled rather than in terms of subtest names.

QUESTIONS FOR CHAPTER REVIEW

1. Reading tests assess six types of comprehension skills. A skill deficit in each type could have significant implications for learning. What are the implications of deficits in listening and lexical comprehension?

2. In assessing reading strengths and weaknesses, what options do teachers have?

3. What are the relative merits and limitations in using criterion-referenced diagnostic reading tests and in using norm-referenced tests?

4. Dierdre, a student in Mr. Albert's fifth-grade class, has considerable difficulty reading. Mr. Albert wants to know at what level to begin reading instruction. Given the state of the art in diagnostic testing in reading, describe some alternative ways for Mr. Albert to identify a starting point.

5. When teachers use criterion-referenced reading tests, they often find that the sequence in which specific individuals learn reading skills differs from the sequence of skills assessed by the test. How might this difference be explained?

PROJECT

Using information found in the text, write a summary for three diagnostic reading tests. Upon completion, compare your summaries with the text summaries. Then go to the *Mental Measurements Yearbooks* (see "Print Resources"), and compare and contrast your summaries with the reviews of the tests you selected. If your summaries differ from the reviews, have the reviewers used information and standards different from those you used?

RESOURCES FOR FURTHER INVESTIGATION

Print Resources

Armbruster, B., & Osborn, J. (2001). *Putting reading first: The research building blocks for teaching children to read.* Jessup, MD: Partnership for Reading. Available from the National Institute for Literacy website: www.nifl.gov.

Arthaud, T. J., Vasa, S. F., & Steckelberg, A. L. (2000). Reading assessment and instructional practices in special education. *Diagnostique, 25*(3), 205–227.

Brown, V., Hammill, D., & Wiederholt, J. L. (1997). *Test of Reading Comprehension–3*. Austin, TX: Pro-Ed.

Conoley, J. C., & Impara, J. C. (1995). *The twelfth mental measurements yearbook* (GORT-3, pp. 422–425). Lincoln, NE: University of Nebraska Press.

Conoley, J. C., & Kramer, J. J. (1989). *The tenth mental measurements yearbook* (WRMT-R, pp. 909–916; TORC, pp. 850–855). Lincoln, NE: University of Nebraska Press.

Elliott, S. N., & Piersel, W. C. (1982). Direct assessment of reading skills: An approach which links assessment to intervention. *School Psychology Review, 11,* 267–280.

Karlsen, B., & Gardner, E. F. (1996). *Directions for administering the Stanford Diagnostic Reading Test, Forms J/K* (pp. 7–8). San Antonio, TX: Harcourt Educational Measurement.

Kramer, J. J., & Conoley, J. C. (1992). *The eleventh mental measurements yearbook* (Gates-MacGinitie, pp. 348–354). Lincoln, NE: University of Nebraska Press.

Mitchell, J. V. (1985). *The ninth mental measurements yearbook* (SDRT, pp. 1462–1465). Lincoln, NE: University of Nebraska Press.

Palincsar, A. M., & Brown, A. L. (1984). Reciprocal teaching of comprehension-fostering and comprehension-monitoring activities. *Cognition and Instruction, 1,* 117–175.

Taylor, B., Harris, L., Pearson, P. D., & Garcia, G. (1995). *Reading difficulties: Instruction and assessment* (2nd ed.). New York: McGraw-Hill.

Tucker, D. L., & Bakken, J. P. (2000). How do your kids do at reading? And how do we assess them? *Teaching Exceptional Children, 32*(6), 14–19.

Woodcock, R. (1997). *Woodcock Diagnostic Reading Battery.* Chicago: Riverside Publishing Company.

Technology Resources

RIVERSIDE PUBLISHING
www.riverpub.com
Go to Product Categories, and then, under Clinical and Special Needs, you will find information on reading tests.

PRO-ED CATALOGUE INFORMATION FOR PRODUCTS
www.proedinc.com
Find product information about reading tests.

CHAPTER 23

Assessment of Mathematics

DIAGNOSTIC TESTING IN MATHEMATICS IS DESIGNED TO IDENTIFY SPECIFIC STRENGTHS and weaknesses in skill development. We have seen that all major achievement tests designed to assess multiple skills include subtests that measure mathematics competence. These tests are necessarily global and attempt to assess a wide range of skills. However, in most cases the number of items assessing specific math skills is insufficient for diagnostic purposes. Diagnostic testing in mathematics is more specific, providing a detailed assessment of skill development within specific areas.

There are fewer diagnostic math tests than diagnostic reading tests, but math assessment is more clear-cut. Because the successful performance of some mathematical operations clearly depends on the successful performance of other operations (for example, multiplication depends on addition), it is easier to sequence skill development and assessment in math than in reading. Diagnostic math tests generally sample similar behaviors. They sample various mathematical contents, concepts, and operations, as well as applications of mathematical facts and principles. Some now also include assessment of students' attitudes toward math.

Why Do We Assess Mathematics?

There are several reasons to assess mathematics skills. First, we are often interested in evaluating a student's competence in math. We may use diagnostic tests in mathematics to assess a student's readiness for instruction (in mathematics and other subjects) or to determine eligibility for employment. Second, all public school programs, with the exception of programs for students with profound disabilities, teach math facts and concepts. Thus teachers need to know whether pupils have mastered those facts and concepts. Diagnostic math tests are intended to provide sufficiently detailed information so that teachers and intervention-assistance teams can plan and evaluate instructional programs. Finally, diagnostic math tests are occasionally used to make exceptionality and eligibility decisions. Individually administered tests are usually required for eligibility and placement decisions. Therefore, we often see diagnostic math tests used to establish special learning needs and eligibility for programs for children with learning disabilities in mathematics.

Behaviors Sampled by Diagnostic Mathematics Tests

The National Council of Teachers of Mathematics (NCTM) has specified a set of standards for learning and teaching in mathematics. The most recent specification of those standards was in a document entitled *Principles and Standards for School Mathematics,* issued in 2000. The NCTM specified five content standards and five process standards. Diagnostic math tests now typically assess knowledge and skill in some subset of those ten standards, or they show how what they assess relates to the NCTM standards. The standards are listed in Table 23.1, and for each of the standards we list the kinds of behaviors or skills identified by NCTM as important.

Some math tests include survey questions asking students about their attitudes toward math. Students are asked the extent to which they enjoy math, the extent to which their friends like math more than they do, and so on.

TABLE 23.1   NCTM Standards for Learning and Teaching in Mathematics

Numbers and Operations

Instructional programs from prekindergarten through grade 12 should enable all students to
- Understand numbers, ways of representing numbers, relationships among numbers, and number systems.
- Understand meanings of operations and how they relate to one another.
- Compute fluently and make reasonable estimates.

Algebra

Instructional programs from prekindergarten through grade 12 should enable all students to
- Understand patterns, relations, and functions.
- Represent and analyze mathematical situations and structures using algebraic symbols.
- Use mathematical models to represent and understand quantitative relationships.
- Analyze change in various contexts.

Geometry

Instructional programs from prekindergarten through grade 12 should enable all students to
- Analyze characteristics and properties of two- and three-dimensional geometric shapes and develop mathematical arguments about geometric relationships.
- Specify locations and describe spatial relationships using coordinate geometry and other representational systems.
- Apply transformations and use symmetry to analyze mathematical situations.
- Use visualization, spatial reasoning, and geometric modeling to solve problems.

(continued)

Measurement

Instructional programs from prekindergarten through grade 12 should enable all students to
■ Understand measurable attributes of objects and the units, systems, and processes of measurement.
■ Apply appropriate techniques, tools, and formulas to determine measurements.

Data Analysis and Probability

Instructional programs from prekindergarten through grade 12 should enable all students to
■ Formulate questions that can be addressed with data and collect, organize, and display relevant data to answer them.
■ Select and use appropriate statistical methods to analyze data.
■ Develop and evaluate inferences and predictions that are based on data.
■ Understand and apply basic concepts of probability.

Problem Solving

Instructional programs from prekindergarten through grade 12 should enable all students to
■ Build new mathematical knowledge through problem solving.
■ Solve problems that arise in mathematics and in other contexts.
■ Apply and adapt a variety of appropriate strategies to solve problems.
■ Monitor and reflect on the process of mathematical problem solving.

Reasoning and Proof

Instructional programs from prekindergarten through grade 12 should enable all students to
■ Recognize reasoning and proof as fundamental aspects of mathematics.
■ Make and investigate mathematical conjectures.
■ Develop and evaluate mathematical arguments and proofs.
■ Select and use various types of reasoning and methods of proof.

Communication

Instructional programs from prekindergarten through grade 12 should enable all students to
■ Organize and consolidate their mathematical thinking through communication.
■ Communicate their mathematical thinking coherently and clearly to peers, teachers, and others.
■ Analyze and evaluate the mathematical thinking and strategies of others.
■ Use the language of mathematics to express mathematical ideas precisely.

Connections

Instructional programs from prekindergarten through grade 12 should enable all students to
■ Recognize and use connections among mathematical ideas.
■ Understand how mathematical ideas interconnect and build on one another to produce a coherent whole.
■ Recognize and apply mathematics in contexts outside of mathematics.

Representation

Instructional programs from prekindergarten through grade 12 should enable all students to
■ Create and use representations to organize, record, and communicate mathematical ideas.
■ Select, apply, and translate among mathematical representations to solve problems.
■ Use representations to model and interpret physical, social, and mathematical phenomena.

SOURCE: The National Council of Teachers of Mathematics (NCTM).

Specific Diagnostic Mathematics Tests

This chapter reviews four diagnostic mathematics tests: the Comprehensive Mathematical Abilities Test (CMAT), the Group Mathematics Assessment and Diagnostic C Evaluation (G·MADE), the Stanford Diagnostic Mathematics Test 4 (SDMT4), and STAR Math.

Comprehensive Mathematical Abilities Test (CMAT)

The Comprehensive Mathematical Abilities Test (CMAT; Hresko, Schlieve, Herron, Swain, & Sherbenou, 2003) is an individually administered, norm-referenced test designed to assess a broad range of mathematical skills in the areas of reasoning, calculation, and application in children ages 7 years 0 months to 18 years 11 months. Four uses are suggested for the test: (1) to determine strengths and weaknesses among a student's mathematical skills, (2) to identify students who deviate from peers (above or below) in mathematical skills, (3) to predict students' future performance in mathematics, and (4) use as a measurement tool in research. The basic testing materials consist of student response booklets and a picture book. For subtests in which the student response booklet does not present the problem, the picture book provides the necessary figures and text to answer the questions. The vast majority of items are free response.

Subtests

The CMAT is comprised of 12 subtests that are divided into two groups: core and supplemental. Although none of the subtests is timed, the test authors estimate that it usually takes 45 to 60 minutes to administer the core subtests. Items become increasingly more difficult as students progress through each subtest. The content of the core subtests is primarily from two NCTM content standards: Number and Operations, and Data Analysis and Probability. The supplemental subtests address the Algebra, Geometry, and Measurement content standards. Content knowledge is assessed through the various NCTM process standards.

Core Subtests

Addition (AD). This 25-item subtest assesses students' computation skills in addition. Items may involve whole numbers, decimals, fractions, or mixed numbers. Some items require regrouping or the addition of numbers with different place values. Items are presented in either vertical or horizontal format.

Subtraction (SU). Students solve 23 subtraction problems. Similar to the addition subtest, items may involve whole numbers, decimals, fractions, or mixed numbers. Some problems require regrouping or subtraction of numbers with different place values. Problems can be presented either vertically or horizontally.

Multiplication (MU). Students solve 26 problems using the multiplication operation, including multiplication of whole numbers, decimals, fractions, and mixed numbers. In addition, problems may require regrouping or multiplying numbers with different place values. Problems are presented either vertically or horizontally.

Division (DI). Students solve 25 problems using the division operation. Items include the division of whole numbers, decimals, fractions, and mixed numbers. Items may require regrouping, division of numbers with different place values, or problems with remainders. Calculators may not be used for this subtest.

Problem Solving (PS). Students solve 24 story problems representing a broad array of real-life scenarios. Students must first translate English text into a mathematical problem and then solve the problem. This may require manipulation or combination of operations and the use of formulas, probability, or calculation of percentages or ratios. Students may use a calculator for this subtest.

Charts, Tables, and Graphs (CTG). This 28-item subtest assesses students' ability to decipher relevant mathematical information from charts, tables, and graphs. Graph items use pie charts, histograms, area graphs, and line graphs. Calculators may be used for this subtest.

Supplemental Subtests Calculators may be used for all supplemental subtests.

Algebra (AL). Items (25) from this subtest require students to solve quadratics and linear equations, and to simplify or factor polynomials.

Geometry (GE). This 24-item subtest assesses skills in Euclidean geometry, including students' understanding of plane geometry, area, volume, surface area, parallel lines, and the geometry of triangles and circles.

Rational Numbers (RN). This 27-item subtest assesses student understanding of rounding principles, the magnitudes of fractions and decimal numbers, and the conversion of fractions or decimals to percents and vice versa.

Time (TI). This 25-item subtest assesses student skill in reading analog clocks and calendars, and in computing time by means of addition or subtraction. Computation items are specifically focused on measuring whether students understand the relationships between days, hours, minutes, and seconds.

Money (MO). This 31-item subtest assesses student skills in recognizing currency value and solving problems related to money. Beginning items require students to identify how much money is represented in coins and bills. Later items consist of problems related to common consumer situations, sales commission, interest, and "relationships between compensation paid across multiple time scales" (p. 4).

Measurement (ME). This 23-item subtest assesses student abilities "to use numbers to represent length, area, and volume" (p. 4). Beginning items ask students to estimate lengths of pictured lines or the size of common items. Later items require students to convert from one unit of measurement to another.

Scores

Raw scores from each subtest can be transformed into standard scores with a mean of 10 and a standard deviation of 3. Normative tables are provided for converting subtest raw scores to both age-based and grade-based standard scores and percentile ranks. The age-based tables are divided into six-month increments. The grade-based tables are divided by the fall and spring of each grade level. Various combinations of subtest standard scores yield six composite scores (described below). The sum of the subtest standard scores in each composite can be converted to a composite quotient with a mean of 100 and a standard deviation of 15. Tables are provided for converting the sum of subtest standard scores into composite quotients and percentile ranks. Additional tables are provided to convert composite quotients into normal-curve equivalents, *z*-scores, *t*-scores, stanines, and age or grade equivalents. The six composite quotients are as follows.

Core Composites

General Mathematics. This composite is a combination of the subtests contributing to both Basic Calculation and Mathematical Reasoning. The most widely used, this composite is an overall measure of basic calculation and reasoning skills.

Basic Calculations. This composite is a measure of basic arithmetic computation and is found by combining the following subtests: Addition, Subtraction, Multiplication, and Division.

Mathematical Reasoning. This core composite is found by combining two subtests: Problem Solving and Charts, Tables, and Graphs.

Supplemental Composites

Advanced Calculations. This supplemental composite measures advanced mathematical computation skills. It is composed of the following subtests: Algebra, Geometry, and Rational Numbers.

Practical Applications. This supplemental composite measures real-world applications of mathematics and is found by combining performance on the Time, Money, and Measurement subtests.

Global Composite

Global Mathematics Ability. This global composite is found by combining the standard scores of all 12 subtests. Although the most comprehensive, it is rarely used.

Norms

The CMAT was standardized on 1,625 students ages 7 to 18 between February 1999 and April 2000. Data for the standardization sample were collected in three different ways. First, one major standardization site was chosen from each of the major U.S. regions (Northeast, South, Midwest, and West). Sites were chosen because the demographic characteristics of students in the site closely matched those of the region. Additionally, professionals who had previously purchased Pro-Ed achievement tests were asked to submit data on students in their area. Finally, professional colleagues of the test authors tested students in their area whose demographic characteristics were representative of their community. A table is provided comparing the following characteristics of the norm sample with that of 2000 U.S. Census data: geographic area, gender, race, residence (urban or rural), ethnicity, family income, educational attainment of parents, and disability status (no disability, learning disability, speech-language disorder, attention deficit disorder, or other handicap). The percentage of the sample in each age bracket (for example, 7, 8, . . . 17, 18) is also provided but is not compared to census information. In addition, the data are stratified by age across geographic region, gender, race, residence, ethnicity, income, and parental education, but comparisons to the U.S. population are provided only for the total participants in each group (U.S. Census comparison information is not provided for the stratified data). When information is provided, the norm sample appears representative of the U.S. population.

Reliability

Reliability coefficients are provided for internal-consistency, test-retest, and interrater reliability. Internal-consistency reliabilities for all the subtests were calculated using Cronbach's coefficient alpha method across each age group. (Algebra and Geometry coefficients could not be calculated for ages 7, 8, and 9 because these students do not take those subtests.) Average coefficients for each subtest all exceed .80. However, internal reliabilities for a small number of subtest-age combinations exceeded only .70. In addition, coefficient alphas for composites were derived using Guilford's formula. The average alphas for the composites range from .93 to .98. Alphas across age groups all exceed .80. To demonstrate reliability across subgroups, coefficient alphas for the following subgroups are presented for each subtest and composite: male, female, European American, African American, Hispanic American, Learning Disabilities, and Attention Deficit Hyperactivity Disorder. All coefficients exceed .80.

Test-retest data were collected on two different groups of students. The first group consisted of 30 normally achieving students (16 male, 12 female) ranging in age from 7 to 12 and attending a school in American Falls, Idaho. The second group consisted of 70 normally achieving students (35 male, 35 female) ranging in age from 13 to 18 and attending classes in Rutland, South Dakota. The time period that elapsed between administrations was approximately two to three weeks. All but one of the subtest coefficients from the first sample exceed .80 (Problem Solving, .79), and subtest coefficients from the second sample range from .84 to .99. Composite coefficients from the first sample range from .92 to .99, and composite coefficients from the second sample range from .95 to .99. The test-retest reliability studies are on very small samples of students selected from relatively remote towns.

Evidence of interrater reliability is based on a high correlation in scoring by two graduate students who independently scored 50 protocols. Coefficients ranged from .95 to .99 for subtests and from .98 to .99 for the composites. Again, the sample is very limited.

Validity

The authors present evidence for content, criterion, and construct validity. The authors present the following qualitative evidence to support the content validity of the CMAT. First, a detailed review of research, curriculum materials (scope and sequence charts from textbooks and state or district curriculum guides), and preexisting nationally standardized tests was conducted. Items included in the CMAT are based on data gathered from all of these sources, supporting the CMAT as a measure of what is taught in classrooms. Moreover, the authors demonstrate a link between CMAT content and the mathematics standards developed by the NCTM (2000). In addition, the authors asked experts to review item placement within the subtests and controlled for item difficulty by selecting vocabulary that was appropriate for the grade level aligned with each item.

Although no details are given on the sample used, evidence for criterion-prediction validity is based on the correlation between CMAT scores and scores on other measures of math skills. Specifically, CMAT scores were compared to scores from the Wechsler Individual Achievement Test (Psychological Corporation, 1992); Diagnostic Achievement Test Battery, Third Edition (Newcomer, 2001); Hammill Multiability Achievement Test (Hammill, Hresko, Ammer, Cronin, & Quinby, 1998); Woodcock-Johnson Psychoeducational Battery–Revised (Woodcock & Johnson, 1989); Woodcock-Johnson III Tests of Achievement (Woodcock, McGrew, & Mather, 2000); and the Young Children's Achievement Test (Hresko, Peak, Herron, & Bridges, 2000). The authors grouped correlations into the following categories: reasoning (median $r = .65$), calculations (median $r = .67$), and composites (median $r = .70$). In addition, the authors argue that the best estimate of how well the CMAT correlates with other measures is the relationship between the CMAT General Mathematics composite and other composites. The following correlations were found when the CMAT General Mathematics composite was compared to other composites: Diagnostic Achievement Test for Adolescents, Second Edition (Newcomer & Bryant, 1993), $r = .60$; Woodcock-Johnson Psychoeducational Battery–Revised, $r = .83$; Stanford Achievement Test Series, Ninth Edition (Harcourt Brace Educational Measurement, 1996a), $r = .65$; Metropolitan Achievement Test, Seventh Edition (Balow, Farr, & Hogan, 1992), $r = .95$.

The authors demonstrate construct validity through a three-step process in which they first identified constructs that should account for test performance, generated hypotheses based on these constructs, and verified these hypotheses by means of logical or empirical methods. They identify and provide evidence for seven constructs that are thought to underlie the CMAT.

Summary

The CMAT is an individually administered, norm-referenced test designed to assess mathematical abilities in children ages 7 years 0 months to 18 years 11 months. The normative sample appears representative of the 2000 U.S. population across geographic area, gender, race, residence, ethnicity, family income, educational attainment of parents, and disability status. Evidence for reliability and validity is good. There is no content in the test manual relating test content to instructional interventions or resources.

The Group Mathematics Assessment and Diagnostic Evaluation (G·MADE; Williams, 2004) is a group-administered, norm-referenced, standards-based test for assessing the math skills of students in grades K–12. It is norm referenced in that it is standardized on a nationally representative group. It is standards based in that the content assessed is based on the standards of the National Council of Teachers of Mathematics (NCTM).

G·MADE is a diagnostic test designed to identify specific math skill development strengths and weaknesses, and the test is designed to lead to teaching strategies. The test provides information about math skills and error patterns of each student, using the efficiencies of group administration. Test materials include a CD that provides a cross-reference between specific math skills and math teaching resources. Teaching resources are also available in print.

There are nine levels, each with two parallel forms. Eight of the nine levels have three subtests (the lowest level has two). The three subtests are Concepts and Communication, Operations and Computation, and Process and Applications. The items in each subtest fit the content of the following categories: numeration, quantity, geometry, measurement, time/sequence, money, comparison, statistics, and algebra. Diagnosis of skill development strengths and needs is fairly broad. Teachers learn, for example, that an individual student has difficulty with concepts and communication in the area of geometry.

Subtests

Concepts and Communication   These subtests measure students' knowledge of the language, vocabulary, and representations of math. A symbol, word, or short phrase is presented with four choices (pictures, symbols, or numbers). It is permissible for teachers to read words to students, but they may not define or explain the words. Figure 23.1 is a representation of the kinds of items used to measure concepts and communication skills.

Operations and Computation   These subtests measure students' skills in using the basic operations of addition, subtraction, multiplication, and division. This subtest is not included at Level R (the readiness level and the lowest level of the test). There are 24 items on this subtest at each level, and each consists of an incomplete equation with four answer choices. An example is shown in Figure 23.2.

Process and Applications   These subtests measure students' skill in taking the language and concepts of math, and applying the appropriate operations and computations to solve a word problem. Each item consists of a short passage of one or more sentences and four response choices. An example is shown in Figure 23.3. At lower levels of the test, the problems are one-step problems; at higher levels, they require application of multiple steps.

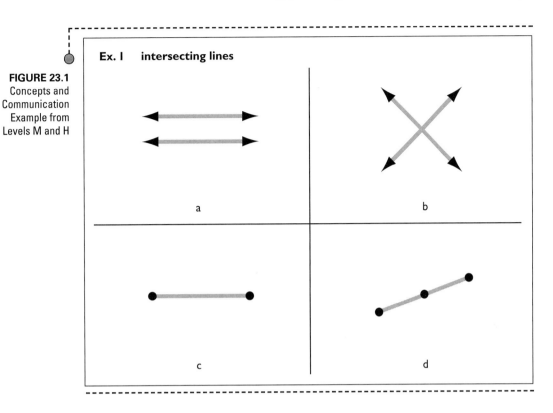

FIGURE 23.1
Concepts and
Communication
Example from
Levels M and H

The G·MADE levels each contain items that are on grade level, items that are somewhat above level, and some that are below level. Each level can be administered on grade level or can be given out of level (matched to the ability level of the student). Teachers can choose to administer a lower or higher level of the test.

FIGURE 23.2
Operations and
Computation Example

Ex. I   943
                   − 812

Work Area

a	136
b	132
c	135
d	131

FIGURE 23.3
Process and Applications
Example

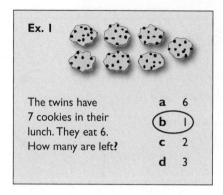

Ex. 1

The twins have	**a**	6
7 cookies in their	**b**	1
lunch. They eat 6.	**c**	2
How many are left?	**d**	3

Scores

Raw scores for the G·MADE can be converted to standard scores (with a mean of 100 and a standard deviation of 15) using fall or spring norms. Grade scores, stanines, percentiles, and normal-curve equivalents are also available. Growth-scale values (GSVs) are provided for the purpose of tracking growth in math skills for students who are given different levels of the test over the years. The G·MADE can be used to track growth over the course of a year or from year to year.

The publisher provides diagnostic worksheets, which consist of cross-tabulations of the subtests with the content areas. The worksheets are used to identify areas in which individual students or whole classes did or did not demonstrate skills. The worksheets are used to prepare reports identifying specific areas of need. For example, the objective assessed by item 28 in Level 1, Form B, is skill in solving a one-step sequence problem that requires the ability to recognize a pattern. When reporting on performance on this item, the teacher might report that "Joe did not solve one-step sequence problems that require the ability to recognize a pattern." He might also indicate that "Two thirds of the class did not solve one-step problems that require the ability to recognize a pattern."

Norms

There were two phases in standardization of the G·MADE. First, a study of bias by gender, race/ethnicity, and region was conducted on more than 10,000 students during a national tryout. In addition, the test was reviewed by a panel of educators who represented minority perspectives, and items they identified as apparently biased were modified or removed.

During the fall of 2002, the G·MADE was standardized on a nationwide sample of students at 72 sites. In spring 2003 the sampling was repeated at 71 sites. Approximately 1,000 students per level per grade participated in the standardization (a total of nearly 28,000 students). The sample was selected based on geographic region, community type (such as rural), and SES (percentage of students on free and reduced-price lunch). Students with disabilities were included in the standardization if they attended regular education classes all or part of the day. Fall and spring grade-based and age-based norms are provided for each level of the G·MADE. Norms that allow for out-of-level testing are available in a G·MADE Out-of-Level Norms Supplement and through the scoring and reporting software. Templates are available for hand scoring, or the test can be scored and reported by computer.

Reliability

Data on internal consistency and stability over time are presented in the G·MADE manual. Internal-consistency reliabilities were computed for each G·MADE subtest and the total test score for each level and form, using the split-half method. All reliabilities exceed .74, with more than 90 percent exceeding .80. The only low reliabilities are at seventh grade for Concepts and Communications and for Process and Applications at all grades beyond grade 4. So, the only really questionable subtest is Process and Applications beyond grade 4. Internal-consistency reliability coefficients are above .90 for the total score at all levels of the test.

Alternate-form reliability was established on a sample of 651 students, and all reliabilities exceeded .80. Stability of the test was established by giving it twice to a sample of 761 students. The test-retest reliability coefficients for this group of students exceeded .80, with the exception of .78 for Level 4, Form A. Overall, there is good support for the reliability of the G·MADE. Internal consistency and stability are sufficient for using the test to make decisions about individuals. The two forms of the test are comparable.

Validity

The content of the G·MADE is based on the NCTM Math Standards, though the test was developed following a year-long research study of state standards, curriculum benchmarks, the score and sequence plans of commonly used math textbooks, and review of research on best practices for teaching math concepts and skills. The author provides a strong argument for the validity of the content of the G·MADE.

Several studies support the criterion-related validity of the test. Correlations with subtests of the Iowa Tests of Basic Skills, the Terra Nova, and the Iowa Tests of Educational Development are reported. Surprisingly, correlations between G·MADE subtests and reading subtests of the ITBS are as high as they are between G·MADE subtests and math subtests of the G·MADE. This was not the case for correlations with the Terra Nova, where those with the math subtests by far exceeded correlations with the reading subtests. In a comparison of performance on Key Math and the G·MADE, all correlations were in excess of .80. The two tests measure highly comparable skills.

Summary

The Group Math Assessment and Diagnostic Evaluation (G·MADE) is a group-administered, norm-referenced, standards-based diagnostic measure of student skill development in three separate areas. There is good evidence for the content validity of the test, and the test was appropriately and adequately standardized. Evidence for reliability and validity of the G·MADE is good. The sole exception to this is the finding that performance on the test is as highly correlated with the reading subtests of some other criterion measures as it is with the math subtests of those measures.

Stanford Diagnostic Mathematics Test 4 (SDMT4)

The Stanford Diagnostic Mathematics Test 4 (SDMT4; Harcourt Brace Educational Measurement, 1996b) is the fourth edition of a widely used test that was first developed and published in 1966. The SDMT4 is a group-administered diagnostic test designed to identify specific strengths and weaknesses in math. It emphasizes general problem-solving and math-specific problem-solving strategies while measuring student competence in those basic math skills and concepts that are prerequisite to mathematics problem solving. The test includes both multiple-choice and free-response items. The test now is more than ten years old and should be restandardized. It reflects only limited portions of the NCTM standards.

Skill Domains

The SDMT4 can be group administered by a classroom teacher. Two skill domains are sampled: concepts and applications, and computation. The following are the kinds of skills assessed in each of the domains.

Concepts and Applications   Items in this domain measure the degree to which students have mastered fundamental concepts and skills, and the extent to which they are able to integrate and apply the skills to solve grade level–appropriate problems. The kinds of concepts assessed include place value, size, geometric properties, math vocabulary, fractions, and decimals. Skills assessed include rounding, measurement, number recognition, recognition and interpretation of alternative representations in graphs and tables, spatial reasoning, and application of math skills and concepts to solve problems.

Computation   Computation items assess the extent to which students have mastered addition, subtraction, multiplication, and division skills.

Scores

The SDMT4 is both norm and criterion referenced. It can be used to assess a pupil's performance relative to the performance of others, and it can be used to pinpoint individual pupils' strengths and weaknesses in specific math skills. Students respond either in the test booklets or on machine-readable answer sheets. The test, therefore, can be either hand scored or machine scored. Six kinds of scores can be obtained; which scores are useful depends on the purpose for which the test has been administered.

   Raw scores are obtained for each subtest and can be transformed into "Progress Indicators," percentile ranks, stanines, grade equivalents, and scaled scores. Progress Indicators are criterion-referenced scores, whereas the other four scores are norm referenced. Progress Indicators are + or – indications as to whether a pupil achieved a predetermined cutoff score in a specific skill domain; they show whether a pupil demonstrates mastery of specific skills important to progress in learning to solve math problems. The manual reports that "in setting the Progress Indicator cutoff scores, the following factors were taken into account: the relative importance of each skill to mathematics, by the location of these skills in the developmental sequence, and by the performance of students at different achievement levels on the items measuring these skills" (Harcourt Brace Educational Measurement, 1996b, p. 15). The manual for each level of the SDMT4 includes an appendix that lists specific instructional objectives assessed by each level of the test.

The norm-referenced scores obtained by administering the SDMT4 can be used for a variety of purposes. The manual includes a detailed table showing the recommended uses of each of the kinds of scores and the extent to which scores are comparable across subtests, forms, levels, and grades. The scores on the test can be used to make setting decisions, identify math strengths and weaknesses, evaluate pupil progress, and identify trends in math achievement at the class, school, and district level.

A number of reports can be generated from the SDMT4 by making use of the publisher's computer-scoring service. Examiners can obtain an individual diagnostic report, which contains a detailed analysis of the performance of a single pupil. They can also obtain a class summary report, which shows the average scores earned by the pupils on each of the subtests. It also provides an analysis of skill development for the class by indicating the number of students in the class who obtained a Progress Indicator of + and the number who obtained a Progress Indicator of −. Examiners can obtain a master-list report, which consists of a listing of scores for all students in a class. They can obtain a parent report, designed specifically for sending test results home to parents. In addition, they can obtain a pupil item analysis, showing the raw scores earned by a particular student on each subtest and cluster, as well as the student's response to each item.

Norms

In preparing this fourth edition of the SDMT, the authors wrote or rewrote all items. Both multiple-choice and free-response items were written. About 3,000 items were tried out on about 27,000 students in 150 districts from 32 states and the District of Columbia. To eliminate bias in assessment, extensive work went into item review and into statistical review of the performance of differing groups of students. In selecting the standardization sample for the SDMT4, the authors used a stratified random-sampling technique. Socioeconomic status (SES), urbanicity, ethnicity, and geographic region were the stratification variables. School system data were obtained from the U.S. Department of Education's 1990 census tapes. Age and gender were not controlled in standardizing the SDMT4.

School districts within each of the stratified cells were invited to participate in standardization of the test. A random sample of consenting districts within each cell was selected. The SDMT4 was standardized during the fall of 1994 and spring of 1995. In the fall standardization (48,000 students), 425 school systems participated. The spring standardization included about 40,000 students, yielding about 88,000 students for both samples. The authors provide a table in their manual showing the relationship of sample characteristics to census characteristics. The numbers are a close match. There is no report of cross-tabulations. Thus we do not know how many low-SES students were from urban versus suburban settings.

Reliability

Three kinds of reliability information for the SDMT4 are provided: internal consistency, alternate forms, and—for the free-response version—interscorer. Internal-consistency reliabilities were computed on the 40,000 students who participated in the spring 1995 standardization. Reliability coefficients are reported by subtest for the six levels of the test and for each of the alternative forms for the three higher levels of the test; about 98 percent (195 of 199) of the reliability coefficients exceed .80.

Alternate-form reliability coefficients are reported based on the performance of 7,000 students in the fall 1994 standardization. Of the 27 coefficients, 21 exceed the desirable .80. Reliabilities for the multiple-choice computation test are consistently in the mid-.70s range at all levels of the test. Interrater reliabilities were all in excess of .97. There is good evidence for the reliability of the SDMT4.

Validity

Data are provided on the content validity, criterion-related validity, and construct validity of the SDMT4. As test items were written, they were reviewed by content experts, who made sure that the items were actually assessing the content objectives they were intended to assess. The manual includes an extensive list of the objectives measured by the items. Criterion-related validity was established by correlating performance on the SDMT3 with that on the SDMT4. There is a strong relationship between performance on the two editions.

Intercorrelations among subtests and between subtests and performance on the Otis-Lennon School Ability Test are provided as evidence for the construct validity of the SDMT4. This does not indicate construct validity but shows the relationship of performance on the SDMT4 and a measure of school ability. Relationships are high. Further evidence of construct validity is provided by showing correlations among performances on the same subtest at adjacent levels. The authors would have done well to correlate performance on the SDMT4 with other measures (such as the Stanford Achievement Test 9) of mathematics achievement.

Summary

The SDMT4 is a group-administered device that is both norm referenced and criterion referenced. The test is now dated. It is reliable enough to be used in pinpointing math strengths and weaknesses. Validity of the test should be judged relative to the content of local curricula.

STAR Math STAR Math (Renaissance Learning, 1998) is designed to provide teachers with quick and accurate estimates of students' math achievement levels relative to national norms. The test also can be used to monitor student progress in math over time. It is appropriate for use with students in grades 3 through 12. Using computer-adaptive procedures, a branching formula matches test items to students' ability and performance level. In other words, the specific test items that students receive depend on how well they perform on previous items. Thus each test is unique, tailored to the individual student, and students can be given the test as many as five times in one year without being exposed to the same item more than once. The test is timed. Students have up to three minutes to solve each item and are given a warning when 30 seconds remain.

Items on STAR Math consist of some of the major strands of math content: numeration concepts, computation, word problems, estimation, statistics, charts, graphs, geometry, measurement, and algebra. Responses are four-item multiple-choice responses. The test consists of two parts: concepts of numeration and computation are addressed in the first part; the other content areas are addressed in the second part.

Scores

Users of STAR Math can obtain grade equivalents, percentile ranks, normal-curve equivalents, and scaled scores. The software provided with the test is used to score the test and give users immediate feedback on student performance.

Norms

STAR Math was standardized on 25,800 students who attended 256 schools in 42 states. Norming was completed in spring 1998, using a sample that was stratified on the basis of geographic region, school location (urban, rural, suburban), gender, and ethnicity. The sample is representative of the U.S. population, as are the proportions of the various kinds of students in the sample.

Reliability

Reliability was calculated using a test-retest method with 1,541 students, who took alternative forms of the test because of its computer-adaptive nature. Reliabilities at grades 3 through 6 are in the high .70s, and at higher grades they are in the .80s. The test has sufficient reliability for use as a screening test, but not for making eligibility and placement decisions.

Validity

Performance on STAR Math was correlated with performance on a number of standardized math tests administered during standardization of the test. An extensive table in the manual reports these results. Comparison tests included the

California Achievement Test, Comprehensive Test of Basic Skills, Iowa Tests of Basic Skills, and Metropolitan Achievement Test. Scores were moderately high and about as would be expected.

Summary

STAR Math is a norm-referenced, computer-adaptive math test that gives teachers information about students' instructional levels as well as their level of performance relative to a national sample. The test was standardized on a large representative sample. It provides teachers with immediate diagnostic profiles on student performance. Evidence for reliability is limited, but evidence for validity is good.

Dilemmas in Current Practice

There are three major problems in the diagnostic assessment of math skills.

The first problem is the recurring issue of curriculum match. There is considerable variation in math curricula. This variation means that diagnostic math tests will not be equally representative of all curricula or even appropriate for some commonly used ones. As a result, great care must be exercised in using diagnostic math tests to make various educational decisions. Assessment personnel must be extremely careful to note the match between test content and school curriculum. This should involve far more than a quick inspection of test items by someone unfamiliar with the specific classroom curriculum. For example, a professional could inspect the teacher's manual to ensure that the teacher assesses only material that has been taught and that there is reasonable correspondence between the relative emphasis placed on teaching the material and testing the material. To do this, the professional might have to develop a table of specifications for the math curriculum and compare test items with that table. However, once a table of specifications has been developed for the curriculum, a better procedure would be to select items from a standards-referenced system to fit the cells in the table exactly.

The second problem is selecting an appropriate test for the type of decision to be made. School personnel are usually required to use individually administered, norm-referenced devices in classification decisions. Decisions about a pupil's eligibility for special services, however, need not be based on detailed information about the pupil's strengths and weaknesses, as provided by diagnostic tests; diagnosticians are interested in a pupil's relative standing. In our opinion, the best mathematical achievement survey tests are subtests of group-administered tests. A practical solution is not to use a diagnostic math test for eligibility decisions but to administer individually a subtest from one of the better group-administered achievement tests.

The third problem is that most of the diagnostic tests in mathematics do not test a sufficiently detailed sample of facts and concepts. Consequently, assessors must generalize from a student's performance on the items tested to his or her performance on the items that are not tested. The reliabilities of the subtests of diagnostic math tests are often not high enough for educators to make such a generalization with any great degree of confidence. As a result, these tests are not very useful in assessing readiness or strengths and weaknesses in order to plan instructional programs. We believe that the preferred practice in diagnostic testing in mathematics is for teachers to develop criterion-referenced achievement tests that exactly parallel the curriculum being taught.

SUMMARY

In this chapter, we have reviewed the kinds of behaviors sampled by diagnostic mathematics tests and have evaluated the most commonly used tests in terms of the kinds of behaviors they sample and their technical adequacy. The four tests reviewed in this chapter are designed to provide teachers and diagnostic specialists with specific information on those math skills that pupils have or have not mastered. Compared with diagnostic testing in reading, diagnostic testing in math puts less emphasis on scores.

The tests described in this chapter differ in their technical adequacy for use in making instructional decisions for students. Knowledge of pupil mastery of specific math skills gained from administration of one or more of the tests, along with knowledge of the general sequence of development of math skills, can help teachers design curricular content for individual students.

QUESTIONS FOR CHAPTER REVIEW

1. How can the diagnostician overcome the problem of curriculum match in the diagnostic assessment of mathematical competence?

2. List and describe the major areas in which behaviors are sampled in diagnostic mathematics tests.

3. Discuss the three major problems in the diagnostic assessment of mathematical competence.

PROJECT

Assume that you wish to use one of the tests reviewed in this text to diagnose strengths and weaknesses in mathematics. Which test would be your first choice? Why? Compare your answer with a classmate's answer. Reconcile any differences.

RESOURCES FOR FURTHER INVESTIGATION

Print Resources

Harcourt Brace Educational Measurement. (1996b). *Stanford Diagnostic Mathematics Test 4.* San Antonio, TX: Psychological Corporation.

Technology Resources

AGS ONLINE PRODUCTS AND SERVICES
www.agsnet.com
Look for product and ordering information about the instruments available from American Guidance Service (AGS). Search for information about KeyMath–Revised/NU: A Diagnostic Inventory of Essential Mathematics–Normative Update.

PRO-ED CATALOGUE INFORMATION FOR PRODUCTS
www.proedinc.com
Find product and ordering information about the Test of Early Mathematical Ability, Second Edition, and the Test of Mathematical Abilities, Second Edition.

NATIONAL COUNCIL OF TEACHERS OF MATHEMATICS (NCTM)
www.nctm.org
This website is designed for teachers of mathematics and contains information and resources related to the subject of math.

CHAPTER 24

Assessment of Language

THE ASSESSMENT OF LANGUAGE COMPETENCE SHOULD INCLUDE EVALUATION OF A student's ability to process, both in comprehension and in expression, language in a spoken or written format. There are four major communication processes: oral comprehension (listening and comprehending speech), written comprehension (reading), oral expression (speaking), and written expression (writing). These are illustrated in Figure 24.1.

In assessing language skills, it is important to break language down into processes and measure each one, because each process makes different demands on the person's ability to communicate. Performance in one modality does not always predict performance in the others. For example, a child who has normal comprehension does not necessarily have normal production skills. Also, a child with relatively normal expressive skills may have problems with receptive language. Therefore, a complete language assessment will include examination of both oral and written reception (comprehension) and expression (production).

Terminology

Educators, psychologists, linguists, and speech-language pathologists often have different perspectives on which skills make up language. These different views have resulted in the development of a plethora of language assessment tests, each with an apparently unique method of assessing language. The terminology used to describe the behaviors and skills assessed can be confusing as well. Terms like *morphology, semantics, syntax, metalinguistics,* and *supralinguistic functioning* are used, and sometimes different test authors use different terms to mean the same thing. One author's vocabulary subtest is another's measure of "lexical semantics."

We define *language* as a code for conveying ideas—a code that includes phonology, semantics, morphology, syntax, and pragmatics. This is how we define these terms:

FIGURE 24.1
The Four Major
Communication
Processes

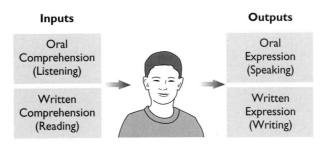

Inputs

Oral
Comprehension
(Listening)

Written
Comprehension
(Reading)

Outputs

Oral
Expression
(Speaking)

Written
Expression
(Writing)

Phonology: the hearing and production of speech sounds. The term *articulation* is considered a synonym for phonology.

Semantics: the study of word meanings. In assessment, this term is generally used to refer to the derivation of meaning from single words. The term *vocabulary* is often used interchangeably with semantics.

Morphology: the use of affixes (prefixes and suffixes) to change the meaning of words used in sentences. Morphology also includes verb tense (John *is* going versus John *was* going).

Syntax: the use of word order to convey meaning. There typically are rules for arranging words into sentences. In language assessment, the word *grammar* is often used to refer to a combination of morphology and syntax.

Pragmatics: the social context in which a sentence occurs. Context influences both the way a message is expressed and the way it is interpreted. For example, the sentence "Can you close the door?" can have different meanings to a student sitting closest to an open door in a classroom and a student undergoing physical therapy to rehabilitate motor skills. According to Carrow-Woolfolk (1995), contexts that influence language comprehension and production include

- Social variables, such as the setting and the age, roles, relationships, and number of participants in a discourse.
- Linguistic variables produced by the type of discourse (which might be a conversation, or narrative, lecture, or text).
- The intention, motivation, knowledge, and style of the sender.

Supralinguistics: a second order of analysis required to understand the meaning of words or sentences. For example, much language must be interpreted in a nonliteral way (sarcasm, indirect requests, and figurative language). Dad may say that the lawn looks like a hay field, when he is actually implying that he wants his child to cut the grass. Mother may say that the weather is "great," when she really means that she is tired of all the cloudy and rainy weather.

Throughout this chapter, we use "comprehension" as a synonym for receptive language and "production" as a synonym for expressive language. In Table 24.1 we define each of the basic language components for receptive and expressive modalities.

| TABLE 24.1 | Language Subskills for Each Channel of Communication |

Language Component	Channel of Communication	
	Reception (Comprehension)	*Expression (Production)*
Phonology	Hearing and discriminating speech sounds	Articulating speech sounds
Morphology and syntax	Understanding the grammatical structure of language	Using the grammatical structure of language
Semantics	Understanding vocabulary, meaning, and concepts	Using vocabulary, meaning, and concepts
Pragmatics and supralinguistics	Understanding a speaker's or writer's intentions	Using awareness of social aspects of language
Ultimate language skill	Understanding spoken or written language	Speaking or writing

Why Assess Oral and Written Language?

There are two primary reasons for assessing language abilities. First, well-developed language abilities are desirable in and of themselves. The ability to converse and to express thoughts and feelings is a goal of most individuals. Those who have difficulties with various aspects of language are often eligible for special services from speech and language specialists or from special educators. Second, various language processes and skills are believed to underlie subsequent development. Students who experience language difficulties have also been shown to experience behavior disorders, learning disabilities, and reading disorders.

Written language and spelling are regularly taught in school, and these areas are singled out for assessment in the Individuals with Disabilities Education Act. Written- and oral-language tests are administered for purposes of screening, instructional planning, entitlement, and progress evaluation.

Considerations in Assessing Oral Language

Those who assess oral language must necessarily give consideration to cultural diversity and the developmental status of those they assess.

Cultural Diversity

Cultural background must be considered in assessing oral-language competence. Although most children in the United States learn English, the form of English they learn depends on where they were born, who their parents are, and so on. For example, in central Pennsylvania, a child might say, "My hands need washed" instead of the standard "My hands need to be washed." In New York City, a child learning Black English might say, "birfday" instead of "birthday" or "He be running" instead of "He is running." These and other culturally determined alternative constructions and pronunciations are not incorrect or inferior; they are just different. Indeed, they are appropriate within the child's surrounding community. Children should be viewed as having a language disorder only if they exhibit disordered production of their own primary language or dialect.

Cultural background is particularly important when the language assessment devices that are currently available are considered. Ideally, a child should be compared with others in the same language community. There should be separate norms for each language community, including Standard American English. Unfortunately, the norm samples of most language tests are heterogeneous, and scores on these tests may not be valid indicators of a child's language ability. Consider Plate 25 of the original Peabody Picture Vocabulary Test. This plate contained four pictures, and the examiner said, "Show me the wiener." There are many places in this country where the only word for that item is *hot dog* or *frankfurter*. Yet, because the test was standardized using *wiener*, the examiner was required to use that term. If a child had never heard "wiener," he or she was penalized and received a lower score, even though the error was cultural and not indicative of a semantic or intellectual deficiency. If there are a number of such items on a language test, the child's score can hardly be considered a valid indicator of language ability.

Developmental Considerations

Age is a major consideration in assessment of the child's language. Language acquisition is developmental; some sounds, linguistic structures, and even semantic elements are correctly produced at an earlier age than others. Thus it is not unusual or indicative of language disorder for a 2-year-old child to say, "Kitty house" for "The cat is in the house," although the same phrase would be an indication of a disorder in a 3-year-old. It is important to be aware of developmental norms for language acquisition and to use those norms when making judgments about a child's language competence.

Considerations in Assessing Written Language

There are two major components of written language: content and form. The content of written expression is the product of considerable intellectual and linguistic activity: formulating, elaborating, sequencing, and then clarifying and revising ideas; choosing the precise word to convey meaning; and so forth. Moreover, much of what we consider to be content is the result of a creative endeavor. Our ability to use words to excite, to depict vividly, to imply, and to describe complex ideas is far more involved than simply putting symbols on paper.

The form of written language is far more mechanistic than its content. For writer and reader to communicate, three sets of conventions or rules are used: penmanship, spelling, and style rules. The most fundamental rules deal with *penmanship*, the formation of individual letters and letter sequences that make up words. Although letter formation tends to become more individualistic with age, there are a limited number of ways, for example, that the letter *A* can be written and still be recognized as an *A*. Moreover, there are conventions about the relative spacing of letters between and within words.

Spelling is also rule governed. Although American English is more irregular phonetically than other languages, it remains largely regular, and students should be able to spell most words by applying a few phonetic rules. For example, we have known since the mid-1960s that about 80 percent of all consonants have a single spelling (Hanna, Hanna, Hodges, & Rudoff, 1966). Short vowels are the major source of difficulty for most writers.

The third set of conventions involves style. *Style* is a catchall term for rule-governed writing, which includes grammar (such as parts of speech, pronoun use, agreement, and verb voice and mood) and mechanics (such as punctuation, capitalization, abbreviations, and referencing).

The conventions of written language are tested on many standardized achievement tests. Spelling is assessed as part of the current forms of the California Achievement Tests, the Iowa Tests of Basic Skills and Tests of Achievement and Proficiency, the Metropolitan Achievement Tests, the Stanford Achievement Test, the Wide Range Achievement Test 3, the Peabody Individual Achievement Test–Revised, and the Woodcock-Johnson Psychoeducational Battery–III. However, the spelling words that students are to learn vary considerably from curriculum to curriculum. For example, Ames (1965) examined seven spelling series and found that they introduced an average of 3,200 words between the second and eighth grades. However, only about 1,300 words were common to all the series; about 1,700 words were taught in only one series. Moreover, those words that were taught in several series varied considerably in their grade placement, sometimes by as many as five grades.

Language *mechanics* (capitalization and punctuation) are also assessed on the current forms of several achievement batteries: the California Achievement Tests, the Iowa Tests of Basic Skills and Tests of Achievement and Proficiency, the Metropolitan Achievement Tests, the Stanford Achievement Test, and the Woodcock-Johnson Psychoeducational Battery–III. Again, standardized tests are not well suited to measuring achievement in these areas because the grade level at which these skills are taught varies so much from one curriculum to another. To be valid, the measurement of achievement in these areas must be closely tied to the curriculum being taught. For example, pupils may learn in kindergarten, first grade, second grade, or later that a sentence always begins with a capital letter. They may learn in the sixth grade or several grades earlier that commercial brand names are capitalized. Students may be taught in the second or third grade that the apostrophe in "it's" makes the word a contraction of "it is" or may still be studying "it's" in high school. Finally, in assessing word usage, organization, and penmanship, we must take into account the emphasis that individual teachers place on these components of written language and when and how students are taught.

The more usual way to assess written language is to evaluate a student's written work and to develop vocabulary and spelling tests that parallel the curriculum. In this way, teachers can be sure that they are measuring precisely what has been taught. Most teacher's editions of language-arts textbook series contain scope-and-sequence charts that specify fairly clearly the objectives that are taught in each unit. From these charts, teachers can develop appropriate criterion-referenced and curriculum-based assessments.

Observing Language Behavior

There has been some disagreement among language professionals about the most valid method of evaluating a child's language performance, especially in the expressive channel of communication. In all, there are three procedures used to gather a sample of a child's language behavior: spontaneous, imitative, and elicited.

Spontaneous Language

One school of thought holds that the only valid measure of a child's language abilities is one that studies the language the child produces spontaneously (for example, see Miller, 1981). Using this approach, the examiner records 50 to 100 consecutive utterances produced as the child is talking to an adult or playing with toys. With older children, conversations or storytelling tasks are often used. The child's utterances are then analyzed in terms of phonology, semantics, morphology, syntax, and pragmatics in order to provide information about the child's conversational abilities. Because the construct of pragmatics has been developed only recently, there are few standard assessment instruments available to sample this domain. Therefore, spontaneous language-sampling procedures are widely used to evaluate pragmatic abilities (see Prutting & Kirshner, 1987). Although analysis of a child's spontaneous language production is not the purpose of any standard oral-language assessment instruments, some interest has been shown in standard assessment of handwriting and spelling skills in an uncontrived, spontaneous situation (for example, the revised *Test of Written Language* by Hammill and Larsen, 1996).

Imitation

Imitation tasks require a child to repeat directly the word, phrase, or sentence produced by the examiner. It might seem that such tasks bear little relationship to spontaneous performance, but some evidence suggests that such tasks are valid predictors of spontaneous production. In fact, many investigators have demonstrated that children's imitative language is essentially the same in content and structure as their spontaneous language (R. Brown & Bellugi, 1964; Ervin, 1964; Slobin & Welsh, 1973). Evidently, children translate adult sentences into their own language system and then repeat the sentences using their own language rules. A young child might imitate "The boy is running and jumping" as "Boy run and jump." Imitation thus seems to be a valuable tool for providing information about a child's language abilities. We note one caution, however: Features of a child's language systems can be obtained using imitation only if the stimulus sentences are long enough to tax the child's memory, because a child will imitate any sentence perfectly if the length of that sentence is within the child's memory capacity (Slobin & Welsh, 1973).

The use of imitation does not preclude the need for spontaneous sampling, because the examiner also needs information derived from direct observation of conversational skills. Rather, imitation tasks should be used to augment the information obtained from the spontaneous sample, for such tasks can be used to elicit forms that the child did not attempt in the conversations. Standardized imitation tasks are widely used in oral-language assessment instruments (such as the Test of Language Development–P:3 and I:3). Assessment devices that use imitation usually contain a number of grammatically loaded words, phrases, or sentences that children are asked to imitate. The examiner records and transcribes the children's responses and then analyzes their phonology, morphology, and syntax. (Semantics and pragmatics are rarely assessed using an imitative mode.) Finally, imitation generally is used only in assessing expressive oral language.

Elicited Language

Using a picture stimulus to elicit language involves no imitation on the part of the child, but the procedure cannot be classified as totally spontaneous. In this type of task, the child is presented with a picture or pictures of objects or action scenes and is asked to do one of the following: (1) point to the correct object (a receptive vocabulary task); (2) point to the action picture that best describes a sentence (receptive language, including vocabulary); (3) name the picture (expressive vocabulary); or (4) describe the picture (expressive language, including vocabulary). Although only stimulus pictures are described in this section, some tests use concrete objects rather than pictures to elicit language responses.

Advantages and Disadvantages of Each Procedure

There are advantages and disadvantages to all three methods of language observation (spontaneous, imitative, and elicited). The use of spontaneous language samples has two major advantages. First, a child's spontaneous language is undoubtedly the best and most natural indicator of everyday language performance. Second, the informality of the procedure often allows the examiner to assess children quite easily, without the difficulties sometimes associated with a formal testing atmosphere.

The disadvantages associated with this procedure relate to the nonstandardized nature of the data collection. Although some aspects of language sampling are stable across a variety of parameters, this procedure shows much wider variability than is seen with other standardized assessments. Additionally, language sampling requires detailed analyses across language domains; such analyses are more time consuming than administering a standardized instrument. Finally, because the examiner does not directly control the selection of target words and phrases, he or she may have difficulty understanding a young child, or there may be several different interpretations of what a child intended to say. Moreover, the child may have avoided, or may not have had an opportunity to attempt, a particular structure that is of interest to the examiner.

The use of imitation overcomes many of the disadvantages inherent in the spontaneous approach. An imitation task will often assess many different language elements and provide a representative view of a child's language system. Also, because of the structure of the test, the examiner knows at all times what elements of language are being assessed. Thus even the language abilities of a child with a severe language disorder (especially a severe phonological disorder) can be quantified. Finally, imitation devices can be administered much more quickly than can spontaneous language samples.

Unfortunately, the advantages of the spontaneous approach become the disadvantages of the imitative method. First, a child's auditory memory may have some effect on the results. For example, an echolalic child may score well on an imitative test without demonstrating productive knowledge of the language structures being imitated. Second, a child may repeat part of a sentence exactly because the utterance is too simple or short to place a load on the child's memory. Therefore, accurate production is not necessarily evidence that the child uses the structure spontaneously. However, inaccurate productions often do reflect a child's lack of mastery of the structure. Thus test givers should draw conclusions only about a child's errors from an imitative test. A third disadvantage of imitative tests is that they are often quite boring to the child. Not all children will sit still for the time required to repeat 50 to 100 sentences without any other stimulation, such as pictures or toys.

The use of pictures to elicit language production is an attempt to overcome the disadvantages of both imitation and spontaneous language. Pictures are easy to administer, are interesting to children, and require minimal administration time. They can be structured to test desired language elements and yet retain some of the impromptu nature of spontaneous language samples, because children have to formulate the language on their own. Because there is no time limit, results do not depend on the child's word-retention skills. Despite these advantages, a major disadvantage limits the usefulness of picture stimuli in language assessment: It is difficult to create pictures guaranteed to elicit specific language elements. Even though it is probably easiest to create pictures for object identification, difficulties arise even in this area. Thus the disadvantage seen in spontaneous sampling is evident with picture stimuli as well—the child may not produce or attempt to produce the desired language structure.

To summarize, all three methods of language observation have advantages and disadvantages. The examiner must decide which elements of language should be tested, which methods of observation are most appropriate for assessing those elements, and which assessment devices satisfy these needs. It should not be surprising that more than one test is often necessary to assess all components of language (phonology, semantics, morphology, syntax, and pragmatics), both receptively and expressively. As noted, standardized instruments should be supplemented with measures of conversational abilities within any oral-language assessment. Additionally, the different language domains are often best assessed by different procedures. For example, picture stimuli are particularly well suited for assessment of phonological abilities, because the examiner should know the intended production. Similarly, imitation tasks are often employed to assess morphological abilities, as the child having difficulty with this component will often delete suffixes and prefixes during imitation. Finally, because assessment of pragmatics involves determining the child's conversational use of language, this domain should be assessed with spontaneous production.

Oral-Language Tests

Goldman-Fristoe Test of Articulation, Second Edition (GFTA-2)

The Goldman-Fristoe Test of Articulation, Second Edition (GFTA-2; Goldman & Fristoe, 2000), is one of the more popular tools developed to assess phonology. It is an individually administered, norm-referenced device in which most consonant sounds and 16 common consonant blends (*st,* for example) are elicited in differing levels of complexity (word, sentence) and in a variety of word positions (beginning, middle, and end of word). Familiarity with the International Phonetic Alphabet and experience in identifying and transcribing disordered speech are useful for administering and scoring the GFTA. Although the device does not specifically measure vowels, the examiner can observe the child's vowel production because all vowels and all but one diphthong are used at least once within the stimulus words. The test is designed to measure articulation for individuals ages 2-0 through 21-11. The authors describe six main uses of the test: (1) to measure articulation at different levels of complexity, (2) to monitor growth, (3) to screen preschool children, (4) to observe vowel and diphthong production, (5) to screen for expressive language difficulties, and (6) to conduct research.

Subtests

Sounds-in-Words   In this subtest, 34 pictures of familiar objects are presented to the child, who must either name the picture or answer questions pertaining to it. In all, 53 responses are elicited, including 77 common consonant blends and single consonant sounds.

Sounds-in-Sentences   This subtest is designed to elicit a sample of a child's speech in a more complex, spontaneous context. The examiner reads two stories aloud to the child while presenting pictures illustrating each story. After the story is read, the examiner again presents the pictures to the child, who recounts the story. The story is loaded with the sounds most commonly misarticulated by children, and the examiner appraises the child's speech-sound production in the more complex context of sentences.

Stimulability   After the first two subtests are completed, the examiner returns to the sounds the child has misarticulated and tries to stimulate correct production by means of a step-by-step procedure explained in the instructions. The purpose of this subtest is to find out how stimulable a child is to intervention. This clinical information then leads to a decision regarding prognosis for and length of intervention.

Unlike some other articulation tests, the GFTA assesses more than one speech sound in many of the test items. This places a greater load on the listening abilities of the examiner, although many individuals using this test seem to have no problem listening for more than one sound in a given word. The stimulus pictures are large and colorful, making the test very motivating for young children. However, older children might find the device too juvenile, especially compared with the black-and-white pictures of a test such as the Arizona Articulation Proficiency Scale (Fudala, 1970).

Scores

Standard scores (mean of 100, standard deviation of 15), 90 and 95 percent confidence intervals, age equivalents, and percentile ranks are available for individuals on the Sounds-in-Words subtest (ages 2-0 through 21-11). Normative scores are not provided for the other subtests.

Norms

Separate GFTA-2 normative samples were developed for males and females. A total of 2,350 individuals (1,175 males and 1,175 females) from 300 sites across the nation were tested. Information on geographic region, mother's education level, and race/ethnicity is compared to that of the U.S. population (as reported by the U.S. Census Bureau, 1998) for each sample according to five age intervals. Additional cross-tabulations of sample characteristics are provided for mother's education level by race/ethnicity and geographic region by race/ethnicity for each sample. Also, information on students receiving special education for particular disabilities is compared to that of the population. Population characteristics are accurately represented in the sample.

Reliability

Coefficient alphas were determined for the Sounds-in-Words subtest using data from the standardization sample. These coefficients were determined for 11 age groups and ranged from .92 to .98 for females, and from .85 to .96 for males. Test-retest reliability was determined by testing a sample of students ($N = 53$) twice with a median of 14 days intervening between administrations (range = same-day administration to 34 days). Percentage of agreement for the presence of error was determined for each consonant and cluster sound tested in Sounds-in-Words. These ranged from 79 to 100 percent agreement, with all but three of the 77 sounds exceeding 90 percent agreement for presence of error across the two administrations. Interrater reliability was somewhat lower. Percentage agreement for presence of error among two raters for a sample of 30 examinees ranged from 63 to 100, with 36 of the 77 sounds exceeding 90 percent agreement for presence of error across the two administrations.

Validity

Content and construct validity are discussed in the manual. The authors argue that, because the test measures nearly all of the consonant sounds and many of the consonant cluster sounds in the English language, it demonstrates content validity. Rationale for the selected items and test format is also provided. Evidence of construct validity was displayed by showing that older individuals had fewer articulation errors than younger individuals, with a notable decrease in errors at the earlier ages. Also, test performance indicated that the correct production of sounds followed the pattern expected due to difficulty in producing particular sounds (for example, *p*, *b*, and *m* sounds were correctly articulated by many young children, whereas *s* and *r* were not correctly articulated by the same number of young children). No evidence of criterion-related validity was provided.

Summary

The GFTA-2 is an individually administered, norm-referenced device for assessing articulation among individuals ages 2-0 to 21-11. The normative sample accurately represents many population characteristics, and reliability data are good. Some validity data are provided, but no evidence of criterion-related validity is identified.

Test for Auditory Comprehension of Language, Third Edition (TACL-3)

The Test for Auditory Comprehension of Language, Third Edition (TACL-3; Carrow-Woolfolk, 1999b), is an individually administered, norm-referenced test designed to measure the auditory language comprehension of children between the ages of 3 years, 0 months, and 9 years, 11 months. Differences between the TACL-R and TACL-3 include an updated norm sample, additional items at the upper levels of the test, and the selection of items demonstrating absence of racial, ethnic, gender, and disability bias. Test results are said to be useful in program planning, early diagnosis, progress monitoring, research, and parent communication.

The TACL-3 consists of 139 items, each of which requires the child to point to one of three pictures that best illustrates the word or phrase read by the examiner. No oral response is required. The test requires an average of 20 to 30 minutes to administer. Test items are divided into three subtests, corresponding to three increasingly complex categories of auditory comprehension. Category I (Vocabulary) assesses the literal meanings of individual words, including nouns, verbs, and modifiers. Category II (Grammatical Morphemes) measures comprehension of simple sentences by requiring children to discriminate among prepositions, noun and verb number, verb tense, noun-verb agreement, suffixes, and pronouns. Category III (Elaborated Phrases and Sentences) assesses comprehension of more complex phrases and sentences, such as interrogative sentences, negative sentences, and embedded sentences. This category also measures the ability to distinguish between active and passive voices as well as between direct and indirect objects within sentences.

Scores

Subtest raw scores can be converted into percentile ranks, standard scores (mean = 10, standard deviation = 3), and age equivalents using tables in the examiner's manual. The 21 different age groups vary from those in three-month intervals for children between 3-0 and 6-11, through six-month intervals for children from 7-0 to 8-11, to a one-year interval for 9-year-olds. Subtest standard scores can be summed and then converted to percentiles, standard scores (called "quotients," which have a mean of 100 and a standard deviation of 15), and age equivalents as estimates of overall performance.

Norms

A stratified sample of 1,102 children from 24 states was selected to correspond to population characteristics as reported by the U.S. Census Bureau (1997). Stratification variables included geographic region, gender, race, ethnicity, residence (urban and rural), disability status, and educational attainment of parents. Projected population percentages for 2000 are also provided for comparison. The sample was additionally stratified within each two-year age group by geographic area, gender, race, residence, and ethnicity. Only one variable in the sample appeared to be disproportionately represented: Approximately equal numbers of children were included from urban and rural areas, whereas 75 percent of the total U.S. school population resides in urban areas. Cross-tabulations across other participant characteristics were not included in the manual.

Reliability

Internal-consistency reliability was estimated using Cronbach's (1951) coefficient alpha for each subtest and total test score at each age level (by year). All subtest alphas exceeded .90, with the exception of the Vocabulary subtest at ages 5 and 9. Alphas for all quotients equaled or exceeded .95. Coefficient alphas are also provided for different gender, ethnic, and disability groups. These also exceeded .90, with the exception of the Vocabulary subtest among students with learning disabilities and attention deficit hyperactivity disorder (alpha = .87). Test-retest reliability (two-week interval) was estimated using 29 second- and third-grade children. The resulting coefficients ranged from .86 to .97.

Validity

The author argues that the variety of items included on the TACL-3 ensures content validity. Criterion-related validity was evaluated by correlating TACL-3 subtest and composite standard scores with the subtest and composite scores of the CREVT. Correlations for subtests ranged from .53 (TACL-3 Vocabulary correlated with CREVT Expressive Vocabulary) to .85 (TACL-3 Grammatical Morphemes correlated with CREVT Expressive Vocabulary). The correlation coefficient for the composite scores (TACL-3 Quotient correlated with CREVT General Vocabulary) was .86. It is interesting to note that the TACL-3 Quotient was more highly correlated with the Expressive Vocabulary component of the CREVT than with the Receptive Vocabulary component; one would anticipate the opposite to be true. Construct validity was investigated in several ways. Factor analysis indicated that a single factor underlies the TACL-3. Items that had gender or ethnic bias were eliminated. In addition, TACL-3 scores correlated positively with age, indicating that the abilities measured by the test are developmental. Additionally, scores for different student groups followed the pattern expected due to language difficulties (students with mental retardation performed more poorly than students who were not native English speakers; they performed more poorly than students with hearing impairments, who performed more poorly than students with delayed speech-language; they performed more poorly than students without disabilities).

Finally, no data are presented to demonstrate that TACL-3 scores are useful for identifying individual children with language problems, for planning educational or therapeutic programs, or for monitoring progress in auditory comprehension.

Summary

The TACL-3 is an individually administered test designed to measure the receptive-language abilities of children ages 3 to 9. Data support the reliability of overall scores on the TACL-3. Some evidence of validity is provided.

Test of Language Development, Primary: Third Edition (TOLD-P:3)

The Test of Language Development, Primary: Third Edition (TOLD-P:3; Newcomer & Hammill, 1999) is a norm-referenced, individually administered test intended to (1) measure children's expressive and receptive competencies in the major components of linguistics, (2) identify children with language problems, (3) provide examiners with a comparative index of children's language strengths and weaknesses, and (4) measure progress in language development. The TOLD-P:3 is designed for use with children aged 4-0 through 8-11. The test contains assessments of semantics (vocabulary), syntax (grammar), and phonology. These competencies are assessed through measures of receptive, expressive, and integrating (mediating) skills. The two-dimensional model used to generate the TOLD-P:3 subtests is shown in Table 24.2.

Subtests

Nine specific subtests make up the TOLD-P:3. Six subtests are considered core or primary, in that their results are combined to form composite scores. These are measures of semantics and syntax. The three phonology subtests are considered supplementary and optional. The authors argue that this was done to provide a clear separation of language (semantics and syntax) and speech (phonology). The nine subtests are described as follows.

Picture Vocabulary   This 30-item subtest requires a child to point to the one picture in a group of four that best represents the stimulus word spoken by the examiner.

TABLE 24.2   The Two-Dimensional Theoretical Model Used to Develop the TOLD-P:3

	Linguistic System		
Linguistic Feature	*Listening (Receptive Skills)*	*Organizing (Integrating-Mediating Skills)*	*Speaking (Expressive Skills)*
Semantics	Picture vocabulary	Relational vocabulary	Oral vocabulary
Syntax	Grammatic understanding	Sentence imitation	Grammatic completion
Phonology	Word discrimination	Phonemic analysis	Word articulation

SOURCE: From Hammill, D., & Newcomer, P., *Test of Language Development–Primary* (Third Edition), Austin, TX: Pro-Ed. Reprinted by permission.

Relational Vocabulary This 30-item subtest requires a child to identify similarities or differences between items or objects whose names are spoken by the examiner. No pictures or other supports are provided.

Oral Vocabulary This 28-item subtest requires a child to define words that are spoken by the examiner. No pictures or other stimulus supports are provided.

Grammatic Understanding This 25-item subtest requires a child to select from a group of three pictures the one that best represents a sentence spoken by the examiner. The task requires no verbalization.

Sentence Imitation This 30-item subtest requires a child to repeat, verbatim, sentences that vary in length from 5 to 12 words and that vary considerably in grammatical form.

Grammatic Completion This 28-item subtest uses a cloze prompting procedure and requires a child to complete sentences by supplying appropriate plurals, possessives, tenses, comparative and superlative adjective forms, and so forth.

Word Discrimination This 20-item subtest requires a child to say whether two words read by the examiner are the same or different. The words differ from each other only in the beginning, middle, or ending phoneme. Six foil items with identical words are included to ensure that the child is not simply responding "different" to all items.

Phonemic Analysis This 14-item subtest is an assessment of a child's skill in breaking words into smaller phonemic units. The child is given specific commands to follow. For example, the examiner says, "Say *government*. Now say it again, but don't say *ment*."

Word Articulation This 20-item subtest uses pictures of familiar things to prompt speech. Phonemic transcriptions of a child's production of the words are completed, and speech errors are noted.

Scores

Subtest raw scores can be transformed into language ages (based on mean performances), percentiles, and standard scores (mean = 10, standard deviation = 3). Each of the subtests of the TOLD-P:3 is made up of a linguistic system (listening, organizing, or speaking) and a linguistic feature (semantics, syntax, or phonology). The subtests can be combined into the following six composites:

1. Listening (Picture Vocabulary and Grammatic Understanding)
2. Organizing (Relational Vocabulary and Sentence Imitation)
3. Speaking (Oral Vocabulary and Grammatic Completion)
4. Semantics (Picture Vocabulary, Relational Vocabulary, and Oral Vocabulary)
5. Syntax (Grammatic Understanding, Sentence Imitation, and Grammatic Completion)

6. Spoken Language (Picture Vocabulary, Relational Vocabulary, Oral Vocabulary, Grammatic Understanding, Sentence Imitation, and Grammatic Completion)

Norms

The TOLD-P:3 was standardized on a sample of 1,000 students in 28 states. This complete renorming of the test is a significant advance over earlier versions, in which a small number of students were added for the new edition rather than restandardizing. The norm sample was chosen on the basis of geographic region, gender, race, residence (rural/urban/suburban), ethnicity, family income, educational attainment of parents, and disabling condition. Tables in the manual show the relationship between sample makeup and the makeup of the 1997 census population. There is good correspondence.

Reliability

Internal-consistency reliability was calculated for both the students in the standardization sample and subgroups (such as boys, students who live in the Northeast). All coefficients exceeded .80. Test-retest reliability was investigated by twice testing 33 students in an elementary school in Austin, Texas, over a four-month interval. Although all but one coefficient exceeded .80, this study is very limited in both sample size and representativeness. Interscorer reliability was studied by having two people in the publisher's research department score the test. Their scoring correlated .99. Evidence for reliability is good, but very limited.

Validity

The authors provide extensive evidence on the content validity of the TOLD-P:3. They show how the procedures they used in selecting test items represent time-honored approaches to assessment of language abilities, and they describe in detail the approaches they used to select items for each subtest. The argument is convincing. They also used classical item-analysis procedures to demonstrate the item characteristics of the final version of the test. The resulting item-discrimination coefficients and item difficulties are reported and provide evidence of content validity.

Correlations of the performance of 30 children from an Austin, Texas, elementary school on the TOLD-P:3 and the Bankson Language Test, Second Edition (Bankson, 1990), are reported. The correlations are significant and as expected. The sample is very small and not representative.

Several indices of construct validity are described and discussed. The authors show that performance on the test is correlated with age, that it differentiates between people known to be average and those known to be below average in linguistic ability, that subtests correlate with one another, that test performance is like that expected based on the way in which the test was developed, and that item performance is correlated with total score. There is good evidence for the construct validity of the test.

Summary

The TOLD-P:3 is an individually administered, norm-referenced test designed to assess expressive, mediating, and receptive semantics, syntax, and phonology. This third edition of the test was completely renormed, and the norms appear representative of the U.S. population of school-age children. Evidence for reliability is limited to data on the internal consistency of the test. There is good evidence for content and construct validity, whereas evidence for concurrent validity is very limited. The test seems most appropriate for identification of students experiencing language difficulty and for intervention planning. The item sample is too limited for the test to be used for either program planning or accountability purposes.

Test of Language Development–Intermediate: 3 (TOLD-I:3)

The Test of Language Development–Intermediate: 3 (TOLD-I:3; Hammill & Newcomer, 1999) is the third edition of this test, originally published in 1977. The TOLD-I:3 is a norm-referenced, individually administered measure designed for use with children between the ages of 8-6 and 12-11. The test is designed to be used in the same ways as the TOLD-P:3: to (1) measure children's expressive and receptive competencies in the major components of linguistics, (2) identify children with language problems, (3) provide examiners with a comparative index of children's language strengths and weaknesses, and (4) measure progress in language development.

A specific theoretical framework was used to develop the TOLD-I:3. The framework is illustrated in Table 24.3. The test includes semantic and syntactic measures of both speaking and listening.

Subtests

The six subtests of the TOLD-I:3 are described as follows.

Sentence Combining   In this 25-item subtest, the child must combine two or more simple sentences into a compound or complex sentence that incorporates all the essential information from the original simple sentences.

TABLE 24.3   The Two-Dimensional Theoretical Model Used to Develop the TOLD-I:3

Linguistic Feature	Linguistic System	
	Listening (Receptive Skills)	*Speaking (Expressive Skills)*
Semantics	Picture vocabulary Malapropisms	Generals
Syntax	Grammatic comprehension	Sentence combining Word ordering

SOURCE: From Hammill, D., & Newcomer, P., *Test of Language Development–Primary* (Third Edition), Austin, TX: Pro-Ed. Reprinted by permission.

Picture Vocabulary   The child is required to make judgments about words presented by the examiner. The examiner says a series of two-word phrases (for example, "telephone user") and the child must identify which of six pictures best represents the stimulus phrase.

Word Ordering   In this 23-item subtest of syntactic ability, a sentence in which the words have been scrambled is presented orally. The child must reorder the words to make a correct English sentence (for example, "party," "fun," "was," "the").

Generals   In this 24-item test, the child must identify the way in which three words read by the examiner are alike. For example, the examiner reads "trout," "perch," and "bass," and the child is expected to identify them as "types of fish."

Grammatic Comprehension   In this 38-item subtest, the child must state whether a sentence presented orally is grammatically correct. The incorrect sentences contain errors in noun-verb agreement, pronouns, comparative and superlative adjectives, negatives, plurals, and adverbs.

Malapropisms   The child is required to identify an incorrect word in each of the 30 sentences on this subtest and to supply the correct form. For example, the child is required to tell the examiner that "photograph" should have been used in the sentence "John took a phonograph of his family." The examiner reads the sentences.

Scores

Subtest raw scores can be transformed into percentiles and standard scores (mean = 10, standard deviation = 3). Subtests can be combined into five composites as follows:

1. Syntax (Grammatic Comprehension, Sentence Combining, and Word Ordering)
2. Semantics (Vocabulary, Generals, and Malapropisms)
3. Speaking (Sentence Combining, Word Ordering, and Generals)
4. Listening (Vocabulary, Grammatic Comprehension, and Malapropisms)
5. Spoken Language (all subtests)

Composites are appropriately obtained by adding the subtest scaled scores and converting this sum to a scaled score with a mean of 100 and a standard deviation of 15.

Norms

The TOLD-I:3 was normed on 779 students in 23 states. This complete renorming of the test is a significant advance over earlier versions, in which a small number of students were added for the new edition rather than restandardizing. The norm sample was chosen on the basis of geographic region, gender, race, residence (rural/urban/suburban), ethnicity, family income, educational attainment of parents, and disabling condition. Tables in the manual show the relationship between sample makeup and the makeup of the 1997 census population. There is good correspondence.

Reliability

Internal-consistency reliability was calculated for both the students in the standardization sample and subgroups (such as boys, students who live in the Northeast). All coefficients exceeded .84. Test-retest reliability was investigated by twice testing 55 students in an elementary school in Austin, Texas, over a four-month interval. Although all coefficients exceeded .80, and coefficients for the composites exceeded .90, this study is very limited in both sample size and representativeness. Interscorer reliability was studied by having two people in the publisher's research department score the test. Their scoring correlated .94. Evidence for reliability is good, but very limited.

Validity

Concurrent validity of the TOLD-I:3 was established by correlating the test performance of 26 elementary school students from Austin, Texas, with their performance on the TOAL-3. Correlations among subtests that measure similar skills were significant. The sample is limited in size and representativeness. Several indices of construct validity are described and discussed. The authors show that performance on the test is correlated with age, that it differentiates between people known to be average and those known to be below average in linguistic ability, that subtests correlate with one another, that test performance is like that expected based on the way in which the test was developed, and that item performance is correlated with total score. There is good evidence for the construct validity of the test.

Summary

The TOLD-I:3 is an individually administered, norm-referenced test designed to assess expressive and receptive semantics and syntax. This third edition of the test was completely renormed, and the norms appear to be representative of the U.S. population of school-age children. Evidence for reliability is limited to data on the internal consistency of the test. There is good evidence for content and construct validity, whereas evidence for concurrent validity is very limited. The TOLD-I:3, like the TOLD-P:3 and the TOAL-3, meets a higher number of psychometric criteria than many tests designed to evaluate oral language. The test seems most appropriate for identification of students experiencing language difficulty and for intervention planning. The item sample is too limited for the test to be used for either program planning or accountability purposes.

Written-Language Tests

Test of Written Language–3 (TOWL-3) The Test of Written Language–3 (TOWL-3; Hammill & Larsen, 1996) is a norm-referenced device designed to assess written-language competence of students between the ages of 7-0 and 17-11. Although the TOWL-3 was designed to be individually administered, the authors provide a series of modifications to allow group administration, with minimal follow-up testing of individual students to assure valid testing. The recommended uses of the TOWL-3 include identifying students who have sufficient difficulty in writing to warrant special help, determining strengths and weaknesses of individual students, evaluating student progress, and conducting research. Two alternative forms (A and B) are available.

The TOWL-3 uses two writing formats (contrived and spontaneous) to evaluate written language. In a contrived format, students' linguistic options are purposely constrained to force the students to use specific words or conventions. The TOWL-3 uses these two formats to assess three components of written language (conventional, linguistic, and cognitive). The conventional component deals with using the rules of Standard American English in spelling, capitalization, and punctuation. The linguistic component deals with syntactic and semantic structures, and the cognitive component deals with producing "logical, coherent, and sequenced written products" (Hammill & Larsen, 1996, p. 3).

Subtests

The first five subtests, eliciting writing in contrived contexts, are briefly described here.

Vocabulary This area is assessed by having a student write correct sentences containing stimulus words.

Spelling The TOWL-3 assesses spelling by having a student write sentences from dictation.

Style Competence in this aspect of writing is assessed by evaluating the punctuation in sentences written by a student from dictation.

Logical Sentences Competence in this area is assessed by having a student rewrite illogical sentences so that they make sense.

Sentence Combining The TOWL-3 requires a student to write one grammatically correct sentence based on the information in several short sentences presented visually.

The last three subtests elicit more spontaneous, contextual writing by the student in response to one of two pictures used as a story starter. After the story has been written (and the other five subtests administered), the story is scored on three dimensions. Each dimension is treated as a subtest. Following are brief descriptions of these subtests.

Contextual Conventions A student's ability to use mechanical conventions (such as punctuation and spelling) in context is assessed using the student's story.

Contextual Language   A student's ability to construct grammatically correct sentences and appropriate vocabulary is assessed from the student's story.

Story Construction   As described by Hammill and Larsen (1996, p. 6), this subtest evaluates a student's story on the basis of the "quality of its plot, prose, development of characters, interest to the reader, and other compositional aspects."

Scores

Raw scores for each subtest can be converted to percentiles or standard scores. The standard scores have a mean of 10 and a standard deviation of 3. Various combinations of subtests result in three composites: contrived writing (Vocabulary, Spelling, Style, Logical Sentences, and Sentence Combining); spontaneous writing (Contextual Conventions, Contextual Language, and Story Construction); and overall writing (all subtests). Subtest standard scores can be summed and converted to standard scores and percentiles for each composite. These quotients have a mean of 100 and a standard deviation of 15.

Raw-score conversions are based on age rather than grade. However, written expression is not a trait that develops independently of schooling; much of the TOWL-3's content (for example, spelling, punctuation, and paragraph usage) is systematically taught in school. Because students of the same age may receive instruction in two or three different grades, grade conversions should also have been provided.

Norms

Two different sampling techniques were used to establish norms for the TOWL-3. First, one site in each of the four geographic regions of the United States was selected, and 970 students were tested. Second, an additional 1,247 students were tested by volunteers who had previously purchased materials from the publisher. The total sample of 2,217 students is distributed somewhat unevenly across the 11 age groups, but no age group has fewer than 105 students. The total sample varies no more than 3 percent from the 1990 census on various demographic variables (that is, gender, urban/rural residence, race, geographic region, ethnicity, family income, educational attainment of parents, and disability). The authors also present data for four age ranges (that is, 7 to 8, 9 to 11, 12 to 14, and 15 to 17), showing that each age range also approximates the 1990 census. However, the comparisons of interest (that is, the degree to which each normative group approximates the census) are absent.

Reliability

Three types of reliability are discussed in the TOWL-3 manual: internal consistencies (both coefficient-alpha and alternate-form reliability), stability, and interscorer agreement.

Two procedures were used to estimate the internal consistency of the TOWL-3. First, a series of coefficient alphas was computed. Using the entire normative sample, coefficient alpha was used to estimate the internal consistency of each score and composite on each form at each age. Of the 176 alphas reported (that is, 2 forms × 11 ages × 8 subtests), 101 are in the .80s. Of the remaining 75 alphas, 25 equal or exceed .90, 46 are in the .70s, and 4 are in the .60s. Alphas are consistently higher on the Vocabulary subtest and lowest on the Contextual Conventions subtest. As is typical, coefficient alpha was substantially higher for the composites. Except for spontaneous writing at ages 7 and 8 years, where all three alphas were in the .80s, all coefficients equaled or exceeded .90. Thus the composites are sufficiently reliable for making important educational decisions about students.

The authors are to be commended for also reporting subtest internal consistencies for several demographic subgroups (that is, males and females, Anglo-Americans, African Americans, Hispanic Americans, and Asian Americans), as well as students with disabilities (that is, learning disabled, speech impaired, and attention deficit hyperactive). The obtained coefficients for the various demographic subgroups are comparable to those for the entire normative sample, while those for the students with disabilities, as should be expected, are somewhat lower.

Second, alternate-form reliability was also computed for each subtest and each composite at each age, using the entire normative sample. These coefficients were distributed in about the same way as were the alphas.

The two-week stability of each subtest and each composite on both forms was estimated with 27 second graders and 28 twelfth graders. Of the 44 coefficients (that is, 11 subtests and composites × 2 forms × 2 age groups), 3 coefficients equaled or exceeded .90, 30 were in the .80s, and 11 were in the .70s. Although these coefficients are somewhat lower than would be desirable, the two age groups selected for study probably provide the most conservative estimates of stability because of potential floor and ceiling effects.

To estimate interscorer agreement, 39 TOWL-3 protocols were selected at random and scored. The correlations between scorers were remarkably consistent. Of the 22 coefficients (that is, 2 forms × 11 subtests and composites), 11 were in the .90s, and 11 were in the .80s. As we discussed in the chapter "Teacher-Made Tests of Achievement," the scoring of written-language samples is quite difficult, and unacceptably low levels of interscorer agreement appear to be the rule rather than the exception. It appears that the scoring criteria contained in the TOWL-3 manual are sufficiently precise and clear to allow for consistent scoring.

Validity

Support for control validity comes from the way the test was developed, the completeness of the dimensions of written language, and the methods by which competence in written language is assessed. The evidence for criterion-related validity comes from a single study in which teacher ratings of writing from the Comprehensive Scales of Student Abilities (Hammill & Hresko, 1994) were correlated with each score on the TOWL-3. Correlations ranging from .34 (story construction) to .69 (spelling) provide quite limited support for the TOWL-3's validity, because teacher ratings for reading, math, and general facts correlated as well as or better than those for writing.

Construct validity is considered at some length in the TOWL-3 manual. First, the authors present evidence to show that TOWL-3 scores increase with age. The correlations with age are substantially stronger for students between the ages of 7 and 13 years than for students from 13 to 18, for whom correlations are negligible. Second, in examining either the subtest intercorrelations or the factor structure, the TOWL-3 appears to assess a single factor both for the sample as a whole and separately for males, females, Anglo-Americans, African Americans, Hispanic Americans, students with learning disabilities, and students with speech impairments. Thus, although individual subtests (or the contrived and spontaneous composites) may be of interest, they are not independent of the other skills measured on the test. Third, scores on the TOWL-3 are moderately (that is, .3 to .6) correlated with scores on the Comprehensive Test of Nonverbal Intelligence (Hammill, Pearson, & Wiederholt, 1996).

The authors were especially careful to examine the possibility of racial or ethnic bias in their assessment of written language. Not only did they examine the factor structure separately for various demographic groups, but they also examined the various reliabilities and the pattern of increasing difficulty of test items for three racial groups. From the data reported, the TOWL-3 does not appear to have racial or ethnic bias.

Summary

The TOWL-3 is designed to assess written-language competence of students aged 7-0 to 17-11. Contrived and spontaneous formats are used to evaluate the conventional, linguistic, and cognitive components of written American English. The content and structure of the TOWL-3 appear appropriate, and the two forms of the test appear to be equivalent.

Although the TOWL-3's norms appear representative in general, the adequacy of the norms at each age cannot be evaluated with the data presented in the test manual. Interscorer reliability is quite good for this type of test. The internal consistencies of composite and total scores are high enough for use in making individual decisions; the stabilities of subtests are incompletely reported and are lower.

Although the test's content appears appropriate and well conceived, the validity of the inferences to be drawn from the scores is unclear. Specifically, group means are the only data to suggest that the TOWL-3 is useful in identifying students with disabilities or in determining strengths and weaknesses of individual students. Students with learning disabilities and speech impairments earn TOWL-3 subtest scores that are only 1 standard deviation (or less) below the mean; they earn composite scores that are no more than 1.2 standard deviations below the mean. However, because we do not know whether these students had disabilities in written language, their scores tell us little about the TOWL-3's ability to identify students with special needs. Given that the TOWL-3 has only two forms and relatively low stability, its usefulness in evaluating pupil progress is also limited.

The Test of Written Spelling–4 (TWS-4; Larsen, Hammill, & Moats, 1999) is a norm-referenced test intended to assess the spelling ability of students ranging in age from 6-0 to 18-11. The TWS-4 uses a dictation format in which the tester reads a word, uses the word in a sentence, and reads the word a second time in isolation. The student then writes the word. Basal and ceiling levels (five consecutive correct responses and five consecutive incorrect responses, respectively) allow the test to be administered quickly, usually in less than 25 minutes. Although used primarily as an individually administered test, the TWS-4 can also be administered to groups, provided the tester uses the ceiling rules to score the tests after all students have completed testing.

Changes to the fourth edition of this test included doing away with the format of having two separate tests, one each for predictable and unpredictable words, and its replacement with two alternative forms. In addition, the authors conducted one reliability study, examined differential item functioning for different racial or ethnic groups, and examined the extent to which the words included in the TWS-4 are still prominent in spelling basal series. No changes were made in items or in norms.

Scores

Raw scores for each form of the TWS-4 may be converted into percentiles and standard scores that have a mean of 100 and a standard deviation of 15. With an apology and a strong warning about the dangers of their use, the authors provide grade and age equivalents because users say they want them.

Norms

Although the test was changed from one with two subtests to one with no subtests, and equivalent forms were developed, the authors did not restandardize the test. The norms are a strange mixture of 3,805 students who made up the TWS-2 norms and 855 students from intact classrooms at only three sites who took the TWS-3. We believe that, given the changes in format and administration procedure, and the fact that the majority of norms are more than 20 years old, the authors should have restandardized this test.

Reliability

With one minor exception, all data on reliability are on former editions of the TWS-4. The authors report reliabilities in excess of .90 for the earlier editions of the TWS-4. For this edition, they went back to original normative data and computed reliabilities for gender and racial subgroups. The test has a reliability of .96 for both forms for every subgroup.

A test-retest study was completed on 41 students at one Texas school. The characteristics of the sample are not described. We know only that there were 14 first-, 14 third-, and 13 sixth-grade students. Reliabilities exceeded .94 for each group.

Validity

With one exception, validity data are on earlier forms of the TWS-4. In the seventh edition of our text, we concluded that evidence for concurrent validity is strong. The new study correlated scores on the TWS-4 with scores on three achievement tests (none with a spelling subtest) for the group of 41 students on whom the reliability study was conducted. Corrrelations were low to moderate.

To investigate the extent to which words on the TWS-4 are still instructionally relevant, the authors examined their status in each of six spelling basal series. The first two thirds of the words on both forms of the test appear in nearly all series. Every word on the TWS-4 is in the Steck-Vaughn EDL Core Vocabulary, a series used to select the words.

Summary

The fourth edition of the Test of Written Spelling differs from earlier editions. The words are the same, but they are arranged in two alternative forms rather than two subtests. The test was not restandardized, the norms are more than 20 years old, and only one small new reliability and validity study was completed. Norms are dated, and although evidence for reliability and validity of the test is good, that evidence is based on a different format of the test. Users are cautioned against making norm-referenced comparisons using this test.

Language Tests That Assess Both Written and Oral Language

Oral and Written Language Scales (OWLS)

The Oral and Written Language Scales (OWLS; Carrow-Woolfolk, 1995) are an individually administered assessment of receptive and expressive language for children and young adults aged 3 through 21. The test includes three scales: Listening Comprehension, Oral Expression, and Written Expression. Test results are used to determine broad levels of language skills and specific performance in listening, speaking, and writing. The scales are described here.

Listening Comprehension   This scale is designed to measure understanding of spoken language. It consists of 111 items. The examiner reads aloud a verbal stimulus, and the student has to identify which of four pictures is the best response to the stimulus. The scale takes 5 to 15 minutes to administer.

Oral Expression   This scale is a measure of understanding and use of spoken language. It consists of 96 items. The examiner reads aloud a verbal stimulus and shows a picture. The student responds orally by answering a question, completing a sentence, or generating one or more sentences. The scale takes 10 to 25 minutes to administer.

Written Expression   This scale is an assessment of written language for students 5 to 21 years of age. It is designed to measure ability to use conventions (spelling, punctuation, and so on), use syntactical forms (modifiers, phrases, sentence structures, and so on), and communicate meaningfully (with appropriate content, coherence, organization, and so on). The student responds to direct writing prompts provided by the examiner.

The OWLS is designed to be used in identification of students with language difficulties and disorders, in intervention planning, and in monitoring student progress.

Norms

The OWLS standardization sample consisted of 1,985 students chosen to match the U.S. Census data from the 1991 Current Population Survey. The sample was stratified within age group by gender, race, geographic region, and socioeconomic status. Tables in the manual show the comparison of the sample to the U.S. population. Cross-tabulations are shown only for age, not for other variables. The 14-to-21 age group is overrepresented by students in the North Central region and underrepresented by students from the West.

Scores

The OWLS produces raw scores, which may be transformed to standard scores with a mean of 100 and a standard deviation of 15. In addition, test age equivalents, normal-curve equivalents, percentiles, and stanines can be obtained. Scores are obtained for each subtest, for an oral-language composite, and for a written-language composite.

Reliability

Internal-consistency reliability was calculated using students in the standardization. Reliability coefficients range from .75 to .89 for Listening Comprehension, from .76 to .91 for Oral Expression, and from .87 to .94 for the oral composite. They range from .77 to .89 for Written Expression. Test-retest reliabilities were computed on a small sample of students who are not described. The coefficients range from .58 to .85 for the oral subtests and composite, and from .66 to .83 for the Written Expression subtest. Reliabilities are sufficient to use this measure as a screening device. They are not sufficient to use it in making important decisions about individual students. This latter, of course, is the use the authors suggest for the test.

Validity

The authors report the results of a set of external validity studies, each consisting of a comparison of performance on the OWLS to performance on other measures. Sample sizes were small, but correlations were in the expected range. The Written Expression subtest was compared to the Kaufman Test of Educational Achievement, the Peabody Individual Achievement Test–Revised, the Woodcock Reading Mastery Test, and the Peabody Picture Vocabulary Test. Student performance on the Oral Expression and Listening Comprehension subtests was compared to performance on the Test for Auditory Comprehension of Language–Revised, the Peabody Picture Vocabulary Test, the Clinical

Evaluation of Language Fundamentals–Revised, and the Kaufman Assessment Battery for Children.

Summary

The OWLS is a language test combining assessment of oral and written language. The test was standardized on the same population, so comparisons of student performance on oral and written measures are enhanced. The manual includes data showing that the standardization sample is generally representative of the U.S. population. Reliability coefficients are too low to permit use of this measure in making important decisions for individuals. Evidence for validity is good, although it is based on a set of studies with limited numbers of students.

Dilemmas in Current Practice

Oral Language

Three issues are particularly troublesome in the assessment of oral language: (1) ensuring that the elicited language assessment is a true reflection of the child's general spontaneous language capacity; (2) using the results of standardized tests to generate effective therapy; and (3) adapting assessment to individuals who do not match the characteristics of the standardization sample. All these dilemmas stem from the limited nature of the standardized tests and must be addressed in practice.

From a practical standpoint, the clinician must use standardized tests to identify a child with a language impairment. Yet, as noted earlier in this chapter, such instruments may not directly measure a child's true language abilities. Thus the clinician must supplement the standard tests with nonstandard spontaneous language sampling. Additionally, if possible, the child should be observed in a number of settings outside the formal testing situation. After the spontaneous samples have been gathered, the results of these analyses should be compared with the performance on the standardized tests.

Selection of targets for intervention is one of the more difficult tasks facing the clinician. Many standardized tests that are useful for identifying language disorders in children may not lend themselves to determining efficient treatment. The clinician must evaluate the results of both the standard and the nonstandard assessment procedures and decide which language skills are most important to the child. Although it is tempting simply to train the child to perform better on a particular test (hence boosting performance on that instrument), the clinician must bear in mind that such tasks are often metalinguistic in nature and will not ultimately result in generalized language skills. Rather, the focus of treatment should be on those language behaviors and structures that are needed for improved language competence in the home and in the classroom.

Authors' Viewpoint

In today's language assessment environment, with a plethora of multicultural and socioeconomic variation within caseloads, a clinician is bound to encounter many children who differ in one or more respects from the normative sample of a particular test. Indeed, clinicians are likely to see children who do not match the normative sample of any standardized test. When this occurs, the clinician must interpret the scores derived from these tests conservatively. Information from nonstandard assessment becomes even more important, and the clinician should obtain reports from parents, teachers, and peers regarding their impressions of the child's language competence. The clinician should also determine whether local norms have been developed for the standard and nonstandard assessment procedures. As noted earlier, it is inappropriate to treat multicultural language differences

(continued)

Dilemmas in Current Practice (*continued*)

as if they were language disorders. However, the clinician performing an assessment must judge whether the child's language is disordered within his or her language community and what impact such disorders may have on classroom performance and communication skills generally.

Written Language
There are two serious problems in the assessment of written language.

Problem
The first problem, assessing the content of written expression, was treated in some detail in the chapter "Portfolio Assessment." The content of written language is usually scored holistically and subjectively. Holistic evaluations tend to be unreliable. When content on the same topic and of the same genre (such as narratives) is scored, interscorer agreement varies from the .50-to-.65 range (as in Breland, 1983; Breland, Camp, Jones, Morris, & Rock, 1987) to the .75-to-.90 range immediately following intensive training (such as Educational Testing Service, 1990). Consistent scoring is even more difficult when topics and genres vary. Interscorer agreement can drop to a range of .35 to .45 when the writing tasks vary (as in Breland, 1983; Breland et al., 1987). In addition, as we noted in the chapter "Assessment Processes and Concerns," subjective scoring and decision making are susceptible to the biasing effects associated with racial, ethnic, social-class, gender, and disability stereotypes.

Authors' Viewpoint
We believe the best alternative to holistic and subjective scoring schemes is to use a measure of writing fluency as an indicator of content generation. Two options have received some support in the research literature: (1) the number of words written (cf. Shinn, Tindall, & Stein, 1988) and (2) the percentage of correctly written words (cf. Isaacson, 1988).

Problem
The second problem is in identifying a match between what is taught in the school curriculum and what is tested. The great variation in the time at which various skills and facts are taught renders a general test of achievement inappropriate. This dilemma also attends diagnostic assessment of written language. Commercially prepared tests have doubtful validity for planning individual programs and evaluating the progress of individual pupils.

Authors' Viewpoint
We recommend that teachers and diagnosticians construct criterion-referenced achievement tests that closely parallel the curricula followed by the students being tested. In cases in which normative data are required, there are three choices. Diagnosticians can (1) select the devices that most closely parallel the curriculum, (2) develop local norms, or (3) select individual students for comparative purposes. Care should be exercised in selecting methods of assessing language skills. For example, it is probably better to test pupils in ways that are familiar to them. Thus, if the teacher's weekly spelling test is from dictation, then spelling tests using dictation are probably preferable to tests requiring the students to identify incorrectly spelled words.

SUMMARY

The primary function of standard oral-language tests is to identify language disorders. Assessment sessions should include nonstandard measures such as language sampling to augment the results obtained from standard instruments. In our review of standardized oral- and written-language measures, we have noted a general lack of application of psychometric principles to the construction of these instruments. Additionally, the mismatch between the standard instruments and the content of instruction remains large.

QUESTIONS FOR CHAPTER REVIEW

1. Identify and describe the three techniques for obtaining a sample of a child's language.

2. Identify and briefly describe two issues that are particularly troublesome in the assessment of oral language.

3. Design an assessment session that includes information about all aspects of language, both comprehension and production. Include a list of specific tests required to complete the session, as well as language sampling.

4. Identify and explain three limitations on analyzing a pupil's English composition to assess skill in spelling, grammar, and punctuation.

PROJECT

Assume that you wish to use one of the tests reviewed in this text to screen for written-language difficulties. Which test would be your first choice? Why? Compare your answer with a classmate's answer. Reconcile any differences.

RESOURCES FOR FURTHER INVESTIGATION

Print Resources

Camarata, S. (1996). On the importance of integrating naturalistic language, social intervention, and speech-intelligibility training (pp. 333–351). In L. Koegel & G. Dunlap (Eds.), *Positive behavior support*. Baltimore, MD: Brookes.

Camarata, S., Nelson, K., & Camarata, M. (1994). A comparison of conversation-based to imitation-based procedures for training grammatical structures in specifically language impaired children. *Journal of Speech and Hearing Research, 37,* 1414–1423.

Hammill, D., & Hresko, W. (1994). *Comprehensive Scales of Student Abilities*. Austin, TX: Pro-Ed.

Hammill, D., & Larsen, S. (1996). *Examiner's manual: Test of Written Language* (3rd ed.). Austin, TX: Pro-Ed.

Hammill, D., Pearson, N., & Wiederholt, L. (1996). *Comprehensive Test of Nonverbal Intelligence.* Austin, TX: Pro-Ed.

Hanna, P., Hanna, J., Hodges, R., & Rudoff, E. (1966). *Phoneme-grapheme correspondence as cues to spelling improvement*. Washington, DC: U.S. Department of Health, Education, and Welfare.

Hillerich, R. L. (1985). *Teaching children to write, K–8* (selected chapters on the evaluation of writing). Englewood Cliffs, NJ: Prentice-Hall.

Isaacson, S. (1988). Assessing the writing product: Quantitative and qualitative measures. *Exceptional Children, 54,* 528–534.

Lahey, M. (1988). *Language disorders and language development*. New York: Macmillan.

Larsen, S., & Hammill, D. (1994). *Test of Written Spelling* (3rd ed.). Austin, TX: Pro-Ed.

Miller, J. (1981). *Assessing language production in children*. Austin, TX: Pro-Ed.

Moss, P., Cole, N., & Khampalikit, C. (1982). A comparison of procedures to assess written language skills at grades 4, 7, and 10. *Journal of Educational Measurement, 19,* 37–47.

Shinn, M., Tindall, G., & Stein, S. (1988). Curriculum-based measurement and the identification of mildly handicapped students: A review of research. *Professional School Psychology, 3*(1), 69–85.

Technology Resources

NATIONAL INFORMATION CENTER FOR CHILDREN AND YOUTH WITH DISABILITIES
www.kidsource.com/NICHCY/speech.html
This site provides information about the nature of speech and language disorders, incidence, characteristics, educational implications, and other topics.

AGS ONLINE PRODUCTS AND SERVICES
www.agsnet.com
Look for product and ordering information about the language assessment instruments available from American Guidance Services (AGS).

PRO-ED CATALOGUE INFORMATION FOR PRODUCTS
www.proedinc.com
Find product and ordering information about the language assessment instruments available from Pro-Ed.

CHAPTER 25

Assessment of Infants, Toddlers, and Preschoolers

WITH THE PASSAGE OF PUBLIC LAW 99-457 IN 1986, STATES WERE REQUIRED TO serve children with disabilities between 3 and 5 years of age. In addition, this law extended services to children from birth to age 3, provided that the children (1) have physical or mental conditions with a high probability of producing developmental delays (for example, cerebral palsy or trisomy); (2) are at risk medically or environmentally for developmental delay; or (3) have developmental delays in cognition, physical development, speech and language, or psychosocial behavior.

Since the law's passage, it has no longer been legally acceptable to delay or deny school admission to children who are developmentally delayed or otherwise disabled. Emphasis has changed from testing young children for school readiness to comprehensively assessing infants, toddlers, and young children to address their educational and developmental needs.

In many important ways, the assessment of young children is quite different from the assessment of older individuals. The types of behavior assessed differ from the behaviors of older individuals. Infants and young children are not miniature adults possessed of adult abilities and behavior. Infant behavior is undifferentiated, molar, and limited; for example, infants fuss with their bodies and their voices. Infant assessment frequently involves neurobiological appraisal in four areas: neurological integrity (for example, reflexes and postural responses); behavioral organization (for example, attention and response to social stimuli); temperament (for example, consolability and responsivity); and state of consciousness (for example, sleep patterns and attention). As infants develop into toddlers and preschoolers, their behavior differentiates, and broad domains of behavior emerge. Assessment of toddlers and preschoolers frequently involves appraisal of communication, cognition, personal-social behavior, and motor behavior.

The evaluation of toddlers and preschoolers generally relies on their attainment of developmental milestones (significant developmental accomplishments), such as using words and walking. Although children's development is quite variable, children are usually considered to be at risk for later problems when their attainment of developmental milestones is delayed. Thus examiners must have a thorough understanding of normal development. Moreover, examiners must understand family systems and the role of culture in child-rearing practices so that they can understand the environments in which infants, toddlers, and preschoolers are developing.

Finally, the procedures used to assess infants, toddlers, and preschoolers differ from those used to evaluate older children and adults. Bailey and Rouse (1989) have reported a number of reasons why infants and young children are difficult to test. Infants between 6 and 18 months are distressed by unfamiliar adults. Although they may have better responses to strangers when held by their caregivers, they may still refuse to respond to an unfamiliar adult. Infants and preschoolers may be very active, inattentive, and distractible; they frequently perform inconsistently in strange situations. Because the language of these children is, by definition, undeveloped, they may not completely understand even simple questions and oral requests. Thus traditional assessment formats in which students respond to examiner questions can be problematic. Not surprisingly, many toddlers and preschoolers are described as untestable.

Why Do We Assess Infants, Toddlers, and Preschoolers?

There are two major reasons to assess young children. First, we use developmental tests with young children much as we use achievement and intelligence tests with students who have enrolled in schools. We use tests to facilitate eligibility decisions. Eligibility for special services and programs is based on criteria, and these criteria are operationalized by tests and rating scales. We also use tests to facilitate programming decisions. Assessments play an integral role in the development of individualized family service plans for eligible students; delayed developmental areas are targeted for intervention. Finally, tests and rating scales are used to facilitate decisions about the effectiveness of intervention programs for children with and without disabilities. Indeed, many measures currently available for use with very young children were developed exclusively for measuring attainment of goals in Head Start programs. Kelley and Surbeck (1985) report that well over 200 assessment instruments were constructed and published between 1960 and 1980, in part as a response to the 1960 congressional mandate to evaluate the programs authorized as the Handicapped Children's Early Education Program.

The second major reason to assess young children is to ascertain the readiness of nondisabled children to enter school. Information from readiness tests may lead educators to recommend delaying school entrance for unready students or to track pupils into various programs. Readiness for kindergarten or first grade refers to both academic and social readiness. Academic readiness is most often thought of in terms of reading readiness but properly includes readiness for all academic instruction. We must also consider children's readiness for the social milieu of school. In school, children must follow the directions of adults other than their parents or caretakers, must enter into cooperative ventures with their peers, must not present a physical threat to themselves or others, must have mastered many self-help skills (such as toileting and feeding), and so forth.

Tests Used with Infants, Toddlers, and Preschoolers

Bayley Scales of Infant Development, Third Edition (Bayley-III)

The Bayley Scales of Infant and Toddler Development, Third Edition (Bayley-III; Bayley, 2006), is a norm-referenced, individually administered test intended to assess the developmental functioning of children ages 1 month to 42 months. The test takes from 30 to 90 minutes to administer depending on the age of the child. The test is available in three formats: the Bayley-III Complete Kit, the Bayley-III Comprehensive Kit (same as the complete kit but with a PDA Administration and Scoring Assistant), and the Bayley-III Screening Test.

The Bayley-III assesses development in five domains: Cognitive, Language, Motor, Socio-Emotional, and Adaptive Behavior. Data for the Cognitive, Language, and Motor domains are obtained by assessing the child; for the other two domains, data are obtained from caregiver responses to a questionnaire. The Language domain includes both receptive and expressive communication subtests, and the Motor subtest includes assessment of both fine and gross motor skills. The Socio-Emotional subtest (Greenspan, 2006) is new to the third edition of this test and is an adaptation of the Greenspan Social-Emotional Growth Chart: A Screening Questionnaire for Infants and Young Children (Greenspan, 2004). The Adaptive Behavior Scale (Harrison, 2006) is composed of items and skill areas from the Adaptive Behavior Assessment System, Second Edition (Harrison & Oakland, 2003). The Adaptive Behavior Scale includes measures of communication, functional preacademics (such as letter recognition and counting), self-direction, leisure time use, social functioning, community use, home living (helping with household tasks), health and safety, self-care, and motor skills (locomotion and getting about in the environment).

Scores

Performance on the Bayley-III can be represented in the form of scaled scores, composite scores, percentile ranks, and growth scores. Developmental age equivalents are available for some subtests. The growth scores are used to plot individual child development over time.

Norms

There were several phases to standardization of the Bayley-III. First, a pilot study was conducted on 353 children. This pilot included items from the second edition of the Bayley, along with a subset of new items. Data were also collected from two clinical groups of children: those born prematurely and children with developmental delays. The data obtained from this pilot were used to construct a preliminary version of the test. This preliminary version was then applied with 1,923 children in a national tryout phase. Data obtained from this national try-out were used to construct a version of the test that was submitted to an additional minipilot with 20 children. Then a final version of the Bayley-III was developed.

The Bayley-III was standardized on a sample of 1,700 children ages 16 days to 43 months, 15 days, and to samples of children from "special groups." The sample was stratified on the basis of gender, geographic region, race/ethnicity, and parent education level. Norms for the Socio-Emotional scale were derived from 456 children in the standardization sample of the Greenspan Social-Emotional Growth Chart, whereas norms for the Adaptive Behavior scale were derived from 1,350 children who participated in the standardization of the Adaptive Behavior Assessment Scale–II. Data in the technical manual for the test show that each age group closely approximates the 2000 U.S. Census in terms of race/ethnicity, geographic region, parental education, and gender.

Reliability

Alphas were used to estimate the internal consistency of the Cognitive, Language, and Motor scales at each age. For the Cognitive scale, alpha ranged from .79 to .97; 10 of the 17 coefficients equaled or exceeded .90. For the Motor scale, alpha ranged from .86 to .96; 14 of the 17 coefficients exceeded .90. Alphas for the Language scale ranged from .82 to .98. Across all three domains, internal-consistency coefficients are lower for children less than 1 year of age than they are for older children. Reliabilities for the Socio-Emotional and Adaptive Behavior scales generally are in the .70s for children less than 1 year and .80s for older children.

Test-retest stability coefficients are generally in the .70s, too low for use in making important decisions for young children (those younger than 26 months of age). Some stability coefficients for children in the age range of 33 to 43 months are barely satisfactory for making important decisions.

Given the fact that it is very difficult to obtain stable performance over time for very young children, the Bayley-III is about as reliable as other measures designed for use with infants and toddlers.

Validity

Data are provided in the technical manual showing evidence for validity based on test content, evidence based on internal structure, and evidence based on relation with other variables. Evidence based on test content is limited to the author's argument that the test measures content consistent with theoretical conceptions of the development of infants and toddlers. Evidence based on internal structure consists of good evidence of the convergent and discriminant validity of the test. Evidence is provided that the Language subtests are more highly correlated with each other than with the Motor subtests and that they are moderately correlated with the Cognitive scale. There is also evidence for moderate correlations between the Motor and Cognitive scales. The author argues that the moderate correlation between scores on the Language and Cognitive scales reflects the close relationship between these domains.

Evidence for validity based on relation with other measures is based on examination of the relationship between performance on the Bayley-III and the second edition of the Bayley Scales of Infant Development, WPPSI-III, Preschool Language Scale 4, Peabody Developmental Motor Scales–II, and the Adaptive Behavior Assessment–2. The data presented provide reasonable evidence for the validity of the test.

There are several studies of the validity of the Bayley-III with special populations of students. Data are provided on the validity of the Bayley-III with children with Down syndrome, children identified as exhibiting "pervasive developmental disorder, children with cerebral palsy, those with specific language impairment, children with motor and physical impairments, those exposed prenatally or at birth to specific risks (asphyxiation at birth, prenatal alcohol exposure), and children born premature or with low birth weight." The scale is sensitive to performance differences between children in the normative sample and samples of children with various conditions that place them at risk for developmental delay.

Summary

The Bayley Scales of Infant and Toddler Development (Bayley-III) is a norm-referenced, individually administered test intended to assess developmental functioning of children between 1 and 42 months of age. The test has five subscales: the Cognitive scale, the Motor scale, the Language scale, a Socio-Emotional scale, and an Adaptive Behavior scale. The scales' norms appear representative in terms of race/ethnicity, geographic region, parental education, and gender, although cross-tabulations are not provided for these variables. There is good evidence for the reliability and validity of the scale, especially for children older than 1 year of age.

Young Children's Achievement Test (YCAT)

The Young Children's Achievement Test (YCAT; Hresko, Peak, Herron, & Bridges, 2000) is an individually administered, norm-referenced test designed to measure the achievement levels of preschool, kindergarten, and first-grade children in a variety of academic areas: general information, reading, mathematics, writing, and spoken language. The test requires between 25 and 45 minutes of administration time. The authors present four uses of the test: (1) to identify children who are developing normally or significantly below their peers in academic achievement, (2) to document educational progress, (3) to accompany other assessment instruments, and (4) to serve as a measure in research projects.

Subtests

General Information   This 20-item subtest measures a child's knowledge of a variety of common and practical concepts. Children are required to give oral answers to questions posed by the examiner and to point to pictures.

Reading   This 21-item subtest requires students to recognize and read letters and words, as well as comprehend short passages read by the examiner.

Mathematics   This 20-item subtest requires students to count and answer basic addition and subtraction questions accompanied by picture stimuli and coins.

Writing   This 20-item subtest requires children to copy basic symbols, letters, and words. Children are also asked to draw symbols, write words and sentences, and answer questions about writing.

Spoken Language   This 36-item subtest asks children to repeat sequences of words, as well as define specific words. Students must also recognize certain sounds in words and identify what groups of words have in common.

Scores

The number of correct items for each subtest is summed, and the sums can then be transformed into percentiles, standard scores (called "quotients," with a mean of 100 and a standard deviation of 15), and age equivalents. Score conversions are based on the child's age in years and months (three- to six-month intervals, depending on the subtest and age). A standard score for the total test, called the Early Achievement Composite (EAC) quotient, is computed by adding standard scores for each subtest and converting the sum into a standard score with a mean of 100 and a standard deviation of 15. The EAC quotient can be converted to a percentile and age equivalent.

Norms

The YCAT norm sample included 1,224 children between the ages of 4-0 and 7-11 from 32 states, who were tested at day care centers, preschools, public schools, and private schools. The sample is representative of the school-age population as reported by the U.S. Census Bureau (1997) according to geographic area, gender, race, residence (urban versus rural), ethnicity, family income, educational attainment of parents, and disability status. Characteristics of the sample are stratified by age (at year intervals) for the variables of geographic region, gender, race, residence, and ethnicity. Further cross-tabulations of sample characteristics are not provided.

Reliability

Internal-consistency coefficients were calculated at yearly intervals for each of the subtest scores and the EAC quotient. The subtest coefficients ranged from .74 (General Information at age 7) to .92 (Reading at age 4). General Information appeared to be the least reliable subtest (coefficients ranged from .74 to .85), whereas Mathematics and Reading were more reliable (coefficients ranging from .84 to .90 for Mathematics and from .85 to .92 for Reading). The composite coefficients ranged from .95 to .97. Test-retest reliability was determined using a sample of 5-year-old children ($N = 77$) and a sample of 113 children ages 4 to 7 who were tested twice, with an average of two weeks between administrations. Reliabilities across ages for the five subtests ranged from .97 to .99. However, these test-retest coefficients were calculated for the entire sample, not for each age group, which results in overestimated stability estimates.

Validity

Sections on content, criterion-related, and construct validity are provided in the manual. Careful selection of test items supports the YCAT's content validity. Criterion-related validity was assessed by correlating the subtest and composite scores of the YCAT with various subtests and composite scores of similar tests. Correlation for the YCAT EAC quotient and the composite score on the Kaufman Survey of Early Academic and Language Skills was .76; similarly, the EAC correlated .75 with the composite score of the Metropolitan Readiness Tests. A lower correlation was identified for the total score of the Gates-MacGinitie Reading Tests and the YCAT EAC quotient (.34). Lower coefficients were also obtained when both the total and subtest scores of the Gates-MacGinitie were correlated with the reading subtest of the YCAT (range of .43 to .54). Correlations for corresponding subtests of the Comprehensive Scales of Student Abilities (for example, Reading correlated with Reading; General Facts correlated with General Information) ranged from .58 to .67. Construct validity was suggested by the corresponding increase in mean subtest scores across ages (at year intervals). Subtest correlations with age ranged from .71 for General Information to .83 for Writing.

YCAT means were also compared for different subgroups of students (males versus females, different ethnic groups, and various disabilities). Subtest and EAC mean scores for students of different gender, different ethnic groups, and students with attention deficit hyperactivity disorder were very close to the overall mean (98 to 103). Reading, Writing, and Spoken Language scores for students with delayed language were lower than average (90 to 92). Subtest scores for students with learning disabilities ranged from 89 to 91, with an EAC quotient average of 85. Subtest scores for students with mental retardation ranged from 73 to 86, with an EAC quotient average of 73. It is important to note that, although a difference in mean scores for students with certain disabilities was found, no information is provided that demonstrates that the YCAT can reliably identify individual students having early achievement significantly below that of their peers.

Summary

The YCAT is intended to measure early reading, math, writing, spoken language, and general information skills among children between the ages of 4 and 7 years. This test is relatively quick and easy to administer. The YCAT composite test score (EAC) is very reliable. Subtest scores are less reliable for students of different ages and do not consistently correlate well with similar subtest scores from other standardized tests. Overall, the YCAT appears to be a useful tool in screening young children for early academic difficulties.

Developmental Indicators for the Assessment of Learning, Third Edition (DIAL-3)

The Developmental Indicators for the Assessment of Learning, Third Edition (Mardell-Czudnowski & Goldenberg, 1998), is an individually administered, 30-minute screening test to assess the development of children between the ages of 3-0 and 6-11. Several new items were developed for this edition of the scale, and a Parental Questionnaire was added to assess self-help, social development, family background, and general developmental information. Finally, a short form (called the Speed Dial) is now available. Both the DIAL-3 and the Speed Dial can be administered in English or Spanish. Although individual children are screened, the testing procedures are designed to handle large numbers of children; different examiners (called operators) administer the Motor, Concepts, and Language subtests to a child, who moves from one testing area (and one tester) to another. There are no special qualifications for operators.

Subtests

Three subtests (called Areas on the DIAL-3) require direct observation of a child's performance on various items that may require multiple responses. The Speed Dial includes eight of the DIAL-3 subtests.[1] Here we describe the subtests, and name and describe the items.

Motor This subtest includes catching a beanbag with one and two hands, jump-hop-skip, building with blocks, touching thumbs and fingers of the same hand in various sequences, cutting with scissors, copying four geometric shapes and four letters, and writing the child's own name.

Concepts This subtest includes pointing to body parts, identification of colors, rapid color naming, rote counting, using blocks to demonstrate relative positions (front, down, and so forth), concepts (for example, "big"), and sorting by shapes.

Language This subtest includes providing personal data (name, age, and so forth), articulation (repeating the names of objects), naming objects and actions, letters and sounds (saying the alphabet, naming letters presented in random order, and producing the sound of a letter), rhyming and "I Spy" (rhyming and alliteration), oral problem solving about social situations, and intelligibility rating by the examiner.

Self-Help Parents rate their children's development of eating, toileting, dressing, and other daily-living skills. Parents indicate whether the child performs the skill most of the time with no help, sometimes or with help, not yet, or not allowed.

Social Development Parents rate the frequency with which their children exhibit feelings and behaviors that are related to successful relationships with family and peers.

Scores

Raw scores for each item are converted to an intermediate score called a Scaled Score for the areas/subtests of Motor, Concepts, and Language, as well as the

---

[1] This item is also used in the Speed Dial.

Speed Dial.[2] The Scaled Scores for each subtest can also be summed into the DIAL-3 Total Score. Testers can look up children's ages (in two-month intervals) in tables to convert Scaled Score sums to percentiles and cutoff levels for potential delay. Raw-score sums for Self-Help and Social Development ratings can also be converted to percentiles and cutoff levels for potential delay.

The authors provide multiple ways to use the DIAL-3 scores to reach a decision and identify a child as needing further assessment. However, they offer users little guidance beyond the fact that more children can be identified with less stringent criteria and fewer children with criteria that are more rigorous.

Norms

The DIAL-3 was standardized on 1,560 children between the ages of 3-0 and 6-11 who were tested between November 1995 and June 1997. The children resided in 36 states, the District of Columbia, Puerto Rico, and Panama. The proportions of individuals in the DIAL-3 norms are comparable to the 1994 census in terms of gender, race/ethnicity, geographic region, and parental educational level.

Reliability

Internal consistency was estimated using coefficient alpha for 8 six-month age groups (3-0 to 3-5, 3-6 to 3-11, and so forth). We consider .80 to be the minimum reliability for a screening device. The Motor, Language, and Self-Help subtests are usually not sufficiently reliable to use for screening decisions: For Motor, none of the alphas for the eight age groups equals or exceeds .80; for Language and Self-Help, two of the eight alphas equal or exceed .80. The remaining two subtests have more age groups for which alphas equal or exceed .80: six age groups for Concepts and all eight for Social Development. The reliability of the Speed Dial equals or exceeds .80 in half of the age groups, and the reliability of the DIAL-3 total exceeds .80 except for the oldest group of children.

To estimate stability, 158 children were divided into two groups. A younger group contained 80 children between 3-6 and 4-5, and an older group contained 78 children between 4-6 and 5-10. The children were retested on average after about 28 days. For the younger group, two subtests had stability estimates that equaled or exceeded .80; stabilities for the DIAL-3 total and the Speed Dial

---

[2] As explained in the chapter "Quantification of Test Performance," "scaled score" usually refers to a standard score with a predetermined mean and standard deviation. However, the DIAL-3 manual defines a Scaled Score as the median of an age distribution, so it is a developmental score. (A Scaled Score of 0 is the median for children younger than 3 years old; 1 is the median for 3-year-olds; 2, for 4-year-olds; 3, for 5-year-olds; and 4, for 6-year-olds.) The manual provides no explanation for the ranges associated with each Scaled Score. For example, in Rapid Color Naming, a Scaled Score of 0 corresponds to raw scores of 0 to 4, a Scaled Score of 1 corresponds to raw scores of 5 to 9, a Scaled Score of 2 corresponds to raw scores of 10 to 19, and so forth. It appears that the Scaled Scores on the DIAL-3 are at best ordinal and cannot provide for equal weighting of items, as claimed on page 70 of the manual.

both exceeded .80. For the older group, Social Development was the only subtest that exceeded .80; stabilities for the DIAL-3 total and the Speed Dial both exceeded .80.

Thus only the DIAL-3 total appears to have sufficient reliability for use in making screening decisions. It should also be noted that the age groups used to estimate reliability are not the same as the age groups used to convert raw scores to percentiles and delay ratings.

Validity

Some claim can be made for the content validity of the DIAL-3 because of the careful selection and field testing of the items. Some evidence for criterion-related validity comes from modest (that is, .25 to .45) correlations with similar subtests on the Early Screening Profile, moderate (that is, .30 to .55) correlations with similar subtests on the Battelle Screening Test, and fairly strong correlations of the total score on the Brigance Preschool Screen with Concepts Language and the DIAL-3 total (that is, .53 to .79), and of Language with the Peabody Picture Vocabulary Test. The Self-Help and Social Development ratings were also correlated with parent ratings of social skills on the Social Skills Rating System. Finally, children with disabilities who were identified by means other than the DIAL-3 earned lower normalized standard scores. However, as interesting as this finding is, it is difficult to interpret because no standard scores are available for the DIAL-3.

The validity of the Speed Dial rests on the validity of the DIAL-3. There is a strong correlation (.94) between the two when scores are converted to normalized standard scores. However, no data are presented about frequency of false negatives and false positives.

Summary

The DIAL-3 is an individually administered screening device assessing development in motor, conceptual, language, self-help, and social development domains. The norms are generally representative, the reliability for the total score is generally adequate (although the reliabilities of the subtests usually are not), and the validity appears clearly established. Users are urged to make screening decisions based on the total score.

STAR Early Literacy Computer-Adaptive Diagnostic Assessment

STAR Early Literacy is a criterion-referenced test designed to provide quick and accurate estimates of the early literacy skills of children in kindergarten through third grade. A computer-adaptive process is used to match test items to the student's ability and performance level; students have up to 90 seconds to answer each item. The specific items that students receive depend on how well they perform on previous items. Each test is uniquely tailored to the individual student. Because students can be tested more than ten times in one year without concern for previous item exposure, the test is suitable for monitoring student progress.

Items on STAR Early Literacy measure literacy skills in seven domains: General Readiness (understanding word boundaries, length, patterns, shapes, and numbers); Phonemic Awareness (the ability to identify sounds in words); Phonics (the ability to pronounce letter and letter-group sounds); Graphophonemic Knowledge (understanding of the relationship between letters and sounds); Structural Analysis (understanding of the relationship between words and word parts); Vocabulary (ability to identify common words and understand antonyms and synonyms); and Reading and Listening Comprehension (ability to read and understand text). Students answer a minimum of two items in each of these domains. All of the items have audio instructions and include three answer choices, with one choice being correct.

Scores

Raw scores are converted to scaled scores that range from 300 to 900 and are intended to roughly indicate the typical age of similar performing students; for example, 300 is a performance of a 3-year-old, and 900 is a performance of a 9-year-old. Students are classified as emergent, transitional, or probable readers based on the scaled score. Domain and skill scores are also calculated and represent an estimated percentage of all the items in the test bank for the given domain or skill that the student would be likely to answer correctly.

Norms

Calibration and pilot studies were conducted based on preliminary versions of the test. The technical manual provides comparisons of various sample characteristics with those of the population; however, very few of the population characteristics were appropriately represented in the samples. Approximate percentile ranks can be obtained for each grade level based on data from these studies.

Reliability

Alternate-form stability was estimated using 9,000 students who had participated in the pilot study. The test-retest interval was several days. These reliability estimates ranged from .63 at prekindergarten to .70 at first grade. Item reliabilities were also estimated using conditional standard errors. These reliability estimates were .85 for each grade except for kindergarten, which was .77. The test's reliability is sufficient for making screening decisions for students.

Validity

Correlations between STAR Early Literacy and performance on a number of standardized reading and early achievement tests are listed in an extensive table in the manual. Comparison tests included the Gates-McGinitie Reading Test, the Iowa Test of Basic Skills, the Metropolitan Readiness Test, the Terra Nova, and STAR Reading, among others. Averages of these correlations were calculated and ranged from .57 to .64 for the different grade levels. Prekindergarten students were not included in these studies. The authors present evidence of construct validity by showing that the scale scores increased with age and grade level in the pilot study sample data.

Summary

STAR Early Literacy is a criterion-referenced, computer-adaptive test of early reading skills that gives teachers information about students' instructional levels and their areas of strength and weakness in seven domains. Norms used in calibrating items appear less than representative.

Test of Early Reading Ability, Third Edition (TERA-3)

The Test of Early Reading Ability, Third Edition (TERA-3; Reid, Hresko, & Hammill, 2001), is an individually administered, norm-referenced test designed to evaluate the emerging literacy skills in children between the ages of 3-6 and 8-6. The test has five purposes: (1) to identify those children who are significantly below their peers in reading development, (2) to identify strengths and weaknesses of individual children, (3) to document children's progress in early reading programs, (4) to serve as a research instrument, and (5) to accompany other assessments. There are two forms of the test, A and B, and each form has three subtests. These are described as follows:

Alphabet. This subtest measures children's knowledge of the alphabet and sound-letter correspondence. It includes assessment of knowledge of letter names, determination of initial and final sounds in printed words, knowledge of the number of sounds and syllables in printed words, and awareness of letters printed in different fonts.

Conventions. The Conventions subtest measures familiarity with the conventions of print (orientation of a book, knowing where to begin reading, letter orientation, knowledge of punctuation, capitalization, and spelling).

Meaning. The Meaning subtest is a test of comprehension of words, sentences, and paragraphs. It includes measures of relational vocabulary, sentence construction, and paraphrasing.

Scores

Raw scores can be converted to percentiles, normal-curve equivalents, subtest standard scores, age and grade equivalents, and reading quotients (that is, a standard score with a mean of 100 and a standard deviation of 15).

Norms

TERA-3 norms are based on the performances of 875 children from 22 states. Three methods were used to standardize the test. First, four major sites were chosen: Philipsburg, Pennsylvania (East); Austin, Texas (South); Madison, South Dakota (Midwest); and Denver, Colorado (West). In addition, Pro-Ed customers were invited to participate in the standardization by administering the test to children in their area. Third, the test authors contacted their professional colleagues and asked them to help by testing children in their area who matched the demographic characteristics of their community. Tables in the test manual show that the demographic characteristics of the norm sample are nearly an identical match to the U.S. Census (1999) demographics. The sizes of the norm groups at specific ages are very small. The norm sample is heavily weighted at the 6-year-old level.

Reliability

Estimates of internal consistency (coefficient alpha) are presented for each age for each form. Internal-consistency reliability coefficients exceed .80, but few of the subtest reliabilities exceed .90. Alternate-form reliability coefficients are consistently high. Test-retest stability evidence is based on the performance of two very small samples of children: one from Okemos, Michigan, and the other from Austin, Texas. Stability coefficients are high (exceeding .88) but based on very limited numbers of children. The authors report "average reliability coefficients" of various types for the subtests and composites. These are averaged across ages and overestimate reliability of the test. The composite score seems reliable enough for use in making important educational decisions. Users should refrain from making such decisions based on subtest performance.

Validity

The major purpose of the TERA-3 is to identify children who are ahead of or behind their age peers in the development of emerging literacy skills. Evidence that the TERA-3 is valid for this purpose comes from several sources. First, considerable work was completed to ensure the content validity of the test. Research, curriculum materials, and other tests were reviewed as sources for items. In addition, the authors solicited expert judgment, completed conventional item analyses, and examined differential item functioning. Evidence of criterion validity is based on predictive relationships between the TERA-3 and subtests of the Woodcock Reading Mastery test; relationships with the TERA-2; and relationships with selected subtests of the Stanford Achievement Test 9. Primarily moderate to high correlations were found. Evidence for construct validity is based on several indices: positive correlation of performance with age, appropriate differentiation of groups, and expected relationships among subtests.

Summary

The TERA-3 is an individually administered, norm-referenced test designed to evaluate emergent literacy skills between the ages of 3-6 and 8-6. It assesses these skills in three areas: alphabet knowledge, knowledge of conventions of print, and reading comprehension. The process for standardization of the test was questionable, but the norms appear representative for single variables. No cross-tabulations are provided indicating the extent to which the norms are representative for specific kinds of individuals (such as white children from urban environments in the Midwest). The test has excellent internal consistency at most ages, and the evidence for stability, although limited, suggests that the TERA-3 has adequate consistency over time. Evidence for content validity may be problematic, depending on the educator's orientation to reading. Clearly, there is some controversy about what are important elements to consider, and the TERA-3's content may not be well received by professionals preferring a skills approach to teaching reading. Evidence for criterion-related and construct validity is good.

Test of Early Mathematics Ability, Third Edition (TEMA-3)

The Test of Early Mathematics Ability, Third Edition (TEMA-3; Ginsburg & Baroody, 2003), is an individually administered, norm-referenced test designed to evaluate the informal and formal mathematical thinking of children between the ages of 3-0 and 8-11. There are two forms of the test, A and B, each containing 72 items. The test consists of an examiner's manual, picture stimulus books and record booklets for each form, manipulatives, and an Assessment Probes and Instructional Activities manual. The TEMA-3 is designed to identify children who are significantly behind or ahead of their peers in development of mathematical thinking, identify strengths and weaknesses in mathematical thinking, suggest instructional practices, and document children's progress in learning math. Items in this test assess either informal or formal mathematical thinking. The items assessing informal mathematical thinking tap children's number skills, number comparison facility, calculation skills, and understanding of concepts. The items assessing formal mathematical thinking evaluate children's numeral literacy, mastery of number facts, calculation skills, and understanding of concepts. The TEMA-3 is not a timed test. On the average, testing time takes about 45 to 60 minutes.

Scores

Raw scores can be converted to percentiles, age and grade equivalents, and math ability scores (standard scores with a mean of 100 and a standard deviation of 15). In addition, the authors claim that the test can be used as a diagnostic or criterion-referenced measure.

Norms

The TEMA-3 was standardized on 1,228 children; 637 took Form A, and 591 took Form B. The norm sample was selected by identifying standardization sites in each of the four major geographic areas, training examiners and testing children, or by having Pro-Ed customers test 10 to 20 children whose demographic makeup matched that of their community. The total sample closely approximates the U.S. Census (1999) demographics for gender, race, ethnicity, family income, educational level of parents, and disabling condition. To get the sample even more proportional to the U.S. school-age population, the sample was weighted during norm development and standardization. However, no data are provided for the representativeness of each age sample—the information that allows a test user to assess the representativeness of the norms for the particular child being assessed. Each norm group consisted of more than 100 children, except for the 3- and 4-year-old groups, which had 62 to 93 children for each form of the test.

Reliability

Estimates of internal consistency (coefficient alpha) are presented for each age; all coefficients exceed .90. Alternate-form reliability exceeded .95. Stability was estimated by testing and retesting 49 children for Form A and 21 children for Form B. The children on whom reliability of Form A is based were from either Putnam Valley, New York, or Mandan, North Dakota, whereas the 21 children tested and retested on Form B were all from Mandan, North Dakota. Coefficients ranged from .82 to .93.

Validity

The major purpose of the TEMA-3 is to identify children who are ahead of or behind their age peers. Evidence that the TEMA-3 is valid for this purpose comes from the careful conceptualization of the domains (such as formal and informal thinking and their components) and from the statistical procedures used to retain items. Additional evidence comes from criterion-related and construct-validity studies. Evidence of relationship to other measures was evidenced by correlating performance on the Basic Concepts and Operations composites from Key Math, the Applied Problems subtest of the Woodcock-Johnson III Tests of Achievement, the Math Reasoning and Math Calculation subtests and the Math Quotient of the Diagnostic Achievement Battery–3, and the Math Quotient from the Young Children's Achievement Test. The obtained coefficients provide evidence that the TEMA-3 has predictive validity. Evidence for construct validity is based on evidence that age is positively related to performance. The test differentiates between individuals who are and are not mathematically proficient, while not differentiating between groups (such as gender or race) whom one would not want the test to differentiate between. Evidence for validity based on internal structure is provided by showing that performance on items is highly correlated with performance on the total test. No evidence is presented that bears on three of the TEMA-3's purposes: identifying strengths and weaknesses in mathematical thinking, suggesting instructional practices, and documenting achievement growth.

Summary

The TEMA-3 is an individually administered, norm-referenced test designed to evaluate the informal and formal mathematical thinking of children from ages 3-0 to 8-11. Raw scores can be converted to four other kinds of scores. The test appears appropriately standardized, and there is good evidence for reliability. Evidence for validity is limited to the TEMA-3's ability to discriminate between high and low levels of mathematical thinking ability.

Dilemmas in Current Practice

There are three major dilemmas in assessing infants, toddlers, and preschoolers. The first is that the performances of children who are very young are so variable that long-term prediction (for example, one year) is not feasible. This inability to predict precisely is particularly pronounced with shorter, quickly administered (and less reliable) measures. Because there is relatively poor predictive validity, most inferences must be drawn with great care. If individuals wish to use these measures to predict school success, they should recognize that the closer the predicted measure (that is, the criterion) is to the predictor measure (that is, the test), the greater is the accuracy of the prediction. For example, language tests predict later language skills better than perceptual-motor tests do.

The second dilemma occurs when using tests of readiness and development as measures of current functioning

and current attainment. If tests are to be used in this way, they must be scrutinized. This is especially true when using developmental measures to document pupil progress at the preschool level. To use developmental measures in this way, educators must make sure that there is appropriate linkage between the curriculum and the content of the test.

The third dilemma is the fact that students must be labeled to be eligible for preschool programs, but the act of labeling may set up expectations for limited pupil performance. Those who assess infants, toddlers, and preschool children need to assess within a context of situational specificity. There is much situational variability in performance, and this must be taken into account when making predictions or planning interventions.

SUMMARY

Tests are used with preschoolers, infants, and toddlers for the purpose of screening. Focus generally is on identification of those children who would profit from early intervention. Assessment is based on the notions of prevention and developmental plasticity. It is assumed that it is a good idea to identify students early, intervene, change them, and prevent later problems. The impetus for preschool assessment is largely a legal one. The most recent major federal legislation to affect early assessment is Public Law 99-457.

There have been major advances in early assessment since the law was enacted in 1986. Educators now assess newborn infants, and that assessment typically involves neurobiological appraisal, consisting of assessment of neurological integrity, behavioral organization and needs, temperament, and state of consciousness. Increasingly, early childhood educators

are engaged in planning interventions for medically high-risk infants and special-needs infants and toddlers, and they develop individualized family service plans (IFSPs).

Readiness measures are a special form of preschool assessment. They are administered for the purposes of predicting who is not ready for formal school entry and who will profit from remedial or compensatory intervention. Specific measures of school readiness were reviewed in the chapter.

There are three major dilemmas in early assessment. First, tests are administered for the purpose of predicting later performance, but at these young ages, performance is so highly variable that prediction is very difficult. Second, it is dangerous to use preschool measures as indexes of current standing. Third, provision of services is dependent on labeling children, but labeling may set up expectations for limited pupil performance.

QUESTIONS FOR CHAPTER REVIEW

1. What two primary factors have contributed to the push for early intervention and associated assessment activities?

2. Describe the assessment-related parts of Public Law 99-457 and the basic components of the IFSP required by the law.

3. Discuss the four major areas of neurobiological assessment.

4. Identify and briefly discuss two features that distinguish readiness assessments from other forms of assessment instruments.

5. Delineate the three major dilemmas in assessing infants, toddlers, and preschoolers.

PROJECT

Using information found in the text, write a summary of three tests used to assess school readiness. Upon completion, compare your summaries with the text summaries. Then go to the *Mental Measurements Yearbook* (see References), and compare and contrast your summaries with the reviews of the tests you selected. If your summaries differ from the reviews, did the reviewers use information and standards different from those that you used?

RESOURCES FOR FURTHER INVESTIGATION

Print Resources

Als, H. (1984). *Manual for the naturalistic observation of newborn behavior (preterm and full-term infants)* (pp. 1–19). Boston: Children's Hospital.

Bracken, B. A. (1988). Limitations of preschool instruments and standards for minimal levels of technical adequacy. *Journal of Psychoeducational Assessment, 5,* 313–326.

Dubowitz, L., & Dubowitz, V. (1981). The neurological assessment of the preterm and fullterm newborn infant (Clinics in developmental medicine, Spastics International Medical Publications, No. 79). Philadelphia: J. B. Lippincott.

Technology Resources

AGS Online Products and Services
www.agsnet.com
Look for product and ordering information about the instruments available from American Guidance Service. Here you can find out information about the Mullen Scales of Early Learning: AGS Edition; Developmental Indicators for the Assessment of Learning–3; and the Kaufman Survey of Early Academic and Language Skills. Just search by product title.

Pro-Ed Catalogue Information for Products
www.proedinc.com
Find product and ordering information about the Developmental Observation Checklist System.

Assessment of Preschool Children
www.ed.gov/databases/ERIC_Digests/ ed389964.html
The authors of this article describe why young children are difficult to assess and make suggestions about good assessment practices with preschool children.

CHAPTER 26

Assessment of Social and Emotional Behavior

SOCIAL AND EMOTIONAL FUNCTIONING OFTEN PLAYS AN IMPORTANT ROLE IN THE development of student academic skills. When students either lack or fail to demonstrate a certain repertoire of expected behavioral, coping, and social skills, their academic learning can be hindered. The reverse is also true: School experiences can impact student social-emotional well-being and related behaviors. To be successful in school, students frequently need to engage in certain positive social behaviors, such as turn taking and responding appropriately to criticism. Other behaviors, such as name calling and uttering self-deprecating remarks, may cause concern and can denote underlying social and emotional problems. In the chapter "Assessing Behavior Through Observation," we noted that teachers, psychologists, and other diagnosticians systematically observe a variety of student behaviors. In the current chapter, we discuss additional methods and considerations for the assessment of behaviors variously called social, emotional, and problem behaviors.

The appropriateness of social and emotional behavior is somewhat dependent on societal expectations, which may vary according to the age of a child, the setting in which the behavior occurs, the frequency or duration of the behavior, and the intensity of the behavior. For example, it is not uncommon for preschool students to cry in front of other children when their parents send them off on the first day of school. However, the same behavior would be considered atypical if exhibited by an eleventh grader. It would be even more problematic if the eleventh grader cried every day in front of her peers at school. Some behaviors are of concern even when they occur infrequently, if they are very intense. For example, setting fire to an animal is significant even if it occurs rarely—only every year or so.

Although some social and emotional problems that students experience are clearly apparent, others may be much less easily observed, even though they have a similar negative impact on overall student functioning. Externalizing problems, particularly those that contribute to disruption in classroom routines, are typically quite easily detected. Excessive shouting, hitting or pushing of class-mates, and talking back to the teacher are behaviors that are not easily over-looked. Internalizing problems, such as anxiety and depression, are often less readily identified. These problems might be manifested in the form of social iso-lation, excessive fatigue, or self-destructive behavior. In assessing both external-izing and internalizing problems, it can be helpful to identify both behavioral excesses (for instance, out-of-seat behavior or interrupting) and deficits (such as sharing, positive self-talk, and other coping skills) that can then become targets for intervention.

Sometimes students fail to behave in expected ways because they do not have the requisite coping or social skills; in other cases, students may actually have the necessary skills but fail to demonstrate them under certain conditions. Bandura (1969) points to the importance of distinguishing between such acquisi-tion and performance deficits in the assessment of social behavior. If students never demonstrate certain expected social behaviors, they may need to be in-structed how to do so, or it may be necessary for someone to more frequently model the expected behavior for them. If the behavior is expected to be demon-strated across all contexts and is restricted to one or few contexts, there may be discriminative stimuli unique to the few environments that occasion the behav-ior, or there may be specific contingencies in those environments that increase or at least maintain the behavior. An analysis of associated environmental variables can help determine how best to intervene. When problematic behavior is gener-alized across a variety of settings, it can be particularly difficult to modify and may have multiple determinants, including biological underpinnings.

Ways of Assessing Problem Behavior

Four methods are commonly used, singly or in combination, to gather informa-tion about social and emotional functioning: observational procedures, interview techniques, situational measures, and rating scales. Direct observation of social and emotional behavior is often preferred, given that the results using this method are generally quite accurate. However, obtaining useful observational data across multiple settings can be time consuming, particularly when the be-havior is very limited in frequency or duration. Furthermore, internalizing prob-lems can go undetected unless specific questions are posited, given that the associated behaviors may be less readily detected. The use of rating scales and interviews can often allow for more efficient collection of data across multiple settings and informants, which is particularly important in the assessment of so-cial and emotional behavior. Observational procedures were discussed in the chapter "Assessing Behavior Through Observation"; the remaining methods are described in the following sections.

Interview Techniques Interviews are most often used by experienced professionals to gain information about the perspectives of various knowledgeable individuals, as well as to gain further insight into a student's overall patterns of thinking and behaving. Martin (1988) maintains that self-reports of "aspirations, anxieties, feelings of self-worth, attributions about the causes of behavior, and attitudes about school are [important] regardless of the theoretical orientation of the psychologist" (p. 230). There are many variations on the interview method—most distinctions are made along a continuum from structured to unstructured or from formal to informal. Regardless of the format, Merrell (1994) suggests that most interviews probe for information in one or more of the following areas of functioning and development: medical/developmental history, social-emotional functioning, educational progress, and community involvement. Increasingly, the family as a unit (or individual family members) is the focus of interviews that seek to identify salient home environment factors that may be having an impact on the student (Broderick, 1993).

Situational Measures

Situational measures of social-emotional behavior can include nearly any reasonable activity (D. K. Walker, 1973), but two well-known methods are peer-acceptance nomination scales and sociometric ranking techniques. Both types of measures provide an indication of an individual's social status and may help describe the attitude of a particular group (such as the class) toward the target student. Peer nomination techniques require that students identify other students whom they prefer on some set of criteria (such as students they would like to have as study partners). From these measurements, sociograms, pictorial representations of the results, can be created. Overall, sociometric techniques provide a contemporary point of reference for comparisons of a student's status among members of a specified group.

Rating Scales

There are several types of rating scales; generally a parent, teacher, peer, or "significant other" in a student's environment must rate the extent to which that student demonstrates certain desirable or undesirable behaviors. Raters are often asked to determine the presence or absence of a particular behavior and may be asked to quantify the amount, intensity, or frequency of the behavior. Rating scales are popular because they are easy to administer and useful in providing basic information about a student's level of functioning. They bring structure to an assessment or evaluation and can be used in almost any environment to gather data from almost any source. The important concept to remember is that rating scales provide an index of someone's perception of a student's behavior. Different raters will probably have different perceptions of the same student's behavior and are likely to provide different ratings of the student; each is likely to have different views of acceptable and unacceptable expectations or standards. Self-report is also often a part of rating scale systems. Gresham and Elliott (1990) point out that rating scales are inexact and should be supplemented by other data collection methods.

One procedure that has been developed to incorporate multiple methods in the assessment of social and emotional behavior is multiple gating (Walker & Severson, 1992). This procedure is evident in the Systematic Screening for Behavior Disorders (SSBD), which involves the systematic screening of all students using brief rating scales. Screening is followed by the use of more extensive rating scales, interviews, and observations for those students who are identified as likely to have social-emotional problems. Multiple gating may help limit the number of undetected problems, as well as target time-consuming assessment methods toward the most severe problems.

Why Do We Assess Problem Behavior?

There are two major reasons for assessing problem behavior: (1) identification and classification, and (2) intervention. First, some disabilities are defined, in part, by inappropriate behavior. For example, the regulations for implementing the Individuals with Disabilities Education Act (IDEA) describe in general terms the types of inappropriate behavior that are indicative of emotional disturbance and autism. Thus, to classify a pupil as having a disability and in need of special education, educators need to assess social and emotional behavior.

Second, assessment of problem behavior may lead to appropriate intervention. For students whose disabilities are defined by behavior problems, the need for intervention is obvious. However, the development and demonstration of social and coping skills, and the reduction of problem behavior, are worthwhile goals for any student. Both during and after intervention, behaviors are monitored and assessed to learn whether the treatment has been successful and the desired behavior has generalized.

Specific Rating Scales of Social-Emotional Behavior

Overview of the Achenbach System of Empirically Based Assessment (ASEBA)

The Child Behavior Checklist (CBCL) series by Achenbach and his colleagues has been used widely in both practice and research settings to examine child and adolescent emotional/behavioral functioning (Achenbach & Rescorla, 2004). This series is now part of a larger system entitled the Achenbach System of Empirically Based Assessment (ASEBA), which includes measures that address functioning across nearly the entire age span (1.5 to over 90 years) and has been translated into 69 different languages. The following section provides a review of the ASEBA tools that can be used in assessing children and adolescents ages 1.5 to 18 years. Table 26.1 includes information on the domains, groupings, and syndromes that are associated with the six forms that are a part of this review.

There are eight school-age forms of the ASEBA, including the following: the CBCL for ages 1.5 to 5 (CBCL/1.5–5); the Caregiver-Teacher Report Form for ages 1.5 to 5 (C-TRF); the CBCL for ages 6 to 18 (CBCL/6–18); the Teacher's Report Form (TRF); the Youth Self-Report (YSR); the Semistructured Clinical Interview for Children and Adolescents, Second Edition (SCICA-2); the Direct Observation Form (DOF); and the Test Observation Form for ages 2 to 18 (TOF). There is also a Language Development Survey (LDS) for ages 1.5 to 5 years, which is included within the CBCL/1.5–5. Altogether, these measures provide a structure for collecting data across multiple settings and sources, and seek to document both the strengths and weaknesses of the same child across different contexts. The instruments are designed to provide behavioral descriptions of students, as opposed to diagnostic inferences.

TABLE 26.1	Domains, Groupings, and Syndromes of the ASEBA (Child Forms)

Test Form	Sections/Domains	Groupings and Syndrome Scales (numbered)
CBCL/1.5–5	Problem items	Internalizing (1) Emotionally Reactive (2) Anxious/Depressed (3) Somatic Complaints (4) Withdrawn Externalizing (5) Attention Problems (6) Aggressive Behavior (7) Sleep Problems
C-TRF	Problem items	Internalizing (1) Emotionally Reactive (2) Anxious/Depressed (3) Somatic Complaints (4) Withdrawn Externalizing (5) Attention Problems (6) Aggressive Behavior
CBCL/6–18	I. Competence items	Activities Social School
	II. Problem items	Internalizing (1) Anxious/Depressed (2) Withdrawn/Depressed (3) Somatic Complaints Externalizing (4) Rule-Breaking Behavior (5) Aggressive Behavior (6) Social Problems (7) Thought Problems (8) Attention Problems
TRF	I. Academic performance II. Adaptive characteristics	Working Hard Behaving Appropriately Learning Happy
	III. Problem items	Internalizing (1) Anxious/Depressed (2) Withdrawn/Depressed (3) Somatic Complaints Externalizing (4) Rule-Breaking Behavior (5) Aggressive Behavior (6) Social Problems (7) Thought Problems (8) Attention Problems

TABLE 26.1	Domains, Groupings, and Syndromes of the ASEBA (Child Forms) (*continued*)

Test Form	Sections/Domains	Groupings and Syndrome Scales (numbered)
YSR	I. Competence items	Activities
		Social
	II. Problem items	Internalizing
		(1) Anxious/Depressed
		(2) Withdrawn/Depressed
		(3) Somatic Complaints
		Externalizing
		(4) Rule-Breaking Behavior
		(5) Aggressive Behavior
		(6) Social Problems
		(7) Thought Problems
		(8) Attention Problems
DOF		On Task
		Problem Behaviors
		Internalizing
		(1) Withdrawn/Inattentive
		(2) Nervous/Obsessive
		(3) Depressed
		Externalizing
		(4) Hyperactive
		(5) Attention Demanding
		(6) Aggressive

Data from multiple sources are the basis for empirically derived, cross-informant syndromes included as part of the ASEBA. A syndrome is composed of items that tend to co-occur within one instrument. Cross-informant syndromes are composed of items that were found to be in a syndrome for two of the instruments for a given age level. As you read the descriptions of the Achenbach scales included here, keep in mind that the different scales share many items. Still, each form has its own research base, protocols, and technical qualities. Achenbach also publishes overviews and integrative guides to assist professionals in using the various scales.

Child Behavior Checklist for Ages 1.5 to 5 (CBCL/1.5–5)

The Child Behavior Checklist for ages 1.5 to 5 (CBCL/1.5–5; Achenbach & Rescorla, 2000) is an individually administered parent (or surrogate) assessment checklist of a child's problem behaviors. The primary purpose of the CBCL/1.5–5 is to provide a set of standardized procedures for assessing behavioral and emotional disorders. The authors indicate that it can be used in combination with other ASEBA tools and related instruments to screen for problems and to plan interventions within educational settings. It represents a revision of previous CBCL versions and is geared for a slightly different age group than earlier forms. The items on the checklist can be read individually by the parent, or the interviewer may read the questions aloud; respondents should have at least a fifth-grade reading level in order to complete the checklist without reading assistance from the interviewer. Informants are asked to rate each item (there are a total of 100 such items) as either representing the child's current behavior or describing the child's behavior over the previous two months. Items include statements similar to "Refuses food" and "Does not share." Each item is rated "not true," "somewhat or sometimes true," or "very true or often true." Some items allow for further elaboration by the rater (for instance, "Is angry often (describe): _____."). The rater is also asked to answer additional open-ended questions and fill out a form on the child's language development (the Language Development Survey [LDS]).

The CBCL/1.5–5 yields information according to seven syndrome scales. These syndromes provide a profile of a child's problem behaviors along two broad groupings of behavior: internalizing and externalizing. The internalizing grouping is comprised of the Emotionally Reactive, Anxious/Depressed, Somatic Complaints, and Withdrawn syndrome scales. The externalizing grouping is comprised of the Attention Problems and Aggressive Behavior syndrome scales. There is an additional scale not included in these groupings: Sleep Problems. There is also an "Other Problems" section that allows for further consideration of behaviors, such as items similar to "Refuses food" or "Very rarely afraid," which can signal that further attention may be warranted. Users can also calculate the extent to which item ratings are consistent with those for certain DSM-IV diagnostic categories. These include the following categories: Affective Problems, Anxiety Problems, Pervasive Developmental Problems, Attention Deficit Hyperactivity Problems, and Oppositional Defiant Problems, which represent DSM-oriented scales.

Scores

The CBCL/1.5–5 can be scored by hand or by computer. Detailed scoring procedures are described in the manual. Scale scores are computed by summing the raw scores of items that compose a separate behavioral grouping or scale. In addition, a Total Problems score is presented on the CBCL/1.5–5. Percentile ranks and *T*-scores can be obtained from a profile for each scale and grouping. Explicit decision rules and scoring criteria are provided in the manual for classifying a child's score, and for determining whether the child falls within the normal, borderline, or clinical range. This information can be pooled with information collected through the C-TRF to allow for comparisons across informants from different contexts (see section on C-TRF for more information).

Explicit directions are provided in the manual for hand-scoring the Language Development Survey. The average length of phrases that the parent recalls the child having used is calculated, as well as the number of vocabulary words out of 310 listed that the parent recalls the child using. These calculations are compared to those for same-age peers from across the nation to obtain percentile ranks for the child.

Norms

Data for the norm sample are based on information collected between 1999 and 2000 from children who were selected from across the 48 contiguous United States. To be selected for inclusion in the sample, individuals had to have no major mental or physical disabilities, as well as a parent or guardian who spoke English. Participants were selected by stratified randomized methods to match national gender-by-age characteristics. Data for any individuals who had received mental health or special education services were removed from the sample. In the end, the standardization sample included information for 700 students from 40 states. The authors argue that, because minimal gender and age differences in scores were identified for the sample, they were justified in basing norms solely on a sample that was combined across these variables. Data on socioeconomic status (SES), ethnicity, and regional characteristics of the normative sample are provided but not compared to national characteristics, which brings into question the overall representativeness of the sample. It appears that individuals from the South are slightly overrepresented, as are African American children. The seven syndromes were originally derived based on factor analyses of data from both the norm sample derived above and from children selected from various mental health and special education settings.

The normative sample for the LDS consisted of 278 children. There were approximately the same number of boys and girls in the LDS sample according to five-month age groups (18 to 23 months, 24 to 29 months, and 30 to 35 months).

Reliability

Interparent Agreement   The CBCL/1.5–5 was administered to both parents of 72 children from a longitudinal study conducted in New York and Vermont, children referred to receive certain clinical services, and children from a preschool in Pennsylvania. Correlations ranged from .48 (for the Anxious/Depressed scale) to .67 (for the Sleep Problems, Externalizing, and Pervasive Developmental Problems scales). All of these correlations were significant at the $p < .01$ level; however, data were aggregated for all age groups.

Test-Retest Reliability   Mothers' ratings of 68 nonreferred children from Massachusetts, Vermont, New York, and Pennsylvania were completed twice, with a mean intervening time of eight days. Reliabilities ranged from .68 (for the Anxious/Depressed scale) to .92 (for Sleep Problems); the Total Problems scale test-retest correlation was .90. Results were not disaggregated for different age groups. The mean r across all scales was .85, and all correlations were significant at the $p < .01$ level.

Long-Term Stability   Long-term stability was examined using 80 individuals from Vermont and New York who were rated twice with a 12-month intervening period. The correlation for Total Problems was .76. Across all scales, the correlations ranged from .52 (for Pervasive Developmental Problems and Attention

Deficit Hyperactivity Problems) to .76 (for Internalizing and Total Problems scales). The mean correlation across scales was .61.

Internal Consistency   Internal consistency using Cronbach's alpha was calculated for referred and nonreferred children combined. The alphas for the seven syndrome and composite scales ranged from .66 (for Anxiety Problems) to .95 (for the Total Problems scale). As with other reliabilities, these were not disaggregated by different age levels.

Reliability for Language Development Survey (LDS)   Several studies were described that involved investigation of the test-retest reliability of the LDS. In a sample ($N = 30$) of students with and without language delays, a .99 test-retest correlation was calculated for the vocabulary score across a seven-day intervening period. A similar study of 66 2-year-olds with a one-month intervening period indicated a correlation of .97 across rating periods.

Validity

Content Validity   The CBCL/1.5–5 is composed of a total of 100 items that were selected based on information from research reviews and consultation with researchers, practitioners, and parents. All, with the exception of two items, discriminated effectively on either the CBCL/1.5–5 or the C-TRF among referred and nonreferred samples. For the two remaining items, evidence of appropriate discrimination was available from past samples of referred and nonreferred children, such that the authors considered it appropriate to maintain inclusion of these items. The author cautions users of the instrument to judge for themselves whether the content is appropriate for their particular purpose.

Criterion-Related Validity   The authors compared the scores for 563 nonreferred children to a set of referred children from 14 different special education and mental health agencies. The nonreferred sample was selected to match the referred group according to age, gender, SES, and ethnicity. Multiple-regression analyses were conducted across the combined samples to examine the variance in scale scores accounted for by referral status. Referral status was found to account for quite a bit of variance in scale scores, such that the associated effect sizes for referral status qualified as medium for 7 of the 15 CBCL scales examined.

Investigations of correlations with the Behavior Checklist (BCL; Richman, Stevenson, & Graham, 1982), the Toddler Behavior Screening Inventory (TBSI), and the Infant-Toddler Social and Emotional Assessment (ITSEA) are limited to studies of the previous version of the CBCL (the CBCL/2–3). These correlations ranged from .56 to .70 from parent ratings. Criterion-related validity of the LDS was determined using correlations with other tests (such as the Reynell Expressive Language and the Bayley Mental Development Index, among others). Correlations ranged from .56 (for the Reynell Receptive Test) to .87 (for a sum of the Bayley objects and Reynell pictures named scores). Categorizations of individuals as delayed or nondelayed in language across the LDS and other language tests were found to be similar.

Other Indices of Validity The authors present odds ratios and results from discriminant analyses that involved examining how well item performance predicted student classification as referred or nonreferred. When conducting discriminant analyses using Problem items as predictors, 84.2 percent of children were correctly classified as referred or nonreferred. The authors also present information on the prediction accuracy of later CBCL/4–18 scores for children ages 4 to 9 years based on previous data from the CBCL/2–3 that were rescored according to the CBCL/1.5–5 scales for these children. Associated correlations across time for the Total Problems scales were greater than .54. A similar prediction study was conducted for the LDS, with correlations between the LDS at 24 to 31 months correlating significantly with performance on grammar, vocabulary, and verbal memory tasks at age 13. The scale composition of the CBCL/1.5–5 was based on a series of exploratory and confirmatory factor analyses that were conducted using data from 1,728 individuals for all items, which identified seven factors corresponding to the seven syndrome scales. Although the measure generally appears to be effective at discriminating between students with and without significant emotional and behavioral problems, more evidence is needed to demonstrate that it is an effective tool for planning interventions.

Summary

The CBCL/1.5–5 is a two-page parent rating form of young children's emotional and behavioral problems, with an additional two-page language development survey. A total of 100 items are scored for the initial two-page form, using a three-point scale. Some items are designed so that parents provide additional written descriptions to add clarity to behavioral concerns. Overall, the CBCL/1.5–5 appears to be an adequate adaptation of a well-known system of evaluation and should contribute greatly to the identification of young children in need of additional emotional and behavioral supports. As the author mentions, however, the CBCL/1.5–5 should not be used as the sole data source when making individual diagnostic or placement decisions.

Caregiver-Teacher Report Form (C-TRF) The Caregiver-Teacher Report Form (C-TRF; Achenbach & Rescorla, 2000) is an individually administered checklist to be completed by teachers or caregivers of children 1.5 to 5 years of age. It parallels the scales of the CBCL/1.5–5 and is intended to allow for comparisons of student behavior across different contexts. Items are very similar to or slightly changed from the CBCL/1.5–5 to apply to peer-group versus home situations. It represents a slight revision of the original C-TRF that was originally used for children ages 2 to 5. The format is very similar to that of the CBCL/1.5–5, and readers are advised to refer to the previous section on the CBCL/1.5–5 for information on purposes, directions for administration, item descriptions, and how items are rated.

Raters who use this form provide additional data on their relationship with the child (such as how often they spend time with and have known the child, where they see the child, and so forth). In contrast to the CBCL/1.5–5, no Language Development Survey is included. The syndrome scales are identical to those for the CBCL/1.5–5, with the exception that there is not a Sleep Problems composite.

Scores

The scoring procedures are identical to those described in the previous section on the CBCL/1.5–5. In addition, cross-informant comparisons can be conducted when both the CBCL/1.5–5 and the C-TRF are completed. Computer scoring is suggested for these calculations. Multiple forms completed by multiple informants, with up to eight total respondents (for example, a child's mother and father both fill out a separate CBCL/1.5–5, and three caregivers fill out separate C-TRF forms) can be entered into a computer-scoring program. The program provides side-by-side comparisons of ratings for each item across informants and illustrates informant differences across scales using side-by-side bar graphs. Correlations across informants (for instance, Q-scores ranging from −1.00 to 1.00) are also provided to assist with interpreting data from multiple informants across multiple settings.

Norms

Of the 700 children who were included in the standardization sample for the CBCL/1.5–5, 203 children had also completed C-TRF forms. Only those who attended either day care or preschool programs and those whose parents had given consent for having the C-TRF completed were included from the original 700. Data from the 203 children were combined with data from the 1997 normative sample, providing a total sample of 604 girls and 588 boys. Data on socioeconomic status (SES), ethnicity, and regional characteristics of the normative sample are provided but not compared with national characteristics, which brings into question the overall representativeness of the sample. Individuals of low SES, Latinos, and those from the Midwest appear to be underrepresented, whereas those of high SES, African Americans, and those from the Northeast appear to be overrepresented.

The six syndromes were originally derived based on factor analyses of data from both the norm sample derived above and from children selected from various mental health, special education, Head Start, preschool, and day care settings.

Reliability

Interrater Agreement   The C-TRF was administered to caregivers and teachers of 102 children from a study conducted in Vermont and the Netherlands. Correlations across informants ranged from .21 (for the Somatic Complaints scale) to .79 (for the Externalizing scale). All of these correlations were significant at the $p < .05$ level, and all but one (the Somatic Complaints scale) were significant at the $p < .01$ level. The mean interrater correlation was .65. These calculations were based on aggregated data for all age groups.

Data were also presented for interrater agreement across the CBCL/1.5–5 and the C-TRF for 226 children. These correlations were somewhat lower, with an average correlation across scales of .40. They ranged from .21 (Affective Problems scale) to .58 (Externalizing scale), with a Total Problems correlation of .50.

Test-Retest Reliability   The C-TRF was administered twice to caregivers and teachers of 59 children from Vermont ($N = 20$) and the Netherlands ($N = 39$) across an eight-day period. Correlations ranged from .57 (for the Anxiety Problems scale) to .91 (for the Somatic Complaints scale), with a Total Problems test-retest correlation of .88. The average correlation for the scales was .81. All of the correlations were significant at the $p < .01$ level; however, data were aggregated for all age groups.

Long-Term Stability   Long-term stability was examined using 32 individuals from Vermont who were rated twice with a three-month intervening period. The correlation for Total Problems was .56. Across all scales, the correlations ranged from .22 (for Somatic Complaints) to .85 (for Affective Problems). The Total Problems correlation was .56, and the mean correlation across scales was .59.

Internal Consistency   Internal consistency using Cronbach's alpha was calculated for referred and nonreferred children combined. The alphas for the seven syndrome scales ranged from .52 (for Somatic Complaints) to .97 (for the Total Problems scale). As with other reliabilities, these were not disaggregated by different age levels.

Validity

Content Validity   The C-TRF is composed of a total of 100 items that were selected based on information from research reviews; consultation with researchers, practitioners, and parents; and studies that involved investigation of the Teacher's Report Form (TRF). All but two items discriminated effectively on either the CBCL/1.5–5 or the C-TRF among referred and nonreferred samples, such that referred samples scored higher than nonreferred samples. For the two remaining items, evidence of appropriate discrimination was available from past samples of referred and nonreferred children, such that the authors considered it appropriate to maintain inclusion of these items.

Criterion-Related Validity   The authors compared the scores for 303 nonreferred children to those of a set of referred children from 11 different mental health and special education agencies. The nonreferred sample was selected to match the referred group according to age, gender, SES, and ethnicity. Multiple-regression analyses were conducted to examine the extent to which referral status could account for variance in the C-TRF scale scores. Results indicated that the variance accounted for by referral status met Cohen's (1988) medium effect size criteria for many of the scales.

Other Indices of Validity   The authors present odds ratios and results from discriminant analyses that involved examining how well item performance predicted student classification as referred or nonreferred. When conducting discriminant analyses using Problem items as predictors, 74.3 percent of children were correctly classified as referred or nonreferred. As was the case for the

CBCL/1.5–5, the scale composition of the C-TRF was based on a series of exploratory and confirmatory factor analyses that were conducted using data from 1,113 individuals for all items, which identified six factors corresponding to the six scales. Although the measure generally appears to be effective at discriminating between students with and without significant emotional and behavioral problems, more evidence is needed to demonstrate that it is an effective tool for planning interventions.

Summary

The C-TRF is a two-page caregiver/teacher rating form of young children's emotional and behavioral problems. A total of 100 items are scored for the initial two-page form, using a three-point scale. Some items are designed so that caregivers and teachers can provide additional written descriptions to add clarity to behavioral concerns. Overall, the C-TRF appears to be an adequate adaptation of a well-known system of evaluation and should contribute greatly to the identification of young children in need of additional emotional and behavioral supports. When combined with information from the CBCL/1.5–5, it can provide a nice overview of student social-emotional functioning across multiple contexts. As the author mentions, however, these tools should not be used as the sole data source when making individual diagnostic or placement decisions.

Child Behavior Checklist for Ages 6 to 18 (CBCL/6–18)

The Child Behavior Checklist for ages 6 to 18 (CBCL/6–18) is an individually administered parent (or surrogate) assessment checklist of a child's competence and problem behaviors (Achenbach & Rescorla, 2001). The primary purpose of the CBCL/6–18 is to provide a set of standardized procedures for assessing behavioral and emotional disorders. It represents the latest revision of *The Manual for the Child Behavior Checklist and Revised Child Behavior Profile* (Achenbach & Edelbrock, 1983). It can be completed in 10 to 20 minutes. The parent may read and rate the items independently (given that the parent has adequate reading skills), or the examiner can read the items aloud for the parent and mark answers if assistance is needed. Parents are asked to rate the child, taking into consideration the child's behavior across the most recent six-month period. The authors claim that this instrument can be used to monitor and guide interventions, and to identify students with behavior and emotional disorders.

The CBCL/6–18 is composed of two main sections: Competence items and Problem items. Discriminations are made between children who are adapting successfully and those in need of additional support to deal with behavioral and emotional problems. The Competence scale includes 16 items that parents rate according to the amount and quality of their child's participation along three dimensions: (1) extracurricular activities (such as participation in sports, hobbies, clubs, and jobs); (2) social interactions; and (3) school functioning. The Problem section includes 113 specific Problem items. Problem items include statements similar to "Argumentative," "Harms own body," and "Appears lonely." On some items, parents are asked to describe the problem behavior in a way similar to the following: "Has unnatural fears (describe): _____" or "Nervous movements or twitching (describe): _____." Two broad groupings of internalizing and externalizing problems, eight syndrome scales, and a Total Problem score are presented on the CBCL/6–18. The eight syndrome scales include the following: Anxious/Depressed, Withdrawn/Depressed, Somatic Complaints, Social Problems, Thought Problems, Attention Problems, Rule-Breaking Behavior, and Aggressive Behavior. The first three of these scales listed comprise the internalizing problems composite, and the last two comprise the externalizing problems composite. There are also DSM-Oriented scales that allow one to examine item endorsement according to various DSM-IV disorder categories (such as Affective Problems, Anxiety Problems, Somatic Problems, Attention Deficit Hyperactivity Problems, Oppositional Defiant Problems, and Conduct Problems).

Scores

The Competence items are scored by having parents estimate their child's engagement (both type and quality) across the 16 items and three scales. For several of these items, a four-point comparative scale ("below average," "average," "above average," or "don't know") is used to make judgments on a child's engagement in comparison with same-age peers. Problem items are scored using a three-point response scale: 0, not true; 1, somewhat or sometimes true; 2, very true or often true. Composite scores are computed by summing the item scores associated with each competence area, syndrome, or DSM-IV diagnostic category. Internalizing, Externalizing, Total Competence, and Total Problems scores are also computed. A child's score is then evaluated according to percentile ranks and normalized T-scores to classify scores within a normal, borderline, or clinical range. Decision rules and scoring criteria are included in the manual. The CBCL/6–18 can be scored by hand or computer.

Cross-informant comparisons can be conducted when more than one respondent completes a form for a child (this can be done in combination with the TRF and the YSR forms). Computer scoring is suggested for these calculations. Multiple forms completed by multiple informants, with up to eight total respondents (for instance, a child's mother and father both fill out a separate CBCL/1.5–5, and three caregivers fill out separate C-TRF forms) can be entered into a computer scoring program. The program provides side-by-side comparisons of ratings for each item across informants and illustrates informant score differences across scales using side-by-side bar graphs. Correlations across informants (Q-scores ranging from −1.00 to 1.00) are also provided to assist with interpreting data from multiple informants across multiple settings.

Norms

The norms for the CBCL/6–18 consist of a national sample that includes children ages 6 through 18 (N = 1,753). Normative data for the CBCL/6–18 are based on children who had not received mental health or special education services within one year of standardization. Subjects were recruited to produce a standardization sample representative of the 48 contiguous states, with respect to socioeconomic status (SES), geographic region, and ethnic status. However, the data are not compared to characteristics of the actual national population. It appears that individuals of lower SES and Latinos are underrepresented, whereas those from the South and of middle SES are overrepresented. The CBCL/6–18 scales are normed separately for each gender for ages 6 to 11 and 12 to 18. However, information on the demographic characteristics of these subgroups is not provided.

The CBCL/6–18 syndrome scales were derived based on factor analyses of item responses for both nonreferred children and those assessed in mental health and other settings (total N = 4,994). Data on the ethnic and gender makeup of this sample are provided. The sample appears overrepresentative of individuals of African descent and underrepresentative of those of non-Latino white backgrounds.

Reliability

Data are reported on interinterviewer reliability, test-retest reliability, and internal consistency. Achenbach uses intraclass correlation coefficients (ICCs) for several reliability measures. ICCs reflect the proportion of total variance present in item scores and are sensitive to differences in rank order and magnitude of scored items. It should be noted that a significant portion of supporting reliability information is based on earlier studies conducted on the earlier version. Also, reliability information is not disaggregated by age or gender.

Interinterviewer Reliability To assess differences that may result if the CBCL/6–18 is self-administered or used as a questionnaire, interinterviewer reliability was computed on results obtained by three interviewers. It is important to note that this analysis is based on the earlier (pre-1991) normative data for non-referred children. A total of 723 children were matched for gender, age, ethnicity, and SES to establish matched triads. ICCs obtained for the 20 Competence items and for the 118 specific Problem items were .93 and .96, respectively.

Interrater Reliability Data were presented on the correlations among scales for CBCL/6–18 forms that were completed independently by mothers and fathers of the same 297 children, all of whom were referred for a variety of mental health services. Correlations ranged from .57 (for Activities) to .88 (for Conduct Problems), with a mean correlation of .69 across Competence scales and .76 across Problem scales.

Data were also presented for interrater agreement across the CBCL/6–18 and the TRF for 1,126 children, and across the CBCL/6–18 and the YSR for 1,038 children. These correlations were lower, with an average correlation of .29 for Problem scales when comparing the CBCL/6–18 to the TRF, and an average correlation across Problem scales of .48 when comparing the CBCL/6–18 with the YSR.

Test-Retest Reliability A single interviewer visited mothers of 72 nonreferred children two times, one week apart. The ICC for the Competence items was 1.00, and that for the Problem items was .95. Mean correlations for 73 children rated twice with an eight-day intervening period were .90 for both the Competence scales and the Problem scales, and the mean correlation for the DSM-Oriented scales was .88.

CBCLs were completed at one- and two-year intervals by mothers during a longitudinal study that included low-birth-weight and normal-birth-weight children (ages 7 to 9 years). Competence scale correlations ranged from .43 to .76, Problem scale correlations ranged from .50 to .82, and DSM-Oriented scale correlations ranged from .31 to .80.

Internal Consistency   Internal consistency, using Cronbach's alpha for Total Competence scales, ranged from .63 to .79. For Problem scales, internal-consistency coefficients ranged from .78 to .94, with a .97 correlation for Total Problems. They ranged from .72 to .91 for the DSM-Oriented scales.

Validity

Several types of validity data are reported on the CBCL/6–18. The primary concern in the development of the CBCL/6–18 was to ensure content validity by assembling items that represented a broad range of competencies and Problem items of clinical concern. Selection of the original item pool and evaluation of item content were extremely rigorous and included clinical research and literature reviews. In addition, consultations with clinical experts, developmental psychologists, psychiatrists, and psychiatric social workers were completed. The initial item pool was then pilot tested. Empirical evidence and professional feedback were used to improve the final measure.

Criterion-Related Validity   The CBCL/6–18 and the Conners Parent Rating Scale (1997) were completed for the same children by 53 parents. Correlations across the CBCL scales examined ranged from .71 to .80. The CBCL/6–18 and the Behavior Assessment System for Children were also completed for the same children among 82 mothers and 68 fathers. Correlations ranged from .38 to .88 across scales, with a Total Problems correlation of .89 and .85 across mothers and fathers, respectively.

Achenbach states that a key index of criterion validity is the ability of a measure to identify individuals whose problems arouse enough concern that they are referred for professional help. Multiple-regression analyses were conducted to examine the variance accounted for in scale scores by referral status. Referral status effects were medium for six of the scales and large for nine of the scales (these included the DSM-Oriented and Problem scales).

Other Indices of Validity   The CBCL/6–18 syndrome scales were derived empirically using exploratory and confirmatory factor analytic methods to construct a taxonomy of childhood disorders. Clinical cutoff points were used to evaluate the discriminant ability of the CBCL/6–18. Overall, more than 80 percent of the referred children scored in the borderline or clinical range for the Total Competence and/or Total Problems scales. This is in contrast to the between 25 and 30 percent of nonreferred children who scored in the borderline or clinical ranges for the Total Competence and/or Total Problems scales. This provides initial evidence that the CBCL/6–18 discriminates between children with and without substantial emotional and behavior problems.

Achenbach also presents relative-risk odds ratios to indicate the odds of an individual's having a particular condition, given a particular risk factor. This ratio is compared with the odds for individuals who do not have the particular risk factor. For the sake of the odds ratio analyses presented for the CBCL, individuals who scored in the borderline or clinical range were identified as having a risk factor, and referred versus nonreferred status served as the condition studied. The odds ratio results provide evidence that the CBCL/6–18 can help in distinguishing between referred and nonreferred individuals. Results from discriminant analyses found that a combination of the CBCL Total Competence and Problem scales could accurately place 85 percent of students in their respective referred or nonreferred groups. Finally, additional factor analytic studies and longitudinal studies have been conducted on samples from a variety of different cultural groups, and have provided additional support for the described structure and predictive validity of the CBCL.

Summary

The CBCL/6–18 is used to record in a standardized manner children's competence and problem behaviors as reported by a parent. Internalizing and externalizing dimensions are used to classify children's emotional and behavioral problems. Eight syndrome scales were derived empirically. Important demographic information on the normative sample is missing, and many reliability analyses were conducted on prior samples of individuals. Adequate validity evidence is provided for identifying students with emotional and behavior problems, although the authors do not provide adequate evidence to support the purpose of planning and monitoring interventions. Altogether, the 2001 revision does generally advance the CBCL assessment system, and it continues to be one of the best available assessments for use by clinicians and psychologists.

Teacher's Report Form (TRF)

The Teacher's Report Form for ages 6 to 18 (TRF; Achenbach & Rescorla, 2001) is modeled on the CBCL/6–18 and is designed to obtain a description of a pupil's behavior as observed by teachers in school environments. Like all the Achenbach instruments, the TRF is not meant to be used as the sole basis for diagnostic inferences. Practitioners are encouraged to verify that the teacher is familiar with the student being evaluated and that the student has been enrolled in the class for at least a two-month period.

Description of the Scales

The TRF is comprised of three major sections. Teachers are asked to rate student functioning across a variety of areas, determined based on interactions with the student across the most recent two months. In the first section, a student's academic performance relative to grade level is rated by the teacher for specific content areas. In the second section, ratings of four Adaptive characteristics (working hard, behaving appropriately, is learning, and is happy) compare the target student with typically developing peers of the same age.

The third section consists of 113 items indicative of childhood and adolescent behavior problems. Problem items include statements similar to "Behaves like a younger child," "Destroys others' things," "Is obsessive about following rules," and "Often appears lonely." As in the CBCL/6–18, several items require additional information from the teacher to provide a description of the problem behavior, in a way similar to the following: "Exhibits irresponsible behavior (describe): _____" and "Exhibits compulsive behavior (describe): _____." Two groupings (internalizing and externalizing), eight syndrome scales, and a Total Problems score are presented on the TRF. The first grouping, internalizing, is comprised of three scales: Withdrawn/Depressed, Somatic Complaints, and Anxious/Depressed. The externalizing grouping is comprised of the Rule-Breaking Behavior and Aggressive Behavior scales. Items have also been organized to allow for an examination of an individual's functioning according to various DSM-IV–oriented scales, including Affective Problems, Anxiety Problems, Somatic Problems, Attention Deficit Hyperactivity Problems, Oppositional Defiant Problems, and Conduct Problems.

Scores

The Academic Performance items are scored on a five-point scale from "far below grade" to "far above grade." Adaptive characteristics are rated on a seven-point comparative scale. Problem Behaviors are scored on a three-point scale (0, not true; 1, somewhat or sometimes true; and 2, very true or often true). Scale scores are computed by summing the item scores for each domain (Academic, Adaptive, Problems, and DSM-Oriented). Scores are plotted by gender and age (6 to 11 years and 12 to 18 years) to provide a graphic display for each scale. Percentile ranks based on nonreferred pupils and *T*-scores are obtained from the profile. Internalizing, Externalizing, and Total Problems scores are also computed. Decision rules and scoring criteria are included in the manual. The TRF can be scored by hand or by computer. ASEBA Web-Link allows data from informants to be submitted electronically. Data from multiple informants across the CBCL/6–18 and the TRF can be compared using side-by-side breakdowns of item responses, as well as through bar graphs of syndrome scale scores. Correlations of responses across different informants can also be calculated using a *Q*-score that ranges from –1 (no agreement) to +1 (complete agreement).

Norms

The standardization sample for the TRF was based on a combined sample from the 1989 standardization and the more recent 1999 sample ($N = 2,319$). The 1999 sample included 976 children who were in school, had parents who provided consent for teachers to fill out the form, and had not received mental health or special education services in the past year. The two samples were selected to be representative of the 48 contiguous states with respect to SES, ethnicity, and region. The 1989 sample was additionally selected to be representative according to urban, suburban, and rural characteristics of students. The TRF scales are normed for each gender separately for ages 6 to 11 and 12 to 18. Information for SES, ethnicity, and region is provided without national information to allow for comparison. In general, lower-SES individuals and Latino students tend to be underrepresented. Non-Latino white students appear to be overrepresented.

Data from a total sample of 4,437 students were used to identify syndromes through factor analysis; this included data from the nonreferred combined samples described above, as well as students from 60 different special education and mental health settings. Information is provided on ethnicity for this sample. As with the standardization sample, this sample appears to be overrepresentative of non-Latino white students, and underrepresentatitive of Latino students.

Reliability

Test-Retest Reliability   Teachers completed TRF ratings twice on 44 students following a mean waiting period of 16 days. Mean correlations between first and second assessments were .90 for Adaptive scales, .90 for the Problem scales, and .85 for the DSM-Oriented scales. These results were not disaggregated by age or gender.

Stability   Teachers completed TRF ratings at two- and four-month intervals for 22 children who were referred for special services due to behavioral and emotional problems. The mean Problem scale correlation was .73 at the two-month interval and .62 at the four-month interval. The mean DSM-Oriented scale correlation was .65 at the two-month interval and .60 at the four-month interval. Results for the Adaptive items were not reported.

Interrater Agreement   A total of 88 children were rated by two teachers who were familiar with each student. The mean correlation was .49 for the Adaptive scales, .60 for the Problem scales, and .58 for the DSM-Oriented scales.

Internal Consistency   Internal-consistency reliability coefficients were reported for demographically matched referred and nonreferred samples ($N = 3,086$). Coefficient alphas ranged from .72 (for the Somatic Complaints and Thought Problems scales) to .97 (for the Total Problems scale). Results were not disaggregated by age or gender.

Validity

Content Validity   All scale items on the TRF are statements of a student's competencies and problems that are identified concerns of parents, mental health providers, and educators. The scales have been subjected to extensive research and clinical application. Most of the items on the TRF are taken directly from the CBCL/6–18. A total of 98 out of 113 items are similar to items presented on the CBCL/6–18; the remaining items are slightly different. Based on analyses showing that certain items were not highly discriminating between demographically similar referred and nonreferred samples, three items from the previous TRF were replaced with new items.

Criterion-Related Validity   In a study to establish criterion-related validity, 46 students were rated by teachers on the TRF and the Conners (1997) Teacher Rating Scale–Revised (CTRS-R). TRF Attention Problems (Inattention and Hyperactivity-Impulsivity scales), Aggressive Behavior, and Oppositional Defiant Problems scales correlated from .77 to .89 with the Conners Rating Scales (teacher form). Scales from the Behavior Assessment System for Children (BASC) were also correlated with the TRF for 51 children. Correlations for related scales on these assessment tools ranged from .40 (Depression) to .87 (Hyperactivity-Impulsivity), with all correlations being significant at the $p < .001$ level. Criterion-related validity of the TRF was also assessed by evaluating two samples of demographically matched referred and nonreferred students who were rated by teachers. Regression analyses were completed to identify the unique effects of referral status on scores for the various scales, when removing effects of various demographic variables. A large effect size associated with referral status identified for 1 Problem scale, medium effect sizes identified for 15 scales, and small effect sizes identified for 5 scales.

Other Indices of Validity   The TRF syndrome scales were derived empirically using exploratory and confirmatory factor analytic methods to construct a taxonomy of childhood disorders; results supported a nine-factor structure for Problem items, including seven associated with the syndrome scales, and two associated with the Attention (one associated with Hyperactivity/Impulsivity, and the other with Inattention).

Achenbach also presents relative-risk odds ratios to indicate the odds of having a particular condition, given that an individual has a particular risk factor. Odds ratio analyses were conducted on TRF scores and referral status. First, students from the matched referred and nonreferred samples were identified as scoring in the borderline or clinical range on any of the TRF scales. Next, calculations were made to determine the odds that a referred student received a borderline or clinical score relative to the odds that a nonreferred student received such a score. Across scales, odds ranged from 2:1 to 9:1, such that referred students tended to earn such scores much more commonly than nonreferred students. Across all of these scales, the proportion of children rated in the clinical range was significantly greater ($p < .01$) for the referred sample than for the nonreferred sample.

One of the most efficient and effective ways to discriminate clinical from nonclinical subgroups is to classify students as deviant if their Academic, Total Adaptive, and Total Problems scores are in the clinical range. Additional findings are presented in the manual that will help practitioners select the most powerful combinations of scale and items to differentiate between clinical and normal samples. The TRF appears relatively successful at discriminating among groups of referred and nonreferred students. Finally, additional factor analytic studies and longitudinal studies have been conducted on samples from a variety of different cultural groups, and have provided additional support for the described structure of the TRF.

Summary

The TRF is a well-developed, empirically based instrument designed to obtain information from teachers about a student's performance on Academic, Adaptive, and Problem items in a standardized manner that can be compared with norms established by gender and age. The standardization sample was selected from the overall CBCL/6–18 sample and combined with a previous sample. Test-retest coefficients were within an acceptable range; stability and interrater reliability were marginal. It is important to note that results were not disaggregated by gender and age, making it difficult to know whether there is variation in the adequacy of reliability for these different demographic groups with which student ratings were compared.

Overall, the TRF is a well-researched instrument that appears to measure what it is supposed to measure: the overall emotional/behavioral status of children and youth. The TRF is an important component of assessment that will serve professionals well in the field.

Youth Self-Report (YSR)

The Youth Self-Report (YSR; Achenbach & Rescorla, 2001) is a self-administered rating scale designed to be completed in approximately 15 minutes by adolescents ages 11 to 18 years. If the adolescent is not an adequate reader, the test may be read aloud by an examiner. The YSR was developed primarily to assess a student's interests, feelings, and behaviors. It is a revision of the Youth Self-Report from the 1991 edition (Achenbach, 1991d). Item revisions and new norms were created for the most recent edition.

Description of the Scales

Two broad areas are assessed: Competence and Problem Behaviors. The Competence scales include activities (such as sports, hobbies, and jobs), social life (such as total number of friends and time spent with friends), and Total Competence, which additionally includes self-ratings of academic performance. Problem scales include two groupings of syndromes: internalizing (Anxious/Depressed, Withdrawn/Depressed, Somatic Complaints) and externalizing (Rule-Breaking Behavior, Aggressive Behavior). Three additional syndrome scales are not part of either the internalizing or the externalizing grouping (Social Problems, Thought Problems, Attention Problems). Scales associated with various DSM-IV categories are also available and can be determined using scores from Problem items. These categories include the following: Affective Problems, Anxiety Problems, Somatic Problems, Attention Deficit Hyperactivity Problems, Oppositional Defiant Problems, and Conduct Problems.

The Problem Behaviors items are very similar to the items from the CBCL/6–18 but are written in the first person; there is a total of 112 Problem items. Items include statements similar to "I get into arguments a lot," "I am often stressed out," and "I destroy things a lot." Some items provide open-ended questions that allow the student to list additional physical problems or to provide further descriptions of scored items. These items are presented in a way similar to the following: "I do a lot of strange things (describe): _____" and "I am often afraid of things of which other people are not afraid (describe): _____." Respondents are encouraged to provide descriptions of these items so that the items will not be scored improperly. Fourteen items that were deemed to reflect socially desirable behavior are included on the Problem items scale.

Scores

Detailed scoring procedures are provided in the administration manual. Students rate their competence across different points of interest, using a three-point scale; that is, they determine whether the amount of time or number of activities is "less than average," "average," or "more than average," as compared with their same-age peers. The 112 Problem items are rated on a three-point scale (0, not true; 1, somewhat or sometimes true; 2, very true or often true).

Raw scores are tallied for all items within individual scales and are plotted on the YSR profile by gender. Percentile rank and normalized *T*-scores are presented for all scales; no differentiation is made by age. As with the other Achenbach instruments, scores may be classified within the normal, borderline, or clinical range.

Norms

A subsample of the CBCL standardization sample was recruited by targeting adolescents between 11 and 18 years of age. To create a normative sample that was representative of general education students, students who had not received mental health services or special education services within the preceding 12 months were selected from this group; the resulting YSR normative sample contained 1,057 subjects. Ethnic distributions were similar to those of the CBCL/6–18. The YSR scales are normed separately for each gender for ages 11 to 18.

In order to identify the syndrome scales, factor analyses were conducted across a more diverse sample of students, which included many students from outpatient and inpatient mental health settings. This group included 2,551 children from 40 states and several countries. Some demographic information for this sample is provided, which is similar to that provided for the CBCL/6–18 factor analysis sample; however, no information is provided on the associated national census data to allow for comparison.

Reliability

Test-Retest Reliability Eighty-nine subjects completed the YSR two times, with an eight-day time lapse. The correlations ranged from .67 (Withdrawn/Depressed) to .91 (School-Behaving). The Competence scale mean correlation was .88, the Problem scale mean correlation was .82, and the DSM-Oriented scale mean correlation was .79. These results were not disaggregated by gender or age.

Long-Term Stability Children selected from the general population sample completed the YSR on two occasions, seven months apart. A total of 144 children (ages 11 to 14 years) participated. Competence scores produced a mean correlation of .54, the Total Problems scales produced a mean correlation of .53, and the DSM-Oriented scales produced a mean correlation of .51.

Internal Consistency   Internal consistency for the Total Competence scale was .75; for the Total Problems scale, alpha was .95. Both the internalizing and the externalizing groupings had internal consistencies of .90. Alphas for all scales ranged from .55 (Social-Working) to .95 (Total Problems).

Validity

Content Validity   A majority of YSR items were taken directly from the previously validated CBCL/6–18. The author describes the process used to add, delete, and revise items.

Criterion-Related Validity   In a study of 1,938 subjects, the author evaluated the relationship between scale scores and concurrent referral status. The sample included nonreferred and referred students who were matched according to gender, age, SES, and ethnicity. Regression analyses were completed to identify the unique effects of referral status on scores for the various scales, when removing effects of various demographic variables. Large effect sizes associated with referral status were identified for one of the Adaptive scales, with medium effects found for the remaining two Adaptive scales examined. Similar analyses were conducted for the Problem scales. Medium effect sizes were identified for five scales. In general, the results for the YSR suggested that this tool is less discriminating than the other two scales (CBCL/6–18 and TRF) with respect to referral status.

Other Indices of Validity   The YSR syndrome scales were derived empirically using exploratory and confirmatory factor analytic methods to construct a taxonomy of childhood disorders; results supported an eight-factor structure. Achenbach presents relative-risk odds ratios to indicate the odds of having a particular condition, given that an individual has a particular risk factor. Odds ratio analyses were conducted on YSR scores and referral status. Students from the matched referred and nonreferred samples were identified as scoring in the borderline or clinical range on any of the YSR scales. Next, calculations were made to determine the odds that a referred student received a score in the borderline or clinical range relative to a nonreferred student. Across scales, odds ranged from 3:1 to 10:1, such that referred students were much more likely to obtain borderline or clinical scores. Across all of these scales, the proportion of children rated in the clinical range was significantly greater ($p < .01$) for the referred sample than for the nonreferred sample.

   One of the most efficient and effective ways to discriminate clinical from nonclinical subgroups is to classify students as deviant if their Competence and Total Problems scores are in the clinical range. Additional findings are presented in the manual that will help practitioners select the most powerful combinations of scale and items to differentiate between clinical and normal samples.

Summary

The YSR is a self-administered report on an adolescent's competence and problem concerns. The instrument's scales provide indications of the student's overall emotional/behavioral status. Because of the empirical underpinnings of the YSR, its technical features are advanced for this particular type of assessment. However, the technical characteristics of this instrument are of lower quality than those found for the other related ASEBA tools. Reliability and validity studies are mixed. Still, the YSF should be considered a useful adjunct in screening and a key component in a multiaxial assessment process.

Direct Observation Form (DOF)

The Direct Observation Form (DOF; Achenbach, 1986) is designed to record behavior problems exhibited by a child during ten-minute observations. No age-range guidelines are given, although the clinical sample included children ages 5 to 14 years. Observations are conducted in group settings, such as in classrooms and at recess. A detailed list of 96 specific problem behaviors and an open-ended item for entering additional problems are provided. In general, observers are asked to describe a child's behavior in a narrative during a ten-minute observation. The observer is advised to refer to the DOF items during the observation to organize the narrative description. In addition, a child's on-task behavior is recorded and included in the final description of his or her performance. After watching a child and completing the narrative, an observer rates the child on each of the 96 items and provides information on the open-ended question. Although the DOF provides supplemental information on a child's performance, direct links with the other Achenbach instruments are enhanced by the fact that 72 of the 96 Problem items have counterparts on the CBCL/6–18, and 83 items directly correspond to items on the TRF. Examples of Problem items include "Acts too young for age," "Argues," "Disturbs other children," "Shows off or clowns," and "Unhappy, sad, or depressed."

Like the other Achenbach instruments, the DOF can be scored by hand or by computer. Detailed rules for scoring each item are printed on the DOF. Scores are provided on four broad scales and six syndromes. Broad scales include On Task, Total Problems, Internalizing, and Externalizing. The syndromes include Withdrawn/Inattentive, Nervous/Obsessive, Depressed, Hyperactive, Attention Demanding, and Aggressive. Unlike those for other instruments, the syndrome scores for the DOF can be obtained only when the computer-scoring program is used, because of the complexity of producing these scores.

Scores

The on-task intervals are tallied at the end of the observation and reported as a score ranging from 0 to 10. The 96 problem behaviors are also rated by the observer on a four-point scale (0 to 3). This four-point scale is different from those used in the other Achenbach instruments in that the author claims that the additional gradation of the scale allows "a slight or ambiguous occurrence" of a behavior to be scored as a 1; "a definite occurrence with a mild to moderate intensity and less than three minutes duration" to be scored as a 2; and "a definite occurrence with severe intensity or greater than three minutes duration" to be scored as a 3.

Mean scores are computed based on the number of observations conducted. Scores can be plotted on the DOF profile, and percentiles and *T*-scores can be obtained to determine whether a target student's performance is within clinical or normal ranges. The same scoring profile is used for both boys and girls. The author suggests that the DOF should be completed on three to six occasions to obtain a stable index of a child's performance. In addition, to provide direct peer comparisons, it is suggested that two randomly selected peers be observed immediately prior to and immediately after observing the target child. The two peer observations can be averaged to provide a standard against which the target child's performance can be compared.

Norms

All scale scores and syndromes identified on the DOF were empirically derived using principal-components analyses on data obtained from a sample of 212 clinically referred individuals (5 to 14 years old). The DOF was then normed on 287 regular education students recruited from 45 schools located in three states (Vermont, Nebraska, and Oregon). No additional demographic characteristics are provided.

Reliability and Validity

Reliability and validity information are not provided in a separate manual for the DOF. Rather, users of the DOF are referred to the following sources for technical data in support of the scale: Achenbach and Edelbrock (1983); McConaughy, Achenbach, and Gent (1988); McConaughy, Kay, & Fitzgerald (1998, 1999); and Reed and Edelbrock (1983).

Summary

The DOF provides practitioners with an observational tool that can be used to record on-task behavior and problem behaviors across 96 items that are highly similar to those included in other Achenbach instruments. Although the correspondence of items across the CBCL/6–18 and the TRF may be helpful in coordinating data, the overall technical adequacy of the DOF by itself is not well substantiated. The norms of the DOF are not well defined, and users of the scale who want information on reliability and validity must seek outside references to obtain this evidence. Overall, the DOF should be considered as an ancillary tool to substantiate behavioral problems in classroom or group settings, rather than as an independent instrument.

Asperger Syndrome Diagnostic Scale (ASDS)   The Asperger Syndrome Diagnostic Scale (ASDS; Myles, Bock, & Simpson, 2001) is a norm-referenced rating scale for use with individuals between the ages of 5 and 18 who are suspected of having Asperger's syndrome. Teachers, parents, caregivers, or others who have sufficient opportunity to observe the target individual can complete the ASDS in about 15 minutes. The scale consists of the following five subtests.

Language This subtest contains 9 items that are typical of individuals with Asperger's syndrome (for example, talks excessively about favorite topics that hold limited interest for others, does not understand subtle jokes, and so forth).

Social Skills This subtest contains 13 items typical of individuals with Asperger's syndrome (for example, avoids or limits eye contact, has difficulty understanding social cues, and so forth).

Maladaptive Behavior This subtest contains 11 behaviors often displayed by individuals with Asperger's syndrome (for example, strong reactions to changes in routines; engaging in behavior that is repetitive, obsessive, and/or ritualistic; and so forth).

Cognition This subtest contains 10 behaviors typical of individuals with Asperger's syndrome (for example, displays an extreme or obsessive interest in a narrow subject, is overly sensitive to criticism, and so forth).

Sensorimotor Development This subtest contains 7 characteristics frequently exhibited by individuals with Asperger's syndrome (for example, frequently stiffens, flinches, or pulls away when hugged; overreacts to smells that are hardly recognizable to others; and so forth).

Scores

Raw scores on each subtest can be converted to standard scores (mean = 10, standard deviation = 3) and percentiles. Total raw scores can also be converted to Asperger Syndrome Quotients (mean = 100, standard deviation = 15) and percentiles. Higher standard scores and percentiles indicate greater likelihood that a person has Asperger's syndrome.

Norms

Norms are based on 115 individuals between the ages of 5 and 18 who resided in 21 states and who had previously been diagnosed with Asperger's syndrome. The sample, although small, is representative in terms of ethnicity. As is typical for individuals diagnosed with the condition, 83 percent of the sample is male. The sample is not representative geographically, but there is no reason (at this time) to believe there are geographic factors in the development of Asperger's syndrome. Separate age norms are not provided because raw scores on the ASDS are not correlated significantly with age.

Reliability

The alpha coefficients for each subtest and the total score are all below .90, with the total score coefficient being .83. The authors correctly caution against using the subtest scores to identify students with Asperger's syndrome. Interrater reliability based on the performances of 14 students is also reported. The correlation among raters (.93) is excellent; mean difference among raters is much less than the standard error of measurement.

Validity

The ASDS has good evidence of content validity because it is based on the criteria from the American Psychiatric Association's DSM-IV; the World Health Organization's *International Classification of Diseases, Tenth Edition*; and descriptions of Asperger's syndrome found in current research. The authors also performed discriminant analyses and found that the ASDS differentiates students with Asperger's syndrome from other students with disabilities with 85 percent accuracy.

Summary

The ASDS provides a quick assessment of students suspected of having Asperger's syndrome who are between 5 and 18 years of age. The ASDS's norms are adequate, and the interrater consistency is excellent. However, internal consistency is too low to use, without corroboration from other indices, to make diagnostic decisions about students. The scale has good content validity, and there is some evidence for other types of validity.

Behavior Assessment System for Children, Second Edition (BASC-2)

The Behavior Assessment System for Children, Second Edition (BASC-2; Reynolds & Kamphaus, 2004), is a "multimethod, multidimensional system used to evaluate the behavior and self-perceptions of children and young adults aged 2 through 25 years" (p. 1). This comprehensive assessment system is designed to assess numerous aspects of an individual's adaptive and maladaptive behavior. The BASC-2 is composed of five main measures of behavior: (1) Teacher Rating Scale (TRS), (2) Parent Rating Scale (PRS), (3) Self-Report of Personality (SRP), (4) Structured Developmental History (SDH), and (5) Student Observation System (SOS). The test authors indicate that the BASC-2 can be used for clinical diagnosis, educational classification, and program evaluation. They indicate that it can facilitate treatment planning and describe how it may be used in forensic evaluation and research, as well as in making manifestation determination decisions.

Behaviors Sampled

The Teacher Rating Scale (TRS) is a comprehensive measure of both adaptive and problem behaviors that children exhibit in school and caregiving settings. Three different forms are available—preschool (2 to 5 years), child (6 to 11 years), and adolescent (12 to 21 years)—with the behavior items specifically tailored for each age range. Teachers, school personnel, or caregivers rate children on a list of behavioral descriptions using a four-point scale of frequency ("never," "sometimes," "often," or "almost always"). Estimated time to complete the TRS is 10 to 15 minutes. The TRS for preschool is composed of 100 items; the TRS for children, 139 items; and the TRS for adolescents, 139 items. Items consist of ratings of behaviors similar to the following: "Has the flu,"

"Displays fear in new settings," "Speeds through assignments without careful thought," and "Works well with others."

The Parent Rating Scale (PRS) is a comprehensive measure of a child's adaptive and problem behavior exhibited in community and home settings. The PRS uses the same four-point rating scale as the TRS. In addition, three forms are provided by age groups, as defined previously. Estimated time to complete this measure is 10 to 20 minutes.

The Self-Report of Personality (SRP) contains short statements that a student is expected to mark as either true or false, or to provide a rating ranging from "never" to "almost always." Three forms are available by age/schooling level: child (8 to 11 years), adolescent (12 to 21 years), and young adult/college (for 18- to 25-year-old students in a postsecondary educational setting). Estimated administration time is 20 to 30 minutes. Spanish translations of the PRS and SRP are available.

The Structured Developmental History (SDH) is a broad-based developmental history instrument developed to obtain information on the following areas: social, psychological, developmental, educational, and medical history. The SDH may be used either as an interview format or as a questionnaire. The organization of the SDH may help in conducting interviews and obtaining important historical information that may be beneficial in the diagnostic process.

The Student Observation System (SOS) is an observation tool developed to facilitate diagnosis and monitoring of intervention programs. Both adaptive and maladaptive behaviors are coded during a 15-minute classroom observation. An electronic version of the SOS is available for use on a laptop computer or personal digital assistant (PDA).

The SOS is divided into three parts. The first section, the Behavior Key and Checklist, is a list of 65 specific behaviors organized into 13 categories (4 categories of positive behavior and 9 categories of problem behavior). Following the 15-minute observation, the coder rates the child on the 65 items, according to a three-point frequency gradation ("never observed," "sometimes observed," and "frequently observed"). The rater can separately indicate whether the behavior is disruptive.

The second part, Time Sampling of Behavior, requires the informant to decide whether a behavior is present during a 3-second period following each 30-second interval of the 15-minute observation. Observers place a check mark in separate time columns next to any of the 13 categories of behavior that occurs during any one interval. The third section, Teacher's Interaction, is completed following the 15-minute observation. The observer scores the teacher's interactions with the students on three aspects of classroom interactions: (1) teacher position during the observation, (2) teacher techniques to change student behavior, and (3) additional observations that are relevant to the assessment process.

Scores

The BASC-2 can be either hand or computer scored. A hand-scored response form can be used for the first three instruments (TRS, PRS, and SRP). The hand-scored protocols are constructed in a unique format, using pressure-sensitive paper that provides the examiner with an immediate translation of ratings to scores. After administration of the different rating forms, the administrator removes the outer page to reveal a scoring key. Scale and composite scores are totaled easily, and a behavior profile is available to represent the data graphically. Validity scores are tabulated to evaluate the quality of completed forms and to guard against response patterns that may skew the data profiles positively or negatively. Detailed scoring procedures that use a ten-step procedure for each of these scales are described in the administration manual.

Raw scores for each scale are transferred to a summary table for each individual measure. T-scores (mean = 50, standard deviation = 10), 90 percent confidence intervals, and percentile ranks are obtained after selecting appropriate norm tables for comparisons. In addition, a high/low column is provided to give the assessor a quick and efficient method for evaluating whether differences among composite scores for the individual are statistically significant.

The TRS produces three composite scores of clinical problems: Externalizing Problems, Internalizing Problems, and School Problems. Externalizing problems include aggression, hyperactivity, and conduct problems. Internalizing problems include anxiety, depression, and somatization. School problems are broken down into attention and learning problems. A broad composite score of overall problem behaviors is provided on the behavioral symptoms index (BSI), which includes several of the subscales listed above, in addition to Atypicality and Withdrawal. In addition, positive behaviors are included in an adaptive skills composite; these include the Leadership, Social Skills, Study Skills, Adaptability, and Functional Communication subscales. An optional content scale can also be used, which provides information according to the following subscales: Anger Control, Bullying, Developmental Social Disorders, Emotional Self-Control, Executive Functioning, Negative Emotionality, and Resiliency. The PRS provides the same scoring categories and subscales, with the exception that the School Problems composite scores, composed of subscales for learning problems and study skills, are omitted, and Activities of Daily Living is added.

The Self-Report of Personality (SRP) produces four composite scores—Inattention/Hyperactivity, Internalizing Problems, Personal Adjustment, and School Problems—and an overall composite score referred to as an Emotion Symptoms Index (ESI). The composite ESI score includes both negative and adaptive scales. Inattention/Hyperactivity includes the Attention Problems and Hyperactivity subscales. The Internalizing Problems composite includes atypicality, locus of control, social stress, anxiety, depression, and sense of inadequacy. Personal Adjustment groupings include relations with parents, interpersonal relations, self-esteem, and self-reliance. The School Problems composite includes attitude to school and attitude to teachers. Additional subscales, including Sensation Seeking, Alcohol Abuse, School Adjustment, and Somatization, are included in the ESI. An optional content scale is also available that includes the following subscales: Anger Control, Ego Strength, Mania, and Test Anxiety.

Three validity scores are provided. To detect either consistently negative bias or consistently positive bias in the responses provided by the student, there is an F index ("fakes bad") and an L index ("fakes good"). The V index incorporates nonsensical items (similar to "Spiderman is a real person"), such that a child who consistently marks these items true may be exhibiting poor reading skills, may be uncooperative, or may have poor contact with reality.

The Structured Developmental History inventory (SDH) and Student Observation System (SOS) are not norm-referenced measures and do not provide individual scores of comparison. Rather, these instruments provide additional information about a child, which may be used to describe his or her strengths and weaknesses.

Norms

Standardization and norm development for the general and clinical norms on the TRS, PRS, and SRP took place between August 2002 and May 2004. Data were collected from over 375 sites. The number of children who received or provided behavioral ratings across the different measures were, for the TRS, $N = 4,650$; for the PRS, $N = 4,800$; and for the SRP, $N = 3,400$. Efforts were made to ensure that the standardization sample was representative of the U.S. population of children ages 2 to 18, including exceptional children. The standardization sample was compared with census data for gender, geographic region, SES (as measured by mother's education level), placement in special education and gifted/talented programs, and race/ethnicity. Several cross-tabulations are provided (for instance, geographic region by gender by age, race by gender by age, and so forth). Data collected through Spanish versions of the PRS and SRP are included in the standardization sample. The authors present data to support mostly balanced norms; however, the 2- to 3-year-old sample tends to vary somewhat from the characteristics of the population. For instance, 2- to 3-year-old students of low SES (mother's education level) tend to be underrepresented, whereas 2- to 3-year-old students of high SES tend to be overrepresented. The authors claim that children with behavioral-emotional disturbances are represented appropriately at each grade level of each instrument, and the data provided in the manual support this claim.

A separate norm sample was collected for the college level of the SRP. This sample consisted of 706 students ages 18 to 25 who were attending various postsecondary educational institutions. Information on the degrees sought by participants is presented, along with information on the frequency by age and gender of participants in this standardization sample. No comparisons to the U.S. population are presented. Females appear to be overrepresented in this sample.

Clinical population sample norms consist of data collected on children receiving school or clinical services for emotional, behavioral, or physical problems. Sample sizes were, for the TRS, $N = 1,779$; for the PRS, $N = 1,975$; and for the SRP, $N = 1,527$. The authors state that the clinical sample was not controlled demographically because this subgroup is not a random set of children. For example, significantly more males were included than females.

Reliability

The manual has a chapter devoted to the technical information supporting reliability and validity for each normed scale (TRS, PRS, and SRP). Three types of reliability are provided within the technical manual: internal consistency, test-retest, and interrater agreement.

Internal Consistency   Coefficient alpha reliabilities are provided for the TRS and PRS by gender according to the following six age levels: ages 2 to 3, ages 4 to 5, ages 6 to 7, ages 8 to 11, ages 12 to 14, and ages 15 to 18. Median reliabilities for the TRS subscales for these age/gender groups range from .84 to .89. Lower reliabilities are evident for subscales associated with the Internalizing Problems scale (including Anxiety, Depression, Somatization) than for those associated with the Externalizing Problems scale. Median reliabilities for the PRS subscales range from .80 to .87 across these age/gender groups; reliabilities tend to be lower at the preschool-and-below ages. SRP coefficient alpha reliabilities are provided according to the following age levels: ages 8 to 11, ages 12 to 14, ages 15 to 18, and ages 18 to 25. Median subscale reliabilities for the SRP range from .79 to .83. The Sensation Seeking, Somatization, and Self-Reliance subscales tended to be particularly low (< .70) at certain age levels. Internal-consistency reliabilities for the composite scales exceeded .80 across all three scales for each age/gender group. Coefficient alphas are also provided for certain disability groups within the clinical sample by gender (such as learning disabilities, ADHD, and all clinical), and for those taking the Spanish version of the SRP and the PRS. Coefficient alpha reliabilities for the clinical groups are similar to those provided for the general norm sample; those for the Spanish version are slightly lower.

Test-Retest Reliability   TRS test-retest reliability was computed by having teachers rate the same child twice, with 8 to 65 days intervening between rating periods; this was done for a total of 240 students. Results are presented by age level (preschool, child, and adolescent) for each subscale and composite. Adjusted reliabilities ranged from .81 to .93 for composites and from .64 to .90 for the subscales. PRS test-retest reliability was determined based on parent ratings of 252 students, with an intervening time period of 9 to 70 days. Adjusted reliabilities for the PRS composites ranged from .78 to .92; those for the subscales ranged from .72 to .88. Test-retest reliabilities for the SRP were based on ratings provided by 279 students, for which there was an intervening time period of 13 to 66 days. Adjusted composite reliabilities ranged from .74 to .93; adjusted subscale reliabilities ranged from .61 to .99.

Interrater Reliability   A total of 170 students were rated according to the TRS by two teachers to determine interrater reliability of the TRS. Adjusted reliabilities ranged from .48 to .81 for the composite scales and from .19 to .82 for the subscales. Parents and caregivers completed the PRS for 134 students, such that two rating scales were completed for each student by different individuals. Adjusted reliabilities for the PRS composite scales ranged from .65 to .86; associated reliabilities for the PRS subscales ranged from .53 to .88. No interrater reliability study was conducted for the SRP, given that the scale is a self-report instrument.

Correlations were calculated across the PRS and the TRS by age level (preschool, child, and adolescent) for students in the standardization samples that had both forms completed (N = 2,324). Correlations for the related composites ranged from .17 to .52 for the preschool forms, from .22 to .50 for the child forms, and from .36 to .51 for the adolescent forms. The internalization composite scale tended to have the lowest correlations across forms. Correlations between the SRP and both the PRS and TRS are also provided; however, the composites are substantially different for the SRP, making the presence of lower correlations among composites difficult to interpret.

Validity

The authors describe the procedures used to develop and select items for inclusion in the BASC-2. Many of the items included on the BASC-2 are taken directly from the original BASC. In the development of the original items, alternate behavior-rating scales and related instruments were examined, and clinicians provided consultation in the selection of items to measure both problem and adaptive behaviors. Students and teachers were also involved in item development. The items went through several cycles of testing via expert and statistical review for inclusion in the original BASC. Several new items were developed for the BASC-2 to replace those with poor technical characteristics. More extensive revisions were conducted for the SRP, in which the item response format was altered from the previous edition, based on results of research studies examining internal consistency and factor loadings across the two formats. Confirmatory factor analysis was used to examine item characteristics to assist with decision making about inclusion in the final instrument. Items that correlated substantially with alternate composite scales that were not intended to be measured with the item, as well as those items that had low factor loadings on the intended composite scale, were eliminated. Analyses of partial correlations and differential item-functioning analyses were conducted to examine whether items were measuring appropriately across various student demographic groups (for instance, females versus males, African Americans versus non-Hispanics, and Hispanics versus non-Hispanics). A total of five items was eliminated based on bias reviews. Both exploratory and confirmatory factor analytic procedures were used to examine the appropriateness of the composite scale structure for the TRS, PRS, and SRP. These analyses supported the three-factor and four-factor child and adolescent composite scores.

Criterion-Related Validity   The TRS was compared with several related behavior-rating scales, including various portions of the Achenbach System of Empirically Based Assessment (ASEBA; Achenbach & Rescorla, 2001); the Conners Teacher Rating Scale–Revised (Conners, 1997); and the original BASC TRS. Ratings from the preschool form of the TRS were compared to an associated form of the ASEBA among 46 children ages 2 to 5 years. Fifty-seven children ages 6 to 11 years and 39 adolescents ages 12 to 18 years similarly had corresponding rating forms from the BASC and the ASEBA compared. Correlations for related subscales were primarily in the .60-to-.90 range, with the exception of Somatization subscales, which tended to be very weakly correlated across rating scales. Correlations across composite scales were higher; however,

Internalizing Problems composites tended to be lower than the other composite scale correlations.

Correlations with the Conners Teacher Rating Scale–Revised were based on teacher ratings for 59 children ages 6 to 11 years and 45 adolescents ages 12 to 18 years. Associated subscale adjusted correlations ranged from .26 (Anxiety scales for adolescents) to .94 (Aggression/Oppositional scales for adolescents). Composite behavior scale correlations (Conners Global Index and the BASC Behavioral Symptoms Index) were .84 at the child level and .69 at the adolescent level. Information is presented on the correlations with ratings from the original BASC for the standardization samples. As expected, the results for the BASC and the BASC-2 were very similar, with correlations exceeding .90 for the majority of composite and subscales.

The PRS was also compared to a variety of similar rating scales, including the following: related forms of the ASEBA, Conners Parent Rating Scale–Revised, the Behavior Rating Inventory of Executive Functioning (Gioia, Isquith, Guy, & Kenworthy, 2000), and the original BASC PRS. The associated parent rating forms for the ASEBA and the BASC-2 were completed for 53 young children, 65 school-age children, and 67 adolescents. Adjusted correlations for associated subscales ranged from .34 to .77; adjusted correlations for associated composites ranged from .67 to .84. Internalizing Problems composites tend to have weaker correlations than Externalizing Problems composites.

Correlations with the Conners Parent Rating Scale were determined based on 60 children ages 6 to 11 and 55 adolescents ages 12 to 18 years. The Conners Global Index and the BASC-2 Behavioral Symptoms Index correlated .79 at the child level and .65 at the adolescent level. Subscale adjusted correlations ranged from .41 to .84 at the child level and .35 to .64 at the adolescent level. The BASC-2 and the Behavior Rating Inventory of Executive Functioning (Gioia et al., 2000) were administered to 51 children ages 6 to 11 and 40 adolescents ages 12 to 18 years. Broad composite scores correlated .67 at the child level and .80 at the adolescent level. Finally, correlations with the original BASC PRS were primarily in the .80 to .95 range, as expected.

Criterion-related validity of the SRP was evidenced through correlations with the associated forms of the ASEBA, the Conners-Wells Adolescent Self-Report Scale (Conners, 1997), the Children's Depression Inventory (Kovacs, 1992), and the Revised Children's Manifest Anxiety Scale (Reynolds & Richmond, 2000). The associated scale of the ASEBA was administered concurrently with the SRP among 51 adolescents. Associated composite adjusted correlations were in the .75 to .80 range. All associated subscales of the Conners-Wells Adolescent Self-Report correlated positively (.52 to .67) with the BASC-2 scales among 54 adolescents, with an exception being the negative correlations showing up as expected for the relationship between "family problems" and "relations with parents" across these scales. Finally, the associated scales of the Children's Depression Inventory and the Children's Manifest Anxiety Scale correlated positively with the Depression and Anxiety scales on the BASC-2 SRP. Correlations for a group ($N = 86$) of students in postsecondary settings who took the college level of the SRP and the ASEBA self-report ranged from .38 to .61 for associated composite and subscales.

Evidence for criterion-related validity of the college level of the BASC-2 SRP is also presented using the Brief Symptom Inventory (BSI; Derogatis, 1993) and the Minnesota Multiphasic Personality Inventory–2 (Butcher, Graham, Ben-Porath, Tellegen, Dahlstrom, & Kaemmer, 2001). Correlations of the BASC-2 SRP with the original BASC SRP were lower than corresponding correlations for the TRS and PRS, but still positive.

Although there appears to be some evidence of validity for using the BASC-2 in making diagnostic decisions, no evidence of validity for the purposes of program evaluation and treatment planning is provided.

Summary

The BASC-2 is a comprehensive instrument that may be used to evaluate the behavior and self-perception of children ages 2 to 25 years. The integrated system comprises five separate measures of behavior: (1) Teacher Rating Scale, (2) Parent Rating Scale, (3) Self-Report of Personality, (4) Structured Developmental History Inventory, and (5) Student Observation Scale. Although the multimethod and multidimensional approach should be commended, the TRS, PRS, and SRP are the only scales for which normative data are provided on which any classification statements can be made. Norms for the BASC are more than adequate, with general and clinical norm data provided. Reliability of the composite scales is good, although the internalizing composites tend to have lower reliability coefficients, along with lower reliability coefficients evident for very young children. The BASC-2, like the ASEBA, provides one of the most comprehensive assessment tools on the market today. Good evidence of reliability and validity is presented via analysis of standardization sample data and correlations with additional behavior rating scales; however, validity evidence is not present for all of the possible uses described by the authors.

Behavioral and Emotional Rating Scale, Second Edition (BERS-2)

The second edition of the Behavioral and Emotional Rating Scale (BERS-2; Epstein, 2004) is a norm-referenced rating scale intended to assess the behavioral and emotional strengths of individuals between the ages of 5 and 18 years, and is used to identify persons with limited strengths, aid in the identification of educational and treatment goals, assess progress toward these goals in areas of strength, and measure strengths in research and evaluation projects. The BERS-2 consists of three components: a Teacher Rating Scale, a Parent Rating Scale, and a Youth Rating Scale. Each scale consists of 52 items and is divided into five subscales. The 15 items on the Interpersonal Strength subscale assess such things as reacting to disappointment calmly, listening to others, and being kind to others. The Family Involvement subscale consists of 10 items, such as maintaining positive family relationships, interacting positively with others, and complying with rules. The Intrapersonal Strength subscale consists of 11 items, such as being self-confident, identifying own feelings, and being enthusiastic about life. The School Functioning subscale consists of 9 items, such as completing tasks on first request, paying attention in class, and studying for tests. The Affective Strength subscale consists of 7 items, such as acknowledging painful feelings, being close with others, and expressing affection for others. The Parent and Youth Rating Scales each have 5 supplementary questions about Career Strength, such as having plans for the future and having selected a career.

Scores

Items are scored on a four-point scale: 3 (the statement is very much like the subject), 2 (the statement is like the subject), 1 (the statement is not much like the subject), and 0 (the statement is not at all like the subject). Scores for each subscale are summed, and each subscale sum is converted to a percentile and scaled score (mean = 10, standard deviation = 3). The total score (called the BERS-2 Strength Index) can be converted to a percentile and standard scores (mean = 100, standard deviation = 15). Separate norms are provided for males and females based on the performance of persons in the normative sample. For example, the ratings on a 6-year-old female student are compared to those for females ranging in age from 5 to 18 years.

Norms

Four sets of norms are available for interpreting the BERS-2 scores: The first is teacher ratings of students not identified with emotional or behavioral disorders; the second is teacher ratings of students identified as having emotional or behavioral disorders; the third is parental ratings of their children; and the fourth is student self-ratings. Each of the four sets has separate norms for males and females. Thus there is a total of eight norm samples, and each one consists of either male or female students who range in age from 5-0 to 18-11.

The normative samples for teacher ratings of students without identified emotional or behavioral disorders is the normative sample for the first edition of the BERS. These data were collected in 1996 on 2,176 students living in 31 states and ranging in age from 5-0 to 18-11. Overall, this norm group is representative in terms of geographic region, gender, race, Hispanic ethnicity, educational attainment of parents, and disability; it slightly overrepresents students from high-income families. The percentage of individuals from each age varies from 4 percent (at 18) to 14 percent (at 8). The representativeness of the sample is not described by gender.

The norms for teacher ratings of students identified as having emotional or behavioral disorders consists of 861 students from the same 31 states. Overall, this norm group is representative in terms of race, Hispanic ethnicity, and educational attainment of parents. It slightly overrepresents individuals from the West and students from high-income families. The percentage of individuals at each age ranges from 2 percent (at 5) to 15 percent (at 15). Although norms appear equally representative at each age, the more important question is the representativeness of the male and female samples, because separate norm tables are provided for males and females—not for ages.

The norms for parent ratings consist of 927 students living in 34 states. Overall, this norm group is representative in terms of geographic region, gender, race, Hispanic ethnicity, family income, educational attainment of parents, and disability. The percentage of individuals at each age ranges from 4 percent (at 5 and 18) to 14 percent (at 12). Although norms appear equally representative at each age, the more important question is the representativeness of the male and female samples, because separate norm tables are provided for males and females—not for ages.

The norms for youth ratings consist of 1,301 students between the ages of 11 and 18. Overall, this norm group is representative in terms of geographic region, gender, race, Hispanic ethnicity, family income, and disability; it somewhat underrepresents parents with less than a college degree. The percentage of individuals at each age ranges from 5 percent (at 18) to 20 percent (at 13). Although norms appear equally representative at each age, the more important question is the representativeness of the male and female samples, because separate norm tables are provided for males and females—not for ages.

Reliability

The most relevant reliability estimates are those associated with each BERS-2 score. Coefficient alpha was calculated separately for males and females for each subscale and the Strength Index. For teacher ratings of students without emotional or behavioral problems, every alpha equaled or exceeded .90 for males and females with one exception (female Affective Strength scores). For parent ratings, the Strength Index and the Interpersonal Strength subscale had reliabilities greater than .90 for males and females. Alphas for other subscales were between .82 and .89 for males and females. For self-ratings, alphas for males and females were .95 for the Strength Index and between .76 and .87 for males and females on all subscales. No estimates of internal consistency are presented for teacher ratings of male and female students with emotional and behavioral problems.

Alpha coefficients and standard errors of measurement were also calculated for each age from 5 to 15 and for students between 16 and 18. Alphas for teacher ratings of students not identified with emotional and behavioral disorders vary by subscale and age, ranging from .79 to .97. About one third of subscale-by-age reliability combinations are less than .90. The reliability of the Composite Strength Index ranges from .96 to .99.

Teacher ratings of students identified with emotional and behavioral disorders also vary by subscale and age, ranging from .71 to .95. About two thirds of subscale-by-age reliability combinations are less than .90. The reliability of the Composite Strength Index ranges from .95 to .98. Parent ratings of students also vary by subscale and age, ranging from .77 to .95. The reliability of the Interpersonal Strength subscale equals or exceeds .90 at every age; none of the other subscale-by-age reliability combinations equals .90. The reliability of the Composite Strength Index ranges from .95 to .97. Youth self-ratings vary little by age or subscale. With one exception, none of the other subscale-by-age reliability combinations equals .90. The reliability of the Composite Strength Index ranges from .94 to .96.

The author also presents the average alphas for selected subgroups within the normative populations—specifically, whites, blacks, Hispanics, and individuals with emotional disturbance. These alphas show only minor (not meaningful) fluctuations among these subgroups, and the obtained alphas parallel those reported above: the Composite Strength Index always exceeds .90, whereas the subscales are generally variable and less reliable.

Stability was estimated in six studies with students of varying ages and retest intervals. Test-retest estimates of reliability for the Composite Strength Index ranged from .87 to .99; subscale reliabilities were lower.

Interrater agreement was also examined in three studies. In the most completely reported study, nine pairs of special education teachers rated 96 males with emotional disturbance. Their ratings were very similar. Correlations between raters for the subscales ranged from .83 to .96; the correlation between raters for the Composite Strength Index was .98. One of the studies with only 20 students is incompletely described; the other study compares youth and parent ratings, and should not be considered an indication of interrater agreement.

Validity

Evidence for the general validity of the BERS-2 comes from several sources. First, the contents of the scales were carefully developed to represent emotional and behavioral strengths. Next, the BERS-2 correlates well with other scales measuring similar skills and abilities (for example, the Walker-McConnell Scale of Social Competence and School Adjustment–Adolescent Version, the System Screening for Behavior Disorders, the Social Skills Rating System, and so forth). Evidence for differentiated validity comes from the scales' ability to distinguish groups of students with severe emotional problems from those without emotional problems. Other indices of validity include absence of bias against African Americans and Hispanics, and factor-analytic that studies support the BERS-2's subscale structure. No evidence is presented that the BERS-2 is useful in identifying educational and treatment goals or in assessing progress toward those goals.

Evidence for the relationships between BERS-2 scores and age has not been reported. This information is important because the norm groups span the entire age range of the test, and it is not intuitively obvious that performance on individual items is not age related. For example, it is unlikely that most 5-year-olds will receive high ratings on items assessing studying for tests and completing homework or that 18-year-olds will score as well as 5-year-olds on such items as getting along well with parents.

Summary

The BERS-2 is a norm-referenced rating scale intended to assess the behavioral and emotional strengths of individuals between the ages of 5 and 18 years of age. The BERS-2 consists of three components: a Teacher Rating Scale, a Parent Rating Scale, and a Youth Rating Scale. Each scale consists of 52 items divided into five subscales: Interpersonal Strength, Family Involvement, Intrapersonal Strength, School Functioning, and Affective Strength. The parent and youth rating scales have 5 supplementary questions each about Career Strength. Two sets of norms are available for interpreting teacher ratings: One consists of ratings of students not identified with emotional or behavioral disorders, and the other consists of ratings of students identified as having emotional or behavioral disorders. There are also norms for parent and self-ratings. Separate norms are provided for males and females within each norm group. Overall, the norms appear representative. The Strength Index has sufficient internal consistency to use in making important educational decisions for males and females; the subscales frequently do not. Stability for males and females combined for the Composite Strength Index ranged from .87 to .99; subscale reliabilities were lower. Estimates of interrater agreement for the Strength Index were excellent for males. Aside from the absence of information about the relationship between BERS-2 scores and age, the general validity is satisfactory. The content of the scales appears appropriate. BERS-2 scores correlate with other similar measures of social skills and discriminate between students with and without emotional and behavior disorders; it does not appear to discriminate against blacks or Hispanics. Evidence of validity of the BERS-2's utility in identifying educational and treatment goals or in assessing progress toward those goals is not presented.

Gilliam Asperger's Disorder Scale (GADS)

The Gilliam Asperger's Disorder Scale (GADS; Gilliam, 2001) is a norm-referenced rating scale for use with individuals between the ages of 3 and 22 years who are suspected of having Asperger's syndrome. The 32-item GADS can be completed in 5 to 10 minutes by teachers, parents, or others who are knowledgeable about the target individual. The scale consists of the following four subtests:

Social Interaction. Ten items assessing problems such as difficulty cooperating in groups, lack of awareness of social conventions or codes of conduct, and so forth.

Restricted Patterns of Behavior. Eight items assessing problems such as having clumsy and uncoordinated gross motor movements, being insensitive to the needs of others, and so forth.

Cognitive Patterns. Seven items assessing problems such as talking about a single subject excessively, using exceptionally precise or pedantic speech, and so forth.

Pragmatic Skills. Seven items assessing problems such as having difficulty knowing when someone is teasing, having difficulty predicting probable consequences of social events, and so forth.

Scores

The items are scored on a four-point scale: never observed (0 points), seldom observed (1 point), sometimes observed (2 points), and frequently observed (3 points). The points for each subtest are summed, and the sums can be converted to percentile ranks and standard scores (mean = 10, standard deviation = 3). The sum of the scaled scores is converted to an Asperger's Disorder Quotient (mean = 100, standard deviation = 15) and percentiles. Higher scores indicate more significant problems.

Norms

The GADS was standardized on 371 individuals who had already been diagnosed with Asperger's syndrome, who were between the ages of 3 and 22, and who resided in 46 states and four foreign countries. Like the population of individuals with Asperger's syndrome, the sample is predominantly male and closely approximates the U.S. population in terms of geographic and urban residence. The sample underrepresents African Americans and Hispanic Americans, although the prevalence of the syndrome does not appear to be related to ethnicity.

Reliability

Coefficient alpha was used to estimate the internal consistency of the GADS for various groups with disabilities (Asperger's, autism, and other) and a group without disability. We believe the most reasonable estimate of the GADS's internal consistency is the one for the pooled sample of all students because this sample would have less restricted ranges of ability than would the specific samples. For the total sample, the subtest reliabilities are all in the .80s and the Asperger's Disorder Quotient's internal consistency is .94. Two-week stabilities, based on the performances of 10 students, are in the .70s for subtests and .93 for the Asperger's Disorder Quotient. Interrater agreement, based on 16 students jointly rated by parents and teachers, ranges from .72 to .84 for the subtests and is .89 for the Asperger's Disorder Quotient.

Validity

The GADS has good evidence of content validity because it is based on the criteria from the American Psychiatric Association's DSM-IV; the World Health Organization's *International Classification of Diseases and Related Health Problems, Tenth Edition;* and descriptions of Asperger's syndrome found in current research. The authors also performed discriminant analyses and found that the GADS differentiates students with Asperger's syndrome from other students with disabilities with 83 percent accuracy.

Summary

The GADS provides a quick assessment of students suspected of having Asperger's syndrome who are between 3 and 22 years of age. The GADS's norms are adequate, and the total score is sufficiently reliable and stable to use in making important diagnostic decisions about individual students. The scale has good content validity, and there is some evidence for other types of validity.

Temperament and Atypical Behavior Scale (TABS)

The Temperament and Atypical Behavior Scale: Early Childhood Indicators of Developmental Dysfunction (TABS; Neisworth, Bagnato, Salvia, & Hunt) is an individually administered, norm-referenced rating scale intended to assess dysfunctional behavior of infants and young children between the ages of 11 and 71 months. The TABS can be administered in about 15 minutes, and the screener (comprised of 15 items from the TABS) takes a third time. The TABS is divided into four factorially derived subtests.

Detached. These 20 items assess the child's connection to the environment and people (for example, looking through people, staring at lights, and playing with toys in strange ways).

Hyper-Sensitive/Active. These 17 items assess emotional needs and lability (for example, getting angry too easily, being easily frustrated, being too "grabby" or impulsive).

Underreactive. These 11 items assess the child's reaction to the environment and people (for example, not paying attention to sights and sounds, not reacting to own name, not enjoying playing with mother or caregiver).

Dysregulated. These 7 items assess sleep habits (for example, being frightened by dreams or nighttime) and ability to self-comfort (for example, cries for too long).

Scores

Each item is scored as yes or no. Yeses are summed for each subtest and the total score (called the Temperament and Regulatory Index, or TRI). Because the scores are not normally distributed on subtests and the TRI, percentiles were calculated separately for each subtest and the TRI. Two types of standard scores are available for subtests and the TRI: actual standard scores and normalized standard scores that give standard scores and percentiles the same relationship they would have if the distributions were normal. Both standard scores have a mean of 100 and a standard deviation of 15.

Norms

The norms consist of 833 children between the ages of 11 and 71 months; 212 of the children were identified as disabled, and 621 students were not classified as disabled. Because the authors believed that the atypical behaviors were unrelated to socioeconomic class, geographic factors, or ethnic/cultural factors, these factors were ignored in developing TABS norms. Also, because TABS scores were not related to sex or age, the norms consist of a single group of boys (53 percent) and girls (47 percent) of all ages covered.

Cutoff scores are also provided for each subtest, TRI, and screener. These cutoffs are based on the overlap of performances of children with and without disabilities. Children are not considered to be at risk when their scores are more likely to be earned by students without disabilities; they are considered to be at risk when their scores are more likely to be earned by children with disabilities. Children are considered disabled when their score is earned by less than 6.9 percent of children not identified as disabled and is earned by more than 74 percent of children with disabilities.

Reliability

Internal consistency was estimated by odd-even correlations corrected by the Spearman-Brown formula separately for the sample of disabled students, the sample of nondisabled students, and the pooled sample of all children. We believe the most reasonable estimate of the TABS's internal consistency is the one for the pooled sample of all students, because this sample would have less restricted ranges of ability than would the specific samples. The TRI, Detached, and Hyper-Sensitive/Active scales have corrected internal consistencies equal to or greater than .90. The authors report a study of TABS stability with 157 children (60 of whom were disabled) who were reevaluated within three weeks of their initial evaluations. Stability coefficients for TRI and Hyper-Sensitive/Active exceed .90.

Validity

The content validity of the TABS is based on the careful development of the scale. Aberrant and atypical items were developed by examining research journals dealing with early intervention, existing scales, and suggestions from clinicians who described behavior-associated developmental disabilities. In addition, the same four factors theorized by the National Center for Infants, Toddlers, and Families (1994) to underlie atypical behavior were found to underlie the content of the TABS. As would be expected, TABS scores are uncorrelated with age. Likewise, TABS scores are uncorrelated with gender in the nondisabled population, but they are with gender in the disabled population. The TABS screener produces 2.4 percent false negatives and 14.5 percent false positives in the normative sample.

Summary

The TABS is an individually administered, norm-referenced rating scale intended to assess dysfunctional behavior of infants and young children between the ages of 11 and 71 months. The TABS can be administered in about 15 minutes, and the screener (comprised of 15 items from the TABS) takes a third time. The TABS is divided into four factorially derived subtests: Detached, Hyper-Sensitive/Active, Underreactive, and Dysregulated. The norms consist of both disabled children ($N = 212$) and children not identified as disabled ($N = 621$). Internal consistency for the total score, Detached subscale, and Hyper-Sensitive/Active subscale is equal to or greater than .90, and the stability for the total score and the Hyper-Sensitive/Active subscale exceeds .90. Satisfactory evidence for content validity is provided; evidence for construct validity is limited.

Dilemmas in Current Practice

Problem

The subjectivity inherent in ratings or self-reports of problem behavior causes two problems. First, raters must know the person being rated in order to make judgments about problem behaviors. Yet familiarity can cloud judgments. Raters may take into account unrelated attributes. For example, a teacher might rate Billy more leniently because he is a bright child, really tries hard to behave, and has parents who seem concerned. Second, raters sometimes have a stake in the decision. Self-ratings or ratings of others may exaggerate or downplay the frequency or severity of problem behavior. For example, parents or teachers who feel that problem behavior reflects badly on themselves may unintentionally downplay the frequency or severity of behavior; on the other hand, parents or teachers who cannot cope with the behavior any longer may unintentionally overestimate the frequency or severity of problem behavior.

Authors' Viewpoint

Diagnosticians can do two things to reduce some of the subjectivity inherent in evaluating problem behavior. First, they can select instruments that are likely to minimize subjectivity. For example, scales that attempt to objectively quantify behavior should be less prone to bias than scales that do not. Scales that ask about observable behavior (such as hitting) should be less prone to bias than scales that require inferences (such as aggressiveness). Second, diagnosticians can obtain information from several people who have had the opportunity to observe in the same contexts.

Scores from rating scales or checklists may not correlate highly with external criteria or measures of behavior. In particular, rating scales that have internalizing dimensions may not be very good at identifying students with depressive disorders and do not agree with clinical or interview data. Therefore, students suspected of being at risk for internalizing disorders such as childhood depression are best served via a comprehensive clinical evaluation.

Finally, all social-emotional assessment is linked to the idea that effective interventions and treatments will be available for the students whom we identify as being in need of service. Some of the instruments reviewed in this chapter have companion manuals that describe interventions based on specific items or groups of items assessed by the rating scales or checklists. Some of these ideas are tried-and-true methods that fit into most useful social-skills training programs. Others are less well documented and lack effective instructional or intervention strategies. Social-emotional and behavioral assessment practices are neatly summed up by L. Brown and Hammill (1990) with the phrase "caveat utilitor." Interventions with students must be based on sound assessment data, and it is up to the users of these devices to evaluate the instruments and plan for instruction. Assessments and rating scales are only as good as the practitioners who use them. It is essential that any sort of treatment based on information gleaned from rating scales or other social-emotional assessment be evaluated in terms of its positive and negative impact on student behavior and social-emotional progress.

SUMMARY

In recent years, the assessment of internalizing and externalizing problem behavior has become more frequent. Most often, assessment is considered for children at risk for emotional/behavioral disorders; however, children with academically based deficits may also be referred for social-skills or behavioral evaluations. Common methods of measurement include rating scales, interviews, and direct observation. Assessment of social-emotional behavior, like most academic assessment, should be conducted with the intention of providing assessment-based interventions to ameliorate identified problems.

QUESTIONS FOR CHAPTER REVIEW

1. What are the major concerns of using rating scales to describe student social-emotional behavior?

2. Design an assessment session that incorporates the concept of multifactor evaluation. Why might some portions of the session be more relevant than others to particular concerns? Which type (or types) of measurement do you believe results in the best assessment data?

3. Assume that you had to assess a student's social-emotional behavior. How would you go about doing so in a way that would be appropriate?

PROJECT

Compare the results obtained from two of the assessments described in the chapter. Note where differences appear, and explain the reasons for the differences.

RESOURCES FOR FURTHER INVESTIGATION

Print Resources

Knoff, H. M. (1986). *The assessment of child and adolescent personality* (Chapter 3: A conceptual model and pragmatic approach toward personality assessment referrals). New York: Guilford Press.

Martin, R. P. (1988). *Assessment of personality and behavior problems: Infancy through adolescence.* New York: Guilford Press.

McCarney, J. (2004a). *Attention-Deficit Disorders Evaluation Scale, Home Version–Third Edition: Technical manual.* Columbia, MO: Hawthorne Educational Services.

McCarney, J. (2004b). *Attention-Deficit Disorders Evaluation Scale, School Version–Third Edition: Technical manual.* Columbia, MO: Hawthorne Educational Services.

McCarney, J. & Arthaud, T. (2005). *The Behavior Evaluation Scale–3, Home Version: Technical manual.* Columbia, MO: Hawthorne Educational Services.

Merrell, K. W. (1994). *Assessment of behavioral, social, and emotional problems.* New York: Longman.

Technology Resources

AGS ONLINE PRODUCTS AND SERVICES
www.agsnet.com
Look for product and ordering information about the instruments available from American Guidance Service (AGS). Here you can find information about the Behavior Assessment System for Children, Second Edition.

PRO-ED CATALOGUE INFORMATION FOR PRODUCTS
www.proedinc.com
Find product and ordering information about the Autism Screening Instrument for Educational Planning–2 and the Behavior Rating Profile, Second Edition.

AUTISM RESOURCES
www.autism-resources.com
Look here to find an index of materials, information, and resources about autism and Asperger's syndrome.

ACHENBACH SYSTEM OF EMPIRICALLY BASED ASSESSMENT
www.aseba.org/index.html
Find product and ordering information about the Child Behavior Checklist.

ATTENTION DEFICIT HYPERACTIVITY DISORDER
www.adhd.com
This website has a list of information about attention deficit hyperactivity disorder and provides many links to related sites.

FUNCTIONAL BEHAVIOR ASSESSMENT AND BEHAVIOR INTERVENTION PLANS
http://www.wrightslaw.com/info/discipl.fab .starin.htm
This site discusses what functional behavior assessments are and why they are done as well as how to observe, analyze, and manipulate behavior in natural environments.

CHAPTER 27

Assessment of Adaptive Behavior

ADAPTIVE BEHAVIOR IS THE WAY INDIVIDUALS ADAPT THEMSELVES TO THE REQUIRE-
ments of their physical and social environment (Schmidt & Salvia, 1984). In
part, adaptation means survival: Adaptive behaviors are those that allow individuals to continue to live by avoiding dangers and by taking reasonable precautions to ensure their safety. Yet adaptivity refers to more than mere survival; it
implies the ability to thrive in both good and adverse times.

Adaptive behavior also requires more than an appropriate response to the
demands of the immediate environment; it requires preparation for responses to
probable future environments. Certain current behaviors (for example, smoking
or high-risk sexual activity) can have life-threatening future consequences. Similarly, acquiring more education or job training and saving money increase the
likelihood of thriving in later years. Adaptive behavior, in the present and for the
future, must also take into account the demands of a person's physical surroundings and the expectations of that person's culture.

Defining Adaptive Behavior

Physical Environment The knowledge and skill required to avoid danger (or to react appropriately
when in danger) vary considerably from environment to environment. For exam-
ple, different environments require different protective clothing and different
precautions against climatic conditions. Living in the desert Southwest in summer requires guarding against dehydration and heat stroke, whereas living in
New England in the winter requires guarding against hypothermia and frostbite.
Different environments have different dangerous wildlife: alligators in southeastern swamps, scorpions and Gila monsters in the Southwest, rats in many urban
areas, and so forth. In addition to natural hazards, different environments present human-made hazards: automobiles, electrical appliances, cutting tools,
chemicals, and so forth.

Social and Cultural Expectations   Social expectations vary considerably from culture to culture, and the ability to thrive in a culture requires some degree of conformity to that society's cultural norms. Societal expectations manifest themselves in language usage (for example, polite or respectful language, speaking distance, and speaking volume), role performance, personal responsibility, and independence.

Age and Adaptation   Sociocultural expectations are also a function of the person's age. In the United States, we have different expectations of infants, children, adolescents, and adults. For infants and young children, expectations center on maturational processes; at some points in these processes, reflexive behavior (for example, sucking) is a necessary component of survival. After infancy, maturational processes merely enable behavior. "Thus, goodness of vision and hearing, intactness of motor skills, neuromotor integrity, and similar characteristics are not adaptive behaviors of the individual; they are biological characteristics of the human species and provide the basis for behavior" (Salvia, Neisworth, & Schmidt, 1990, p. 57). Thus, for older individuals, adaptive behavior is learned behavior.

We expect youngsters to use language socially, to play appropriately, to assume limited responsibilities (for example, picking up toys), and to function in increasingly independent ways (for example, self-feeding, self-dressing, and moving around in their homes and neighborhoods). As children get older, the expectations for independence and responsibility increase, both at home and in school. With adolescence come demands for making the transition to adulthood (for example, preparing for employment and accepting more complete personal responsibility).

Performance Versus Ability   The ability to behave in expected ways is not synonymous with the performance of adaptive behavior. Knowing how to survive and thrive does not ensure that people will behave accordingly. For example, children may know that they should look both ways before crossing streets, and they may know how to do so; however, the important consideration is whether they do look both ways. Not only must a behavior be performed regularly (habitually and customarily), but it must also be performed without prompting or assistance.

Maladaption   In their definitions of adaptive behavior, some theorists include an absence of marked maladaption. Although such a position may have intuitive appeal, there are at least two conceptual problems with including maladaptive behavior on formal tests. First, the absence of maladaptive behavior does not imply the presence of adaptive behavior. Second, except for suicidal behavior and a very few universally taboo behaviors (for example, adolescents' or adults' smearing human excrement on themselves), maladaptive behavior is determined by context, as well as by frequency and amplitude.

Context   The context of behavior refers to both social tolerance and the specific situation in which a behavior occurs. Social tolerance is an important qualifier, because very few behaviors are universally taboo. For example, certain types of hallucinations may be prized as religious experiences in some societies but seen as psychotic in others; homosexuality is accepted in some societies but punished in others. The list of potential examples is very long. Within a society, taboo behavior is codified by custom, religion, and law.

Some behaviors are evaluated solely on the basis of context. For example, disrobing is usually considered deviant in a classroom full of students but normal before bathing; failure to disrobe is normal in classrooms but abnormal before bathing. Even when certain behaviors are proscribed, the circumstances in which those behaviors are demonstrated is important. For example, in the United States, killing another person is not necessarily murder. The context in which the death occurred determines whether it is a crime (murder or voluntary manslaughter) or not (self-defense or accidental death).

Finally, for a behavior to be considered deviant, either the behavior or its consequence must be observed. If no one witnesses the act or its consequence, it will not be considered maladaptive. Moreover, the person observing the behavior (or consequence) must be willing and must have the authority to label the behavior as deviant.

Frequency and Amplitude

The frequency and amplitude of behavior are also important in labeling a behavior as maladaptive. Some behavior will be tolerated or condoned if it occurs infrequently. For example, occasional drunkenness may be ignored, but chronic drunkenness is considered alcoholism. The boundaries separating tolerated occasional misbehavior from deviance vary with context, status of the person, and consequences of the behavior. The amplitude of behavior also affects social and cultural tolerance. For example, fingernail biting is seldom, in and of itself, considered significant. However, when fingernail biting produces bleeding, scarring, and deformity, the behavior has crossed a line into self-mutilation.

Assessing Adaptive Behavior

Historically, the assessment of adaptive behavior has relied on the report of a third person (typically designated as a "respondent"). Thus we do not assess an individual's adaptive behavior directly; an examiner does not test or observe the individual being assessed. Instead, the examiner relies on the cumulative observations of a respondent who is both truthful and sufficiently familiar with the subject of the assessment to make a judgment about that subject's behavior.

This method of administration is susceptible to a variety of errors and biases. The student being evaluated may generally conceal behavior that is culturally taboo, or the student may conceal behavior from the respondent if the student knows that the respondent disapproves of the behavior. The student being evaluated may selectively demonstrate the behavior. For example, when the respondent (a parent or teacher) is present, the student may behave appropriately; when the respondent is absent, the student may not. Finally, when respondents have a stake in the outcome, they may be less than truthful or objective. For example, if a parent respondent does not want a student classified as mentally retarded, that parent may give the child the benefit of the doubt in every response.

Why Do We Assess Adaptive Behavior?

There are two major reasons for assessing adaptive behavior: (1) identification of mental retardation and (2) program planning. First, mental retardation is generally defined, in part, as a failure of adaptive behavior. In theory, in order to classify a pupil as having mental retardation, for example, an evaluator needs to assess adaptive behavior. More important, however, are the federal regulations and state school codes requiring that adaptive behavior be assessed before a pupil can be considered mentally retarded.

Second, for program planning, educational objectives in the domain of adaptive behavior are frequently developed for individuals with moderate to severe retardation, as well as for students with other disabilities. Adaptive behavior is often important in planning habilitative and transition services for various students. Thus scales of adaptive behavior are often the source of educational goals.

Specific Tests of Adaptive Behavior

The seven devices reviewed in the pages that follow are used most often in assessment of handicapped individuals: the Vineland Adaptive Behavior Scales, Second Edition (VABS II); the American Association on Mental Deficiency (AAMD) Adaptive Behavior Scale: Residential and Community Scale, Second Edition (ABS-RC2); the AAMR Adaptive Behavior Scale–School 2 (ABS-S2); and the Scales of Independent Behavior–Revised (SIB-R).

Vineland Adaptive Behavior Scales, Second Edition (VABS II)

The Vineland Adaptive Behavior Scales, Second Edition (VABS II; Sparrow, Cicchetti, & Balla, 2005), is an individually administered adaptive behavior scale for use with individuals from birth through 90 years of age. The VABS II is intended for use in diagnostic evaluations, monitoring a student's progress, planning educational and treatment plans, and research. The scale is completed by respondents (that is, parents or guardians[1]) who are familiar with the target individual's behavior. Respondents can either complete a rating form or participate in a structured third-party interview. The VABS II authors recommend using the interview form for diagnostic decisions and the rating form for program planning and evaluation. A Spanish translation is available, and available computer software can convert raw scores to derived scores and generate score reports.

The Survey Interview Form consists of 413 questions distributed among five domains.

■ *Communication.* This domain has two subdomains. Expressive Communication consists of 54 items, such as crying when wet or hungry and saying one's complete home address when asked. Written Communication consists of 25 items, such as recognizing one's own name and writing business letters.

■ *Daily Living Skills (DLS).* This domain has three subdomains. Personal DLS has 41 items, such as opening mouth when food is offered and making appointments for regular medical and dental checkups. Domestic DLS consists

---

[1] A form for use with teachers was not available at the time this review was prepared.

of 24 items, such as being careful with hot objects and planning and preparing the main meal of the day. Community DLS consists of 44 items, such as talking to familiar people on the telephone and budgeting for monthly expenses.

- *Socialization.* This domain has three subdomains. Interpersonal Relationships has 38 items, such as looking at parent's (caregiver's) face and going on single dates. Play and Leisure Time has 31 items, such as responding to playfulness of a parent (or caregiver) and going to places in the evening with friends. Coping Skills consists of 30 items, such as apologizing for unintended mistakes and showing respect for coworkers.

- *Motor Skills.* This domain has two subdomains. Gross Motor consists of 40 items, such as holding head up for 15 seconds and pedaling a tricycle for six feet. Fine Motor consists of 36 items, such as reaching for a toy and using a keyboard to type ten lines.

- *Maladaptive Behavior.* This domain has three subdomains. Internalizing consists of 11 items, such as being overly dependent and avoiding social interaction. Externalizing consists of 10 items, such as being impulsive and behaving inappropriately. Other Maladaptive Behavior consists of 15 items, such as sucking one's thumb, being truant, and using alcohol or illegal drugs during the school or work day. Critical Items consists of 14 items, such as engaging in inappropriate sexual behavior, causing injury to self, and being unable to complete a normal school or work day because of psychological symptoms.

The Parent/Caregiver Rating Form consists of 433 questions distributed among six domains.

- *Communication.* This domain has three subdomains. Listening and Understanding consists of 20 items, such as responding to one's spoken name and listening to informational talk for 30 minutes. Talking consists of 54 items, such as crying or fussing when hungry or wet, using possessives in phrases or sentences, and describing long-range goals. Reading and Writing consists of 25 items, such as recognizing one's name when printed and editing or correcting one's written work before handing it in.

- *Daily Living.* This domain has three subdomains. Caring for Self has 41 items, such as eating solid foods and keeping track of medications and refilling them as needed. Caring for Home has 24 items, such as cleaning up play or work area at the end of an activity and performing routine maintenance tasks. Living in the Community consists of 44 items, such as being aware and demonstrating appropriate behavior when riding in a car and holding a full-time job for a year.

- *Social Skills and Relationships.* This domain has three subdomains. Relating to Others consists of 38 items, such as showing two or more emotions, recognizing the likes and dislikes of others, and starting conversations about things that interest others. Playing and Using Leisure Time consists of 31 items, such as playing simple interaction games (for example, peekaboo), showing good sportsmanship, and planning fun activities requiring arrangements for two or more things. Adapting has 30 items, such as saying thank you and controlling anger or hurt feelings when not getting one's way.

■ *Physical Activity.* This domain has two subdomains. Using Large Muscles has 40 items, such as climbing on and off an adult-sized chair and catching a tennis ball from 10 feet. Using Small Muscles has 36 items, such as picking up small objects, holding a pencil in proper position for writing or drawing, and tying a bow.

■ *Maladaptive Behavior Part 1.* This domain contains 36 items divided into three parts: Internalizing, Externalizing, and Other Behaviors. Maladaptive behaviors include both states (for example, being overly anxious or nervous) and behaviors (for example, tantruming and being truant).

■ *Problem Behaviors Part 2.* This domain has 14 "critical" items, such as obsessing with objects or activities and being unaware of things happening around oneself.

Scores

Individual items are scored on a four-point scale: 2 = usually, 1 = sometimes or partially, 0 = never, and DK = don't know.[2] To speed administration of the VABS II, basal and ceiling rules are used in all subtests except those assessing maladaptive behavior.

Raw scores are converted to v-scale scores, a standard score with a mean of 10 and a standard deviation of 3. Summed v-scale scores can be converted to normalized standard scores (mean = 100, standard deviation = 15) and stanines for subdomains; subdomain scores can be summed and converted to domain indexes and to an Adaptive Behavior Composite. Raw scores can also be converted to age equivalents.[3] Percentiles are available for domain scores and the Adaptive Behavior Composite. Percentiles are based on the relationship between standard scores and percentiles in normal distributions.

Norms

Regardless of the method of assessment (that is, interview or rating scale), one set of norms is used to interpret VABS II scores. The decision to use a single set of norms was based on the results of a study comparing the results from both interviews and rating scales for 760 individuals. Three of the four analyses performed by the authors support the decision to use a single set of norms. However, the analysis of correlations between the two methods of assessment does not support that conclusion. For individuals 6 years of age or older, less than 10 percent of the correlations between the two assessment methods equal or exceed .90; almost half are less than .80. Clearly, the scores are not interchangeable.

---

[2] If the number of items scored DK is greater than two, the subdomain should not be scored.

[3] Age equivalents are defined on the VABS II as representing "the age at which that score is average." It is unclear whether the average refers to the mean, the median, or the mode.

The normative sample consists of 3,695 individuals selected to represent the U.S. population. The manual offers only the most cursory explanation of how these individuals were selected from a larger pool of potential subjects: Selections were made electronically "in a way that matched the demographic variable targets within each age group" (p. 93).

The number of persons within each age group varies considerably from age to age. Samples of children under 2 years of age, the sample of children 4 to 4.5 years, the sample of individuals between 19 and 21, and samples of adults more than 31 years of age each contain fewer than 100 individuals. The norms are generally representative in terms of ethnicity (African American, Hispanic, and Caucasian), educational level of the respondents, and geographic region.

Reliability

Split-half estimates of internal consistency for adaptive behavior are provided for 19 age groups: one-year age groups from 0 through 11 years, two-year groups from 12 to 21 years, and four multiyear ranges from 22 through 90 years. The reliability of 18 of the 19 Adaptive Behavior Composites equals or exceeds .90; the exception is the 32-to-51 age group. Domain scores are generally less reliable. In 6 of the 19 age groups, the reliability of the Communication domain is less than .90; in 9 of the 19 age groups, the reliability of the Daily Living Skills domain is less than .90; in 7 of the 19 age groups, the reliability of the Socialization domain is less than .90; and in 5 of the 9 age groups, the reliability of the Motor Skills domain is less than .90. Coefficient alpha is also reported for Part 1 Maladaptive Behavior for five age groups: 3 to 5, 6 to 11, 12 to 18, 19 to 30, and 40 to 90. No alpha for the Internalizing composite reaches .90, and only one (for 12- to 18-year-olds) equals .90. Only the alphas for the Maladaptive Behavior Index for individuals 6 to 11 (.90) and for individuals 12 to 18 (.91) are large enough to use in making important individual decisions.

Test-retest estimates of reliability for adaptive behavior are provided for six age ranges.[4] Except for the 14-to-21 age group, the obtained stability[5] of the Adaptive Behavior Composite equals or exceeds .90; stability for the same group is .81. Stabilities of domains are lower; 11 of the 18 reported stability coefficients are less than .90. Stabilities of subdomain scores are generally less than those for the domains; 45 of the 50 subdomain stabilities reported are less than .90. Test-retest estimates are also provided for Part 1 Maladaptive Behavior for five age groups: 3 to 5, 6 to 11, 12 to 18, 19 to 39, and 40 to 71. Only the Externalizing and Maladaptive indexes for individuals between 40 and 71 years old reach the .90 level. All estimates of internalizing behavior and all other estimates of externalizing and the Maladaptive Behavior Index are between .72 and .89.

---

[4] Although it appears that standard scores were used to estimate the stability of domain scores, it is unclear what scores were used to estimate the stability of subdomain scores. We note that the use of raw scores would inflate stability estimates.

[5] The authors report both obtained and adjusted stability estimates. We prefer interpreting the reliability estimates that were actually obtained and therefore do not discuss adjusted estimates.

Interinterviewer reliability was also evaluated for the interview form. Two interviewers interviewed the same respondent at different times. For adaptive behavior, two age ranges were used: 0 to 6 years and 7 to 18 years. No VABS II score had an estimated reliability of .90 or higher, and most estimates were in the .40-to-.60 range. For Part 1 Maladaptive Behavior, three age ranges were used: 3 to 11, 12 to 18, and 19 to 70. Estimated interinterviewer reliabilities ranged from .44 to .83.

Interrespondent reliability was evaluated by having two respondents rate the same individual. For adaptive behavior, two age ranges were again used: 0 to 6 years and 7 to 18 years. In neither age group did the Adaptive Behavior Composite or any domain score reach an estimated reliability of .90. Most estimates were in the .60-to-.80 range. For Part 1 Maladaptive Behavior, three age ranges were again used: 3 to 11, 12 to 18, and 19 to 70. Estimated interrater reliabilities ranged from .32 to .81.

Validity

Five types of information about the VABS II validity is included in the manual: test content, response process, test structure, clinical groups, and relationship with other measures. The description of content development lacks sufficient detail to allow a systematic analysis of that process. Similarly, the description of how items were selected is vague. In contrast, factor-analytic studies support the existence of separate domains and subdomains, whereas the examination of test content for sex bias, SES bias, and ethnic bias indicates a lack of bias. Also, VABS II raw scores show a consistent developmental pattern, as would be expected with any measure of adaptive behavior.

Previously identified groups of individuals with mental retardation, autism, attention deficit hyperactivity disorder, emotional disturbance, learning disability, and vision and hearing impairments each earned the types of scores that would be expected for persons with those disabilities. For example, individuals with mental retardation all showed significant deficits on the Adaptive Behavior Composite and domain scores.

The VABS II correlates well with the previous edition of the scale. Correlations vary by age and domain, ranging from .65 (Communication for children 0 to 2 years of age) to .94 (Socialization for children 3 to 6 years of age). The VABS II correlates moderately with the Adaptive Behavior Assessment System, Second Edition, and the Behavior Assessment System for Children, Second Edition.

Summary

The VABS II is an individually administered, norm-referenced scale for evaluating the adaptive behavior of individuals from birth to 90 years of age. The scale can be administered as a structured interview or as a rating scale, but these two methods appear to yield somewhat different results (that is, they are not so highly correlated that they can be used interchangeably). Despite the differences in the results of the two administrations, one set of norms is used to convert raw scores to derived scores. Thus, although norms appear representative, their use for both methods of administration is problematic.

Reliability is generally inadequate for making important individual decisions about students, especially adolescents. Both interinterviewer and interrespondent reliability are too low to use the VABS II with confidence. The internal consistency of the Adaptive Behavior Composite is generally reliable enough to use in making important educational decisions for students. Domain, subdomain, and maladaptive reliabilities are not. Except for adolescents, the stability of the Adaptive Behavior Composite is adequate; the domain, subdomain, and maladaptive items stabilities are usually too low for making important individual decisions.

General indications of validity are adequate. However, no data are presented to indicate that the VABS II is valid for monitoring a student's progress or planning educational and treatment plans.

AAMD Adaptive Behavior Scale: Residential and Community Scale, Second Edition (ABS-RC2)

The AAMD Adaptive Behavior Scale: Residential and Community Scale, Second Edition (ABS-RC2; Nihira, Leland, & Lambert, 1993b), is an individually administered, norm-referenced scale designed for use with individuals between 18 and 79 years of age. Since its introduction in 1969, this scale has undergone numerous modifications. For this latest version, items from previous editions were selected because of their interrater reliability and effectiveness in discrimination among various levels of adaptation.

The scale is divided into two parts. Part I focuses on ten domains related to independent and responsible functioning, physical development, language development, and socialization. Three factors underlie these domains: personal self-sufficiency, community self-sufficiency, and personal–social responsibility.

Two administration formats are used in this part. In the first format, responses to items consist of a series of statements denoting increasingly higher levels of adaptation. These items are scored by circling the highest level of functioning demonstrated by the client. For example, in the domain of Physical Development, the response to item 25 (vision) has four levels: has no difficulty seeing, has some difficulty seeing, has great difficulty seeing, and has no vision at all.

In the second format, each item consists of a series of statements that are answered either yes or no. A socially desirable response is awarded 1 point. For example, item 62 (persistence) in the Self-Direction domain consists of five statements: "Cannot organize task," "Becomes easily discouraged," "Fails to carry out tasks," "Jumps from one activity to another," and "Needs constant encouragement to complete task." For this item, "No" is the socially desirable response; each time a statement does not apply to the subject, the subject is awarded 1 point. Thus a subject may receive between 0 and 5 points on this item. Students can earn from 3 to 9 points on each item scored in this format.

The items in Part II of the scale are concerned with maladaptive behaviors that are manifestations of personality and behavior disorders. These items are grouped into eight domains, and only one administration format is used. Two factors underlie these eight domains: Social Adjustment and Personal Adjustment. Each item consists of multiple statements and is scored on a 3-point scale (never, 0; occasionally, 1; frequently, 2). See Table 27.1 for a list of domains and factors.

| TABLE 27.1 | Domains and Factors in Parts I and II of the ABS-RC2 |

	Domains (number of items in each)	Factors
Part I	1. Independent Functioning (24)	Personal Self-Sufficiency
	2. Physical Development (6)	Community Self-Sufficiency
	3. Economic Activity (6)	Personal–Social Responsibility
	4. Language Development (10)	
	5. Numbers and Time (3)	
	6. Domestic Activity (6)	
	7. Prevocational/Vocational Activity (3)	
	8. Self-Direction (5)	
	9. Responsibility (3)	
	10. Socialization (7)	
Part II	11. Social Behavior (7)	Social Adjustment
	12. Conformity (6)	Personal Adjustment
	13. Trustworthiness (6)	
	14. Stereotyped and Hyperactive Behavior (5)	
	15. Sexual Behavior (4)	
	16. Self-Abusive Behavior (3)	
	17. Social Engagement (4)	
	18. Disturbing Interpersonal Behavior (6)	

Scores

All raw scores from the ABS-RC2 can be converted to percentiles, standard scores for domains (mean = 10, standard deviation = 37), and quotients for factors (mean = 100, standard deviation = 15). Age equivalents are also available for scores from Part I; Part II scores are not related to age, so no age equivalents are available. Derived scores for an adaptive-behavior total or composite are not available.

Domain scores provide measures of relative standing in each topical domain. In addition, five factor scores (based on previous research and a confirmatory factor analysis) can be obtained for the three factors in Part I (Personal Self-Sufficiency, Community Self-Sufficiency, and Personal–Social Responsibility) and the two factors in Part II (Social Adjustment and Personal Adjustment). The factor scores are obtained by summing item raw scores and converting the totals to derived scores.

Norms

The ABS-RC2 was standardized on 4,103 individuals with developmental disabilities. Participants in the standardization were stratified on living arrangements: those living in the community (for example, living at home or in small community-based residences) and those living in institutions. Some subjects were selected by site coordinators in Connecticut, Florida, Ohio, and California; other subjects were located through a mailing to members of the American Association on Mental Deficiency who were asked to participate in the standardization.

These techniques for finding subjects resulted in a sample drawn from 46 states and the District of Columbia. Subjects in the normative sample were predominantly between the ages of 18 and 39; there were 1,339 individuals between 18 and 29, 1,254 individuals between 30 and 39, 759 individuals between 40 and 49, 418 individuals between 50 and 59, and 333 individuals 60 or older. The sample is generally representative of the nation in terms of geographic region, race, and ethnicity; however, it overrepresents males and individuals living in urban areas. The extent to which this sample represents the population of individuals with mental retardation is unclear: 18 percent of the sample had an IQ less than 20, 43.2 percent had an IQ between 20 and 49, and 38.8 percent had an IQ between 50 and 70. Professionals who conduct assessments with the ABS-RC2 must be very aware that the percentiles and standard scores are based on the performances of individuals with mental retardation. Thus the usual score interpretations are not correct. A person earning a percentile of 50 on this test has performed equal to or greater than 50 percent of the individuals in the normative sample.

Reliability

Reliability of the ABS-RC2 was estimated for items (using coefficient alpha), for times (stability), and for raters.[6] In Part I, alphas for domains ranged from a low of .80 (for ages 18 to 29 on Prevocational/Vocational Activity) to a high of .98 (Independent Functioning for ages 18 to 29 and 30 to 39); of the 50 domain alphas, 41 equaled or exceeded .90. Alphas for Part I factors were all quite high, ranging from .96 to .99. In Part II, alphas for domains ranged from a low of .80 (Sexual Behavior for ages 60 and older and Self-Abusive Behavior for ages 35 to 39 and 40 to 49) to a high of .95 (Social Behavior for ages 18 to 29 and 50 to 59). Of the 40 alphas for Part II domains, only 13 equaled or exceeded .90. Alphas for Part II factors all exceeded .90. The reason alphas were higher for factor scores than for domain scores is probably because there are more items in factor scores, and the factor scores are more homogeneous than domain scores.

Two-week stability was estimated based on scores of 45 individuals working in a sheltered workshop. The individuals ranged in age from 24 to 61 years, but it is unclear whether standard scores or other methods of controlling for age range were used. Uncorrected correlations between test and retest for Part I domains ranged from .86 to .98; seven of the ten coefficients equaled or exceeded .90. Uncorrected correlations for factors ranged from .93 to .98. For Part II, uncorrected correlations ranged from .81 to .97 for domain scores; four of the eight coefficients equaled or exceeded .90. Part II factor scores were .94 and .82.

The authors also provide information about interrater agreement (which they called "ecological validity") for 45 employees of a sheltered workshop.

---

[6] The authors provide information about what they call "interscorer reliability." In the study they cite, two graduate students tabulated completed protocols. Because the tabulation of scores is not particularly complicated on this scale, the high correlations are not surprising.

Supervisors and the parents of the employees were independently rated. For Part I domain scores, agreement ranged from .31 (Prevocational/Vocational Activity) to .87 (Physical Development); the agreement for Part I factor scores ranged from .47 (Personal–Social Responsibility) to .88 (Personal Self-Sufficiency). For Part II domain scores, agreement ranged from .07 (Social Behavior) to .85 (Sexual Behavior); for Part II factors, agreement was .31 (Social Adjustment) and .39 (Personal Adjustment).

Validity

Content Validity   The content of the revised scale remains quite similar to the content of previous versions of this device. In previous editions of this text, we questioned the content validity of the scale because the authors presented no conceptualization of the domain used to guide inclusion and exclusion of items. We were also troubled because many of the items assess physical and emotional states (not behaviors) and because many items that appeared in Part II probably should not be considered maladaptive (for example, "Gossips about others," "Is always in the way," "Bites fingernails"). We still find the rationale for item selection and the scale's content to be troubling.

Criterion-Related Validity   Two criterion-related validity studies are reported. In the first, 63 individuals were tested using the ABS-RC2 and the Vineland Adaptive Behavior Scales. In the second study, 30 individuals were tested using the ABS-RC2 and the Adaptive Behavior Inventory.[7] In both studies, the correlations between the Part I ABS-RC2 scores and the other measures were generally moderate to high; the correlations between Part II ABS-RC2 scores and the other measures were generally not significantly different from zero. These findings strongly suggest that Part II is not measuring what is typically measured on other measures of adaptive behavior. The findings also provide some support for the criterion-related validity of Part I scores.

Construct Validity   Although several indexes of construct validity are provided in the ABS-RC2 manual, three seem most pertinent to our discussion. The first evidence comes from the relationship between age and both Part I and Part II of the scale. As expected for a valid measure of adaptive behavior, Part I scores show some relationship to age for normally developing children and youth, but no relationship to age for adults with mental retardation. Part II scores are unrelated to age—also as would be expected of a valid measure.

Second, the empirical factor structure of the ABS-RC2 supports the hypothesis of three factors for Part I (as is typically found in factor-analytic studies of adaptive behavior) and two factors for Part II. Thus, not only do Parts I and II measure different things, but Part I also appears to be measuring constructs simi-

---

[7] The same study appears to have been reported in the examiner's manual for the school version of the ABS. (Identical correlations are reported, and the subject description is similar.) In that manual, the subjects are described as attending school. At worst, these individuals fall outside the age range with which the ABS-RC2 is intended to be used; at best, these individuals represent only one extreme of the age range with which the ABS-RC2 is intended to be used.

lar to those assessed by other measures of adaptive behavior. The meaning of Part II is not clarified by these results.

Third, scores on the ABS-RC2 differentiate youngsters with and without disabilities, and both these groups of youngsters perform differently than adults with mental retardation. Although these results are suggestive of the construct validity of the scale, we note that the ABS-RC2 is not intended for use with children and youth. As expected, scores frequently discriminated individuals living in community placements from those living in residential settings.

Summary

The ABS-RC2 is an individually administered, norm-referenced scale designed for use with individuals between 18 and 79 years of age. The scale is divided into two parts. Part I focuses on ten domains that assess three factors: personal self-sufficiency, community self-sufficiency, and personal–social responsibility. Part II focuses on eight domains that assess (the lack of) social adjustment and personal adjustment. The ABS-RC2 represents a substantial improvement over previous editions of the ABS. The norming is far more comprehensive and appears much more representative. However, given the elusive nature of mild retardation, the identification of which is affected by economic and social circumstances, conclusions about the population of reference must be tentative.

The information about the scale's reliability is far more extensive than in previous editions. The internal consistency of factor scores on both parts of the scale is excellent; the domain alphas are not nearly as high. The factor scores also appear to be quite stable. Interrater agreement (called "ecological validity" by the authors) is weak, however. Thus examiners should expect the ABS-RC2 to produce internally consistent scores that are stable over time but that vary according to who provides the information. Evidence of the scales' validity is emerging. The content of specific items is troubling, but there is no indication that the scale lacks criterion-related or construct validity.

AAMR Adaptive Behavior Scale– School 2 (ABS-S2) [8]

The revised school version of the AAMR Adaptive Behavior Scale (ABS-S2; Nihira, Leland, & Lambert, 1993a) is an individually administered, norm-referenced scale designed for use with children and youth ages 3 to 21 years. The 1993 revision is the latest version of the 1969 and 1974 AAMR Adaptive Behavior Scales. Like the residential and community version of this scale, the ABS-S2 has undergone numerous modifications since its introduction in 1969. In this edition, items from previous editions were selected because of their interrater reliability and effectiveness in discriminating among various levels of adaptation.

The items and scoring procedures of the school version of the ABS are identical to those used with the residential and community edition, with two exceptions. On the school version, one domain has been deleted from each part of the scale: Domestic Activity from Part I and Sexual Behavior from Part II. Otherwise,

[8] The ABS-RC2 and the ABS-S2 are highly similar devices. Even though much of the material is redundant, we have treated them as separate scales to facilitate the use of this text as a reference work.

the two scales appear to be identical. (Readers familiar with the community and residential version of the ABS should skip to the sections dealing with technical characteristics of this version.)

Thus the scale is divided into two parts. Part I focuses on nine domains related to independent and responsible functioning, physical development, language development, and socialization. Three factors underlie these domains: personal self-sufficiency, community self-sufficiency, and personal–social responsibility. In this part, two administration formats are used. In the first format, items consist of a series of statements denoting increasingly higher levels of adaptation. These items are scored by circling the highest level of functioning demonstrated by the client. For example, in the domain of Physical Development, item 25 (vision) has four levels of functioning: has no difficulty seeing, has some difficulty seeing, has great difficulty seeing, and has no vision at all. In the second format, each item consists of a series of statements that are answered either yes or no. A socially desirable response is awarded 1 point. For example, item 62 (persistence) in the Self-Direction domain consists of five statements: "Cannot organize task," "Becomes easily discouraged," "Fails to carry out tasks," "Jumps from one activity to another," and "Needs constant encouragement to complete task." For this item, "No" is the socially desirable response; each time a statement does not apply to the subject, the subject is awarded 1 point. Thus a subject may receive between 0 and 5 points on this item. Students can earn from 3 to 9 points on each item scored in this format.

The items in Part II of the scale are concerned with maladaptive behaviors that are manifestations of personality and behavior disorders. These items are grouped into seven domains that form two factors: Social Adjustment and Personal Adjustment. Only one administration format is used in Part II. Each item consists of multiple statements and is scored on a 3-point scale (never = 0, occasionally = 1, frequently = 2). See Table 27.2 for a list of domains and factors.

Scores

Raw scores from the ABS-S2 can be converted to standard scores and percentiles for domains (mean = 10, standard deviation = 3) or to quotients for factors (mean = 100, standard deviation = 15), and factor standard scores can be converted to percentiles on the basis of the normal curve. Age equivalents are also available for scores from Part I; Part II scores are not related to age, so no age equivalents are available. Derived scores for an adaptive-behavior total or composite are not available.

Norms

As with the ABS-RC2, two different sampling procedures were used to develop norms for the ABS-S2. First, standardization sites were established in Connecticut, Florida, Ohio, and California. A site coordinator with experience in collecting standardization data was selected for each location and trained with the ABS-S2. Second, individual educators were contacted and asked to complete 10 to 20 evaluations. Individuals selected under either procedure were pooled into two normative samples. One sample consisted of 2,074 individuals with mental

TABLE 27.2	Domains and Factors in Parts I and II of the ABS-S2

	Domains (number of items in each)	Factors
Part I	1. Independent Functioning (24)	Personal Self-Sufficiency
	2. Physical Development (6)	Community Self-Sufficiency
	3. Economic Activity (6)	Personal–Social Responsibility
	4. Language Development (10)	
	5. Numbers and Time (3)	
	6. Prevocational/Vocational Activity (3)	
	7. Self-Direction (5)	
	8. Responsibility (3)	
	9. Socialization (7)	
Part II	10. Social Behavior (7)	Social Adjustment
	11. Conformity (6)	Personal Adjustment
	12. Trustworthiness (6)	
	13. Stereotyped and Hyperactive Behavior (5)	
	14. Self-Abusive Behavior (3)	
	15. Social Engagement (4)	
	16. Disturbing Interpersonal Behavior (6)	

retardation; these individuals ranged in age from 3 to 21 and resided in 40 different states. The second sample consisted of 1,254 individuals without mental retardation, who ranged in age from 3 to 18 and resided in 44 states and the District of Columbia.

Both samples adequately approximate the demographic makeup of the United States in terms of race, ethnicity, gender, and geographic region. Both normative samples are more urban than the nation is. Table 27.3 indicates the number of individuals from each group at each age. About two thirds of the time, the number of people in the age groups is less than 100. Thus some care must be exercised when interpreting derived scores based on these samples. They are too small to allow a full range of scores.

The authors offer no guidance on when an examiner should use one set of norms or the other. However, it seems logical to use the norms based on individuals without retardation when the purpose of assessment is to establish entitlement to services. Interpretations based on the norm group of individuals with retardation should be made most carefully, because these individuals have very limited intellectual ability (that is, 60 percent have an IQ below 50).

Reliability

Reliability of the ABS-S2 was estimated separately for each normative group. The authors present reliability estimates for items (coefficient alpha), for times (stability), and for raters.[9] For the sample with mental retardation, alphas for the

---

[9] Refer back to footnote 3.

TABLE 27.3   Norm Samples Used for the ABS-S2

Age	Individuals Without Retardation	Individuals with Retardation
3	72	74
4	65	74
5	96	91
6	79	90
7	83	83
8	110	98
9	85	143
10	108	134
11	85	133
12	93	132
13	81	123
14	69	146
15	69	123
16	66	126
17	48	94
18	45	114
19		101
20		105
21		90

171 domain-age reliabilities in Part I ranged from a low of .81 to a high of .98; 42 of the 171 coefficients (primarily associated with the Prevocational/Vocational and Responsibility domains) were below .90. The reliability of factor scores at all ages equaled or exceeded .95. In Part II, alphas for the 133 domain-age reliabilities ranged from a low of .80 to a high of .96; 49 of the 133 coefficients were below .90. With one exception, the reliability of factor scores at all ages equaled or exceeded .90. For the sample without mental retardation, in Part I, alphas for the 144 domain-age reliabilities ranged from a low of .79 to a high of .97; 100 of the 144 coefficients were below .90. The reliability of the factor scores at the 16 ages ranged from .80 to .97, and 14 of the 32 coefficients were below .90. In Part II, alphas for the 112 domain-age reliabilities ranged from a low of .80 to a high of .98; 69 of the 112 coefficients were below .90. Reliability of the factor scores was higher. Only 7 of the 32 factor-age alphas were below .90.

In summary, for both samples, domain scores should be used with some caution because their reliabilities frequently are below .90, especially for the normative sample without mental retardation. Factor scores had more consistently acceptable reliability. The reason alphas were higher for factor scores than for domain scores is probably because there are more items in factor scores, and the factor scores are more homogeneous than the domain scores.

Two-week stability was estimated based on scores of 45 students with emotional disturbance in ninth through eleventh grades. Uncorrected correlations between test and retest for Part I domains ranged from .42 to .79; none of the nine coefficients equaled or exceeded .90. Uncorrected stability estimates for factors ranged from .61 to .72. For Part II, uncorrected test-retest correlations ranged from .72 to .89 for domain scores; Part II factor scores were .84 and .81. Thus none of the stabilities reached .90.

The authors also provide information about interrater agreement ("ecological validity") for 50 students with emotional disabilities. The students' teacher and the teacher's aide each completed an ABS-S2. For Part I domain scores, agreement ranged from .51 (Physical Development) to .92 (Numbers and Time); the reliability of only one domain score reached or exceeded .90. For Part I factor scores, the reliabilities were .80, .66, and .76. For Part II domain scores, agreement ranged from .55 (Social Engagement) to .88 (Conformity); for Part II factors, agreement was .61 (Social Adjustment) and .53 (Personal Adjustment).

Validity

Content Validity   The content of the revised scale remains quite similar to the content of previous versions of this device. In previous editions of this textbook, we questioned the content validity of the scale because the authors presented no conceptualization of the domain used to guide inclusion and exclusion of items. We were also troubled because many of the items assess physical and emotional states (not behavior) and because many items that appeared in Part II probably should not be considered maladaptive (for example, "Gossips about others," "Is always in the way," "Bites fingernails"). We still find the rationale for item selection, as well as the scale's content itself, to be troubling.

Criterion-Related Validity   One criterion-related validity study dealing specifically with the ABS-S2 is reported. In this study, 30 students with mental retardation were tested using the ABS-S2 and the Adaptive Behavior Inventory (ABI). The correlations between the Part I ABS-S2 scores and the ABI were generally moderate to high; the correlations between Part II ABS-S2 scores and the ABI were generally not significantly different from zero. These findings strongly suggest that Part II is not measuring what is typically measured on other measures of adaptive behavior. They also provide some support for the criterion-related validity of Part I scores.

Construct Validity   Although several indexes of construct validity are provided in the ABS-S2 manual, three seem most pertinent to our discussion. The first evidence comes from the relationship between age and Parts I and II of the scale. As expected for a valid measure of adaptive behavior, most scores from Part I show some relationship to age for normally developing children and youth; however, they do tend to flatten out around age 15 or 16 years, depending on the particular score. Part II scores show a much weaker developmental trend to about age 15 or 16, but then tend to decline. This observation suggests that students with maladaptive behavior were lost, possibly because they dropped out of school. These data generally appear consistent with the developmental domains being assessed.

Second, the factor structure of the ABS-S2 supports the notion of three factors for Part I (as is typically found in factor-analytic studies of adaptive behavior) and two factors for Part II. Thus, not only do Parts I and II measure different things, but Part I also appears to be measuring constructs similar to those assessed by other measures of adaptive behavior. The meaning of Part II is not clarified by these results.

Third, scores on the ABS-S2 differentiate children and youth with and without mental retardation. Thus individuals with mental retardation earn lower scores than individuals without mental retardation.

Summary

The ABS-S2 is an individually administered, norm-referenced scale designed for use with individuals between 3 and 18 years of age. The scale is divided into two parts. Part I focuses on nine domains that assess three factors: personal self-sufficiency, community self-sufficiency, and personal–social responsibility. Part II focuses on seven domains that assess (the lack of) social adjustment and personal adjustment. The ABS-S2 represents a substantial improvement over previous editions. The norming is far more comprehensive and appears much more representative.

The information about the scale's reliability is far more extensive than in previous editions. The internal-consistency estimates vary by norm group, score, and age. Surprisingly, the scale is more reliable with the sample of individuals who have mental retardation; generally, reliability estimates based on the performance of extreme populations are lower, for reasons we can only speculate about. For all subjects, factor scores are generally more reliable than domain scores. However, examiners are cautioned that specific age-score combinations frequently fail to meet minimum standards (.90) recommended when making important educational decisions. Similarly, neither the domain nor the factor scores appear to be sufficiently stable to be used as the basis for important educational decisions. Interrater agreement ("ecological validity") is weak. Evidence of the scales' validity is emerging. Specific content items are troubling, but there is no indication that the scale lacks criterion-related or construct validity.

Scales of Independent Behavior–Revised (SIB-R)

The Scales of Independent Behavior–Revised (SIB-R; Bruininks, Woodcock, Weatherman, & Hill, 1996) is an individually administered, norm-referenced device suitable for use with infants to individuals 90 years old. The SIB-R is intended to be used to identify individuals who lack independence in various settings (home, school, community, work, and so forth), provide instructional and training goals, contribute to placement decisions, and provide evidence for program evaluation, as well as to be used in research and training. The SIB-R can be administered to a respondent who is thoroughly familiar with the subject being assessed. The SIB-R may be completed as an interview or a checklist.

The 259 adaptive-behavior items are arranged into 14 subscales; subscales are grouped into four clusters. The motor skills cluster consists of two subscales: Gross Motor Skills and Fine Motor Skills. The social interaction and communication skills cluster consists of three subscales: Social Interaction, Language Comprehension, and Language Expression. The personal living skills cluster consists of five subscales: Eating and Meal Preparation, Toileting, Dressing, Personal Self-Care, and Domestic Skills. The community living skills cluster consists of four subscales: Time and Punctuality, Money and Value, Work Skills, and Home and Community Orientation. Cluster scores are combined into a total score (Broad Independence). Each item is evaluated on the same scale:

0　The person never or rarely performs the skill even if asked.

1　The person performs the skill. However, the person does not perform the task well or performs the task about a quarter of the time. The person may need to be asked to perform.

2　The person performs the skill fairly well or about three quarters of the time. The person may need to be asked to perform the skill.

3　The person performs the skill very well (always or almost always) without being asked.

Three forms are available to assess adaptive behavior: the full-scale form, the short form, and the early development form. The full-scale form uses all 14 adaptive subscales. The short form, intended as a screening device, consists of 40 items culled from the 259 adaptive items. The early development form also consists of 40 items that are "particularly suitable for assessing the development of preschoolers and the adaptive skills of youths or adults with serious disabilities" (Bruininks et al., 1996, p. 16).

Maladaptive behavior is assessed by interviewing the respondent about areas of problem behavior, rather than asking about specific behaviors.[10] There are three broad clusters of maladaptive behavior. The internalized maladaptive cluster consists of three areas: behavior that is hurtful to self, unusual or repetitive habits, and withdrawn or inattentive behavior. The externalized maladaptive cluster also consists of three areas: behavior that is hurtful to others, destruction of property, and disruptive behavior. The asocial maladaptive cluster consists of two areas: socially offensive behavior and uncooperative behavior. Each area is assessed on two dimensions: a frequency scale and a severity scale. The frequency scale is a 5-point scale:

1　Less than once a month

2　1 to 3 times a month

3　1 to 6 times a week

4　1 to 10 times a day

5　1 or more times an hour

---

[10] We believe this format is a distinct improvement over other formats used to assess problem behavior. (Typical respondents are asked to rate the subject on a long list of problem behaviors that may or may not contain the specific behavior that is causing problems.) The SIB-R format also avoids the dilemma of differing importance of maladaptive behavior (for instance, is nail biting as important or significant as eye gouging?).

The severity scale is also a 5-point scale (beginning at zero):

0   Not serious (not a problem)
1   Slightly serious (a mild problem)
2   Moderately serious (a moderate problem)
3   Very serious (a severe problem)
4   Extremely serious (a critical problem)

Scores

Except for age equivalents for adaptive-behavior subscales, obtaining commonly used scores on the SIB-R is unnecessarily complicated. Seven steps are required to find standard scores or percentiles for each adaptive-behavior cluster. (Computer scoring disks are available.) Other norm-referenced scores are arcane.

Norms

SIB-R norms are a composite of the first edition norms ($N = 1,764$) and an additional 418 individuals added from a separate standardization conducted for the second edition. Considering both norming groups, SIB-R norms are based on the performances of 2,182 individuals ranging in age from 3 months to 90 years. These individuals came from more than 60 cities and 15 states. The total sample approximates the 1990 U.S. Census in terms of gender, race, and community size. More than half of the sample comes from the Midwest, although less than 25 percent of the U.S. population lives in that region. However, the comparisons of interest (that is, the degree to which each normative group approximates the U.S. Census) are absent. Nonetheless, the statistical values obtained for the combined sample were then adjusted. Three hundred twenty-five individuals who participated in the 1995 standardization of the SIB-R also participated in the standardization of the Woodcock-Johnson Psychoeducational Battery–Revised (WJ-R). Based on the performances of these 325 individuals in comparison with the entire standardization sample of the WJ-R, the SIB-R norms were altered.

Reliability

Internal consistencies of the adaptive-behavior subscales and clusters were estimated using corrected split-half correlations. Estimates of the internal consistency of each subscale are provided for ten age ranges: 3 to 11 months, 1 year, 2 years, 3 years, 4 years, 5 to 7 years, 8 to 9 years, 10 to 12 years, 13 to 19 years, and 20 to 90 years. Reliability coefficients for subscales range from .40 to .96; about 15 percent of the coefficients equal or exceed .90. As is typically the case, cluster reliabilities are substantially higher, ranging from .67 to .97; 25 of the 40 cluster-by-age coefficients equal or exceed .90. Broad Independence (the total score) equals or exceeds .90 for each age group. The internal consistency of the short form equals or exceeds .90 in only one age group (3 to 11 months). The internal consistency of the early development form is less than .90 from ages 2 through 7.

The stabilities of adaptive-behavior subscales and clusters, as well as mal-adaptive-behavior clusters and Broad Independence, were also examined in several studies. In one study, 31 individuals between the ages of 6 and 13 years were retested within a four-week period. Subscale stabilities ranged from .83 to .94; 11 of the 14 coefficients equaled or exceeded .90. Cluster and Broad Independence stabilities all exceeded .90. The stabilities of the three maladaptive indexes and the general maladaptive score were in the low .80s. The stability of the short form was .97. The authors report additional studies examining the stability of the maladaptive indexes. The results of these studies are consistent with the previously reported study.

The authors report four studies examining interrater agreement. In the first study, mothers and fathers of 26 individuals without disabilities (between the ages of 6 and 13 years) were interviewed separately. For adaptive subscales, the correlations between mother's report and father's report ranged from .58 (Toileting) to .94 (Language Expression). Three of the four coefficients of agreement for the clusters were in the .80s; one was .93. The agreement for Broad Independence was .95, and the agreement for the short form was .93. Agreements for the maladaptive indexes were somewhat lower: One coefficient was in the .70s, and the rest were in the .80s.

In the second study, teachers and teacher's aides rated 30 students with moderate mental retardation between the ages of 6 and 13 years. For adaptive subscales, the correlations between teacher report and teacher's aide report ranged from .71 (Domestic Skills) to .96 (Gross Motor Skills and Language Expression). Three of the four coefficients of agreement for the clusters were in the .90s; one was .88. The agreement in Broad Independence score was .96, and the agreement for the short form was .95. Agreements for the maladaptive indexes were substantially lower: .57, .87, and .78; the consistency for the general maladaptive index was .84.

In the third study, teachers and teacher's aides rated students with moderate to severe retardation between the ages of 12 and 21. Agreement on each cluster ranged from .74 to .86, and agreement for Broad Independence was .80. The consistency of ratings of the maladaptive indexes ranged from .69 to .81; the consistency for the general maladaptive index was .80.

In the last study, teachers and teacher's aides rated 63 children between the ages of 2 and 5 years. The consistency of Broad Independence (early development form) was .91. The agreement for the maladaptive indexes ranged from .68 to .83, and the agreement for the general maladaptive index was .79.

Validity

The validity of the SIB-R rests largely on the validity of the first edition, although the items on the two editions differ somewhat. Some new items were prepared for the SIB-R, and some old items from the SIB were dropped. Nonetheless, scores from the two forms are reported to be highly correlated. Content validity for the SIB was established through delineation of the domain and through careful item selection.

Construct validity was established in several ways. On the SIB-R, adaptive-behavior scores increase with age (although maladaptive behavior is essentially unrelated to age). SIB-R scores are also moderately correlated with intelligence (as measured by the cognitive portion of the Woodcock-Johnson Psychoeducational Battery). Several studies are reported in which the adaptive (or maladaptive) behavior of individuals with disabilities is compared with the behavior of individuals without disabilities. In one such study, the SIB-R early development form was used with 30 children with disabilities or delays and 30 children of the same age but without disabilities. The children with disabilities earned substantially lower scores on the adaptive items and on two of the four maladaptive scores. The remaining comparison studies were conducted with the SIB. In these studies, the scores earned by individuals from special populations (for example, trainable individuals with mental retardation) were compared with the scores earned by nonhandicapped persons drawn at random from the normative sample. The comparisons showed that individuals with disabilities earned consistently lower SIB scores when compared with persons without disabilities. Moreover, differences in adaptive behavior were on expected dimensions. For example, hearing-impaired individuals earned significantly lower scores on the Social Interaction and Language Comprehension subscales.

Criterion-related validity of the SIB was previously investigated in two studies in which SIB scores were correlated with scores from the AAMD Adaptive Behavior Scale (school edition). Correlations between SIB-R cluster scores and ABS-S2 factor scores ranged from .33 to .86. Maladaptive indexes of the SIB were correlated with results of the Revised Problem Behavior Checklist (RPBC; Quay & Peterson, 1987); the pattern of correlations supports the validity of the SIB-R (for example, the asocial maladaptive behavior index of the SIB-R correlates better with scores on the Socialized Aggression, Attention Problems, and Motor Excess scales of the RPBC than with scores on the other subscales of the RPBC). A study comparing the SIB-R early development form with the Early Screen Profiles was also conducted. The two measures were highly correlated.

Summary

The SIB-R is an individually administered, norm-referenced adaptive-behavior scale that is useful with individuals ranging in age from infancy through adulthood. The SIB-R includes four clusters of adaptive behavior (motor skills, social interaction and communication skills, personal living skills, and community living skills) and four maladaptive-behavior indexes (general maladaptive behavior, internalized maladaptive behavior, asocial maladaptive behavior, and externalized maladaptive behavior). The SIB-R's norms are difficult to evaluate. They are a mixture of old and new norms that have been adjusted, and they do not appear representative of the United States as a whole. Reliability estimates for each age are not presented. Internal consistencies of the adaptive-behavior subscales, early development form, and short form are generally too low to use in making important educational decisions about students. The internal consistencies of cluster scores are variable, but the internal consistency of the total score (that is,

Broad Independence) exceeds .90 for all ages reported. No stability data are presented for individuals older than 13 years. For individuals 13 years or younger, stabilities are moderate. However, no data are presented for individual ages. Interrater agreement for students between the ages of 6 and 13 years was quite variable. Given the data reported in the technical manual, the Broad Independence score is probably reliable at any age; other scores should be interpreted cautiously. Evidence for the SIB-R's validity suggests that the scale indeed measures adaptive behavior.

Dilemmas in Current Practice

There are three severe problems in the use of currently available instruments to assess adaptive behavior: (1) lack of internal consistency, (2) poor norms, and (3) lack of interrater agreement.

Problem

First, there is no theoretical reason that adaptive behavior scales should not be internally consistent. That some scales are not homogeneous can reasonably be attributed to the lack of a clear definition of adaptive behavior, a problem to which we alluded earlier in this chapter. There is no professional consensus about the types of behavior that are indicative of adaptation. Indeed, inspection of the behaviors sampled by the various devices suggests a lack of agreement about what adaptive behavior is—there is a broad range of behaviors sampled and of orientations toward measurement. Without a more precise concept of adaptive behavior, we should probably expect heterogeneous operationalizations of the definition (that is, heterogeneous scales of adaptive behavior) to continue.

Authors' Viewpoint

One solution to this problem is for test authors to rely more heavily on factor-analytic studies of adaptive behavior. If scores on adaptive behavior scales represent underlying factors, the scores will be more homogeneous and therefore more reliable. This point is clearly illustrated by the ABS-RC2, for which domain scores are less reliable than factor scores. Therefore, whenever possible, test users should rely on scores that represent the underlying factors that make up adaptive behavior, rather than using scores that describe interrelated surface performances (for example, eating or dressing).

Problem

The second problem is that scales of adaptive behavior frequently are poorly normed (sometimes normed only on individuals with disabilities). If its norm samples are unrepresentative, a scale should not be used.

Authors' Viewpoint

An alternative to using unrepresentative norms is simply to identify one or two students to use for social comparison. Teachers or parents can be asked to nominate individuals of the same age and gender as those in the norm group, whom they believe have "adapted" successfully. The behavior of these adaptive peers can then be used to make rather simple comparisons. Although one or two children certainly are no substitute for a normative sample, they may prove adequate for some comparisons.

Problem

The third and most vexing problem, both theoretically and practically, is the lack of agreement among raters. When reported at all for adaptive-behavior scales, interrater agreement is often poor. The interpretation of such findings can proceed along two lines. First, poor agreement can suggest lack of reliability. Thus we would suspect at least three potential problems: (1) The specific items are difficult to understand or interpret; (2) the criteria used to rate the behavior are subjective; or (3) one or both of the raters are insufficiently familiar with the student.

Lack of interrater agreement can also suggest lack of validity, in addition to lack of reliability. Thus we would suspect at least two potential problems: (1) One of the raters may have distorted perceptions or may not be entirely truthful, or (2) the student's behavior may vary in

Dilemmas in Current Practice (*continued*)

different contexts. In practice, examiners have few options for dealing with rater disagreement.

Authors' Viewpoint

Assessors should select as the respondent the person who is most familiar with the student, who has seen the student in the most contexts, and who will provide the most truthful and objective responses. Examiners should also guard against conveying their own expectations to the respondent. Finally, when behavior clearly varies across contexts, examiners should consider elements in those contexts that may set the occasion for behavior, because such elements may have importance in educational interventions.

SUMMARY

In the assessment of adaptive behavior, we are interested in what an individual regularly does, not what the individual is capable of doing. Ultimately, the behaviors of interest in adults are those that allow individuals to manage their affairs sufficiently well that they do not require societal intervention to protect them or others. The behaviors that are believed to be important vary from time to time and from theory to theory. In general, in the United States, adults are expected to take reasonable care of themselves (by managing their own health, dressing, eating, and so on), to work, and to engage in socially acceptable recreational or leisure activities. In children and adolescents, the behaviors of interest are those that are believed to enable the development or acquisition of desired adult behaviors and skills.

The assessment of adaptive behavior usually takes the form of a structured interview with a person (for example, a parent or teacher) who is very familiar with the person being assessed (the subject of the interview). The assessment of adaptive behavior has been plagued by inadequate instruments—scales that lack reliability and are poorly normed. Assessors must select scales (or parts of scales) with great care.

QUESTIONS FOR CHAPTER REVIEW

1. How does the assessment of adaptive behavior differ from most other types of assessment discussed in this textbook?

2. Describe some of the factors that help determine whether a behavior is considered adaptive.

3. The current state of the art in adaptive-behavior instruments presents a number of problems for examiners. Briefly discuss two of them.

4. How might a teacher or psychologist overcome the problems associated with the inadequate norms of adaptive-behavior scales when assessing a child?

5. With the increasing use of computers and robots in American industry, what do you think will happen to current definitions of adaptive behavior?

PROJECT

Using information found in the text, write a summary for two tests used in the assessment of adaptive behavior. Upon completion, compare your summaries with the text summaries. Then go to *The Fourteenth*

Mental Measurements Yearbook (see References; Plake & Impara, 2002), and compare and contrast your summaries with the reviews of the tests you selected. If your summaries differ from the reviews, did the reviewers use information and standards different from those that you used?

RESOURCES FOR FURTHER INVESTIGATION

Print Resources

American Association on Mental Retardation. (2002). *Mental retardation: Definition, classification, and systems of support* (10th ed.). Washington, DC: Author.

Balboni, G., Pedrabissi, L., Molteni, M., & Villa, S. (2001). Discriminant validity of the Vineland Scales: Score profiles of individuals with mental retardation and a specific disorder. *American Journal on Mental Retardation, 106*(2), 162–172.

Bruininks, R., Woodcock, R., Weatherman, R., & Hill, B. (1996). *Scales of Independent Behavior, Revised, comprehensive manual.* Chicago: Riverside Publishing Company.

Kamphaus, R. W. (1987). Conceptual and psychometric issues in the assessment of adaptive behavior. *Journal of Special Education, 21,* 27–35.

McCarney, S. B. (1995). *Adaptive Behavior Evaluation Scale, Home Version, Revised.* Columbia, MO: Hawthorne Educational Services.

Sattler, J. M. (2001). *Assessment of children: Cognitive applications.* San Diego, CA: Jerome Sattler.

Schmidt, M., & Salvia, J. A. (1984). Adaptive behavior: A conceptual analysis. *Diagnostique, 9*(2), 117–125.

Technology Resources

AGS ONLINE PRODUCTS AND SERVICES
www.agsnet.com
Look for product and ordering information about the instruments available from American Guidance Service (AGS). Search by product title to find information about the Vineland Adaptive Behavior Scales.

PSYCHOLOGICAL ASSESSMENT RESOURCES
www.clsphila.org/Maladaptive%20Behavior.htm
The site provides a discussion of maladaptive behavior, provides examples of maladaptive behavior, lists some disorders that are always accompanied by maladaptive behavior, and discusses how maladaptive behavior is evaluated.

PART 5

Decision Making

Assessment is a process of collecting data for the purpose of making decisions about students. The fifth part of this text is about using assessment information to make decisions.

We began this text by developing the basic foundations of assessment. In the first part, we provided an overview of assessment in special and inclusive education (assessment of students, assessment processes and concerns, and legal and ethical considerations). In the second part, we provided the basics of psychometric theory (descriptive statistics, test scores, norms, reliability, and validity) before turning to the very special considerations of adapting tests for use with students with disabilities and testing students with limited English proficiency. In the third part, we discussed how assessment is conducted in classrooms. We considered how students were assessed using observation techniques, teacher-made tests, and portfolios; how the instructional setting (rather than the student) is assessed; and how to evaluate tests themselves. In the fourth part, we discussed commercially available tests that are commonly used with students with disabilities. These tests and procedures dealt with testing psychological processes (that is, intelligence, sensory acuity, perceptual-motor skills, and language), as well as achievement (that is, reading, mathematics, achievement batteries, problem behavior, and adaptive behavior). Because the behavior of infants and toddlers tends to be undifferentiated and its measurement fraught with difficulties, we provided a separate chapter on this topic.

Part 5 returns to the assessment of students. It contains four chapters that discuss how, in practice, various decisions are made. In Chapter 28, various instructional decisions and the assessment information used to make those decisions are discussed. In Chapter 29, we discuss decisions related to special education eligibility and how they are made. Specifically, we discuss how to determine whether a student has a disability and whether a disabled student needs special education. We provide examples of how specific test results are used in making these decisions. In Chapter 30, we discuss assessment of response to instruction (RTI). RTI is part of the Individuals with Disabilities Education Improvement Act and may be used in the identification of students with learning disabilities—the category of disability with by far the largest number of students. This chapter provides an overview of what is meant by the term, where and how it has been used successfully, and questions that remain unanswered. The fourth chapter in this part discusses making accountability decisions: establishing important educational outcomes for all students and alternate or modified achievement standards for some students with disabilities, developing standards-based accountability systems, the current state of assessment and accountability practices, and important assessment considerations in making accountability decisions. We conclude with an epilogue: "The Evolution of Assessment Practice: Where Are We Headed?"

CHAPTER 28

Teacher Decision Making

EACH REGULAR AND SPECIAL EDUCATION TEACHER MAKES LITERALLY HUNDREDS OF professional decisions every day. Some decisions affect classroom management; others affect instructional management. Some types of decisions occur infrequently; others occur several times each day. In this chapter, we are concerned with the decisions that teachers make about the adequacy and appropriateness of instruction for students who need special assistance, students who are at risk, and students who are exceptional.

Both general and special educators share responsibility for students who are exceptional. General educators are largely responsible for identifying students with sufficiently severe learning or behavior problems to be referred for special education services. General and special educators share responsibility for the education of students with disabilities who are included in general education classrooms. Special educators are responsible for students whose disabilities are so severe that they cannot be educated in general education settings.

Decisions Prior to Referral

The vast majority of students are presumed to be normal, or nondisabled, when they begin school and most complete their schooling under the same presumption. However, approximately 40 percent of all students will experience difficulty during their school career, and approximately 10 to 12 percent of all students who actually enter school will experience sufficient difficulty to be identified as having a disability at some time during their school career. Most of these students will receive special education services because they need special instruction. Some students with disabilities (such as students with certain chronic health impairments) will not need special education but will require special related services that must be provided under Section 504 of the Rehabilitation Act of 1973.

In this portion of the chapter, we deal with those decisions that precede entitlement to special education. Before referring students for possible identification as exceptional, general educators take several steps, some of which are mandated by state regulations. The first step is to recognize that a problem exists; the remaining steps may vary in sequence, depending on the state or district.

Decision: Is There a Problem?   At some point in the school year, general educators may come to believe that some students have such different academic or behavioral needs that they will require special assistance if they are to achieve desired educational outcomes. The threshold of recognition varies from teacher to teacher and may be a function of several factors: teacher skill and experience, class size, availability of alternative materials and curriculum, ability and behavior of other students in the class, and the teacher's tolerance for atypical progress or behavior. Generally, when a student is performing at a rate that is between 20 and 50 percent of the rate of other students, a teacher has reason to be concerned.

Academic Needs   A teacher's recognition of academic need is usually triggered in one of two ways. First, the teacher may recognize that a student has special academic needs when that student cannot be maintained in the lowest instructional groups in a class—that is, the student becomes an instructional isolate. Second, the teacher may recognize that a student has special academic needs when that student performs adequately in most academic areas but has extreme difficulty in one or more important core skills.

Example 1. Alex is a third grader whose teacher is worried that he is falling behind his peers. Assessment information is of two types. First, his teacher notices that he has not kept up with the slowest students in the class and that he has not acquired reading skills as fast as those students. Second, his teacher assesses Alex and some of his peers, and finds that the students in the lowest reading group are reading preprimer materials orally at a rate of 70 words per minute or more, with no more than 2 errors per minute. Alex reads the same materials at a rate of 30 words per minute with 4 errors per minute. The reading materials used by the lowest group are too hard for Alex; easier reading materials are needed for effective instruction.

Example 2. Jenna is a fourth grader whose teacher is concerned about her writing skills. Assessment information is of two types. First, her teacher notes that Jenna has been placed in the classroom's highest instructional group for arithmetic, reading, social science, and music, where her performance is among the best in the class. However, her teacher notices that she struggles in her written work. Her writing is messy and often indecipherable. Her written work is like that of the least able students in the class. Second, her teacher assesses Jenna and some of her peers using timed writings with story starters. Jenna's writings contain relatively few words (7 words per minute), whereas the writings of peers judged to be progressing satisfactorily write almost twice as many (13) words per minute. Jenna has frequent misspellings (about 30 percent of her words), whereas peers progressing satisfactorily misspell about 7 percent of their words. Although not quantified, Jenna's writing demonstrates poor graphomotor skills (for example, letter formation, spacing within and between words, and text lines that move up and down as they go across the page), whereas her peers' writing is much neater and more legible.

Why a student is having difficulty is seldom clear at this point in the decision-making process. Obviously, not all achievement problems require special education. There are multiple reasons for school failure, and these reasons may often interact with one another. Generally, these reasons may be classified as being related to ineffective instruction or individual differences.

Ineffective Instruction

Some students make progress under almost any instructional conditions. When students with emerging skills and a wealth of information enter a learning situation, such students merely need the opportunity to continue learning and developing skills. These students will learn in spite of ineffective instructional methodology.

However, many students enter a learning situation with far less developed skills and require much better instruction. Without effective instruction, these students are in danger of becoming casualties of the educational system because they make progress only when they have sufficient opportunity to learn and when the approaches used to teach them are effective. Some of these students may fail to learn because they are given only limited opportunity to learn. This situation can occur in at least five ways.

1. *Students' lack of prerequisite knowledge or skill.* Some students may lack the prerequisites for learning specific content. In such cases, the content to be learned may be too difficult because the student must learn the prerequisites and the new content simultaneously. For example, Mr. Santos may give Alex a reader in which he knows only 70 percent of the words. Alex will be forced to learn sight vocabulary that he lacks while trying to comprehend what he is reading. The chances are that he will not comprehend the material because he must read too many unknown words (Salvia & Hughes, 1990).

2. *Insufficient instructional time.* The school curriculum may be so cluttered with special events and extras that sufficient time cannot be devoted to core content areas. Students who need more extensive and intensive instruction in order to learn may suffer from the discrepancy between the amount of instruction (or time) they need and the time allocated to teaching them.

3. *Teachers' lack of subject-matter knowledge.* The teacher may lack the skills to teach specific subject matter. For example, in some rural areas, it may not be possible to attract physics teachers, so the biology teacher may have to teach the course and try to stay one or two lectures ahead of the students.

4. *Teachers' lack of pedagogical knowledge.* A teacher may lack sufficient pedagogical knowledge to teach students who are not independent learners. Although educators have known for a long time about teaching methods that promote student learning (see Stevens & Rosenshine, 1981), this informa-

tion is not as widely known to teachers and supervisors as one would hope. Thus some educators may not know how to present new material, structure learning opportunities, provide opportunities for guided and independent practice, or give effective feedback. Also, given the number of families in which all adults work, there is less opportunity for parents to provide supplementary instruction at home to overcome faulty instruction at school.

5. *Teachers' use of ineffective methods.* A teacher may be committed to ineffective instructional methods. A considerable amount of effort has gone into the empirical evaluation of various instructional approaches. Yet much of this research fails to find its way into the classroom. For example, a number of school districts have rejected systematic instruction in phonics. However, the empirical research is more than clear that early and systematic phonics instruction leads to better reading (Adams, 1990; Foorman, Francis, Fletcher, Shatschneider, & Mehta, 1998; Pflaum, Walberg, Karegianes, & Rasher, 1980; Stanovich, 1986).

Before investing in expensive and extensive assessment of the student, it is almost always preferable to examine the effectiveness of the curriculum and the instruction. If a student begins to make better progress with more effective instructional procedures, there is no need to refer her or him. A few students make little progress in spite of systematic application of sound instructional principles that have been shown to be generally effective. These are the students who should be considered for special instruction.

Individual Differences

The best general teaching methods and curricula may not work well with each and every student. There are at least three reasons for this. First, student ability may affect instruction. Obviously, instruction that relies heavily on visual or auditory presentation will be less effective with students who have severe visual or auditory impairments.[1] Just as obviously, slow learners require more practice to acquire various skills and knowledge. Second, some students may find a particular subject inherently interesting and be motivated to learn, whereas other students may find the content to be boring and require additional incentives to learn. Third, cultural differences can affect academic learning and behavior.

For example, reading is an interactive process in which an author's writing is interpreted on the basis of a reader's experience and knowledge. To the extent that students from different cultures have different experiences, their comprehension of some written materials may differ. Thus students from different cultural groups may have different understandings of, for example, "all men are created equal." Similarly, cultural norms for instructional dialogues between

---

[1] The instructional importance of other abilities has been asserted; however, there is scant evidence to support such assertions. There is limited and dated support for the notion that intelligence interacts with teaching methods in mathematics. Maynard and Strickland (1969) found that students with high IQs tended to learn mathematics somewhat better when discovery methods were used, although more direct methods were equally effective with students with lower IQs.

teacher and student may also vary, especially when the teacher and student are of different genders. Boys and girls may be raised differently, with different expectations, in some cultures. Thus it may be culturally appropriate for women and girls to be reticent in their responses to male teachers. Similarly, teachers may feel ill equipped to teach students from different cultures. For example, teachers may be hesitant to discipline students from another culture, or they may not have culturally relevant examples to illustrate concepts and ideas.

Behavioral Needs   General educators may also come to believe that a student has such different behavioral needs that he or she will require special assistance to achieve desired educational outcomes. As discussed in the chapter "Assessing Behavior Through Observation," any behavior that falls outside the range typically expected—too much or too little compliance, too much or too little assertiveness, too much or too little activity, and so forth—can be problematic in and of itself. In other cases, a behavior may be problematic because it interferes with learning.

> *Example 3.* Nick is a fifth grader who is earning unsatisfactory grades in all instructional areas. Assessment data are again of two types. First, his teacher notices that Nick frequently does not understand new material and seldom turns in homework. His teacher notices that he frequently stares into space or watches the tropical fish in the class aquarium at inappropriate times. He occasionally seems startled when his teacher calls on him. Although he usually begins seatwork, unlike the other students in class, he usually fails to complete his assignments. He seldom brings his homework to school even when his mother says that he has done it. Second, his teacher systematically observes Nick and two of his peers who are progressing satisfactorily for their attention to task. Specifically, once each minute during language arts and arithmetic seatwork, the teacher notes if the boys are on task (that is, looking at their work, writing, or appear to be reading). After a week of observation, the teacher summarizes the data and finds that Nick is off task in both language arts and arithmetic about 60 percent of the time. His peers are off task less than 5 percent of the time. It is not surprising, given Nick's lack of attention, that he is doing poorly in school.

As is true with academic learning problems, why a student is having difficulty may be unclear. The problem may lie in the teacher's inability to manage classroom behavior, the individual student's distinctive behavior, or a combination of both.

Ineffective Classroom Management

A teacher may lack sufficient knowledge, skill, or willingness to structure and manage a classroom effectively. Many students come to school with well-developed interpersonal and intrapersonal skills, and such students are well behaved and easily directed or coached in almost any setting. Other students enter the classroom with far less developed skills. For these students, a teacher needs much better management skills. In a classroom in which the teacher lacks these skills, the behavior of such students may interfere with their own learning and the learning of their peers. Thus a teacher must know how to manage classroom behavior and be willing to do so.

Classroom management is one of the more emotional topics in education, and often teachers' personal values and beliefs affect their willingness to control their classrooms. Although for some time there has been extensive empirical research supporting the effectiveness of various management techniques (see Alberto & Troutman, 1995; Sulzer-Azaroff & Mayer, 1986), these techniques may be rejected by some teachers on philosophical grounds. Occasionally, teachers may know how to manage behavior and be willing to do so generally but be unwilling to deal with specific students for some reason. For example, some European American teachers may be hesitant to discipline minority students.

Individual Differences

Even when teachers use generally effective management strategies, they may be unable to control some students effectively. For example, some students may be difficult to manage because they have never had to control their behavior before, because they reject women as authority figures, or because they seek any kind of attention—positive or negative. Other students may not get enough sleep or nutritious food to be alert and ready to participate and learn in school.

Thus generally effective management strategies may be ill suited to a particular student. Because there is seldom a perfect relationship between undesirable behavior and its cause, it is impossible to know a priori whether a student's difficulties are the result of different values, lack of learning, or flawed management techniques without modifying some of the management strategies and observing the effect of the modifications. If a student begins to behave better with the modifications, the reasons for the initial difficulties are not particularly important (and no one should assume that the teacher has found the cause of the difficulty).

Prereferral Decisions

Early on, special educators adopted the term *referral* to designate a request that a student be evaluated for special education eligibility and entitlement. Subsequently, an additional step was added to the process. Because referral had already gained widespread acceptance, the new step was called "prereferral," although this step clearly involves referral, too. We use the term *prereferral* to describe assessment and intervention activities that occur prior to formal referral to determine eligibility for special education.

Decision: Does the Student Need Extra Help? Because so many academic and behavioral problems can be remediated or eliminated by classroom teachers, the first decision that a teacher should make is to provide students who are experiencing difficulties with a little extra help. Frequently, this special assistance will take the form of more of the same instruction and attempts to obtain parental help; occasionally, assistance involves informal consultation with other teachers or building specialists. The special help can also take the form of Title I services. If the student responds to the extra help and the problems are solved, no further action is required (with the exception of perhaps more careful monitoring).

Example 4. Because Nick has trouble paying attention, his teacher moves him to the front of class and away from the class aquarium. When his attention seems to wander, she taps his desk unobtrusively with her index finger; this usually brings him back to task. The teacher also has a conference with Nick's mother, and they agree that the teacher will send the parents each homework assignment via e-mail. The mother agrees to check Nick's book bag each morning to make sure that his completed homework is taken to school. It is important that the teacher monitors the effect of these interventions on Nick's attention and learning; that is, sees if the intervention improves Nick's behavior. The assessment data used by the teacher consist of the frequency of homework turned in before and after the homework intervention is introduced. The teacher also notes the duration of Nick's redirected attention.

Decision: Should the Student Be Referred to an Intervention Assistance Team?

When teachers are unable to address a student's academic or behavioral problems effectively, they often seek formal help from a specialist or staff support team to discuss issues related to their specific needs or the student's, to get suggestions, or to obtain follow-up assistance.

Example 5. The data on the effectiveness of the interventions on Nick's on-task behavior showed mixed results. Nick's rate of homework completion immediately jumped to 100 percent. Thus Nick's completion problem was solved by providing the parents with each homework assignment and having them make sure that Nick actually brought his homework to school. Moving Nick to the front of the class, nearer to the teacher, stopped him from staring at the aquarium but had little effect on his staring into space in general. The tapping cue to redirect Nick's attention worked 100 percent of the time, but the duration of his redirected attention was short, averaging about 30 seconds. Moreover, the teacher found that harder and harder tapping was required, and that this intervention had become intrusive and distracting to the students seated next to Nick. Because the teacher's classroom interventions had met with little success and because Nick's lack of attention was still affecting his learning, the teacher decided to consult with the building's child study team to see if they had other suggestions.

The team can respond to requests in a variety of ways. It can provide immediate crisis intervention, short-term consultation, continuous support, or the securing of information, resources, or training for those who request its services. By providing problem-specific support and assistance to individuals and groups, the team can help teachers and other professionals to become more skillful, gain confidence, and feel more efficacious in their work with students. Although the team's makeup and job titles vary by state, team members should be skilled in areas of learning, assessment, behavior management, curriculum modification, and interpersonal communication.

Obviously, students should not receive special education simply because they are casualties of a certain teaching style or curriculum. Nor should students receive special education when better teaching or management would allow them to make satisfactory progress in regular education. Thus, when a teacher seeks help in addressing the special needs of a student, the first form of help offered should be providing the general education classroom teacher with additional strategies and materials. The goals of prereferral assessment and intervention are (1) to remediate, if possible, student difficulties before they become disabling; (2) to provide remediation in the least restrictive environment; and (3) to verify that, if the problems cannot be resolved effectively, they are not caused by the school (that is, to establish that the problems reside within the child or the family). Typically, there are five stages of prereferral activities (Graden, Casey, & Bonstrom, 1983): (1) making a formal request for services, (2) clarifying the problem, (3) designing the interventions, (4) implementing the interventions, and (5) evaluating the interventions' effects.

Making the Request

Because prereferral intervention is a formalized process, a formal request for services may be required and might be made on a form similar to that shown in Figure 28.1. When a prereferral form is used, it should contain identifying information (such as teacher and student names), the specific problems for which the teacher is seeking consultation, the interventions that have already been attempted in the classroom, the effectiveness of those interventions, and current academic instructional levels. This information allows those responsible for providing consultation to decide whether the problem warrants their further attention.

Clarifying the Problem

In the initial consultation, the team works with the classroom teacher to specify the nature of a problem or the specific areas of difficulty. These difficulties should be stated in terms of observable behavior, not hypothesized causes of the problem. For example, the teacher may specify a problem by saying that "Jenna does not write legibly" or that "Nick does not complete homework assignments as regularly as other students in his class." The focus is on the discrepancy between actual and desired performance.

The team may seek additional information. For example, the referring teacher may be asked to describe in some detail the contexts in which problems occur, the student's curriculum, the way in which the teacher interacts with or responds to the student, the student's interactions with the teacher and with classmates, the student's instructional groupings and seating arrangements, and antecedents and consequences of the student's behaviors. The referring teacher may also be asked to specify the ways in which the student's behavior affects the teacher or other students and the extent to which the behavior is incongruent

FIGURE 28.1
Request for Prereferral
Consultation

Request for Prereferral Consultation

Student _____ Gender _____ Date of Birth _____

Referring Teacher _____ Grade _____ School _____

Specific Educational/Behavioral Problems:

_____

_____

_____

_____

Current Level or Materials in Deficit Areas:

_____

_____

_____

Specific Interventions to Improve Performance in Deficit Areas and
Their Effectiveness:

_____

_____

_____

_____

What Special Services Does the Student Receive
(e.g., Title I Reading, Speech Therapy)?

_____

_____

Most Convenient Days and Times for Consultation:

_____

_____

with the teacher's expectations. When multiple problems are identified, they may
be ranked in order of importance for action.

Finally, as part of the consultation, a member of the staff support team may
observe the pupil in the classroom to verify the nature and extent of the problem. In relevant school settings, a designated member of the team observes the
student, notes the frequency and duration of behaviors of concern, and ascertains the extent to which the student's behavior differs from that of classmates.
At this point (or later in the process), the perceptions of the student and the student's parents may also be sought.

Designing the Interventions

Next, the team and the referring teacher design interventions to remediate the most pressing problems. The team may need to coach the referring teacher on how to implement the interventions. Initially, the interventions should be based on empirically validated procedures that are known to be generally effective. In addition, parents, other school personnel, and the student may be involved in the intervention.

A major factor determining whether an intervention will be tried or implemented by teachers is feasibility. Those who conduct assessments and make recommendations about teaching must consider the extent to which the interventions they recommend are doable. (Unfortunately, too often feasibility is determined on the basis of how much of a hassle the intervention planning will be or how much work it will take to implement a given program.) Phillips (1990) identifies eight major considerations in making decisions about feasibility, which we suggest that assessors address.

1. *Degree of disruption.* How much will the intervention the teacher recommends disrupt school procedures or teacher routines?
2. *Side effects.* To what extent are there undesirable side effects for the student (for example, social ostracism), peers, home and family, and faculty?
3. *Support services required.* How readily available are the support services required, and are the costs reasonable?
4. *Prerequisite competencies.* Does the teacher have the necessary knowledge, motivation, and experience to be able to implement the intervention? Does the teacher have a philosophical bias against the recommended intervention?
5. *Control.* Does the teacher have control of the necessary variables to ensure the success of the intervention?
6. *Immediacy of results.* Will the student's behavioral change be quick enough for the teacher to be reinforced for implementing the intervention?
7. *Consequences of nonintervention.* What are the short- and long-term prognoses for the student if the behaviors are left uncorrected?
8. *Potential for transition.* Is it reasonable to expect that the intervention will lead to student self-regulation and generalize to other settings, other curriculum areas, or even other students who are experiencing similar difficulties?

The intervention plan should include a clear delineation of the skills to be developed or the behavior to be changed, the methods to be used to effect the change, the duration of the intervention, the location of the intervention, and the names of the individuals responsible for each aspect of the intervention. Moreover, the criterion for a successful intervention should be clear. At a minimum, the intervention should bring a student's performance to an acceptable or tolerable level. For academic difficulties, this usually means accelerating the rate of acquisition. For an instructional isolate, achievement must improve sufficiently to allow placement in an instructional group. For example, if Bernie currently cannot read the material used in the lowest reading group, the team would need to know the level of the materials used by the lowest instructional group. In addition, the team would need to know the probable level of materials that the group will be using when Bernie's intervention has been completed. For students with more variable patterns of achievement, intervention is directed toward improving performance in areas of weakness to a level that approximates performance in areas of strength.

Setting the criterion for a behavioral intervention involves much the same process as setting targets for academic problems. When the goal is to change behavior, the teacher should select two or three students who are behaving appropriately. These students should not be the best-behaved students but those in the middle of the range of acceptable behavior. The frequency, duration, latency, or amplitude of their behavior should be used as the criterion. Usually the behavior of the appropriate students is stable, so the team does not have to predict where they will be at the end of the intervention.

Implicit in this discussion is the idea that the interventions will reach the criterion for success within the time allotted. Thus the team not only desires progress toward the criterion, but also wants that progress to occur at a specific rate—or faster. Finally, it is generally a good idea to maintain a written record of these details. This record might be as informal as a set of notes from the team meeting, or it might be a formal document such as the Prereferral Intervention Plan shown in Figure 28.2.

Implementing the Interventions

The interventions should then be conducted as planned. Occasionally, to ensure that the intervention is being carried out faithfully, a member of the team will observe the teacher using the planned strategy or special materials.

Evaluating the Effects of the Interventions

The effects of the interventions should be evaluated frequently enough to allow fine-tuning of the teaching methods and materials. Frequently, student performance is graphed to create learning pictures (Salvia & Hughes, 1990). Effective programs designed to increase desired behavior produce results like those shown in Figure 28.3: The student usually shows an increase in the desired behavior (correct responses) and a decrease in the number of errors (incorrect responses). It is also possible for successful programs to produce only increasingly correct responses or only a decrease in errors. Ineffective programs show no increase in the desired correct responses, no decrease in the unwanted errors, or both.

To assess a student's rate of behavior change, we graph the acceleration of a desired behavior (or the deceleration of an undesired behavior) as a separate line, called an "aimline," as shown in Figure 28.4. The aimline connects the student's current level of performance with the point that represents both the desired level of behavior and the time at which the behavior is to be attained. The student's progress is compared with the aimline. When behavior is targeted for

FIGURE 28.2
Prereferral
Intervention Plan

Prereferral Intervention Plan

Complete one form for each targeted problem.

Student _____ Gender _____ Date of Birth _____

Referring Teacher _____ Grade _____ School _____

Intervention Objectives

Behavior to be changed:

Criterion for success/termination of intervention:

Duration of intervention:

Location of intervention:

Person responsible for implementing the intervention:

Strategies

Instructional methods:

Instructional materials:

Special equipment:

Signatures

_____   _____
(Referring Teacher)   (Date)

_____   _____
(Member, Teacher Assistance Team)   (Date)

increase, we expect the student's progress to be above the aimline (as shown in Figure 28.4); when behavior is targeted for decrease, we expect the student's progress to be below the aimline (not shown). Thus a teacher, the intervention assistance team, or the student can look at the graph and make a decision about the adequacy of progress.

When adequate progress is being made, the intervention should obviously be continued until the criterion is reached. When better-than-anticipated progress is being made, the teacher or team can decide to set a more ambitious goal (that is, raise the level of desired performance) without changing the aim date, or they

FIGURE 28.3
A Successful
Learning Intervention

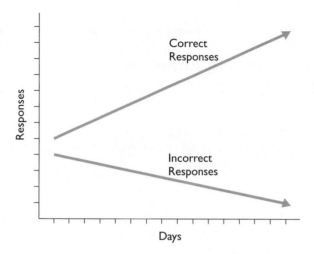

Correct
Responses

Incorrect
Responses

Days

can set an earlier target for achieving the criterion without changing the level of performance.

When inadequate progress is being made, teachers can take several steps to fine-tune the student's program. Salvia and Hughes (1990, pp. 121–122) offer various suggestions for instructional modification, depending on the pattern of student performance in relation to the aimline. Although a discussion of instructional methods is beyond the scope of this text, some examples can illustrate the kinds of things a teacher might do when faced with inadequate progress. When a student demonstrates no correct responses (or too few), the goal may be too difficult; the team should consider changing the goal to include attainment of a prerequisite skill. When a student demonstrates correct responses but too many errors, the teacher should consider modeling or prompting and more closely monitoring practice. When a student demonstrates accurate but slow responding, the teacher can encourage faster performance by providing incentives or ad-

FIGURE 28.4
Student Progress
with an Aimline

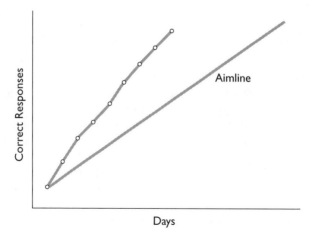

Aimline

Days

ditional practice. When performance is consistently below the aimline (three days is generally considered a significant amount of time), the teacher might consider varying the instructional methods or incentives. Finally, when a student's performance worsens, the teacher should question the motivational value of the task, vary any drill or practice activities, or discuss the performance directly with the student.

Decision: Should the Student Be Referred for Multidisciplinary Evaluation?

When several attempted interventions have not led to sufficient success, the student is likely to be referred for psychoeducational evaluation to ascertain eligibility for special education.

Example 6. Alex's teacher found an easier reader for him and read individually with him for five minutes each day. During this time, Mr. Santos corrected his errors and showed him how to sound out words. Although Alex could read the lower-level materials more fluently, he was unable to advance to more grade-appropriate reading materials (that is, his fluency and error rate were below an instructional level). The building assistance team recommended that the teacher assess Alex's knowledge of letter-sound associations. Alex was found to know all long vowel sounds, the short *a* sound, and hard consonant sounds. Consequently, the team developed a program that targeted the sounds of the consonants and vowels that he had not yet mastered. One of the district's reading specialists administered the intervention daily and evaluated his progress every other day. Assessment data to ascertain the effectiveness of the intervention consisted of Alex's progress in learning letter-sound associations and his oral reading fluency. The reading specialist administered a letter-sound probe after each day's instruction. After four weeks of intervention, Alex had learned half of the unknown soft consonant sounds as well as the short *e* and *i* sounds. A retest of his oral reading fluency indicated that he had become fluent in the next higher reading level. At the rate he was improving, he would fall at least another half-year behind his peers at the end of the current school year. Because the intervention selected had support in the research literature but had not proved sufficiently effective with Alex, he was referred for multidisciplinary evaluation to ascertain if there were nonschool factors that could be impeding his learning (for example, a disability).

Determination of eligibility requires further assessment by specialists, such as school psychologists, who use commercially prepared instruments. These instruments are discussed in the chapters "Assessment of Intelligence: Individual Tests" and "Assessment of Adaptive Behavior." Eligibility and related decision making are discussed in the chapters "Assessment of Intelligence: An Overview" and "Making Entitlement Decisions."

Decisions Made in Special Education

After students have been determined to be eligible for special education, special education decisions revolve around design and implementation of their individualized education plans (IEPs). An IEP is a blueprint for instruction and specifies the goals, procedures, and related services for an individual eligible student. Assessment data are important for such planning. Numerous books and hundreds of articles in professional and scientific journals discuss the importance of using assessment data to plan instructional programs for students. The Individuals with Disabilities Education Act requires a thorough assessment that results in an IEP. Pupils are treated differentially on the basis of their IEPs. Moreover, most educators would agree that it is desirable to individualize programs for students in special and remedial education because the general education programs have not proved beneficial to them.

Decision: What Should Be Included in a Student's IEP?

The Individuals with Disabilities Education Act of 1997 and regulations published in June 1999 set forth the requirements for IEPs. Instructionally, an IEP is a road map of a student's one-year trip from point A to point B. This road map is prepared collaboratively by an IEP team composed of the parents and student (when appropriate), at least one general education teacher, at least one of the student's special education teachers, a representative of the school administration, an individual who can interpret the instructional implications of evaluation results, and other individuals who have knowledge or special expertise regarding the student.

The IEP begins with a description of the student's current educational levels—the starting point of the metaphoric trip. Next, the IEP specifies measurable, annual, academic and functional goals (the student's destination). The IEP must include a description of how progress toward meeting annual goals will be measured and when progress reports will be provided to parents. The IEP must identify the special education and related services that are based on peer-reviewed research (to the extent practicable) needed by the student in order to reach the goals (the method of transportation and provisions that make the trip possible). Finally, the IEP requires measurement, evaluation, and reporting of the student's progress toward the annual goals (periodic checks to make sure the student is on the right road and traveling fast enough).

Current Levels

A student's current level of performance is not specifically defined in the regulations. However, because current levels are the starting points for instruction, a current level must be instructionally relevant and expressed quantitatively. Although legally permissible, scores from standardized achievement are not particularly useful. The fact that a student is reading less well than 90 percent of students in the grade is not useful information about where the teacher should begin instruction. If a student is physically aggressive in the third-grade classroom, that alone is too vague to allow a teacher, parents, and the student to tell whether progress toward acceptable behavior is being made. We think a current educational level in an academic area should be the level at which a student is appropriately instructed.

Example 7. For the sake of this example, assume that Alex has been found eligible for special education services as a student with a learning disability in reading. To ascertain Alex's current level of performance in oral reading, he was again assessed by having him read from the materials actually used in his school. Two passages of 300 to 400 words that were representative of the beginning, middle, and end of each grade-level reading text were selected. Because Alex was already known to be reading only slightly above the preprimer level, he was asked to start reading at that level. He read passages of increasing difficulty until he was no longer reading at an instructional level (that is, reading with 85 to 95 percent accuracy[2]). Alex read beginning first-grade materials with 95 percent accuracy, but he read middle second-grade material with only 87 percent accuracy. Thus his current instructional level in oral reading was determined to be middle second grade.

Current educational level in behavioral areas should also be quantified. Frequency, duration, latency, and amplitude can be quantified, and the results compared to those of a peer who is performing satisfactorily on the target skill or behavior.

Example 8. For the sake of this example, assume that Nick has also been found eligible for special education services as a student with other health impairments (attention deficit disorder without hyperactivity). To ascertain the duration of Nick's attention to task during academic instruction, the school counselor systematically observed Nick and another student who was not reported to be having attention problems. Observations occurred between 10:00 and 10:45 for a week during reading and arithmetic instruction. Nick's teacher did not use the tapping cue during this time period. The counselor sat in behind and to Nick's side, and used an audio signal tape with beeps at a fixed interval of 30 seconds. The counselor calculated that Nick was on task 35 percent of the time, while during the same times, his peer was on task 93 percent of the time. Nick's current level of attention to academic tasks is 35 percent.

Goal IEPs must contain a statement of measurable annual goals, including benchmarks or short-term objectives, which meet each educational need arising from the student's disability and ensure the student's access to the general education curriculum (or appropriate activities, if a preschooler). Thus, for each area of need, parents and schools must agree on what should be a student's level of achievement after a year of instruction.

The Context of Goal Setting

In part, the selection of long-term goals is based on the aspirations and prognosis for a student's postschool outcomes. Although these are not formally required until a special education student reaches 14 years of age, the expected or desired postschool outcomes shape the special education a student receives. For students

---

[2] To calculate accuracy, first find the number of words with two or more letters. Then count the number of errors; for example, words a reader cannot decode correctly and words a reader incorrectly adds to the text. See the chapter "Assessment of Reading" for a discussion of errors in oral reading.

with pervasive and severe cognitive disabilities, the prognosis may be assisted living without employment. With this prognosis, educational goals are likely to be daily living and leisure rather than academic areas. For students with more moderate disabilities, the prognosis may be independent living and unskilled or semi-skilled employment. With this prognosis, educational goals are likely to be academic and vocational. For students with mild disabilities, the prognosis may be professional or highly skilled employment. For these students, educational goals are likely to lead to the college or technical preparatory curriculum.

In part, the selection of long-term goals is based on the degree to which the educational deficit caused by the disability is remediable. All students receiving special education will lag significantly behind their nondisabled peers.[3] Except when students have severe and pervasive disabilities, special educators and parents generally try to remediate the educational deficits first. The benefit of this approach is that it allows the student the fullest access to later school and postschool opportunities. When remediation repeatedly fails, parents and teachers usually turn to compensatory mechanisms so that the student can attain the more generally desired educational outcomes. For example, if Cliff just cannot learn math facts, he may be allowed to use a calculator. The advantage of this option is that it allows Cliff to move to higher curricular goals; the disadvantage is that the deficits will always be with Cliff, and he will always behave to compensate for them. When a student cannot master the curriculum with compensatory mechanisms, parents and teachers may adapt the curriculum by reducing the complexity of some components. For example, in social studies all students might be required to learn about taxes, but Lashaun might not have to learn about the constitutional issues surrounding the creation of the federal income tax. If reducing the complexity is not appropriate, areas of the curriculum may be eliminated for individual students with disabilities.

Obviously, this option is the last resort, but it may be appropriate when a child's disabilities are profound. For example, we would not expect all deaf students to be fluent oral communicators, although we would expect them to attain other generally prescribed educational outcomes; we would not expect quadriplegics to pass a swimming test, although we might well expect them to meet other educational outcomes.

Specific Goals

Annual goals are derived directly from a student's curriculum and a student's current instructional levels. When continued academic integration is the desired educational outcome, a student's goals are mastery of the same content at the same rate as nondisabled peers. Thus, after one year, the student would be expected to be instructional in the same materials as his or her peers. When reintegration is the desired educational outcome, a student's goal depends on where the regular class peers will be in one year. For students pursuing alternative cur-

---

[3] Some gifted students have learning disabilities. Thus these gifted students will also have significant deficits.

ricula, the IEP team makes an educated guess about where the student will be after one year of instruction.

Example 9. Alex is finishing third grade, so his annual goal specifies his desired performance near the end of fourth grade. If he were to be completely caught up with his peers, Alex would read independently in his fourth-grade materials. (If his teacher or school uses different levels of reading materials for different tracks of students, he would need to read independently the materials used by the lowest track in regular education.) For the sake of this example, let us assume that the lowest group will use reading materials written at the middle third-grade level at the end of fourth grade. Thus, for Alex to be "caught up" with his peers, he would need to complete about 3.3 years in 1 year. Because this much growth in reading could not likely be attained without omitting instruction in other key curricular areas (such as science and written language), the IEP team decides to take two years to try to catch Alex up to his age peers. Thus his annual goal becomes "At the end of one year of instruction in oral reading Alex will read material written at the end of second-grade difficulty level with 95 percent accuracy."

Specially Designed Instruction

The Individuals with Disabilities Act defines special education, in part, as specially designed instruction that is provided in classrooms, the home, or other settings (see §300.26). It includes the adaptation of instructional content, methods, or delivery to meet the needs of a student with disabilities.

Historically, psychologists and educators have been interested in how a student's abilities affect instructional methods, in the belief that, if instruction can be matched to specific abilities, students will learn better. In special education, this approach led to a search for test-identified strengths and weaknesses and, subsequently, to the development of instructional procedures that capitalized on areas of strength or avoided weaker abilities. For example, test scores from the first edition of the Developmental Test of Visual Perception (Frostig, Maslow, Lefever, & Whittlesey, 1964), the Illinois Test of Psycholinguistic Abilities (Kirk, McCarthy, & Kirk, 1968), and the Purdue Perceptual-Motor Survey (Roach & Kephart, 1966) were at one time believed to have instructional meaning. In part because test-identified abilities were frequently unreliable and in part because special instructional methods did not result in better learning, this approach to instruction gradually lost favor, although some educators today still cling to a belief in it.

In the 1980s, attempts to match instruction to specific student attributes resurfaced. However, hypothetical cognitive structures and learning processes replaced the hypothetical abilities of the 1960s (for example, see Resnick, 1987). Although this approach offered promise, it has yet to be validated. One advocate of this approach has noted, "Widespread adoption and application will require much more work and is likely more than a few years away" (Bruer, 1993, p. 263). His opinion is still correct: Much more work is needed, and application, if it comes, is likely a few decades away.

At present, the best way to teach handicapped learners appears to rely on generally effective procedures. Teachers can do several things to make it easier for their pupils to learn facts and concepts, skills, or behavior. They can model the desired behavior. They can break down the terminal goal into its component parts and teach each of the steps and their integration. They can teach the objective in a variety of contexts with a variety of materials to facilitate generalization. They can provide time for practice, and they can choose the schedule on which practice is done (in other words, they can offer distributed or massed practice). Several techniques that are under the direct control of the teacher can be employed to instruct any learner effectively. To help pupils recall information that has been taught, teachers may organize the material that a pupil is to learn, provide rehearsal strategies, or employ overlearning or distributed practice. There are also a number of things that teachers can do to elicit responses that have already been acquired: Various reinforcers and punishers have been shown to be effective in the control of behavior.

Assessment personnel can help teachers identify specific areas in which instructional difficulties exist, and they can help teachers plan interventions in light of information gained from assessments. Certain procedures (Ysseldyke & Christenson, 1987b; Ysseldyke, Christenson, & Kovaleski, 1994) can aid assessment personnel in determining the nature of students' instructional environments. Procedures such as the Instructional Environment System–II (Ysseldyke & Christenson, 1993) may be used both to pinpoint the extent to which a student's academic or behavioral problems are a function of factors in the instructional environment and to identify likely starting points for designing appropriate interventions for individual students. Yet there is just no way to know for certain ahead of time how best to teach a specific student.

We recommend that teachers first rely on general principles that are known and demonstrated to be effective in facilitating learning for students with disabilities. However, we can seldom find validated translations of these principles into actual classroom activities and procedures. Moreover, even if we did find studies that demonstrated that a particular application of a learning principle worked for a research sample, we still could not be certain that it would work for specific students in a specific classroom. The odds are that it will, but we cannot be sure. Consequently, we must treat our translation of these principles, known to be effective, as tentative. In a real sense, we hypothesize that our treatment will work, but we need to verify that it has worked. The point was made years ago by Deno and Mirkin (1977, p. 11) and remains true today:

> At the present time we are unable to prescribe specific and effective changes in instruction for individual pupils with certainty. Therefore, changes in instructional programs that are arranged for an individual child can be treated only as hypotheses that must be empirically tested before a decision can be made about whether they are effective for that child.

Teaching is experimental in nature. Generally, there is no database to guide our selection of specific tasks or materials. Decisions are made about particular strategies, methods, and materials to use in instruction, but these decisions must be tentative. The decision maker makes some good guesses about what will work and then implements an instructional program. We do not know whether a decision is correct until we gather data on the extent to which the instructional program actually works. We never know the program will work until it has worked.

Tests do provide some very limited information about how to teach. Tests of intelligence, for example, yield information that gives a teacher some hints about teaching. Generally, the lower a pupil's intelligence, the more practice the student will require for mastery. A score of 55 on the Wechsler Intelligence Scale for Children–III does not tell the teacher whether a pupil needs 25 percent or 250 percent more practice, but it does alert the teacher to the likelihood that the pupil will need more practice than the average student will. Other tenuous hints can be derived, but we feel that it is better to rely on direct observation of how a student learns in order to make adjustments in the learning program. Thus, to see whether we had provided enough practice, we would observe Sally's recall of information rather than looking at Sally's IQ. We cannot do anything about Sally's IQ, but we can do something about the amount of practice she gets.

Example 10. The assessment data pointed to areas where Nick needed specially designed instruction. Although Nick's physician prescribed Ritalin, Nick also needed systematic behavioral intervention to minimize the effects of his attention deficit disorder on school functioning.[4] The team developed a program of specially designed instruction that included systematic reinforcement for appropriate attention and systematic instruction in self-monitoring his attention. The district behavior management specialist will be responsible for training Nick to self-monitor accurately, and Nick's teacher will be trained to implement the plan developed by the district specialist.

Example 11. The assessment data also indicated that Alex needs specially designed instruction in reading. Although he had now mastered all of the sounds of consonants and vowels, he was slow and inaccurate in reading grade-appropriate materials. To improve Alex's accuracy, the IEP team decided that Alex should be taught the basic site vocabulary needed to read the words in his language arts text as well as content-area curricula. To improve Alex's reading fluency, the IEP team decided to use the strategy of rereading.

Least Restrictive Appropriate Environment   Federal law expresses a clear preference for educating students with disabilities as close as possible to their home and with their nondisabled peers to the maximum extent appropriate. Education in "special classes, separate schooling or other removal of children with disabilities from the regular educational environment occurs only if the nature or severity of the disability is such that education in regular classes with the use of supplementary aids and services cannot be achieved satisfactorily" (*Federal Register,* 1999, §300.550).

---

[4] Assume that Nick's psychoeducational evaluation did not reveal other intellectual, physical, or cognitive problems beyond his lack of attention.

Placement Options

A hierarchy of placements ranges from the least restrictive (educating students with disabilities in a general education classroom with a general education teacher who receives consultative services from a special education teacher) to the most restrictive (educating students with disabilities in segregated residential facilities that provide services only to students with disabilities). Between these two extremes are at least five other options:

1. *Instructional support from a special education teacher in the general education classroom.* In this arrangement, eligible students remain in the general education classroom in their neighborhood schools, and the special education teacher comes to the student to provide whatever specialized instruction is necessary.

2. *Instructional support from a special education teacher in a resource room.* In this arrangement, eligible students remain in a general education classroom for most of the day. When they need specialized instruction, they go to a special education resource room to receive services from a special education teacher. Because districts may not have enough students with disabilities in each school to warrant establishing a resource room program at each school, a student may be assigned to a general education classroom that is not in the student's neighborhood school.

3. *Part-time instruction in a special education classroom.* In this arrangement, eligible students have some classes or subject matter taught by the special education teacher and the rest taught in the general education classroom. As is the case with resource rooms, the general education classroom may not be in the student's neighborhood school.

4. *Full-time instruction in a special education classroom, with limited integration.* In this arrangement, eligible students receive all academic instruction from a special education teacher in a special classroom. Eligible students may be integrated with nondisabled peers for special events or activities (such as lunch, recess, and assemblies) and nonacademic classes (such as art and music).

5. *Full-time instruction in a special education classroom, without integration.* In this arrangement, eligible students have no interaction with their nondisabled peers, and their classrooms may be in a special day school that serves only students with disabilities.

Factors Affecting the Placement Choice

The selection of a particular option should be based on the intensity of education needed by the eligible student: the less intensive the intervention needed by the student, the less restrictive the environment; the more intensive the intervention needed by the student, the more restrictive the environment. The procedure for determining the intensity of an intervention is less than scientific. Frequently, there is some correspondence between the severity of disability and the intensity of service needed, but that correspondence is not perfect. Therefore, special education teachers and parents should consider the frequency and duration of the needed interventions. The more frequent an intervention is (for instance, every morning versus one morning per week) and the longer its duration (for example, 30 minutes versus 15 minutes per morning), the more likely it is that the intervention will be provided in more, rather than less, restrictive settings. When frequent and long interventions are needed, the student will have less opportunity to participate with nondisabled peers, no matter what the student's placement. Obviously, if students require round-the-clock intervention, they cannot get what they need from a resource room program.

In addition to the nature of needed interventions, parents and teachers may also reasonably consider the following factors when deciding on the type of placement:

1. *Disruption.* Bringing a special education teacher into or pulling a student out of a general education classroom may be disruptive. For example, some students with disabilities cannot handle transitions: They get lost between classrooms, or they forget to go to their resource rooms. When eligible students have a lot of difficulty changing schedules or making transitions between events, then less restrictive options may not be appropriate.

2. *Well-being of nondisabled individuals.* Eligible students will seldom be integrated when they present a clear danger to the welfare of nondisabled peers or teachers. For example, assaultive and disruptive students are likely to be placed in more restrictive environments.

3. *Well-being of the student who has a disability.* Many students with disabilities require some degree of protection—in some cases, from nondisabled peers who may tease or physically abuse a student who is different; in other cases, from other students with disabilities. For example, the parents of a seriously withdrawn student may decide not to place their child in a classroom for students with emotional disabilities when those students are assaultive.

4. *Labeling.* Many parents, especially those of students with milder handicaps, reject disability labels. They desire special education services, but they want these services without having their child labeled. Such parents often prefer consultative or itinerant services for their children.

5. *Inclusion.* Some parents are willing to forgo the instructional benefits of special education for the potential social benefits of having their children educated exclusively with nondisabled peers. For such parents, full inclusion is the only option.

There are also pragmatic considerations in selecting the educational setting. One very real consideration is that a school district may, for economic reasons, not be able to provide a full range of options. In such districts, parents are offered a choice among existing options unless they are willing to go through a due-process hearing or a court trial. A second consideration is instructional efficiency. When several students require the same intervention, the special education teacher can often form an instructional group. Thus it will probably cost less to provide the special education services. A third consideration is the specific teachers. Some teachers are better than others, and parents may well opt for a more highly regarded teacher who works in a more restrictive setting.

Parents and special education teachers must realize that selecting a placement option is an imprecise endeavor. Thus, although federal regulations are clear in their preference for less restrictive placements, the criteria that guide the selection of one option over another are unclear. Choices among placement options should be regarded as best guesses.

Example 12. Although Nick's behavior was not disruptive or detrimental to the learning of his peers, the interventions that his regular class teacher had used were distracting to the other students. However, the team felt that the specially designed instruction (systematic reinforcement for appropriate attention and self-monitoring) that had been approved by the team would be much less intrusive. Therefore, the team felt that the impact of the intervention on Nick's peers would not be a consideration in where the special education services would be provided.

The positive reinforcement can be administered correctly by the classroom teacher once properly trained by the behavior management specialist. Although the behavior management specialist will remove Nick from class when teaching him to self-monitor, Nick's use of the self-monitoring system will be evaluated in his classroom by the special education teacher and the behavior specialist. Thus Nick's needs can readily be met in the regular classroom; he will not be instructed in a special education setting.

Example 13. Because the reading interventions designed by the IEP team were not being used in Alex's classroom and because Alex required more instruction in reading than could be provided in his regular classroom, the IEP team recommended placement in a special education resource room for one hour per day. The team decided that Alex would go to the resource room when the rest of his class was being instructed in social studies and art.

Related Services

In addition to special instruction, eligible students are entitled to developmental, corrective, and other supportive services if such services are needed in order for the students to benefit from special education; federal legislation uses the term *related services*, which has been widely adopted by states and school districts. Related services include both those not typically provided by schools and those typically provided (*Federal Register,* 1999, §300.24).

Types of Services

Schools must provide to students with disabilities a variety of services to which nondisabled students are seldom entitled. Services include, but are not limited to, the following types:

1. *Audiology.* Allowable services include evaluation of hearing, habilitation (for example, programs in auditory training, speech reading, and speech

conservation), amplification (including the fitting of hearing aids), and hearing conservation programs.

2. *Psychological services.* Psychological services allowed include testing, observation, and consultation.

3. *Physical and occupational therapy.* These therapies can be used to (a) improve, develop, or restore functional impairments caused by illness, injury, or deprivation; and (b) improve independent functioning. These therapies may also be used with preschool populations to prevent impairment or further loss of function.

4. *Recreational therapy.* Allowable programs include those located in the schools and community agencies that provide general recreation programs, therapeutic recreation, and assessment of leisure functioning.

5. *Counseling services.* Either group or individual counseling may be provided for students and their parents. Student counseling includes rehabilitation counseling that focuses on career development, employment preparation, achievement of independence, and integration in the workplace and community; it also includes psychological counseling. Parental counseling includes therapies addressing problems in the student's living situation (that is, home, school, and community) that affect the student's schooling. Parental counseling also includes assistance to help parents understand their child's special needs, as well as information about child development.

6. *Medical services.* Diagnostic and evaluative services required to determine medically related disabilities are allowed.

The schools must also provide to students with disabilities the services they typically provide to all children. Thus schools must provide to students with disabilities, as needed, speech and language services, school health and school social work services, and transportation. School-provided transportation includes whatever is needed to get students to and from school, as well as between schools or among school buildings, including any required special equipment, such as ramps. Although these related services are mandatory for students who need them to profit from their special education, there is nothing to prohibit a school from offering other services. Thus schools may offer additional services free of charge to eligible students.

Establishing Need for Related Services

Although federal law is very clear about the need to provide related services to students with disabilities, how that need should be established remains unclear. In practice, most schools or parents seek an evaluation by a specialist. The specialist notes a problem and expresses a belief that a specific therapy could be successful and benefit the student. Thus need is frequently based on professional opinion.

We must also note that related services can be very costly, and some school districts try to avoid providing them. We have heard of districts maintaining that they do not offer a particular service, even though that service is mandated by law for students who need it.

SUMMARY

Both general educators and special educators have responsibilities for students with disabilities. These responsibilities vary as a function of the severity of a student's disability and the way in which individual states and school districts provide educational services. However, both general and special education personnel will necessarily be involved in decision making with regard to students with exceptional needs. General educators may be involved in identifying students with severe learning or behavioral problems who are believed to be in need of special education services. They may be involved in providing extra assistance to students who are experiencing difficulties in the general education classroom. When the extra assistance is insufficient to meet the students' needs, regular educators are involved in referrals for psychoeducational evaluation.

When this evaluation indicates that a student is entitled to special education or related services, a number of other decisions must be made. All students receiving special education must have IEPs. As part of the process of developing an IEP, educators and parents (as well as other individuals) participate on decision-making teams to select appropriate educational or habilitative goals, instructional methods, related services, and the setting in which the student will receive special education. The decisions made by educators should be based on accurate and meaningful data.

QUESTIONS FOR CHAPTER REVIEW

1. Give five examples of why classroom instruction may be ineffective for a specific student.

2. Explain the concept of "least restrictive environment." What are the most important components of this concept, and on what types of information would educators base decisions regarding their choice of environment?

3. List three related services that a special education student might need to receive.

4. Jerome is a second-grade student who has enrolled in Blake School during early December. He has moved into the area from another state. No records were sent from the school his mother said that he previously attended, and calls by Blake School personnel to that school indicate that he was not enrolled there. Within the first few weeks of his entry into her class, Ms. Jones has noticed that Jerome is far behind his classmates in reading and math skills. Describe what would be the best practice in addressing this problem.

PROJECT

Talk to two teachers, each of whom is from a different school district, about the prereferral process and how it works in their schools. Explore whether each process is formalized or informal. Ask parents, students, or teachers at each school for their opinions about how well that school's process works.

RESOURCES FOR FURTHER INVESTIGATION

Print Resources

Farlow, L. J., & Snell, M. E. (1989). Teacher use of student performance data to make instructional decisions: Practices in programs for students with moderate to profound disabilities. *Journal of the Association for Persons with Severe Handicaps, 14*(1), 13–22.

Pretti-Frontczak, K., & Bricker, D. (2000). Enhancing the quality of individualized education plan (IEP) goals and objectives. *Journal of Early Intervention, 23*(2), 92–105.

Rosenshine, B. (1995). Advances in research on instruction. *Journal of Educational Research, 88,* 262–268.

Salvia, J., & Hughes, C. (1990). *Curriculum-based assessment: Testing what is taught* (Chapter 2, Specify Reasons for Assessment). New York: Macmillan.

Technology Resources

IEP: INVOLVING THE STUDENT IS IMPORTANT
FOR A SUCCESSFUL PLAN
www.nfb.org/involve.htm
This article discusses the benefits of involving students in the planning of their own IEP.

INVOLVING PARENTS IN THE IEP PROCESS
**www.ed.gov/databases/ERIC_Digests/
ed455658.html**
This article discusses how to facilitate meaningful parent participation in the IEP process.

CHAPTER 29

Making Entitlement Decisions

ENTITLEMENT GIVES RIGHTS TO INDIVIDUALS BASED ON THEIR CLASSIFICATION. INDIviduals who meet various disability criteria are entitled to special benefits as specified in state and federal law. Individuals who do not meet the criteria are not entitled to those benefits. Although the rationale for policies to provide special help to only some students with special needs is seldom made explicit, there are clearly political and scientific components to the decision. First, new disabilities must be recognized within the scientific and professional communities. For example, psychologists and educators were aware that some otherwise bright and capable children had major difficulties in learning to read, write, spell, or learn the basic math facts. Many of these students were motivated and tried hard to learn, but they just could not master even the basics. Educators and psychologists studied these children and learned that many had difficulties with perception, motor skills, or language that were believed to cause the learning problems. They began to classify these behavioral symptoms into syndromes such as perceptual handicap, minimal brain dysfunction, developmental aphasia, learning disability, and so forth. By the early 1970s, parents joined with educators and other professionals to successfully lobby the federal government to recognize learning disability as a disability under the Education for All Handicapped Children Act (Public Law 94-142) and to provide various protections and entitlements, including special education. More recently, autism spectrum disorder has followed a similar path to recognition as a disability with special protections and entitlements. Until the late 1980s, attention deficits were not considered a separate disability and were not specifically covered in the education regulations. Parents lobbied legislatures and argued successfully in court that their children should be entitled to special protections and entitlements. In 1999, attention deficit disorder was specifically included in the regulations for the Individuals with Disabilities Education Act (IDEA). To our knowledge, once a disability has been recognized and entitled under the law, that entitlement has never been removed.

Official Student Disabilities

Students are classified as disabled under several laws; three are particularly important. The Americans with Disabilities Act (Public Law 101-336) defines a disability as a physical or mental impairment that substantially limits one or more of the major life activities of an individual. The act defines physical or mental impairment as any physiological disorder, including cosmetic disfigurement, or anatomical loss affecting one or more body systems. Specifically included as mental and psychological disorders are orthopedic, visual, speech, and hearing impairments; cerebral palsy; epilepsy; muscular dystrophy; multiple sclerosis; cancer; heart disease; diabetes; mental retardation; emotional illness; specific learning disabilities; HIV disease; tuberculosis; drug addiction; and alcoholism. Section 504 of the Rehabilitation Act of 1973 defines a physical or mental impairment as a physiological disorder or condition, cosmetic disfigurement, or anatomical loss, or a mental or psychological disorder, such as mental retardation, organic brain syndrome, emotional or mental illness, and specific learning disabilities. In the schools and other educational settings, the disabilities enumerated in regulations of the IDEA (34 CFR §300.7) are the most frequently used. The following disabilities are recognized in the IDEA: autism, mental retardation, specific learning disability, emotional disturbance, traumatic brain injury, speech or language impairment, visual impairment, deafness and hearing impairment, orthopedic impairments, other health impairments, deaf–blindness, multiple disabilities, and developmental delay.

Entitlements

With governmental recognition of a disability comes entitlement to special treatment in the schools. The special treatment consists of four types: procedural safeguards, special services, altered outcome expectancies, and special fiscal arrangements.

Procedural Safeguards

Students who are disabled (or are believed to be disabled) are afforded several procedural safeguards beyond those offered to any other students. These safeguards are discussed in detail in the chapter "Legal and Ethical Considerations in Assessment." Here, we only reiterate the safeguards usually associated with disability:

- Notice prior to identification, evaluation, or educational placement[1]
- Parental participation in multidisciplinary teams to determine disability
- Parental participation in team meetings to ascertain eligibility and to plan educational programs
- Protection from unfair, biased, and inappropriate evaluation

[1] If the parent of a child does not consent to an initial evaluation (or the parent fails to respond to a request to provide the consent), some states allow a school district to use the due-process hearing procedures to obtain authority for evaluation. See §614(a)(1)(D)(ii)(I).

■ Right to independent evaluations

■ Recourse to administrative due-process proceedings to redress specifically enumerated grievances

Special Services   The federal and state governments extend special benefits to disabled students. All students with disabilities are entitled to access to an appropriate educational program. Access includes providing a disabled student with specialized transportation (for example, using a van that can accommodate a student in a wheelchair) and an accessible classroom (for example, replacing stairs with ramps to accommodate a student who cannot negotiate stairs). Access also includes the provision of related services; that is, developmental, corrective, and other supportive services required to assist a student with a disability to derive benefit from an educational program. Almost any type of educational or psychological service could qualify as a related service in the right circumstance: speech-language audiology services, psychological services, physical and occupational therapy, therapeutic recreation, counseling (including rehabilitation counseling), orientation and mobility services, medical services for diagnostic or evaluation purposes, school health services, school social work services, and parent counseling and training. For example, consider Alice, a bright and capable student who is paraplegic and requires regular catheterization. If Alice cannot self-catheterize, she cannot attend school unless someone there can do the catheterization. Because catheterization is not a medical service (it can be performed by someone with minimal instruction), it is considered a related service, and the school would be required to provide that service so that Alice can come to school and get access to an education.

Disabled students are also entitled to a variety of curricular, instructional, and testing adaptations and accommodations (see the chapter "Adapting Tests to Accommodate Students with Disabilities"). For example, David, a student with attention deficit disorder, may be too distractible to be tested in the regular classroom. Because testing him in a smaller, quieter environment is necessary for valid test results, David is entitled to this accommodation. Table 29.1 contains some commonly used accommodations and adaptations for students with disabilities in general education classrooms. It is the intent of the law that, with few exceptions (such as coaching and reading the reading test), students with disabilities are to receive the same accommodations in assessment that they receive in instruction.

Students who are disabled and also need specialized curricular and instructional procedures are entitled to special education. Specifically, they are entitled to a free and appropriate public education that includes specially designed instruction (as detailed in each student's individualized education plan [IEP]) and, when needed, special materials, equipment, and technology. Students who are entitled to special education are also entitled to the related services that are necessary for them to profit from their special education. Other benefits for students entitled to special education include (1) formal education continuing until the student graduates or reaches 21 years of age; (2) instruction by teachers

---

TABLE 29.1	Common Accommodations and Adaptations

Instructional Accommodations and Adaptations

Writing key points of a lesson on board or overhead projector
Providing study guides with key concepts and vocabulary
Providing uncluttered handouts and worksheets
Furnishing the student with a peer's class notes
Providing alternative reading materials (e.g., texts written at a lower reading level)
Providing alternatives to reading (e.g., peer reader, talking books)
Allowing alternate responses to homework assignments (e.g., oral responses)
Allowing extra time (in or out of class) to complete work
Forming study groups
Providing immediate feedback to correct errors and strengthen correct responses
Providing periodic feedback about progress toward instructional and behavioral goals
Giving the student's homework log (assignments, timelines) to parents
Giving copies of instructional materials (texts, workbooks, etc.) to parents
Supplementing lectures with other materials
Reducing length or complexity of written assignments
Simplifying written directions (fewer steps, fewer words)
Using cooperative learning
Providing sufficient repetition to ensure retention
Providing manipulables and concrete examples
Systematically providing for generalization
Teaching additional skills not ordinarily taught (e.g., study skills, organizational skills, note taking, test taking, and learning strategies)

Testing Accommodations and Adaptations

Using alternative questions and response modes (e.g., questions on tape, oral responses)
Using untimed tests
Retaking unsatisfactory examinations
Testing in less distracting environments (e.g., library, resource room)
Providing study guides for test
Simplifying tests (e.g., reduced "supply" options)
Using alternative demonstrations of knowledge (e.g., oral reports, diagrams)

---

who have had special coursework and practicum experiences, and may have special certification; and (3) instruction in smaller classes than those for general education.

Altered Outcome Expectancies

Students receiving special education are frequently exempted from various curricular requirements that are established for students in general education. For example, students who complete their individual transition plans are eligible for a high school diploma regardless of whether they have completed all of the general graduation requirements mandated for all other students. Further, these students may be asked to achieve the graduation outcomes in different ways, or they may even have different outcomes. For example, students with more severe disabilities may be taught skills associated with navigating daily living, using public transportation, building and maintaining interpersonal relationships, and using social services.

Special Fiscal Arrangements

The education of students who are disabled and require special education is generally more costly than the general education provided to students who are not disabled. Part or all of the additional costs associated with special education are borne by the state with federal assistance.[2] Determining that Johnny is eligible for special education dictates that part of his special education will be paid for under special provisions of federal and state law. Thus, in the schools, eligibility decisions are also decisions about whether a child is entitled to additional help paid for by special funds earmarked for special education.[3]

Definitions of Disability Under the IDEA

Under the IDEA, the term *child with a disability* means a child

> having mental retardation, a hearing impairment including deafness, a speech or language impairment, a visual impairment including blindness, serious emotional disturbance (hereafter referred to as emotional disturbance), an orthopedic impairment, autism, traumatic brain injury, another health impairment, a specific learning disability, deaf-blindness, or multiple disabilities, and who, by reason thereof, needs special education and related services.

The definitions in the IDEA excluding the need for special education are generally used for entitlements under Section 504.

Autism

Autistic students are those who demonstrate "developmental disability significantly affecting verbal and nonverbal communication and social interaction, generally evident before age 3, which adversely affects the child's educational performance. Other characteristics often associated with autism are engagement in repetitive activities and stereotyped movements, resistance to environmental change or change in daily routines, and unusual responses to sensory experiences. The term *autism* does not apply if a child's educational performance is adversely affected primarily because the child has an emotional disturbance."

Students with suspected autism are usually evaluated by speech and language specialists and psychologists after it has been determined that some aspects of their educational performance fall outside the normal range and that various attempts to remedy the educational problems have failed. Frequently, a speech and language specialist would look for impaired verbal and nonverbal

---

[2] Because the federal government does not pay for all of the extra costs associated with a student's special education, special education is a partially funded mandate.

[3] Under the requirements of Section 504 of the 1973 Rehabilitation Act, students with disabilities are entitled to related services even when they do not need special education. In such cases, a school district is required to provide the needed services, but the funding for these services does not come from special education budgets.

communication. A large proportion of autistic children are mute, a condition that is readily apparent. Autism in students with speech and language might manifest itself as overly concrete thinking. For example, an autistic student might react to a statement like "Don't cry over spilled milk" quite literally ("I didn't spill any milk."). Another manifestation would be a lack of conversational reciprocity (usually long, often tedious, orations about a favorite subject) and failure to recognize a listener's waning interest. Moreover, this impaired social communication would be a consistent feature of the student's behavior rather than an occasional overexuberance. A psychologist looks for behavior that defines the condition: repetitive activities (for example, self-stimulating behavior, spinning objects, aligning objects, smelling objects), stereotyped movements (for example, hand flapping, rocking, head banging), and resistance to change (for example, eating only certain foods or tantruming when activities are ended). A psychologist may also administer a behavior rating scale (for example, the Gilliam Autism Rating Scale) as an aid to diagnosis. Finally, a psychologist rules out emotional disturbance as a cause of the student's behavior and impairments.

Mental Retardation   Mentally retarded pupils are those who demonstrate "significantly subaverage intellectual functioning, existing concurrently with deficits in adaptive behavior and manifested during the developmental period, which adversely affects the child's educational performance." Students who are eventually labeled "mentally retarded" are often referred because of generalized slowness: They lag behind their age mates in most areas of academic achievement, social and emotional development, language ability, and, perhaps, physical development.

Students suspected of being mentally retarded are evaluated by a psychologist after it has been determined that some aspects of their school performance fall outside the normal range and that various attempts to remedy the educational problems have failed. Whenever possible, a psychologist will administer a test of intelligence that is appropriate in terms of the student's age, acculturation, and physical and sensory capabilities. In most states, students must have an IQ that is two standard deviations or more below the mean (usually 70 or less) on a validly administered test. However, a test of intelligence is not enough. The pupil must also demonstrate impairments in adaptive behavior. There is no federal requirement that a test or rating scale be used to assess adaptive behavior psychometrically. In practice, most school psychologists will administer an adaptive-behavior scale (for example, the Vineland Adaptive Behavior Scales–II). However, when it is not possible to do so appropriately, a psychologist will interview parents or guardians and make a clinical judgment about a student's adaptive behavior. Thus an assessment for mental retardation must always contain an assessment of achievement, intelligence, and adaptive behavior.

Specific Learning Disability   Learning-disabled pupils are those who demonstrate "a disorder in one or more of the basic psychological processes involved in understanding or in using language, spoken or written, which may manifest itself in the imperfect ability to listen, think, speak, read, write, spell, or do mathematical calculations, including conditions such as perceptual disabilities, brain injury, minimal brain dysfunction, dyslexia, and developmental aphasia. The term does not include learning problems that are primarily the result of visual, hearing, or motor disabilities; of mental retardation; of emotional disturbance; or of environmental, cultural, or economic disadvantage." Students who are eventually labeled "learning disabled" are often referred because of inconsistent performance; they are likely to have pronounced patterns of academic and cognitive strengths and weaknesses. For example, Jason may grasp mathematics and social concepts quite well, but he may not learn to read, no matter what his teacher tries. Jeanine may be reading at grade level, be a good speller, and have highly developed language skills, but not be able to master addition and subtraction facts.

Students suspected of being learning disabled are evaluated after it has been determined that their educational performance in the specified areas (that is, oral expression, listening comprehension, written expression, basic reading skill, reading comprehension, mathematics calculation, or mathematics reasoning) falls outside the normal range and that various attempts to remedy the educational problems have failed. Such students may be evaluated by a speech and language specialist who would look for manifestations of a disorder in producing or understanding language. This specialist may conduct an assessment of a student's spontaneous or elicited language during an interview or play situation; the specialist may administer a formal test such as the Test for Auditory Comprehension of Language, Third Edition, or the Test of Language Development, Primary: Third Edition. There are no quantitative guidelines in the regulations to indicate a language disorder, but a child with a disability in language would be expected to earn scores that are substantially below average.

Students suspected of being learning disabled must be evaluated by psychologists. Some psychologists may administer tests to assess basic psychological processes, such as visual perception (for example, the Developmental Test of Visual Perception). All psychologists will probably search for manifestations of a disorder in the areas specified in the IDEA. In the past, the search required the results from a current test of intelligence. These results were necessary to rule out mental retardation (as required by the federal definition of learning disability) and establish the level of ability that was needed to ascertain whether a student had a significant discrepancy between ability and achievement. Psychologists usually administered a standardized achievement test like the Woodcock-Johnson Psychoeducational Battery–III: Tests of Achievement or the Wechsler Individual Achievement Test in all areas of possible learning disability. The results of the achievement tests served two purposes. First, they verified that the student was indeed having difficulties in oral expression, listening comprehension, written expression, basic reading skill, reading comprehension, mathematics calculation, or mathematics reasoning. Second, the standard scores in these areas were systematically compared to the student's IQ to determine whether a significant discrepancy existed between the scores. Because the IDEA does not specify the number of standard score points required for a difference in scores to be considered a significant discrepancy, practice is inconsistent from state to state—and sometimes from district to district within a state.[4] The current version of the IDEA allows states to replace severe discrepancy as a defining criterion for learning disability with evidence that a student has failed to be responsive to intervention. At the time this is being written, there are no federal or state guidelines for making this determination.

Finally, the committee responsible for making the actual determination that a student has a learning disability must rule out other causes for poor achievement in oral expression, listening comprehension, written expression, basic reading skill, reading comprehension, mathematics calculation, or mathematics reasoning. The IDEA specifically forbids that the student's achievement problem be the result of a visual, hearing, or motor impairment; mental retardation; emotional disturbance; or environmental, cultural, or economic disadvantage.

Emotional Disturbance

Emotionally disturbed pupils exhibit "one or more of the following characteristics over a long period of time and to a marked degree that adversely affects the child's educational performance: (1) an inability to learn that cannot be explained by intellectual, sensory, or health factors; (2) an inability to build or maintain satisfactory interpersonal relationships with peers and teachers; (3) inappropriate types of behavior or feelings under normal circumstances; (4) a general pervasive mood of unhappiness or depression; or (5) a tendency to develop physical symptoms or fears associated with personal or school problems." Emotional disability includes students with schizophrenia but excludes students who are socially maladjusted unless they also have an emotional disability. Students who are eventually labeled as having an emotional disturbance are often referred for problems in interpersonal relations (for example, fighting or extreme noncompliance) or unusual behavior (for example, unexplained episodes of crying or extreme mood swings).

Students suspected of being emotionally disturbed are evaluated by a psychologist after it has been determined that some of their school performance falls outside the normal range and that various attempts to remedy the school problems have failed. Requirements for establishing a pupil's eligibility as a student with emotional disturbance vary among the states. That said, multidisciplinary teams usually obtain a developmental and health history from a student's parent or guardian to rule out sensory and health factors as causes of a student's inability to learn. A parent or guardian is usually interviewed about the student's relationships with peers, feelings (for example, anger, alienation, depression, and fears), and physical symptoms (for example, headaches or nausea). Parents or guardians may also be asked to complete a behavior rating scale such as Achenbach's Child Behavior Checklist to obtain normative data on the student's

---

[4] Some psychologists will define a severe discrepancy as a difference greater than chance fluctuation. Psychologists who use this approach may use the reliability of an obtained difference or the reliability of the predicted difference to reach their decision. Some psychologists will use the rarity of a difference, which is often provided by test authors when they have normed both the intelligence and the achievement tests on the same sample.

behavior. Teachers will likely be interviewed about their relationships with the student and the student's relationships with peers at school. They may also be asked to complete a rating scale (for example, the Walker-McConnell Scale of Social Competence and School Adjustment) to obtain normative data for in-school behavior. In addition, a psychologist might be asked to administer a norm-referenced achievement battery to verify that the student's educational performance has been negatively affected by the student's emotional problems.

Traumatic Brain Injury

Students with traumatic brain injury have "an acquired injury to the brain caused by an external physical force, resulting in total or partial functional disability, psychosocial impairment, or both, which adversely affects the child's educational performance. The term applies to open or closed head injuries resulting in impairments in one or more areas, such as cognition; language; memory; attention; reasoning; abstract thinking; judgment; problem solving; sensory, perceptual, and motor abilities; psychosocial behavior; physical functions; information processing; and speech. The term does not apply to brain injuries that are congenital or degenerative, or brain injuries induced by birth trauma." Students with traumatic brain injury have normal development until they sustain a severe head injury. As a result of this injury, they are disabled. Most head injuries are the result of an accident (frequently an automobile accident), but they may also occur as a result of physical abuse or intentional harm (for example, being shot).

Traumatic brain injury will be diagnosed by a physician, who is usually a specialist (a neurologist). The need of a student with brain injury for special education will be based first on a determination that the student's school performance falls outside the normal range and that various attempts to remedy the educational problems have failed. Next, a school psychologist will likely administer a standardized achievement battery to verify that the student's achievement has been adversely affected.

Speech or Language Impairment

A student with a speech or language impairment has "a communication disorder such as stuttering, impaired articulation, a language impairment, or a voice impairment that adversely affects the child's educational performance." Many children will experience some developmental problems in their speech and language. For example, children frequently have difficulty with the *r* sound and say "wabbit" instead of "rabbit." Similarly, many children will use incorrect grammar, especially with internal plurals; for example, children may say, "My dog has four foots." Such difficulties are so common as to be considered a part of normal speech development. However, when such speech and language errors continue to occur beyond the age when most children have developed correct speech or language, there is cause for concern. Not all students who require intervention for speech or language problems are eligible for special education. A student may be eligible for speech or language services but not have a problem that adversely affects his or her school performance. Thus, for a student to be eligible for special education as a person with a speech or language impairment, that student must not only have a speech-language impairment, but also need special education.

The identification of students with speech and language impairments proceeds along two separate paths. School personnel identify the educational disability in the same way that other educational disabilities are identified. When extra help from a teacher does not solve the problem, the student is referred to a child study team for prereferral intervention. If those interventions fail to remedy the achievement problem, the student is referred for multidisciplinary evaluation. A psychologist or educational diagnostician will likely administer a norm-referenced achievement test to verify the achievement problem. At the same time, speech and language specialists will use a variety of assessment procedures (norm-referenced tests, systematic observation, and criterion-referenced tests) to identify the speech and language disability. If the student has both need and disability, the student will be eligible for special education and related services.

Visual Impairment

A student with a visual impairment "has an impairment in vision that, even with correction, adversely affects a child's educational development." Visual impairment includes both partial sight and blindness. Students with severe visual impairments are usually identified by an ophthalmologist before they enter school. Some partially sighted students may not be identified until they reach school age, when visual demands increase. Severe visual impairment is always presumed to adversely affect educational development, and students with this disability are presumed to require special education services and curricular adaptations (for example, mobility training, instruction in Braille, talking books, and so forth). A vision specialist usually assesses functional vision through systematic observation of a student's responses to various types of paper, print sizes, lighting conditions, and so forth.

Deafness and Hearing Impairment

Deafness is an impairment in hearing "that is so severe that the child is impaired in processing linguistic information through hearing, with or without amplification, and that adversely affects the child's educational performance." A student with a hearing impairment has an impairment in hearing, whether permanent or fluctuating, that adversely affects educational performance but is not included under the definition of deafness.

Most students classified as deaf will be identified before they enter school. Deafness will be presumed to adversely affect a student's educational development, and students with this disability are presumed to require special education services and curricular adaptations. However, even severe hearing impairments may be difficult to identify in the first years of life, and students with milder hearing impairments may not be identified until school age. Referrals for undiagnosed hearing-impaired students may indicate expressive and receptive language problems, variable hearing performance, problems in attending to aural tasks, and perhaps problems in peer relationships. Diagnosis of hearing impairment is usually made by audiologists, who identify the auditory disability, in conjunction with school personnel, who identify the educational disability.

Orthopedic Impairments

An orthopedic impairment is a severe impairment that "adversely affects a child's educational performance. The term includes impairments caused by congenital anomaly (such as clubfoot or absence of some member), impairments caused by disease (such as poliomyelitis or bone tuberculosis), and impairments from other causes (such as cerebral palsy, amputations, and fractures or burns that cause contractures)."

Physical disabilities are generally identified prior to entering school. However, accidents and disease may impair a previously nondisabled student. Medical diagnosis establishes the presence of the condition. The severity of the condition may be established in part by medical opinion and in part by systematic observation of the particular student. For many students with physical disabilities, ability to learn is not affected. These students may not require special education classes, but they will need accommodations and modifications to the curriculum—and perhaps the school building—which can be managed through a 504 plan. For example, a student may require a personal care aide to help with positioning, braces, and catheterization; another student may require educational technology (for example, a voice-activated computer) and school transportation that can accommodate a wheelchair. When such adaptations and accommodations are insufficient to allow adequate school progress, special education is indicated. The specially designed instruction can include alternative assignments, alternative curricula, alternative testing procedures, and special instruction.

Other Health Impairments

"Other health impairment means having limited strength, vitality, or alertness, including a heightened alertness to environmental stimuli, which results in limited alertness with respect to the educational environment and which (1) is due to chronic or acute health problems, such as asthma, attention deficit disorder or attention deficit hyperactivity disorder, diabetes, epilepsy, a heart condition, hemophilia, lead poisoning, leukemia, nephritis, rheumatic fever, and sickle cell anemia, and (2) adversely affects the child's educational performance." Diagnosis of health impairments is usually made by a physician, who identifies the health problem, and school personnel, who identify the educational disability. For some students with other health impairments, ability to learn is not affected. These students may not require special education classes, but they will need accommodations and modifications to the curriculum, which can be managed through a 504 plan. For example, a student may require nursing services to administer medication, times and places to rest during the day, and provisions for instruction in the home. When health impairments adversely affect educational progress even with curricular adaptations and modifications, special education is indicated.

Deaf-Blindness

"Deaf-blindness means concomitant hearing and visual impairments, the combination of which causes such severe communication and other developmental and educational needs that they cannot be accommodated in special education programs solely for children with deafness or for children with blindness."

Only a small number of students are deaf-blind, and that assessment is typically complex. Tests that compensate for loss of vision usually rely on auditory processes, and tests that compensate for loss of hearing usually rely on visual processes. Psychological and educational evaluations of students who are both deaf and blind rely on observations as well as interviews of and ratings by individuals sufficiently familiar with the students to provide useful information.

Multiple Disabilities

"*Multiple disabilities* means concomitant impairments (such as mental retardation–blindness, mental retardation–orthopedic impairment, and so forth), the combination of which causes such severe educational needs that they cannot be accommodated in special education programs for only one of the impairments. The term does not include deaf-blindness."

Developmental Delay

Although not mandated by the IDEA, states may use the category of developmentally delayed for children between the ages of 3 and 9 who need special education and are "experiencing developmental delays, as defined by the state and as measured by appropriate diagnostic instruments and procedures, in one or more of the following areas: physical development, cognitive development, communication development, social or emotional development, or adaptive development." Diagnosis of developmental delay is usually made by school personnel, who identify the educational disability, and other professionals (such as speech and language specialists, physicians, and psychologists), who identify the delays in the developmental domains.

Establishing Educational Need for Special Education

In addition to having one (or more) of the disabilities specified in the IDEA, a student must experience a lack of academic success. This criterion is either implicit or explicit in the IDEA definitions of disabilities. Autism, hearing impairment, mental retardation, and six other disabling conditions are defined as "adversely affecting a child's educational performance." Multiple disabilities (such as deaf-blindness) cause "severe educational needs." Learning disability results in an "imperfect ability" to learn basic academic skills.

Most students without obvious sensory or motor disabilities are presumed to be nondisabled when they enter school. However, during their education, it becomes clear to school personnel that these students have significant problems. They demonstrate marked discrepancies from mainstream expectations or from the achievement and behavior of typical peers. These discrepancies are usually verified by normative comparisons (that is, use of norm-referenced assessment devices) or peer referencing.[5] The magnitude of the discrepancy necessary to consider a student for special education is not codified, and there are many opinions on this issue. Whereas some say that a student should be performing at half the level of his or her peers, others believe that only a 20 percent discrepancy demonstrates educational need. Marston and Magnusson (1985) recommend that students receive special education services when they are two years behind their peers.

The presence of a discrepancy alone does not establish need, because there are many causes for a discrepancy. Thus school personnel usually should engage in a number of remedial and compensatory activities designed to reduce or eliminate

---

[5] In peer referencing, a target student's performance is compared with the performance of satisfactorily performing peers. See the chapter "Teacher Decision Making" or Deno (1985).

the discrepancy. As discussed in the chapter "Teacher Decision Making," interventions initially may be designed and implemented by the classroom teacher. When the teacher's interventions are unsuccessful, then the student is referred to a teacher assistance team that designs and may help implement further interventions. Need for special education services for students is established when one of two conditions is met. First, if a student fails to respond to validated and carefully implemented interventions, need for special education is indicated. We address the specifics of making decisions about response to intervention in the chapter "Assessing Response to Instruction." Second, successful interventions may be too intensive or extensive for use in regular education. In other words, the interventions needed to remediate the student's academic or behavioral deficits are so intrusive, labor intensive, or specialized that a general education classroom teacher cannot implement them without the assistance of a special education teacher or without seriously detracting from the education of other students in the classroom.

Some students have such obvious sensory or motor problems that they are identified as disabled before they enter school. From accumulated research and professional experience, educators know that students with certain disabilities (for example, blindness, deafness, and severe mental retardation) will not succeed in school without special education. Thus educators (and relevant regulations) assume that the presence of a severe disability is sufficient to demonstrate the need for special education services.

Determining That a Student Is Disabled

The determination that a student has a disability is made by a team of professionals called a multidisciplinary team (MDT). The team conducts a multidisciplinary evaluation (MDE) by collecting, assembling, and evaluating information to determine whether a student meets the conditions that define a handicap as set forth in the IDEA and state law.

Composition of the MDT

The IDEA requires that the team have members with the same qualifications as those who must serve on IEP teams and "other qualified professionals, as appropriate" (34 CFR §300.533). Thus the team must include the student's parents (and the student, if appropriate), a general education teacher, a special education teacher, a representative of the school administration, and an individual who can interpret the instructional implications of evaluation results. If the student is suspected of having a learning disability, the team must also include "at least one person qualified to conduct individual diagnostic examinations of children, such as a school psychologist, speech-language pathologist, or remedial reading teacher" (34 CFR §300.540). In practice, school psychologists are usually members of most MDTs.

Responsibilities of the MDT

The team is responsible for gathering information and determining whether a student is disabled. In theory, the decision-making process is straightforward. The MDT assesses the student to see whether he or she meets the criteria for a specific disability. Thus the MDT must collect, at minimum, information required by the definition of the disability being considered. Moreover, federal regulations (34 CFR §300.532) require that a student be "assessed in all areas related to the suspected disability, including, if appropriate, health, vision, hearing, social and emotional status, general intelligence, academic performance, communicative status, and motor abilities." Regulations (34 CFR §300.535) also require the team to do the following:

- Draw on information from a variety of sources, including aptitude and achievement tests, teacher recommendations, physical condition, social or cultural background, and adaptive behavior.

- Ensure that information obtained from all these sources is documented and carefully considered.

Determining Eligibility

To identify a student as disabled, MDTs compare the assessment data to the state and federal standards for the suspected disability. For example, if Charles's referral suggested a possible classification as a person who is mentally retarded, the school psychologist would select tests of intelligence and adaptive behavior (the abilities specified in the definition of mental retardation).

In practice, deciding whether a student is entitled to special education can be complex. Sometimes, the problems a student is experiencing can suggest a specific disability to team members. For example, having problems maintaining attention, being fidgety, and being disorganized may suggest the possibility of attention deficit disorder; persistent and major difficulties learning letter-sound correspondences despite many interventions could suggest a learning disability. MDTs must do more than simply confirm a disability. MDTs must adopt a point of view that is, in part, disconfirmatory—a point of view that looks to disprove the working hypothesis.

Many behaviors are indicative of different disabilities. For example, stereotypies such as hand-flapping are associated with autism, severe retardation, and some emotional disturbances. Assessors must be open to alternative explanations for the behavior and, when appropriate, collect information that will allow them to reject a working hypothesis of a particular disability. For example, if Tom was referred for inconsistent performance in expressive language, even though his other skills—especially math and science—are average, an MDT might suspect that he could have a learning disability. What would it take to reject the hypothesis that he has such a disability? If it could be shown that his problem was caused by a sensorineural hearing loss, he would not be considered learning disabled; if his problem arose because his primary language is a dialect of English, he would not be learning disabled; if he suffered from recurrent bouts of otitis media (middle-ear infections), he would not be learning disabled. Therefore, the MDT would have to consider other possible causes of his behavior. Moreover, when there is some evidence that something other than the hypothesized disability was the cause of the educational problems, the MDT would need to collect additional data that would allow them to evaluate these other explanations. Thus MDT evaluations frequently (and correctly) go beyond the information required by the entitlement criteria, to rule out other possible disabling conditions or to arrive at a different diagnosis.

Finally, in attempting to establish that a student should be classified with a disability, we often must choose among competing procedures and tests. However, as we show in the chapter "Assessment of Intelligence: Individual Tests," individual tests of intelligence are not interchangeable. They differ significantly in the behaviors they sample, in the adequacy of their norms and reliability, and slightly in their standard deviations. A dull, but normal, person may earn an IQ of less than 70 on one or two tests of intelligence but earn scores greater than 70 on two others. Thus, if we had to assess such a student, we could be caught in a terrible dilemma of conflicting information.

The routes around and through the dilemma are easier to state than to accomplish. First, we should choose (and put the most faith in) objective, technically adequate (reliable and well-normed) procedures that have demonstrated validity for the particular purpose of classification. Second, we must consider the specific validity. For example, we must consider the culture in which the student grew up and how that culture interacts with the content of the test. A test's technical manuals may contain information about the wisdom of using the test with individuals of various cultures, or the research literature may have information for the particular cultural group to which a student belongs. Often, theory can guide us in the absence of research. Sometimes it is just not possible to test validly, and we must also recognize that fact. Finally, when we find ourselves in a swamp of conflicting data, we must remember why we gathered the data. In this example, we would have gathered the data to learn whether a student met the eligibility requirement: an IQ equal to or less than 69. (Note that the reason for giving an intelligence test was not to see whether the student needed help; we already knew that.)

Problems in Determining Special Education Eligibility

Four problems with the criteria used to determine eligibility for special services are especially noteworthy. First, we find the prevalent (but mistaken) belief that special education services are for students who could benefit from them. Thus, in many circles, educational need is believed to be sufficient for entitlement. Clearly, this belief is contradicted by pertinent law, regulations, and litigation. Students must need the services *and* meet the criteria for a condition. Nonetheless, some educators have such strong humanitarian beliefs that, when they see students with problems, they want to get those students the services that they believe are needed. Too often, the regulations may be bent so that students fit entitlement criteria.

Second, the definitions that appear in state and federal regulations are frequently very imprecise. The imprecision of federal regulations creates variability in standards among states, and the imprecision of state regulations creates variability in standards among districts within states. Thus students who are eligible in one state or district may not be eligible in other states or districts. For example, some states and school districts may define a learning disability as a severe discrepancy between measured intellectual ability and actual school achievement. However, there is no consensus about the meaning of "severe discrepancy"; certainly, there is no widely accepted mathematical formula to ascertain severe discrepancy. To some extent, discrepancies between achievement and intelligence are determined by the specific tests used. Thus one test battery might produce a significant discrepancy, whereas another battery would not produce such a discrepancy for the same student. Other states and school districts may define a learning disability by an inadequate response to intervention. Yet what constitutes an inadequate response is ambiguous.

Third, the definitions treat disabilities as though they were discrete categories. However, most diagnosticians are hard pressed to distinguish between primary and secondary mental retardation or between primary and secondary emotional disturbance. Also, for example, distinctions between individuals with autism and individuals with severe mental retardation and autisticlike behaviors are practically impossible to make with any certainty.

Fourth, parents may often prefer the label associated with one disability (for example, autistic or learning disabled) over the label associated with another (for example, mentally retarded). Because of the procedural safeguards afforded students with special needs and their parents, school districts may become embroiled in lengthy and unnecessarily adversarial hearings in which each side has an expert testifying that a particular label is correct, even though those labels are contradictory and sometimes mutually exclusive. School personnel find themselves in a no-win situation because the definitions and their operationalizations are so imprecise. As a result, school districts frequently give parents the label they want, rather than what educators, in their best professional judgments, believe to be correct. There are two reasons for this. First, districts may be reluctant to risk litigation; parents can frequently find an expert to contradict the district staff members. Second, in some states, special education services are noncategorical. In these states, a label qualifies a student for special education but does not determine the nature of the special education; that is determined by the individual student's needs, not by a label.

SUMMARY

Assessment data are collected to make decisions about a student's need for special education services and the student's exceptionality. When students are disabled and have such intense or special instructional needs that these needs cannot be met in a general education setting, they can be classified as eligible for and entitled to special education. Entitlement is an administrative act. Federal and most state special education laws contain provisions specifying that students must be classified before they receive services. Criteria for establishing the existence of handicapping conditions are specified in rules or guidelines, and assessment data are used to ascertain the extent to which the criteria are met.

QUESTIONS FOR CHAPTER REVIEW

1. List and explain three benefits of classifying disabled students.

2. How would you go about selecting an assessment battery to see whether a boy (age 8) should be eligible for special education classes?

3. In establishing educational need for services, it is necessary to document a discrepancy between expected performance and the performance of peers. Discuss two other criteria that must be met for the documentation of need for special education services.

4. What criteria should be used to select the assessment device for collecting data to make a decision about eligibility or classification?

PROJECT

Talk to a parent of a student who receives special education services. Have the parent tell you about the multidisciplinary team and the process of determining eligibility for services and developing an individualized education plan.

RESOURCES FOR FURTHER INVESTIGATION

Print Resources

Cromwell, R. L., Blashfield, R. K., & Strauss, J. S. (1975). Criteria for classification systems. In N. Hobbs (Ed.), *Issues in the classification of children* (Vol. 1). San Francisco: Jossey-Bass.

Nelson, J. R., Smith, D. J., Taylor, L., Dodd, J. M., & Reavis, K. (1991). Prereferral intervention: A review of the research. *Education and Treatment of Children, 14,* 243–253.

Reynolds, M. C., & Lakin, K. C. (1987). Noncategorical special education: Models for research and practice. In M. C. Wang, M. C. Reynolds, & H. J. Walberg (Eds.), *The handbook of special education: Research and practice.* Oxford, England: Pergamon Press.

Technology Resources

SPECIAL EDUCATION SERVICES
www.ed.gov/about/offices/list/osers/index.html
Look here for information about a wide array of supports for parents, individuals, school districts, and states in special education, vocational rehabilitation, and research. Also find information about No Child Left Behind and the New Freedom Initiative as they relate to special education.

INTRODUCTION TO MENTAL RETARDATION
www.aamr.org
Visit the American Association on Mental Retardation's website to find information about mental retardation across the lifespan. The site provides information about classification of individuals, educational and community supports, current research, and advocacy.

LEARNING DISABILITIES
www.teachingld.org
Look here to learn more about students with learning disabilities. The website describes the characteristics of students and the accommodations that teachers can implement in the classroom.

ATTENTION DEFICIT HYPERACTIVITY DISORDER
www.nimh.nih.gov/publicat/adhd.cfm
This comprehensive site provides information about symptoms, diagnosis, causes, and treatment of ADHD. There is also information about ADHD and families, school, childhood, the teenage years, and adulthood.

CHAPTER 30

Assessing Response to Instruction

A MAJOR PURPOSE OF ASSESSMENT HAS BEEN TO MONITOR PUPIL PROGRESS; THIS means assessing and documenting a student's achievement—that is, responses to or responsiveness to instruction. We have learned that standardized tests are not satisfactory instruments for monitoring response to instruction. They are time consuming, are insensitive to small but important changes, are expensive, are not suitable for repeated administrations, and fail to match a student's curriculum and instruction. Over time, demands to develop new ways to monitor response to instruction have increased.

The acronym *RTI* currently is used to refer to *response to instruction* or *response to intervention*. We believe it is important to differentiate between these two terms, and we do so in this chapter. We use the terminology *response to instruction* to refer to response to core instruction or universal programming (the everyday instruction that occurs for students). Assessment of response to core instruction occurs for all students. Sometimes the assessment is continuous, sometimes it is periodic (occurring three to ten times per month), and sometimes it is a one-time assessment occurring once per year.

We use the term *response to intervention* to refer to a student's response when substantial changes are made in regular programming (for the large group, the small group, or individual students). Over time, students who experience academic or behavioral difficulties in school receive increasingly intensive instruction. Those who demonstrate at-risk performance receive enhanced instruction, and those who do not respond to enhanced instruction are given intensive instruction. In Figure 30.1 we illustrate with a triangle the three levels, phases, or tiers of instruction. Core instruction is for all students, enhanced instruction is for some students, and intensive instruction is for few students. Those who are familiar with the intervention model proposed by Horner, Sugai, and their colleagues (Horner, Sugai, & Horner, 2000) will recognize the parallel to their model. Horner and Sugai use the terms *primary, secondary,* and *tertiary* in describing interventions in the three phases or levels.

FIGURE 30.1
Three Levels
of Instruction

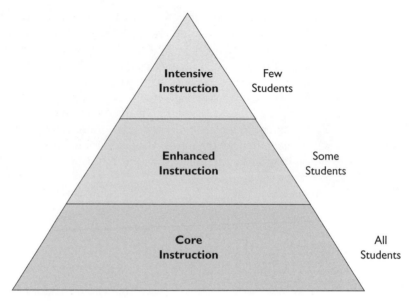

Measurement is done similarly for the two RTIs, but one (response to intervention) involves a substantive change to instruction, and the other does not. In this chapter, the use of the term *response to intervention* is reserved for situations in which an instructional change is implemented and the corresponding effects on student achievement are measured. Assessing response to intervention goes slightly beyond assessing response to instruction and involves comparing rate of learning during an intervention to the rate of learning during general instruction to determine whether the given change was helpful. Response to instruction and response to intervention are measured in both general and special education, so do not assume that the distinction is related to a specific setting.

Beginning in the 1970s, assessment methodologies called curriculum-based measurement, curriculum-based assessment, curriculum-based evaluation, and problem solving were developed, and these improved on earlier models of precision teaching (Lindsley, 1990), criterion-referenced assessment (Boehm, 1973), behavioral consultation (Bergan, 1977), data-based program modification (Deno & Mirkin, 1977), and formative evaluation (Bloom, Hastings, & Madaus, 1971). The assessment methodologies of the 1970s have been refined and expanded over time, and now are proposed as methods for making all kinds of assessment decisions, including entitlement (eligibility) and accountability decisions (see the 2004 reauthorization of the Individuals with Disabilities Education Act, 34 CFR §300.7).

This chapter is about assessing response to instruction. Before getting down to an analysis of current practices and procedures, we need to introduce two cautions and considerations. First, implicit in assessing RTI is the notion of effective instruction. After all, who wants to measure the extent to which pupils profit from inadequate or ineffective instruction? We want to know the extent to which instruction that generally works for individuals and groups is effective with specific individuals and groups. For instance, does the reading program that has been shown to be effective with third graders work with Joe, who is in Ms. Harvey's third-grade class, and does it work for the other students who are in the class? We need a system that is sensitive enough to find this out in a timely fashion. Thus school personnel talk about direct and frequent measurement of student progress toward specific goals or standards, or they talk about measuring the extent to which students become more competent over time.

A second consideration is what educational personnel do with the data they obtain by assessing response to instruction. Data that are collected are useful only to the extent that they are used to make decisions that lead to enhanced student competence or to building the capacity of systems to meet students' needs and enhance their competencies. It is implicit not only that the data will be collected, but also that they will be used for the purpose of making decisions about students.

RTI Conceptualizations

Definition of Response to Instruction

Response to instruction (RTI) is a concept with multiple meanings but without definition as yet in state or federal laws or regulations. Sometimes it is defined simply as collecting data on student performance and progress toward some goal; invariably it has to do with progress monitoring. The general notion is to monitor student progress (continuously, periodically, annually, or with some other degree of frequency) in order to spot deviance, ascertain skill development, or check the efficacy of academic or behavioral interventions being used with the student. Some would say it is all about catching children early so that they do not get left behind. Reports of assessments of response to instruction could consist of report cards every six weeks, simple statements that a student's overall progress is satisfactory, or more formal, highly specific statements such as "In two weeks, she has increased her single-digit addition accuracy from four out of ten problems correct to eight out of ten problems correct." Obviously, these different kinds of reports have different meanings and differ in their usefulness for instructional decision making.

Assessment of response to instruction and progress monitoring are now encountered by educators in many different ways. The No Child Left Behind Act requires that schools implement "evidence-based instruction"; most often this is interpreted to mean that someone has monitored the extent to which an instructional program "works" in general; that is, the extent to which students who receive the instruction make progress toward grade-level standards. And the ramifications of RTI assessment are seen when state departments of education punish schools where students are failing to make adequate yearly progress.

The extent to which any given program or intervention will be effective within a given educational context cannot be known until it is applied. Generally effective instruction may not work because of unique characteristics of the children or their teachers. Teachers need to know how to choose interventions that address individual students' needs. Yet, even when that happens, differences exist across school settings that may influence the efficacy of a given intervention.

For instance, instructional materials vary across schools in terms of the extent to which they cover certain skills. A supplemental program with strong support in the research literature may not necessarily address the skills with which students at a particular school are struggling. It is therefore important to consider contextual factors when selecting a program that is supported in the research literature. Furthermore, it is important to monitor student progress over time to know whether a program or intervention, when applied, has the intended positive impact on student learning.

The federal government has funded a National Center on Student Progress Monitoring (NCSPM), a center charged with evaluating progress-monitoring practices, reporting on effective practices, and providing the necessary technical assistance to states to enable them to implement effective progress-monitoring methodologies. The NCSPM has a website (www.studentprogress.org) where it periodically posts assessment devices that are shown to be scientifically validated and where it answers questions about curriculum-based measurement and progress monitoring.

Most formal definitions of RTI have addressed its use in making eligibility decisions. Recent changes in federal legislation have noted the possibility of using RTI procedures to identify students with disabilities who are in need of special education services. Section 614b6B of IDEA 2004 states:

> In determining whether a child has a specific learning disability, a local educational agency may use a process that determines if the child responds to scientific, research-based intervention as a part of the evaluation procedures described in paragraphs 2 and 3.

Vaughn and Fuchs (2003) describe a model for this use of RTI. They state that "A response to intervention model measures the individual child's learning along a continuum of academic responding to the instructional environment and designates disability as a fixed point on that continuum" (p. 142). They describe three phases of measuring response to intervention:

Phase 1. Measuring rate of growth for all students in a class in order to provide evidence for the contention that the overall rate of responsiveness of students in a classroom is sufficient to indicate that the instructional environment is nurturing enough to expect progress (We call such Phase 1 assessments measures of response to instruction.)

Phase 2. Identification of a subset of students in a class who are at risk for failure to achieve outcomes as evidenced by their lack of responsiveness to instruction

Phase 3. Measurement of responsiveness to classroom adaptations that are implemented in an effort to make the student more responsive to the general classroom environment and the instruction occurring therein

We refer to this as measuring response to intervention because it involves assessing what happens after a change is made. Special education services might be considered if the adaptations needed for the student to make progress do not appear viable through general education services alone.

The approach to learning disability identification advocated by Vaughn and Fuchs (2003) is often labeled the "treatment validity model," and many researchers consider it "the most fully developed conceptualization of how response to intervention may be applied to LD identification" (Speece, Case, & Molloy, 2003). As these authors state,

> In this model, curriculum based measures (CBM) are used in general education classrooms to identify children whose level and rate (slope) of performance are below those of their classmates. This "dual discrepancy" of level and slope becomes the marker by which to judge responsiveness to instruction. Dually-discrepant children then receive general education instruction that is redesigned to meet their needs. This instruction and continued placement in general education would be "treatment valid" for children who demonstrate improvement and are no longer dually discrepant. For children who continue to demonstrate a dual discrepancy, the instruction and placement would not be valid, leading to a trial placement in special education to determine responsiveness and, hence, treatment validity, under more intensive instructional parameters. (p. 148)

D. Fuchs and colleagues (2003) describe RTI in terms of the steps that educational professionals go through. They list these as follows. (We have modified steps 5 and 6 for purposes of this text.)

1. Students are provided with "generally effective" instruction by their classroom teachers.

2. Their progress is monitored.

3. Those who do not respond get something else, or something more, from their teacher or someone else. The "something else" should be an intervention for which there is evidence of a high probability of success.

4. Again, their progress is monitored.

5. Decisions about resource allocation and entitlement for supplemental programs (e.g., Title I, Special Education) are made.

6. Steps 1–4 are repeated until the teacher uses instruction that enables the student to reach desired levels of performance.

Fundamental Assumptions in Assessing Response to Instruction

There are seven assumptions that underlie the practice of assessing RTI.

1. *Instruction occurs.* When we assess response to instruction, we assume that instruction actually occurs. However, some philosophies of education explicitly eschew direct or systematic instruction and value a student's discovering content, skills, and behavior.[1] Thus it is likely that some students

---

[1] Most parents would prefer that this procedure not be used to teach their children to swim.

could spend their time in instruction-free environments and would stand no
chance of being instructed.

2. *Instruction occurs as intended.* It is assumed that instruction is implemented
   in the way in which it is intended to be implemented and that students are
   actively engaged in the instruction. Over the past decade, researchers have
   become increasingly interested in intervention integrity (also sometimes
   called treatment integrity or fidelity of treatment). For example, when we assess the extent to which a student responds to phonics instruction, we are assuming that the phonics instruction is implemented as the teacher intended
   and that the student is actively engaged in responding to the instruction.

3. *The instruction that is assessed is known to be generally effective.* There
   needs to be empirical evidence that the instruction that is implemented
   works for students in general and, more specifically, for students who are
   the same age and grade as the pupil being assessed.

4. *The measurement system is adequate to detect changes in student learning
   as a result of instruction.* There are four subcomponents to this assumption.

   a. The measurement system reflects the curriculum or assesses the effect of instruc-
      tion in that curriculum. It is axiomatic that response to instruction must reflect
      the content being instructed.

   b. The measurement system can be used frequently. Frequent measurement is impor-
      tant to avoid wasting a student's and a teacher's time when instruction is not
      working. It is also important to prevent a student from practicing (and mastering)
      errors and making them more difficult to correct.

   c. The measurement system is sensitive to small changes in student performance. If
      measurement is conducted frequently, it is unlikely that there will be large
      changes in student learning. Thus, to be effective, the measurement system must
      be capable of detecting small, but meaningful, changes in student learning or per-
      formance.

   d. The measurement system actually assesses pupil performance, not simply what the
      teacher does. Clearly, what a teacher does is important because it goes directly to
      treatment fidelity. However, we are interested in whether the student is learning.

5. *There are links between the assessment data and modifications in instruction.* This is the concept of data-driven decision making and reiterates our
   earlier point that data collected and not used to make decisions are useless.
   It is assumed that the data are both useful and usable for purposes of instructional planning. Student failure to respond appropriately to instruction,
   as determined by the formative measures used, should trigger a change in instruction. Additional data may need to be collected to determine what
   change has the highest probability of leading to student success; nevertheless, a change would be needed in the type of instruction, amount of instruction, or instructional delivery method.

6. *There are consequences that sustain (a) improved student outcomes and
   (b) continued implementation of the measurement system.* It is assumed not

only that the system is good, but that it is worth keeping in place. In our experience we have learned that the collection of direct frequent data on student performance is considered both time consuming and arduous by some teachers. At the same time, teachers tell us that they and their students are "better off" when data are collected. Although many teachers are motivated by their students' progress, it is sometimes necessary to provide rewards to others for data collection if we want them to engage in direct and frequent measurement. These teachers have told us that, if it does not matter to someone that they monitor student progress, they will stop doing so.

7. *Assessment of RTI is not setting specific.* It is assumed that response to instruction can be assessed in both general and special education settings.

Measurement Concepts in RTI Models

There are several measurement concepts that are important to understanding application of RTI models. These include progress monitoring, curriculum-based measurement, curriculum-based assessment, and curriculum-based evaluation. In this section we define these and distinguish between them. We refer to texts where they are covered in more depth. The increased use of curriculum-based measurement, curriculum-based assessment, and other techniques involved in assessing response to intervention is due at least in part to the recognition that traditional norm-referenced methods of assessment are not useful for instructional decision making.

Assessment of response to instruction consists of monitoring student progress toward specific instructional outcomes or toward state standards. Remember that, if substantive changes are made in instruction and we measure the response to those changes, the term *response to intervention* is used. We like to think that progress monitoring is an ongoing process that involves (1) collecting and analyzing data to ascertain student progress toward mastery of specific skills or general outcomes and (2) using the data collected to make instructional decisions. When applied in educational settings, the term often used as a synonym for progress monitoring is *data-driven decision making.* Progress monitoring and data-driven decision making require both data collection *and* use. The following is how the National Center on Student Progress Monitoring describes progress monitoring:

> To implement progress monitoring, the student's current levels of performance are determined and goals are identified for learning that will take place over time. The student's academic performance is measured on a regular basis (at least weekly). Progress toward meeting the student's goals is measured by comparing expected and actual rates of learning. Based on these measurements, teaching is adjusted as needed. Thus, the student's progression of achievement is monitored and instructional techniques are adjusted to meet the individual student's learning needs. (www.studentprogress.org)

Although the NCSPM includes weekly or daily measurement in its notion of progress monitoring, progress can be monitored on a continuum of time intervals ranging from minute by minute to annual. Student deficits in skill level and progress may dictate how frequently measurement should occur: Students with substantial deficits are monitored more frequently to ensure that instructional methods are effective. Those who want to know more about how the expected rate is set or the specific procedures used to monitor student progress are referred to Hosp and Hosp (2003) or Shinn (1989).

Typically, the terms *curriculum-based measurement, curriculum-based assessment,* and *curriculum-based evaluation* are used to describe the assessment methodologies that are used to collect and evaluate student achievement data in order to monitor student progress. The term *curriculum-based assessment (CBA)* was first used by Gickling and Havertape in 1980 to refer to assessment practices in which the instructional needs of students were determined by measuring the ratio of known to unknown material in the curriculum. The term *CBA* was used over time to refer to assessment of accuracy and a system of monitoring student progress through the curriculum. Multiple models of CBA emerged over time, and eventually the originators of the term switched to using the term *instructional assessment*. This term was used most in the Pennsylvania Instructional Support Team Model to refer to an accuracy-based approach (Burns, MacQuarrie, & Campbell, 1999).

Curriculum-based measurement is the term used by Deno and his associates (Deno, 1985; Fuchs & Deno, 1991) to refer to the periodic assessment of the annual goals in a subject matter. Brief tests (samples of the material contained in the annual goal) are administered frequently and regularly. Assuming that progress in the curriculum is linear, test scores can be compared to expected progress and thus serve as an indication of progress. CBM uses specific decision rules to determine whether progress is sufficient and to adapt instruction when it is not. CBMs are useful for decisions about placement in instructional materials, long-term goal setting, and progress monitoring.[2]

Curriculum-based evaluation (CBE), a term coined by Howell and Morehead (1987), is a strategy for collecting and using data to make decisions about individual students or groups. Howell and Morehead offer a decision-making framework that can guide data collection and analysis within a particular content area. This process allows one to link assessment information to a potentially highly effective intervention. CBE is useful for determining what instructional sequences or skills need to be taught.

In summary, CBM most often refers to measuring response to a set of terminal goals and objectives (maybe even standards), whereas CBA refers to actual task analysis of the curriculum followed by frequent samplings of student performance on those curricular tasks. CBE is a decision-making framework that assists with the identification of interventions that are likely to lead to student success and may include CBM and other informal measures. Data from one or

---

[2] CBM has expanded over time, and now people talk about the use of stimulus materials drawn from sources other than the curriculum. The terms *general outcomes measurement* (GOM; Fuchs & Deno, 1994) and *dynamic indicators of basic skills* (DIBS; Shinn, 1998) have been used to describe these materials. The notion of general outcomes measurement is applied most vividly in the new technology-enhanced systems (Accelerated Math and Standards Master) that are used to monitor student progress in math, reading, writing, and so forth, independent of a specific curriculum.

more of these assessment methodologies are used to evaluate student progress through the curriculum; hence the term *curriculum-based evaluation*.

Dimensions of Assessment of RTI

Assessments of student response to educational interventions vary along two dimensions: specificity and frequency. Technically adequate measures of RTI are those that are highly specific and very frequently administered. This concept is illustrated in Figure 30.2. Along the vertical axis, measures vary in their specificity from those that are global to those that are highly specific. Along the vertical axis we illustrate that measures differ in frequency of assessment, from those that are given very infrequently to those that are administered daily, hourly, or even continuously. The "best" measures, those that are most technically adequate for decision making, are in the upper right-hand quadrant (highly sensitive or specific and frequently administered).

Specificity   Assessments differ along a continuum of specificity. This is illustrated in Figure 30.3.

The more specific the assessment and the more specific the information collected by or reported to the teacher, the more precise the teacher can be in planning instructional interventions. Think about where you would begin teaching a student who is "doing fine in reading."

Frequency   Assessments also vary along a continuum of frequency. As illustrated in Figure 30.3, assessments range from annual assessments to daily assessments. In school settings, many measures (such as large-scale achievement tests) are given annu-

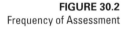

FIGURE 30.2
Frequency of Assessment

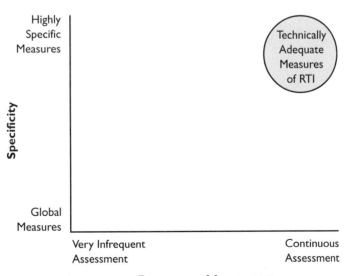

Frequency of Assessment

FIGURE 30.3
Continuum of Specificity

Given 10 consonant-vowel-consonant words with the short e sound, Bill says 8 correctly.

Bill has mastered short vowel sounds.

Bill is at the 70th percentile in decoding skills.

Bill passed the unit test.

Bill earned a B in reading.

Bill is doing fine in reading.

ally. These are broad assessments that must cover considerable content (material learned over an entire school year). Thus they must either be very general or be a limited sample of more specific content. In either case, the results of such assessments do not provide sufficiently detailed information about what a student knows and does not know to plan specific lessons. The results of unit tests or report cards are provided more frequently than standardized tests, but they are still inadequate to learn what a student specifically knows and does not know.

Increasingly, educators are measuring performance and progress very frequently. Many of the new measurement systems, such as those employing technology-enhanced assessments, call for continuous measurement of pupil performance and progress. They provide students with immediate feedback on how they are doing, give teachers daily status reports indicating the relative standing of all students in a class, and pinpoint the skills missing among students who are experiencing difficulty. The more frequent the measurement, the quicker you can adapt instruction to ensure that students are making optimal progress. However, frequent measurement is only helpful when it can immediately direct teachers as to what to teach or how to teach next. To the extent that teachers can use data efficiently, frequent assessment is valuable; if it consists simply of frequent measurement with no application, then it is not valuable.

The Purposes of Assessing Response to Intervention

School personnel assess response to intervention for many different reasons. To organize thinking about the use of RTI approaches, we provide the purposes we identified in Chapter 1 here.

Prereferral Classroom Decisions

Most models of assessing response to instruction include a significant assessment of response to general classroom instruction. We refer to this as assessing response to instruction. This is a formal part of the Iowa Problem-Solving Model and is Phase 1 of the model advocated by Vaughn and Fuchs (2003). The goal here is to identify students who are at risk for failure so that an alternative intervention can be put in place. Once the alternative is put in place, student progress is monitored to ascertain response to the new intervention (thus referred to as measuring response to intervention). By comparing students' rate of learning during an intervention to their rate of learning solely from regular instruction, you can determine whether an intervention is effective. In many RTI models, students are referred to child study teams for more in-depth evaluation when they demonstrate lack of progress for a specified time period.

Entitlement Decisions   In making entitlement decisions, school personnel need to determine whether a student is exceptional. Exceptionality is defined as difference or deviance from a standard. Students who are shown to be performing below a specified cutoff are considered exceptional. States or districts specify cutoffs, and there are some differences among states in the cutoffs they use. For example, students who perform more than 2 standard deviations below the mean on an individually administered test of intelligence may be considered mentally retarded in one state, whereas another state may require a criterion of 1.5 standard deviations below the mean. With the new RTI methods specified by the 2004 reauthorization of the IDEA, eligibility decisions for students thought to be learning disabled are being based on response to intervention. Students are declared eligible for service when they score below a cutoff level and do not respond to increasingly intense interventions.

Recently, many educators have been advocating the use of a "dual discrepancy" to identify students with disabilities in need of special education. They argue that students should be considered entitled to special education services when they are (1) performing poorly relevant to grade-level goals or standards and (2) making less progress than their classroom peers following the implementation of adaptations to general instruction. Some RTI entitlement decision-making approaches consider such a dual discrepancy sufficient for entitlement (Fuchs, Fuchs, & Speece, 2002); others additionally include the need to demonstrate what the student's instructional needs are and that these needs go beyond what can be met through general education services (Grimes & Kurns, 2003).

The following is an example of how a student might be entitled to receive special education services through the Heartland problem-solving model.[3]

> Johnny, a second-grader, performed below the tenth percentile among second-graders at his school on the mid-year administration of the Dynamic Indicators of Basic Early Literacy Skills (DIBELS) oral reading fluency measure. Based on a comparison with his beginning-of-year oral reading fluency DIBELS performance, Johnny had improved an average of 0.5 words correct per minute per week across the course of the first semester, which was substantially below the 1.5 words correct per minute per week median progress level of his second-grade peers. The school psychologist was asked to assist with individual problem

---

[3] It is important to note that the Heartland problem-solving model is intended to address a variety of student problems; it is not meant merely to help make entitlement decisions.

solving, given that Johnny demonstrated a dual discrepancy. Using the CBE framework, the school psychologist analyzed Johnny's curriculum, instruction, environment, and learning characteristics, and found that he did not accurately and fluently identify common sight words. Sight-word practice was not included in his current instructional programming and would not be addressed again until the fall of his third-grade year. Prior to intervention development and implementation, a goal was set for Johnny to be at the associated DIBELS benchmark by spring (90 words correct per minute); he was currently reading 53 words correct per minute. A sight-word instruction and practice intervention was then developed and implemented by an adult classroom volunteer five days a week for 30 minutes at a time. The DIBELS oral reading fluency progress-monitoring measures were administered twice a week to Johnny throughout the intervention. After three and a half weeks (7 data points), Johnny was found to be making progress at the rate of 0.7 words correct per minute per week. Given his limited progress, the team decided to increase the intervention to include two 20-minute sessions five days a week. After four more weeks, Johnny was making progress at the rate of 1 word correct per minute per week, which was not sufficient for him to meet the predetermined goal and was a level of progress substantially below that of his peers. An individualized education plan (IEP) was then developed to include a reading goal and a description of the special education services that would address his specific reading skill deficits.

Postentitlement Classroom Decisions

Special education services are intended to target individualized learning needs among students with disabilities. Monitoring a student's response to special education and related services is mandated by the IDEA. Students are expected to make more than *de minimis* progress. Student progress toward their IEP goals is used to make decisions about when to make a change in type of instruction, when to increase the level of special education support, and when to consider a more restrictive placement. RTI is useful in meeting this legal mandate as well as in making special education exit and general education reintegration decisions when students no longer have skill deficits that require special education services.

Accountability/ Outcome Decisions

To date there has been limited use of RTI methodologies in making accountability/outcome decisions. Yet this is envisioned by some (Ysseldyke, 2005). If school systems have in place continuous monitoring systems, then it is possible to aggregate data on student progress and to use those data to make accountability decisions. It would be possible, for example, to define grade-level standards in terms of these measures and to count and report the numbers of students who are at, above, or below grade level, or who meet grade-level standards. We think that this practice would be a bit unwieldy unless one was able to use technology-enhanced assessment systems like Renaissance Place (Renaissance Learning, 2004), DIBELS (Good & Kaminski, 2002), Yearly Progress Pro (McGraw-Hill Digital Learning, 2004), and AIMSweb (Edformation, undated). These can be used to engage in continuous or periodic measurement of student progress; the systems collect and store data on the performance and progress of individual students, and those data can be used to make accountability decisions. Technology-enhanced systems like Yearly Progress Pro and Standards Master can be given periodically and are matched to the state standards for many states. Performance on the monitoring systems tells educational personnel the extent to which students are making instructional progress. The technology-enhanced systems will alert school administrators to the performance and progress of individual students, individual classrooms, individual schools, or the entire district.

Examples of RTI Assessment Models

You can expect that over time there will be claims that many activities that actually look very different from one another are RTI models. At the time we write this text, there are some models of RTI that have been in place long enough to gather some data on their effectiveness and long enough to work out a variety of challenges. In this section, we review briefly four models that others (D. Fuchs et al., 2003; Burns & Ysseldyke, 2005) use to illustrate RTI practices. These include the models used in the Heartland Area Education Agency in Iowa, the Instructional Support Team model used in Pennsylvania, Ohio's Intervention-Based Assessment model, and the Problem-Solving Model used in the Minneapolis, Minnesota, schools. First, though, we start with an overview of the Sacajawea Project conducted in the Great Falls, Montana, school district. That project was based on the earlier work of Ogden Lindsley, a University of Kansas faculty member who developed and expanded on a method that he called "precision teaching."

Great Falls, Montana, Schools Sacajawea Project

In the late 1960s and early 1970s, educational professionals in the Great Falls, Montana, schools implemented an instructional intervention based on the principles of precision teaching specified by Lindsley. The program was designed to help students build and maintain basic skills in math, reading, and spelling, and it focused on students in both general and special education. Five elements guided the process used in the Great Falls schools: (1) setting high academic expectations, (2) slicing the curriculum into small steps, (3) providing one-minute practice exercises, (4) monitoring daily progress, and (5) making data-based decisions based on the magnitude of student progress. The project was on two separate occasions in 1975 and 1979 approved by the U.S. Department of Education, National Diffusion Network, as a validated program to help elementary students in general and those in special education to build and maintain basic skills. The one-minute Basic Skill Builders developed as part of the Great Falls project look much like the curriculum-based assessments we defined earlier, which are used so heavily in several of today's problem-solving models. The fundamental concept in the Great Falls project was to track student progress through the curriculum, spot those who were not making desired progress, and implement interventions to get them back on track. A number of studies were completed as part of the Great Falls Sacajawea Project, which demonstrated the validity of this model. The studies are summarized in a paper by Beck (1979) and in a National Diffusion Network product (National Diffusion Network, 1995).

Heartland, Iowa, Problem-Solving Model

School personnel in the Heartland Education Agency in central Iowa were among the first in the nation to implement a formal model of problem solving that included direct and frequent assessment of student response to instruction. The model began to be implemented around 1990 as part of an effort by the Iowa Department of Education to move away from a traditional service delivery model, in which students were served in either general or special education and eligibility for individualized intervention services was dependent on formal identification of students as having a particular disability and needing special education. The problem-solving model was initially implemented with individual students, but now many Iowa schools are additionally using problem solving to analyze and target intervention toward schoolwide problems.

The Iowa problem-solving model had its origins in early work on behavioral consultation (Bergan, 1977; Tharp & Wetzel, 1969), and formal steps in problem solving were used with individual students. The steps are illustrated in Figure 30.4. When students experience academic difficulties, education professionals conduct an assessment to ascertain the difference between expected and actual student behavior or performance. Data are collected in an effort to clearly define the problem, determine why it is occurring, and identify an intervention that has a high likelihood of success. A plan is developed for addressing the problem, the plan is implemented, and the plan is evaluated. "The process of defining problems, developing plans, implementing plans, and evaluating effectiveness is used with a greater degree of specificity and with additional resources as the intensity and severity of problems increases" (Grimes & Kurns, 2003).

In the past, this process has been applied at four different levels to address individual student problems of varying severity and need for resources. More recently, the model has been refined to address problems from a schoolwide

FIGURE 30.4
Problem-Solving Process

SOURCE: Grimes, J., & Kurns, S. (2003). An intervention-based system for addressing NCLB and IDEA expectations: A multiple-tiered model to ensure every child learns. Paper presented at a Responsiveness to Intervention Symposium sponsored by the National Center on Learning Disabilities. Kansas City, MO, December 4–5, 2003.

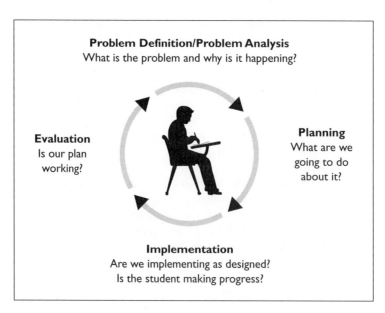

Problem Definition/Problem Analysis
What is the problem and why is it happening?

Evaluation
Is our plan working?

Planning
What are we going to do about it?

Implementation
Are we implementing as designed?
Is the student making progress?

perspective using a three-tier overlay to the traditional four-tier model. Core instruction (as we specified earlier in describing assessment of response to instruction) is considered the "universal intervention," or the set of experiences that students receive in general education. It is argued that "the most efficient manner of improving student performance is through the provision of an effective core curriculum and then early determination of performance gaps for students whose performance is not keeping pace with expectations" (Grimes & Kurns, 2003).

Tier 2, sometimes called "secondary intervention" (we labeled it "enhanced instruction"), consists of implementation of specific educational interventions for students experiencing academic and behavior problems, and systematic assessment of the extent to which those interventions are successful in enabling the student to improve in functioning and to be more like his or her peers. Tier 3 interventions are intensive interventions for students who do not profit from Tier 2 interventions, and they may include special education services. The Heartland problem-solving approach is shown in Figure 30.5.

Assessment within the Heartland problem-solving model typically consists of periodic measurement of the progress of all students in general education settings (Assessment of Response to Instruction). Devices like the Dynamic Indicators of Basic Early Literacy Skills (DIBELS; Good & Kaminski, 2002) are administered periodically (several times a year), and students who fail to perform as well as their peers are identified for problem-solving intervention within Tier 2 or Tier 3 of the schoolwide model. It is possible at Tier 1 to engage in continuous assessment of the progress of all students toward state or district standards. The technology exists for enabling school personnel to do this (for

FIGURE 30.5
Heartland Problem-Solving Approach

SOURCE: Heartland Area Education Agency, Johnston, Iowa. Reprinted by permission.

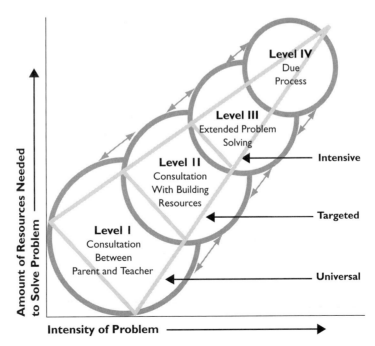

example, using Accelerated Math or Yearly Progress Pro) on a continuous rather than a periodic basis. Within Heartland, school teams are developed to systematically examine schoolwide student performance data in relationship to the school curriculum, instruction, and environment, in order to identify whether intervention is needed, and how intervention could most effectively be targeted.

The needs of many students who fail to demonstrate satisfactory performance and progress according to Tier 1 schoolwide data collection devices are referred for additional assessment at Tier 2. This typically includes about 10 to 15 percent of the school population. Interventions are selected by school personnel to target identified needs, and progress is monitored on a biweekly or monthly basis using tools such as the DIBELS or curriculum-based measurement methodologies derived from the early work of Deno, D. Fuchs, L. Fuchs, and Shinn (Deno, 1985; Deno & Fuchs, 1987; Shinn, 1989; L. Fuchs, Deno, & Mirkin, 1984). Teams working through the problem-solving process at Tier 2 may include professionals with greater expertise in CBE to assist with analyzing problems and developing interventions.

Assessment at Tier 3 involves the expertise of a specialist (school psychologist, educational consultant, social worker) in the given area of concern. Curriculum-based evaluation is used to more systematically examine the nature of the individual pupil's problem and to collect data that can link to a potentially highly effective intervention. Progress is measured very frequently (at least once weekly) using curriculum-based measurement techniques, and the intervention is modified as needed. Special education support may be considered for students requiring a continued high level of support.

Pennsylvania Instructional Support Team Model

The Pennsylvania Instructional Support Team (IST) model also came about in response to a perceived need by the Pennsylvania Department of Education to develop supports for students with disabilities in general education classes rather than to classify them and move them to set-aside placements like self-contained classes and resource rooms. The ISTs are now in place in Virginia, Delaware, Illinois, and elsewhere. The model is put in place at the prereferral level and consists of collaborative team problem solving in an effort to identify instructional approaches that move struggling students forward. The Pennsylvania ISTs are much like the problem-solving teams in Iowa. An important difference is the assessment methodology used. The Pennsylvania teams use curriculum-based assessment based on the early work of Gickling and Havertape (1980). All of these approaches focus on a team of teachers and specialists consulting with classroom teachers on individual students through a problem-solving process. The goal is to craft adaptations to the instructional program in the general education classroom that are intended to resolve the "problem" presented by the target student, while having a positive impact on the instructional program for all students. In Figure 30.6 we show the current model used in the Pennsylvania IST system. The current model is an adaptation of the earlier model used and incorporates initial assessment, systematic tryout of interventions, formal assessment of the effectiveness of those interventions, and continuous monitoring of student performance and progress.

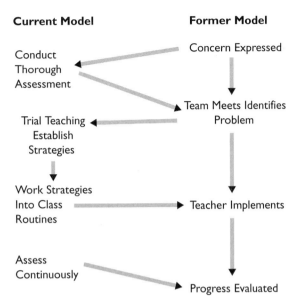

FIGURE 30.6
Addition of Program
Features to the Current
Problem-Solving Team
Model

SOURCE: Kovaleski, J.
(2003, December). The
three-tier model for identifying learning disabilities: Critical program
features and system is-
sues. National Research
Center on Learning Dis-
abilities Responsiveness
to Intervention Sympo-
sium, Kansas City, MO.

Ohio Instructionally Based Assessment (IBA) Model

Ohio's IBA program began in the early 1990s in selected Ohio school districts. Schools that already had multidisciplinary teams in place became part of a project in which teams gathered data on instructional performance and used the data to plan instructional interventions for individual students who were suspected of disability. The Ohio model was patterned on premises of behavioral consultation and functional analysis. Members of multidisciplinary teams work together to design interventions and to monitor student progress toward specific instructional goals. There are no specific phases in IBA, and continuous instruction and assessment occur until effective approaches are identified or the student is declared eligible for special education services. The Ohio model includes continuous assessment of student progress and use of the information collected to make instructional, and eventually eligibility, decisions. The model includes both assessment of response to instruction and assessment of response to intervention.

Minneapolis Problem-Solving Model

Educational personnel in the Minneapolis Public Schools actually use the assessment term *curriculum-based measurement* to refer to their model of problem solving. They describe their model as one in which there are repeated assessments of student progress across time, and these assessments are used to evaluate the impact of instructional modifications. In Minneapolis, students are declared eligible for special education services and are usually referred to as "students needing alternative programming" (SNAP students) when they fail to make progress after being exposed to increasingly intensive regular education instructional adaptations.

Issues and Considerations

Given that school personnel are engaged in increased response to intervention, it is important that you think about factors that will be critical in making decisions about the extent to which assessment of RTI procedures are effective. In this section we review a number of those factors or issues.

Intervention Integrity

As school personnel assess response to intervention, it will be critical to demonstrate that intervention is occurring and that it is occurring in ways that it was intended. Imagine assessing student response to treatment, concluding that the student did not respond to the treatment, and then learning later that the treatment either was never put in place or was poorly implemented. Or imagine that a student starts to make substantial progress, but you are not sure what made the difference and thus are not sure what to maintain or change in a student's program. More than for other forms of assessment, RTI assessment models are dependent on effective instruction's being implemented with good integrity.

There are likely a number of ways to make sure that interventions are put in place with good integrity. First, teachers need to learn the nuances of implementing an intervention. If, for example, teachers are to implement the Success for All program with their classes, it would be important that they know the specifics of doing so. They might attend specific training in Success for All, read extensively about implementation of the program, or work for a time alongside another teacher in a setting where Success for All is being implemented. If teachers are to work with individual students on phonemic awareness, it is important that they know how to do so and that they do so with implementation integrity.

Assessors can examine the extent to which interventions are implemented with integrity by specifically listing the steps in the intervention. Then they can directly observe the extent to which the teacher implements the intervention.

Upah and Tilley (2002) identify a 12-component quality indicator model that can be used to indicate best practices in designing, implementing, and evaluating quality interventions. These quality indices are as follows:

Problem identification. The problem is defined as the difference between what is expected and the actual student behavior or performance.

- *Behavioral definition.* The behavior must be defined in observable and measurable terms.
- *Baseline data.* Current level of performance must be measured.
- *Problem validation.* The student's behavior must be shown to deviate from peers' behavior or classroom expectations.

Problem analysis. The team or teacher examines why the problem is occurring.

- *Problem analysis steps.* The team identifies relevant known and unknown information, generates a hypothesis, validates the hypothesis, and links the assessment information to the intervention design.

Plan implementation. The plan is put into place.

- *Goal setting.* Goals are stated clearly in a measurable way and indicate what the student's performance will look like if the intervention is successful.
- *Intervention plan development.* An intervention plan is developed.
- *Measurement strategy.* A way to gather progress data is identified.
- *Decision-making plan.* The team specifies how data will be used to drive improved instruction.

Program evaluation. The team analyzes the extent to which the program worked.

- *Progress monitoring.* The team decides whether to use CBM procedures, observations, frequency counts, checklists, portfolios, or rating scales.
- *Formative evaluation.* An assessment of the extent to which the intervention plan is working
- *Treatment integrity.* An assessment of the extent to which the plan is being implemented as intended and as desired
- *Summative evaluation.* An assessment of the extent to which the plan worked

Intervention Efficacy

When examining response to intervention for individual students, there should be good evidence that the treatment itself is generally effective with students who are at the same age and grade as the student being assessed. This is especially true in models that require normative peer comparisons (examinations of pupil progress relative to that of classmates). Under the requirements of NCLB, school personnel are expected to be putting in place evidence-based treatments. Information about the extent to which treatments are generally effective is found by reviewing the research evidence in support of the treatments.

The What Works Clearinghouse (WWC) can provide direction as to what treatments might be particularly effective. You can go to the WWC website, look up interventions for middle school math, and find a topic report listing the kinds of interventions that the clearinghouse reviewed on middle school math. Information on the extent to which there is good empirical support for a particular intervention can be obtained from the website.

However, always remember that efficacy is local. It is highly recommended that you consider the characteristics of the student and teachers when selecting an intervention, rather than rely solely on what has been shown to be most effective in the research literature. If an intervention is not targeted appropriately to an individual child's or school's needs, it may not be effective. What works in general might not work for Billy. That is why we monitor Billy's performance to see if the treatment is efficacious for him, too.

Response Stability

In assessing response to intervention, it is important to document the extent to which the student's response varies over content and over time. We expect that in nearly all instances it will. Few students respond to the content of different subject matter in the same way, and their responses are seldom consistent over time. We are interested in the usual response to instruction, not response to instruction on a bad day.

It is said that we all "get sick of too much of a good thing." It is often the case that an intervention that "works" and is effective in moving a student toward an instructional goal will work for only a limited period of time. Students get satiated with specific instructional approaches or interventions. Indeed, one of the evidence-based principles of effective instruction is that variety in instructional presentation and in response demand enhances instructional outcomes.

FIGURE 30.7A, B, AND C
Alternative Ways of Presenting Data

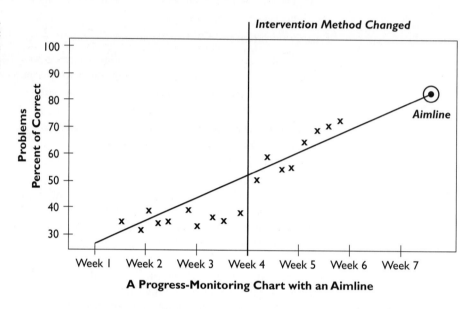

A Progress-Monitoring Chart with an Aimline

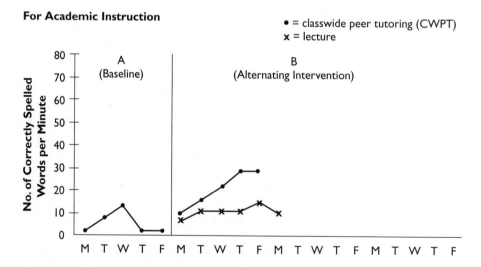

Goal: Improve Robin's spelling accuracy.

Intervention: Alternate between classwide peer tutoring and lecture formats to determine which is most effective.

Across Behaviors

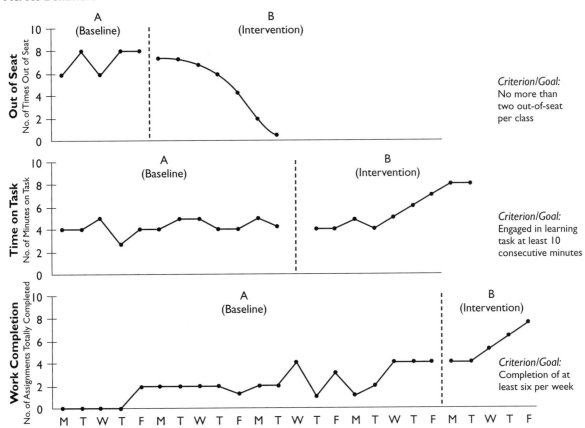

Goal: Reduce out-of-seat behavior and increase time on task and work completion.

Intervention: Lottery ticket system.

This presents significant challenges for those who teach students with learning and behavior problems. They must not only identify instructional approaches that work, but must also identify multiple competing instructional approaches that work. You may need to work to identify several different approaches to achieve the same instructional goals.

Data Presentation for Decision Making

Assessment of response to intervention involves more than collecting data. The data must be *used*. Typically data are presented visually in a format that enables communication among educational professionals about the extent to which a student is responding to intervention. There are several alternative ways of presenting data, and these different ways are best for communicating different kinds of information. In Figure 30.7 we illustrate three different ways of presenting data. Fuchs and Fuchs (1986a) found that graphing student progress resulted in better student achievement than the use of record sheets.

Interventions Are Not Linear. School-based interventions do not occur in a linear, well-specified sequence. Many interventions (or components of interventions) occur simultaneously or spiral back on themselves. School personnel should not think of instruction as following a "do A, then B, then C, then D" approach. A more realistic picture of what actually occurs is something like "Do A, do B, do A, do A again, do C, do A, do B, do C, do D." Students who are difficult to teach require repetition and reteaching.

What Cutoff? When one assesses response to intervention, the goal is to find interventions that work or do not work. So, at what point does one decide that an intervention is not working or does not work? How long does a student have to fail at a set of tasks before we conclude that he or she cannot do the task? At what point on a continuum is a student considered eligible for or entitled to special education services? What is a good response to instruction? Should local norms or a universal standard be used to decide when response to intervention is adequate? Although we have some guidelines for modifying instruction based on common-sense considerations in the precision teaching and CBM literature, there are no validated cutoffs for what is sufficiently unresponsive to instruction to be considered disabled.

Can't Do It Versus Won't Do It When we assess student response to intervention, we learn one of two things: The student demonstrates the skill (she or he does it) or does not demonstrate the skill (she or he does not do it). It is always critical that assessment personnel consider carefully whether failure to respond correctly is indicative of a skill deficit or a performance deficit. Some students have skills that they simply choose not to demonstrate. This distinction has important implications for how interventions should be designed to improve student functioning. If you think a student does not have the skill, but they actually do, and you spend time teaching the skill, this will be a serious waste of time and energy. Likewise, if you implement an intervention that merely rewards skill demonstration, the intervention will have no effect for a student who does not actually have the skill to begin with.

Old Wine in New Bottles Some teachers cannot or will not do CBA, CBM, or IBA. And some teachers will continue to do what they have always done but use the current terminology (RTI) to describe their practices, even though they are doing nothing remotely like what is needed. It will be necessary to demonstrate the value of RTI to teachers who currently are not using it and also necessary to find practices that educators currently are using but that are not useful so that these may be eliminated and replaced with RTI. This keeps RTI from becoming "one more thing on my plate."

How Well Can We Monitor Progress in All Content Areas? Although the quality of available progress-monitoring procedures has improved greatly in recent years, they are largely limited to measurement within a few content areas, such as reading decoding, writing, and math facts and computation at the elementary level. Measures that are sensitive to progress in other areas and at the secondary level will need to be developed and tested in order to appropriately apply RTI procedures in additional areas. Right now measures are not available that are highly sensitive to growth in social skills, study skills, and reading comprehension. Effective application of RTI in these areas will require the development of more technically adequate formative measures.

Avoiding Intervention Smorgasbords Throughout this chapter we have attempted to stress the fact that assessment of response to instruction or response to intervention requires that the interventions being implemented are ones for which there is good evidence of their effectiveness. School personnel need to be implementing evidence-based interventions rather than simply "tossing" a variety of interesting interventions at students.

Technology-Enhanced Progress-Monitoring Systems

Application of RTI assessment methods in school settings is labor intensive. Educational professionals need to be committed to a problem-solving approach to assessment of student performance and progress, and they need to be provided with tools that will enable them to do the job of collecting massive amounts of data in the process of progress monitoring. In fact, without the aid of technology we believe it will be impossible for school personnel to engage in RTI.

Concluding Comments

The practice of gathering data on student performance and progress and then using those data for purposes of making subsequent instructional decisions clearly has merit and appeal. The process also brings with it a significant amount of work for classroom teachers. They, or those who assist them, must have a clear understanding of precisely what educational outcomes are desired and then decide what measures to use. They may choose to build their own assessment procedures, select from available measures on now-common websites that provide them with such assessments (for instance, list of graded words or word passages), or use the measures developed by CBM and CBA research projects. No matter how they build their measures, the collection, maintenance, and use of data on student performance and progress can be a "records-intensive" and time-consuming process. It need not be that way, however. There are now commercially available progress-monitoring systems that can be used to monitor student performance and progress in any curriculum on a direct and continuous basis. Programs like Accelerated Math (AM) are progress-monitoring systems that perform a number of important functions for the teacher:

1. They assign academic work matched to the student's current level of skill development.
2. They provide the student with relevant practice exercises, scan in student responses, score the responses, and provide feedback on accuracy to the student.

3. They provide the teacher with a daily printout showing the current standing and progress of every student in a class. This printout includes a flagging system to identify students who are experiencing difficulty with their practice exercises and who need instructional assistance. Additional reports show the teacher the specific skills that students are having difficulty mastering.

4. They notify teachers when students have been demonstrating sufficient mastery of daily practice exercises that they are ready for a test. The teacher approves computer generation of the test. The student scans his or her responses into the computer, and the test is scored by the computer. The computer signals mastery or nonmastery of the specific instructional objective and assigns new work for the student.

Systems like AM can be used to monitor progress in any math curricula, and they tell teachers whether or not students are mastering the material and making progress. The measures used in AM are similar to the kinds of measures that Deno has referred to as "general outcome measures."

Technology-enhanced systems like Standards Master can be used to measure student progress toward mastery of state standards. The system measures student progress periodically (typically three to ten times per year) and lets school personnel know the extent to which all students in a teacher's class are on target to master the state standards for a given level. Again, the measures are generated and scored by the computer, and feedback is immediate.

We believe that technology-enhanced systems (we can refer here to AIMSweb, AM, AW [Accelerated Writer], DIBELS, Yearly Progress Pro, and the new systems being developed by Microsoft and IBM) can make RTI more acceptable and useful.

SUMMARY

For many years educational professionals have gathered data on student performance and progress. They just have not done so systematically. Data on student progress have been used primarily to "see how students are doing" and to make judgments about whether, how, and when to change what is being done with the student. Now, the process is becoming more prevalent, and it is being extended to the making of eligibility decisions. School personnel engage

in two kinds of progress monitoring: they monitor day-to-day progress in regular instruction, and, when they develop specialized interventions for individual students, they monitor response to those interventions. We differentiated response to instruction and response to intervention. We described ways in which people gather data on RTI, and we described the steps in doing so. When response to intervention is assessed, one must always make sure that the intervention assessed was actually implemented as intended. This is called intervention integrity. We concluded the chapter by raising a set of issues about assessing response to intervention.

QUESTIONS FOR CHAPTER REVIEW

1. State the difference between response to instruction and response to intervention. Then indicate why an educational professional would be concerned about each.

2. Get together with one or more of your classmates and discuss the relative merits and limitations of a test-based approach and an RTI approach in making decisions about whether students are eligible for special education.

3. Why is it important always to check on intervention integrity in assessing response to intervention?

PROJECT

Put "response to intervention" in a search engine on your computer. This will yield several school district websites where the district's RTI practices are described. Select two school districts and compare their approaches.

RESOURCES FOR FURTHER INVESTIGATION

Print Resources

Batsche, G., Elliott, J., Graden, J., Grimes, J., Kovaleski, J., Prasse, D., et al. (2005). *Response to intervention: Policy considerations and implementation.* Alexandria, VA: National Association of State Directors of Special Education.

Christ, T., Burns, M., & Ysseldyke, J. (in press). Conceptual confusion within response-to-intervention vernacular: Clarifying meaningful differences. *Communique.*

Technology Resources

AIMSweb
www.edformation.com
This is the website for AIMSweb, a progress-monitoring and instructional management system. Included at this website is a section on AIMSweb RTI. The site includes a description of the steps school teams need to go through in conducting RTI, and copies of forms to use in the process of completing an assessment of RTI.

RESEARCH INSTITUTE ON PROCESS MONITORING
www.progressmonitoring.net
The research institute focuses on the development of a seamless and flexible system of progress monitoring that can be applied across students and curricula. This system of progress monitoring will be used to evaluate the effects of individualized instruction on access to and progress in the general education curriculum for students with disabilities and will result in improved instructional decision making, which will in turn result in more successful instructional programs in general education for students with disabilities.

The research conducted through the Research Institute on Progress Monitoring will involve Minnesota and Iowa students of varying ages (3–21 years) and disability levels (from students without disabilities to students with mild, moderate, and severe disabilities, including students who are blind, deaf, hard of hearing, or who have autism). Research will involve varying curriculum areas (reading, mathematics, written expression, and science), topics (from the development of measures to the use of those measures for instructional evaluation), and languages (development of measures in English and Spanish).

CHAPTER 31

Making Accountability Decisions

ARE OUR SCHOOLS PRODUCING THE RESULTS WE WANT? TO WHAT EXTENT ARE INDIvidual students meeting the goals, standards, or outcomes that their schools have set for them? What goals or standards should we expect students and schools to meet? How should we assess progress toward meeting standards? Over the past 15 years there has been an increased focus on the results of education for all students, including students with disabilities. In this chapter we examine the collection and use of assessment information for the purpose of making accountability decisions.

A powerful idea dominates policy discussions about schools: the notion that "students should be held to high, common standards for academic performance and that schools and the people who work in them should be held accountable for ensuring that students—all students—are able to meet those standards" (Elmore, 2002). It has not always been that way. Until the early to mid-1990s, school personnel focused on the *process* of providing services to students. They provided evidence that they were teaching students and, often, evidence that they were teaching specific types of students (such as Title I, mentally retarded, or disadvantaged students). When administrators were asked about special education students or services, they typically described the numbers and kinds of students who were tested or taught, the settings in which they were taught, or the numbers of special education teachers who tested and taught them (for instance, "We have 2,321 students with disabilities in our district; 1,620 are educated in general education classes with special education supports, and the remainder are in resource rooms, self-contained classes, and out-of-school settings; the students are served by 118 special education teachers and 19 related services personnel."). Few administrators could provide evidence for the results or outcomes of the services being provided. Since the early 1990s there has been a dramatic shift in focus from serving students with disabilities to measuring the results of the services provided. This shift has paralleled the Total Quality Management (TQM; Deming, 1994, 2000), Results-Based Management, and Management by

Objectives (Olson, 1964) movements in business, and more recently in federal and state government.

Much of the impetus for this shift to a focus on results was the publication of *A Nation at Risk: The Imperative for Educational Reform* (National Commission of Excellence in Education, 1983). In this document, the then-secretary of education revealed the low status of U.S. schoolchildren relative to their counterparts in other nations and reported that "the educational foundations of our society are presently being eroded by a rising tide of mediocrity that threatens our very future as a nation and a people" (p. 5). In this report, the secretary argued that the nation was at risk because mediocrity, not excellence, was the norm in education. Recommendations included more time for learning, better textbooks and other materials, more homework, higher expectations, stricter attendance policies, and improved standards, salaries, rewards, and incentives for teachers. The entire nation began to focus on raising educational standards, measuring performance, and achieving results. Policy makers and bureaucrats, who had been spending a great deal of money to fund special education, began demanding evidence of its effectiveness. In essence, they employed the old saw "The proof of the pudding is in the eating"—arguing that it matters little what you do if it does not produce what you want.

In 1994 the Clinton administration specified a set of national education goals. Called Goals 2000, these were a list of goals that students should achieve by the year 2000. The 1994 reauthorization of the Elementary and Secondary Education Act (ESEA), known as the Improving American Schools Act or IASA, included a requirement that, in Title I schools, disadvantaged students should be expected to attain the same challenging standards as all other students. The 1997 reauthorization of the Individuals with Disabilities Education Act (IDEA) included provisions specifying that students with disabilities should participate in states' assessment and accountability systems, that states needed to specify standards to be attained by *all* students, and that states would report each year on the extent to which *all* students, including students with disabilities, met state-specified standards. In 2004 Congress again amended the IDEA and reaffirmed those requirements.

The No Child Left Behind Act of 2001 (a portion of the Improving America's Schools Act) included requirements that states report annually on the performance and progress of *all* students. All states now have accountability systems and are required by law to report on the participation and performance of students with disabilities on their state assessments. Within state or district systems, there may be two kinds of accountability. One kind assigns responsibility to the student (*student accountability*) and the other assigns responsibility to the educational system or to individuals within that system (*system accountability*). System accountability is designed to improve educational programs, whereas student accountability is designed to motivate students to do their best. System accountability is the focus of federal education reform efforts. All states have some type of system accountability, but not all states have student accountability. Accountability systems hold schools responsible for helping all students reach high, challenging standards, providing rewards to schools that reach those standards and sanctions to schools that do not. They are used to achieve specific educational goals by attaching to performance indicators certain consequences meant to bring about change in specific areas of functioning. States or school districts specify goals they aim to achieve and then apply certain positive or negative consequences meant to promote reform to schools that meet certain performance criteria in specific areas (Marion & Gong, 2004).

Today the consequences of accountability systems are becoming more significant, often referred to as "high stakes." States are relying on evidence from state and district assessments to determine high stakes. The most common high-stakes use of assessment evidence for individual students is to determine whether a student receives a standard high school diploma or some other type of document. Another type of student accountability, appearing with increasing frequency, is the use of test scores to determine whether a student will move from one grade to another.

All states are required to have an accountability system with sanctions and rewards. Imposing sanctions on schools or administrators is slightly more prevalent than providing rewards. Among the sanctions that states commonly use are assigning negative labels to schools, removing staff, and firing principals. Rewards include assigning positive labels to schools and giving extra funding to schools or cash awards to staff.

Legal Requirements

The 1997 reauthorization of the IDEA challenged all states to develop accountability systems that were sensitive to the educational progress of all students. The law was based on the beliefs that all children can learn, that all students are to be held to the same high standards, and that schools should be held accountable to ensure that all students are achieving to the same high standards. IDEA 1997 introduced the requirement for alternate assessments. The law led to a push for specification of standards, development of assessments to measure student progress toward standards, and annual reporting on how schools and students are doing. It required alternate assessments for all students unable to participate in statewide assessments even with accommodations. The 2004 reauthorization of the IDEA contains those same requirements.

The No Child Left Behind Act included the requirement that states have assessment and accountability systems, report annually on the performance and progress of all students, and have alternate assessments in place for reporting on annual yearly progress of all students in reading, math, and science. In 2003 the U.S. Department of Education issued a set of guidelines for alternate assessments that included the concept of alternate achievement standards. School personnel are required by law to measure the performance and progress of all students, and they need to know much about how to use assessment information to make accountability decisions. The law requires that school systems look not only at how their students are doing as a whole, but at how particular groups of students are doing. To be considered successful, schools must succeed with all students.

Important Terminology

The standards-based assessment and accountability movement has brought with it a new assessment vocabulary that includes terms like *alternate achievement standards* and *adequate yearly progress*. Some of these terms are used in many different ways in the professional and popular literature. In fact, the multiple uses of the terms cause confusion. The Council of Chief State School Officers publishes a *Glossary of Assessment Terms and Acronyms Used in Assessing Special Education*. This glossary is a good source of definitions for terms used in assessment and accountability systems.

We include an adapted version of this glossary in Table 31.1.

TABLE 31.1   Glossary of Assessment Terms Used Within Accountability Systems

---

Academic standards There are two types of standards: content and performance.

- *Academic content standards.* Statements of the subject-specific knowledge and skills that schools are expected to teach students, indicating what students should know and be able to do
- *Academic achievement (performance) standards.* Indices of qualities that specify how adept or competent a student demonstration must be and that consist of the following four components:
  1. Levels that provide descriptive labels or narratives for student performance (i.e., advanced, proficient, etc.)
  2. Descriptions of what students at each particular level must demonstrate relative to the task
  3. Examples of student work at each level illustrating the range of performance within each level
  4. Cut scores clearly separating each performance level

Accommodations Changes in the administration of an assessment, such as setting, scheduling, timing, presentation format, response mode, or others, including any combination of these that does not change the construct intended to be measured by the assessment or the meaning of the resulting scores. Accommodations are used for equity, not advantage, and serve to level the playing field. To be appropriate, assessment accommodations must be identified in the student's individualized education plan (IEP) or Section 504 plan and used regularly during instruction and classroom assessment.

Accountability The use of assessment results and other data to ensure that schools are moving in desired directions. Common elements include standards, indicators of progress toward meeting those standards, analysis of data, reporting procedures, and rewards or sanctions.

Accountability system A plan that uses assessment results and other data outlining the goals and expectations for students, teachers, schools, districts, and states to demonstrate the established components or requirements of accountability. An accountability system typically includes rewards for those who exceed the goals and sanctions for those who fail to meet the goals.

Adaptations A generalized term that describes a change made in the presentation, setting, response, or timing or scheduling of an assessment that may or may not change the construct of the assessment

(*continued*)

TABLE 31.1 Glossary of Assessment Terms Used Within Accountability Systems (*continued*)

Adequate yearly progress (AYP) A provision of the federal No Child Left Behind (NCLB, 2001) legislation requiring schools, districts, and states to demonstrate on the basis of test scores that students are making academic progress based on test scores. Each state was required by NCLB to submit by January 31, 2003, a specific plan for monitoring AYP.

Alignment The similarity or match between or among content standards, performance standards, curriculum, instruction, and assessments in terms of knowledge and skill expectations

Alternate achievement standards Expectations for performance that differ in complexity from a grade-level achievement standard, but are linked to the content standards. "When designed appropriately, these alternate achievement standards represent high academic standards for students with the most significant cognitive disabilities" (U.S. Department of Education, 2005, p. 8).

Alternate assessment An instrument used in gathering information on the standards-based performance and progress of students whose disabilities preclude their valid and reliable participation in general assessments. Alternate assessments measure the performance of a relatively small population of students who are unable to participate in the general assessment system, with or without accommodations as determined by the IEP team. When used as part of state assessment programs, alternate assessments must have an explicit structure, guidelines for which students may participate, clearly defined scoring criteria and procedures, and a report format that communicates student performance in terms of the academic achievement standards defined by the state (U.S. Department of Education, 2005).

Baseline data The initial measures of performance against which future measures will be compared

Benchmarks A specific statement of knowledge and skills within a content area's continuum that a student must possess to demonstrate a level of progress toward mastery of a standard

Body of evidence Information or data that establish that a student can perform a particular skill or has mastered a specific content standard and that were either produced by the student or collected by someone who is knowledgeable about the student

Cut score A specified point on a score scale. Scores at or above that point are interpreted differently from scores below that point.

Disaggregation The collection and reporting of student achievement results by particular subgroups (e.g., students with disabilities, limited-English-proficient students) to ascertain the subgroup's academic progress. Disaggregation makes it possible to compare subgroups or cohorts.

Modification A change to the testing conditions, procedures, and/or formatting so that measurement of the intended construct is no longer valid

Modified achievement standards Expectations for performance that are lower than the grade-level achievement standards, but linked to or aligned with the content standards. This term will be further defined by policy makers in the near future.

Norm-referenced tests (NRT) A standardized test designed, validated, and implemented to rank a student's performance by comparing that performance to the performance of that student's peers

Opportunity to learn The provision of learning conditions, including suitable adjustments, to maximize a student's chances of attaining the desired learning outcomes, such as the mastery of content standards

Out-of-level testing (off-grade or off-level) Administration of a test at a level above or below a student's present grade level to enable the student to be assessed at the level of instruction rather than the level of enrollment

---

| **TABLE 31.1** | Glossary of Assessment Terms Used Within Accountability Systems (*continued*) |

Student accountability Consequences exist for individual students, and are based on their individual assessment performance. For example, students might not be promoted to the next grade or graduate if their assessment results do not meet a prespecified level.

System accountability Consequences exist for school systems, and are based on the assessment performance of a group of individuals (e.g., school building, district, or state education agency). For example, a school might receive a financial award or special recognition for having a large percent of students meeting a particular assessment performance level.

SOURCE: Adapted from Copyright © 2003 by Council of Chief State School Officers. *Glossary of assessment terms and acronyms used in assessing special education.* Policy to Practice Study Group: Assessing Special Education Students.

It's All About Meeting Standards

Assessments completed for accountability purposes involve measuring the extent to which students are learning what we want them to learn or the extent to which school systems are accomplishing what we want them to accomplish. To do this, school personnel must specify what it is that students are to learn. They typically do so by specifying a set of *academic content standards*—statements of the subject-specific knowledge and skills that schools are expected to teach students, indicating what students should know and be able to do. States must also specify *academic achievement standards* (sometimes called *performance standards*)—statements of the levels at which or the proficiency with which students will show that they have mastered the academic content standards. Academic achievement standards use language drawn directly from the NCLB law, and they have the force of law. The law requires that all students be assessed related to the state content and achievement standards, and that the state must provide for reasonable adaptations and accommodations for students with disabilities necessary to measure the academic achievement of such students relative to state academic content and state student academic achievement standards.

Two other kinds of standards apply specifically to students with disabilities: alternate achievement standards and modified achievement standards. *Alternate achievement standards* are expectations for performance that differ in complexity from a grade-level achievement standard, but they are linked to those general education standards. In August 2005, the U.S. Department of Education issued a document providing *Non-Regulatory Guidance on Alternate Achievement Standards for Students with the Most Significant Cognitive Disabilities* (U.S. Department of Education, 2005). States are permitted to define alternate achievement standards to evaluate the achievement of students with the most significant cognitive disabilities. *Modified achievement standards* are as yet undefined but are designed for students who are on IEPs and who demonstrate "persistent academic difficulties."

Standards-based assessment is characterized by specifying what all students can be expected to learn and then expecting that time will vary, but that all will achieve the standards. States are required to have in place assessments of student proficiency relative to academic content standards.

The following is a set of reasons why school personnel would want to assess student performance and progress relative to standards.

■ To ascertain the extent to which individual students are meeting state standards; that is, accomplishing what it is society wants them to accomplish

■ To ascertain the extent to which specific schools within states are providing the kinds of educational opportunities and experiences that enable their students to achieve state-specified standards

■ To provide data on student or school performance that can be helpful in making instructional policy decisions (curricula or instructional methodologies to use)

■ To decide who ought to receive a diploma as indicated by performance on tests that measure whether standards are met

■ To inform the public on the performance of schools or school districts

■ To know the extent to which specific subgroups of students are meeting specified standards

Alternate Assessment and Alternate Achievement Standards

Regardless of where students receive instruction, all students with disabilities should have access to, participate in, and make progress in the general curriculum. Thus all students with disabilities must be included in state assessment systems and in state reporting of *adequate yearly progress* (AYP) toward meeting the state's standards. We have noted that states must specify academic content standards and academic achievement standards, and must have assessments aligned to those standards. To address the needs of students with substantial concerns, states may choose to develop alternate achievement standards and modified achievement standards that are linked to the expectations for all students.

States must include all students in their assessment and accountability systems. But not all students can participate in state assessments, even with assessment accommodations designed to compensate for their specific needs. IDEA 1997 included a provision that by the year 2000 states would have in place alternate assessments intended for use with those students who evidenced severe cognitive impairments. In August 2002, the U.S. secretary of education proposed a regulation to allow states to develop and use alternate achievement standards for students with the most significant cognitive disabilities for the purpose of determining the AYP of states, local education agencies, and schools. In August 2003, the secretary specified that the number of students considered proficient using alternate assessments toward alternate achievement standards could not exceed 1 percent of all students, and on April 7, 2005, the secretary of education issued a new rule that states could have an alternate assessment for an additional 2 percent of students who evidence persistent academic difficulties and thus are working toward "modified achievement standards." Most recently, a federal decision was made to no longer call the assessments linked to modified achievement standards alternate assessments. Rather, they are to be called modified assessments. Neither of the terms modified achievement standards nor modified assessments were defined. States thus may include 1 percent of students in the alternate assessment intended for students with significant cognitive disabilities who are working toward alternate achievement standards, and 2 percent of students in a modified assessment intended for students with "persistent academic difficulties" who are working toward modified achievement standards. The significance of the new ruling is not clear. More alternate and modified assessment scores can be counted as proficient to determine AYP.

An *alternate assessment* is defined in the NCLB federal regulations as "an assessment designed for the small number of students with disabilities who are unable to participate in the regular state assessment, even with appropriate accommodations." It is indicated further that "an alternate assessment may include materials collected under several circumstances, including (1) teacher observation of the student, (2) samples of student work produced during regular classroom instruction that demonstrate mastery of specific instructional strategies…, or (3) standardized performance tasks produced in an 'on demand' setting, such as completion of an assigned task on test day" (p. 7). The assessments must yield results separately in both reading/language arts and mathematics, and must be designed and implemented in a manner that supports use of the results as an indicator of AYP.

Alternate assessments are not simply compilations of student work, sometimes referred to as box or folder stuffing. Rather, they must have a clearly defined structure, specific participation guidelines, clearly defined scoring criteria and procedures, and a reporting format that clearly communicates student performance in terms of the academic achievement standards specified by the state. Alternate assessments may be needed for students with a broad array of disabling conditions, so a state may use more than one alternate assessment.

Alternate assessments can be designed to measure student performance toward either grade-level standards or alternate achievement standards. Recall that an alternate achievement standard is an expectation of performance that differs in complexity from a grade-level standard. For example, the Massachusetts Curriculum Frameworks include the following content standard: "students will identify, analyze, and apply knowledge of the purpose, structure, and elements of nonfiction or informational materials and provide evidence from the text to support their understanding." A less complex demonstration of this standard is "to gain information from signs, symbols, and pictures in the environment"; a more complex demonstration is to "gain information from captions, titles, and table of contents in an informational text" (Massachusetts Department of Education, 2001).

As previously mentioned, modified standards and assessments are a very new concept, and at the time we were writing this section, many were only in the very beginning stages of considering what these standards and assessments might look like.

Developing Alternate Achievement Standards

As this book was being written, many states were in the beginning stages of developing alternate achievement standards. To create these, it is important to first clarify the intended student population. According to federal regulations, only students with the most significant cognitive disabilities are to participate in alternate assessments toward alternate achievement standards. Rather than defining this category to include only students with a particular disability type, it can be helpful to make the definition more general. Those students who need to be tested against alternate achievement standards are typically those students who require extensive support to meaningfully access grade-level content knowledge, in addition to intensive individualized instruction to obtain, maintain, and generalize that knowledge.

Alternate achievement standards are to be developed so that they are linked to the general content standards. They represent levels of performance on academic-related tasks that correspond to the academic skills measured among all other same-grade students. However, they involve measurement of student performance on less complex activities. Performance descriptors (such as "advanced," "satisfactory," "limited knowledge," "unsatisfactory") for alternate achievement standards can be similar to those used to describe performance toward the regular achievement standards. Methods used to determine performance levels can also be similar to those used to determine regular achievement standards, but the individuals involved in determining performance levels should be very familiar with the population assessed. The process may involve the selection of a panel of knowledgeable judges who examine sample student alternate assessment data across multiple iterations, eventually reaching consensus about the data needed to constitute performance at various levels. Cut scores should be set to represent meaningful levels of performance, and procedures for scoring student performance should be carefully described, with training provided to those who will be involved in the scoring process. The development of exemplars can assist with communicating cut scores and performance levels to those who will be involved in scoring alternate assessments toward alternate achievement standards.

Developing Standards-Based Accountability Systems

Nationally, there is no consensus on educational standards. States have been developing standards-based accountability systems, and these are revised and rewritten regularly. There is also much debate about whether alternate assessments must be aligned with the general education standards or simply linked to those standards. The National Center on Educational Outcomes developed a self-study guide for states and school districts to use in the development of accountability systems (Ysseldyke & Thurlow, 1993). In this section of this chapter, we rely on the content of the self-study guide and describe the process that a school or school district would go through in developing a system to assess the extent to which it is achieving desired results. We describe ways to accomplish the following:

◼ Establish a solid foundation for educators' assessment efforts.

◼ Develop, adopt, or adapt a conceptual model of outcomes and indicators.

◼ Establish a data collection and reporting system.

◼ Install a standards-based accountability system.

Establish a Solid Foundation for Assessment Efforts

Accountability systems must be carefully thought out and comply with current federal legislation. It is important that stakeholders be involved up front and throughout the entire process, with their involvement carefully documented and reported, and that they give considerable thought to why they want to measure and report results. Considerable confusion exists in this field, so it is very important to define terms and consider the assumptions that underlie efforts to account for educational results. Finally, it is critical to resolve some fundamental issues before beginning.

Involve Stakeholders Up Front

Stakeholders are those individuals in a community who have a personal interest in the measurement of educational results: teachers, supervisors, providers of related services, parents, representatives of community agencies, and students. Involving stakeholders up front in the process of developing standards and desired results enhances their feeling of investment in the assessment process and their desire to participate in it. Involvement up front empowers these individuals or groups to chart their own activities and futures.

Decide Why We Measure and Account for Results

There are four major reasons that stakeholders want to measure educational results: instructional improvement, public accountability, public information, and policy formulation. First, data on the results of service provision can be useful in improving instructional programs for students. In fact, to improve instructional practices, it is imperative that school personnel have data illustrating the extent to which what they are doing is achieving the desired results. For example, school personnel might want to know the extent to which the math curriculum they are using is resulting in students' earning high scores on math tests. Knowledge of results enables professionals to consider making changes in instructional programs. For instructional improvement, it is important that stakeholders reach agreement on assessment goals.

Second, data on results are important for accountability: to document for people in authority that desired goals are being met. Tests are regularly given to students, and data indicating how pupils are doing are provided to state agencies and school districts within states. The test scores can be used by legislators and policy makers to decide whether they are getting their money's worth from funds invested in education.

Third, data on educational results are useful in providing public information on the outcomes of schooling. You may have seen reports in newspapers indicating how the nation's youth is doing in math, reading, science, and other forms of literacy.

Fourth, data on results are useful in policy formulation. Those who formulate educational policy repeatedly indicate the need to have information about outcomes of schooling in order to allocate resources and establish instructional processes.

Consider the Assumptions That Underlie an Accountability System

Any accountability system is based on a number of assumptions. Those who want to assess educational results will have to consider carefully the assumptions that underlie the system they develop. There is general agreement on the following:

- Accountability systems are needed for all students and, at the broadest level, should apply to all students, regardless of the characteristics of individuals.
- Accountability systems should focus primarily on intended outcomes but be sensitive to unintended outcomes of schooling.
- Indicators of results for students receiving special education services should be related, conceptually and statistically, to those identified for students without disabilities.
- Indicators should reflect the diversity of gender, culture, race, and other characteristics of the students in today's school population.
- An accountability system should provide the data needed to make policy decisions at the national, state, and local levels.
- An accountability system should be flexible, dynamic, and responsive to review and criticism. It should also change to meet identified needs and future developments in the measurement of educational inputs, contexts, processes, and results.

Develop, Adopt, or Adapt a Conceptual Model of Outcomes and Indicators

Specify Content Domains for Data Collection

School personnel typically restrict data collection to academic content domains. In some instances, states specify both academic and functional literacy domains.

Specify Rewards and Sanctions

Educational professionals must decide the kinds of rewards that will be provided for students, teachers, schools, and districts who provide evidence of making annual yearly progress for all students. And they must specify the kinds of sanctions that will be provided to those who fail to show progress.

Establish a Data Collection and Reporting System

Stakeholders should give considerable thought to sources of information or data that can be used to illustrate educational results. Decisions need to be made about where data will come from, how they will be collected, and how results will be reported to and used by the general community.

Identify Data Sources

Those who engage in standards-based accountability will necessarily have to identify sources from which they can get data or the extent to which results are being met. A fundamental premise to guide the data collection process is that it should rely as much as possible on use of existing information.

Develop or Adapt Data Collection and Analysis Mechanisms

School personnel find that they have to create new data collection mechanisms to address new indicators or to include new populations that have not been included before. Data collection systems must be designed in such a way that they are sensitive to cultural differences during sampling, instrument development, data collection, and data analysis.

Decide How Information Will Be Reported and Used

Information on educational results (accountability systems) needs to be reported in ways that are meaningful to the intended audience. It is important to ask members of the audience (for instance, administrators, school board members) what would help them make decisions consistent with the stated purpose of the accountability system (such as program improvement, public information, or policy formulation). Probably the most important decision to be made is how the data will be used. Will rewards and consequences be given as a result of educational outcomes? Other reporting decisions to be made include levels of reporting (system versus individual), formats and types of reports, types of comparisons to be reported, ways of presenting and grouping data, and vehicles for dissemination of information.

Install a Standards-Based Accountability System

An accountability system cannot be installed overnight. Those who use the information on results will need to see personal and programmatic benefits before the system can be considered fully in place. There must be incentives for the teachers, parents, and administrators who will ultimately ensure the success of the system.

Two commonly used incentives are public comparisons and sanctions for failure to meet standards or goals. Public comparisons formally display schools, districts, or states side by side. Sanctioning involves negative techniques such as withdrawal of accreditation, takeovers of schools, and reduction of funding based on identification of inadequate outcomes. Both comparisons and sanctions are high-stakes uses of any accountability system. They can lead to overemphasis on appearances, without substantive changes.

Change in measurement and accountability systems occurs in the same way that it occurs in any other system. State or government agencies fund research and demonstration projects, establish networking and recognition systems, and provide resources for use of outcomes-based accountability systems. Personnel in state departments of education provide technical assistance to local school districts that are trying to implement accountability systems.

Once an outcomes-based accountability system is in place and being used, we may be able to identify the extent to which the interventions used with individuals who have disabilities are working as we would like them to work. Systemwide accountability assessment should enable us to make judgments about the extent of the system's success.

Current State Assessment and Accountability Practices

With the exception of Iowa, all state education agencies have specified standards that they expect students to achieve (standards in Iowa are specified at the district or Area Education Agency level). Over the past decade, states have been busy developing assessments to measure student progress toward standards and guidelines to provide direction on those students who are to participate and how they are to participate.

Accountability systems and assessments for the purpose of accountability differ considerably from state to state. Most states convene panels of stakeholders to reach agreement on state education standards in specific content areas (usually reading/language arts, mathematics, writing, social studies, and science). States then typically contract with test publishers to develop tests that assess the content of their state standards. When publishers build state-specific tests, the standards-referenced tests they build are usually referred to as "custom made." In some instances (as noted above), off-the-shelf norm-referenced tests (such as the Stanford Achievement Test 10 or the Iowa Tests of Basic Skills) are used as state tests. We include in this section a description of the statewide accountability systems in California, Texas, Michigan, Iowa, and Nebraska to illustrate the variability in assessment systems across the various states. We selected states that differed significantly in their approaches, rather than states that were representative in size, geographic region, or demographic makeup.

California

The California Department of Education refers to its statewide testing program as the Standardized Testing and Reporting (STAR) program. Three kinds of statewide tests are administered in California. The California Standards Tests (CSTs) and the California Alternate Performance Assessment (CAPA) are criterion-referenced tests. Results are based on how well students achieve identified state-adopted content standards, not how student results compare with results of other students taking the same tests. The California Department of Education also administers the California High School Exit Exam (CAHSEE), an exam built for the state by the Educational Testing Service. Beginning in 2005–2006, all students must pass this exam to get a high school diploma. The California Department of Education computes an Academic Performance Index (API) to measure the performance and growth of individual schools in the state. The API is a numeric index (or scale) that ranges from a low of 200 to a high of 1,000. A school's score on the API is an indicator of a school's performance level. The statewide API performance target for all schools is 800. A school's growth is measured by how well it is moving toward or past that goal. A school's base-year API is subtracted from its growth API to determine how much the school improved in a year.

Texas

The statewide testing program in Texas has four components. The major statewide test is called the Texas Assessment of Knowledge and Skills (TAKS™). Texas has a statewide curriculum (most states do not), and the TAKS is used to measure performance in the statewide curriculum. Texas also has a State-Developed Alternative Assessment II (SDAA II), which is used to assess students who are receiving instruction in Texas Essential Knowledge and Skills, but for whom TAKS is an inappropriate measure of their academic performance. The Reading Proficiency Tests in English (RPTE) are administered as a measure of annual growth in the English-reading proficiency of English-language learners. Students with limited English proficiency in grades 3 through 12 take the RPTE until they achieve a reading level of advanced. Like California, Texas requires that students pass an exit exam to receive a standard high school diploma. At this time, the exit exam is the Texas Assessment of Academic Skills (TAAS), which will remain the graduation test for students who were enrolled in grade 9 or higher on January 1, 2001.

Michigan

The statewide assessment system in Michigan is called the Michigan Educational Assessment System (MEAS). It has three components: the Michigan Educational Assessment Program (MEAP), MI-Access, and ELL-Access. MI-Access is designed for students for whom the IEP team has determined that the MEAP assessments, even with assessment accommodations, are not appropriate for the student. ELL-Access is designed for use with students whose primary language is not English. The Michigan Educational Assessment Program tests were developed for the purpose of determining what students know and what they are able to do, as compared to state standards at key checkpoints during their academic career. The state standards are specifications of what Michigan educators believe all students should know and be able to achieve in five content areas: reading, mathematics, science, social studies, and writing. Beginning in 2007, the MEAP for high school students is known as the Michigan Merit Exam (MME). No other tests may be used to assess student performance or progress relative to Michigan Standards.

Michigan has a unique practice of awarding monetary rewards to students who demonstrate outstanding performance on the MEAP or MME. The award provides $2,500 to individual students.

Iowa and Nebraska

Not all states have mandated state tests. Iowa and Nebraska are examples of exceptions. In Iowa, there are no statewide standards. Rather, the individual local education agencies in Iowa specify local standards. The districts then report to the state how their students and schools do relative to the district standards.

The Nebraska Department of Education has specified a set of state standards, but there is no statewide test in Nebraska. Rather, individual districts (there are more than 400 of these in Nebraska) report on the performance and progress of students relative to the state standards. The Nebraska accountability system is referred to as the School-Based Teacher-Led Assessment and Reporting System (STARS). The system is grounded in the belief that decisions about student learning should be standards based and based on classroom knowledge of the student. The system relies on the professional expertise of Nebraska educators who use locally designed assessments in combination with national tests and a statewide writing assessment to determine the performance of students on the academically rigorous content standards. The tests developed by local school districts must meet six criteria:

1. They must match and measure the standards.
2. They must provide opportunity for students to have learned the content.
3. They must be free of bias.
4. They must be written at the appropriate level.
5. They must be reliable and consistently scored.
6. Districts must determine appropriate mastery levels.

Important Considerations in Assessment for the Purpose of Making Accountability Decisions

As a result of accountability system implementation, student assessment data have become much more readily available to the public. Although this public reporting is intended to promote better student instruction and learning, it is important that those who have access to the data know how to appropriately interpret the information. Without these skills, poor judgments and decisions may be made that are harmful to students. For instance, it is important for consumers of accountability information to understand that most tests used for accountability purposes are intended to measure performance of an entire group of students and that the tests do not necessarily provide reliable data on the skills of individual students. Without this knowledge, consumers may make unwarranted judgments and decisions about individual students based on their test scores.

In addition, it is important for people to recognize that not all students need to be tested in the same way; it is often important for students to be tested using different formats. Some students have special characteristics that make it difficult for them to demonstrate their knowledge on content standards in a traditional paper-and-pencil format. These students may need accommodations to demonstrate their true knowledge. What is most important is that students' knowledge and skill toward the identified achievement standards are measured. Those with assessment expertise can help determine what accommodations or alternate assessments might be necessary for students to best demonstrate their skills and knowledge.

Best Practices in High-Stakes Assessment and Accountability

It is critical that accountability systems include and report on the performance of all students, including those with disabilities and limited English proficiency. Personnel at the National Center on Educational Outcomes (Thurlow, Quenemoen,

Thompson, & Lehr, 2001) specified a set of principles and characteristics of inclusive assessment and accountability systems. These are listed in Table 31.2. The principles and characteristics address who should participate, the kinds of guidelines states should have, how scores should be reported, the use of scores in accountability systems, and the fundamental belief system that should guide practice.

TABLE 31.2	NCEO Best Practices in Inclusive Assessment and Accountability

Principle 1. All students with disabilities are included in the assessment and accountability system.

Characteristics

1. All students in all settings who receive educational services are included in the assessment and accountability system.
2. Alternative ways to participate in assessment—other than the same way as other students, with accommodations, or in an alternate assessment—are allowed only to the extent that they are allowed for other students, and only after they have been carefully reviewed by stakeholders and policy makers, and their use and impact have been carefully studied.
3. Exemptions or exclusions from assessment are allowed for students with disabilities only to the extent that they are allowed for other students.

Principle 2. Decisions about how students with disabilities participate in the assessment and accountability system are the result of clearly articulated participation, accommodations, and alternate assessment decision-making processes.

Characteristics

1. Decisions about how students participate in the assessment and accountability system are based on the student's ability to show what she or he knows and is able to do in the assessment formats available to all students—not on the student's instructional program, current level of functioning, or expectations about how well a student will perform.
2. Accommodations are available to all students, and decisions about use are based on student need and use in instruction.
3. The IEP (individualized education plan) team makes assessment participation, accommodation, and alternate assessment decisions on an individual student basis for each state and district assessment.
4. The IEP team documents assessment participation, accommodation, and alternate assessment decisions and the rationale for them on the IEP, and reviews the decisions made for individual students and the rationale for these decisions at least annually.
5. There are clear and efficient procedures for collecting, compiling, and transferring assessment decision information from each student's IEP to state and district assessment planners and administrators.

Principle 3. All students with disabilities are included when student scores are publicly reported, in the same frequency and format as all other students, whether they participate with or without accommodations, or in an alternate assessment.

Characteristics

1. All students in all placement settings who receive educational services are accounted for in the reporting system.
2. The number and percentage of students not in the assessment system in any way (with or without accommodations, or via an alternate assessment) are reported and an explanation given for their nonparticipation.
3. Scores that are not aggregated because of technical issues are still reported.
4. Reports are provided to educators, parents, students, policy makers, and journalists, with a clear explanation of results and implications.

(*continued*)

Principle 4. The assessment performance of students with disabilities has the same impact on the final accountability index as the performance of other students, regardless of how the students participate in the assessment system (i.e., with or without accommodations, or in an alternate assessment).

Characteristics

1. Performance data for all students, regardless of how they participate, have the same impact as all other student performance data in accountability indices.
2. There are incentives for including all students in the accountability system, such as including participation rates or increase in participation rates in the accountability index.
3. There are phase-in and appeals processes for student accountability for students who have not had access to the general curriculum, but systems are held accountable immediately.

Principle 5. There is improvement of both the assessment system and the accountability system over time, through the processes of formal monitoring, ongoing evaluation, and systematic training in the context of emerging research and best practice.

Characteristics

1. All decisions about student participation, accommodations, and alternate assessment are collected, compiled, and reported, and the data are used to improve the quality of the assessment process at the school, district, and state levels.
2. The consequences of student assessment decisions are identified, compiled, and reported, and the data are reviewed by multiple stakeholders and are used to improve the quality of the accountability processes at the school, district, and state levels.
3. Based on the results of the monitoring and evaluation of the assessment and accountability systems, training is provided to multiple audiences to increase the understanding of the purpose, options, procedures, and implications of assessment options, including consequences for promotion and graduation.
4. Appropriate training for IEP teams and other key personnel is provided through collaboration of state, district, higher education (both preservice and inservice), and advocacy organizations.

Principle 6. Every policy and practice reflects the belief that *all students* must be included in state and district assessment and accountability systems.

Characteristics

1. There is broad support in the governor's office, at the state legislature and state agencies, and among professional groups for inclusion of all students in state school reform efforts linked to assessments and accountability, demonstrated by sufficient funding and resources (e.g., staff development) designed to ensure the capacity in every school for every student to succeed.
2. All students are included in every aspect of assessment and accountability systems, including the assessments, the reporting of data, the determination of accountability measures, and the use of data for school improvement.
3. All aspects of assessment and accountability systems are designed and reviewed collaboratively, with input from other stakeholders (e.g., parents, advocacy groups, related service providers, community members), as well as general education, special education, curriculum, assessment, and administrative personnel.

SOURCE: Thurlow, M., Quenemoen, R., Thompson, S., & Lehr, C. (2001). *Principles and characteristics of inclusive assessment and accountability systems* (Synthesis Report 40). Minneapolis, MN: National Center on Educational Outcomes, University of Minnesota, Table 1.

Technology-Enhanced Assessment and Accountability Systems

In May 2004, the U.S. Department of Education convened a working conference on Using Technology to Enhance Assessment and Accountability Systems. The meeting was in response to the fact that many publishers were developing technology-enhanced assessments that could be used to provide data as part of statewide assessment and accountability systems. Technology-enhanced assessments are continuous or periodic assessments of student progress toward state standards. Some systems, like Renaissance Place, Ease-e, Cognos, and Microsoft Achieve are data warehousing systems. They are used to store test data, student demographic data, grades, transportation data, attendance data, and so forth. More recently, publishers have been developing continuous progress-monitoring systems like Accelerated Math, Accelerated Writer, and AIMSweb. Still others have been developing periodic (three to ten times per year) measures of student performance and progress (DIBELS, STAR Math, Yearly Progress Pro, Standards Master, STAR Early Literacy, and STAR Reading). The national Center on Student Progress Monitoring maintains a website with information about progress-monitoring systems that have been found to be effective in monitoring the progress of individual students (www.studentprogress.org).

There now is an increased push to use the data collected as part of continuous or periodic monitoring of student performance and progress as part of statewide accountability systems. The argument goes something like this:

> If we monitor student progress frequently (continuously or periodically), we should be able to put the assessment data into a data warehouse and know at any point in time precisely where individual students are performing and how teachers are doing with the students in their classes, and use the information for the purpose of making instructional and policy decisions. We also should be able to use this information to make predictions about how students will perform on standards-referenced state tests. If researchers are able to show that it is indeed possible to aggregate data on student performance and progress in order to make high-stakes accountability decisions, then continuous and periodic progress monitoring could replace the use of large-scale tests.

The shift to using progress-monitoring tools for the purpose of making accountability decisions would be a shift from a top-down (trying to use the results of large-scale tests to make both accountability and instructional planning decisions) to a bottom-up (using the results of progress monitoring to make both accountability and instructional planning decisions) approach.

SUMMARY

Today, much activity is directed toward demonstrating the extent to which education is working for students with disabilities. This has been part of a larger focus on the results of education. State departments of education now are required to specify standards for all students, including students with disabilities. States and districts must assess students annually, and must report to the U.S. Department of Education the extent to which students are making progress toward state or district standards. States must also have alternate assessments in place for students with severe cognitive disabilities and can have additional modified assessments developed to measure the performance of students with persistent academic difficulties who are working toward modified achievement standards. There is considerable variability in the kinds of assessment and accountability practices in individual states. We illustrated this by describing the accountability systems in five states. We described the steps to go through in developing standards-based accountability systems, and important considerations in assessment and accountability.

Clearly, there have been major advances in school system accountability practices. Students with disabilities are much more a part of the picture than they were even five years ago. This has resulted in accountability data that are more comparable across states and useful in policy decision making.

QUESTIONS FOR CHAPTER REVIEW

1. What fundamental assumptions underlie the use of accountability systems?
2. What do we know about current state practices in assessment for the purpose of making accountability decisions?
3. What steps should state and school district personnel go through as they develop standards-based accountability systems?
4. Why is it important that students with disabilities be included in assessment and accountability systems?

PROJECTS

1. Go to the link for approved state accountability plans on the U.S. Department of Education website (www.ed.gov/admins/lead/account/stateplan03/index.html). Look up the system for your state, and describe the ways in which assessment data are collected.
2. Go to the website for your state department of education. Find the section on state assessments, and review the kinds of tests given, the areas tested, and the grade levels at which tests are administered. Then go to the website for any other state department of education. Describe how the assessment and accountability system in that state is the same or different from the one used in your state.

RESOURCES FOR FURTHER INVESTIGATION

Print Resources

Thurlow, M. L., Quenemoen, R., Thompson, S., & Lehr, C. (2001). *Principles and characteristics of inclusive assessment and accountability systems* (Synthesis Report 40). Minneapolis, MN: National Center on Educational Outcomes, University of Minnesota.

Thurlow, M. L., & Ysseldyke, J. E. (2002). *Including students with disabilities in assessments.* Washington, DC: National Education Association.

Thurlow, M. L., Elliott, J. L., & Ysseldyke, J. E. (2003). *Testing students with disabilities: Procedures for complying with district and state requirements.* Thousand Oaks, CA: Corwin Press.

Thurlow, M. L., Ysseldyke, J. E., Vanderwood, M. L., & Spande, G. (1994). A guide to developing and implementing a system of outcomes and indicators. *Special Services in the Schools, 9,* 115–126.

Ysseldyke, J. E., Krentz, J., Erickson, R., & Moore, M. (1998). *NCEO framework for educational accounta-*

bility. Minneapolis, MN: National Center on Educational Outcomes, University of Minnesota.

Technology Resources

NO CHILD LEFT BEHIND
www.nochildleftbehind.gov
This website provides information about the No Child Left Behind Act, which was signed on January 8, 2002.

NATIONAL INSTITUTE ON STUDENT ACHIEVEMENT, CURRICULUM, AND ASSESSMENT
www.ed.gov/offices/OERI/SAI
This website reports on the coordinated and comprehensive program of research and development of the National Institute on Student Achievement, Curriculum, and Assessment.

NATIONAL ASSESSMENT GOVERNING BOARD
www.nagb.org
Learn about the National Assessment of Education Progress, the only ongoing test of academic progress.

NATIONAL CENTER ON EDUCATIONAL OUTCOMES
www.education.umn.edu/NCEO
This website describes the focus of NCEO activities on educational outcomes for all students, including students with disabilities. Also offered are summaries of the center's publications and links to related websites.

OUTCOMES-BASED EDUCATION
www.eric.ed.gov/ERICDocs/data/ericdocs2/ content_storage_01/0000000b/80/2a/1f/d8.pdf
This document explains the basis of outcomes-based education, including suggestions for districtwide implementation.

The Evolution of Assessment Practice: Where Are We Headed?

VERY LITTLE STAYS CURRENT FOR VERY LONG IN ASSESSMENT. THE REAL CHANGES IN assessment practice are more evolutionary than revolutionary. Here, we provide a picture of what is currently happening in assessment and where we think assessment practices in schools might go.

We start with the notion of assessment as a dynamic, changing field and its great impact on those involved. We also cover the recent expansion of assessment practices, their increased focus on prevention and early identification, the push for accountability, the issue of whom standards are for, and matters of diversity. Increasingly, school personnel are using a problem-solving approach with less emphasis on testing formally and more focus on implementing evidence-based interventions and monitoring their effectiveness with individual students.

Assessment as a Dynamic and Dynamite Practice

Assessment practices are a function of history, training of assessment personnel, changing social needs (as reflected in laws, guidelines, and regulations), and social, political, and educational tolerance. Assessment practices are dynamic because they are evolving even as you read this book. For example, a president's commission on excellence in special education recently specified a number of recommendations about assessing students. And a national joint committee on learning disabilities recommended that IQ-achievement discrepancies no longer be used in identification of students with learning disabilities. Government and professional organizations are continually proposing changes that they hope will improve assessment practice.

Assessment practices are also dynamite; that is, they are potentially explosive. As we noted in the chapter "Assessment of Students," testing practices play a major role in social decision making. Tests are used to decide whether schools get more resources, teachers get merit pay increases, people are hired for jobs, and students graduate, get into college or graduate school, or are eligible for special education. When the tests have perceived negative consequences, people often blame the tests.

Expansion of Assessment Practices

The history of assessment of students with disabilities and those who are at risk is one of documentation of deviance, deficits, and disabilities. School personnel have been engaged extensively in giving tests for the purpose of documenting that students meet the state-specified criteria for declaring them eligible for special education or related services. It has been presumed that classification and identification of specific deficits would lead to interventions with known results. Research findings have not always supported these presumptions.

More recently, assessment practices have expanded to focus on competence enhancement. Assessors increasingly are working to identify student skill levels and desired skill levels, and to develop instructional interventions designed to move students from where they are to where we want them to be. Assessors are required to meet the legal mandates of demonstrating that students are eligible for services, while still focusing on specification of treatments based on assessment results.

Increased Focus on Prevention and Early Identification

Assessment practices are changing from those designed to predict student behavior and performance or merely name a deficit (which is often a limited view of the problem at hand) to those designed to make a difference in students' lives. This move, too, reflects the focus on intervention. Assessors increasingly work to identify academic, physical, and behavioral difficulties at early ages or early in the course of the development of difficulties. They do so for the purpose of planning interventions that can be implemented to move students toward desired outcomes. Given that the bottom line is development of interventions that will make a difference in students' lives, the focus is on assessment for instructional planning.

The Significant Push for Accountability

As discussed in the last chapter, since the early 1990s there has been a significant push to hold schools accountable for student progress and to hold students accountable for meeting specified state educational standards. State education agencies in all states except Iowa have specified state educational standards (the Iowa standards are at the district level) and have developed or are developing tests matched to the standards. By law, states are required to assess students each year, include all students in assessments, and report annually on the performance and progress of all students. The National Education Association (NEA, 2001) recently issued a set of requirements for the development of tests to support instruction and accountability. The requirements are listed in Table 1.

| **TABLE 1** | NEA Requirements for Development of Tests to Support Instruction and Accountability |

1. A state's content standards must be prioritized to support effective instruction and assessment. State personnel need to identify a small number of content standards (rather than a lengthy list) suitable for large-scale assessment which represent the most important or enduring skills and knowledge students need to learn in school.
2. A state's high-priority content standards must be clearly and thoroughly described so that the knowledge and skills students need to demonstrate competence are evident.
3. The results of a state's assessment of high-priority content standards should be reported standard by standard for each student, school, and district.
4. A state must ensure that all students have the opportunity to demonstrate their achievement of state standards; consequently, it must provide well-designed assessments appropriate for a broad range of students, with accommodations and alternate methods of assessment available for students who need them.
5. A state should secure evidence that supports the ongoing improvement of its state assessments to ensure those assessments are (a) appropriate for the accountability purposes for which they are used, (b) appropriate for determining whether students have attained state standards, (c) appropriate for enhancing instruction, and (d) not the cause of negative consequences.

SOURCE: National Education Association. (2001). *Building tests to support instruction and accountability.* Washington, DC: Author.

The push for accountability will not go away. The 1997 amendments to the Individuals with Disabilities Education Act and the 2002 Elementary and Secondary Education Act and its No Child Left Behind provisions specify that states and districts must report annually on the performance and progress of all students. There is still, however, considerable resistance among many school personnel to notions of accountability. This is due in part to difficulty in demonstrating progress for all students and in part to resistance among school personnel to be held accountable for their work.

Standards for All and All for Standards

When states specify their state standards, they indicate that the standards are for all students, including students with disabilities and limited English proficiency. And it seems that everyone is for standards, although not for the same standards for all. Students with disabilities have specific procedural safeguards (due process, the right to a free and appropriate education, protection in evaluation procedures) and individualized education plans (IEPs). Periodically, there are moves to make these same safeguards and IEPs available to all students.

Diversity and Limited English Proficiency (LEP): Being Responsive and Responsible

Increased language and cultural diversity clearly is the pattern in U.S. schools. The majority of classrooms in large urban school districts and in other districts in specific states (such as California, Florida, Texas, and Arizona) include students whose first language is not English. Of those whose first language is not English, most speak Spanish. The publishers of most tests that are widely used have developed or are developing Spanish versions of their tests. Yet school personnel are faced with a number of significant issues. As we noted in the chapter "Testing Students with Limited English Proficiency," language and culture interact. Not all students who speak a given language have similar experiential backgrounds. For example, students who speak Spanish may have Spanish, Mexican, Puerto Rican, South American, or Cuban backgrounds. In some school districts today, the big assessment difficulty is the increased numbers of students whose primary language is neither Spanish nor English. For example, in St. Paul, Minnesota, the schools have a very large Hmong population, whereas in neighboring Minneapolis, large numbers of students are from Somalia or from former Soviet states (such as Ukraine and Romania). University teacher-training programs typically do not prepare teachers and assessment personnel to assess students from language backgrounds other than English. Students who do not speak English and who are suspected of having a disability have the right to be assessed in ways that reflect their abilities rather than their language differences. School personnel must identify ways to do so absent instruments designed for appropriate assessments.

Schools and researchers only recently have begun to conduct research on appropriate assessment of students who have both LEP and a disability. This is certainly a new and evolving area in assessment. Several projects have begun since 2000, and additional projects have begun within just months preceding the writing of this text. The website for the National Center on Educational Outcomes (www.coled.umn.edu/nceo) includes information on the latest research findings, as well as tracking of practices in assessment of students with LEP.

The Promise of the Problem-Solving Model

Many states and school districts are moving to put a problem-solving model into their special education assessment and decision-making process. The problem-solving approach used in the Heartland Educational Service Area in Iowa is depicted in Figure 1. It illustrates the steps that assessment/intervention personnel go through as they work to solve a student's educational difficulties. This system is based on rigorous interventions that are made prior to any referral to special education services. Problem solving involves systematic application of effective instruction and collection of data on student performance. It includes the use of data on student performance to make decisions about what and how to teach. And intensity of service varies in accord with student need.

This figure illustrates four levels of service, ranging in intensity from individual consultation between teachers and parents to special education team IEP consideration. The focus at Level I is on identifying strategies that might work to alleviate problems and then implementing interventions and keeping track of what happens. This most basic form of problem solving has been going on for decades in our nation's schools. Level II consultation involves bringing other resources to bear on the problem. In most schools, there are teacher assistance teams—groups of educators who meet to discuss individual student difficulties

FIGURE 1
Heartland Area
Education Agency Problem-
Solving Model

SOURCE: Heartland
Area Education Agency,
Johnston, Iowa. Reprinted
by permission.

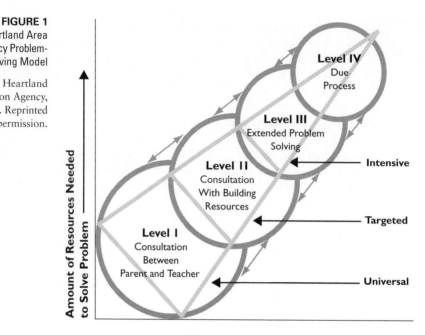

and to work together to identify ways to intervene and remediate those difficulties. Levels III and IV represent increased involvement of other personnel and increased intensity of intervention. Level IV usually involves entitlement consideration. At all four levels, school personnel work together to identify and specify the problem (an activity called "problem clarification"), hypothesize why the problem is occurring, specify what should be done about the problem, do it, and evaluate the extent to which the intervention worked.

Assessment practices change very quickly. Changes are being brought about by factors such as increased focus on prevention and early intervention, linking of assessment to instruction, limited English proficiency, increased cultural diversity, and the intense push for accountability. Assessment is becoming as important as instruction in today's schools. This simply highlights the need for prospective and current school personnel to be highly trained in measurement and assessment, and to be highly informed consumers of assessment information.

Thinking About Assessment Practice

We encourage you to research and think about these assessment issues, to be aware of current proposals and changes in assessment practice. As a way to begin this inquiry, consider tracking your local newspaper for one week and summarizing articles that are written about assessment or student performance on tests. Identify at least two issues that are raised by the articles. In addition, take a closer look at the assessment issues raised in this chapter and at the "Dilemmas in Current Practice" features throughout this text. Identify two alternative perspectives on addressing each of the issues raised.

APPENDIX 1

AREAS OF THE NORMAL CURVE

Area equals the proportion of cases between the z-score and the mean; extreme area equals .5000 less the proportion of cases between the z-score and the mean.

z	.00	.01	.02	.03	.04	.05	.06	.07	.08	.09
0.0	.0000	.0040	.0080	.0120	.0160	.0199	.0239	.0279	.0319	.0359
0.1	.0398	.0438	.0478	.0517	.0557	.0596	.0636	.0675	.0714	.0753
0.2	.0793	.0832	.0871	.0910	.0948	.0987	.1026	.1064	.1103	.1141
0.3	.1179	.1217	.1255	.1293	.1331	.1368	.1406	.1443	.1480	.1517
0.4	.1554	.1591	.1628	.1664	.1700	.1736	.1772	.1808	.1844	.1879
0.5	.1915	.1950	.1985	.2019	.2054	.2088	.2123	.2157	.2190	.2224
0.6	.2257	.2291	.2324	.2357	.2389	.2422	.2454	.2486	.2517	.2549
0.7	.2580	.2611	.2642	.2673	.2704	.2734	.2764	.2794	.2823	.2852
0.8	.2881	.2910	.2939	.2967	.2995	.3023	.3051	.3078	.3106	.3133
0.9	.3159	.3186	.3212	.3238	.3264	.3289	.3315	.3340	.3365	.3389
1.0	.3413	.3438	.3461	.3485	.3508	.3531	.3554	.3577	.3599	.3621
1.1	.3643	.3665	.3686	.3708	.3729	.3749	.3770	.3790	.3810	.3830
1.2	.3849	.3869	.3888	.3907	.3925	.3944	.3962	.3980	.3997	.4015
1.3	.4032	.4049	.4066	.4082	.4099	.4115	.4131	.4147	.4162	.4177
1.4	.4192	.4207	.4222	.4236	.4251	.4265	.4279	.4292	.4306	.4319
1.5	.4332	.4345	.4357	.4370	.4382	.4394	.4406	.4418	.4429	.4441
1.6	.4452	.4463	.4474	.4484	.4495	.4505	.4515	.4525	.4535	.4545
1.7	.4554	.4564	.4573	.4582	.4591	.4599	.4608	.4616	.4625	.4633
1.8	.4641	.4649	.4656	.4664	.4671	.4678	.4686	.4693	.4699	.4706
1.9	.4713	.4719	.4726	.4732	.4738	.4744	.4750	.4756	.4761	.4767
2.0	.4772	.4778	.4783	.4788	.4793	.4798	.4803	.4808	.4812	.4817
2.1	.4821	.4826	.4830	.4834	.4838	.4842	.4846	.4850	.4854	.4857
2.2	.4861	.4864	.4868	.4871	.4875	.4878	.4881	.4884	.4887	.4890
2.3	.4893	.4896	.4898	.4901	.4904	.4906	.4909	.4911	.4913	.4916
2.4	.4918	.4920	.4922	.4925	.4927	.4929	.4931	.4932	.4934	.4936
2.5	.4938	.4940	.4941	.4943	.4945	.4946	.4948	.4949	.4951	.4952
2.6	.4953	.4955	.4956	.4957	.4959	.4960	.4961	.4962	.4963	.4964
2.7	.4965	.4966	.4967	.4968	.4969	.4970	.4971	.4972	.4973	.4974
2.8	.4974	.4975	.4976	.4977	.4977	.4978	.4979	.4979	.4980	.4981
2.9	.4981	.4982	.4982	.4983	.4984	.4984	.4985	.4985	.4986	.4986
3.0	.4987	.4987	.4987	.4988	.4988	.4989	.4989	.4989	.4990	.4990

Source: From *Statistics: An Intuitive Approach*, by G. H. Weinberg and J. A. Schumaker. Copyright © 1981, 1974, 1969, 1962 Brooks/Cole Publishing Company, Pacific Grove, California 93950. A division of International Thompson Publishing, Inc. By permission of the publisher.

APPENDIX 2

EQUATIONS USED IN THE TEXT

Location in Text	Term Defined	Equation
Ch. 4, p. 76	Mean	$\bar{X} = \dfrac{\Sigma X}{N}$ (Equation 4.1)
Ch. 4, p. 77	Variance	$s^2 = \dfrac{\Sigma(X - \bar{X})^2}{N}$ (Equation 4.2) or $s^2 = \dfrac{\Sigma X^2}{N} - \left(\dfrac{\Sigma X}{N}\right)^2$
Ch. 4, p. 82	Pearson product-moment correlation coefficient, where X and Y are scores on two tests	$r = \dfrac{N \Sigma XY - (\Sigma X)(\Sigma Y)}{\sqrt{N \Sigma X^2 - (\Sigma X)^2} \sqrt{N \Sigma Y^2 - (\Sigma Y)^2}}$
Ch. 5, p. 93	Percentile rank for a particular score	%ile = Percentage of people scoring below the score plus one half the percentage of people obtaining the score
Ch. 5, p. 95	z-score	$z = (X - \bar{X}) \div S$ (Equation 5.1)
Ch. 5, p. 96	Any standard score	$SS = \bar{X}_{ss} + (S_{ss})(z)$ (Equation 5.2)
Ch. 7, p. 125	Coefficient alpha	$r_{aa} = \dfrac{k}{k-1}\left(1 - \dfrac{\Sigma S^2_{items}}{S^2_{test}}\right)$ (Equation 7.2)
Ch. 7, p. 126	Point-to-point agreement	$\dfrac{(100)\text{number of agreements on occurrence and nonoccurrence}}{\text{number of observations}}$ (Equation 7.3)
Ch. 7, p. 127	Percent agreement on occurrence	$\dfrac{(100)\text{number of agreements on occurrence}}{\text{number of observations} - \text{number of agreements on nonoccurrence}}$ (Equation 7.4)
Ch. 7, p. 128	Cohen's coefficient of agreement	$\text{Kappa} = \dfrac{P_{occurrence} - P_{expected}}{1 - P_{expected}}$ (Equation 7.5)

Location in Text	Term Defined	Equation
Ch. 7, p. 129	Spearman-Brown formula to correct for test length	$r_{xx} = \dfrac{2r_{(\frac{1}{2})(\frac{1}{2})}}{1 + r_{(\frac{1}{2})(\frac{1}{2})}}$ (Equation 7.6)
Ch. 7, p. 133	Standard error of measurement	$\text{SEM} = S\sqrt{1 - r_{xx}}$ (Equation 7.7)
Ch. 7, p. 134	Estimated true score	$X' = \bar{X} + \left(r_{xx}\right)\left(X - \bar{X}\right)$ (Equation 7.8)
Ch. 7, p. 137	Lower and upper limits of a confidence interval, where z-score determines level of confidence	Lower limit = X' − (z-score)(SEM) Upper limit = X' + (z-score)(SEM) (Equation 7.9)
Ch. 7, p. 139	Reliability of a predicted difference	$\hat{D} = \dfrac{r_{bb} + \left(r_{aa}\right)\left(r^2_{ab}\right) - 2r^2_{ab}}{1 - r^2_{ab}}$ (Equation 7.10)
Ch. 7, p. 139	Standard deviation of a predicted difference	$S_{\hat{D}} = S_b \sqrt{1 - r^2_{ab}}$ (Equation 7.11)
Ch. 7, p. 139	Reliability of a difference of obtained scores	$r_{\text{dif}} = \dfrac{\frac{1}{2}\left(r_{aa} + r_{bb}\right) - r_{ab}}{1 - r_{ab}}$ (Equation 7.12)
Ch. 7, p. 139	Standard deviation of obtained difference	$S_{\text{dif}} = \sqrt{S^2_a + S^2_b - 2r_{ab}S_a S_b}$ (Equation 7.13)
Ch. 7, p. 140	Standard error of measurement of a difference	$\text{SEM}_{\text{dif}} = \sqrt{S^2_a + S^2_b - 2r_{ab}S_a S_b} \sqrt{1 - \dfrac{\frac{1}{2}\left(r_{aa} + r_{bb}\right) - r_{ab}}{1 - r_{ab}}}$ (Equation 7.14)
Ch. 7, p. 140	Estimated true difference	(obtained difference)(r_{dif}) (Equation 7.15)

GLOSSARY

abscissa   The horizontal axis of a graph, representing the continuum on which individuals are measured

access   Availability of an assessment to consumers

accommodation   Change in testing materials or procedures that enables students to participate in assessments in ways that reflect their skills and abilities rather than their disabilities

accommodative ability   The automatic adjustment of the eyes for seeing at different distances

accountability, accountability system   The use of assessment results and other data to ensure that schools are moving in desired directions. Common elements include standards, indicators of progress toward meeting those standards, analysis of data, reporting procedures, and rewards or sanctions

acculturation   A child's particular set of background experiences and opportunities to learn in both formal and informal educational settings

accuracy   Usually the percentage of a student's attempted responses that are correct; accuracy is most important during a student's acquisition of new information

achievement   What has been learned as a result of instruction

achievement test   Measure of what students have been taught and learned

adaptations   A generalized term that describes a change made in the presentation, setting, response, or timing or scheduling of an assessment that may or may not change the construct of the assessment

adaptive behavior   Behavior that allows individuals to adapt themselves to the expectations of nature and society

adequate yearly progress (AYP)   A provision of the federal No Child Left Behind (NCLB, 2001) legislation requiring schools, districts, and states to demonstrate that students are making academic progress based on test scores. Each state was required by NCLB to submit by January 31, 2003, a specific plan for monitoring AYP

age equivalent   A derived score that expresses a person's performance as the average (the median or mean) performance for that age group; age equivalents are expressed in years and months, with a hyphen used in age scores (for example, 7-1 is 7 years, 1 month); an age-equivalent score is interpreted to mean that the test taker's performance is equal to the average performance of an X-year-old

aid   An error in oral reading, recorded when a student hesitates for more than ten seconds and the word or words are supplied by the teacher

algorithm   The steps, processes, or procedures used for solving a problem or reaching a goal

alignment   The similarity or match between or among content standards, performance standards, curriculum, instruction, and assessments in terms of knowledge and skill expectations

alternate assessment   Substitute way of gathering data, often by means of portfolio or performance measures; alternate assessments are intended for students with significant disabilities that keep them from participating in the regular assessment

alternate forms   Two tests that measure the same trait or skill to the same extent and that are standardized on the same population; alternate forms offer essentially equivalent tests; sometimes, in fact, they're called "equivalent forms"

alternative achievement standard   Expectations for performance that differ in complexity from a grade-level achievement standard, but are linked to the content standards

amplitude   The intensity of a behavior

assessment   The process of collecting data for the purpose of (1) specifying and verifying problems, and (2) making decisions about students

attainment   What an individual has learned, regardless of where it has been learned

audiogram   A graph of the results of the pure-tone threshold test

basal   That item in a test below which it is assumed the student will get all items correct

behavioral observation   Observation of spontaneous behavior, which has not been elicited by a predetermined and standardized set of stimuli (that is, not test behavior)

behavioral topography   The way in which a behavior is performed

benchmark   A specific statement of knowledge and skills within a content area's continuum that a student must possess to demonstrate a level of progress toward mastery of a standard

bimodal distribution   A distribution that has two modes

biserial correlation coefficient   An index of association between two variables, one of which has been forced into an arbitrary dichotomy (for example, smart/dull) and one of which is equal interval (for example, grade point average)

body of evidence   Information or data that establish that a student can perform a particular skill or has mastered a specific content standard and that was either produced by the student or collected by someone who is knowledgeable about the student

cash validity   The notion that frequently used tests are valid tests

Category A data   The basic, minimum information schools need in order to operate an educational program, including identifying information, as well as information about a student's educational progress

Category B data   Test results and other verified information useful to the schools in planning a student's educational program or maintaining a student safely in school

Category C data   Information that may be potentially useful to schools, including any unverified information, scores on personality tests, and so forth

ceiling   That item in a test above which it is assumed the student will fail all items

classification   A type of decision that concerns a pupil's eligibility for special services, special education services, remedial education services, speech services, and so forth

coefficient alpha   The average split-half correlation based on all possible divisions of a test into two parts; coefficient alpha can be computed directly from the variances of individual test items and the variance of the total test score

concurrent criterion-related validity   A measure of how accurately a person's current test score can be used to estimate a score on a criterion measure

conductive hearing loss   Abnormal hearing associated with poor air-conduction sensitivity but normal bone-conduction sensitivity

confidence interval   The range of scores within which a person's true score will fall with a given probability

construct validity   A measure of the extent to which a test measures a theoretical trait or characteristic

consultation   A meeting between a resource teacher or other specialist and a classroom teacher to verify the existence of a problem, specify the nature of the problem, and develop strategies that might relieve the problem

content standard   Statement of the specific content or skills that students are expected to have mastered at a specific point in time

content validity   A measure of the extent to which a test is an adequate measure of the content it is designed to cover; content validity is established by examining three factors: the appropriateness of the types of items included, the comprehensiveness of the item sample, and the way in which the items assess the content

correlation   A measure of the degree of relationship between two or more variables; a correlation indicates the extent to which any two variables go together—that is, the extent to which changes in one variable are reflected by changes in the second variable

correlation coefficient   Numerical index of the relationship between two or more variables

criterion-referenced test   Test that measures a person's skills in terms of absolute levels of mastery

criterion-related validity   A measure of the extent to which a person's score on a criterion measure can be estimated from that person's score on a test of unknown validity

crystallized intelligence (*gc*)   General knowledge and skill that an individual acquires over time (compare with **fluid intelligence**)

curriculum-based assessment   Use of assessment materials and procedures that mirror instruction in order to ascertain whether specific instructional objectives have been accomplished and monitor progress directly in the curriculum being taught

cut score   A specified point on a score scale. Scores at or above that point are interpreted differently from scores below that point. Also called a cutoff score.

decile   Band of percentiles that is ten percentile ranks in width; each decile contains 10 percent of the norm group

derived score   A general term for a raw score that is transformed to a developmental score or to a score of relative standing

descriptive statistics   Numerical values, such as mean, standard deviation, or correlation, that describe a data set

developmental age   A test score expressed as an age equivalent; the score represents the average score earned by individuals of a specific age

developmental equivalent A type of derived score in which raw scores are converted to the mean or median for a particular age or grade (For example, a grade equivalent expresses a test taker's raw score as the mean of a school grade; a grade equivalent of 7.0 means that the raw score was the mean of students in the beginning of seventh grade. An age equivalent of 7-0 means that the raw score was the mean of seven-year-old test takers. Age equivalents are also sometimes divided by chronological age to create a developmental quotient.)

developmental score Raw score that has been transformed into age equivalent (AE) (mental age, for example), grade equivalent, or developmental quotient

deviation IQ Standard score with a mean of 100 and a standard deviation of 15 or 16 (depending on the test)

deviation score The distance between an individual's score and the average score for the group, such as z-scores and T-scores

disaggregation The collection and reporting of student achievement results by particular subgroups (e.g., students with disabilities, limited-English-proficient students) to ascertain the subgroup's academic progress. Disaggregation makes it possible to compare subgroups or cohorts

discriminative stimulus Stimulus that is consistently present when a behavior is reinforced and that elicits the behavior even in the absence of the original reinforcer

disregard of punctuation An error in oral reading in which a student fails to give appropriate inflection in response to punctuation; for example, a student may not pause for a comma, stop for a period, or indicate voice inflection at a question mark or exclamation point

distractor Incorrect option contained in a response set

distribution The way in which scores in a set array themselves; a distribution may be graphed to demonstrate visually the relations among the scores in the group or set

duration The length of time a behavior lasts

ecobehaviorial assessment Observations of functional relationships between student behavior and ecological or environmental factors (What environmental factors are related to specific student behaviors?); ecobehavioral assessment enables educators to identify natural instructional conditions that are associated with academic success, behavioral competence, or problem behaviors

ecobehavioral observation Observation targeting the interaction among student behavior, teacher behavior, time allocated to instruction, physical grouping structures, the types of tasks being used, and instructional content

ecology Mutual relationships between organisms and their environments

efficiency The speed and economy with which data are collected

entitlement In special education, the right to a free and appropriate education, related services, and due process

equal-interval scale Scale in which the differences between adjacent values are equal, but in which there is no absolute or logical zero

error Misrepresentation of a person's score as a result of failure to obtain a representative sample of times, items, or scorers

ethnographic observation Observation in which the observer does not participate in what is occurring

etiology Cause of a disorder

expectancy The tendency of an observer to see behaviors consistent with her or his beliefs about what should happen

expressive language The production of language

fluid intelligence (*gc*) The efficiency with which an individual learns and completes various tasks (compare with **crystallized intelligence**)

formative evaluation Ongoing frequent evaluation as the thing being evaluated is occurring; in instructional evaluation, collection of data as instruction is occurring

free operant A test situation that presents more problems than a student can answer in the given time period

frequency The tabulation of the number of behaviors with discrete beginnings and endings that occur in a predetermined time frame; when the time periods in which the behavior is counted vary, frequencies are usually converted to rates

frustration level Usually accuracy that is less than 85 percent correct; when a student is performing at frustration level, the material is too difficult

grade equivalent A derived score that expresses a student's performance as the average (the median or mean) performance for a particular grade; grade equivalents are expressed in grades and tenths of grades, with a decimal point used in grade scores (for example, 7.1 is grade 7 and one tenth)

gross mispronunciation An error in oral reading in which a student's pronunciation of a word is in no way similar to the word in the text

halo effect The tendency of an observer to make subjective judgments on the basis of general attributes, such as race or social class

hesitation An error in oral reading in which a student pauses for two or more seconds before pronouncing a word

histogram A representation of frequency distribution by means of rectangles whose widths are class intervals and whose areas are proportional to corresponding frequencies

historical information Information that describes how a person has functioned in the past

independent level Usually accuracy that is 95 percent or higher

indicator Symbolic representation of one or more outcomes that can be used to make comparisons among students or schools

individual consent Consent by parent (or pupil) required for the collection of family information (religion, income, occupation, and so on), personality data, and other noneducational information

individualized education plan (IEP) A document that specifies the long-term and short-term goals of an instructional program, where the program will be delivered, who will deliver the program, and how progress will be evaluated

informal assessment Any assessment that involves collection of data by anything other than a norm-referenced (standardized) test

informal reading inventory (IRI) Usually a test without normative sample that consists of graded reading passages and vocabulary words that span a wide range of skill levels; IRIs are used to assess decoding and comprehension in order to locate the level at which a student reads at an instructional level (with about 90 percent accuracy)

informed consent Consent that a parent or a student gives for the collection or dissemination of information not directly relevant and essential to the child's education; the assumption underlying the notion of informed consent is that the parent (or pupil) is "reasonably competent to understand the nature

and consequences of his [or her] decision" (Goslin, 1969, p. 17)

insertion An error in oral reading in which a student inappropriately adds one or more words to the sentence being read

instructional ecology Relationships between students and their instructional environments

instructional environment Those contexts in which learning takes place (schools, classrooms, homes), as well as the interface of essential contexts for children's learning (home-school relationships)

instructional level Usually accuracy that is between 85 and 95 percent correct

intelligence An inferred ability; a term or construct used to explain differences in present behavior and to predict differences in future behavior

internal consistency A measure of the extent to which items in a test correlate with one another

interscorer reliability An estimate of the degree of agreement between two or more scores on the same test

intervention assistance team (IAT) A group of teachers (and sometimes other professionals, such as school psychologists or speech-language pathologists) who meet to review student difficulties, try to ascertain the kinds of interventions to implement to try to alleviate difficulties in the regular classroom, and monitor the extent to which the interventions work; sometimes called "mainstream assistance team" or "prereferral team"

inversion An error in oral reading in which a student says the words in an order different from the order in which they are written

keyed response Correct answer in a response set

KR-20 An estimate of the internal consistency of a test when test items are scored dichotomously

kurtosis The peakedness of a curve, or the rate at which a curve rises

language A code for conveying ideas; although there is some variation, language theorists propose five basic components to describe the code: phonology, semantics, morphology, syntax, and pragmatics

language mechanics Punctuation and capitalization

latency The amount of time between a signal to initiate the behavior and the actual beginning of the behavior

leptokurtic curve Fast-rising curve; tests that do not spread out (or discriminate among) those taking the test are typically leptokurtic

Likert scale   A technique in which a set of attitude statements is presented and respondents are asked to express degree of agreement or disagreement, usually on a five- or seven-point scale usually ranging from strongly agree to strongly disagree; each degree of agreement is given a numerical value, and a total numerical value can be calculated from all the responses

mastery   Usually accuracy that equals or exceeds 90 to 95 percent correct

mean   The arithmetic average of scores in a distribution

median   A score that divides the top 50 percent of test takers from the bottom 50 percent; the point on a scale above which 50 percent of the cases (not the scores) occur and below which 50 percent of the cases occur

metalinguistic   Relating to the direct examination of the structural aspects of language

mixed hearing loss   Abnormal hearing attributed to abnormal bone conduction and even more abnormal air conduction

mode   The most frequently obtained score in a distribution

modified achievement standards   Expectations for performance that are lower than the grade-level achievement standards, but linked to or aligned with the content standards. This term will be further defined by policy makers in the near future

momentary time sampling   A procedure used in systematic observation to determine when observations will occur; a behavior is scored as an occurrence if it is present at the last moment of an observation interval; if the behavior is not occurring at the last moment of the interval, a nonoccurrence is recorded

morphology   The use of affixes (prefixes and suffixes) to change the meaning of words used in sentences

multiple-skill battery   Test that measures skill development in several achievement areas

negatively skewed distribution   An asymmetric distribution in which scores tail off to the low end; a distribution in which there are more scores above the mean than below it

nominal scale   A scale of measurement in which there is no inherent relationship among adjacent values

nonsystematic observation   Observation in which the observer notes behaviors, characteristics, and personal interactions that seem of significance

normal-curve equivalent   Standard score with a mean equal to 100 and a standard deviation equal to 21.06

normative sample (norm group)   A group of subjects of known demographic characteristics (age, gender, grade in school, and so on) to whom a person's performance may be compared

norm group   See **standardization sample**

norm-referenced device   Test that compares an individual's performance to the performance of his or her peers

objective-referenced assessment   Tests referenced to specific instructional objectives rather than to the performance of a peer group or norm group

observation   The process of gaining information through one's senses—visual, auditory, and so forth; observation can be used to assess behavior, states, physical characteristics, and permanent products of behavior (such as a child's poem)

omission   An error in oral reading in which a student skips a word or a group of words

operationalize   To define a behavior or event in terms of the operations used to measure it; for example, an operational definition of intelligence would be a score on a specific intelligence test

ordinal scale   Scale on which values of measurement are ordered from best to worst or from worst to best; on ordinal scales, the differences between adjacent values are unknown

ordinate   The vertical axis of a graph of a distribution, showing the frequency (or the number) of individuals earning any given score

outcome   The result of interactions between individuals and schooling experiences

out-of-level test   A lower- or higher-level test that is judged appropriate for the student's developmental level rather than the student's age/grade level

partial-interval recording   A procedure used in systematic observation in which an occurrence is scored if the behavior occurs during any part of the interval

partial mispronunciation   One of several kinds of errors in oral reading, including partial pronunciation, phonetic mispronunciation of part of the word, omission of part of the word, or insertion of elements of words

participant-observer observation   Observation in which the observer joins the target social group and participates in its activities

Pearson product-moment correlation coefficient (*r*) An index of the straight-line (linear) relationship between two or more variables measured on an equal-interval scale

penmanship The formation of individual letters and letter sequences that make up words

percentile rank (percentile) Derived score that indicates the percentage of people whose scores are at or below a given raw score; percentiles are useful for both ordinal and equal-interval scales

performance standard Statement of the degree of mastery (such as "with 80 percent accuracy") students are expected to demonstrate

phi coefficient An index of linear correlation between two sets of naturally dichotomous variables (for example, male/female, dead/alive)

phonology The hearing and production of speech sounds

platykurtic curve Curve that is flat and slow rising

point biserial correlation coefficient An index of linear correlation between one naturally occurring dichotomous variable (such as gender) and a continuous, equal-interval variable (such as height measured in inches)

portfolio A collection of products that provide a basis for judging student accomplishment; in school settings, portfolios typically contain extended projects and may also contain drafts, teacher comments and evaluations, and self-evaluations

positively skewed distribution An asymmetrical distribution in which scores tail off to the higher end of the continuum; a distribution in which there are more scores below the mean than above it

power test The test is untimed, and our interest is in how many items a student can complete correctly

pragmatics The social context in which language occurs

predictive criterion-related validity A measure of the extent to which a person's current test scores can be used to estimate accurately what that person's criterion scores will be at a later time

prereferral Activities that occur prior to formal referral, assessment, and consideration for placement; the goal of prereferral and intervention is twofold: (1) verification and specification of the nature of a student's difficulties and (2) provision of services in the least restrictive environment

probe A special testing format that is well suited to the assessment of direct performances; probes are brief (usually three minutes or less), timed, frequently administered assessments that can be used for any purpose

prognosis A prediction of future performance

qualitative data Information consisting of nonsystematic and unquantified observations

qualitative observation A description of behavior, its function, and its context; the observer begins without preconceived ideas about what will be observed and describes behavior that seems important

quantitative data Observations that have been tabulated or otherwise given numerical values

quartile Band of percentiles that is 25 percentile ranks in width; each quartile contains 25 percent of the norm group

random error In measurement, sources of variation in scores that make it impossible to generalize from an observation of a specific behavior observed at a specific time by a specific person to observations conducted on similar behavior, at different times, or by different observers

range The distance between the extremes in a set of scores, including those extremes; the highest score less the lowest score, plus one

rate The number of responses per minute; rate measures are thought to indicate a student's fluency or automaticity of response

rating scale A standardized assessment procedure whereby behavior, states, or feelings are quantified; most rating scales rely on ordinal measurement of recalled observations

ratio IQ A derived score based on mental age (MA), in relation to chronological age (CA), in which IQ equals

$$\frac{\text{MA (in months)}}{\text{CA (in months)}} \times 100$$

ratio scale Scale of measurement in which the difference between adjacent values is equal and in which there is a logical and absolute zero

raw score The quantified evaluation of a test item or group of test items such as right or wrong on a specific item or the number of right or wrong items on a student's test; in standardized testing, raw scores are usually transformed to derived scores

readiness Extent of preparation to participate in an activity; the term most often refers to readiness to enter school but applies to all levels

receptive language The comprehension of language

referral A request for help from a specialist; for example, a teacher or parent may refer a student to a specialist who can provide the student with an appropriate educational program

reliability In measurement, the extent to which it is possible to generalize from an observation of a specific behavior observed at a specific time by a specific person to observations conducted on similar behavior, at different times, or by different observers

reliability coefficient An index of the extent to which observations can be generalized; the square of the correlation between obtained scores and true scores on a measure r_{xt}^2

repetition An error in oral reading in which a student repeats words or groups of words

representational consent Consent to collect data, given by appropriately elected officials, such as members of a state legislature

RTI (response to instruction) Response to instruction refers to how students respond to core instruction or universal programming (the everyday instruction that occurs for students)

response to intervention Response to intervention refers to students' responses when substantial changes are made in regular classroom instruction

retention The percentage of correct responses recalled following learning; also called "maintenance," "recall," or "memory"

sample A representative subset of a population

scoring rubric An ordinal scale used to rate a product. Rubrics typically use verbal descriptions to anchor the end intermediate points of the scale

scotoma A visionless spot in the eye

screening An initial stage of assessment in which those who may evidence a particular problem, disorder, disability, or disease are discriminated from the general population

selection format A method of presenting test questions in which students indicate their choice from an array of the possible test answers (usually called "response options"); true-false, multiple-choice, and matching are the three most common selection formats

semantics The study of word meanings; although the scope of the term can extend beyond individual words to include sentence meaning, the term generally applies to words

sensitivity An assessment procedure's capacity to detect small differences among or within students

sensorineural hearing loss Abnormal hearing associated with both poor bone-conduction sensitivity and poor air-conduction sensitivity

setting event Environmental event that sets the occasion for the performance of an action

single-skill test Test designed to measure skill development in one specific content area (for example, reading)

skew Asymmetry in a distribution; the distribution of scores below the mean is not a mirror image of the distribution above the mean

social comparison Observing a peer whose behavior is considered to be appropriate and using the peer's rate of behavior as the standard against which to evaluate the target student's rate of behavior

social tolerance The threshold above which behaviors are viewed as undesirable by others

social validity A consumer's access to and satisfaction with an intervention or assessment

Spearman rho An index of correlation between two variables measured on an ordinal scale

speed test Timed test

spelling The formation of words from letters according to accepted usage

split-half reliability estimate An estimate of internal-consistency reliability derived by correlating people's scores on two halves of a test

stability coefficient Stability coefficient is another name for test-retest reliability coefficient. The stability coefficient quantifies the consistency of scores over time

standard deviation A measure of the degree of dispersion in a distribution; the square root of the variance

standard error of measurement (SEM) The standard deviation of error around a person's true score

standardization sample The group of individuals on whom a test is standardized; also called "the norm group"

standard score The general name for a derived score that has been transformed to produce a distribution with a predetermined mean and standard deviation

stanine Short for *standard nines;* standard-score band that divides a distribution into nine parts; the middle seven stanines are each 0.50 standard deviation wide, and the fifth stanine is centered on the mean

stem In selection formats, the part of a problem that contains the question

student accountability Consequences exist for individual students, and are based on their individual assessment performance. For example, students might not be promoted to the next grade or graduate if their assessment results do not meet a pre-specified level

substitution An error in oral reading in which a student replaces one or more words in the passage with one or more meaningful words (synonyms)

supply format A method of presenting test questions in which a student is required to produce a written or oral response; this response can be as restricted as a number or a word and can be as extensive as a sentence, a paragraph, or several pages of written response

supralinguistics A second order of analysis required to understand the meaning of words or sentences

syntax Word order of sentences; includes a description of the rules for arranging the words into a sentence

system accountability Consequences exist for school systems, and are based on the assessment performance of a group of individuals (e.g., school building, district, or state education agency). For example, a school might receive a financial award or special recognition for having a large percent of students meeting a particular assessment performance level

systematic error Consistent error that can be predicted; bias

systematic observation Observation in which an observer specifies or defines the behaviors to be observed and then counts or otherwise measures the frequency, duration, magnitude, or latency of the behaviors

test A predetermined set of questions or tasks to which predetermined types of behavioral responses are sought

testing Administering a particular set of questions to an individual or group of individuals in order to obtain a score

test-retest reliability An index of stability over time

tetrachoric correlation coefficient An index of correlation between two arbitrarily dichotomized variables (for example, tall/short, smart/dull)

transformed score Special form of z-score that allows the transformation of a z-score to a distribution defined by the user

Transformed score = Mean +
(z * Standard deviation)

where the z-score is computed from existing data and the mean and standard deviation are defined according to the needs of the user

true score The score that a student would earn if the entire domain of items was assessed

T-score A standard score with a mean of 50 and a standard deviation of 10

tunnel vision Normal central visual acuity with a restricted peripheral field

validity The extent to which a test measures what its authors or users claim it measures; specifically, test validity concerns the appropriateness of the inferences that can be made on the basis of test results

validity coefficient A coefficient that measures the correlation between a test of unknown validity and an established criterion measure

variance A numerical index describing the dispersion of a set of scores around the mean of the distribution; specifically, the average squared distance of the scores from the mean

visual acuity The clarity or sharpness with which a person sees

whole-interval recording A procedure used in systematic observation in which an occurrence is scored if the behavior is present throughout the entire observation interval

writing style Rule-governed writing, which includes grammar (for example, verb tense and use) and mechanics (for example, punctuation and capitalization)

z-score Standard score with a mean of 0 and a standard deviation of 1

Achenbach, T. M. (1986). *The Direct Observation Form (DOF)*. Burlington: University of Vermont, Department of Psychiatry.

Achenbach, T. M. (1991a). *Integrative guide to the 1991 CBCL, YSR, and TRF profiles*. Burlington: University of Vermont, Department of Psychiatry.

Achenbach, T. M. (1991b). *Manual for the Child Behavior Checklist/4–18*. Burlington: University of Vermont, Department of Psychiatry.

Achenbach, T. M. (1991c). *Teacher's Report Form (TRF)*. Burlington: University of Vermont, Department of Psychiatry.

Achenbach, T. M. (1991d). *Youth Self-Report (YSR)*. Burlington: University of Vermont, Department of Psychiatry.

Achenbach, T. M. (1992). *Child Behavior Checklist/2–3 Years (CBCL/2–3)*. Burlington: University of Vermont, Department of Psychiatry.

Achenbach, T. M., & Brown, J. S. (1991). *Bibliography of published studies using the Child Behavior Checklist and related materials* (1991 ed.). Burlington: University of Vermont, Department of Psychiatry.

Achenbach, T. M., & Edelbrock, C. (1983). *Manual for the Child Behavior Checklist and Revised Child Behavior Profile*. Burlington: University of Vermont, Department of Psychiatry.

Achenbach, T. M., & Edelbrock, C. (1987). *Manual for the Youth Self-Report and Profile*. Burlington: University of Vermont, Department of Psychiatry.

Achenbach, T. M., & Rescorla, L. A. (2000). *Manual for the ASEBA Preschool Forms and Profiles*. Burlington: University of Vermont, Department of Psychiatry.

Achenbach, T. M., & Rescorla, L. A. (2001). *Manual for the ASEBA School-Age Forms and Profiles*. Burlington: University of Vermont, Department of Psychiatry.

Achenbach, T. M., & Rescorla, L. A. (2004). The Achenbach System of Empirically Based Assessment (ASEBA) for Ages 1.5 to 18 years. In M. R. Maruish (Ed.), *The use of psychological testing for treatment planning and outcomes assessment* (3rd ed., Vol. 2, pp. 179–213). Mahwah, NJ: Lawrence Erlbaum Associates.

Adams, D. (1991). Writing portfolios: A powerful assessment and conversation tool. *Writing Teacher, 12–15.*

Adams, M. (1990). *Beginning to read: Thinking and learning about print*. Cambridge, MA: MIT Press.

Alberto, P. A., & Troutman, A. C. (1999). *Applied behavior analysis for teachers* (5th ed.). Upper Saddle River, NJ: Prentice-Hall.

Algozzine, B. A., Christenson, S. L., & Ysseldyke, J. E. (1982). Probabilities associated with the referral to placement process. *Teacher Education and Special Education, 5,* 19–23.

Algozzine, B. A., & Ysseldyke, J. E. (1992). *Strategies and tactics for effective instruction*. Longmont, CO: Sopris West.

Algozzine, B. A., Ysseldyke, J. E., & Elliott, J. L. (1997). *Strategies and tactics for effective instruction* (2nd ed.). Longmont, CO: Sopris West.

Als, H. (1984). *Manual for the naturalistic observation of newborn behavior (preterm and full-term infants)* (pp. 1–19). Boston: Children's Hospital.

American Association for the Advancement of Science. (1987). *Science for all Americans*. New York: Oxford University Press.

American Association for the Advancement of Science. (1993). *Benchmarks for science literacy*. New York: Oxford University Press.

American Association on Mental Retardation. (1992). *Mental retardation: Definition, classification, and systems of supports* (9th ed.). Washington, DC: Author.

American Association on Mental Retardation. (2002). *Mental retardation: Definition, classification, and systems of support* (10th ed.). Washington, DC: Author.

American Educational Research Association (AERA), American Psychological Association, & National Council on Measurement in Education. (1985). *Standards for educational and psychological testing*. Washington, DC: American Psychological Association.

American Educational Research Association (AERA), American Psychological Association, & National Council on Measurement in Education. (1997). *Standards for educational and psychological testing*. Washington, DC: American Educational Research Association.

American Educational Research Association (AERA), American Psychological Association, & National Council on Measurement in Education. (1999). *Standards for educational and psychological testing.* Washington, DC: American Educational Research Association.

American Psychiatric Association. (1995). *Diagnostic and statistical manual of mental disorders* (4th ed.). DSM-IV Primary Care Version. Washington, DC: Author.

American Psychological Association. (1992). *Ethical principles of psychologists and code of conduct.* Washington, DC: Author.

American Psychological Association, American Educational Research Association, & National Council on Measurement in Education. (1974). *Standards for educational and psychological tests.* Washington, DC: American Psychological Association.

American Speech-Language-Hearing Association. (1990). Guidelines for audiometric symbols. *ASHA, 32* (Suppl. 2), 25–30.

Ames, W. (1965). A comparison of spelling textbooks. *Elementary English, 42,* 146–150, 214.

Anastasi, A. (1980). *Psychological testing* (4th ed.). New York: Macmillan.

Anastasi, A. (1988). *Psychological testing* (5th ed.). New York: Macmillan.

Archbald, D., & Newman, F. (1988). *Beyond standardized testing: Assessing authentic academic achievement in the secondary school.* Reston, VA: National Association of Secondary Principals.

Armbruster, B., & Osborn, J. (2001). *Put reading first: The research building blocks for teaching children to read.* Jessup, MD: Partnership for Reading. Available from the National Institute for Literacy website: www.nifl.gov.

Aronson, E., Blaney, N., Stephan, C., Sikes, J., & Snapp, M. (1978). *The jigsaw classroom.* Beverly Hills, CA: Sage.

Arreaga-Mayer, C., Carta, J. J., & Tapia, Y. (1992). *ESCRIBE: Ecobehavioral system for the contextual recording of interactional bilingual environments.* Kansas City, KS: Juniper Gardens Children's Project, University of Kansas.

Arreaga-Mayer, C., Carta, J. J., & Tapia, Y. (1995). Ecobehavioral assessment: A new methodology for evaluating instruction for exceptional culturally and linguistically diverse students. In S. B. Garcia (Ed.), *Shaping the future: Defining effective services for exceptional culturally and linguistically diverse learners (Monograph 1).* Washington, DC: CEC-DDEL.

Arreaga-Mayer, C., Utley, C. A., Perdomo-Rivera, C., & Greenwood, C. R. (2003). Ecobehavioral assessment of instructional contexts in bilingual special education programs for English language learners at risk for developmental disabilities. *Focus on Autism and Other Developmental Disabilities, 18*(1), 28–40.

Arter, J., & Jenkins, J. R. (1979). Differential diagnosis—prescriptive teaching: A critical appraisal. *Review of Educational Research, 49,* 517–556.

Arter, J., & Spandel, V. (1992, May). Using portfolios of student work in instruction and assessment. *Instructional Topics in Educational Measurement,* 36–44.

Arthaud, T. J., Vasa, S. F., & Steckelberg, A. L. (2000). Reading assessment and instructional practices in special education. *Diagnostique, 25*(3), 205–227.

Atkinson, R. L., Atkinson, R. C., Smith, E. E., & Bem, D. J. (1993). *Introduction to psychology* (11th ed.). Fort Worth, TX: Harcourt Brace Jovanovich.

Ayers, A. (1981). *Sensory integration and the child.* Los Angeles, CA: Western Psychological Services.

Bachor, D. (1990). The importance of shifts in language level and extraneous information in determining word-problem difficulty: Steps toward individual assessment. *Diagnostique, 14,* 94–111.

Bachor, D., Stacy, N., & Freeze, D. (1986). *A conceptual framework for word problems: Some preliminary results.* Paper presented at the conference of the Canadian Society for Studies in Education, Winnipeg, Manitoba.

Bagnato, S., & Neisworth, J. (1990). *System to plan early childhood services.* Circle Pines, MN: American Guidance Service.

Bailey, D. B., & Rouse, T. L. (1989). Procedural considerations in assessing infants and preschoolers with handicaps. In D. B. Bailey & M. Wolery (Eds.), *Assessing infants and preschoolers with handicaps.* Columbus, OH: Merrill.

Baker, E., O'Neil, Jr., H., & Linn, R. (1993). Policy and validity prospects for performance-based assessment. *American Psychologist, 48*(12), 1210–1218.

Balboni, G., Pedrabissi, L., Molteni, M., & Villa, S. (2001). Discriminant validity of the Vineland Scales: Score profiles of individuals with mental retardation and a specific disorder. *American Journal on Mental Retardation, 106*(2), 162–172.

Balow, I. H., Farr, R. C., & Hogan, T. P. (1992). *Metropolitan Achievement Test 7*. San Antonio, TX: Psychological Corporation.

Bandura, A. (1969). *Principles of behavior modification*. Oxford: Holt, Rinehart, & Winston.

Bangert-Drowns, R. L., Kulik, J. A., Kulik, C.-L. (1991). Effects of frequent classroom testing. *Journal of Educational Research, 85*(2), 89–99.

Bankson, N. W. (1990). *Bankson Language Test* (2nd ed.). Austin, TX: Pro-Ed.

Barraga, N. (1976). *Visual handicaps and learning: A developmental approach*. Belmont, CA: Wadsworth.

Barsch, R. (1966). Teacher needs—motor training. In W. Cruickshank (Ed.), *The teacher of brain-injured children*. Syracuse, NY: Syracuse University Press.

Batsche, G., Elliott, J., Graden, J., Grimes, J., Kovaleski, J., Prasse, D., et al. (2005). *Response to intervention: Policy considerations and implementation*. Alexandria, VA: National Association of State Directors of Special Education.

Baumgardner, J. C. (1993). *An empirical analysis of school psychological assessments: Practice with students who are deaf and bilingual*. Unpublished doctoral dissertation, University of Minnesota, Minneapolis.

Baxter, G., Shavelson, R., Goldman, S., & Pine, J. (1992). Evaluation of procedure-based scoring for hands-on science assessment. *Journal of Educational Measurement, 29*(1), 1–17.

Bayley, N. (1993). *Manual: Bayley Scales of Infant Development* (2nd ed.). San Antonio, TX: Psychological Corporation.

Bayley, N. (2006). *Bayley Scales of Infant and Toddler Development*. San Antonio, TX: Psychological Corporation.

Beck, R. (1979). *Great Falls Precision Teaching Project: Report for Joint Dissemination and Review Panel*. Great Falls, MT: Great Falls Public Schools.

Beery, K. E. (1982). *Revised administration, scoring, and teaching manual for the Developmental Test of Visual-Motor Integration*. Cleveland, OH: Modern Curriculum Press.

Beery, K. E. (1989). *The Developmental Test of Visual-Motor Integration*. Cleveland, OH: Modern Curriculum Press.

Beery, K. E. (1997). *Developmental Test of Visual-Motor Integration*. Cleveland, OH: Modern Curriculum Press.

Beery, K. E., & Beery, N. (2004). *Beery VMI*. Minneapolis, MN: NCS Pearson.

Bender, L. (1938). *Bender Visual-Motor Gestalt Test*. New York: Grune & Stratton.

Bennett, R. (1993). On the meanings of constructed responses. In R. Bennett & W. Ward (Eds.), *Constructive versus choice in cognitive measurement: Issues in constructed response, performance testing, and portfolio assessment*. Hillsdale, NJ: Lawrence Erlbaum Associates.

Bentz, J., & Pavri, S. (2000). Curriculum-based measurement in assessing bilingual students: A promising new direction. *Diagnostique, 25*(3), 229–248.

Bergan, J. R. (1977). *Behavioral consultation*. Columbus, OH: Merrill.

Bess, F. H., & Hall, J. W. (1992). *Screening children for auditory function*. Nashville, TN: Bill Wilkerson Center Press.

Bielinski, J., Thurlow, M., Callender, S., & Bolt, S. (2001). *On the road to accountability: Reporting outcomes for students with disabilities* (Technical Report 32). Minneapolis: University of Minnesota, National Center on Educational Outcomes.

Bielinski, J., Ysseldyke, J. E., Bolt, S., Friedebach, M., & Friedebach, J. (2001). Prevalence of accommodations for students with disabilities participating in a statewide testing system. *Assessment for Effective Intervention, 26*(2), 21–28.

Black, L., Daiker, D. A., Sommers, J., & Stygall, G. (Eds.). (1994). *New directions in portfolio assessment: Reflective practice, critical theory, and large-scale scoring*. Portsmouth, NH: Boynton/Cook.

Blackshire-Belay, C. (Ed.). *Current issues in second language acquisition and development*. Lanham, MD: University Press of America.

Bleckman, E. (1985). *Solving child behavior problems at home and at school*. Champaign, IL: Research Press.

Bloom, B. (1956). *Taxonomy of educational objectives: The classification of educational goals: Handbook 1. Cognitive domain*. New York: McKay.

Bloom, B., Hastings, J., & Madaus, G. (1971). *Handbook of formative and summative evaluation of student learning*. New York: McGraw-Hill.

Boehm, A. E. (1973). Criterion-referenced assessment for the teacher. *Teacher's College Record, 75*(1), 117–126.

Boehm, A. E. (1986). *Boehm Test of Basic Concepts–Revised*. San Antonio, TX: Psychological Corporation.

Boehm, A. E., & Weinberg, R. A. (1997). *The classroom observer: A guide for developing observation skills* (3rd ed.). New York: Teachers College Press.

Bond, G., & Dykstra, R. (1967). The cooperative research program in first-grade reading instruction (1967). *Reading Research Quarterly, 2,* 5–142.

Bower, E. M. (1981). *Early identification of emotionally handicapped children in school* (3rd ed.). Springfield, IL: Charles E. Thomas.

Bowers, P., & Wolf, M. (1993). Theoretical links between naming speed, precise timing mechanisms and orthographic skill in dyslexia. *Reading and Writing: An Interdisciplinary Journal, 5,* 69–85.

Bracken, B. A. (1988). Limitations of preschool instruments and standards for minimal levels of technical adequacy. *Journal of Psychoeducational Assessment, 5,* 313–326.

Bracken, B., & McCallum, R. S. (1998). *Universal Nonverbal Intelligence Test.* Itasca, IL: Riverside Publishing Company.

Bradbury, R. (1953). *Fahrenheit 451.* New York: Ballantine Books.

Brannigan, G., & Decker, S. (2003). *Bender Visual-Motor Gestalt Test* (2nd ed.). Itasca, IL: Riverside Publishing.

Breland, H. (1983). *The direct assessment of writing skill: A measurement review* (College Board Report No. 83-6). New York: College Entrance Examination Board.

Breland, H., Camp, R., Jones, R., Morris, M. M., & Rock, D. (1987). *Assessing writing skill.* New York: The College Board.

Briggs, A., & Underwood, G. (1984). Phonological coding in good and poor readers. *Reading Research Quarterly, 20,* 54–66.

Broderick, C. B. (1993). *Understanding family process: Basics of family systems theory.* Newbury Park, CA: Sage.

Bronfenbrenner, U. (1979). *The ecology of human development.* Cambridge, MA: Harvard University Press.

Brown, L., & Hammill, D. (1978). *Behavior Rating Profile.* Austin, TX: Pro-Ed.

Brown, L., & Hammill, D. (1983). *Behavior Rating Profile.* Austin, TX: Pro-Ed.

Brown, L., & Hammill, D. (1990). *Behavior Rating Profile* (2nd ed.). Austin, TX: Pro-Ed.

Brown, L., Hammill, D., & Wiederholt, J. L. (1995). *Test of Reading Comprehension–3.* Austin, TX: Pro-Ed.

Brown, L., & Leigh, J. (1986a). *Adaptive Behavior Inventory.* Austin, TX: Pro-Ed.

Brown, L., & Leigh, J. (1986b). *The Adaptive Behavior Inventory manual.* Austin, TX: Pro-Ed.

Brown, L., Sherbenou, R., & Johnsen, S. (1997). *Test of Nonverbal Intelligence–3.* Austin, TX: Pro-Ed.

Brown, R., & Bellugi, U. (1964). Three processes in the child's acquisition of syntax. *Harvard Educational Review, 34,* 133–151.

Brown, V., Cronin, M., & McEntire, E. (1994). *Test of Mathematical Abilities–2.* Austin, TX: Pro-Ed.

Bruer, J. (1993). *School for thought: A science of learning in the classroom.* Cambridge, MA: MIT Press.

Bruininks, R., Woodcock, R., Weatherman, R., & Hill, B. (1996). *Scales of Independent Behavior, Revised, comprehensive manual.* Chicago: Riverside Publishing Company.

Burns, M. K., MacQuarrie, L. L., & Campbell, D. T. (1999). The difference between Curriculum-Based Assessment and Curriculum-Based Measurement: A focus on purpose and result. *Communiqué, 27*(6), 18–19.

Burns, M. K., & Ysseldyke, J. E. (2005). Questions about responsiveness to intervention implementation: Seeking answers from existing models. *California School Psychologist, 10,* 9–20.

The Buros Institute. *The mental measurements yearbook.* Lincoln: University of Nebraska Press.

Butcher, N. N., Graham, J. R., Ben-Porath, Y. S., Tellegen, Y. S., Dahlstrom, W. G., & Kaemmer, B. (2001). *Minnesota Multiphasic Personality Inventory–2.* Minneapolis, MN: University of Minnesota Press.

Caldwell, J., & Goldin, J. (1979). Variables affecting word problem difficulty in elementary school mathematics. *Journal of Research in Mathematics Education, 10,* 323–335.

Calfee, R., & Perfumo, P. (1993). Student portfolios: Opportunities for a revolution in assessment. *Journal of Reading, 36*(7), 532–537.

Camarata, S. (1996). On the importance of integrating naturalistic language, social intervention, and speech-intelligibility training. In L. Koegel & G. Dunlap (Eds.), *Positive behavior support* (pp. 333–351). Baltimore, MD: Brookes.

Camarata, S., Nelson, K., & Camarata, M. (1994). A comparison of conversation-based to imitation-based procedures for training grammatical structures in specifically language impaired children.

Journal of Speech and Hearing Research, 37, 1414–1423.

Camp, R. (1993). The place of portfolios in our changing views of writing assessment. In R. Bennett & W. Ward (Eds.), *Constructive versus choice in cognitive measurement: Issues in constructed response, performance testing, and portfolio assessment.* Hillsdale, NJ: Lawrence Erlbaum Associates.

Campbell, D., & Fiske, D. (1959). Convergent and discriminate validation by the multi-trait–multi-method matrix. *Psychological Bulletin, 56,* 81–105.

Cannell, J. J. (1988). Nationally normed elementary achievement testing in America's public schools: How all 50 states are above the national average. *Educational Measurement: Issues and Practice,* 7(2), 5–9.

Carr, E. (1994). Emerging themes in functional analysis of problem behavior. *Journal of Applied Behavioral Analysis, 27,* 393–400.

Carroll, J. B. (1963). A model of school learning. *Teachers College Record, 64,* 723–733.

Carroll, J. B. (1985). The model of school learning: Progress of an idea. In L. W. Anderson (Ed.), *Perspectives on school learning: Selected writings of John B. Carroll* (pp. 82–102). Hillsdale, NJ: Lawrence Erlbaum Associates.

Carroll, J. B., & Horn, J. L. (1981). On the scientific basis of ability testing. *American Psychologist, 36,* 1012–1020.

Carroll, J. G. (1993). *Human cognitive abilities: A survey of factor-analytic studies.* New York: Cambridge University Press.

Carrow-Woolfolk, E. (1985). *Test for Auditory Comprehension of Language, examiner's manual* (rev. ed.). Allen, TX: Developmental Learning Materials.

Carrow-Woolfolk, E. (1995). *Manual for the Listening Comprehension and Oral Language Subtests of the Oral and Written Language Scales.* Circle Pines, MN: American Guidance Service.

Carrow-Woolfolk, E. (1996). *Manual for the Written Expression Subtest of the Oral and Written Language Scales.* Circle Pines, MN: American Guidance Service.

Carrow-Woolfolk, E. (1999a). *Comprehensive Assessment of Spoken Language.* Circle Pines, MN: American Guidance Service.

Carrow-Woolfolk, E. (1999b). *Test for Auditory Comprehension of Language* (3rd ed.). San Antonio, TX: Harcourt.

Chalfant, J., Pysh, M. V., & Moultrie, R. (1979). Teacher assistance teams: A model for within-building problem solving. *Learning Disability Quarterly, 2,* 85–96.

Chall, J. (1967). *Learning to read: The great debate.* New York: McGraw-Hill.

Chase, J. B. (1985). Assessment of the visually impaired. *Diagnostique, 10,* 144–160.

Christenson, S. L., & Ysseldyke, J. E. (1989). Assessing student performance: An important change is needed. *Journal of School Psychology, 27,* 409–426.

Cohen, G. (1972). Hemispheric differences in a letter classification task. *Perception and Psychophysics, 11,* 139–142.

Cohen, J. (1960). A coefficient of agreement for nominal scales. *Educational and Psychological Measurement, 20,* 37–46.

Cohen, J. (1988). *Statistical power analysis for the behavioral sciences* (2nd ed.). Hillsdale, NJ: Lawrence Erlbaum Associates.

Collins, A. (1993). Alternative assessment in undergraduate science education, with emphasis on portfolios. *Proceedings of the National Science Foundation workshop on the role of faculty from the scientific disciplines in the undergraduate education of future science and mathematics teachers.* Washington, DC: National Science Foundation.

Columba, L., & Dolgos, K. A. (1995). Portfolio assessment in mathematics. *Reading Improvement, 32*(3), 174–176.

Conners, C. K. (1989). *Conners Teacher Rating Scales.* North Tonawanda, NY: Multi-Health Systems.

Conners, C. K. (1997). *Conners Parent Rating Scale–Revised.* New York: Psychological Corporation.

Connolly, A. (1998). *KeyMath–Revised: A diagnostic inventory of essential mathematics.* Circle Pines, MN: American Guidance Service.

Conoley, J. C., & Impara, J. C. (1995). *The twelfth mental measurements yearbook* (GORT-3, pp. 422–425). Lincoln, NE: University of Nebraska Press.

Conoley, J. C., & Kramer, J. J. (1989). *The tenth mental measurements yearbook* (WRMT-R, pp. 909–916; TORC, pp. 850–855). Lincoln, NE: University of Nebraska Press.

Cooper, C. (1977). Holistic evaluation of writing. In C. Cooper & L. Odell (Eds.), *Evaluating writing: Describing, measuring, judging.* Buffalo, NY: National Council of Teachers of English.

Corn, A. (1983). Visual function: A theoretical model for individuals with low vision. *Journal of Visual Impairment and Blindness, 77,* 373–377.

Crocker, L., & Algina, J. (1986a). *Introduction to classical and modern test theory* (Chapter 7: Procedures for estimating reliability). New York: Holt, Rinehart, & Winston.

Crocker, L., & Algina, J. (1986b). *Introduction to classical and modern test theory* (Chapter 10: Introduction to validity). New York: Holt, Rinehart, & Winston.

Crocker, L. M., Miller, M. D., & Franks, E. A. (1989). Quantitative methods for assessing the fit between test and curriculum. *Applied Measurement in Education, 2*(2), 179–194.

Cromwell, R. L., Blashfield, R. K., & Strauss, J. S. (1975). Criteria for classification systems. In N. Hobbs (Ed.), *Issues in the classification of children* (Vol. 1). San Francisco: Jossey-Bass.

Cronbach, L. (1951). Coefficient alpha and the internal structure of tests. *Psychometrika, 16,* 297–334.

Cronbach, L., & Snow, R. (1977). *Aptitudes and instructional methods: A handbook for research on interactions.* New York: Irvington.

CTB/Macmillan/McGraw-Hill. (1992). *California Achievement Tests/5: Technical bulletin 1.* Monterey, CA: Author.

CTB/Macmillan/McGraw-Hill. (1993). *California Achievement Tests/5.* Monterey, CA: Author.

CTB/McGraw-Hill. (1997). *Terra Nova.* Monterey, CA: Author.

CTB/McGraw-Hill. (2001). *InView.* Monterey, CA: Author.

CTB/McGraw-Hill. (2002). *Terra Nova* (2nd ed.). Monterey, CA: Author.

Cummins, J. (1984). *Bilingual special education: Issues in assessment and pedagogy.* San Diego, CA: College Hill.

Das, J., Kirby, J., & Jarman, R. (1975). Simultaneous and successive syntheses: An alternative model for cognitive abilities. *Psychological Bulletin, 82,* 87–103.

Davilla, R. R. (1989). Letter to Mr. Robert Dawson, November 17, signed by Michael Vader, Acting Assistant Secretary of the U.S. Department of Education.

Davis, A., & Felknor, C. (1994). The demise of performance-based graduation in Littleton. *Educational Leadership, 51*(6), 64–65.

Deming, W. E. (1994). *The new economics for industry, government and education.* Cambridge, MA: MIT, Center for Advanced Educational Services.

Deming, W. E. (2000). *The new economics for industry, government and education* (2nd ed.). Cambridge, MA: MIT Press.

Deno, S. L. (1985). Curriculum-based assessment: The emerging alternative. *Exceptional Children, 52,* 219–232.

Deno, S. L. (1986). Formative evaluation of individual school programs: A new role for school psychologists. *School Psychology Review, 15,* 358–374.

Deno, S. L. (2004). Curriculum-based measures: Development and perspectives. Unpublished paper. Available on the RIPM website: www.progress monitoring.net

Deno, S. L., & Fuchs, L. S. (1987). Developing curriculum-based measurement systems for data-based special education problem solving. *Focus on Exceptional Children, 19,* 1–16.

Deno, S. L., & Mirkin, P. (1977). *Data-based program modification: A manual.* Reston, VA: Council for Exceptional Children.

Derogatis, L. R. (1993). *Brief Symptom Inventory.* Minneapolis, MN: National Computer Systems.

Diana v. State Board of Education, 1970 (*Diana v. State Board of Education,* C-70: 37RFT) (N.D. Cal., 1970).

Doggett, R., Edwards, R., & Moore, J. (2001). An approach to functional assessment in general education classroom settings. *School Psychology Review, 30*(3), 313–328.

Doman, R., Spitz, E., Zuckerman, E., Delacato, C., & Doman, G. (1967). Children with severe brain injuries: Neurological organization in terms of mobility. In E. C. Frierson & W. B. Barbe (Eds.), *Educating children with learning disabilities.* New York: Appleton-Century-Crofts.

Dorans, N., & Schmitt, A. (1993). Constructed response and differential item functioning: A pragmatic approach. In R. Bennett & W. Ward (Eds.), *Constructive versus choice in cognitive measurement: Issues in constructed response, performance testing, and portfolio assessment.* Hillsdale, NJ: Lawrence Erlbaum Associates.

Down, A. L. (1969; original work published 1866). Observations on an ethnic classification of idiots. In R. Vollman (Ed.), *Down's syndrome (mongolism), a reference bibliography.* Washington, DC: U.S. Department of Health, Education, and Welfare.

Dubowitz, L., & Dubowitz, V. (1981). The neurological assessment of the preterm and fullterm newborn infant (Clinics in developmental medicine, Spastics International Medical Publications, No. 79). Philadelphia: J. B. Lippincott.

Dunn, L. M., & Dunn, M. (1997). *Peabody Picture Vocabulary Test–III.* Circle Pines, MN: American Guidance Service.

Dunn, L. M., & Markwardt, F. C. (1970). *Peabody Individual Achievement Test.* Circle Pines: MN: American Guidance Service.

Dwyer, C. (1993). Innovation and reform: Examples from teacher assessment. In R. Bennett & W. Ward (Eds.), *Constructive versus choice in cognitive measurement: Issues in constructed response, performance testing, and portfolio assessment.* Hillsdale, NJ: Lawrence Erlbaum Associates.

Edformation (undated). *AIMSweb.* Available at www.edformation.com.

Educational Testing Service. (1990). *Exploring new methods for collecting students' school-based writing: NAEP's 1990 portfolio study* (ED 343154). Washington, DC: U.S. Department of Education.

Egeland, personal communication, March 30, 1994.

Elliott, J. L., Algozzine, B. A., & Ysseldyke, J. E. (1998). *Timesavers for educators.* Longmont, CO: Sopris West.

Elliott, J. L., Thurlow, M. L., & Ysseldyke, J. E. (1996). *Assessment guidelines that maximize the participation of students with disabilities in large-scale assessments.* Minneapolis, MN: University of Minnesota, National Center on Educational Outcomes.

Elliott, S. N., & Piersel, W. C. (1982). Direct assessment of reading skills: An approach which links assessment to intervention. *School Psychology Review, 11,* 267–280.

Elmore, R. (2002). *Bridging the gap between standards and achievement.* Washington, DC: The Albert Shanker Institute.

Englemann, S., Granzin, A., & Severson, H. (1979). Diagnosing instruction. *Journal of Special Education, 13,* 355–365.

Englert, C., Cullata, B., & Horn, D. (1987). Influence of irrelevant information in addition word problems on problem solving. *Learning Disabilities Quarterly, 10,* 29–36.

Epstein, M. H. (2004). *Examiner's manual for the Behavioral and Emotional Rating Scale* (2nd ed.). Austin, TX: Pro-Ed.

Ervin, S. M. (1964). Imitation and structural change in children's language. In E. H. Lenneberg (Ed.), *New directions in the study of language.* Cambridge, MA: MIT Press.

Farlow, L. J., & Snell, M. E. (1989). Teacher use of student performance data to make instructional decisions: Practices in programs for students with moderate to profound disabilities. *Journal of the Association for Persons with Severe Handicaps, 14*(1), 13–22.

Feagans, L., Sanyal, M., Henderson, F., Collier, A., & Appelbaum, M. I. (1986). The relationship of middle ear disease in early childhood to later narrative and attention skills. *Journal of Pediatric Psychology, 12,* 581–594.

Feldt, L. S., Forsyth, R. A., Ansley, T. N., & Alnot, S. D. (1996). *Iowa Tests of Educational Development.* Chicago: Riverside Publishing Company.

Figueroa, R. (1990). Assessment of linguistic minority group children. In C. R. Reynolds & R. W. Kamphaus (Eds.), *Handbook of psychological assessment of children.* New York: Guilford Press.

Flanagan, D. P., Genshaft, J. L., & Harrison, P. L. (1997). *Contemporary intellectual assessment: Theories, tests, and issues.* New York: Guilford Press.

Flanagan, D. P., & Harrison, P. L. (2005). *Contemporary intellectual assessment: Theories, tests, and issues* (2nd ed.). New York: Guilford Press.

Fleischer, K. (1997). *The effects of structured rating paradigms on the reliability of teacher ratings of written language samples over time.* Unpublished doctoral dissertation, Pennsylvania State University, State College, PA.

Flesch, R. (1955). *Why Johnny can't read.* New York: Harper & Row.

Fodness, R. (1987). *Test-retest reliability of the Test of Language Development–Intermediate.* Unpublished master's thesis, Central Michigan University, Mt. Pleasant, MI.

Foorman, B., Francis, D., Fletcher, J., Schatschneider, C., & Mehta, P. (1998). The role of instruction in learning to read: Preventing reading failure in at-risk children. *Journal of Educational Psychology, 90,* 1–13.

Forsyth, R. L., Ansley, T., Feldt, L., & Alnot, S. (2002). *Iowa Tests of Educational Development.* Chicago: Riverside Publishing Company.

Frazier, D., & Paulson, F. (1992). How portfolios motivate reluctant writers. *Educational Leadership,* 62–65.

Fredricksen, J., & Collins, A. (1989). A systems approach to educational testing. *Educational Researcher, 18*, 27–32.

Freeland, J., Skinner, C., Jackson, B., McDaniel, C., & Smith, S. (2000). Measuring and increasing silent reading comprehension rates: Empirically validating a related reading intervention. *Psychology in the Schools, 37*(5), 415–429.

Friel-Patti, S., & Finitzo, T. (1990). Language learning in a prospective study of otitis media with effusion in the first two years of life. *Journal of Speech and Hearing Research, 33*, 188–194.

Frostig, M. (1968). Education for children with learning disabilities. In H. Myklebust (Ed.), *Progress in learning disabilities*. New York: Grune & Stratton.

Frostig, M., Maslow, P., Lefever, D. W., & Whittlesey, J. R. (1964). *The Marianne Frostig Developmental Test of Visual Perception: 1963 standardization*. Palo Alto, CA: Consulting Psychologists Press.

Fuchs, D., & Fuchs, L. S. (1989). Effects of examiner familiarity on black, Caucasian, and Hispanic children: A meta-analysis. *Exceptional Children, 55*(4), 303–308.

Fuchs, D., Mock, D., Morgan, P. L., & Young, C. (2003). Responsiveness to intervention: Definitions, evidence, and implications for the learning disabilities construct. *Learning Disabilities Research and Practice, 18*(3), 157–171.

Fuchs, L. S., & Deno, S. L. (1991). Paradigmatic distinctions between instructionally-relevant measurement models. *Exceptional Children, 57*(6), 488–499.

Fuchs, L. S., & Deno, S. L. (1994). Must instructionally useful performance assessment be based in the curriculum? *Exceptional Children, 61*(1), 15–24.

Fuchs, L. S., Deno, S. L., & Mirkin, P. (1984). The effects of frequent curriculum based measurement and evaluation on pedagogy, student achievement and student awareness of learning. *American Educational Research Journal, 21*, 449–460.

Fuchs, L. S., & Fuchs, D. (1986a). Effects of systematic formative evaluation: A meta-analysis. *Exceptional Children, 53*, 199–208.

Fuchs, L. S., & Fuchs, D. (Eds.). (1986b). Linking assessment to instructional intervention: An overview. *School Psychology Review, 15*(3).

Fuchs, L. S., & Fuchs, D. (2003). Curriculum-based measurement: A best practice guide. *NASP Communique, 32*(2), unpaged insert.

Fuchs, L. S., Fuchs, D., & Maxwell, L. (1988). The validity of informal reading comprehension measures. *Remedial and Special Education*, 20–28.

Fuchs, L. S., Fuchs, D., & Speece, D. L. (2002). Treatment validity as a unifying construct for identifying learning disabilities. *Learning Disability Quarterly, 25*, 33–45.

Fudala, J. (1970). *Arizona Articulation Proficiency Scale*. Los Angeles: Western Psychological Services.

Gardner, M. (1990). *Expressive One-Word Picture Vocabulary Test*. Novato, CA: Academic Therapy Publications.

Gearhart, M., Herman, J., Baker, E., & Whittaker, A. (1992). *Writing portfolios at the elementary level: A study of methods for writing assessment* (CSE Technical Report No. 337). Los Angeles: University of California, Center for the Study of Evaluation.

Gearhart, M., Herman, J., Baker, E., & Whittaker, A. (1993). *"Whose work is it?" A question for the validity of large-scale portfolio assessment* (CRESST/CSE Technical Report No. 363). Los Angeles: University of California, Center for the Study of Evaluation.

Gelfer, J., & Perkins, P. (1998). Portfolios: Focus on young children. *Teaching Exceptional Children, 31*(2), 44–47.

Gersten, R., & Baker, S. (2000). What we know about effective instructional practices for English-language learners. *Exceptional Children, 66*(4), 454–470.

Gickling, E., & Havertape, E. (1980). *Curriculum-based assessment*. Minneapolis: National School Psychology Inservice Training Network.

Gillespie, C. S., Ford, K. L., Gillespie, R. D., & Leavell, A. G. (1996). Portfolio assessment: Some questions, some answers, some recommendations. *Journal of Adolescent & Adult Literacy, 39*, 480–491.

Gilliam, J. E. (2001). *Manual for the Gilliam Asperger Disorder Scale*. Circle Pines, MN: American Guidance Service.

Ginsburg, H., & Baroody, A. (1990). *Test of Early Mathematics Ability* (2nd ed.). Austin, TX: Pro-Ed.

Ginsburg, H., & Baroody, A. (2003). *Test of Early Mathematics Ability* (3rd ed.). Austin, TX: Pro-Ed.

Gioia, G. A., Isquith, P. K., Guy, S. C., & Kenworthy, L. (2000). *Behavior Rating Inventory of Executive Functioning (BRIEF)*. Lutz, FL: Psychological Assessment Resources.

Gitomer, D. (1993). Performance assessment and educational measurement. In R. Bennett & W. Ward (Eds.), *Constructive versus choice in cognitive measurement: Issues in constructed response, performance testing, and portfolio assessment.* Hillsdale, NJ: Lawrence Erlbaum Associates.

Goldman, R., & Fristoe, M. (1986). *Goldman-Fristoe Test of Articulation.* Circle Pines, MN: American Guidance Service.

Goldman, R., & Fristoe, M. (2000). *Goldman-Fristoe Test of Articulation* (2nd ed.). Circle Pines, MN: American Guidance Service.

Good, R. H., Gruba, J., & Kaminski, R. A. (2002). Best practices in using Dynamic Indicators of Basic Early Literacy Skills (DIBELS) in an outcomes-driven model. In A. Thomas & J. Grimes (Eds.), *Best practices in school psychology IV* (pp. 699–720). Washington, DC: National Association of School Psychologists.

Good, R. H., & Kaminski, R. A. (Eds.). (2002). *Dynamic Indicators of Basic Early Literacy Skills* (6th ed.). Eugene, OR: Institute for the Development of Educational Achievement. Available at dibels.uoregon.edu. Also available in print form from Sopris West Educational Publishers (sopriswest.com).

Good, R. H., & Salvia, J. A. (1989). Curriculum bias in published norm-referenced reading tests: Demonstrable effects. *School Psychology Review, 17*(1), 51–60.

Gordon, C. (1990). Students' and teachers' criteria for quality writing: Never the twain shall meet? *Reflections on Canadian Literacy, 8,* 74–81.

Goslin, D. A. (1969). *Guidelines for the collection, maintenance, and dissemination of pupil records.* Troy, NY: Russell Sage Foundation.

Gottesman, I. (1968). Biogenics of race and class. In M. Deutsch, I. Katz, & A. Jensen (Eds.), *Social class, race, and psychological development.* New York: Holt, Rinehart, & Winston.

Goyette, C. H., Conners, C. K., & Ulrich, R. F. (1978). Normative data on the revised Conners Parent and Teacher Rating Scales. *Journal of Abnormal Child Psychology, 6,* 221–236.

Grace, C., & Shores, E. (1992). *The portfolio and its use: Developmentally appropriate assessment of young children.* Little Rock, AR: Southern Association of Children Under Six.

Graden, J., Casey, A., & Bonstrom, O. (1983). *Prereferral interventions: Effects on referral rates and teacher attitudes* (Research Report No. 140). Minneapolis: Minnesota Institute for Research on Learning Disabilities.

Greenspan, S. I. (2004). *Greenspan Social Emotional Growth Chart: A Screening Questionnaire for In-*fants and Young Children. San Antonio, TX: Harcourt Educational Measurement.

Greenspan, S. I. (2006). *Bayley Scales of Infant and Toddler Development: Socio-Emotional Subtest.* San Antonio, TX: Harcourt Educational Measurement.

Greenwood, C. R., Abbott, M., & Tapia, Y. (2003). Ecobehavioral strategies: Observing, measuring, and analyzing behavior and reading interventions. In S. Vaughn & K. L. Briggs (Eds.), *Reading in the classroom: Systems for observing teaching and learning* (pp. 53–82). Baltimore: Brookes.

Greenwood, C. R., Carta, J. J., & Atwater, J. (1991). Ecobehavioral analysis in the classroom: Review and implications. *Journal of Behavioral Education, 1,* 59–77.

Greenwood, C. R., Carta, J. J., Kamps, D., & Arreaga-Mayer, C. (1990). Ecobehavioral analysis of classroom instruction. In S. R. Schroeder (Ed.), *Ecobehavioral analysis and developmental disabilities: The twenty-first century* (pp. 33–63). New York: Springer-Verlag.

Greenwood, C. R., Carta, J. J., Kamps, D., & Delquadri, J. (1995). *Ecobehavioral Assessment System Software.* Kansas City, KS: Juniper Gardens Children's Center.

Greenwood, C. R., Carta, J. J., Kamps, D., Terry, B., & Delquadri, J. (1994). Development and validation of standard classroom observation systems for school practitioners: Ecobehavioral Assessment System Software (EBASS). *Exceptional Children, 61,* 197–210.

Greenwood, C. R., Delquadri, J., & Hall, V. (1978). *The code for instructional structure and student academic response.* Kansas City, KS: Juniper Gardens Children's Center.

Greenwood, C. R., Horton, B. T., & Utley, C. A. (2002). Academic engagement: Current perspectives on research and practice. *School Psychology Review, 31*(3), 328–349.

Gresham, F., & Elliott, S. N. (1990). *Social Skills Rating System.* Circle Pines, MN: American Guidance Service.

Gresham, F., Watson, T., & Skinner, C. (2001). Functional behavioral assessment: Principles, procedures, and future directions. *School Psychology Review, 30*(2), 156–172.

Grimes, J., & Kurns, S. (2003, December). Response to intervention: Heartland's model of prevention and intervention. National Research Center on Learning

Disabilities Responsiveness to Intervention Symposium, Kansas City.

Griswold, P. (1990). Assessing relevance and reliability to improve the quality of teacher-made tests. *NASSP Bulletin, 74*(523), 18–24.

Gronlund, N. E. (1976). *Measurement and evaluation in teaching* (3rd ed.). New York: Macmillan.

Gronlund, N. E. (1982). *Constructing achievement tests*. Englewood Cliffs, NJ: Prentice-Hall.

Gronlund, N. E. (1985). *Measurement and evaluation in teaching* (5th ed.; Part 2: Constructing classroom tests). New York: Macmillan.

Gronlund, N. E., Linn., R., & Davis, K. (1999). *Measurement and assessment in teaching*. Englewood Cliffs, NJ: Prentice-Hall.

Guilford, J. (1936). *Psychometric methods*. New York: McGraw-Hill.

Guilford, J. P. (1967). *The nature of human intelligence*. New York: McGraw-Hill.

Gustafson, J. E. (1984). A unifying model for the structure of intellectual abilities. *Intelligence, 8*, 179–203.

Hacker, J., & Hathaway, W. (1991, April). *Toward extended assessment: The big picture*. Paper presented at the annual conference of the American Educational Research Association, Chicago.

Hammill, D. (1998). *Examiner's manual: Detroit Tests of Learning Aptitude*. Austin, TX: Pro-Ed.

Hammill, D. D. (1991). *Detroit Tests of Learning Aptitude* (3rd ed.). Austin, TX: Pro-Ed.

Hammill, D., Brown, L., & Bryant, B. (1992). *A consumer's guide to tests in print* (2nd ed.). Austin, TX: Pro-Ed.

Hammill, D., Brown, V., Larsen, S., & Wiederholt, J. (1994). *Test of Adolescent and Adult Language* (3rd ed.). Austin, TX: Pro-Ed.

Hammill, D., & Hresko, W. (1994). *Comprehensive Scales of Student Abilities*. Austin, TX: Pro-Ed.

Hammill, D., & Larsen, S. (1996). *Test of Written Language* (3rd ed.). Austin, TX: Pro-Ed.

Hammill, D., Mather, H., & Roberts, R. (2001). *Illinois Test of Psycholinguistic Abilities* (3rd ed.). Austin, TX: Pro-Ed.

Hammill, D., & Newcomer, P. (1999). *Test of Language Development–Intermediate* (3rd ed.). Austin, TX: Pro-Ed.

Hammill, D., Pearson, N., & Voress, J. (1993). *Examiner's manual: Developmental Test of Visual Perception* (2nd ed.). Austin, TX: Pro-Ed.

Hammill, D., Pearson, N., & Voress, J. (1996). *Test of Visual-Motor Integration*. Austin, TX: Pro-Ed.

Hammill, D., Pearson, N., & Wiederholt, L. (1996). *Comprehensive Test of Nonverbal Intelligence*. Austin, TX: Pro-Ed.

Hammill, D. D., Hresko, W. P., Ammer, J. J., Cronin, M. E., & Quinby, S. S. (1998). *Hammill Multiability Achievement Test*. Austin, TX: Pro-Ed.

Hanna, P., Hanna, J., Hodges, R., & Rudoff, E. (1966). *Phoneme-grapheme correspondence as cues to spelling improvement*. Washington, DC: U.S. Department of Health, Education, and Welfare.

Hansen, J. (1992). Literary portfolios emerge. *The Reading Teacher, 45*(8), 604–607.

Harcourt Assessment, Inc. (2004). *Stanford Achievement Test series, Tenth Edition technical data report*. San Antonio, TX: Author.

Harcourt Brace Educational Measurement. (1996a). *Stanford Achievement Test* (9th ed.). San Antonio, TX: Psychological Corporation.

Harcourt Brace Educational Measurement. (1996b). *Stanford Diagnostic Mathematics Test 4*. San Antonio, TX: Psychological Corporation.

Harcourt Brace Educational Measurement. (1996c). *Stanford Early School Achievement Test*. San Antonio, TX: Psychological Corporation.

Harcourt Brace Educational Measurement. (1996d). *Test of Academic Skills*. San Antonio, TX: Psychological Corporation.

Harcourt Educational Measurement. (2002). *Metropolitan Achievement Test* (8th ed.). San Antonio, TX: Author.

Harcourt Educational Measurement. (2003). *Otis Lennon School Ability Test, Eighth Edition*. San Antonio, TX: Author.

Harrison, P. (1985). *Vineland Adaptive Behavior Scales: Classroom edition manual*. Circle Pines, MN: American Guidance Service.

Harrison, P. (2006). *Bayley Scales of Infant and Toddler Development: Adaptive Behavior Subtest*. San Antonio, TX: Harcourt Educational Measurement.

Harrison, P., & Oakland, T. (2003). *Adaptive Behavior System, Second Edition*. San Antonio, TX: Harcourt Educational Measurement.

Hathaway, S., & McKinley, J. (1970). *Minnesota Multiphasic Personality Inventory*. Minneapolis: University of Minnesota Press.

Hebert, E. (1992, May). Portfolios invite reflection from students and staff. *Educational Leadership*, 58–61.

Herbert, E., & Schlutz, L. (1996). The power of portfolios. *Educational Leadership, 53*(7), 70–71.

Herrnstein, R., & Murray, C. (1994). *The bell curve: Intelligence and class structure in American life.* New York: The Free Press.

Hieronymus, A. N., Hoover, H. D., & Lindquist, E. F. (1986). *Iowa Tests of Basic Skills.* Chicago: Riverside Publishing Company.

Hillerich, R. L. (1985). *Teaching children to write, K–8* (selected chapters on the evaluation of writing). Englewood Cliffs, NJ: Prentice-Hall.

The Hispanic population in the United States, March 2000, Current Population Reports (P20-535). Washington, DC: U.S. Census Bureau.

Hoover, H. D., Dunbar, S. B., & Frisbie, D. A. (2001). *Iowa Tests of Basic Skills.* Chicago: Riverside Publishing Company.

Hoover, H. D., Hieronymus, A. N., Frisbie, D. A., & Dunbar, S. B. (1996). *Iowa Tests of Basic Skills.* Chicago: Riverside Publishing Company.

Horn, E. (1967). *What research says to the teacher: Teaching spelling.* Washington, DC: National Education Association.

Horner, R. H., Sugai, G. H., & Horner, H. F. (2000). A schoolwide approach to student discipline. *School Administrator, 57*(2), 20–23.

Hosp, M. K., & Hosp, J. L. (2003). Curriculum-based measurement for reading, spelling, and math: How to do it and why. *Preventing School Failure, 48*(1), 10–17.

Howell, K. W. (1986). Direct assessment of academic performance. *School Psychology Review, 15,* 324–335.

Howell, K. W. (1991). Curriculum-based evaluation: What you think is what you get. *Diagnostique, 16*(4), 193–203.

Howell, K. W., & Morehead, M. K. (1987). *Curriculum-based evaluation for special and remedial education.* Columbus, OH: Merrill.

Hresko, W., Peak, P., Herron, S., & Bridges, D. L. (2000). *Young Children's Achievement Test.* Austin, TX: Pro-Ed.

Hresko, W. P., Schlieve, P. L., Herron, S. R., Swain, C., & Sherbenou, R. J. (2003). *Comprehensive Mathematical Abilities Test.* Austin, TX: Pro-Ed.

Hurlin, R. G. (1962). Estimated prevalence of blindness in the U.S.–1960. *Sight Saving Review, 32,* 4–12.

Ireton, H., & Thwing, E. J. (1974). *Minnesota Child Development Inventory.* Minneapolis: Behavior Science Systems.

Isaacson, S. (1988). Assessing the writing product: Qualitative and quantitative measures. *Exceptional Children, 54,* 528–534.

Jenkins, J., & Pany, D. (1978). Standardized achievement tests: How useful for special education? *Exceptional Children, 44,* 448–453.

Jensen, A. R. (1974). Interaction of level I and level II abilities with race and socioeconomic status. *Journal of Educational Psychology, 66,* 99–111.

Jensen, A. R. (1980). *Bias in mental testing.* New York: The Free Press.

Johnson, D., & Myklebust, H. (1967). *Learning disabilities: Educational principles and practices.* New York: Grune & Stratton.

Jose, R. T., Smith, A. J., & Shane, K. G. (1988). Evaluating and stimulating vision in multiply impaired children. In J. Erin (Ed.), *Dimensions: Selected papers from the Journal of Visual Impairment and Blindness.*

Kampfer, S., Horvath, L., Kleinert, H., & Kearns, J. (2001). Teachers' perceptions of one state's alternative assessment: Implications for practice and preparation. *Exceptional Children, 67*(3), 361–374.

Kamphaus, R. W. (1987). Conceptual and psychometric issues in the assessment of adaptive behavior. *Journal of Special Education, 21,* 27–35.

Kamphaus, R. W. (1994). *Clinical assessment of children's intelligence.* Boston: Allyn & Bacon.

Kaplan, E., Fein, D., Kramer, J., Morris, R., Delis, D., & Maerlender, A. (2004). *Wechsler Intelligence Scale for Children* (4th ed., Integrated). San Antonio, TX: Psychological Corporation.

Kappauf, W. E. (1973). Studying the relationship of task performance to the variables of chronological age, mental age, and IQ. In N. Ellis (Ed.), *International review of research in mental retardation* (Vol. 6). New York: Academic Press.

Karlsen, B., & Gardner, E. F. (1996). *Directions for administering the Stanford Diagnostic Reading Test, Forms J/K.* San Antonio, TX: Harcourt Educational Measurement.

Katz, C., & Johnson-Kuby, S. (1996). Like portfolios for assessment. *Journal of Adolescent and Adult Literacy, 39,* 508–511.

Kaufman, A., & Kaufman, N. (1983). *Kaufman Assessment Battery for Children, interpretive manual.* Circle Pines, MN: American Guidance Service.

Kaufman, A., & Kaufman, N. (1985). *Kaufman Test of Educational Achievement, comprehensive form manual.* Circle Pines, MN: American Guidance Service.

Kaufman, A., & Kaufman, N. (1990). *Kaufman Brief Intelligence Test.* Circle Pines, MN: American Guidance Service.

Kaufman, A., & Kaufman, N. (1998a). *Kaufman Test of Educational Achievement–Normative update–Brief form manual.* Circle Pines: MN: American Guidance Service.

Kaufman, A., & Kaufman, N. (1998b). *Kaufman Test of Educational Achievement–Normative update–Comprehensive form manual.* Circle Pines: MN: American Guidance Service.

Kearns, J., Kleinert, H., Clayton, J., Burdge, M., & Williams, R. (1998). Principal supports for inclusive assessment: A Kentucky story. *Teaching Exceptional Children, 31*(2), 16–23.

Keefe, C. (1995). Portfolios: Mirrors of learning. *Teaching Exceptional Children, 27*(2), 66–67.

Keith, T. Z. (1994). Intelligence *is* important, intelligence *is* complex. *School Psychology Quarterly, 9,* 209–221.

Kelley, M. F., & Surbeck, E. (1985). History of preschool assessment. In K. D. Paget & B. Bracken (Eds.), *The psychoeducational assessment of preschool children.* New York: Grune & Stratton.

Kephart, N. (1971). *The slow learner in the classroom.* Columbus, OH: Merrill.

Kirk, S., & Kirk, W. (1971). *Psycholinguistic disabilities.* Urbana: University of Illinois Press.

Kirk, S., McCarthy, J., & Kirk, W. (1968). *Illinois Test of Psycholinguistic Abilities.* Urbana: University of Illinois Press.

Knoff, H. M. (1986). *The assessment of child and adolescent personality* (Chapter 3: A conceptual model and pragmatic approach toward personality assessment referrals). New York: Guilford Press.

Knowlton, M. (1988). *Minnesota Functional Vision Assessment.* Minneapolis: University of Minnesota. Unpublished paper.

Koening, A. J., & Holbrook, M. C. (1993). *Learning-media assessment.* Austin: Texas School for the Blind and Visually Impaired.

Koppitz, E. M. (1963). *The Bender Gestalt Test for Young Children.* New York: Grune & Stratton.

Koppitz, E. M. (1975). *The Bender Gestalt Test for Young Children. Volume II: Research and application, 1963–1973.* New York: Grune & Stratton.

Koretz, D. (1993). New report on Vermont Portfolio Project documents challenges. *National Council on Measurement in Education Quarterly Newsletter, 1*(4), 1–2.

Koretz, D., Klein, S., McCaffrey, D., & Stecher, B. (1993). *Interim report: The reliability of Ver-mont portfolio scores in the 1992–93 school year* (CRESST/CSE Technical Report No. 370). Los Angeles: University of California, Center for the Study of Evaluation.

Koretz, D., Lewis, E., Skewes-Cox, T., & Burstein, L. (1992). *Omitted and not-reached items in mathematics in the 1990 National Assessment of Educational Progress* (CSE Tech. Rep. 357). Los Angeles: University of California, National Center for Research on Evaluation, Standards, and Student Testing.

Kovacs, M. (1992). *Children's Depression Inventory: Manual.* North Tonawanda, NY: Multi-Health Systems.

Kramer, J. J., & Conoley, J. C. (1992). *The eleventh mental measurements yearbook* (Gates-MacGinitie, pp. 348–354). Lincoln, NE: University of Nebraska Press.

Kratochwill, T. R., & Bergan, J. R. (1990). *Behavioral consultation in applied settings: An individual guide.* New York: Plenum.

Krug, D. A., Arick, J. R., & Almond, P. A. (1993). *Autism Screening Instrument for Educational Planning* (2nd ed.). Austin, TX: Pro-Ed.

Kubiszyn, T., & Borich, G. (2003). *Educational testing and measurement: Classroom application and practice* (7th ed.). New York: Wiley.

LaBerge, D., & Samuels, S. (1974). Toward a theory of automatic information processing in reading. *Cognitive Psychology, 6,* 293–323.

Lachar, D. (1982). *Personality Inventory for Children–Revised.* Los Angeles: Western Psychological Services.

Lahey, M. (1988). *Language disorders and language development.* New York: Macmillan.

Langley, B., & DuBose, R. F. (1989). Functional vision screening for severely handicapped children. In J. Erin (Ed.), *Dimensions: Selected papers from the Journal of Visual Impairment and Blindness.*

Language Spoken at Home for the Citizen Population 18 Years and Over Who Speak English Less Than "Very Well" (STP194), 2000 Census of Population. Washington, DC: U.S. Bureau of the Census.

Larsen, S., & Hammill, D. (1994). *Test of Written Spelling* (3rd ed.). Austin, TX: Pro-Ed.

Larsen, S., Hammill, D. D., & Moats, L. (1999). *Test of Written Spelling–4.* Austin, TX: Pro-Ed.

LeMahieu, P., Eresh, J., & Wallace, Jr., R. (1992). Using student portfolios for public accounting. *The School Administrator, 49*(11), 8–15.

Lentz, F. E., & Shapiro, E. S. (1986). Functional assessment of the academic environment. *School Psychology Review, 15,* 346–357.

Lidz, C. (1991). *Practitioner's guide to dynamic assessment.* New York: Guilford.

Lindsley, O. (1990). Precision teaching: By teachers for children. *Teaching Exceptional Children, 22*(3), 10–15.

Lindsley, O. R. (1964). Direct measurement and prosthesis of retarded behavior. *Journal of Education, 147,* 68–81.

Linn, R., & Baker, E. (1993, Fall). Portfolios and accountability. *The CRESST Line: Newsletter of the National Center for Research on Evaluation, Standards, and Student Testing.* Los Angeles: NCRESST, 1, 8.

Linn, R., Graue, E., & Sanders, N. (1990). Comparing state and district test results to national norms: The validity of claims that "everyone is above average." *Educational Measurement: Issues and Practice, 9*(3), 5–14.

Linn, R. L., & Gronlund, N. E. (2000). *Measurement and assessment in teaching* (8th ed.). Columbus, OH: Merrill.

Loeding, B. L., & Crittenden, J. B. (1993). Inclusion of children and youth who are hearing impaired and deaf in outcomes assessment. In J. E. Ysseldyke & M. L. Thurlow (Eds.), *Views on inclusion and testing accommodations for students with disabilities.* Minneapolis: University of Minnesota, National Center on Educational Outcomes.

Lohman, D., & Hagan, E. (2001). *Cognitive Abilities Test.* Chicago: Riverside Publishing.

Luria, A. (1966). *Higher cortical functions in man.* New York: Basic Books.

Madaus, G. (1993). A national testing system: Manna from above? A historical/technological perspective. *Educational Assessment, 1,* 9–26.

Maddox, T. (Ed.). (2003). *Tests: A comprehensive reference for assessments in psychology, education, and business* (5th ed.). Austin, TX: Pro-Ed.

Maeroff, G. (1991, December). Assessing alternative assessment. *Phi Delta Kappan,* 272–281.

Mann, L. (1971). Perceptual training revisited: The training of nothing at all. *Rehabilitation Literature, 32,* 322–335.

Mardell-Czudnowski, C., & Goldenberg, D. (1998). *Manual: Developmental indicators for the assessment of learning* (3rd ed.). Circle Pines, MN: American Guidance Service.

Marion, S., & Gong, B. (2003, October). *Evaluating the validity of state accountability systems.* Paper presented at the Ed Reidy, Jr. Interactive Lecture Series, Nashua, NH.

Markwardt, F. (1998). *Peabody Individual Achievement Test–Revised–Normative update.* Circle Pines, MN: American Guidance Service.

Marston, D., & Magnusson, D. (1985). Implementing curriculum-based measurement in special and regular education settings. *Exceptional Children, 52,* 266–276.

Marston, D., Muyskens, P., Lau, M., & Canter, A. (2003). Problem-solving model for decision making with high-incidence disabilities: The Minneapolis experience. *Learning Disabilities Research and Practice, 18*(3), 187–200.

Martin, R. P. (1988). *Assessment of personality and behavior problems: Infancy through adolescence.* New York: Guilford Press.

Massachusetts Department of Education. (2001). *Resource Guide to the Massachusetts Curriculum Frameworks for Students with Significant Disabilities–English Language Arts Section.* Retrieved April 5, 2005, from www.doe.mass.edu/mcas/alt/rg/ela.pdf

Mather, N., Hammill, D., Allen, E., & Roberts, R. (2004). *Test of Silent Word Reading Fluency.* Austin, TX: Pro-Ed.

Mather, N., & Woodcock, R. W. (2001). *Woodcock-Johnson III Tests of Cognitive Abilities: Examiner's manual.* Itasca, IL: Riverside Publishing.

Maynard, F., & Strickland, J. (1969). *A comparison of three methods of teaching selected mathematical content in eighth and ninth grade general mathematics courses* (ED 041763). Athens, GA: University of Georgia.

McCarney, J. (1994). *The Behavior Evaluation Scale–2, Home Version: Technical manual.* Columbia, MO: Hawthorne Educational Services.

McCarney, J. (1995a). *Attention-Deficit Disorders Evaluation Scale, Home Version–Second Edition: Technical manual.* Columbia, MO: Hawthorne Educational Services.

McCarney, J. (1995b). *Attention-Deficit Disorders Evaluation Scale, School Version–Second Edition: Technical manual.* Columbia, MO: Hawthorne Educational Services.

McCarney, S. B. (1992a). *Early Childhood Behavior Scale: Technical manual.* Columbia, MO: Hawthorne Educational Services.

McCarney, S. B. (1992b). *Preschool Evaluation Scale.* Columbia, MO: Hawthorne Educational Services.

McCarney, S. B. (1995). *Adaptive Behavior Evaluation Scale, Home Version, Revised.* Columbia, MO: Hawthorne Educational Services.

McCarney, S. B., & Leigh, J. E. (1990). *Behavior Evaluation Scale–2.* Columbia, MO: Hawthorne Educational Services.

McConaughy, S. H. (1993a). Advances in the empirically based assessment of children's behavioral and emotional problems. *School Psychology Review, 22,* 285–307.

McConaughy, S. H. (1993b). Evaluating behavioral and emotional disorders with the CBCL, TRF, and YSR cross-informant scales. *Journal of Emotional and Behavioral Disorders, 1,* 40–52.

McConaughy, S. H., Achenbach, T. M., & Gent, C. L. (1988). Multiaxial empirically based assessment: Parent, teacher, observational, cognitive, and personality correlates of Child Behavior Profiles for 6–11-year-old boys. *Journal of Abnormal Child Psychology, 16,* 485–509.

McConaughy, S. H., Kay, P. J., & Fitzgerald, M. (1998). Preventing SED through parent-teacher action. Research and social skills instruction: First-year outcomes. *Journal of Emotional and Behavioral Disorders, 6,* 81–93.

McConaughy, S. H., Kay, P. J., & Fitzgerald, M. (1999). The Achieving Behaving Caring Project for preventing ED: Two-year outcomes. *Journal of Emotional and Behavioral Disorders, 7,* 224–239.

McGraw-Hill Digital Learning. (2004). *Yearly Progress Pro.* Columbus, OH: Author.

McGrew, K., Thurlow, M. L., Shriner, J., & Spiegel, A. N. (1992). *Inclusion of students with disabilities in national and state data collection programs* (Technical Report 2). Minneapolis: University of Minnesota, National Center on Educational Outcomes.

McGrew, K., Werder, J., & Woodcock, R. (1991). *Woodcock-Johnson Psychoeducational Battery–Revised: Technical manual.* Chicago: Riverside Publishing.

McGrew, K. S., & Woodcock, R. W. (2001). *Woodcock-Johnson III: Technical manual.* Itasca, IL: Riverside Publishing Company.

Meisels, S. J., Bickel, D. D., Nicholson, J., Xue, Y., & Atkins-Burnett, S. (1998). *Pittsburgh work sampling achievement validation study.* Ann Arbor, MI: School Restructuring Evaluation Project.

Meisels, S. J., Jablon, J., Marsden, D. B., Dichtelmiller, M. L., & Dorfman, A. (1994). *The Work Sampling System.* Ann Arbor, MI: Rebus.

Meisels, S. J., Marsden, D. B., Wiske, M. S., & Henderson, L. W. (1997). *Early Screening Inventory–Revised.* Ann Arbor, MI: Rebus.

Meisels, S. J., & Wiske, M. S. (1975). *Eliot-Pearson Screening Inventory.* Medford, MA: Tufts University, Department of Child Study.

Mercer, C., & Mercer, A. (1985). *Teaching students with learning problems* (2nd ed.). Columbus, OH: Merrill.

Merrell, K. W. (1994). *Assessment of behavioral, social, and emotional problems.* New York: Longman.

Messick, S. (1980). Test validity and the ethics of assessment. *American Psychologist, 35,* 1012–1027.

Messick, S. (1989). Meaning and values in test validation: The science and ethics of assessment. *Educational Researcher, 18*(2), 5–11.

Messick, S. (1993). Validity. In R. L. Linn (Ed.), *Educational measurement* (4th ed., pp. 13–103). New York: ACE/Macmillan.

Meyer, C. (1992). What's the difference between *authentic* and *performance* assessment? *Educational Leadership, 49*(8), 39–40.

Miller, J. (1981). *Assessing language production in children.* Austin, TX: Pro-Ed.

Mills, R. (1989). Portfolios capture rich array of student performance. *The School Administrator, 46*(11), 8–11.

Mitchell, J. V. (1985). *The ninth mental measurements yearbook* (SDRT, pp. 1462–1465). Lincoln, NE: University of Nebraska Press.

Moss, P., Cole, N., & Khampalikit, C. (1982). A comparison of procedures to assess written language skills at grades 4, 7, and 10. *Journal of Educational Measurement, 19,* 37–47.

Mullen, E. (1989). *Infant Mullen Scales of Early Learning manual.* Circle Pines, MN: American Guidance Service.

Mullen, E. (1992). *Mullen Scales of Early Learning manual.* Circle Pines, MN: American Guidance Service.

Myles, B., Bock, S., & Simpson, R. (2001). *Examiner's manual for the Asperger Syndrome Diagnostic Scale.* Circle Pines, MN: American Guidance Service.

Naglieri, J. (1997). *Naglieri Nonverbal Ability Test.* San Antonio, TX: Harcourt Brace Educational Measurement.

Naglieri, J. (1999). *Essentials of CAS assessment.* New York: Wiley.

Naglieri, J. A. (1985). *Matrix Analogies Test.* San Antonio, TX: Psychological Corporation.

Naglieri, J., & Das, J. (1997). *Cognitive Assessment System.* Itasca, IL: Riverside Publishing.

Naglieri, J., LeBuffe, P., & Pfeiffer, S. *Devereux Behavior Rating Scale–School Form.* San Antonio, TX: Psychological Corporation.

National Association of School Psychologists. (1997). *Principles for professional ethics.* Bethesda, MD: Author.

National Association of School Psychologists. (2000). *Principles for professional ethics.* Bethesda, MD: Author.

National Association of School Psychologists. (2002). *Principles for professional ethics.* Bethesda, MD: Author.

National Association of State Boards of Education. (1992). *Winners all: A call for inclusive schools.* Washington, DC: Author.

National Commission of Excellence in Education. (1983). *A nation at risk: The imperative for educational reform.* Washington, DC: U.S. Government Printing Office.

National Council of Teachers of Mathematics. (1993). *Assessment standards for school mathematics, working draft.* Reston, VA: Author.

National Council of Teachers of Mathematics. (2000). *Principles and standards for school mathematics.* Reston, VA: Author.

National Education Association. (2001). *Building tests to support instruction and accountability.* Washington, DC: Author.

National Institute of Child Health and Human Development. (2000a). Report of the National Reading Panel. *Teaching children to read: An evidence-based assessment of the scientific research literature on reading and its implication for reading instruction* (NIH Publication 00-4). Washington, DC: U.S. Government Printing Office.

National Institute of Child Health and Human Development. (2000b). Report of the National Reading Panel. *Teaching children to read: An evidence-based assessment of the scientific research literature on reading and its implication for reading instruction: Reports of the Subgroups* (Chapter 2, Part II). Available at www.nichd.hih.gov/publications/nrp/ch2-II.pdf

National Society for the Prevention of Blindness. (1961). *Vision screening in the schools.* New York: Author.

Neisworth, J., Bagnato, S., Salvia, J. A., & Hunt, F. (1999). *Temperament and Atypical Behavior Scale.* Baltimore, MD: Paul H. Brookes.

Nelson, J. R., Smith, D. J., Taylor, L., Dodd, J. M., & Reavis, K. (1991). Prereferral intervention: A review of the research. *Education and Treatment of Children, 14,* 243–253.

Newcomer, P. (1983). *Diagnostic Achievement Battery.* Austin, TX: Pro-Ed.

Newcomer, P. (1986). *Standardized Reading Inventory.* Austin, TX: Pro-Ed.

Newcomer, P. (1990). *Diagnostic Achievement Battery–2.* Austin, TX: Pro-Ed.

Newcomer, P. (1999). *Standardized Reading Inventory* (2nd ed.). Austin, TX: Pro-Ed.

Newcomer, P. (2001). *Diagnostic Achievement Battery* (3rd ed.). Austin, TX: Pro-Ed.

Newcomer, P., & Bryant, B. (1993). *Diagnostic Achievement Battery–3.* Austin, TX: Pro-Ed.

Newcomer, P., & Hammill, D. (1988). *Test of Language Development–Primary* (2nd ed.). Austin, TX: Pro-Ed.

Newcomer, P., & Hammill, D. (1999). *Test of Language Development–Primary* (3rd ed.). Austin, TX: Pro-Ed.

Nihira, K., Leland, H., & Lambert, N. (1993a). *AAMR Adaptive Behavior Scale–School* (2nd ed.). Austin, TX: Pro-Ed.

Nihira, K., Leland, H., & Lambert, N. (1993b). *Examiner's manual, AAMR Adaptive Behavior Scale–Residential and Community* (2nd ed.). Austin, TX: Pro-Ed.

Northern, J. L., & Downs, M. P. (1991). *Hearing in children* (4th ed). Baltimore, MD: Williams & Wilkens.

Nunnally, J. (1967). *Psychometric theory.* New York: McGraw-Hill.

Nunnally, J. (1978). *Psychometric theory* (2nd ed.). New York: McGraw-Hill.

Nunnally, J., & Bernstein, I. (1994). *Psychometric theory* (3rd ed.). New York: McGraw-Hill.

Nurss, J., & McGauvran, M. (1995). *The Metropolitan Readiness Tests: Norms book* (6th ed.). San Antonio, TX: Harcourt Brace.

Nuttall, D. (1992). Performance assessment: The message from England. *Educational Leadership, 49*(8), 54–57.

O'Leary, K., & O'Leary, S. (1972). *Classroom management: The successful use of behavior modification.* New York: Pergamon.

Olson, D. (1964). *Management by objectives.* Auckland, NZ: Pacific Book Publishers.

Otis, A. S., & Lennon, R. T. (1989). *Otis-Lennon School Ability Test.* San Antonio, TX: Psychological Corporation.

Otis, A. S., & Lennon, R. T. (1996). *Directions for Administering the Otis-Lennon School Ability Test.* San Antonio, TX: Harcourt Educational Measurement.

Palincsar, A. M., & Brown, A. L. (1984). Reciprocal teaching of comprehension-fostering and comprehension-monitoring activities. *Cognition and Instruction, 1,* 117–175.

Pandey, T., & Smith, R. (Eds.). (1991). *A sampler of mathematics assessment* (ED 341553). California Assessment Program. Sacramento, CA: California Department of Education.

Paul, D., Nibbelink, W., & Hoover, H. (1986). The effects of adjusting readability on the difficulty of mathematics story problems. *Journal of Research in Mathematics Education, 17,* 163–171.

Paulson, F., Paulson, P., & Meyer, C. (1991). What makes a portfolio a portfolio? *Educational Leadership, 48*(5), 60–64.

Pflaum, S., Walberg, H., Karegianes, M., & Rasher, S. (1980). Reading instruction: A quantitative analysis. *Educational Researcher, 9,* 12–18.

Phillips, K. (1990). *Factors that affect the feasibility of interventions.* Workshop presented at Mounds View Schools, unpublished.

Phillips, S. (1992). *Testing condition accommodations for handicapped students.* Paper presented at the annual meeting of the American Educational Research Association, San Francisco.

Plake, B., & Impara, J. (2002). *The fourteenth mental measurements yearbook.* Lincoln, NE: Buros Institute.

Polin, L. (1991, January/February). Writing technology, teacher education: K–12 and college portfolio assessment. *The Writing Notebook,* 25–28.

Porter, R. B., & Cattell, R. (1975). *Children's Personality Questionnaire.* Champaign, IL: Institute for Personality and Ability Testing.

Pretti-Frontczak, K., & Bricker, D. (2000). Enhancing the quality of individualized education plan (IEP) goals and objectives. *Journal of Early Intervention, 23*(2), 92–105.

Prutting, C., & Kirshner, D. (1987). A clinical appraisal of the pragmatic aspects of language. *Journal of Speech and Hearing Disorders, 52,* 105–119.

Psychological Corporation. (1992). *Wechsler Individual Achievement Test.* San Antonio, TX: Harcourt Brace Jovanovich.

Psychological Corporation. (1999). *Wechsler Abbreviated Scale of Intelligence.* San Antonio, TX: Author.

Psychological Corporation. (2001). *Wechsler Individual Achievement Test* (2nd ed.). San Antonio, TX: Author.

Psychological Corporation. (2002). *Wechsler Preschool and Primary Scale of Intelligence–III.* San Antonio, TX: Author.

Quality Education Data. (2001). *State school guide.* Denver, CO: Author.

Quay, H., & Peterson, D. (1987). *Revised Behavior Problem Checklist.* Coral Gables, FL: University of Miami.

Rasch, G. (1980). *Probabilistic models for some intelligence and attainment tests (Expanded Edition).* Chicago: University of Chicago Press.

Rayner, K., Foorman, B., Perfetti, C., Pesetsky, D., & Seidenberg, M. (2001). How psychological science informs the teacher of reading. *Psychological Science in the Public Interest, 2,* 31–73.

Reed, M. L., & Edelbrock, C. (1983). Reliability and validity of the Direct Observation Form of the Child Behavior Checklist. *Journal of Abnormal Child Psychology, 11,* 521–530.

Reid, D., Hresko, W., & Hammill, D. (1989). *Test of Early Reading Ability* (2nd ed.). Austin, TX: Pro-Ed.

Reid, D., Hresko, W., & Hammill, D. (2001). *Test of Early Reading Ability* (3rd ed.). Austin, TX: Pro-Ed.

Renaissance Learning. (1997). *Standardized Test for the Assessment of Reading.* Wisconsin Rapids, WI: Author.

Renaissance Learning. (1998). *STAR Math.* Wisconsin Rapids, WI: Author.

Renaissance Learning. (2004). Renaissance Place. Available at www.renlearn.com

Reschly, D. (1993). Consequences and incentives: Implications for inclusion/exclusion decisions regarding students with disabilities in state and national assessment programs. In J. E. Ysseldyke & M. L. Thurlow (Eds.), *Views on inclusion and testing accommodations for students with disabilities.*

Minneapolis: University of Minnesota, National Center on Educational Outcomes.

Reschly, D., & Ysseldyke, J. E. (2002). Paradigm shift: The past is not the future. In A. Thomas & J. Grimes (Eds.), *Best practices in school psychology IV* (pp. 3–20). Bethesda, MD: NASP.

Resnick, L. (1987). *Education and learning to think.* Washington, DC: National Academy Press.

Reynolds, C. R., & Kamphaus, R. W. (2004). *Behavior Assessment System for Children–Second Edition–Manual.* Circle Pines, MN: American Guidance Service.

Reynolds, C. R., & Richmond, B. O. (2000). *Revised Children's Manifest Anxiety Scale.* Los Angeles: Wester Psychological Services.

Reynolds, M. C., & Lakin, K. C. (1987). Noncategorical special education: Models for research and practice. In M. C. Wang, M. C. Reynolds, & H. J. Walberg (Eds.), *The handbook of special education: Research and practice.* Oxford, England: Pergamon Press.

Richman, N., Stevenson, J., & Graham, P. J. (1982). *Preschool-to-school: A behavioural study.* New York: Academic Press.

Roach, E. F., & Kephart, N. C. (1966). *The Purdue Perceptual-Motor Survey.* Columbus, OH: Merrill.

Roid, G. (2003). *Stanford-Binet Intelligence Scale* (5th ed.). Chicago, IL: Riverside Publishing.

Roid, G., & Miller, N. (1997). *Leiter International Performance Scale–Revised.* Chicago: Stoelting.

Rosenshine, B. (1995). Advances in research on instruction. *Journal of Educational Research, 88,* 262–268.

Rubin, S. (1969). A re-evaluation of figure-ground pathology in brain-damaged children. *American Journal of Mental Deficiency, 74,* 111–115.

Sabers, D., Feldt, L., & Reschly, D. (1988). Appropriate and inappropriate use of estimated true scores for normative comparisons. *Journal of Special Education, 22*(3), 355–358.

Sage, D. D., & Burrello, L. C. (1988). *Public policy and management in special education.* Englewood Cliffs, NJ: Prentice-Hall.

Salend, S. (1998). Using portfolios to assess student performance. *Teaching Exceptional Children, 31*(2), 36–43.

Salvia, J. A., Algozzine, R., & Sheare, J. (1977). Attractiveness and school achievement. *Journal of School Psychology, 15*(1), 60–67.

Salvia, J. A., & Good, R. H. (1982). Significant discrepancies in the classification of pupils: Differentiating the concept. In J. T. Neisworth (Ed.), *Assessment in special education.* Rockville, MD: Aspen Systems.

Salvia, J. A., & Hughes, C. (1990). *Curriculum-based assessment: Testing what is taught.* New York: Macmillan.

Salvia, J. A., & Hunt, F. (1984). Measurement considerations in program evaluation. In B. Keogh (Ed.), *Advances in special education* (Vol. 4). New York: JAI Press.

Salvia, J. A., & Meisel, J. (1980). Observer bias: A methodological consideration in special education research. *Journal of Special Education, 14*(2), 261–270.

Salvia, J. A., Neisworth, J., & Schmidt, M. (1990). *Examiner's manual: Responsibility and Independence Scale for Adolescents.* Allen, TX: DLM.

Salvia, J. A., Sheare, J., & Algozzine, R. (1975). Facial attractiveness and personal-social development. *Journal of Abnormal Child Psychology, 3*(7), 171–178.

Sattler, J. M. (2001). *Assessment of children: Cognitive applications.* San Diego, CA: Jerome Sattler.

Scannell, D. P. (1996). *Tests of Achievement and Proficiency.* Chicago: Riverside Publishing.

Scannell, D. P., Haugh, O. M., Lloyd, B. H., & Risinger, C. F. (1993). *Tests of Achievements and Proficiency.* Chicago: Riverside Publishing.

Schmidt, M., & Salvia, J. A. (1984). Adaptive behavior: A conceptual analysis. *Diagnostique, 9*(2), 117–125.

Schrank, F. A., & Woodcock, R. W. (2001). *WJ-III Compuscore and Profiles Program.* Itasca, IL: Riverside Publishing.

Shapiro, E. S. (1996). *Academic skills problems: Direct assessment and intervention* (2nd ed.). New York: Guilford Press.

Shapiro, E. S., & Derr, T. (1987). An examination of overlap between reading curricula and standardized reading tests. *Journal of Special Education, 21*(2), 59–67.

Shapiro, E. S., & Kratochwill, T. (Eds.). (2000). *Behavioral assessment in schools: Theory, research, and clinical foundations* (2nd ed.). New York: Guilford Press.

Shapiro, E. S., & Kratochwill, T. R. (Eds.). (1988). *Behavioral assessment in schools: Conceptual founda-*

tions and practical applications. New York: Guilford Press.

Share, D., & Stanovich, K. (1995). Cognitive processes in early reading development: A model of acquisition and individual differences. *Issues in Education: Contributions from Educational Psychology, 1,* 1–57.

Sharpe, M., McNear, D., & McGrew, K. (1996). *Braille Assessment Inventory.* Columbia, MO: Hawthorne Educational Services.

Shavelson, R., Baxter, G., & Pine, J. (1991). Performance assessment in science. *Applied Measurement in Education, 4*(4), 347–362.

Shavelson, R., Gao, X., & Baxter, G. (1991). *Design theory and psychometrics for complex performance assessment: Transfer and generalizability* (Interim Report). Los Angeles: University of California, Center for Research on Evaluation, Standards, and Student Testing.

Shinn, M. (1998). *Advanced applications of curriculum-based measurement.* New York: Guilford Press.

Shinn, M. R. (Ed.). (1989). *Curriculum-based measurement: Assessing special children.* New York: Guilford.

Shinn, M. R. (1995). Best practices in curriculum-based measurement and its use in a problem-solving model. In J. Grimes & A. Thomas (Eds.), *Best practices in school psychology III* (pp. 547–568). Silver Spring, MD: National Association of School Psychologists.

Shinn, M., Tindall, G., & Stein, S. (1988). Curriculum-based measurement and the identification of mildly handicapped students: A review of research. *Professional School Psychology, 3*(1), 69–85.

Shriner, J., & Salvia, J. A. (1988). Content validity of two tests with two math curricula over three years: Another instance of chronic noncorrespondence. *Exceptional Children, 55,* 240–248.

Siegler, R. (1989). Strategy diversity and cognitive assessment. *Educational Researcher, 18*(9), 15–20.

Sindelar, P., Monda., L., & O'Shea, L. (1990). Effects of repeated readings on instructional- and mastery-level readers. *Journal of Educational Research, 83*(4), 220–226.

Slobin, D. I., & Welsh, C. A. (1973). Elicited imitation as a research tool in developmental psycholinguistics. In C. Ferguson & D. Slobin (Eds.), *Studies of child language development.* New York: Holt, Rinehart, and Winston.

Snow, C., Burns, M., & Griffin, P. (1998). *Preventing reading difficulties in young children.* Washington, DC: National Academy Press.

Snow, R. (1993). Construct validity and constructed response tests. In R. Bennett & W. Ward (Eds.), *Constructive versus choice in cognitive measurement: Issues in constructed response, performance testing, and portfolio assessment.* Hillsdale, NJ: Lawrence Erlbaum Associates.

Sopris West. (1995). *Educational programs that work.* National Diffusion Network project (U.S. Department of Education). Longmont, CO: Author.

Sparrow, S., Balla, D., & Cicchetti, D. (1984a). *Interview edition, expanded form manual, Vineland Adaptive Behavior Scales.* Circle Pines, MN: American Guidance Service.

Sparrow, S., Balla, D., & Cicchetti, D. (1984b). *Interview edition, survey form manual, Vineland Adaptive Behavior Scales.* Circle Pines, MN: American Guidance Service.

Sparrow, S., Cicchetti, D., & Balla, D. (2005). *Vineland Adaptive Behavior Scales* (2nd ed.). Circle Pines, MN: American Guidance Service.

Special Education Rules, Iowa Department of Education, 1998.

Speece, D., Case, L. P., & Molloy, D. E. (2003). Responsiveness to general education instruction as the first gate to learning disabilities identification. *Learning Disabilities Research and Practice, 18*(3), 147–156.

Stake, R., & Wardrop, J. (1971). Gain score errors in performance contracting. *Research in the Teaching of English, 5,* 226–229.

Stanovich, K. (1986). Matthew effects in reading: Some consequences of individual differences in the acquisition of literacy. *Reading Research Quarterly, 21,* 360–406.

Stanovich, K. (2000). *Progress in understanding reading: Scientific foundations and new frontiers.* New York: Guilford Press.

Stevens, R., & Rosenshine, B. (1981). Advances in research on teaching. *Exceptional Education Quarterly, 2*(1), 1–9.

Stevens, S. S. (1951). Mathematics, measurement, and psychophysics. In S. S. Stevens (Ed.), *Handbook of experimental psychology* (p. 23). New York: Wiley.

Stiggins, R. (1997). *Student-centered classroom assessment* (2nd ed.). Upper Saddle River, NJ: Prentice-Hall.

Stokes, S. (1982). *School-based staff support teams: A blueprint for action.* Reston, VA: Council for Exceptional Children.

Suen, H., & Ary, D. (1989). *Analyzing quantitative behavioral observation data.* Hillsdale, NJ: Lawrence Erlbaum Associates.

Sulzer-Azaroff, B., & Roy Mayer, G. (1986). *Achieving educational excellence: Using behavior strategies.* New York: Holt, Rinehart, and Winston.

Sweetland, R., & Keyser, D. (1991). *Tests: A comprehensive reference for assessments in psychology, education, and business.* Austin, TX: Pro-Ed.

Taylor, B., Harris, L., Pearson, P. D., & Garcia, G. (1995). *Reading difficulties: Instruction and assessment* (2nd ed.). New York: McGraw-Hill.

Terman, L., & Merrill, M. (1916). *Stanford-Binet Intelligence Scale.* Boston: Houghton Mifflin.

Terman, L., & Merrill, M. (1937). *Stanford-Binet Intelligence Scale.* Boston: Houghton Mifflin.

Terman, L., & Merrill, M. (1973). *Stanford-Binet Intelligence Scale.* Chicago: Riverside Publishing.

Tharp, R. G., & Wetzel, R. J. (1969). *Behavior modification in the natural environment.* New York: Academic Press.

Therrien, M., & Ramirez, R. (2000). Cited in *Diversity of the country's Hispanics highlighted in U.S. Census Bureau Report.* U.S. Department of Commerce News, March 6, 2001. Washington, DC: USGPO.

Thompson, S., & Thurlow, M. (2001). *State special education outcomes: A report on state activities at the beginning of the new decade.* Minneapolis: University of Minnesota, National Center on Educational Outcomes.

Thorndike, R. L. (1963). *The concepts of over- and underachievement.* New York: Columbia University Press.

Thorndike, R. L. (1982). *Applied psychometrics.* Boston: Houghton Mifflin.

Thorndike, R. L. (1997). *Measurement and evaluation in psychology and education* (6th ed.). Upper Saddle River, NJ: Prentice-Hall.

Thorndike, R. L., & Hagen, E. (1978). *Measurement and evaluation in psychology and education.* New York: Wiley.

Thorndike, R. L., & Hagen, E. (1994). *Cognitive Abilities Test* (2nd ed.). Chicago: Riverside Publishing.

Thorndike, R. L., Hagen, E., & Sattler, J. (1985). *Stanford-Binet Intelligence Scale.* Chicago: Riverside Publishing.

Thorndike, R. L., Hagen, E., & Sattler, J. (1986). *Technical manual: The Stanford-Binet Intelligence Scale* (4th ed.). Chicago: Riverside Publishing.

Thurlow, M. L. (2001). *Use of accommodations in state assessments: What databases tell us about differential levels of use and how to document the use of accommodations* (Technical Report 30). Minneapolis: University of Minnesota, National Center on Educational Outcomes.

Thurlow, M. L., & Bolt, S. (2001). *Empirical support for accommodations most often allowed in state policy* (Synthesis Report 41). Minneapolis: University of Minnesota, National Center on Educational Outcomes.

Thurlow, M. L., Elliott, J. L., & Ysseldyke, J. E. (1998). *Testing students with disabilities: Practical strategies for complying with district and state requirements.* Thousand Oaks, CA: Corwin Press.

Thurlow, M. L., Elliott, J. L., & Ysseldyke, J. E. (2003). *Testing students with disabilities: Practical strategies for complying with district and state requirements* (2nd ed.). Thousand Oaks, CA: Corwin Press.

Thurlow, M. L., Elliott, J. L., & Ysseldyke, J. E. (2003). *Testing students with disabilities: Procedures for complying with district and state requirements.* Thousand Oaks, CA: Corwin Press.

Thurlow, M. L., House, A. L., Scott, D. L., & Ysseldyke, J. E. (2000). Students with disabilities in large-scale assessments: State participation and accommodation policies. *Journal of Special Education, 34*(3), 154–163.

Thurlow, M. L., Olsen, K., Elliott, J. L., Ysseldyke, J. E., Erickson, R., & Ahearn, E. (1997). *Alternate Assessment* (Policy Directions Paper, No. 9). Minneapolis: University of Minnesota, National Center on Educational Outcomes.

Thurlow, M. L., Quenemoen, R., Thompson, S., & Lehr, C. (2001). *Principles and characteristics of inclusive assessment and accountability systems* (Synthesis Report 40). Minneapolis, MN: National Center on Educational Outcomes, University of Minnesota.

Thurlow, M. L., Seyfarth, A., Scott, D., & Ysseldyke, J. E. (1997). *State policies on participation and accommodations in state assessments for students with disabilities* (Synthesis Report No. 31). Minneapolis: University of Minnesota, National Center on Educational Outcomes.

Thurlow, M. L., & Thompson, S. (2004). *2003 state special education outcomes.* Minneapolis: University of Minnesota, National Center on Educational Outcomes.

Thurlow, M. L., & Ysseldyke, J. E. (2002). *Including students with disabilities in assessments.* Washington, DC: National Education Association.

Thurlow, M. L., Ysseldyke, J. E., & Silverstein, B. (1993). *Testing accommodations for students with disabilities: A review of the literature* (Synthesis Report 4). Minneapolis: University of Minnesota, National Center on Educational Outcomes.

Thurlow, M. L., Ysseldyke, J. E., Vanderwood, M. L., & Spande, G. (1994). A guide to developing and implementing a system of outcomes and indicators. *Special Services in the Schools, 9,* 115–126.

Thurstone, T. G. (1941). Primary mental abilities in children. *Educational and Psychological Measurement, 1,* 105–116.

Tierney, R., Carter, M., & Desai, L. (1991). *Portfolio assessment in the reading and writing classrooms.* New York: Christopher-Gorelon.

Tilly, D. (2002). Best practices in school psychology as a problem-solving enterprise. In A. Thomas & J. Grimes (Eds.), *Best practices in school psychology IV* (pp. 21–36). Bethesda, MD: NASP.

Tilly, III, W. D. (2003). *How many tiers are needed for successful prevention and early identification? Heartland Area Education Agency evolution from four to three tiers.* Paper presented at the National Center on Learning Disabilities Symposium, Kansas City, MO.

Tindal, G., & Fuchs, L. (1999). *A summary of research on test changes: An empirical basis for determining testing accommodations.* Lexington, KY: University of Kentucky, Mid-South Regional Resource Center.

Tindal, G. A., & Marston, D. B. (1990). *Classroom-based assessment: Evaluating instructional outcomes* (Chapter 15: Individual-referenced evaluation). Columbus, OH: Merrill.

Torgesen, J., & Bryant, B. (2004). *The Test of Phonological Awareness, Second Edition: Plus, Examiner's Manual.* Austin, TX: Pro-Ed.

Torgesen, J., Morgan, S., & Davis, C. (1992). Effects of two types of phonological awareness training on word learning in kindergarten children. *Journal of Educational Psychology, 84,* 364–370.

Tucker, J. (1985). Curriculum-based assessment: An introduction. *Exceptional Children, 52,* 199–204.

Tunmer, W., Herriman, M., & Nesdale, A. (1988). Metalinguistic abilities and beginning reading. *Reading Research Quarterly, 23,* 134–158.

U.S. Census Bureau. (1991). *Current population survey.* Washington, DC: Author.

U.S. Census Bureau. (1994). *Current population survey.* Washington, DC: Author.

U.S. Census Bureau. (1997). *Current population survey, October 1997: School enrollment supplement.* Washington, DC: Author.

U.S. Census Bureau. (1998). *Current population survey.* Washington, DC: Author.

U.S. Census Bureau. (1999). *U.S. Census 1990.* Washington, DC: Author.

U.S. Census Bureau. (2000). *Census of population.* Washington, DC: Author.

U.S. Department of Education. (1983). *A nation at risk: The imperative for school reform.* Washington, DC: Author.

U.S. Department of Education. (2005). *Alternate achievement standards for students with the most significant cognitive disabilities: Non-regulatory guidance.* Washington, DC: Author.

U.S. Public Health Service. (1971). *Vision screening of children* (PHS Document No. 2042). Washington, DC: Author.

Upah, K. R., & Tilly, W. D. (2002). Best practices in designing, implementing, and evaluating quality interventions. In A. Thomas & J. Grimes (Eds.), *Best practices in school psychology IV.* Bethesda, MD: National Association of School Psychologists.

Vaughn, S., & Fuchs, L. (2003). Redefining learning disabilities as inadequate response to instruction: The promise and potential problems. *Learning Disabilities Research and Practice, 18*(3), 137–146.

Voress, J., & Maddox, T. (1998). *Developmental Assessment of Young Children.* Austin, TX: Pro-Ed.

Wagner, R., Torgesen, J., & Rashotte, C. (1999). *Comprehensive Test of Phonological Processing.* Austin, TX: Pro-Ed.

Walberg, H. J. (1984). Families as partners in educational productivity. *Phi Delta Kappan, 65,* 397–400.

Walker, D. K. (1973). *Socioemotional measures for preschool and kindergarten children.* San Francisco: Jossey-Bass.

Walker, H. M. (1983). Assessment of behavior disorders in school settings: Issues, problems, and strategies. In M. Noel & N. Haring (Eds.), *Progress or change? Issues in educating the mildly emotionally disturbed.* Washington, DC: U.S. Department of Education, USOSE Monograph Series.

Walker, H. M., Hops, H., & Greenwood, C. R. (1984). The CORBEH research and development model: Programmatic issues and strategies. In S. Paine, G. Bellamy, & B. Wilcox (Eds.), *Human services that work* (pp. 57–78). Baltimore, MD: Brookes.

Walker, H. M., & McConnell, S. R. (1988). *Walker-McConnell Scale of Social Competence.* Austin, TX: Pro-Ed.

Walker, H. M., & Severson, H. H. (1992). *Systematic screening for behavior disorders* (2nd ed.). Longmont, CO: Sopris West.

Walker, H. M., Severson, H., Stiller, B., Williams, G., Haring, N., Shinn, M., & Todis, B. (1988). Systematic screening of pupils in the elementary age range for behavior disorders: Development and trial testing of a multiple-gating model. *Remedial and Special Education, 9*(3), 8–14.

Wallace, G., & Hammill, D. (1994). *Comprehensive Receptive and Expressive Vocabulary Test.* Austin, TX: Pro-Ed.

Wallace, G., & Hammill, D. (2002). *Comprehensive Receptive and Expressive Vocabulary Test* (2nd ed.). Austin, TX: Pro-Ed.

Wechsler, D. (1939). *Wechsler-Bellevue Intelligence Scale.* New York: Psychological Corporation.

Wechsler, D. (1967). *Manual for the Wechsler Preschool and Primary Scale of Intelligence.* Cleveland: Psychological Corporation.

Wechsler, D. (1974). *Manual for the Wechsler Intelligence Scale for Children–Revised.* Cleveland, OH: Psychological Corporation.

Wechsler, D. (1989). *Manual for the Wechsler Preschool and Primary Scale of Intelligence–Revised.* San Antonio, TX: Psychological Corporation.

Wechsler, D. (2002). *Wechsler Intelligence Scale for Children–IV.* San Antonio, TX: Psychological Corporation.

Wechsler, D. (2003). *Wechsler Intelligence Scale for Children* (4th ed.). San Antonio, TX: Psychological Corporation.

Wechsler, D. (2003). *Wechsler Intelligence Scale for Children, Fourth Edition–Integrated: Administration and scoring manual.* San Antonio, TX: Psychological Corporation.

Wechsler, D. (2004). *Wechsler Intelligence Scale for Children, Fourth Edition–Integrated: Technical and interpretive manual.* San Antonio, TX: Psychological Corporation.

Werner, H., & Strauss, A. A. (1941). Pathology of figure-background relation in the child. *Journal of Abnormal and Social Psychology, 36,* 236–248.

Wiederholt, L., & Bryant, B. (2001). *Gray Oral Reading Tests–4.* Austin, TX: Pro-Ed.

Wiederholt, L. (1986). *Formal Reading Inventory.* Austin, TX: Pro-Ed.

Wiederholt, L., & Bryant, B. (2001). *Examiner's manual: Gray Oral Reading Tests–3.* Austin, TX: Pro-Ed.

Wiley, J. (1971). A psychology of auditory impairment. In W. Cruickshank (Ed.), *Psychology of exceptional children and youth.* Englewood Cliffs, NJ: Prentice-Hall.

Wilkinson, G. (1993). *Wide Range Achievement Test–3.* Wilmington, DE: Jastak Associates.

Williams, C., & Wang, J. J. (1997). *Technical References to the Peabody Picture Vocabulary Test–III.* Circle Pines, MN: American Guidance Service.

Williams, K. (2001). *Group reading assessment and diagnostic evaluation.* Circle Pines, MN: American Guidance Service.

Williams, K. T. (2004). *Group Mathematics Assessment and Diagnostic Evaluation.* Circle Pines, MN: AGS Publishing.

Winograd, P., & Gaskins, R. (1992). Improving the assessment of literacy: The power of portfolios. *Pennsylvania Reporter, 23*(2), 1–6.

Wolf, D. (1989). Portfolio assessment: Sampling student work. *Educational Leadership, 46*(7), 35–39.

Wolf, M. (1991). Naming speed and reading: The contribution of the cognitive neurosciences. *Reading Research Quarterly, 26,* 123–141.

Woodcock, R. W. (1997). *Woodcock Diagnostic Reading Battery.* Allen, TX: DLM.

Woodcock, R. W. (1998). *Woodcock Reading Mastery Tests–Revised: Normative update.* Circle Pines, MN: American Guidance Service.

Woodcock, R. W., & Johnson, M. B. (1989). *Woodcock-Johnson Psychoeducational Battery–Revised.* Allen, TX: DLM.

Woodcock, R., McGrew, K., & Mather, N. (2000). *Woodcock-Johnson 3: Tests of Achievement.* Chicago: Riverside Press.

Woodcock, R. W., McGrew, K. S., & Mather, N. (2001). *WJ-III Tests of Cognitive Abilities and Tests of Achievement.* Itasca, IL: Riverside Publishing.

Woodcock, R. W., McGrew, K., & Werder, J. (1994). *Mini-Battery of Achievement.* Chicago: Riverside Publishing.

Yell, M. (1998). *The law and special education.* Upper Saddle River, NJ: Prentice-Hall.

Ysseldyke, J. E. (1973). Diagnostic-prescriptive teaching: The search for aptitude-treatment interactions. In L. Mann & D. A. Sabatino (Eds.), *The first review of special education.* New York: Grune & Stratton.

Ysseldyke, J. E. (2005, March). *Technology tools for enhancing progress monitoring.* Presentation at the annual meeting of the National Association of School Psychologists, Atlanta, GA.

Ysseldyke, J. E., Algozzine, B., & Thurlow, M. L. (1999). Legal issues in special education. In *Critical issues in special education* (3rd ed.; ch. 8). Boston: Houghton Mifflin.

Ysseldyke, J. E., & Christenson, S. L. (1987a). Evaluating students' instructional environments. *Remedial and Special Education, 8,* 17–24.

Ysseldyke, J. E., & Christenson, S. L. (1987b). *The Instructional Environment Scale.* Austin, TX: Pro-Ed.

Ysseldyke, J. E., & Christenson, S. L. (1993). *The Instructional Environment System–II.* Longmont, CO: Sopris West.

Ysseldyke, J. E., & Christenson, S. L. (2002). *Functional assessment of academic behavior: Creating successful learning environments.* Longmont, CO: Sopris West.

Ysseldyke, J. E., Christenson, S. L., & Kovaleski, J. F. (1994). Identifying students' instructional needs in the context of classroom and home environments. *Teaching Exceptional Children, 26*(3), 37–41.

Ysseldyke, J. E., Krentz, J., Erickson, R., & Moore, M. (1998). *NCEO framework for educational accountability.* Minneapolis: National Center on Educational Outcomes, University of Minnesota.

Ysseldyke, J., & Olsen, K. (1999). Putting alternative assessments into practice: What to measure and possible sources of data. *Exceptional Children, 65*(2), 175–185.

Ysseldyke, J. E., & Salvia, J. A. (1974). Diagnostic-prescriptive teaching: Two models. *Exceptional Children, 41,* 181–186.

Ysseldyke, J. E., & Thurlow, M. L. (1993). *Self-study guide to the development of educational outcomes and indicators.* Minneapolis: University of Minnesota, National Center on Educational Outcomes.

Ysseldyke, J. E., Thurlow, M. L., Bielinski, J., House, A., Moody, M., & Haigh, J. (2001). The relationship between instructional and assessment accommodations in an inclusive state accountability system. *Journal of Learning Disabilities, 34*(3), 212–220.

Ysseldyke, J. E., Thurlow, M. L., McGrew, K. S., & Shriner, J. G. (1994). *Recommendations for making decisions about the participation of students with disabilities in statewide assessment programs* (Synthesis Report 15). Minneapolis: University of Minnesota, National Center on Educational Outcomes.

Ysseldyke, J. E., Vanderwood, M., & Shriner, J. (1997). Changes over the past decade in special education referral to placement probability: An incredibly reliable practice. *Diagnostique, 23*(1), 193–201.

Zerkel, P., & Richardson, S. N. (1988). *A digest of Supreme Court decisions affecting education* (2nd ed.). Bloomington, IN: Phi Delta Kappa Educational Foundation.

ZERO TO THREE: National Center for Infants, Toddlers, and Families. (1994). *Diagnostic Classification: 0–3.* Washington, DC: Author.

CREDITS

P. 8, Table 1.1: Adapted from *Special Education Rules*, Iowa Department of Education, 1998. Reschly and Ysseldyke, 2002; Tilly 2002.

P. 112, Table 6.1: Salvia J., Neisworth, J. and Schmidt, M. (1990) *Examiner's Manual: Responsibility and Independence for Adolescents*. Allen, TX: DLM.

P. 130, Figure 7.1: Source: *Psychological Testing*, 6/e by A. Anastasi, © 1988. Reprinted by permission of Prentice-Hall, Inc., Upper Saddle River, NJ.

P. 166, Table 9.1: From *Synthesis Report 41* by M.L. Thurlow and S. Bolt, National Center on Educational Outcomes, University of Minnesota. Reprinted by permission.

P. 168, Making Decision About Groups: "Practical Strategies for Complying with District and State Requirements" from *Testing Students with Disabilities*, 2/e by Thurlow, Elliot and Ysseldyke, pp. 46–47. Copyright © 2003. Reprinted by permission of Sage Publications, Inc.

P. 210, Figure 12.1: "Carroll's Model of School Learning" from "A Model of School Learning" by John B. Carroll in *Teaching College Record*, Vol. 64, pp. 723-733, © 1963. Reprinted by permission of John B. Carroll.

P. 212, Table 12.1: Reprinted with permission from Algozzine, B. and Ysseldyke, J. (1997). *Strategies and Tactics for Effective Instruction* (2nd ed.). Longmont, CO: Sopris West.

Pp. 223–224, Table 12.5: Reprinted with permission of Sopris West from Ysseldyke, J.E. & Christenson, S.L. (2002), *Functional Assessment of Academic Behavior: Creating Successful Learning Environments*. Longmont, CO: Sopris West.

P. 309, Table 17.1: Copyright © 2001 by The Riverside Publishing Company. "Table 2.2. Broad and Narrow Abilities Measured by the WJ III COG and WJ III ACH" from the *Woodcock-Johnson® III (WJ III®) Technical Manual* reproduced with permission of the publisher. All rights reserved.

Pp. 326–327, Figure 17.2: Source: From *Test of Non-Verbal Intelligence (TONI-3)*. Copyright © 1997 by Pro-Ed. Reprinted by permission of the publisher.

P. 353, Figure 19.1: Source: "Guidelines for Audiometric Symbols," Figure 1. ASHA, 32, 25–30, 1990. Reprinted by permission of the American Speech-Language-Hearing Association.

P. 354, Figure 19.2: Source: Adapted from "Guidelines for Audiometric Symbols," Table 1. ASHA, 32, 25–30, 1990. Reprinted by permission of the American Speech-Language-Hearing Association.

P. 355, Figure 19.3: From H.S. Bess and L. E. Humes, *Audiology: The Fundamentals*, 1st edition, Copyright Williams and Wilkins, 1990. Reprinted by permission of Lippincott Williams & Wilkins.

P. 362, Figure 19.7: From H.S. Bess and L. E. Humes, *Audiology: The Fundamentals*, 1st edition, Copyright Williams and Wilkins, 1990. Reprinted by permission of Lippincott Williams & Wilkins.

P. 410, Table 21.6: "Grade-Equivalent Scores Obtained by Matching Specific Reading Test Words to Standardized Reading Test Words" from "Standardized Achievement Tests: How Useful for Special Education?" by J. Jenkins & D. Pany in *Exceptional Children*, 44 (1978), p. 450. Copyright © 1978 by The Council for Exceptional Children. Reprinted with permission.

Pp. 423, Figure 22.2: Copyright © 1997 by The Riverside Publishing Company. "The Reading Performance Model" from the *Woodcock Diagnostic Reading Battery (WDRB) Examiner's Manual* reproduced with permission of the publisher. All rights reserved.

Pp. 424, Figure 22.3: Copyright © 1997 by The Riverside Publishing Company. "Selective Testing Table" from the *Woodcock Diagnostic Reading Battery (WDRB) Examiner's Manual* reproduced with permission of the publisher. All rights reserved.

Pp. 426, Table 22.1: Copyright © 1997 by The Riverside Publishing Company. "Median Reliabilities for WDRB Subtests and Clusters" from the *Woodcock Diagnostic Reading Battery (WDRB) Examiner's Manual* reproduced with permission of the publisher. All rights reserved.

INDEX

Note: Page numbers followed by *n* indicate footnotes

AAMD Adaptive Behavior Scale: Residential and Community Scale, Second Edition (ABS-RC2), 567–571
  technical data for, 568–571
AAMR Adaptive Behavior Scale—School 2 (ABS-S2), 571–576
  technical data for, 572–576
Abbott, M., 216
Ability, performance versus, 560
Abscissa, 72
Absent desirable behavior, 197
Absolute standards, 30–32
Abstract reasoning, assessment by intelligence tests, 288–289
Academic achievement standards, 659
Academic content standards, 659
Academic needs, teacher recognition of, 587–590
Academic problems
  as assessment domain, 19
  factors contributing to, 208–215
Accommodation in testing, 158–169
  current practice in, 166–167
  environmental considerations for, 164
  factors affecting accurate assessment and, 162–164
  legal considerations for, 164–165
  need for, 158–160
  participation and, 160–161
  participation decisions and, 165
  recommendations for making decisions about, 167–168
  types of accommodations and, 161
Accountability
  assumptions underlying, 664
  current state practices and, 666–668
  push for, 675–676
  student, 655
  system, 655
Accountability decisions, 8, 17–18, 654–672
  accountability and, 17–18
  assessment for purpose of making, 668
  best practices in high-stakes assessment and accountability and, 668–670
  legal requirements and, 656
  program evaluation and, 17

response to instruction assessment for, 640–641
standards and, 659–662
standards-based accountability system development and, 662–668
technology-enhanced assessment and accountability systems and, 671
terminology related to, 657–659
Acculturation, 44
  educational prognosis and, 36
  intelligence tests and, 283–284
  of norm sample, 108
Accuracy, 100
  concern about, 42
  need for, 160
Achenbach, T. M., 519, 521, 525, 528, 532, 536, 539, 540, 547
Achenbach System of Empirically Based Assessment (ASEBA), 519–521
Achievement, 16
  assessing in limited English proficiency students, 182
Achievement standards, alternate, 657, 659, 661–662
Achievement tests, 379–411
  categories of, 380–381
  getting the most out of, 410–411
  practical dilemmas regarding, 409, 410
  reasons for using, 382–383
  selection of, 381–382
  teacher-made, *see* Teacher-made achievement tests
Adams, M., 413, 414, 589
Adaptive behavior, definition of, 559–561
Adaptive behavior assessment, 561–582
  practical dilemmas regarding, 581–582
  reasons for, 562
  tests for, 562–581
Adequate yearly progress (AYP), 657, 660
Adjusting instruction, 215
Administration errors, validity and, 155
Administration instructions, writing, 234
Admission, review, and dismissal (ARD) teams, 13
Age
  adaptive behavior and, 560
  chronological, correlation between test scores and, 152–153

developmental, 92
  intelligence tests and, 284
  of norm sample, 106
Age equivalents, 90
Air-conduction hearing, 350
Alberto, P. A., 189, 193, 591
Algozzine, B. A., 13, 18, 209–210, 210, 214
Algozzine-Ysseldyke Model of Effective Instruction, 209–215, 221
Allen, E., 431
Alnot, S., 337
Altered outcome experiences as entitlement, 615–616
Alternate achievement standards, 657, 659, 661–662
Alternate assessments, 661
Alternate-form reliability, 123
American Association for the Advancement of Science, 396
American Association on Mental Retardation (AAMR), 114
American College Testing Program, accommodations and, 166
American Educational Research Association (AERA), 21, 105, 107, 114, 116, 143, 144, 144*n*, 145, 155, 163, 256, 269, 272, 273, 274
American Psychological Association, 21, 58, 105, 116, 143, 163, 256, 272
American Speech-Language-Hearing Association, 353, 354
Americans with Disabilities Act (ADA) of 1990 (Public Law 101-336), 50, 51, 53, 164, 613
Ames, W., 474
Ammer, J. J., 459
Amplitude of behaviors, 193, 195, 561
Analogical reasoning, assessment by intelligence tests, 288
Analytic tests, 227–229
Anecdotal records, 33–34
Ansley, T., 337
Appelbaum, M. I., 358
Armbruster, B., 414
Arreaga-Mayer, C., 208, 216, 217
Arter, J., 252, 255, 256
Ary, D., 188, 189, 196*n*
Asperger Syndrome Diagnostic Scale (ASDS), 540–542
  subtests of, 541
  technical data for, 541–542

Acronyms Used in Special Education

ABA: Applied Behavioral Analysis

ABC: Antecedent-Behavior-Consequence

ADA: Americans with Disabilities Act

ADC: Aid to Dependent Children Program

ADHD: Attention Deficit Hyperactivity Disorder

APD: Auditory Processing Disorder

APE: Adaptive Physical Education

ARD: Admission, Review, and Dismissal Committee

AS: Asperger's Syndrome

ASD: Autistic Spectrum Disorder

ASL: American Sign Language

AT: Assistive Technology

AYP: Adequate Yearly Progress

BD: Behavioral Disorder

BD/ED: Behavior Disordered / Emotionally Disturbed

BIA: Bureau of Indian Affairs

BIP: Behavior Intervention Plan

BP: Bi-Polar Disorder

CAPD: Central Auditory Processing Disorder

CBA: Curriculum-Based Assessment

CBE: Curriculum-Based Evaluation

CBM: Curriculum-Based Measurement

CD: Conduct Disorder

CEC: Council for Exceptional Children

CNS: Central Nervous System

CP: Cerebral Palsy

CSE: Committee for Special Education (called "MDT" in some states)

CSPD: Comprehensive System for Personnel Development

CST: Child Study Team (also called Child Find Team)

DB: decibel

DD: Developmental Disabilities

DEC: Division of Early Childhood of the Council for Exceptional Children

DODDS: Department of Defense Dependent Schools

DOE: Department of Education

DSM-IV: Diagnostic and Statistical Manual of Mental Disorders (4th Edition)

ECSE: Early Childhood Special Education

ED: Emotionally Disturbed

EH: Emotionally Handicapped

EHA: Education of All Handicapped Children Act

EI: Early Intervention

ELL: English Language Learner

EPSDT: Early Periodic Screening Diagnosis and Treatment

ESE: Exceptional Student Education

ESEA: Elementary and Secondary Education Act

ESL: English as a Second Language

ESY: Extended School Year Services

FAPE: Free Appropriate Public Education

FAS: Fetal Alcohol Syndrome

FBA: Functional Behavioral Assessment

FERPA: Federal Educational Rights and Privacy Act

FOIA: Freedom of Information Act

G/T: Gifted and Talented (see also TAG)

HoH: Hard of Hearing

IAT: Intervention Assistance Team

IDEA: Individuals with Disabilities Education Act

IEE: Independent Educational Evaluation

IEP: Individualized Education Plan

IFSP: Individualized Family Service Plan

IHP: Individual Habilitation Plan

ITED: Iowa Tests of Educational Development

ITP: Individualized Transition Plan

LD: Learning Disability

LEA: Local Education Agency (the school district)

LEP: Limited English Proficiency

LLD: Language-based Learning Disability

LRE: Least Restrictive Environment

MBD: Minimal Brain Dysfunction